KU-681-020

BRENDAN SIMMS

# Unfinest Hour

## BRITAIN AND THE DESTRUCTION OF BOSNIA

PENGUIN BOOKS

PENGUIN BOOKS

Published by the Penguin Group
Penguin Books Ltd, 80 Strand, London WC2R 0RL, England
Penguin Putnam Inc., 375 Hudson Street, New York, New York 10014, USA
Penguin Books Australia Ltd, 250 Camberwell Road, Camberwell, Victoria 3124, Australia
Penguin Books Canada Ltd, 10 Alcorn Avenue, Toronto, Ontario, Canada M4V 3B2
Penguin Books India (P) Ltd, 11, Community Centre, Panchsheel Park, New Delhi – 110 017, India
Penguin Books (NZ) Ltd, Cnr Rosedale and Airborne Roads, Albany, Auckland, New Zealand
Penguin Books (South Africa) (Pty) Ltd, 24 Sturdee Avenue, Rosebank 2196, South Africa

Penguin Books Ltd, Registered Offices: 80 Strand, London WC2R 0RL, England

www.penguin.com

First published by Allen Lane The Penguin Press 2001
Published in Penguin Books with a new Preface 2002
4

Copyright © Brendan Simms, 2001, 2002

All rights reserved

The moral right of the author has been asserted

Printed in England by Clays Ltd, St Ives plc

Except in the United States of America, this book is sold subject
to the condition that it shall not, by way of trade or otherwise, be lent,
re-sold, hired out, or otherwise circulated without the publisher's
prior consent in any form of binding or cover other than that in
which it is published and without a similar condition including this
condition being imposed on the subsequent purchaser

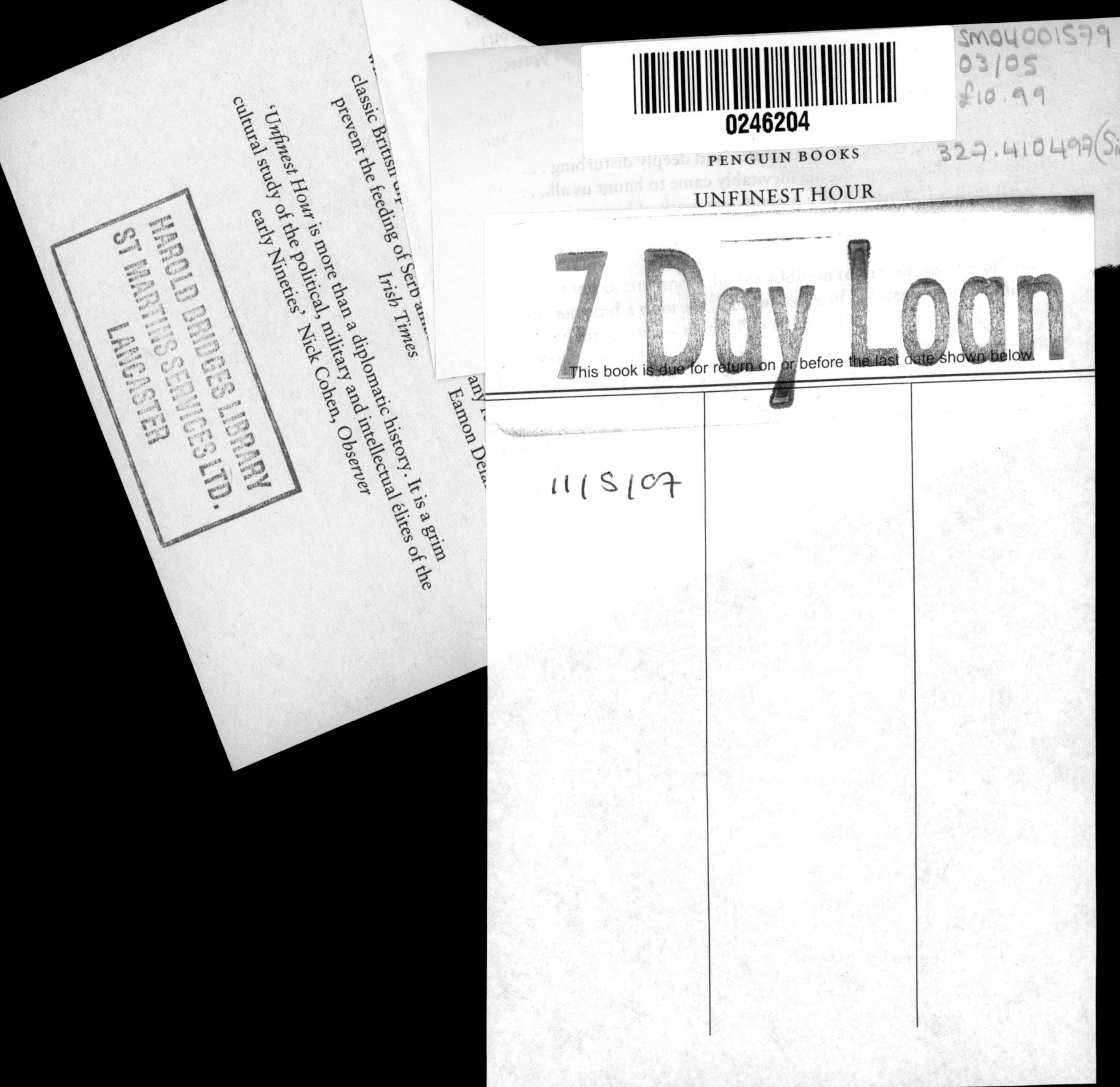

0246204

SM04001579
03/05
£10.99
327.410497 (Sim)

PENGUIN BOOKS

UNFINEST HOUR

7 Day Loan

This book is due for return on or before the last date shown below.

11/5/07

Irish Times

'*Unfinest Hour* is more than a diplomatic history. It is a grim cultural study of the political, military and intellectual élites of the early Nineties' Nick Cohen, *Observer*

HAROLD BRIDGES LIBRARY
ST MARTINS SERVICES LTD.
LANCASTER

'An i…
the pol…
moral a…

'Simms shows ho…
consensus' Si…

ABOUT THE AU…

Brendan Simms is Director of Studies in Hist… Newton Sheehy Lecturer in International Relat… for International Studies, University of Cambridge. … author of *The Impact of Napoleon* and *The Struggle fo…* *Germany, 1779–1850*.

For Sophie
23.3.1999–23.8.1999

If you have shown yourself weak at a time of crisis, how limited is your strength!
Rescue those being dragged away to death, and save those being hauled off to execution.
If you say, 'But this person I do not know', God, who fixes a standard for the heart, will take note; he who watches you will know; he will repay everyone according to what he does.

Proverbs 24: 10–12

# *Contents*

# *Preface to the Paperback Edition*

*Unfinest hour* was published in the immediate aftermath of the 11 September attacks and the resulting war in Afghanistan. It was reviewed or discussed in all the major broadsheets, almost always in very positive terms.[1] The resonance in Bosnia, Croatia and even Serbia was very warm and extensive. The author was inundated by letters of support, reams of additional evidence, revealing videos and invitations to participate in television documentaries. His attention was also drawn to a number of stories from the world of the secret services, some of them exotic, others one fears less so.

In short, there was no wave of public obloquy and head-shaking. To an extent that was both gratifying and disconcerting, it became clear that *Unfinest hour* was battering an open door. With the arrival of the Labour government in 1997, the whole tone and content of British Balkan policy had begun to change. But the interpretative context had changed too. After the success of operations 'Deliberate Force', when NATO air power helped to defeat the Bosnian Serbs in the autumn of 1995, and – eventually – 'Allied Force', when the alliance took on Milosevic in Kosovo, nobody needed to be persuaded of the efficacy of air power. After the Srebrenica massacre and the expulsion of the Albanians from Kosovo, the contours of the Greater Serb project were not in doubt. And, of course, *Unfinest hour* benefitted from the institutional amnesia of the press. As the *Sunday Times* reviewer Alan Judd wrote: 'One thing we can be sure of: the papers and magazines that will rightly praise this book were, almost to an issue, supporters of our Bosnian policy.'[2]

The start of the trial of the Serbian leader Slobodan Milosevic before the International War Crimes Tribunal in The Hague triggered a fresh wave of interest and caused further embarrassment to the British foreign policy establishment.[3] Even a cursory glance at the indictment showed how comprehensively the old paradigm had been discredited. Far from viewing Milosevic as a valid partner in the peace process, the prosecutors sought to establish his 'individual criminal responsibility' on counts of Genocide, Crimes against Humanity and War Crimes. Far from seeing the horrors of Bosnia as the result of haphazard – if asymmetrical – escalation, the prosecutors refer specifically and uniquely to Milosevic's 'participation in a joint criminal enterprise as co-perpetrator'.[4] 'The purpose of this joint criminal enterprise,' point 6 of the indictment continues, 'was the forcible and permanent removal of the majority of non-Serbs, principally Bosnian Muslims and Bosnian Croats, from large areas of the Republic of Bosnia and Herzegovina.' And far from accepting the argument that Bosnia was essentially a civil war, the prosecutors claimed in point 47 of their indictment that: 'At all times relevant to this indictment, a state of international armed conflict and partial occupation existed in Bosnia and Herzegovina.' It would be difficult to find a more comprehensive refutation of all the presuppositions on which British policy between 1992 and 1995 rested.

Of course, the idea that Milosevic's widespread contacts with Western – especially British – elites somehow constitute a defence in law is ludicrous. Even more eccentric is the suggestion that his Western interlocutors should be standing beside him in the dock. Whether, on the strength of the arms embargo, they might plausibly be charged with being accomplices to genocide is a more interesting issue of international law, which the Bosnian government itself briefly explored in 1993; this was not, however, an argument made in *Unfinest hour*. What the book did do was provide a timely reminder of the fact that John Major's government and the EU mediator, Lord Owen, had done all they could to neuter the Tribunal at birth, and to 'coopt' the Serbian leader into the 'peace process'.[5] The result had been perhaps not an explicit deal, but certainly an implicit understanding at Dayton in November 1995 that Milosevic would not be prosecuted. Otherwise Milosevic's cavalier recognition of the Tribunal at Dayton – now rescinded – and his unfulfilled promise to deliver indicted war criminals to The Hague,[6] made no sense. Milosevic must also have felt that his role in winding up the war, and as a legitimate and sought-after interlocutor, had put him in good standing. Milosevic would have been further encouraged by the fact that the former Foreign Secretary, Douglas Hurd, and Pauline Neville-Jones, who had attended Dayton in her capacity as Political Director of the Foreign Office, came to Belgrade a year later in pursuit of a lucrative contract to advise on the privatization of Serbian utilities. It was only in 1998–9 that the penny finally dropped that Milosevic was the principal cause of instability in the Balkans, not part of the solution. To see Milosevic before a British judge, Richard May, and being confronted by a British co-prosecutor, Geoffrey Nice QC, was thus an irony indeed, though a welcome one.

Today, some of the roles of the early 1990s are reversed. Under the new Labour administration, Britain played a crucial role in defeating Milosevic, and remained firm when US President Clinton appeared to wobble; it is American rather than British foot-dragging that now impedes the pursuit of war criminals in Bosnia; and it is Britain that wholeheartedly supports a permanent international criminal court over American objections. Yet without the Americans, there would have been no Tribunal in the first place. Without the Americans, the Bosnian Serbs would never have been defeated in 1995, and without American firepower the international coalition would never have prevailed over Milosevic in Kosovo. To that extent humanitarian intervention and international stability rely on a large degree of – often unilateral – US military assertiveness. An international criminal court which placed American commanders at the mercy of Third Worldist axe-grinders would have killed at birth any US appetite to subdue Milosevic. It is easy to sneer at victors' justice, but without victory there would have been no justice at all.

At the same time, *Unfinest hour* resonated in the post-11 September debate. The book dispelled the notion that the United States was somehow intrinsically anti-Muslim in its foreign policy. It showed that the American government had pursued a courageously pro-Bosnian course in 1992–5, even at the risk of a split in the Western alliance. Tens of thousands of Muslims – Bosniacs and Kosovar Albanians – would now be dead, and a million more still homeless if it had not been for the United States. It also showed how the patronizing view of a world divided between sophisticated Europeans and irresponsibly gung-ho Americans had been prefigured during the Bosnian War. And, of course, events in Afghanistan showed that cooperation between US air power and local proxies could achieve specific political objectives, in this case the defeat of the Taliban. Once again, the assorted pundits had got it wrong. They cheerfully assured us – as they had during the early stages of the Kosovo campaign – that air power and the Americans had had their comeuppence at last. They will never learn.

In other ways, however, the appearance of *Unfinest hour* was inopportune. The general spirit of brotherhood and unity which, quite properly, followed 11 September in Whitehall and Washington was not propitious for a full discussion of recent transatlantic splits. Equally reasonably, the middle of a war involving large-scale deployment of British special forces was not deemed to be the best moment to conduct a searching investigation of the Gorazde crisis. Nor was it, all things considered, a good time to draw attention to a period when a British government – albeit a Conservative one – had willy-nilly abandoned a Muslim-populated state to its fate, and when senior British officers had demonstrated a palpably 'orientalist' mindset. At the same time, *Unfinest hour* discomfited those on the left who lamented the alleged partiality of current US policy in the Middle East; these were sometimes the very same intellectuals and pundits who had criticized the Americans for going to the aid of embattled Muslims in Europe. That the Conservative leadership, which spent the autumn of 2001 putting it about that the Tories were somehow more pro-American and more reliable on defence, showed little interest in the book, needs no further elaboration.

For equally obvious reasons, Douglas Hurd and David Hannay (the former British representative on the United Nations Security Council) did not like the book at all, while the *Economist*, which had followed a relentlessly fake 'realist' line until an embarrassingly late point in the war, was positively scornful. Air Marshal Professor Sir Timothy Garden, who had served as Assistant Chief of the Air Staff for the first six months of the war, was equally unimpressed.[7]

The most sustained and intelligent engagement with the book was undertaken by Sir Ivor Roberts, formerly the British Chargé d'Affaires in Belgrade and a prominent executor of the British government's strategy of engagement with Milosevic.[8] He put the author right on a number of minor points. In particular, Roberts understandably took exception to the sentence that he 'was even reputed [*sic*] once to have fallen asleep in the company of the leader of the Albanian passive resistance in Kosovo, Ibrahim Rugova'. Far from sensing any reserve towards peripheral nationalisms, Roberts writes, Rugova not merely presented him with expensive jewels on the last meeting but also kissed him on the lips; both men remained fully sentient throughout. For the rest, one can only sympathize with Roberts's frustration at being unable to publish his eagerly awaited memoirs, *Conversations with Milosevic*. The author is as keen to learn the inside story of the strategy of engagement with Milosevic as the Foreign Office is to see it buried.

The author has two principal regrets. One is his underestimation of the extent and importance of Croatian expansionism, and especially the role played by the Croatian President, Franjo Tudjman. The other lies in his assessment of the Liberal leader Paddy Ashdown. When all is said and done, Paddy Ashdown did far more than any other party leader to keep Bosnia on the agenda, and his appointment as UN High Representative in Bosnia is to be warmly welcomed. He made no response to the book, but if he had he might reasonably have objected to the lack of generosity with which the author had exposed some of his misconceptions. These remarks had been intended to show just how pervasive the governmental discourse had been, even among those rightly reckoned to have had a 'good war'. The author was also – though this is no excuse – led astray by an anxiety to avoid any suggestion of political partisanship.[9] In the end, Paddy Ashdown, as Tony Blair once told the House of Commons, 'was [largely] right about Bosnia before we were'.

Interestingly, none of the reviewers adverted to *Unfinest hour*'s account of the controversial circumstances surrounding the siege of the UN Safe Area Gorazde in 1994. Here my argument that the UNPROFOR commander General Sir Michael Rose had systematically minimized the threat from Serb forces to the Safe Area in April 1994 was resoundingly vindicated by Gillian Sandford.[10] Through a series of fortunate coincidences she had come into possession of the reports of the SAS observation team that was directly instructing General Rose in Sarajevo by satellite phone. On 10 April, they informed him that 'the situation in Gorazde deteriorated into crisis proportions. There were heavy artillery and tank impacts around the city, which culminated with shells landing in the city centre.' Five days later, after heroic efforts by the Bosnian defenders, the team reported that 'the Bosnian Muslims are abandoning their posts. Given the Serb momentum and Bosnian Muslim lack of ordinance, the Serbs could be in the immediate vicinity in the next couple of hours.' They were reporting from a bank building in the town itself.

Yet after the Serb advance was halted by the very NATO air ultimatum he had resisted for so long, Rose visited Gorazde and publicly accused Major Pat Stogran, the Canadian commander of the United Nations Military Observers (UNMOS), of losing his nerve and sending exaggerated reports from the enclave. In his memoirs Rose wrote that 'the chief UNMO [Stogran] in the bank building had been responsible for some of the inaccurate reporting from Gorazde. I told him that his misleading reports had done damage to the credibility of the United Nations' mission.' In a subsequent interview Rose even went so far as to claim that the secret reports sent by his SAS team were 'completely and utterly different' from those of Stogran. As Gillian Sandford observes, 'these reports have now come to light and they show the SAS agreed with Lt.-Col. Stogran that the town was about to fall'.

As *Unfinest hour* makes clear, there is so much about Rose's behaviour that remains questionable that a proper government inquiry – not merely into Gorazde, but into the whole handling of the Bosnian crisis – remains imperative. We cannot plead the principle of 'unripe time' for ever.

Peterhouse, Cambridge, 1.3.2002

# *Preface*

Between April 1992 and October 1995 a European country was destroyed. Tens of thousands of its inhabitants were murdered. More than a million were expelled, deported, or fled in fear of their lives. An unknown number were raped, humiliated, and traumatized. Bosnians of all ethnic origins – Muslim, Serb, and Croat – both suffered and inflicted suffering, particularly as the war dragged on. The Croatian government of President Franjo Tudjman, and his Croat nationalist henchmen in Bosnia, played an extremely sinister role, even more so than previously expected. But the primary and original transgressors were the Serb radical nationalists led by Radovan Karadzic and General Ratko Mladic, and their sponsors in Belgrade. Unlike the Bosnian government side, which never entirely lost its distinctive multi-ethnic complexion, these Serbs aimed to create an ethnically pure state, from which all trace of its former Muslim heritage had been eradicated. *All* the mosques in Serb-occupied areas were destroyed; the majority of Catholic and Orthodox churches in Bosnian-held territory survived more or less intact. And whereas many Serbs and Croats, particularly in urban areas, loyally supported the Bosnian government throughout the war, virtually all Croats and Muslims were expelled from Serb-held Bosnia. There was no equivalence between the Bosnian government and its Serb nationalist assailants.

The campaign of ethnic cleansing that overwhelmed Bosnia's Muslims, particularly in north-west and north-eastern Bosnia, was not the outcome of a gradual escalation of communal tensions. It was not the by-product of war or civil breakdown. Rather, ethnic cleansing was the *purpose* of the war. Indeed, the most comprehensive and brutal ethnic cleansing – such as that in Banja Luka, Prijedor, Foca, Zvornik, and Bjeljina – took place without any significant fighting at all. Throughout much of 1992 in Bosnia, there was no war, but a massacre, in which a well-armed and organized Serb military establishment pressed home its advantage against largely defenceless civilians.

This massacre was the result of a savage war of secession waged by Serb nationalists against the very federal structures which enabled them to live within the same state. From the mid-1980s, the Serbian leader, Slobodan Milosevic, seeing the global decline of communism, and taking advantage of Albanian nationalist unrest in the province of Kosovo, relegitimated his rule through a new form of national-socialist synthesis. He sought, in fact, to reorganize Yugoslavia as a Greater Serbia. In 1989, Milosevic overturned the old federal constitution by abolishing the autonomy of Kosovo and Vojvodina. The protests of the other constituent republics were met by economic blockades and intimidation. By 1990, both Slovenia and Croatia, disgusted by Belgrade's behaviour, and increasingly themselves in the grip of nationalist fervour, prepared to hold referenda on independence.

The wars of the Yugoslav secession began in farce and ended in tragedy. After the fiasco in Slovenia in June 1991, when the Yugoslav People's Army made a half-hearted attempt to subdue the Slovene territorial defence forces, the focus shifted to Croatia and to a completely new agenda. This war was not about the preservation of Yugoslavia within an equal federation. Slobodan Milosevic was no Balkan Abraham Lincoln. Nor was it primarily about whether all Serbs could remain in one state. It was not even any longer about creating the kind of Serb domination in Bosnia and Croatia which had already been effected in Kosovo and the Vojvodina. Instead, to the Bosnian Serb leadership in Pale – less so to their sponsors in Belgrade – the war was about ensuring that *only* Serbs would live in the new order west of the Drina river which separated Bosnia from Serbia proper.

In the autumn of 1995 this work of destruction was completed by the Dayton peace accord. In practice, Dayton confirmed the partition of Bosnia into three ethnic mini-states. The crucial clauses on the return of refugees have not been implemented to date. The pursuit of indicted war criminals has speeded up, but it is still painfully slow, and the two most notorious individuals, the Bosnian Serb political leader throughout the war, Radovan Karadzic, and his military counterpart,

Ratko Mladic, still remain at large. Bosnia-Herzegovina today remains a profoundly traumatized country, a land damaged to a degree unique in Europe since 1945.

Britain played a particularly disastrous role in the destruction of Bosnia, more so even than France. Her political leaders became afflicted by a particularly disabling form of conservative pessimism which disposed them not only to reject military intervention themselves, but to prevent anybody else, particularly the Americans, from intervening either. A one-sided arms embargo, which unfairly disadvantaged the Bosnian government, was maintained to the bitter end; the use of sustained Nato airpower was resisted for three long years at the United Nations Security Council in New York and the North Atlantic Council in Brussels. At the same time, British statesmen and diplomats seemed to regard a 'strong' Serbia as the best guarantee of peace in the Balkans. British mediators deferred to the Serbs, bullied the Bosnians and did all they could to sabotage US plans for military intervention. The recent claim by Milosevic's lawyers that Lords Hurd, Carrington and Owen gave him a 'green light' thus comes as no surprise.[1]

As we shall see, the Bosnian crisis undermined Britain's international standing and brought the country to the edge of a calamitous transatlantic split. British officers 'on the ground' became mired in a debilitating 'stag fight' with Nato. Throughout this fiasco, British experts routinely and systematically misjudged the fighting power of the Bosnian Serbs. Parliament repeatedly showed itself to be in the grip of harrumphing squires, paranoid Germanophobes and barrack-room historians. And neither the press nor the intelligentsia proved capable of mounting a serious challenge to the prevailing consensus. Indeed, the recent decision by the playwright Harold Pinter to lend his name to the 'International Committee to Defend Slobodan Milosevic' shows that the *trahison des clercs* over Bosnia persists.[2] Yet it would be wrong to seek explanations in conspiracy theories or ethical deficiencies. Britain's response to the Bosnian crisis reflected a failure not so much of morality, as of judgement.

All this matters, because the consequences of failure in Bosnia are still with us today. The roots of the current transatlantic tension over Nato go back to the Franco-British *entente* forged in 1992–5. The senior ranks of the army and the officer corps are still riddled with anti-Americanism. Many in the upper echelons of the Foreign and Commonwealth Office remain profoundly Serbophile and suspicious of the Americans. Indeed, a disconcertingly high number of those interviewed for this study gave a strong impression of having learned nothing from the Bosnian fiasco. In short, the questions thrown up by the Bosnian experience are highly relevant. Unless the collective failure of government, the Foreign Office, the military, and indeed the whole advisory process is satisfactorily confronted, the risk of repetition remains acute.

A number of interesting publications have appeared on the international response to the Bosnian war, but this is the first detailed study of British policy. Like most contemporary history, it is based on an incomplete range of sources. Many of the most important records – such as those of the Foreign Office, the Cabinet Office, and the Ministry of Defence – will remain closed to researchers for the next twenty-five years, perhaps longer. The author has therefore had to rely on memoirs, journal and newspaper articles, and, of course, interviews. He has spoken to hundreds of people in the course of his research, many of whom wished to remain anonymous. A respectable number of the major protagonists were prepared to speak 'on the record', some of them for the first time, and to that extent this study breaks fresh ground empirically. This book, however, is not conceived as a narrative, or a series of revelations, but as an *argument*. Wherever possible, therefore, sources in the contemporary public domain have been used in order to illustrate how much was known and knowable *at the time*.

Inevitably, a book of this length can only scratch the surface. It could not have been written without the kind collaboration of many people. My largest debt is to my wife, Anita Bunyan, whose advice and rigour were essential at every stage of research and writing. I am also extremely grateful to a generation of Cambridge graduate students whose work I have supervised. I thank Alan Mendoza for generously sharing his expertise on American politics and fascinating interview transcripts. I am obliged to Benedikte Petersen for the use of her transcripts on the 'Lessons of Bosnia and Kosovo', mostly as background material. Joseph Pearson was kind enough to let me cite from his fascinating PhD dissertation on British press responses to the outbreak of war in Bosnia, and to comment on various parts of the manuscript. Joel Dowling was extremely generous with his expertise on the British army in Bosnia. Finally, I thank Slobodan Markovic – currently Programme Director at the Belgrade Open School – for sharing his knowledge of Serbian politics under Milosevic and for many introductions. I was not able to speak with as many of the Serb *ancien régime* as I would have liked during my trip to Belgrade: they were feeling shy, and in any case, some of them were wanted elsewhere. It was a far cry from the bad old days of the early 1990s, when they would confidently beard us in Britain with their lies.

Jessica Fugate, an expert on Nato enlargement at the Council for Foreign Relations in Washington, made very useful comments on the sections relating to Nato and the US, so did Kristina Spohr at Nato headquarters. Gillian Sandford kindly put much of her knowledge of the British army in Bosnia at my disposal and saved me from error. Her forthcoming study of the Gorazde enclave in 1994–5, *Wheel of fire*, will surely be definitive. Mary McLaughlin, now of GOAL Ireland, kindly shared some of her experiences as a doctor in Gorazde during the siege of 1994, and read Chapter 5. Calin Trenkov-Wermuth and Gabriel Citron were very capable research assistants when this project was in its infancy.

Many people were kind enough to supply me with unpublished material. Among them were Lord Renwick of Clifton, who let me cite from his forthcoming memoirs, and Sir Reginald Hibbert, who let me have various drafts and memoranda, as did Tim Winter, formerly President of the UK Friends of Bosnia–Herzegovina.

I am grateful to numerous institutions for giving me the chance to present my ideas to various military, political, and academic audiences. A number of senior officers, who wish to remain anonymous, commented on various chapters. I also profited immensely from the advice of Richard Caplan, Quintin Hoare, Lynne Jones, Irina Nikolic, Holly Palubiak, David Simms, Daniel Simms, Andy Olson, Valerie Hughes, Peter Walsh, Lee Bryant and Chris Clark. Miranda Long and Hazel Dunn performed heroic efforts preparing interview transcripts, while Bobbie Elsom uncomplainingly sent messages and fielded calls from all manner of individuals. My colleagues at the Centre for International

Studies at Cambridge, particularly Philip Towle, Paul Cornish, and Marc Weller, made very helpful comments. Neither they, nor anybody else thanked here, is responsible for the argument put forward in this book.

Naturally, I thank all those soldiers, diplomats, and politicians who spoke to me, both on and off the record, particularly those who knew that my approach was likely to be critical. Here I would like to single out Lord Owen, who was generous with his time and courteously answered all my questions.

This book is dedicated to my god-child Sophie Mamaine Carleton Paget, who was much loved during her short life.

# *Abbreviations*

| | |
|---|---|
| CIA | Central Intelligence Agency |
| DIS | Defence Intelligence Staff |
| EU | European Union |
| JNA | Yugoslav People's Army |
| Nato | North Atlantic Treaty Organization |
| OSCE | Organization for Security and Cooperation in Europe (previously CSCE: Conference on Security and Co-operation in Europe) |
| SACEUR | Supreme Allied Commander Europe |
| UN | United Nations |
| UNHCR | United Nations High Commissioner for Refugees |
| UNMO | United Nations Military Observer |
| UNPROFOR | United Nations Protection Force |
| VOPP | Vance–Owen peace plan |
| WEU | Western European Union |

# *Acknowledgements*

The author and publisher would like to thank the following for permission to use copyright material: Victor Gollancz/The Orion Publishing Group Ltd for extracts from David Owen's *Balkan Odyssey*; The Harvill Press for extracts from General Sir Michael Rose's *Fighting for Peace* copyright © The Rose Partnership, 1998; Robert Hale for extracts from Major Vaughan Kent-Payne's *Bosnia Warriors*; HarperCollins for extracts from Milos Stankovic's *Trusted Mole*; Michael Joseph/Penguin UK for extracts from Cameron Spence's *All Necessary Measures* copyright © Cameron Spence, 1998; Little, Brown & Co. (UK) for extracts from Douglas Hurd's *The Search for Peace*, *Collected Stories* and *Ten Minutes to Turn the Devil*.

# Maps

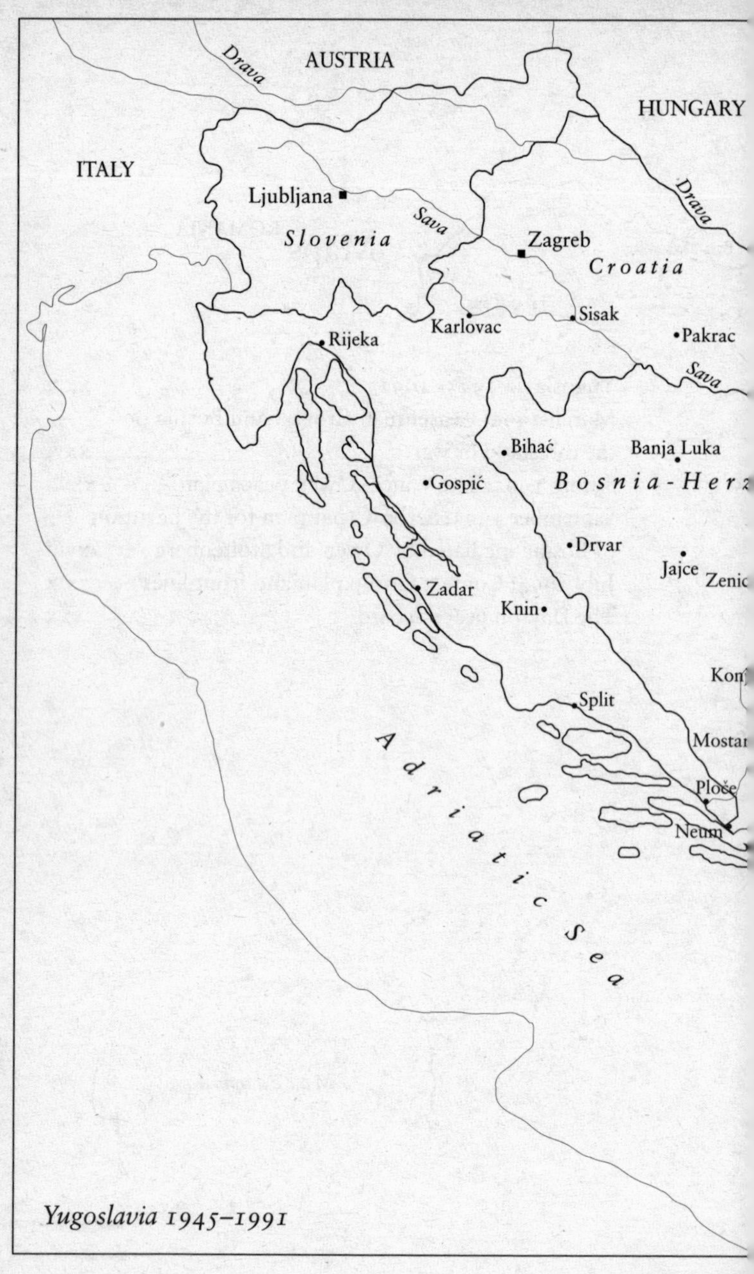


*Yugoslavia 1945–1991*

Source: Laura Silber and Allan Little, *The death of Yugoslavia* (London, 1995)

N
Tisa
Danube
Subotica
ROMANIA
Beli Manastir
Vojvodina
Osijek
Vukovar
Novi Sad
Belgrade
Brčko
Sava
Požarevac
ovina
Tuzla
Morava
Zvornik
Srebrenica
Danube
Serbia
Užice
Sarajevo
Drina
Foča
Niš
Neretva
Montenegro
Dubrovnik
Priština
BULGARIA
Podgorica
Kosovo
Skopje
Bar
ALBANIA
Macedonia
GREECE

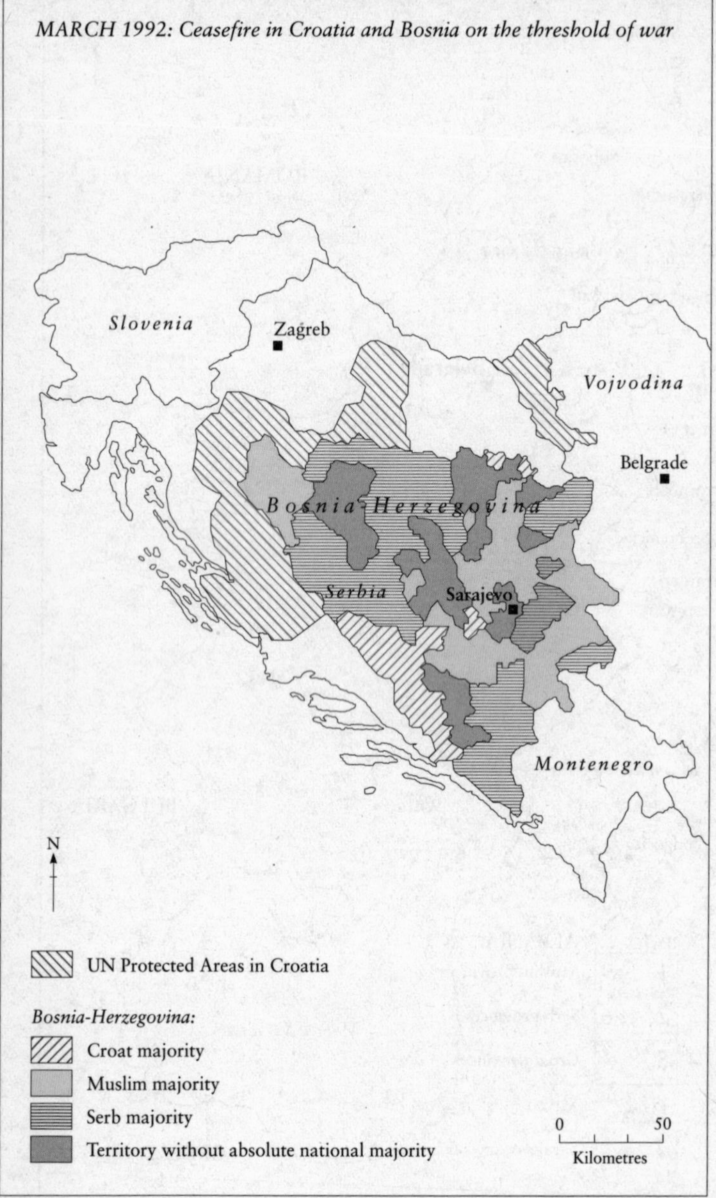
MARCH 1992: Ceasefire in Croatia and Bosnia on the threshold of war
Slovenia
Zagreb
Vojvodina
Belgrade
Bosnia-Herzegovina
Serbia
Sarajevo
Montenegro
N
UN Protected Areas in Croatia
Bosnia-Herzegovina:
Croat majority
Muslim majority
Serb majority
Territory without absolute national majority
0
50
Kilometres

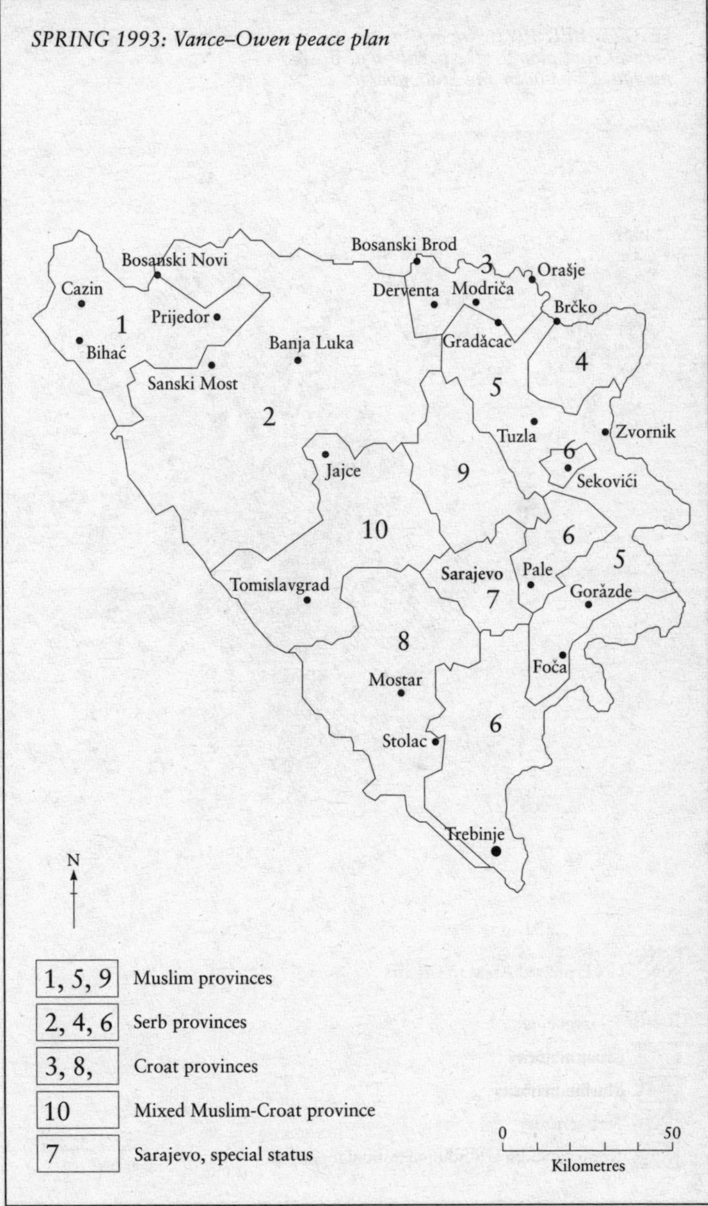
SPRING 1993: Vance–Owen peace plan
Bosanski Brod
Bosanski Novi
Cazin
Orašje
Derventa
Modriča
Prijedor
Brčko
Bihać
Banja Luka
Gradăcac
Sanski Most
Tuzla
Zvornik
Jajce
Sekovići
Sarajevo
Pale
Goražde
Tomislavgrad
Foča
Mostar
Stolac
Trebinje
1
2
3
4
5
6
7
8
9
10
N
1, 5, 9 Muslim provinces
2, 4, 6 Serb provinces
3, 8, Croat provinces
10 Mixed Muslim-Croat province
7 Sarajevo, special status
0
50
Kilometres

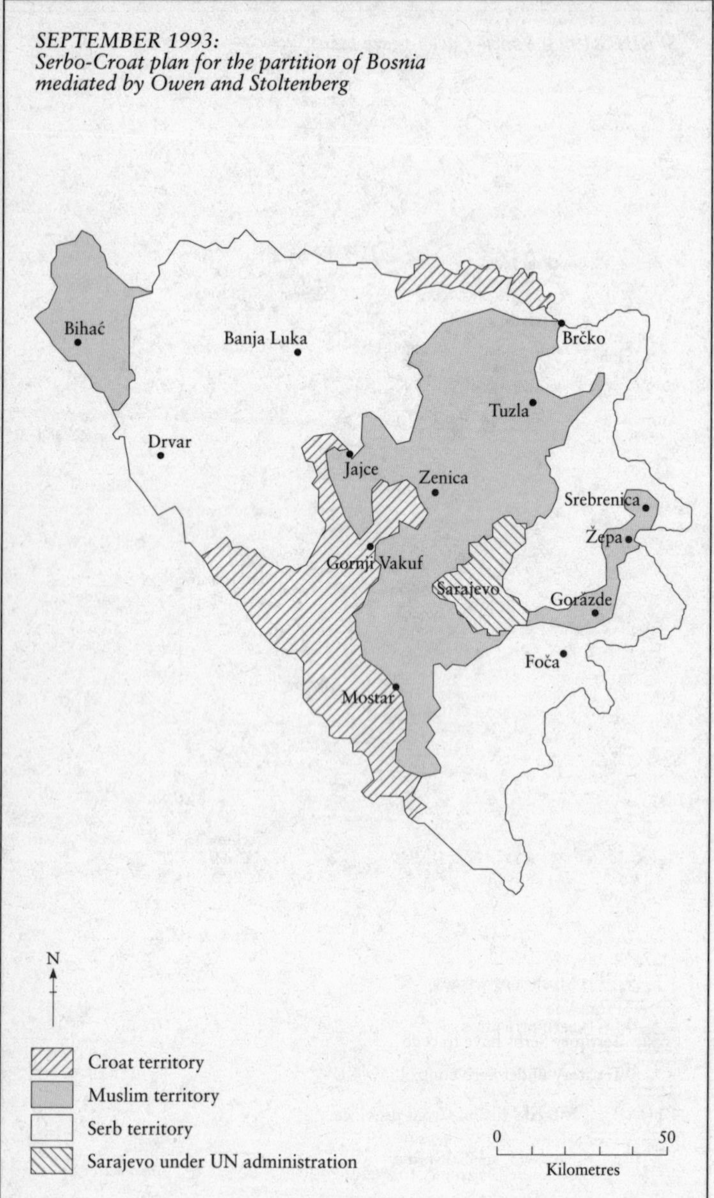
*SEPTEMBER 1993:*
*Serbo-Croat plan for the partition of Bosnia mediated by Owen and Stoltenberg*
Bihać
Banja Luka
Brčko
Tuzla
Drvar
Jajce
Zenica
Srebrenica
Žepa
Gornji Vakuf
Sarajevo
Goražde
Foča
Mostar
N
Croat territory
Muslim territory
Serb territory
Sarajevo under UN administration
0
50
Kilometres

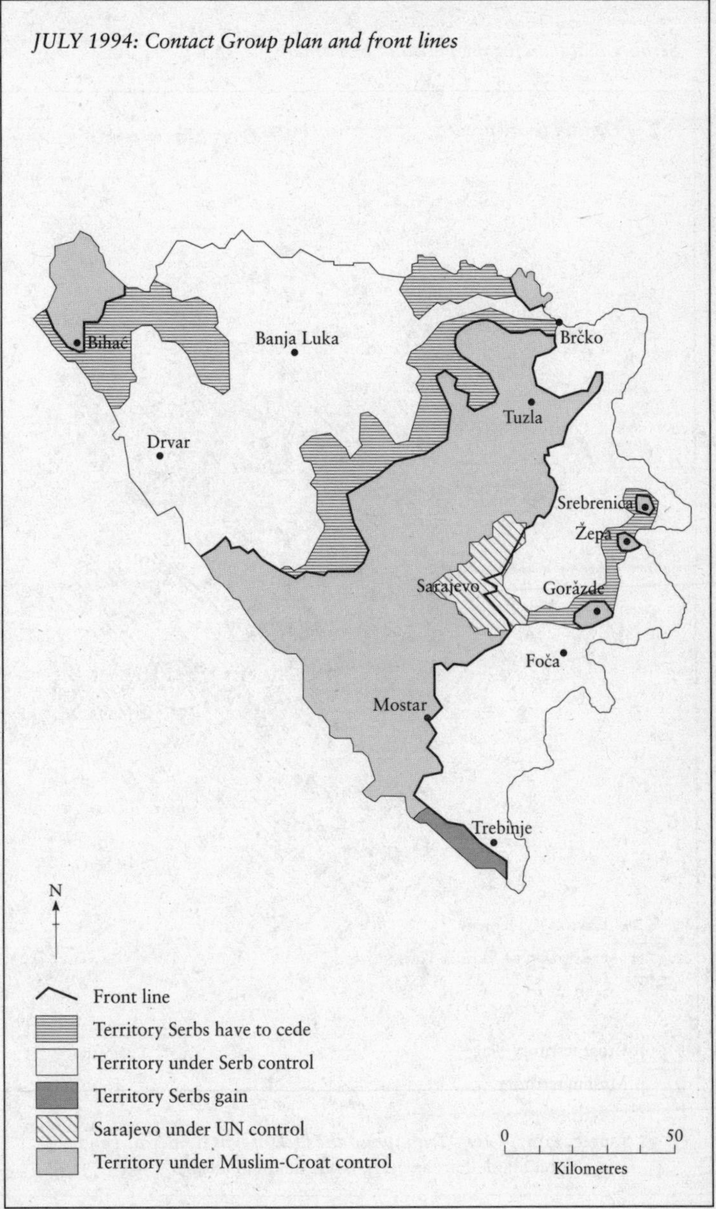
JULY 1994: Contact Group plan and front lines
Bihać
Banja Luka
Brčko
Tuzla
Drvar
Srebrenica
Žepa
Sarajevo
Goražde
Foča
Mostar
Trebinje
N
Front line
Territory Serbs have to cede
Territory under Serb control
Territory Serbs gain
Sarajevo under UN control
Territory under Muslim-Croat control
0
50
Kilometres

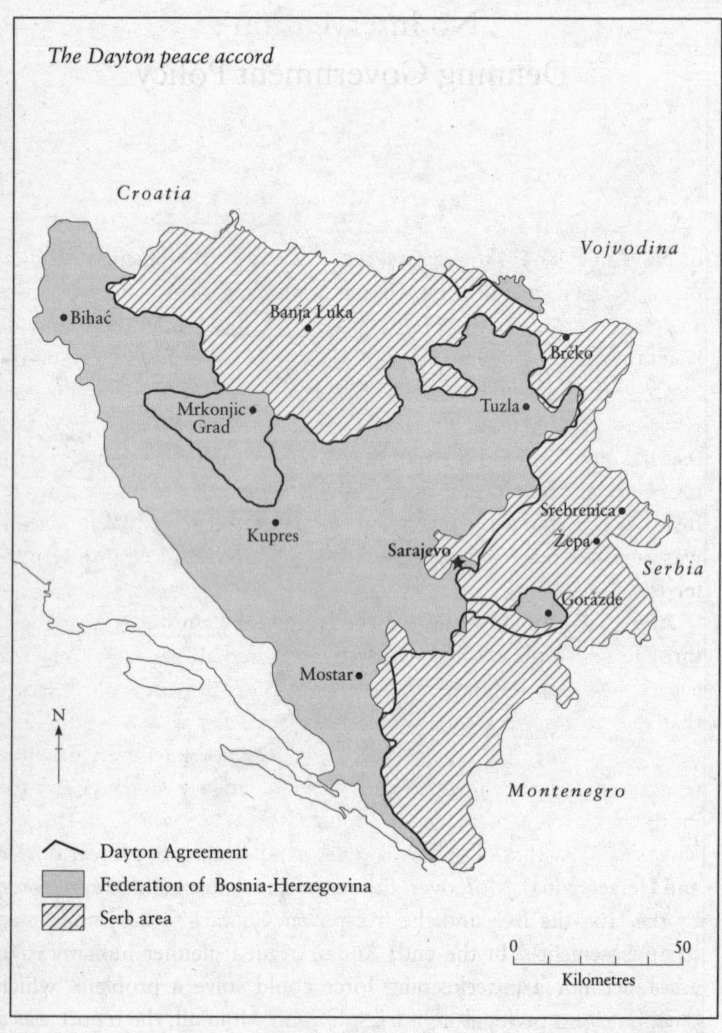


Source: James Gow, *Triumph of the lack of will* (London, 1997)
Note: Shaded areas mark lands held in October 1995

CHAPTER I

# 'No Intervention': Defining Government Policy

In November 1999, four years after the end of the Bosnian conflict, the Secretary General of the United Nations, Kofi Annan, released a 155-page report on the Srebrenica massacre of July 1995 and its background. He made no attempt to disguise either his own responsibility as the former UN Under-Secretary-General for Peacekeeping Operations, or that of the United Nations as a whole.[1] He firmly rejected any notion of blaming the Bosnians for their fate, both with regard to the Srebrenica massacre in particular and the war in general. Instead, he pointed the finger directly at the Serbs and their 'central war aim: to create a geographically contiguous and ethnically pure territory'.

Above all, Annan criticized the 'prism of "amoral equivalency" through which the conflict was seen [by] international observers and actors'.[2] For too long, there had been a 'general tendency to assume that the parties were equally responsible for the transgressions that occurred'.[3] 'The [UN] arms embargo' against the internationally-recognised government of Bosnia-Herzegovina', he noted, 'did little more than freeze in place the military balance within the former Yugoslavia'[4] without honouring 'the attendant duty to protect Bosnia and Herzegovina'. Moreover, the various mediatory efforts sponsored by the UN, the EC, and the five-power Contact Group 'amounted to appeasement'.[5] In the end, Annan argued, neither humanitarian assistance nor a peacekeeping force could solve a problem 'which cried out for a political-military solution'. All in all, the report was a remarkably honest piece of self-criticism which went some way towards correcting the view of the UN as merely a vast system of outdoor relief for Third World elites.

In the summer of 1995, by contrast, the outgoing British Foreign Secretary, Douglas Hurd, commissioned an internal report on the handling of the Bosnian crisis, which has remained strictly confidential ever since. It is easy to see why. Any investigation written with even a modicum of the candour and self-criticism which characterized Annan's report would have exposed the way in which the Foreign Office and British government failed to grasp the essence of the Bosnian conflict. It would show how Britain obstructed efforts to aid Bosnia militarily, and tried to pressure the Bosnian government into an unjust peace. It would show how Britain's international standing, so high in the aftermath of the Gulf War, plummeted across the Atlantic to levels not seen since the Suez crisis. In short, it would show that the Europe which Douglas Hurd bequeathed to his successor in the summer of 1995 was a much less safe place than it had been when the Yugoslav crisis first erupted four years earlier. It was his and Britain's unfinest hour since 1938.

But the men and women who implemented this policy were not tub-thumping isolationists, rabid Eurosceptics, little Englanders, or knee-jerk anti-Americanists. Nor were they simply fools or knaves. It is true, of course, that Serb nationalists sought to influence parliament and the cabinet through the lobbyist Ian Greer; and that they tried to manipulate the Defence Secretary, Malcolm Rifkind, through his Serbophile Personal Private Secretary, Henry Bellingham MP.[6] It is also true that for much of the war the Ministry of Defence was politically exposed to Serb sympathizers including Rifkind's maverick former Thatcherite advisor, David Hart. But there is no evidence that all this had any effect on British policy, which for the most part was conducted by men and women of personal honesty and financial probity. As Lady Olga Maitland, the Conservative MP and defence expert, observed about these lobbyists: 'They knew they had a route to Rifkind. It is not that they instructed Rifkind, but they confirmed his views.'[7] If British statesmen and diplomats clung tenaciously to a policy of non-intervention, it was because they were intellectually convinced, not because they had been bought.

And far from being fools, these men and women were reckoned the best and brightest of their generation. In the Defence Secretary Malcolm Rifkind, for example, the government possessed a man of formidable forensic ability: tragically, the damage he was to inflict on British standing and the Bosnian cause was in direct proportion to his skill in parliament and the international conference chamber. In Douglas Hurd, Britain enjoyed what was routinely described as a 'Rolls-Royce' of a Foreign Secretary.[8] He was a man of 'the right expertise and a proper air of gravitas', he 'cut a civilised figure in an uncivilised world . . . a paragon of Establishment virtues – those virtues inculcated so ineradicably by Eton, Cambridge and the FO itself', he 'exude[d] calm authority'. In short, he had 'what they call "grip"'.[9]

At the outset of the crisis, therefore, few would have disagreed with *The Times'* leader writer's description of Douglas Hurd as a 'foreign secretary whose diplomatic experience and intellect are equal to the task'.[10] What is striking – and ironic in view of Hurd's own quarrel with the press – is the deference with which his handling of the crisis was often reported, at least in the early stages. This shines through the humour of Robert Hardman's 'Commons sketch' of 26 September 1992: 'The Foreign Secretary was in his element delivering a cool overview of the world's battlegrounds. Such was his authority that he did not even pretend that this was a debate . . . There was no point-scoring against the opposition but dry explanations prefaced with knowing phrases like "one must go back several years to understand how . . ." Even Labour MPs found themselves nodding as they grasped each point.'[11] In the same way, Peter Riddell described Hurd's handling of parliamentary questions as the Foreign Secretary 'at his most authoritative, in effect conducting an hour-long seminar to educate the Commons in the difficulties of the various options'.[12]

Nor – as some of their wilder critics alleged – were British policy-makers for the most part in the grip of outlandish prejudices. They were not, in their public pronouncements at least, racists; and their policies were not obviously driven by Islamophobia. Nor did British policy-makers conspicuously share the anti-Catholicism which informed the stance of some intellectuals. Nor – whatever their reservations about the recognition of Slovenia and Croatia – did they nourish any serious fears of German expansionism. No conspiracy theory, in short, explains Britain's peculiarly disastrous policy towards aggression and ethnic cleansing in Bosnia.

British statesmen and diplomats were fully informed of events on the ground and the magnitude of the human rights violations taking place. They knew about the camps and the mass rapes, generally before these outrages became public knowledge. In an unguarded moment Malcolm Rifkind acknowledged that these were the worst crimes in Europe since the Holocaust and the Second World War. Similarly, Douglas Hogg, the Minister of State in the Foreign Office, acknowledged that there were 'clearly close parallels in moral terms between what has happened in Bosnia and what happened in Germany as a result of Nazi policy'.[13] This statement may even – from a purist standpoint – have been something of an exaggeration. In any case, all the information was there: British statesmen simply refused to fit it together and draw the right conclusions. British policy on Bosnia was thus not a failure of information in the conventional sense.

The guilty men of the Bosnian crisis were in no sense isolationist or neutralist. They passionately believed there was a global and European role for Britain. They attached great importance to her permanent seat on the Security Council of the United Nations and the prominent role she played in international organizations. As Douglas Hurd observed on New Year's Day 1992, in a formulation which was later to take on a life of its own: 'In recent years Britain has punched above her weight in the world. We intend to keep it that way.'[14] It was therefore a considerable irony that Britain spent virtually the whole of the Bosnian crisis punching much below her actual weight, and preventing heavierweights from connecting with a vastly overrated adversary. Britain could have been a contender, if only she had wanted to be.

Right from the beginning of the Yugoslav crisis, Britain sought to sabotage any kind of international political – and later military – intervention to curb Serb aggression and ethnic cleansing. In September 1991 it was Britain which decisively opposed the French idea of a Western European Union (WEU) interposition force in Croatia.[15] At the crucial and bad-tempered emergency meeting of EC foreign ministers at The Hague, Douglas Hurd warned his colleagues that the dispatch of such a force would lead Europe into a quagmire without an exit. At the same time, British officials briefed the press that 'there is no peace to keep. It would mean sending in a force to hold the parties apart. Public opinion isn't ready for it yet. It is too drastic.'[16] Instead, Douglas Hurd proposed an oil embargo not merely against

Serbia but on the whole of Yugoslavia, 'to bring the country to its senses'. This puzzled many. 'No-one in Yugoslavia', a senior EU official observed, 'is thinking about their economy. Sanctions would be pointless.'[17] The final declaration of the summit, which stated the common 'understanding that there will be no military intervention',[18] was a triumph for British diplomacy and Hurdian advocacy.

Six months later, in early July 1992, Britain was alone in opposing the idea of armed intervention to safeguard the passage of humanitarian aid in the Bosnian conflict.[19] Then, throughout late 1992 and early 1993, Britain resisted the imposition of a 'no-fly zone' principally directed against the Bosnian Serbs and their Yugoslav backers for as long as it could; thereafter, Britain obstructed the actual implementation of that ban for as long as possible. At the same time, Britain dismissed US plans for aid flights to isolated Bosnian government enclaves as mere gimmicks likely to provoke the Serbs to yet more terrible retaliation which might endanger the whole aid effort.[20] Britain abstained on a UN General Assembly resolution in December 1992 comparing ethnic cleansing to genocide, and opposed a similar motion at a session of the UN Human Rights Commission in 1993.[21] And throughout 1993–5, as we shall see in chapters 2 and 3, Britain was the single most virulent opponent of the American strategy of 'lift and strike', that is, of lifting the arms embargo on the Bosnian government and using massive air strikes to even the odds on the ground.

In short, almost until the very end of the war, Britain worked to wreck any initiative on behalf of the Bosnian government which it regarded as 'rash' or 'unhelpful', particularly those involving a military dimension.[22] In time, large sections of European and American opinion, ranging from the President of the European Commission, Jacques Delors, to the leader of the American Republican Party, Senator Bob Dole, came to identify Britain as the greatest obstacle to collective action on Bosnia. As Tadeusz Mazowiecki, the first democratically elected prime minister of Poland, and UN rapporteur on human rights, observed in May 1993: 'Any time there was a likelihood of effective action, a particular western statesman [Hurd] intervened to prevent it.'[23] The international financier and philanthropist George Soros likewise singled out Britain. 'The British government', he wrote in October 1993, 'has played a particularly insidious role.'[24]

This was certainly the perception of the Bosnians themselves: in December 1992, President Izetbegovic stated that the British were the 'biggest brake on any progress'.[25] In December 1994, as the Serb attack on the 'safe area' of Bihac was raging, the Bosnian Information Centre in London noted how 'Through its leading position in the UN peace process, the UNPROFOR mission, NATO and the UN Security Council, Britain has sought to contain Bosnian resistance to aggression and has proved eager to draw up new ethnic partition maps every time rebel Serb forces render the previous "peace plan" obsolete by occupying more Bosnian territory.' Dr Mirko Pejanovic, a visiting member of the Bosnian presidency and leader of the Serb Civic Council, which represented Serbs loyal to the Bosnian government, was told by British officials that they hoped the fall of Bihac would inject a note of 'realism' into the position of the Bosnian government.[26] And very shortly afterwards, President Izetbegovic told the summit of the Conference on Security and Cooperation in Europe (CSCE) at Budapest that 'Paris and London have from the very beginning taken the role of Serbia's protectors; they have blocked the Security Council and Nato and prevented all attempts at stopping Serbia's aggressive war'.

Indeed, so frustrated were the Bosnians with British policy and with her vigorous maintenance of the arms embargo against the legitimate government in Sarajevo, that they threatened to charge Britain before the International Court of Justice as an accomplice to genocide. A letter to that effect was sent to the Security Council in late November 1993.[27] 'This is not something we have come up with overnight,' Sulejman Suljic, the Undersecretary at the Bosnian Foreign Ministry, commented, 'We have been thinking about it for a very long time . . . It's a question of whether the British government is willing to accept its responsibilities under the UN charter's clauses against genocide.' However understandable, this was an ill-judged move, which had little chance of success in the climate of the time. Inevitably, the Bosnians were accused of 'biting the hand that fed them'.[28]

The key to understanding the foreign policy of the British government of the early 1990s in general, and its stance towards Bosnia in particular, lies in the profoundly conservative philosophical realism of its practitioners. James Rubin, who dealt with many British diplomats and statesmen throughout the Bosnian crisis, and who subsequently became US Assistant Secretary of State, saw them as 'hyper-realists' of 'the traditional British kind'.[29] This found its starkest expression in the rhetoric of Malcolm Rifkind, Defence Secretary for most of the conflict, whose very first speech on becoming Foreign Secretary in the summer of 1995 embraced Palmerston's dictum that 'the furtherance of British interests ought to be the sole object of a British foreign secretary'.[30] What distinguished this view from the more 'Gladstonian' universalism of Margaret Thatcher and the 'Wilsonianism' of many Americans was a deep scepticism about the viability – even the desirability – of the 'New World Order' proclaimed by President Bush in 1990, and Britain's role in it. 'Britain has every interest in and commitment to greater regional and global security,' Douglas Hurd argued in July 1993. 'This is a matter of building, brick by brick, not pretending that a great structure of a new world order already exists.'[31] 'We do not have a new world order,' he repeated in April 1994. 'We have a traditional set of world disorders and we are trying, case by case and institution by institution, to equip ourselves to deal more adequately with those disorders.'[32] Indeed, the Foreign Secretary provocatively stated, 'there is no such thing as "the international community"'.[33] The echo of Margaret Thatcher, who had famously denied that there was such a thing as 'society', was surely intentional.

Underlying this was an acute sense of the limitations of British power. 'The UK,' Malcolm Rifkind argued, 'is [only] a medium sized power.' 'I do not believe,' Douglas Hurd told the House of Commons in mid-July 1993, 'and have never used rhetoric that would lead anyone to believe, that it was part of Britain's interests to pretend that we could sort out every man-made disaster in the world, of which there are many at the moment . . . It is in our interest to do our bit, but we should not over-pretend, or let rhetoric get in the way of reality.'[34] Two months later he picked up on this theme in an address to the United Nations in New York: 'It is empty to pretend that we can impose peace with justice on every disorder or dispute outside our national borders.'[35] The net result of all this, as Douglas Hurd told the Royal Institute of International Affairs, was that 'We shall probably have to say "no" more often than "yes".'[36]

This stance could only be reinforced by the systematic reduction of military expenditure to cash in on the 'peace dividend' after the end of the Cold War. Indeed, the onset of the wars of the Yugoslav secession came at precisely the moment that the government was engaged in 'Options for Change', a wide-ranging defence review of British resources and potential commitments in the coming decade. Full-scale military intervention against the Bosnian Serbs would clearly mean halting or even reversing such cuts. Whether the Major administration used the defence cuts to deflect demands for intervention, or the other way around, is unclear;[37] more recently, Ministry of Defence (MoD) officials were not willing to comment on this link. It is certainly remarkable that a senior MoD official, Bill Reeves, was prepared to go on record at the time – a sure sign of political approval – with the argument that even the dispatch of peacekeeping forces, let alone peace-making forces, to Yugoslavia would mean either the end to Options for Change or the reduction of other global commitments.[38] In any case, after some hesitation, the government decided that the defence review should go ahead. Thus the Leader of the House of Commons, Tony Newton, reiterated the need to 'achieve balanced and well-considered reductions in the armed forces'. However, he assured the House that 'Of course, there is no question of anybody becoming redundant while in Bosnia.'[39] What this meant, it transpired, was that they would not be sacked in Bosnia but remain in the Queen's uniform until they had completed their tour. After all, Newton pointed out, 'It would be much more unfair to leave troops serving in Bosnia in a state of continuing uncertainty when the position is being clarified elsewhere.'[40] This was, as some opposition figures hinted, a case of bringing the boys home and putting them on the dole.

Yet it was not simply a matter of what Britain could do, it was also a question of what she *should* do. The notion that Britain should support the imposition of universal values for their own sake provoked a kind of conservative anti-imperialism in Douglas Hurd. 'At first sight,' he warned an audience of young Conservatives at the beginning of the war, 'the concept of benevolent international interventionism might be attractive. But we should not wander down the new road without serious thought.'[41] 'We have no right, power or appetite,' he told the European Parliament in July 1992, 'to establish protectorates in Eastern Europe in the name of a European Order. We must not exaggerate our power to remove those agonies.'[42] Almost exactly a year later he elaborated on this theme to the Carlton Club Political Committee: 'We must not promise more than we can deliver . . . We must not let rhetoric run ahead of reality in this new [post-Cold War] world. Nato is not a world policeman. It is certainly not an army of crusaders marching forward to separate combatants by force or to plant the flag of conquest [sic] on foreign soil . . . Nato cannot be expected to solve all the problems on its borders, and it must not be blamed for failing to do so . . . A new world order does not exist. It can only be built painfully.'[43] In late December 1994, he described the task of imposing by massive ground force an 'imperial role . . . The legions might have had to stay for years.'[44]

It is no accident that the formative years of many British protagonists – certainly those of Douglas Hurd (born 1930) himself – were in the shadow of the Suez débâcle and the American predicament in Vietnam. In the first case, they were scarred by the fallout from a futile grand gesture which exceeded the capabilities of British power and led the country into conflict with her closest ally, the United States. Vietnam, on the other hand, showed the costs of an ideological crusade confronted with local realities. Over Bosnia, the fear was that the pressure for intervention would give way to domestic unrest as the body bags came home. Much better and more humane, the argument went, to recognize the limits of British power and those of the international community as a whole, to help where one could, but to dash any hopes on the part of the Bosnians that Britain might support the imposition of peace with justice.

But, of course, the cautionary tale which instantly sprang to mind was that of Northern Ireland. Such comparisons had a long pedigree in Britain. During the Eastern Crisis of 1876–8, the Prime Minister, Benjamin Disraeli, had observed: 'fancy autonomy for Bosnia with a mixed population, autonomy for Ireland would be less absurd'. The link between Disraeli and the conservative pessimism of Hurd and Rifkind is obvious, and would probably be acknowledged. Throughout the early stages of the Yugoslav wars in 1991–2, British statesmen and diplomats repeatedly invoked the lessons of the Northern Irish 'Troubles', where British troops had found themselves attacked by the very people they had been deployed to protect: the Catholics. Thus

Douglas Hurd told the emergency EC meeting at The Hague in September 1991 that 'We have experience of fighting from village to village and street to street. We have been in Northern Ireland for 22 years.'[45] Two years later he claimed that 'The only thing which would have guaranteed peace with justice would have been an expeditionary force, creating if you like a new Northern Ireland, being there for how many years?'[46]

The Foreign Secretary developed this analogy further after the conflict was over. In a seminar on the 'Lessons of Bosnia', held in 1996, he stated that the 'parallel with Carson and the passing of the Home Rule Bill in 1911–14 . . . is the nearest that I have come up with'.[47] Here the Foreign Secretary was referring to the campaign by Irish Unionists, concentrated in Ulster, to dissociate themselves from the scheme for limited Irish self-government based in Dublin, much in the same way as West Virginia had remained within the Union after Virginia had seceded at the start of the American Civil War. 'I believe,' Hurd explains, 'the essence of the conflict was the unwillingness of the Bosnian Serbs . . . to live within a country called Bosnia with a non-Serb majority, separated from Serbia.'[48] Two years later, in *The search for peace*, Douglas Hurd returned to this theme. 'The parallels with Ireland are worth a closer glance,' he wrote. 'During the years of turmoil in Bosnia I was often reminded of a big sheet which used to hang in my office in Stormont Castle when I was Secretary of State for Northern Ireland in 1984–1985. It was a street plan of the city of Belfast mapped out in a confusion of Orange and Green. It looked like one of those modern paintings which consist of two pots of paint thrown at a canvas . . . No redrawing of the map would produce a neat line combining geography and politics, with each community living in tribal purity within its own boundaries.'[49] This parallel was disquieting, for it suggested that four years on the Foreign Secretary had still not understood the difference between secession – or a secession within a secession – and a campaign of ethnic cleansing designed to create an ethnically pure Greater Serbia. The Bosnian Serbs were no Carsons, they were not Balkan West Virginians committed to the maintenance of the Union, and Slobodan Milosevic was no Lincoln.

Comparisons with the recent conflict in the Gulf and the Falklands, on the other hand, were firmly rejected. As Douglas Hurd told the

Commons in mid-April 1993, 'The aggression of Iraq against Kuwait was a simple act of aggression by one sovereign state against another. In Bosnia, we have a war in which the overwhelming majority of those fighting are Bosnians – Bosnian Serbs, Bosnian Croats and Bosnian Muslims . . . the position is different from that which produced Desert Storm.'[50] Hurd stuck to this view even after the war ended. 'The parallel with Bosnia will not wash . . . the source of that crisis was not foreign aggression but the unwillingness or inability of the different communities inside Bosnia to live together.'[51] This theme was echoed by Malcolm Rifkind when he told the House of Commons that 'The crucial point to be borne in mind is that because the vast majority of those taking part in the actual fighting are Bosnian Serbs, Bosnian Muslims and Bosnian Croats – until a year ago, they were living in the same villages, streets and communities – we cannot treat this in exactly the same way as an invasion of one country by another. That is why the parallels sometimes drawn with the Gulf or the Falklands, with respect to military intervention, are utterly wrong . . . no Bosnian Serb, Muslim or Croat can be expelled from Bosnia by a United Nations Army or other forces.'[52]

Besides, at a very early stage of the crisis, the British government came to the view that the Yugoslav crisis was *sui generis*, and not symptomatic of an imminent general post-communist or nationalist explosion across eastern Europe. 'Although there are possible areas where it could spill over,' the Foreign Office Minister Douglas Hogg told the House Foreign Affairs Committee in November 1991, at the height of the siege of the Croatian town of Vukovar, 'we do not think it will. We think it will be contained within the frontiers of Yugoslavia.' Indeed, he added somewhat priggishly, the events of the past six months might serve *pour encourager les autres*, particularly Czechs and Slovak separatists: 'that is where the example of Yugoslavia has worked towards stability'.[53] In short, the more painful the separation, the more obvious the deterrent value.

Underlying this was a deeply 'realist' hostility towards fragmentation in the international state system. The British were unwilling to 'roll with the punch' and accept the creation of new sovereign entities in Europe.[54] As Douglas Hogg stated in November 1991, 'We have an enormously strong presumption in favour of existing boundaries . . .

We have an interest in boundaries not being disturbed save by agreement.'[55] Even after Bosnia was internationally recognized, Britain refused to set up an embassy in Sarajevo for almost two years. This fed suspicions of governmental Serbophilia. 'Ministers don't say so in public,' one journalist observed at the height of the conflict, 'but the fundamental British view remains that only a strong Serbia can ultimately guarantee security in the Balkans.'[56] This was certainly the view of the EU mediator, Lord Carrington, who as a former Foreign Secretary and Nato Secretary General was a pillar of the British political establishment. The British, he recently admitted, were 'to some extent' pro-Serb for historical reasons, and remained so for pragmatic ones: 'The point was that Serbia, being infinitely the biggest of the republics, was clearly the most important, and unless you somehow managed to keep Serbia onside, there wasn't very much chance of getting an agreement.'[57]

Perhaps the most striking and inexplicable illustration of the tendentially pro-Serb confusion reigning in the Foreign Office is the Diplomatic List for 1993, which lists a British embassy in Serbia, rather than Yugoslavia.[58] The chronological listing at the back refers to the embassy in 'Yugoslavia, now see Serbia'. Indeed, Sir Peter Hall, the former ambassador to Belgrade, is still featured in the *List* for 2000 as the ambassador to 'Serbia' in 1992.[59] This is very odd, because, of course, no country by the name of Serbia actually existed, even by its own lights, though Serb nationalists often talked of the need to carve a 'Greater Serbia' out of the ruins of the old Yugoslavia. Nor were there embassies listed in the other constituent parts of the rump Yugoslavia, such as Montenegro. Despite a formal enquiry, I have not been able to obtain a satisfactory answer as to how this embassy in Serbia – which mysteriously vanished a year later – came about.[60] The informal suggestion that we are dealing with an administrative error is hardly persuasive. The former Chargé to Yugoslavia, Ivor Roberts, speculated that 'the administration officer in 1992 . . . may well have said, "Well as these other places have left, we'd better rename it on the list as Serbia" . . . that wouldn't have been a policy decision taken by anyone'.[61] Nor was the Foreign Secretary able to shed any light on this extraordinary lapse.[62] We are left with the curious fact that in 1993 Britain enjoyed diplomatic relations with a country that did not exist, but did not maintain an embassy in a country – Bosnia and Herzegovina – which did exist.

There was certainly an initial determination to keep Yugoslavia together even after its essentially Serbocentric and repressive character had become obvious. 'I believe,' Mark Lennox-Boyd, the Parliamentary Undersecretary for Foreign and Commonwealth Affairs, told the Commons in late June 1991, 'that the Slovene and Croat leaderships should seek their future in the framework of a single reformed Yugoslav state based on consent . . . We and our western partners have a clear preference for the continuation of a single Yugoslav political entity.' He deplored the use of force, but added that 'the Yugoslav Federal army might have, under the constitution, a role in restoring order if there were widespread civil unrest'.[63] These unfortunate words were spoken without sinister intent, but they could reasonably be interpreted as a 'green light' for the JNA to suppress Croat and Slovene independence. In practice, as Sir Reginald Hibbert, a former ambassador to Paris who fought with Special Operations Executive (SOE) in the Balkans, pointed out, the policy of 'holding together' Yugoslavia inevitably 'favoured the Serbs, because the Serbs too insisted that Yugoslavia should remain united'.[64]

As one might expect, the contemporary Bosnian problem was seen through the prism of the old 'Eastern Question', which every English schoolboy used to know about. This was not just – as we shall see later – a matter of the obvious comparisons between Gladstone's preoccupation with the Turkish atrocities in Bulgaria in 1876 and the public agitation for intervention in Bosnia. It was also about the neuralgic associations which the words 'Sarajevo' and 'Bosnia' formed for generations of diplomats and statesmen schooled to believe that the First World War had been triggered by an obscure Balkan spat. 'I believe,' Douglas Hurd observed, 'the history of this century, and I am reading the life of Sir Edward Grey at the present time, shows what happens if you go down this line of the European Community having their clients and their favourites and supporting them financially and in other ways and this ends up in ruins. That, I think, was the story of the Balkans before the First World War.'[65] When the chairman of the Foreign Affairs Committee, David Howell, expressed the hope that 'there is no analogy between Sir Edward Grey's experience of the

Balkan instability in 1914 and your own', Hurd responded: 'We are trying to avoid it.'

What this meant was that British preoccupation was with international unity on policy towards Bosnia, rather than the content of that policy. Hurd admitted as much in an article penned at the height of the war: 'We have at each stage of the Yugoslav crisis agreed on what we should do – that is, we Europeans have avoided the disastrous rivalries of western powers in the Balkans which caused such harm in the first years of this century.' Even if the problem remained unsolved, that should be reckoned a success. 'The decision to end the war,' he added lamely, 'will be taken by those doing the fighting.'[66] The upshot was a flat denial that any British national interest was at stake in Bosnia. As Douglas Hurd subsequently wrote in *The search for peace* (1998): 'On any calculation of national interest, the Gulf War was more important for Britain than Bosnia . . . Bosnia was intellectually and ethically tangled.'[67] 'By the test of the narrow national interest,' he elaborated further, 'Bosnia could not rate high for the British. No one sitting down calmly in Whitehall to assess where in Britain's interests we should deploy British troops or focus British economic aid would have picked Bosnia as a recipient. There was a British interest in preventing a general Balkan War, a substantial quarrel between the west and Yeltsin's reforming Russia, or a serious rift within NATO or within the EU . . . But they were consequent, not central to Bosnia itself . . . The instinct of the realist was stay out.'[68] The notion that a manifest inability to deal with aggression and ethnic cleansing in an area firmly within the British sphere of influence might be a severe blow to British national interests was apparently unrealistic.

This policy of non-intervention should not be interpreted as mere callous insouciance on the part of its protagonists. With a few exceptions, British statesmen and diplomats were not brazen Machiavellians who delighted in what was to become an increasingly casuistic and untenable position. On the contrary, they were vexed and tortured by the problem. As one observer remarked at the time, Bosnia would be engraved on Douglas Hurd's tombstone; another witness, who was particularly close to the Foreign Secretary during the second half of the war, described him as being obsessed to the point of paralysis with Bosnia. This was most obviously reflected in his fiction, which Hurd encouraged readers to regard as a sort of surrogate memoir. 'I shan't produce my memoirs early,' he told an interviewer in July 1993. 'Yes, I keep a diary but not in a form which anyone could conceivably publish. I'll put it all into fiction meanwhile.'[69] 'The novelist,' he recently wrote in the introduction to a collection of short stories, 'can use the imagination to press home a point or argue passionately for a particular outcome. Or (more relevant in my case) he can point to a predicament of human behaviour without being compelled, as a politician or leader writer is, to point a dogmatic way out of that predicament.'[70] His fiction is not really self-critical in intent – 'penance' in Hurd's own words – but self-exculpatory. But it is, none the less, self-revealing.

The reader of 'Ten minutes to turn the devil', a short story penned in January 1993, at the height of the Bosnian war, will be struck by the undercurrent of self-doubt and moral quandary. The plot centres on Richard Smethwick, Defence Secretary after a spell in Northern Ireland, and his speech to the Conservative Party Conference at Brighton. The event is taking place against the background of the savage civil war in Caucasia, which a couple of years ago had been seen merely as 'a dispute between unimportant and unpronounceable politicians thousands of miles away'.[71] Now, however, it was the subject of a large-scale British humanitarian intervention, and the mounting casualties had fuelled an anti-war movement of TON, 'Troops out now'. When Smethwick/Hurd runs the gauntlet of protesters, he speculates that 'the owners of those twisted faces might well last Christmas have been among those shouting for intervention in Caucasia'.[72] This was a reference surely to Walpole's famous comment on the public agitation for war with Spain in 1739: 'They are ringing the bells now, but soon they will be wringing their hands.'

Beset on all sides for allowing soldiers to be killed in this tangled conflict, Smethwick/Hurd sets aside most of his speech, eschews all partisan reference to the opposition, and launches a passionate defence of the policy of intervention: 'He was not going to talk about expenditure and cost effectiveness, because all the money, all the efficiency in the world could not make up for a lack of will.'[73] But he 'believed that the heart of the party and the heart of the country were sound. We had not lost our courage, we were still prepared to work for a more decent world.' Even if the British serviceman was not directly engaged in the defence of the realm, 'He was doing something new, something in a way more daring and ambitious. He was joining with others in an attempt to deal with wickedness and cruelty, to establish decency and order, not just where the Union Jack flew but throughout the world . . . The question was whether Britain should join in the attempt or leave it to others. Were we interested in the new chapter, or simply in thumbing endlessly through the old chapters, constantly recalling the past while others shaped the future?'[74] This enunciation of the 'doctrine of international community', which was later to underpin Tony Blair's successful intervention in Kosovo, carries the debate and the vote. It is the speech Douglas Hurd himself never made.

Throughout the formative early stages of the war, the Prime Minister was largely eclipsed, and was to remain so (with some exceptions, notably the hostage crisis of 1995), throughout the war. At first sight, this may seem surprising, as it was John Major who had taken the lead on the question of the Kurds against Saddam Hussein. The tidy mind of Douglas Hogg had to accept in November 1991 that, somewhat contrary to current government rhetoric, the case of Iraq showed 'a willingness to deploy, to intervene in the internal affairs of nations where major humanitarian issues have been brought into play'.[75] Indeed, throughout 1992, as Bosnia was torn apart by Serb aggression, and Britain fought to delay the imposition of a no-fly zone, Major continued to breathe fire against Iraq. 'We will instruct the Iraqis not to fly in that area,' he announced in August 1992. 'If they do, they will be perfectly well aware we are likely to attack.' When asked what would happen if the Iraqis resisted, John Major responded, 'We have seen in the past that they will lose.'[76] And in early 1993, almost as if to taunt the citizens of Sarajevo, British and American aircraft launched a round of air strikes against Iraq.

This belligerence was not repeated in Bosnia. In fact, the Gulf aside, John Major was profoundly diffident about his handling of international affairs. 'Of all the roles in government,' he later wrote about his elevation to Foreign Secretary in July 1989, 'the Foreign Office . . . was the one for which I was least prepared.'[77] And being, as he candidly admitted, a 'relative novice in foreign affairs', he wrote that he was 'fortunate in . . . having Douglas Hurd . . . and Malcolm Rifkind' to guide him as Prime Minister.[78] During late 1991 and early 1992, this deference, and Major's own confusion, was palpable. 'The conflict in Bosnia,' he wrote in his autobiography, 'crept up on us while our attention was on the turmoil in the Soviet Union, and took us almost unawares . . . Its roots were bewildering.'[79] Nor did it help that the cabinet was profoundly divided about the wisdom of military engagement, with the President of the Board of Trade, Michael Heseltine, the Social Security Secretary, Peter Lilley, the Scottish Secretary, Ian Lang, and the Chancellor of the Exchequer, Kenneth Clarke, opposed to further involvement.[80] The division, it should be stressed, was between those who favoured a limited humanitarian operation and those who wanted to stay out altogether; there was no voice raised on behalf of military intervention, however limited, in favour of the Bosnian government.

In order to justify and sustain such a policy of non-intervention, the government fell back on a series of palliative diplomatic and rhetorical strategies. The first was to sponsor the search for an agreed settlement conducted by the EC negotiator, the former Foreign Secretary and Secretary General of Nato, Lord Carrington. As the mediator of the Lancaster House agreement which brought Zimbabwe into being, he was a man of proven experience; but his grasp of the real dynamics of the Yugoslav situation proved slender. Carrington's strategy hinged on a flawed presumption and a flawed tactic. From the outset he held all sides to be more or less equally responsible for the violence. They were, he subsequently claimed, 'all impossible people . . . all as bad as each other, and there are just *more* Serbs'. Indeed, he felt that the war in Croatia was 'really Tudjman's fault', for declaring independence without adequate guarantees for the Serb population.[81]

The specific premeditated quality of Serb ethnic cleansing, and Belgrade's responsibility for it, entirely passed Carrington by. In September 1991 he merely noted that 'It does depend on the will of the people concerned as to whether they want to find a solution.'[82] Later he was to speak of the 'gross over-reaction' of the JNA, and a pattern of 'provocation, or perceived provocation, followed by massive Serbian retaliation'.[83] At the same time, Carrington sought to use the recognition of Croatia and Slovenia as a bargaining counter with which to agree an overall settlement. 'The position of the European Community,' he stated in October 1991, at the height of the siege of Dubrovnik, 'has been that nobody is going to recognise the independence and sovereignty of any of the republics until there is a solution to the whole problem.'[84] He was therefore highly critical of the German decision to push the recognition of Slovenia and Croatia through the EC in December 1991. 'As a result of that December decision,' he subsequently claimed, 'the original concept of the Peace Conference had unravelled and we had no real leverage.' Later, others were to argue that recognition precipitated the outbreak of war in Bosnia-Herzegovina, and that there was at least an 'informal understanding' between Britain and Germany to trade recognition for British 'opt-outs' at Maastricht.[85]

This was palpable nonsense. It was not true that Germany had precipitated the war in Bosnia by forcing through the recognition of Slovenia and Croatia as part of a broader hegemonic design. Throughout the early stages of the crisis, in fact, most German politicians and commentators had argued strongly *against* the break-up of the federation; the German Foreign Minister, Hans-Dietrich Genscher, did so at the CSCE summit in Berlin only five days before the outbreak of hostilities.[86] This should come as no surprise: the essentially post-nationalist German elite saw no need to create new divisions at a time when 'the walls were coming down and Europe was uniting'. All that Germany did was to react rather more quickly and sharply to Yugoslavia's manifest destruction by Greater Serb nationalists than some other European powers. Interestingly, the Foreign Secretary himself showed some understanding for the German position. 'Germany,' he noted in January 1992, 'held back for a considerable time', and had been as castigated for its passivity in the Gulf as for its present activism.[87]

Nor is it true that recognition wrecked Lord Carrington's attempts to broker an overall solution. In fact, Carrington had already presented his 'take it or leave it' plan – which guaranteed 'special status' to all minorities – to the six republican leaders at The Hague in mid-October 1991. This was accepted by all involved, *except Slobodan Milosevic*,[88] who rejected the notion of ceding the same rights to minorities within Serbia that he claimed for Serbs elsewhere. If proof was needed that the war was not about legitimate Serb concerns, but about ethnic cleansing and annexation, this was it. Why the Serbs – whom Carrington himself and the Foreign Office identified as the principal obstacle to the 'draft convention for an overall settlement'[89] – would feel pressured if the international community withheld recognition *from Croatia*, he did not explain. Indeed, he admitted himself that once the peace conference reconvened in January 1992 after recognition had been announced, the Serbian attitude became 'more constructive'.[90]

The policy of withholding recognition, in fact, only made sense as a strategy of bludgeoning the weaker side, the Croats, into territorial concessions. Douglas Hogg revealingly stated in November 1991, as Croatia was under incessant attack, that 'If the parties wanted to make adjustments to frontiers, by your prior recognition you actually have an obstacle in the way of that.'[91] Translated, this meant that the Croatians might be able to buy an agreed independence package by shedding a few feathers, for it was clear from the existing military balance, which the arms embargo could only perpetuate, that any 'frontier adjustments' would be entirely one-sided.

The simple truth is that Bosnian Serb extremists – supported by Belgrade – were driven by a murderous dynamic of their own. Already in September 1991, the US Secretary of State, James Baker, no alarmist when it came to Yugoslavia, had warned the United Nations Security Council of aggressive preparations by the Bosnian Serbs.[92] While the Bosnian government was still genuinely trying to work out a new Yugoslav federal framework in 1991, the Bosnian Serbs were already setting up their own – illegal – autonomous regions, stockpiling arms and drawing up lists of Muslim community leaders for murder or deportation. The very most that can be said is that the German move influenced the timing of a genocide, which was long planned and which not negotiation but only resolute pre-emptive military intervention, could have forestalled.

Carrington proved no more successful in understanding or resolving the war in Bosnia. Once again, Carrington made his generalized disdain for all the 'parties' clear; he resolutely refused to make any distinction between the underlying dynamic towards a Greater Serbia, Bosnian self-defence, and Croat separatist opportunism. This was reflected in his memorable comment right at the outset of the war in late April 1992: 'Everybody is to blame for what is happening in Bosnia and

Hercegovina and, as soon as we get the ceasefire, there will be no need to blame anybody.'[93] Three months later, at the height of the initial phase of Serb aggression in the summer of 1992, Carrington was still speaking even-handedly of 'factional leaders' and 'warlords'.[94] One of the great problems, Carrington argued more recently, was 'the demonisation of the Serbs'. Indeed, he believed that President Izetbegovic 'was responsible for some of the atrocities in order to get the Americans interested. He was a dreadful little man.'[95]

Once again, Carrington placed his faith in a 'negotiated' partitionist solution. 'Peace,' Carrington claimed in July 1992, 'will not come to Bosnia until there is a de facto partition.'[96] Just as the Croatian government was supposed to buy recognition through territorial concessions, the Sarajevo government was encouraged to trade land for peace. President Izetbegovic refused, not simply because of the monstrous injustice of the proposition, but because he knew well that any agreement with the Bosnian Serbs would not be worth the paper it was written on, so long as the Bosnian Serbs enjoyed a massive military advantage. The truth of this assertion was to be proven by the events of the lamentable London conference in August 1992.

Throughout the early stages of the Bosnian war, the British government steadfastly maintained – officially – that ethnic cleansing and aggression should not be allowed to stand. 'We need to make it clear that we don't accept the partition of Bosnia by force,' Hurd claimed. 'The idea that simply because you or your friends have occupied swathes of territory, the world simply packs up and accepts that, will be shown to be wrong . . . You cannot just ratify what has happened, valley by valley, village by village, in the past few weeks.'[97] In practice, however, the British government did nothing beyond maintaining the arms embargo and obstructing the – albeit feeble – efforts of others to come to the aid of the Bosnian government. But as the sense of popular and political outrage mounted in the course of the summer – with revelations about the camps and mass expulsions – the need to do something to defuse the pressure for military intervention grew. This obligation was felt the more keenly by London while Britain held the presidency of the EU in the second half of 1992.

The resulting London conference was a sham. Given the urgency of the situation, the decision to announce it three weeks in advance was widely interpreted as an invitation to the Serbs to maximize their gains before having them ratified by the international community.[98] Moreover, as Pauline Neville-Jones, then head of the Defence and Overseas Secretariat in the Cabinet Office, recalls, 'The Foreign Office, having decided to hold this thing and ask[ed] the Prime Minister to chair it, then decided to go on holiday, all of them, Political Director, the lot, leaving almost nobody to prepare this mammoth conference.'[99] When the various statesmen and diplomats finally convened, the British ensured that there was no outright condemnation of the Serbs in the communiqué. Indeed, John Major later freely admitted that he blunted Dutch attempts to single out Belgrade through a procedural stratagem.[100] All that was secured was an agreement on 'principles of civilized conduct' and a *unilateral* commitment by the Bosnian Serbs – in a separate understanding between the Bosnian Serb Vice-President Nikola Koljevic and the Minister of State in the FCO, Douglas Hogg – not to fire their heavy weapons around Sarajevo and three other cities and to submit these to international control and inspection.[101] As Victor Jackovitch, a senior official in the US State Department and subsequently the first ambassador to Bosnia, observed, 'We had difficulties finding out what London was trying to do. When we got there we realised what was happening: a pressure valve. Allow the Serbs to make promises and accept them knowing they had no intention of keeping them. It was a landmark in handling the war and brilliant by the Brits.'[102] The London conference also marked the first appearance of Lord Owen, who replaced Lord Carrington as the EU negotiator.

Very soon it was clear that the conference had achieved nothing. The shelling of Sarajevo and other towns continued; the campaign of ethnic cleansing escalated. Later, Douglas Hurd was to say that 'the corralling of heavy weapons was agreed in principle at the London conference in August. It has not happened, partly because the Bosnian Serbs have not agreed to it and partly as a result of the difficulties of arranging it.'[103] One suspects that the two reasons were related. The Defence Secretary was more honest. 'What has happened so far,' he said in September 1992, 'is that a very small number of pieces of artillery have been collected together but I must add the qualification that those who were in control of those weapons before are still in control of them and are still firing with them. All that the United

Nations has been allowed to do is to monitor that particular operation. I cannot believe that that is an honouring of the spirit of the promise that was given by those who felt it appropriate to make that commitment.'[104] These remarks – a classic example of the new understated conservative realism – must surely rank as among the most pathetic of any made by a senior government minister of a power permanently seated at the UN Security Council.

By the autumn of 1992 it was clear both that a negotiated solution was not imminent and that the war would not end with an early Serb victory. This forced the British government to rethink its original strategy. Whereas ground troops had initially been firmly ruled out, the growing humanitarian crisis now led to the dispatch of substantial British forces to Bosnia as part of the UN Protection Force (UNPROFOR) tasked with the delivery and protection of international aid. The political purpose of the deployment was not stated, but quite transparent: to head off demands for a politico-military commitment to the Bosnian government by the pre-emptive dispatch of ground forces for purely humanitarian purposes. The troops, as the head of UNHCR in central Bosnia, Larry Hollingsworth, later argued, were 'sent in not to be tough but simply to look tough'.[105] In case anybody was in any doubt about this, the Armed Forces Minister, Archie Hamilton, told the Commons that they would be withdrawn if they suffered 'heavy casualties'.[106]

All this was part of a strategy to relativize and depoliticize the conflict and turn it into a purely humanitarian problem. Instead of ethnic cleansing and aggression, the watchwords of British statesmen and diplomats were 'ethnic strife' and 'humanitarian relief'. On this reading, Bosnia became no more than an inconveniently conspicuous but essentially routine civil war and humanitarian crisis. It is telling that, in an overview of the problems facing the EU in September 1992, Douglas Hurd identified not Bosnia but migration as the greatest challenge facing the EU. In a curious spell of amnesia about the ethnically cleansed Native American Indians, he added helpfully that, unlike nineteenth-century America, 'ours is not an empty continent'.[107] A year later, he told a foreign policy symposium in the German capital that 'Sudan, Bosnia, Angola, Liberia, Georgia, Afghanistan, Rwanda, Somalia, Tajikistan and Azerbaijan are all racked by civil war . . .

Some are televised, some are not. They are usually civil wars simmering with centuries of mutual hatred, sustained by people with no will for peace . . . It is empty to pretend that we can impose peace with justice on every disorder outside our own borders.'[108] This argument was echoed by Malcolm Rifkind when he told parliament in April 1993 that he was 'not aware of any ethical distinction between a war in Bosnia and a war in Angola or Cambodia'.[109]

Indeed, he elaborated on this theme a fortnight later, by standing the moral argument on its head and hurling it back at his critics. 'I listened,' he told the House of Commons, 'to the argument that we have a special responsibility in the former Yugoslavia that does not apply in other parts of the world. I can understand that, at a political level, we in the United Kingdom clearly have a security interest in stability in Europe. However, I hope that hon. members will not advance that argument on moral grounds when they demand at the same time that any action must be taken in the name of the United Nations. The UN can make no moral distinction between intervening in Bosnia and intervening in Angola or Cambodia – its responsibility is to the global community. Those hon. members who called for UN intervention, but sought to imply that it must be made in Bosnia even if not elsewhere, displayed an inappropriate inconsistency.'[110] This was a domino theory in reverse: Britain should not resist aggression and ethnic cleansing in one part of the world – even in an area which obviously fell within Britain's sphere of influence on the UN Security Council – because that would somehow commit her to doing the same in all other parts of the globe.

Such attempts to equate a major politico-military crisis in the middle of Europe with more remote African or Asian quarrels – and thus to dismiss it – found an echo, in this case a more understandable one, in the Third Worldist resentments of the UN leadership. The Egyptian Secretary General, Dr Boutros Boutros-Ghali, was quick to contrast the international humanitarian and peacekeeping commitments in Bosnia, which he dismissed as a 'white man's war', with inaction in the Caucasus and Somalia. Unsurprisingly, Boutros-Ghali's visit to Sarajevo in October 1994 was greeted with widespread derision. He responded by reminding the traumatized inhabitants of that city of the plight of black Africa and contrasting the thousands of UN troops in the former Yugoslavia with the totally inadequate provision for Rwanda.[111] It was an unusual spectacle: a Conservative British government – and, as we shall see, Conservative MPs – found common ground with professional anti-colonialists on the basis of the universal brotherhood of man – and of inaction. Throughout the Bosnian war, indeed, men who prided themselves on their innate pragmatism suddenly became afflicted with an abstract and disabling pseudo-universalism.

At the same time, British officials did everything they could to play down the gravity of the situation on the ground. Thus, in May 1993, at the height of the first siege of the Bosnian enclave of Zepa, British diplomatic sources briefed journalists to the effect that 'reports should be treated with caution as Muslims could be expected to do anything to provoke Western military intervention, a goal throughout the Vance–Owen peace process . . . One British source said the Muslims had a history of provoking a disturbance and exaggerating its extent.'[112] More than a year later, in November 1994, British 'sources' were at it again, playing down the threat to the Bihac enclave from advancing Bosnian Serb forces. One briefing claimed that 'London believed that the Serbs were not planning to take Bihac but wanted to tie down the Bosnian Army's Fifth Corps there.'[113] Similarly, after the fall of the enclave of Srebrenica and the massacre of thousands of its menfolk in July 1995, John Sweeney reported how 'the British Ministry of Defence went on the offensive working to deny and play down evidence of a massacre'. Indeed, Sweeney quotes a 'senior UN source in the former Yugoslavia as saying 'The anti-Muslim spin from MI6 is a constant feature. They're always doing it.'[114]

Very often, this British agenda found an echo with a resentful United Nations bureaucracy frantic to avoid offending the Serbs as the strongest power in the region. Thus, some UN officials tried to argue that Sarajevo was not technically under siege, that Serb shelling was often provoked by 'Muslim' initiatives, and that the Bosnian government routinely shelled or sniped its own people in order to precipitate western intervention.[115] This became strikingly obvious immediately after the market-place massacre of February 1994 when UN forensic teams swung into action to obscure the overwhelming likelihood that the round had been fired from Serb positions. At local level, of course, the UN felt it sometimes had no choice but to accommodate the overwhelming power of the Serbs in order to carry out its mandate. This was the case, for example, in Serb-held Sector North in the Krajina (Croatia), where UN troops quickly found themselves overawed by and in league with contemptuous Serbs. 'It is the old problem,' a UN official in Zagreb remarked in December 1994, 'Sector North are tormented by the Serbs – so they've fallen in love with them. They've gone native.'[116]

But it was not enough simply to relativize and minimize the Bosnian war, it was also necessary to blur the distinction between aggressor and victim. It is, of course, true that the Bosnian government side committed atrocities, but these were essentially reactive and quantitatively and qualitatively distinct from the systematic campaign of ethnic cleansing waged by the Croatian and Bosnian Serbs.[117] Yet what is striking is the way in which the argument of moral equivalence went right back to the beginning of the conflict; indeed, to the Croatian war of 1991. 'If,' Douglas Hurd remarked in early July 1991, 'at the end of the day they [the peoples of Yugoslavia] have decided that what they want is civil war, it will be a reproach to Europe but we cannot prevent it.'[118] As Douglas Hogg told the Commons in October 1991, at the height of the sieges of the Croatian towns of Vukovar and Dubrovnik, 'Sadly, there have been repeated ceasefire violations – on both sides.'[119] Not long afterwards, Lord Brabazon of Tara, the Minister of State at the Department of Transport, claimed that '12 successive ceasefire agreements collapsed because of a lack of will on either side to respect them'.[120] This alleged symmetry took no account of the asymmetry in weaponry: at this time Croatian transgressions generally involved small arms, whereas the Serbs brought the full force of their artillery to bear. In mid-December 1991, Hogg was still pronouncing in vague terms that 'A long-term solution will be possible only when the Yugoslavs themselves show a genuine political will to reach a peaceful settlement.'[121]

The same rhetorical strategies were deployed in Bosnia. Here the insistence on referring to aggressor and victim, legitimate government and separatist rebel alike as the 'parties' or 'factions', became almost ritualized. The undifferentiated emphasis on the need for the peoples of the former Yugoslavia to find their own way out of the conflict was if anything accentuated. 'The decision for peace or further fighting,' one British diplomat told the Security Council in August 1993, 'now rests with the Bosnian parties to the conflict.'[122] 'At the end of the day,' Douglas Hurd observed in early 1994, 'as we can see very clearly in Bosnia, the only people who can stop the fighting are the people doing the fighting. You have at the moment, alas, three parties in Bosnia, who each of them believe that some military success awaits them.'[123] One needed, Malcolm Rifkind told parliament in April 1994, 'in a slow, painful, but determined way, to find a way in which each of the factions will realise that military means alone will not produce a lasting peace in Bosnia'.[124] 'Where people are determined to go on fighting,' Baroness Chalker observed at the end of that year, 'it is very difficult to stop them.'[125]

Very often the notion of a moral equivalence, inherent in the language of 'parties' and 'factions', was made explicit. When Jeremy Hanley, the genial but flailing Armed Forces Minister, was asked by Patrick Cormack whether 'the thrust of the blame should be directed at Serbia', he responded that 'I do not believe that it is desirable to try to apportion blame in an area where horrendous acts are carried out by all sides.'[126] Similarly, Sir Nicholas Bonsor, the new Undersecretary of State at the FCO, made his debut by claiming, not long after the hostage crisis and in the same month as the Srebrenica massacre, that 'this is not a one-sided conflict in which there are white hats and black hats at war. It is a conflict in which the depth of bestiality is incomprehensible in a civilised world and it is not confined wholly to the Serbs.'[127]

Sometimes government ministers even took their lead from UNPROFOR – including British officers – and implied that the Bosnians were shelling their own people, particularly after the marketplace massacre in February 1994. Thus the Minister for Overseas Development, Baroness Chalker, found it 'impossible' to tell an MP 'who is responsible for the shelling in Sarajevo. All I can tell him is that the investigations by UNPROFOR have been going on. While it cannot be said with certainty who was responsible for the 70 or so deaths that were caused, we certainly know that there were many people who could have been doing it on both sides in Sarajevo.'[128] Subsequently, the Prime Minister stated that, although he thought the Serbs the most obvious culprits, a later report had implicated Bosnian government forces. In his view, either side was fully capable of perpetrating such an act.'[129] John Major, of course, did not need certainty, he merely needed sufficient doubt to blur the issue and dilute the call for an international response. Alistair Goodlad, the Minister of State at the FCO, advanced the same argument in more general terms. He observed after the market-place massacre of February 1994 that 'We are looking for effective action – if necessary, muscular action – to protect the civilian population of Sarajevo. They have been subjected to mortar attacks from both Serbian and Bosnian forces.'[130] Of course, the notion that the siege of Sarajevo – surrounded on all sides by Serb heavy weapons and defended by undergunned Bosnians – was somehow a joint effort between 'the parties', was quite absurd.

Sometimes, the argument for equivalence was insidiously *a priori*. When challenged by one MP to 'recognise that the conflict is clearly part of the campaign for the creation of a greater Serbia', the Defence Secretary in turn called upon him to 'accept that the Croatians have been seeking to control as much territory as possible in Bosnia . . . and I have no doubt that the Bosnian Muslims [sic], given the opportunity, would also be seeking to do so.'[131] In short, the Bosnian government might not have committed comparable atrocities to Serb separatists, but they *would* surely do so if they had half a chance, particularly if the international arms embargo were to be lifted. This insistence on moral equivalence stemmed in part from ignorance and intellectual laziness. In part, as Reginald Hibbert points out, the language of 'warring factions' served government 'as a means of evading the real issue of the war, which is how to contain an expansionist Serbia'.[132] But it also corresponded to a profound psychological necessity. Confronted with the results of their action, British statesmen felt not shame but irritation. They needed to knock the Bosnians down from their pedestal of victimhood and thus excuse non-intervention. They had done the Bosnians a bad turn and they never forgave them for it.

If the British government acknowledged the primary responsibility of the Bosnian Serbs and their backers in Belgrade, this was generally expressed in the context of a more generalized culpability of 'all the parties'. Thus the Minister for Defence Procurement, Jonathan Aitken, told parliament in early April 1993, that 'It is probably true that Serbian planes have committed most of the violations of the no-fly zone. However, the situation is a complex and confusing situation and there have been some other violations.'[133] In October 1993, the Minister for Overseas Development, Baroness Chalker, observed that 'ethnic cleansing has not only been carried out by the Serbs, although they have probably [sic] done more than the Moslems [sic] or Croatians. All ethnic cleansing must be brought to an end.'[134] A few months later, Malcolm Rifkind engaged in a similar exercise when he responded to a massive Serb assault on a 'safe area' with the observation that 'The events in Gorazde of the past few days have undoubtedly been the consequence of Serb aggression, but there are still a number of warring factions in Bosnia. One of the British soldiers who lost their lives in the past week was killed by Serbian action; a Bosnian government soldier shot the other one dead.'[135] And in late June 1995, Douglas Hogg told the House of Commons that 'the Serbs have committed most of the atrocities. However, all parties have been responsible for acts of this kind.'[136] The structure of such pronouncements generally followed a distinctive pattern of obfuscation: no sooner would the aggressor be identified than some qualifying clause would put responsibility in doubt, and vice versa.

Perhaps the classic example of this was Douglas Hurd's longwinded, superficially considered and precise, but obfuscatory characterization of the conflict in a speech to the House of Commons in February 1994: 'Bosnia is full of civilians who are suffering. Some of them are Bosnian Serbs, some of them are Bosnian Croats and some of them are Bosnian Muslims. Essentially, it is a civil war that originated from Belgrade and the Bosnian Serbs, which is why they carry the heaviest responsibility, sustained to some extent by the old JNA – the Yugoslav National [sic] Army – sustained now to some extent by Croat regular units, and sustained to a smaller extent by people who have come in from the Middle East to help the Bosnian Muslims.'[137] Moreover, Hurd had insisted the day before, that there was a pattern of Muslim provocation within which Serb actions should be understood.[138]

In confidential FCO and MoD briefings, of course, all this was rendered simply as 'all sides are equally guilty'. One American, who was given a 'top-level briefing' at the MoD, reported that 'the whole purpose of the briefing seemed to be to lay as much blame as possible on the Bosnian Muslims. There was nothing about who had started the war, or who had committed most of the atrocities. Instead, it was all about a few recent incidents where the Muslims had "provoked" the "Serbs".'[139] And when two UN soldiers were shot by snipers in Sarajevo, one of them certainly by the Serbs, the other possibly by Bosnian government forces, FCO officials confidently told journalists that *both* of them had been murdered by troops loyal to the Sarajevo government.

Similarly, Patrick Bishop of the *Sunday Telegraph* describes how 'a senior Foreign Office official stretched back in his armchair and told journalists that the pattern of violence in Sarajevo was not as simple as it seemed. It was not all the Serbs' fault. Bombardments tended to be started by the Muslims, triggering a massive Serb response.' 'One of the most depressing aspects of the war in Bosnia,' Bishop observed, 'is the way that relatively straightforward situations have been distorted by officials desperate to twist events to fit their gospel of impotence and inaction. An essential part of that strategy has been to try to establish a moral equivalence between the combatants, the view that basically they are all as bad as each other.'[140] Just how successful this strategy proved was shown by Patrick Bishop's own article on the Bihac crisis later that year. The 'Bosnian Muslims', he argued, 'only had themselves to blame'. 'Lately,' he continued, the 'convenient division between aggressors and sufferers has become blurred, and the claim that all parties in the conflict are as bad as each other is becoming more valid.' The Muslims, in fact, 'would do well to co-operate in the carve-up of the country proposed by international negotiators and give up trying to change things on the battlefield'.[141]

Having spun their way out of taking sides against the aggressor, the British government felt free to pressure the victims into a punitive 'negotiated' settlement. Their trump card, or so they thought, was the policy of non-intervention itself. Already in July 1992, Douglas Hurd had told Bosnian leaders on a visit to Sarajevo not to expect western military intervention and to work towards an agreement instead.[142] He repeated this injunction a year later, when he told an embattled President Izetbegovic, 'Do not suppose that there will be military intervention in your favour.'[143] Even when Britain seemed to tilt against the Bosnian Serbs with the threat of air strikes in February 1994, Douglas Hurd was at pains to stress that the ultimatum was 'addressed to all parties, not to one party alone . . . We do not and will not pretend that by armed force we can impose a settlement. Those in any of the warring parties who wish to draw outside governments and armed forces into the conflict to resolve it will find themselves disappointed.'[144] A year later Malcolm Rifkind warned that 'One of the greatest mistakes of the past three years has been for the United Nations, NATO and individual governments to use a rhetoric that implies a capability that has never been provided. It does no good service to the people of Bosnia-Herzegovina to create expectations that cannot be delivered.'[145]

But it was Douglas Hogg who rammed this message home time and again, often with rather more gusto than seemed appropriate. In August 1992 he boasted to the journalists at Sarajevo airport of how he had explained 'very clearly' to President Izetbegovic 'that there was no cavalry coming over the hill. There is no international force coming to stop this.'[146] A year later Hogg told the House of Commons that since nobody had any intention of sending combat troops to Bosnia, 'people must not encourage the Bosnian Muslims to suppose something different'.[147] A month afterwards he wrote that 'If an acceptable peace settlement can be achieved, that surely must be better for the Bosnian people than prolonged war. They must not continue to hold out in the vain hope of Western military intervention on their side.'[148] And in the following year, Hogg argued in the *Journal of the Royal United Services Institute* that the Bosnian government 'have to recognise defeat when it stares them in the face, that land has been seized by force, and that there has to be a degree of acceptance of that fact . . . The other thing that they must accept is that the military option has to be abandoned.' This, he said, however 'unpalatable even for us to proclaim' and for the Bosnians 'to accept', was a 'major objective' of British policy.[149] Senior Bosnian officials who dealt with Hogg on his visit to Sarajevo and subsequently, still recall the uniquely dispiriting effect he had on them.

The other lever available to the British government was the threat of withdrawal and the termination of humanitarian aid. This notion first surfaced in the summer of 1993, and reflected exasperation at the failure of the Bosnian government to agree to a territorial carve-up. 'If the UN effort collapsed,' Douglas Hurd warned in July 1993, 'if it was simply not possible to go on keeping people alive, if our forces and other forces were withdrawn, if all negotiations came to an end, then it might be a situation in which the friends of each side said: "Here's the kit. Fight it out".'[150] 'If the present political vacuum and lack of cooperation persists,' Hurd repeated in November 1993, 'the parties cannot expect the humanitarian commitment, which many of us undertake, to continue indefinitely. It is unrealistic to suppose that this effort can be expected to go on for ever and ever and ever when it is not receiving local co-operation and there is no progress towards a political settlement.'[151] This warning was echoed by Douglas Hogg in a transparent attempt to force the Bosnian government to accept the Owen–Stoltenberg partition plan, the only international plan that year amenable to the Bosnian Serbs,[152] and indeed throughout much of 1994.[153] Liberal Democrat leader Paddy Ashdown hit the nail on the head when he commented that he 'never thought to hear a British Foreign Minister use humanitarian aid to blackmail the victim of aggression into capitulation'.[154]

The bizarre thing about this was that the victim *had* capitulated. In the spring of 1993, the Bosnians agreed – albeit reluctantly – to the Vance–Owen plan, even though it left the Serbs in clear control of much of the land they had seized. Just over a year later, equally reluctantly, they accepted the Contact Group peace plan, which guaranteed the Serbs almost 50 per cent of Bosnia with 30 per cent of the population. The Bosnians, in short, had done exactly what Douglas Hurd and Douglas Hogg had wanted them to do, which was to swallow the fact that the Bosnian Serbs would withdraw only from around 20 per cent of their ill-gotten territory,[155] rather than disgorge the lot, as 'unrealistic' critics demanded. What British government policy therefore amounted to in practice was maintaining the arms embargo and stalling international intervention for as long as was necessary to depress Bosnian government expectations to the point that the Serbs might actually fulfil them.

An integral part of this strategy was the systematic delegitimization of the internationally recognized Bosnian presidency in Sarajevo. The most effective way of doing this was by routinely referring to a government which included many Catholic Croats and Orthodox Serbs, as 'the Muslims', and therefore by implication merely another ethnic 'faction'. Thus, when the Bosnians accepted Vance and Owen's map in the New York negotiations, John Major told the House of Commons in March 1993 that he very much welcomed 'the Muslim agreement to a document on the cessation of hostilities'.[156] Similarly, at a meeting of the United Nations Security Council in June 1993, the British representative, Sir David Hannay, opposed the lifting of the arms embargo as 'a solution of despair [which] would in practice fail to help the people it is designed to assist, the Bosnian Muslims'.[157] A week later, Douglas Hogg referred in a debate to discussions 'on the lifting of the arms embargo for the Bosnian Muslims'.[158] And in March 1994, Douglas Hurd spoke of American 'efforts, which I support, to reach agreement among the Croats, the Bosnian Croats and the Bosnian Muslims'.[159]

This rhetorical sleight of hand did not go unremarked upon. Patrick Cormack, for example, challenged the Foreign Secretary to 'accept that Bosnia still has a government in which Croats, Serbs and Muslims serve together. Will he admit that the British government recognise that as the legitimate government of Bosnia? In that context, is it not unfair to treat it merely as a warring faction?' Douglas Hurd's response was revealing: 'We regard the Bosnian government as one of the parties that need to reach a negotiated settlement. We believe that the Serbs are mainly responsible for the fighting, but the Croats joined in later and are also to blame. All three sides have committed atrocities.'[160] The Bosnian war thus became a strange beast: a perpetratorless crime, in which all were victims and all more or less equally guilty.

Of course, the longer Bosnia was left to its fate, the more radical and self-consciously Islamic the Muslim population became. Abandoned by the west, and persecuted for their religion, many Bosnians turned to Islam for solace, and to Islamic countries for the practical military assistance denied to them by the arms embargo. Muslim refugees, many from conservative rural backgrounds, most of them traumatized and radicalized by their experiences at the hands of Serb, and later Croat, paramilitaries flooded into the cosmopolitan multi-ethnic centres. Islamic states, themselves under strong domestic pressure, became vociferous defenders of the Bosnian cause at the UN and in the Organisation of the Islamic Conference.[161] In time, press stories of Afghan Mujahedeen fighters, veiled women and the prohibition of alcohol proliferated.[162] Culturally and confessionally, the Bosnians made unconvincing Muslims, but it is certainly true that the Bosnian state and the Bosnian army, which had a strong multi-ethnic component, did indeed become largely 'Muslim' in the political sense by the end of the war.

If British policy helped to erode the multi-ethnic complexion of the Sarajevo government, it also inadvertently encouraged the 'factionalization' of the political landscape. Once it became clear that no western military intervention would materialize, the Bosnian Croats felt emboldened to embark on their own separatist project. Indeed, they were almost forced to do so by the influx of Muslim victims of unchecked Serb aggression in north-western and eastern Bosnia into mixed areas of central Bosnia and western Herzegovina. Not only had aggression been seen to pay, but failure to bail out of the disintegrating Bosnian state would leave the Croats to share a shrinking rump with a growing and ever more radicalized Muslim majority. The latent tension between Croats and the Sarajevo government was finally ignited by the Vance–Owen plan in the spring of 1993. Now, as the journalist Alec Russell wrote, 'With the Croats of Herzegovina killing and cleansing away, the argument of the Foreign Office was becoming a self-fulfilling prophecy. Bosnia had at last become a place where village fought village – but only because we had sat on the sidelines while the anarchy gathered pace.'[163]

The collapse of the Croat–Bosnian government alliance – which seemed to postpone a negotiated solution indefinitely – was not welcomed by British statesmen. But in rhetorical terms, it could only buttress obfuscatory government arguments about 'faction' and 'complexity'; and the unexpected successes of the embattled 'Muslim' forces in central Bosnia, which were inevitably attended by atrocities, provided grist to that mill. Here the government was helped by the fact that because British forces on the ground were stationed in the middle of the Croat–Bosnian government faultline, the Serbs began to recede in public consciousness. Thus, Douglas Hogg warded off demands for action against the Serbs in August 1993 by pointing out that 'the main obstacle to the aid convoys . . . is not the Serbs, but the fighting between the Croats and Muslims in central Bosnia'.[164] When British troops perished in the crossfire, this only strengthened the argument. 'We should remember,' Malcolm Rifkind told parliament, 'that the Serbs in Bosnia are not uniquely guilty, although they bear the main responsibility for current events in Bosnia. The other parties too have committed crimes. Indeed, the British soldier who was killed in January while escorting a convoy of sick and wounded did not fall to a Serbian bullet.'[165]

Likewise, Baroness Chalker observed that 'this is a very complicated civil war. On my own visits there I found Croats fighting Moslems, Moslems fighting Serbs, Croats and Serbs fighting within Bosnia, and battles being played out even within those groups.'[166] Douglas Hurd was able to use parliamentary interventions to blur the necessary distinctions. When challenged to acknowledge that British forces 'went in because of Serbian aggression, yet the young soldier who was killed the other day died not from Serbian bullets but from bullets fired between Muslim and Croatian forces', the Foreign Secretary merely responded that 'it is often extremely difficult, particularly in Sarajevo, to establish who is firing and for what reason'.[167] Three months later he was told by Michael Ancram that the 'situation in Bosnia is anything but simple and, although Serbs are committing appalling atrocities against Muslims, at the same time Muslims and Croats are committing appalling atrocities against each other, sometimes under the noses of the British forces'. Douglas Hurd replied that 'My hon. Friend has the balance quite right. We must take account of events where the cameras are not. The heaviest fighting of the past day or so has been between Muslims and Croats.'[168]

A parallel but related strand of government policy was the attempt to 'humanitarianize' rhetoric and policy. Since all 'sides', 'parties', or 'factions' were more or less equally to blame, the only true victims could be the suffering population. Any sort of action on behalf of the Bosnian government risked 'jeopardizing the humanitarian aid effort': in this way, a palliative and substitutive measure became a stated objective of British policy. This was repeatedly justified with reference to 'expert' advice and the pleas of the 'men on the ground'. Yet the humanitarian effort left the fundamental military-political problem and inequality unresolved. This was strikingly illustrated by the journalist Alec Russell, who visited the embattled Bosnian government enclave of Gorazde in the late summer of 1992 and describes being 'haunted by the closing words of the town's commander: "Send a message to your governments, Thank them for their food and medicines. Tell them that at least we will die with full stomachs".'[169] Ironically, aid workers were relatively rarely killed or taken hostage, while the troops sent to protect often were.

Of course, when the UN commanders on the ground called for military intervention, British statesmen did not rush forward to endorse them. 'There is no ceasefire,' the UN commander General Abdulrazek complained in December 1992. 'We are not making any progress. This situation is deteriorating . . . All our efforts here to save lives and restore utilities [have] failed.'[170] He demanded a deadline against the Bosnian Serbs to be accompanied by the threat of force. 'It is now no longer possible,' the *Guardian* observed of military action, 'to argue complacently that all those "on the spot" are against it.'[171] Nothing happened. Nor was there any movement when the French UN commander, General Cot, called for air strikes in early 1994, and was promptly sacked by the Secretary General.

Moreover, it was the aid agencies themselves which were the most resistant to the 'humanitarianization' of the problem, and clearest about its politico-military causes. Thus Alain Destexhe, the Secretary General of Médecins sans Frontières, observed in December 1992 that 'Europe's foremost political concern, mainly to hide its political inaction behind humanitarian action in the field, now amounts to no more than a shameful farce as civilian recipients of aid are left unprotected against attacks . . . The situation has reached a point of such absurdity that it is no longer the UN which dissuades the aggressor, but rather the aggressor who intimidates governments that have [sent] troops to the war-torn country . . . UN troops and humanitarian organisations . . . are being made the alibi for the lack of political action by European governments.'[172] He expanded on this theme in his book *Yugoslavie: la politique de la bande velpeau*, in 1993. 'Humanitarianism,' he wrote, 'has served as an alibi for political impotence. It has never been further removed from what it asserts itself to be: a significant gesture of fraternity and hope. When the accounts are drawn up, when we finally know Bosnia's fate, humanitarianism will find itself in the dock with the accused . . . a companion to the territorial conquest and ethnic cleansing, even, to a certain extent, making them possible.'[173] Similarly, in August 1993 Oxfam called for 'firm political and military measures' in Bosnia, even at the risk of temporarily halting humanitarian aid. Its eastern Europe coordinator, Tony Vaux, stressed that the need for aid in Bosnia was much lower than in Africa: 'we are dealing with a war and stopping the war is the overwhelming priority – getting aid through is secondary'.[174] In July 1995, David Grubb, the executive director of Feed the Children, demanded that 'Peacekeeping in Bosnia needs to change from "observing" and "monitoring" to actually "defending".'[175] And it was no less than the head of Central Bosnian Operations of the United Nations High Commission for Refugees (UNHCR), Larry Hollingsworth, who demanded tougher military action.[176] As Calum MacDonald reminded the House of Commons in July 1993, Hollingsworth 'has said that force should be used to try to deliver . . . aid. It is not just the armchair theorists who are saying that; it is also being said by the people on the ground.'[177]

The most striking example of the 'humanitarianization' of the war was the case of little Irma Hadzimuratovic. Fragments from the Serb shell which had killed her mother smashed into Irma's spine and sent her into a life-threatening coma. There was nothing special about her case: countless children of her age group had suffered similar wounds over the past year. But thanks to the efforts of the BBC and the tabloid press, Irma's fate briefly became a national preoccupation in Britain. After swift intervention by the Prime Minister, the young girl was flown out with maximum publicity, at vast and disproportionate expense. The aid agencies 'on the ground', who knew the British government's lamentable record on the evacuation of injured adults, were understandably contemptuous. Sylvana Foa, the UNHCR spokeswoman, pointed out that Sarajevo was no supermarket for patients: 'Does that mean Britain wants only children? Maybe you want only blond and blue-eyed children, maybe only children under six, only orphans?'[178] All of this would have been excusable if it had been part of a consciousness-raising exercise to herald politico-military action to lift the siege of Sarajevo. But, of course, 'Operation Irma' was not an overture to such action, but, as ever, a substitute. The

British government had indulged in precisely the kind of grandstanding gesture which it affected to despise.

Irma died quietly in her sleep in 1995, with no end to the siege of Sarajevo in sight.[179] Thousands of children had been killed and maimed since then. Her death made few headlines.

The flurry of activity on the Irma front was in marked contrast to Britain's highly restrictive policy towards refugees. Before the war, Yugoslav nationals did not need a visa to travel to Britain. In late July 1992, the Home Secretary, Kenneth Clarke, boasted that Britain had 'no visa requirement for nationals of former Yugoslavia and we have no plans to impose one'. Less than four months later, such a requirement was imposed. By that time, the four countries adjoining the theatre of conflict, Germany, Austria, Switzerland and Hungary, had welcomed 413,000 refugees; Britain a modest 4,500.[180] Visa applications from former detainees who could automatically claim the status of political victims were routinely turned down. In purely formal terms, of course, the Home Office was entirely within its rights. By the book, refugees were supposed to apply for visas in the country from which they were trying to flee: in the absence of a British embassy in Bosnia, travel to Vienna, Zagreb and even Belgrade (!) was recommended. At the same time, the Home Office insisted that refugees must apply for asylum in the first 'safe' country reached. In this way, the Home Office could claim with a straight face that virtually no 'legitimate' applications found their way through to Britain. But this bureaucratic sophistry took no account of the broader political responsibility which Britain faced in coming to terms with a major crisis in Europe.

A variety of rhetorical strategies was developed to cover British policy on refugees. 'Evacuation,' Douglas Hurd argued in September 1992, 'is often more harmful than helpful, especially to children. The trauma of being separated from the family is often greater than the trauma of remaining with the family in an area affected by conflict.'[181] Moreover, evacuation 'would be helping the aggressors, whose aim is ethnic cleansing; you do the job for them; you legitimise an infamous policy'. Besides, 'If all Yugoslavs are to be evacuated, then why not victims from all other war zones . . . Why Yugoslavs and not Somalis or Afghans or Mozambicans?' 'Moreover,' Hurd continued, 'the civilians have an effect on combatants; their interests put pressure on warring parties to treat for peace. Our aim is not for all civilians to leave in order to create a free fire zone for the military.' Since he could hardly imagine that the plight of refugees would soften the hard hearts of the ethnic cleansers, this curious passage unwittingly suggests that Douglas Hurd saw the humanitarian misery in Bosnia as yet another pressure point on the Sarajevo government which he had no intention of relieving.[182] At the very least, it is a sloppy and meaningless argument.

There was in fact some sense in official circles that the best solution was precisely to recognize the results of ethnic cleansing and ratify them with comprehensive population exchanges. This emerges very clearly from a letter written in June 1993 by Richard Wilkinson of the Foreign Office's Policy Planning Staff to the pro-Serb activist Nora Beloff: 'You know of course that planners are not always representative of the thinking of their governments and that their influence is at best patchy . . . The trouble is that we are in the position of the traveller who was told by the Irishman that if he wanted to reach his intended destination then he should not be starting from where he was. We should never have accepted the dismemberment of Yugoslavia without first having settled the problem of minorities and frontiers, and *probably not before having put in hand a humane programme of population exchange. The recognition of Bosnia, and indeed the incitement to them to proclaim their independence, was the ultimate act of thoughtlessness. We are now having to try to salvage what we can.*'[183] These remarkable words were penned just after the Bosnian Serbs rejected the Vance–Owen plan. In this context, the phrase 'salvage what we can' glosses a largely one-sided movement of population which was neither humane nor an exchange.

In order to dash Bosnian hopes – and to stave off demands for further action – British politicians and diplomats systematically exaggerated the military hazards of intervention. 'The difficulty with all the military options,' Douglas Hurd argued in September 1992, 'is that in such terrain, with the intermingling of military personnel and of civilians and of Serbs, Bosnians and Croats, it is hard to work out a practical scheme which would not merely add to the number killed without ending the fighting.'[184] He regularly denied that there was any compromise between massive intervention by ground forces, which was out of the question and advocated by no one, and complete military inaction. 'Once we cut away . . . rhetorical pretension,' he remarked in July 1993, 'we are left with a whole range of middle paths. Even some of these middle paths have been puffed up by excess expectation. Those who know that comprehensive military intervention is not practicable pretend that lesser measures will guarantee the same result. It is a cruel pretence.'[185] Cruel, so the argument went, because it merely put off the evil day when the Bosnians would have to see sense and agree to the truncation of their country. 'If one comes, however reluctantly, to the judgment that there is not a military solution to the problem we face,' Malcolm Rifkind argued in April 1993 at the height of the first Srebrenica crisis, 'it will not do any service either to the victims of aggression or to the wider moral and ethical issues to take action which one believes is foredoomed to failure.'[186]

This systematic shrinking of the practical military options available was deployed to great effect against domestic critics. In April 1993, Malcolm Rifkind dismissed the Liberal Democrat leader, Paddy Ashdown, in mocking terms: 'He is trying to persuade the House of the crucial importance for moral reasons, the peace of the world and the future of Europe of bringing the war in Bosnia to an end. Why is he prepared to call for what is by any definition only partial measures to bring that about? If he believes in the arguments that he is advancing, why is he not using his authority to call for the total deployment of massive ground forces, including British forces, in Bosnia? If he believes in his own rhetoric, why does he seek to draw back from that position?'[187] Almost exactly a year later – during the Gorazde crisis of April 1994 – Rifkind attempted to see off the Labour MP David Winnick as follows: 'I notice that the hon. Gentleman has been careful to avoid saying what his especial remedy would be for resolving that predicament. Unless he is calling for many thousands of British and other soldiers to be sent in a combat role to Bosnia, frankly, his words are no more than the words of a windbag.'[188] Rifkind's own estimate of the force needed was very large: 'To bring this war to an end militarily would require the commitment of hundreds of thousands of men, equipment and armaments, at enormous risk.'[189] Similarly, Douglas Hogg, the Foreign Office Minister, told the House of Commons in May 1993 that 'Unless we – all nations – are prepared to deploy ground troops in a combat role, perhaps we should not embark on too much bluster.'[190] But such a commitment, he warned, would be very costly, and here he went well beyond Rifkind's most dire predictions. 'When one is considering the cost in terms of human lives of trying to make peace by force,' he claimed, 'one must come to the conclusion that it would take about half a million men.'[191] Not a half a million strong ground force, not half a million casualties, but half a million *dead*, apparently.

What was striking about the intervention debate was the uncharacteristic discourtesy expressed by some government figures during the exchanges. It was not unusual for the Defence Secretary, one of the more abrasive performers in the House, to dismiss David Winnick as a 'windbag'. But it was certainly not in character for the Prime Minister to accuse the Liberal Democrat leader, Paddy Ashdown, of being 'heroic with other people's lives' and 'talk[ing] glibly about bombing from the air'.[192] Two years later, evidently goaded beyond endurance by Ashdown's critique of his Bosnia policy, Major accused him of having 'done nothing but grandstand on this issue from the commencement of the matter. If he really understood a little more about it, he might say a little less about it.'[193]

Serious military and political alternatives – of which more later – were dismissed as little more than juvenile war games and armchair speculations. 'It is very easy', Baroness Chalker told the House of Lords in December 1994, 'to be an armchair critic of this highly complicated situation . . . There are far too many armchair critics in this country who think that they know best.'[194] Later John Major was to fulminate in his memoirs about the 'abuse from politicians and others who wished to grandstand from the safety of their armchairs'.[195] The result was a preposterously high estimate of the force levels required to reverse ethnic cleansing and the numbers of casualties that were likely to result, coupled with a markedly dismissive view of the capabilities of the Croat and Bosnian armies. Curiously, none of the military experts publicly broke ranks with this assessment, even though it helped to justify cuts in defence expenditure. At every stage, in fact, the case for a limited military intervention on behalf of the Bosnian government was denied, ignored and suppressed by Douglas Hurd, Malcolm Rifkind, Douglas Hogg, and a whole host of other British politicians, diplomats and experts.

At the diplomatic level, the government tried to hide behind the alleged limitations of the United Nations mandate. 'I do not believe,' Douglas Hogg told parliament in November 1991, 'that at present the Security Council would authorise the use of force.'[196] 'My Lords,' Baroness Chalker claimed in December 1994, 'the mandate does not entitle UNPROFOR or NATO to use force to stop one party against another. The mandate is absolutely clear.'[197] The mandate was indeed clear. UN resolution 770 of 13 August 1992, passed under Chapter VII of the United Nations Charter as an 'enforcement' mandate, had authorized the use of 'all measures necessary' to ensure the safe passage of humanitarian aid. This was significant because, in all previous peacekeeping operations, as the international lawyers Paul Williams and Michael Scharf have pointed out, the UN had 'not chosen to base . . . the mandate on any particular Charter provisions, let alone on chapter VII'.[198] The phrasing of the resolution was intended to remind the Serbs of the famous resolution of 1990 by which the UN sanctioned 'all necessary means' to expel Saddam Hussein from Kuwait.[199] Moreover, the Bosnian resolution called on 'states to take [the necessary action] nationally or through regional agencies', stipulating only that such actions be coordinated with the Secretary General.[200] At this stage, of course, there were no British forces yet on the ground. There is no doubt that the resolution would have covered a more robust intervention by Britain or a British-led 'coalition of the willing' to open access routes to Srebrenica and Gorazde, or to lift the siege of Sarajevo. Yet if one looks at the Foreign Office briefing paper of November 1992 on 'Former Yugoslavia: the UN mandate', references to Chapter VII are nowhere to be found, and for good reason; the briefing also contrived to make no *specific* mention of resolution 770 on the passage of humanitarian aid.[201]

The UN mandate further expressly authorized – in resolution 836 of 4 June 1993, passed under Chapter VII – the use of force to 'deter attacks on the safe areas' and to 'promote the withdrawal of military or paramilitary units *other than those of the government of Bosnia and Herzegovina* [my italics]'. It also 'Decides that . . . member states, acting nationally or through regional organisations or arrangements, may take, under the authority of the Security Council and subject to close coordination with the Secretary General and UNPROFOR, all necessary measures, through the use of air power, in and around the safe areas . . . to support UNPROFOR' in deterring attacks.[202] There was thus no need to seek additional Security Council approval to enforce the Nato ultimatum in February 1994, which threatened the Serbs with massive air strikes if they failed to withdraw their heavy weapons. 'United Nations Security Council resolution 836,' as John Major told parliament, 'authorises the use of air power in support of UNPROFOR in and around the safe areas in Bosnia-Herzegovina. There is no need for further decisions by the Security Council.'[203] This was a view with which the UN Secretary General himself concurred.[204] Indeed, Sir David Hannay, who served as British ambassador to the UN Security Council throughout the war, agreed that the mandate in Bosnia – which was substantially made up of resolutions passed under Chapter VII – was always open to an 'enforcement' interpretation.[205] For when full-scale intervention finally did come about in the late summer of 1995, it went ahead without the passage of any qualitatively new Security Council resolutions specifically authorizing enforcement action. The root of the problem lay not with any lack of international legal authorization, but in a failure of political will.

Another stratagem hinged on alleged Russian objections. Thus in April 1993 Baroness Chalker told the House of Lords that 'We have had more backing through resolutions in the United Nations in this matter than I believe even over the situation in Kuwait. But because of old alliances between the Serbs, Russians and others, it has been difficult to achieve intervention in what started out certainly as an internal war.'[206] More decisive action, so the argument went, would offend the Russians and impale itself on their veto in the United Nations Security Council. Yet in reality pretended Russian objections were simply a shield for government policy. Russia used its Security Council veto on only one occasion when it blocked a resolution sponsored by Muslim countries in 1994 aimed at cutting off the supply of fuel to the Bosnian Serbs from Serbia.[207] At no point did the Russians ever take on western policy on Bosnia at the United Nations directly. When it came to a vote on mandatory sanctions on Yugoslavia (resolution 757, 30 May 1992), only China and Zimbabwe abstained; on 13 August 1992, only India, China and Zimbabwe abstained from resolution 770 authorizing 'all necessary measures'. As for the safe areas resolution, it was the Russian representative on the Security Council, Mr Vorontsov, who remarked that 'Henceforth, any attempted military attacks, shooting and shelling of safe areas, any armed incursions into those areas, and any hindrance of delivery of humanitarian assistance will be stopped by United Nations forces using all necessary measures, including the use of armed force.'[208]

Last but not least, the government sought to hide behind 'public opinion'. 'I do not detect,' John Major stated in August 1992, 'any support in Parliament or in public opinion for operations which would tie down large numbers of British forces in difficult and dangerous terrain for a long period.'[209] Likewise, Douglas Hogg told parliament in early 1993 that 'We cannot use United Kingdom ground troops . . . in a combat role unless the country is solidly behind such a venture. The truth is that it is not, and there is not such an opinion in this House either.' Any effort, he later elaborated, would have to be 'underpinned by national will. I do not believe that that will exists in this case.'[210]

But, according to Annika Savill, the diplomatic correspondent of the *Independent*, this view was based on little more than intuition. 'In mid-May 1992,' she wrote, 'a senior diplomat asked me – I thought this was taking market research on such grave matters a bit frivolously – whether I thought "public opinion would accept British soldiers being killed in a relatively obscure place like Yugoslavia". By July of the same year, the same diplomat was able to say: "John Major is personally convinced that public support could not be sustained for sending troops to die in Bosnia".'[211] This has been confirmed by a very senior Foreign Office figure: 'His worry was would he have political support in the country because there is nothing [more] serious than engaging in military activity without public support or support by your own party.'[212] Douglas Hurd was to observe retrospectively that 'Although public opinion could not force a government to undertake an enterprise against its better judgment, it can powerfully influence that judgment. On Bosnia no such influence was exerted.'[213] What this plea overlooks is the obligation on government to show leadership and mould opinion, as it successfully had in the Gulf, and was later to do over Kosovo.

The government paid close attention to Foreign Office reports on public opinion, which were based on MPs' questions, ministers' postbags, and leading articles in the national press. What they found in the first year of the war was that there was considerable public concern at events in Bosnia. At certain key points, such as the news of Serb detention camps, mass rapes and the first siege of Srebrenica in 1993, there was intense concern. But – in their judgement – it never developed into the kind of 'cumulative concern' which compelled the west to set up 'safe havens' for the Kurds in northern Iraq. Indeed, as the *Independent on Sunday* reported, the highest level of anger officials noted 'was when Lance-Corporal Wayne Edwards was killed delivering humanitarian aid in Bosnia in January [1993]: anger not against his killers but against the British government for putting troops at risk'.[214] Ironically, a government which was so critical of American and subsequent Labour obsession with 'spin' was itself deeply concerned to stay in tune with public opinion.

Yet public opinion was by no means as opposed to military intervention against the Bosnian Serbs as the government claimed. It is true that early polls suggested caution: a NOP poll in August 1992 found only 33 per cent of respondents supportive of the Bosnian government, with almost 60 per cent unwilling to back any side.[215] Yet at the same time, there was widespread dissatisfaction with the government's handling of the crisis: more than half of those asked were unhappy, a figure which compared badly with the 60 per cent satisfaction rating during the Gulf crisis. But as the war dragged on and the evidence of (primarily) Bosnian Serb atrocities mounted, public opinion became ever more concerned and militant. Indeed, recent research by Joseph Pearson of Cambridge University has shown that popular and press outrage over the camps and rapes in the late summer of 1992 led to a – temporary – consensus on the need for military intervention.[216] This moment passed, because the government deliberately allowed it to. But as the conflict reached a new climax in the spring of the new year, popular opinion once again shifted towards intervention. By mid-1993, MORI polls were showing that, in Peter Riddell's words, 'government was lagging behind public opinion'.[217] More than two-thirds of respondents now wanted the dispatch of British troops to 'stop the fighting'. And in a NOP poll carried out during the Eastleigh by-election of February 1994, more than half of respondents supported air strikes against the Bosnian Serbs to lift the siege of Sarajevo, while nearly three-quarters agreed that such attacks should be carried out 'even if it leads to Britain becoming involved in the Bosnian civil war'.[218] And by the summer of 1995, as government policy was visibly disintegrating, MORI polls showed 65 per cent dissatisfaction with the government and 59 per cent supporting air strikes against the Bosnian Serbs.[219]

According to John Coles, the former head of the diplomatic service, Bosnia was 'for weeks at a time the issue uppermost in the minds of ministers'.[220] This is confirmed by the Minister for Overseas Development, Baroness Chalker. 'I have probably spent more hours on the situation in Bosnia,' she observed in April 1993, 'than on any other single situation at this present time, and the same is true for every member of the government involved.'[221] 'Bosnia,' Douglas Hurd recalled, 'was my main concern during the second half of my period as Foreign Secretary . . . it actually consumed more intellectual and – let's put it this way – *ethical* effort than any other subject running at the time.'[222] Yet when he went to Sarajevo in mid-summer 1992, Hurd notoriously showed no desire either to meet its suffering inhabitants or to get to grips with the reality of the war. Instead of the planned trip to the hospital he went straight from his meeting with President Izetbegovic to UN headquarters and thence to the airport and home.[223] It is certainly revealing that Douglas Hurd saw no need between July 1992 and January 1994 – not throughout the whole traumatic year of 1993 – to visit the country. There does not seem to have been any practical reason for this absence.[224] Moreover, as Annika Savill claims, he 'usually decline[d] television interviews requested on the subject of Bosnia alone: the way to get him [was] to choose another topic and tack on a few Bosnian questions at the end.'[225] At the same time, Hurd kept his meetings with members of the Bosnian government to a bare minimum. He did everything possible to reduce public awareness and debate.

Imagine, therefore, his irritation with the continued topicality of Bosnia as the Bosnian Serbs – and increasingly the Bosnian Croats, too – intensified their policy of ethnic cleansing. But rather than turn on the perpetrators, Hurd's fury was reserved for the messengers of the media and his critics. In March 1993, the Foreign Secretary drew attention – in general terms, without mentioning Bosnia – to the 'tension between *achievers* and *critics*' in society. 'There are signs,' he added, 'that we do not at the moment in Britain have the balance right.'[226] Five months later, at a famous speech given in the Travellers' Club, Douglas Hurd became more specific. He attacked 'most of those who report for the BBC, *The Times*, the *Independent*, the *Guardian*, [who] have all been in different ways enthusiasts for pushing military intervention in Bosnia. They are founder members of the "something must be done" school.'[227] He criticized the 'selectivity' of the 'media searchlight': 'Bosnia has been selected by Europeans from among the world's tragedies for television coverage. This is natural for it is a European tragedy – so long as we realise that several other, bloodier tragedies are being played elsewhere in the world without an audience . . . For every incident in the tragedy there are at least two explanations. But of mangled limbs, hideous deprivation, ruined lives, there is no doubt.' 'The light shone by the media,' the Foreign Secretary later observed, 'is not the regular sweep of the lighthouse, but a random searchlight directed at the whim of its controllers.'[228] This clever blend of relativism and one-worldism was echoed by Archie Hamilton, an erstwhile armed forces minister. He accused the media of having provided saturation coverage of Bosnia, while ignoring equally terrible situations in other parts of the world, such as Angola. Indeed, Hamilton claimed, media coverage had prolonged the war by obstructing a diplomatic endgame based on a local solution.[229]

In reality, much BBC news coverage was remote from the 'something must be done' caricature painted by Douglas Hurd and other government critics. Far from being a fully paid-up supporter of the Bosnians in their quest for international intervention, the Corporation often unconsciously or uncritically absorbed Whitehall rhetoric and became easy prey to FCO and MoD briefings. The most obvious and insidious sign of this was the persistent reference to 'all three warring sides' or the 'three warring factions', thus equating the internationally recognized authorities in Sarajevo with Serb and Croat rebels. The Bosnian government forces, which in some theatres included substantial Catholic Croat and Orthodox Serb contingents, were routinely – and not quite accurately – described by the BBC as 'the Muslims' or 'Muslim forces'. In time, this elision became second nature: when an ethnic Croat – who had been clearly identified as such prior to the programme – appeared on *Newsnight* as a spokesman for the Bosnian government, he was described on air by the presenter Kirsty Wark as a 'Muslim'. Subsequent protests elicited the response that viewers believed the terms 'Muslim' and 'Bosnian' so synonymous that departure from this rule would only confuse them.[230] Moreover, in the attempt to provide 'balance', the BBC gave exaggerated exposure to the Serb viewpoint. As Lee Bryant, the press officer at the Bosnian embassy for much of the war, remarked in August 1995, it was almost impossible to get *Newsnight* to interview his ambassador. 'Many editors and journalists at the BBC,' he said, 'get bored of hearing the Bosnian case because it is so simple. So they'll take Serbs every time because they've always got something extreme to say and it's good television.'

Even more egregious was the way in which straightforward news reports on the World Service were 'spun' by officials in Whitehall. As Vladimir Lojen, an employee of the BBC Croatian Service throughout most of the war, observed, 'The sad fact is: Ministry of Defence and Foreign Office Briefings have been seeping in an undiluted form into the World Service programmes.'[231] This was reflected in the tendency to conceal the extent of Bosnian Serb atrocities and suggest a moral equivalence between the 'warring sides'. Thus in March 1993, the UN stated that the aircraft which had bombed the enclave of Srebrenica had not been formally identified but were seen flying off in the direction of Serbia. In the BBC broadcast this was rendered as: 'British sources say checks are being made to determine where the planes had come from.' In June 1995, three years into the siege of the Bosnian capital, one news bulletin reported that 'Targeting of residential districts of Sarajevo with mortars and rockets, apparently fired from Bosnian Serb positions, is a relatively new development.' In August 1995, an American official was quoted by dispatches and agencies as saying that although both Bosnian government forces and Croats were responsible for isolated outrages, 'The vast majority of ethnic cleansing since 1992 can be attributed to the Bosnian Serbs.' In the subsequent World Service news broadcast this was rendered as 'An American official said that Croatian and Muslim forces had also carried out atrocities' without any mention of the original distinction on which the thrust of the original story rested. As Lojen observes, 'The effort to obscure the obvious, question the indisputable and balance the unbalanceable, [was] one of the cornerstones' of World Service coverage throughout the war. As such, it had become a mere extension of a British policy designed to blur the distinction between aggressor and victim and to keep demands for international military intervention at bay.

CHAPTER 2

# 'The Lowest Common Denominator': Britain Stifles America, 1991–1993

Unlike some of the other defining issues of the decade – such as the exchange rate mechanism and European integration generally – Douglas Hurd and Malcolm Rifkind's Bosnian policy commanded a remarkable consensus within the British administration and the Conservative Party.[1] Throughout the crisis, there was no significant pressure within from the Major government, the Conservative Party or Whitehall for a change of heart. One of the few voices raised in protest was that of Sir John Nott, Defence Secretary during the Falklands War. 'I am ashamed to say,' he wrote in December 1994, 'that the British government, by a huge miscalculation, has been an unwitting accomplice to . . . a policy of such incompetence and arrogance that it is akin to the appeasement of the Nazis.'[2] This critique was echoed – in slightly more restrained form – by a small number of former Foreign Office grandees such as Sir Anthony Parsons, Sir Antony Duff, Sir Donald Maitland, Lord Bridges, Lord Greenhill, Sir Antony Acland and Sir Reginald Hibbert.

The figure who came closest to challenging the government on Bosnia was the former Prime Minister, Margaret Thatcher. She had already been a staunch supporter of Croatian statehood during the Serbian invasion of 1991.[3] In the summer of 1992, in response to a personal appeal from the Bosnian Vice-President, Ejup Ganic, Thatcher made a public appeal for military intervention against the Bosnian Serbs. Throughout the war, Thatcher never wavered in her conviction that a multi-ethnic Bosnia was worth saving; that the rescue could be effected through the massive use of air power combined with lifting the arms embargo on the Bosnian government; and that the failure to intervene was damaging to western credibility in general and that of Britain in particular.[4] 'Nato,' she argued in mid-1992, 'is the most practical instrument to hand, [and] must deal with the crisis. It is not "out of area".'[5] Two years later she noted that 'the credibility of our international stance on every security issue from nuclear non-proliferation to the Middle East is now at stake . . . would-be aggressors are waiting to see how we deal with the Serbs.'[6]

Thatcher was scathing about the inadequacy of British policy and the premises on which it was based. 'We could have stopped this,' she argued in December 1992. 'We could still do so. We have sent a small number of our brave and highly professional servicemen to accompany inadequate supplies to feed some Bosnians before the Serbs and the winter kill them.' 'But for the most part,' she continued, 'we in the west have actually given comfort to the aggressor. We have continued to treat this war of aggression by Serbia as if it were a "civil war". We have repeatedly stated in public that we will not intervene militarily, so removing even a nagging uncertainty from the minds of the generals in Belgrade. We have accepted the flouting of successive Security Council resolutions by Serbia, whose aircraft are still free to drop cluster bombs on women and children.'[7]

But Thatcher's most effective intervention by far was in April 1993, at the height of the first Srebrenica crisis.[8] Rejecting as 'disgraceful', the notion that lifting the arms embargo would create a 'level killing field', she pointed out that Bosnia was already a 'killing field the like of which I thought we would never see in Europe again [and was] not worthy of Europe, not worthy of the west and not worthy of the United States'. 'This,' she stressed, 'is happening in the heart of Europe and we have not done any more to stop it. It is in Europe's sphere of influence. It should be in Europe's sphere of conscience . . . We are little more than an accomplice to massacre.'[9] In private conversation, it seems, Thatcher was even blunter. 'Douglas, Douglas,' she told the Foreign Secretary, 'you would make Neville Chamberlain look like a warmonger.'[10]

Under the impact of this onslaught, which was warmly supported in parts of the press, public approval for military action mounted. A Gallup poll – which had been conducted shortly before her spectacular intervention – showed that 60 per cent of the public supported the dispatch of an international force to impose peace in Bosnia, while 67 per cent wanted British participation.[11] This was, if nothing else, a sign that domestic consensus to reverse or at least contain ethnic cleansing could be built, provided sufficient leadership were shown. Elements within the Conservative Party, such as the Chairman of the Foreign Affairs Committee, David Howell, appeared to break ranks.[12] Of this, more later, but the Major administration dug in. The Prime Minister told the Commons that nobody 'has the monopoly of concern or conscience about this matter', while the Defence Secretary took on Margaret Thatcher directly, and dismissed her claim that Britain had become 'an accomplice to genocide' as 'emotional nonsense'. Some MPs were even more scathing: Robert Adley, the Conservative MP for Christchurch, advised the Prime Minister to ignore 'this former Finchley fishwife'; another suggested that 'The unofficial view is that she has flipped – gone completely mad. It was good Dog and Duck stuff for a Friday afternoon in the pub.'[13]

In the end, like many British supporters of the Bosnian cause, Thatcher became a foreign-political pilgrim. 'After many fruitless conversations with the Foreign Office,' she recalled in her memoirs, 'I despaired of a hearing in Britain. I therefore focused on the United States, seeking to awaken the conscience of the west.'[14] Help would come from across the Atlantic, or it would not come at all.

The British political system never generated within itself the momentum or clarity to reverse a disastrous policy. Instead, this pressure was to come from the force of events themselves, and – more particularly – from the very different interpretation being put on them in the United States. John Major noted how concerned both America and Britain became from 1993 onwards with the Bosnian war.[15] As the debate progressed, disagreements over Bosnia were to culminate in what was, in Major's opinion, the most worrying Anglo-American rift since Suez.[16] This view was shared by the diplomats and officials responsible for the formulation and execution of British policy. Sir Robin Renwick, who had to defend British policy as ambassador in Washington, writes that 'the Bosnia crisis provoked sharp transatlantic differences and one of the most serious disagreements between the British and American governments since Suez'.[17] Sir David Hannay, who was in the line of fire as the British permanent representative on the United Nations

Security Council, admits that Bosnia, though not comparable to Suez, was the most 'sustained and damaging rift' with the United States for the past forty years.[18] Even such a restrained and seasoned observer as Sir Percy Cradock, John Major's foreign policy advisor for many years, was to write that 'Western prestige and alliance solidarity suffered. Yugoslavia must have been one of the first instances of Britain siding with Europe against the United States in a major international crisis . . . the wrangling between London and Washington over Yugoslavia would be costly and would contribute significantly to the decline in the special relationship in the later Major years.'[19]

American views were, if anything, even starker. As Richard Holbrooke, the US Assistant Secretary of State for European Affairs who later brokered the Dayton accords, subsequently observed, 'By the spring of 1995 it had become commonplace to say that Washington's relations with our European allies were worse than at any time since the 1956 Suez crisis. But this comparison was misleading: because Suez came at the height of the Cold War, the strain then was containable. Bosnia, however, had defined the first phase of the post-Cold War relationship between Europe and the United States, and seriously damaged the Atlantic relationship.'[20] Nor was this just self-serving exaggeration, designed to highlight Holbrooke's subsequent negotiating skills. Tony Lake, the National Security Advisor from early 1993, also observed that, whereas the Bosnian Crisis 'wasn't as bad as Suez, it was the worst since Suez [and was] potentially a crisis worse than Suez'.[21] Even Raymond Seitz, the American ambassador in London, himself a sympathizer with the British position, conceded that 'The policy gap was so deep you could sometimes smell a whiff of Suez.'[22] The resulting atmosphere of mistrust and recrimination was subsequently summed up by an official of the US State Department: 'I learned to treat Britain as a hostile power. Britain was prepared to go to the wall against us on Bosnia – out to block anything, everything. I came to think of the British like having the Russians around the State Department.'[23]

By a terrible irony all this was visited on a British administration which prided itself on its 'Atlanticist' credentials. Indeed, Britain had entered the 1990s with a considerable reserve of goodwill built up by the Reagan–Thatcher relationship of the 1980s and consolidated by

Britain's steadfast and unfrivolous performance during the Gulf crisis, when she had twice intervened to strengthen US resolve, first after the invasion of Kuwait itself, and then during the humanitarian disaster brought on by the collapse of the Kurdish revolt in northern Iraq.

At first, all seemed quiet across the Atlantic. It was not that the US government was entirely uninformed or uninterested in Bosnia. Both President Bush's National Security Advisor, Brent Scowcroft, and his last Secretary of State, Lawrence Eagleburger, knew Yugoslavia well; and the CIA had been issuing regular warnings of imminent warfare there since the late 1980s. But like the British government, the Bush administration still had its eye very much on the massive transformations taking place in the former Eastern Bloc and within the Soviet Union itself. For obvious reasons, it had no stomach for making Gorbachev's life more difficult than it already was by creating precedents in Slovenia and Croatia through early recognition of claims to national self-determination. At the same time, whatever strategic significance Yugoslavia had enjoyed in the Cold War had disappeared with the revolutions of 1989–90. A Yugoslav implosion, once the potential trigger for a Third World War, now seemed strangely irrelevant to US national security. The United States, as the Secretary of State James Baker memorably observed, had 'no dog in that fight'. Moreover, a ritualized late Cold War Atlanticism and the not entirely undeserved mutual satisfaction of a job well done in the Gulf, militated against any early confrontation with allied Britain over the situation in the former Yugoslavia.

In fact, the Americans shared key aims of early British policy, particularly the need to keep Yugoslavia together for as long as possible.[24] Like London, the US State Department initially tried to defuse demands for intervention by suppressing the accounts of Serbian camps and atrocities which surfaced in the late summer of 1992;[25] for the same reason, initially upbeat military assessments of the viability of air strikes against Bosnian Serb forces besieging Sarajevo were ignored and revised.[26] Indeed, during the first stages of the EU-sponsored talks in that year, James Baker underlined his distance from the problem by refusing to send an observer.[27] Not least among President George Bush's concerns was to avoid a foreign intervention during an election year. For the first six months of the Bosnian war, therefore, US policy – not unlike British policy – was based on the 'Yellowstone theory', by which the brush fires in the region should be allowed to burn themselves out.

Underlying this were two mutually reinforcing tendencies within the Bush administration. The first was a strong view that – particularly after American exertions in the Gulf – it was up to Europe to take the lead on a major and manageable security issue within its own bailiwick. 'Our point,' as Bruce Jackson, a leading voice in the Republican Party on security issues, recalls, 'was that the Europeans should do it themselves, because this was a small brush fire that was clearly within their ambit of responsibilities and if they let it burn out of control it's going to suck us in.'[28] So when the Luxembourgeois Foreign Minister Jacques Poos memorably declared the early stages of the Yugoslav crisis 'The hour of Europe', the Americans were more relieved than offended. 'We were quite happy,' as Reagan's former Assistant Secretary of State for Defense, Richard Perle, recalls, 'to let the Europeans have a go at it.'[29] But there were also darker sentiments at work. As one note-taker present at State Department meetings testifies, James Baker and Lawrence Eagleburger both felt that the 'European bluff should be called'. Indeed, they had a two-way bet on the outcome. If the Europeans succeeded it would simplify an agenda already dominated by Iraq and the disintegration of the Sovet Union; if they failed, it would bring the Europeans down a peg. 'They will screw it up,' Eagleburger argued, 'and this will teach them a lesson' and 'teach them to burden-share'. This forecast turned out to be only half wrong.

In short, to any informed observer in 1992, the notion that the Bosnian conflict would lead to the greatest transatlantic rift since Suez would have seemed incredible. And yet, even then, some of the tension which was to explode into open conflict in 1993–5 was already evident. For one thing, the Bush administration, whatever the private sympathies and connections of Scowcroft and Eagleburger, did not long remain in doubt about the prime culprits. From mid-1992 onwards, the US government went – rhetorically – well beyond the British in placing the blame on the Bosnian Serbs and their sponsors in Belgrade.[30] Already at the end of May, the Americans singled out the Serbs for censure at the summit of the Conference on Security and

Cooperation in Europe (CSCE), and promised to withhold recognition from a state built on ethnic cleansing.[31] At the same time, the American Secretary of State, James Baker, heavily criticized his European counterparts for failing to contain the fighting. The sanctions imposed on rump Yugoslavia in May 1992 – in the face of Anglo-French misgivings – were largely at the behest of the US.[32]

What is little known, though no secret, is that James Baker seriously considered military intervention against the Bosnian Serbs in May–June 1992. The military was ready. As far back as the siege of Dubrovnik in late 1991, the Supreme Allied Commander Europe, General John Galvin, had prepared plans which envisaged, as he recalled, sending the fleet into the Adriatic and 'just sweeping those [Serb] vessels out of there, and taking care of the artillery as well. We could have achieved that objective, I believe, at very little or no cost.'[33] Likewise, Colonel Karl Lowe, a military planner working on the area at the time, felt that the Yugoslav People's Army was highly vulnerable to air attack, particularly if 'very concentrated and concerted for a number of days [to] home in on the command and control apparatus'.[34] The sanctions of May 1992 were thus only a first step. 'Their intention,' the former State Department official John Fox relates, 'was to escalate into a sort of mini-Iraq thing, not to do it on the ground, but just to escalate to an air campaign.'[35] As the British ambassador in Washington recalls, the UN resolution authorizing 'all necessary measures' to effect the transit of humanitarian aid, 'was intended by Bush to permit the use of air power'.[36] This would have taken advantage of the psychologically opportune moment after news of Bosnian Serb concentration camps had made world headlines. However, as John Fox recalls, the idea 'then got snuffed', primarily because Baker's successor, Lawrence Eagleburger, was still firmly opposed to intervention, as were the Europeans.

Throughout 1992, the American sense of outrage was to mount as more and more Republicans, including the White House Press Spokeswoman, Margaret Tutwiler, the Senate minority leader, Bob Dole, and numerous figures within the administration began to lean towards some form of military intervention on behalf of the Bosnian government. The parting shots of the outgoing Bush administration in December 1992 were two warnings to Belgrade: Lawrence Eagleburger's public denunciation of Serbian President Milosevic's responsibility for war crimes in Bosnia, and George Bush's famous 'Christmas warning' not to precipitate a crisis in Kosovo on pain of a US intervention; this was, as one indignant British diplomat put it, 'a unilateral warning given by the US administration, without consultation as far as I know, and certainly without seeking to get our support . . . and it had no UN validation'. Indeed, by 1994, Eagleburger was calling for air strikes on Serbia itself in order to restore the credibility of Nato and the west.[37]

There were a number of reasons for this shift. First of all, far from burning itself out, the war seemed to bring daily fresh tales of (principally) Serbian expulsions, atrocities, and rapes. Secondly and relatedly, the Democratic presidential candidate, Governor Bill Clinton, cast aside his initial hesitation and made Bosnia an issue in the election campaign. In July 1992, Clinton had argued that 'We have to be very careful. We don't want this to be another Beirut. We don't want America to get into a quagmire that is essentially a civil war that we can't solve and that may not be worth the lives of Americans.'[38] But within a month he had staked out his public policy – or appeared to – when he called for the use of 'air power against the Serbs to try to restore the basic conditions of humanity'.[39] A few days later he promised in a campaign speech to 'make the United States the catalyst for a collective stand against aggression' in Bosnia.[40] In private, however, Clinton remained very cautious.

Yet it would be wrong to see Bosnia as simply an electoral football, or the shifts in American policy as a purely media-driven reaction to the humanitarian crisis on the television screens: the 'CNN factor'. In fact, throughout the Bosnian crisis, polls indicated that US popular revulsion at Serb atrocities did not translate into a consensus even for air action against the Bosnian Serbs. In August 1992, for example, research by *Newsweek* showed that only 53 per cent of the public wanted the US to take the lead in the United Nations-sponsored air strikes against the Bosnian Serbs. There was never more than a bare majority for even such minimal military involvement, which in any case quickly evaporated after the American excursion into the Somalia civil war ended with eighteen dead Rangers in the autumn of 1993.[41] In early May 1993, at the height of the first Srebrenica crisis and the 'lift and strike' debate, an NBC/*Wall Street Journal* poll showed that 58 per cent of respondents thought that 'all ethnic groups were equally responsible' for the fighting, with 21 per cent unsure, and only 16 per cent who blamed the Serbs. As Lee Hamilton, the Democratic Chairman of the House of Representatives Foreign Affairs Committee, observed, the figures were 'all over the place'.[42]

But whereas both American governments were conscious of the polls on Bosnia, particularly the Clinton administration, they were not – as some British critics liked to claim – mesmerized by them. President Clinton's chief pollster, Stan Greenberg, pointed out that whereas there was currently no support for unilateral US military action among the public, polls on foreign policy issues were unhelpful as they could give no indication on popular views *after* the President had given a lead. According to Elizabeth Drew, a journalist who made an intimate study of the first Clinton administration, Greenberg 'also told Clinton that on the basis of his findings, Bosnia was a subject on which public opinion could be shaped'.[43] And so far from being stampeded by selective media images, interventionist opinion and US policy was driven by the events themselves, rather than by the way they were reported; individual atrocities such as the market-place massacre of February 1994 merely hastened the change in direction and did not fundamentally cause it.[44]

Rather, the key to the change in US policy lies in the development of *elite* opinion on Bosnia. It was from individual members of Congress, from the op-ed pages of the mainstream press, particularly the *New York Times*, the *Washington Post*, and the *Wall Street Journal*, from intellectuals, and from the foreign policy think tanks that first George Bush and then Bill Clinton came under sustained attack for their failure to support the Bosnian government. This was, as Bruce Jackson recalls, 'very much a revolution from above'. The men and women who drove this revolt, he adds, were 'people who could afford State Department careers and also afford to quit', and 'reporters who were secure enough in their careers', as well as 'Congressional aides who were animated by this and the editorial writers. So the people who brought this to world attention were probably two or three hundred people world-wide.'[45] As James Rubin, a confidant to Madeleine Albright, recalls: 'We were getting creamed in the papers every day for Bosnia . . . You couldn't mistake the pressure coming from newspapers and the media . . . it was real, it was relentless, it had an effect.'[46] Moreover, the relationship between Congressional and press opinion was fluid and direct: it was routine for Congressional debates on Bosnia to refer to important articles in the broadsheets, and for these to be entered on to the record either extensively or in full.

This debate was never entirely free from electoral or domestic ramifications, but the alignments were essentially bipartisan.[47] Thus the Republican critique of the policy of non-intervention began well before the election in November 1992. By the late summer of 1992, for example, Senator Richard Lugar, the Senior Republican on the Senate Foreign Relations Committee, was calling for air strikes on Serbian positions around Sarajevo and indeed on Serbia itself. The Republican leader in the Senate, Bob Dole, attacked his own administration directly in the summer of 1992, when he asked, 'Why didn't we respond to this aggression 12 months ago?'[48] (that is, when the Serbs were besieging Dubrovnik and levelling Vukovar). Similarly, some of the most tenacious critics of the Clinton administration were themselves Democrats, particularly Senators Joe Lieberman and Joe Biden. The US debate on Bosnia, which was to escalate in intensity from the summer of 1992, eventually ended in July 1995 with a major constitutional crisis: the direct confrontation between a bipartisan majority in the Senate and the Clinton White House over the ending of the arms embargo against the Bosnian government. Of this, more later.

The misgivings that broad sections of the American foreign-political and national security establishment entertained towards US policy towards Bosnia were to be extensively aired throughout the first three years of Clinton's first term, both publicly and in private. Already in the spring of 1992, the former Undersecretary of State for Asian Affairs Richard Holbrooke had telephoned the Bosnian ambassador to the United Nations, Mohamed Sacirbey, to offer his support.[49] In late August of that year he wrote a confidential memorandum to the democratic presidential candidate Bill Clinton and his running mate Al Gore. 'This is not a choice between Vietnam and doing nothing, as the Bush administration has portrayed it,' Holbrooke wrote. 'There are many actions that might be done now, including: dropping the arms embargo against the Bosnians, stationing UN observers along the Kosovo and Macedonia borders . . . Doing nothing now risks a far greater and more costly involvement later.'[50] A month later he publicly attacked the Bush administration in *Newsweek*. 'By its inadequate reaction so far,' he wrote, 'the United States and, to an even greater extent, the European Community may be undermining not only the dreams of a post-Cold War "European House" but also laying the seeds for another era of tragedy in Europe.'[51] He concluded the piece with a call to consider the lifting of the arms embargo against the Bosnian government and the use of air strikes against the Bosnian Serbs.

What is certainly not true is the claim that Europe, effectively Britain and France, had to fill a void left by the absence of US engagement. British objections to limited American intervention against the Bosnian Serbs *predated* the dispatch of British troops. As John Fox recalls, 'the most active lobbying from the [British] embassy [in Washington] came in the spring/summer of 1992 [i.e., before the arrival of British UNPROFOR personnel later that year], when there were some fairly significant attempts from the side of people who worked for Baker to mount an intervention, and this was essentially recommendations for a bombing campaign. And [there] was a very hard line coming out of the [British] embassy against this, very targeted at people in the State Department who were advocating it.'[52] The notion that Britain was somehow 'waiting for America' does not stand up to examination.

The incoming Clinton administration was determined to take a fresh look at western policy towards Bosnia. Many of the new faces, such as Tony Lake, the National Security Advisor, Madeleine Albright, the ambassador to the United Nations, and Al Gore, the Vice-President, were committed supporters of the Bosnian government.[53] During her confirmation hearings, Madeleine Albright announced that Bosnia was 'clearly the highest priority of the President in the National Security Council's agenda'.[54] On the other hand, the new Secretary of State for Foreign Affairs, Warren Christopher, and the Defense Secretary, Les Aspin, were known sceptics on Bosnia. Clinton himself promised just before his inauguration that 'the legitimacy of ethnic cleansing cannot stand',[55] a statement which was widely interpreted as a manifesto for the rollback of Bosnian Serb gains. For many in the new administration, the Bosnian cause was first and foremost a moral one; but amongst experienced figures like Tony Lake, there was also a deep-seated concern about the broader strategic implications of western inaction for the US position in Europe, the Aegean and even the Middle East. He thought the distinction between 'humanitarian' and 'strategic' concerns mistaken. 'The reason it [Bosnia] was topic A for us,' he recalls, 'was precisely because it did involve interests and very real humanitarian concerns as well.'[56] As Richard Holbrooke put it in a memorandum in mid-January 1993: 'Bosnia will be the key test of American policy in Europe . . . Continued inaction carries long-term risks which could be disruptive to US–European relations, weaken NATO, increase tension in Greece and Turkey, and cause havoc with Moscow.'[57]

Relations between Britain and the new man in the White House were already a little tense. 'The Anglo-Saxons,' as the *Telegraph* journalist Ambrose Evans-Pritchard put it, 'are now the skunks at the garden party.'[58] Tellingly, Bill Clinton had been unable to find time to see the Prime Minister on his visit to Washington in the winter of 1992, nor did the President respond to an invitation to an early visit to London. Part of this coolness was due to the immense ideological and cultural gulf which separated even the desiccated Toryism of John Major from the po-faced multiculturalism of the new Clinton administration. More specifically, there was considerable ill feeling about the assistance rendered by Conservative Central Office to the vanquished Republicans during the election. 'The reports of a personal battle between Clinton and Major,' as Tony Lake recalls, 'were greatly overblown.' Nevertheless, he admits, 'there was tension between political advisors over the [election campaigns]'.[59] Moreover, the increased importance of the Irish lobby and Irish vote in Washington was regarded with profound suspicion in London. But the biggest bone of contention was Bosnia.

The first tentative signs of a more activist US policy elicited stiff British opposition. In January and February 1993, American plans to air-drop relief supplies to the hard-pressed Bosnian eastern enclaves of Srebrenica, Cerska and Kamenica, were heavily criticized by London. The British also blocked – for much longer than they decently could – US plans for the creation and the enforcement of a 'no-fly zone' principally directed against Serb aircraft.[60] In both cases, London argued that the risks to the air crews and the danger of provoking Serb retaliation against British forces serving with the United Nations 'on the ground' were too great. And in both cases, in a way which was to become depressingly familiar over the next two years, the British position was presented with a heavily hostile 'spin' against the Americans. 'America might get the glory for shooting down the Serbs,' one government source said, 'but our soldiers would be soft targets if they fire back.'[61] 'There is,' another source claimed, 'a sharp distinction between the doers [i.e., the British] and the spectators [i.e., the Americans].'[62] It was all very well, the Defence Secretary told BBC radio in mid-December 1992, for the Americans to demand enforcement of the no-fly ban, when they had no troops on the ground. 'The Rifkind view,' as one Ministry of Defence source put it in late February 1993, 'is that the Americans are pushing for something that is basically pretty futile but will look very telegenic.'[63]

Moreover, the military relevance of the Serbian violations of the no-fly zone was hotly denied.[64] Indeed, the government took the unusual step of publishing extracts from the report of Tim Lankester, the Permanent Secretary, Overseas Development Administration, who visited Bosnia in late November 1992 and stayed with UNPROFOR. 'Concern was expressed,' he wrote, 'that the security situation was worsening, and also that the UN might move to enforce the no-fly ban. Such aircraft movements as there were, were said not to be causing a significant problem for the Bosnians and any move to enforce the ban would put the air operation and UNPROFOR forces at greater risk.'[65] The British ambassador in Washington, on the other hand, did not share these fears. He told a meeting on Bosnia convened by the Prime Minister that 'a no-fly zone could and should be enforced and that the Serbs were unlikely to challenge this'.[66]

As it happened, the air drops went ahead, and the no-fly zone was eventually enforced, without provoking any Serbian reaction. But, as the former State Department lawyer Michael Scharf recalls, British obstructionism took its toll: whereas the original no-fly proposal was as severe as that imposed on Iraq in 1991, the British succeeded in watering down the final resolution – which spoke only of 'monitoring' the zone – to such an extent that another resolution was needed in the new year to allow for enforcement.[67]

At the same time, Britain and the United States crossed swords over the creation of a United Nations War Crimes Tribunal for the former Yugoslavia. In some respects, British reservations about the viability and legitimacy of such a body were reasonable and longstanding. Already at Nuremberg, British lawyers had been concerned about questions of precedent, evidence, and fairness; they were also generally wary of the global penchant for seeking legal solutions to what were essentially political problems. But in 1992–3, British obstructionism went well beyond such honourable considerations. At almost every stage of its gestation at the UN, British diplomats and lawyers strove to stifle the War Crimes Tribunal at birth. Thus, when the Security Council established a Commission of Experts to investigate breaches of humanitarian law in the former Yugoslavia in October 1992, Britain successfully opposed a demand by the US State Department that the body should be called a 'War Crimes Commission'.[68] Britain also resisted supplying the commission with evidence from debriefed former camp detainees who had found refuge in the United Kingdom.[69] As Frits Klashoven, the Dutch head of the Geneva Commission on War Crimes, subsequently remarked: 'Britain hasn't done anything for us – nothing at all.'[70]

British attempts to subvert the War Crimes Tribunal culminated in the famous 'non-paper' of March 1993. This document – entitled 'Former Yugoslavia: War Crimes Implementation of Resolution 808. Comments and Observations of the United Kingdom', was never formally submitted as a Security Council paper, and British diplomats deny all knowledge of it. On the surface, it expressed confidence in the aims and legitimacy of the Tribunal, but the thrust of the argument suggested otherwise. Even the opening contention that 'The most appropriate basis for establishing an international criminal tribunal would be a treaty between the successor states of former Yugoslavia and other concerned states' under which 'the successor states would cede jurisdiction to the tribunal', was open to question;[71] the notion that Milosevic would agree to a measure which would allow the prosecution of Belgrade-based paramilitary formations – or indeed of himself – was fanciful. The document also expressed serious doubts about the nature of the law to be applied by the Tribunal, queried the competence of the Security Council in that matter, and suggested limiting the tribunal to a 'modest' size until the number of trials was known; it was recommended that 'the judges, including the President, should not be full-time'.[72]

But perhaps the most insidious passage referred to the question of revoking immunity for heads of state: 'It may . . . be undesirable politically to include any provision on the subject in the draft statutes or any reference to it in the report.' Clearly, British thinking went, there could be no peace agreement if one side had the threat of prosecution hanging over their heads.[73] This was openly admitted by the Minister of State in the Foreign Office, Douglas Hogg, who observed to the House of Commons in February 1993 that 'If the authority – the responsibility for those crimes goes as high as the hon. gentleman and I expect, we must ask ourselves what is the priority: is it to bring people to trial or is it to make peace? That is the sort of tension with which we must deal.'[74] Likewise, the number two at the British mission in New York, Tom Richardson, recalls that 'underlying [British attitudes on the War Crimes Tribunal] was a general feeling that at some stage we were going to have to talk to the Serbs. It wasn't going to help very much if all of them were going to be in fear of arrest at The Hague.'[75]

It is no wonder, therefore, that the British did all they could to avoid an activist Chief Prosecutor. When the United States, many Muslim states and the non-aligned states proposed Cherif Bassiouni, an Egyptian-American professor of law at DePaul University near Chicago, Britain, France, Russia and China objected. The British argued that the appointment should be by consensus and canvassed views about the distinguished Scotch lawyer, John Duncan Lowe, though he was never formally proposed.[76] 'Bassiouni', as the Venezuelan ambassador to the UN, Diego Arria, observed, 'was seen as a threat to the peace process.'[77] This was also the reason why Bassiouni refused to serve beneath the British nominee Duncan Lowe. He later remarked that 'I felt that the number two spot would have no say in deciding the strategy for investigations and prosecutions, and feared that Lowe might follow the British line and subordinate prosecutions to Lord Owen's elusive quest for peace.'[78]

Subsequently, the British permanent representative to the UN Security Council, Sir David Hannay, agreed that there might have been a tension between peace and justice in Bosnia.[79] At the time, he told BBC news that the War Crimes resolution was not meaningless rhetoric: 'I think that this is very important assurance for all those who have suffered in the former Yugoslavia that their sufferings are not going to be set on one side simply because there is some diplomatic deal.'[80] He himself has consistently denied any intention to block or delay the Tribunal.

What was particularly remarkable about British objections to US activism on Bosnia was the style in which they were made, and the assumptions underlying them. John Fox, who was on the receiving end for much of 1992 and early 1993, recalls the 'vigour and even desperation with which these lines [were] pushed'.[81] 'I never saw in my lifetime of dealing with these folks in and out of government . . . that kind of, I would almost call it passion, except it wasn't passion, it was interest . . . expressed in such a determined way, no holds barred.'[82] As a 'born and bred Anglophile', who had spent part of his education at a British public school, he 'discovered to [his] consternation . . . that British policy was . . . not just indifferent . . . but actively hostile to the steps that could prevent . . . ethnic cleansing'. 'This became apparent' to him, 'principally through the efforts of the [Washington] embassy . . . but also [from] various US [diplomatic] posts that they were aggressively lobbying against any response to ethnic cleansing'.[83] The impulse, he was told, came directly from Douglas Hurd.

Of course, as John Fox relates, this was all 'done with bluff and bravado and style . . . avuncular, Athens to Rome'.[84] But underlying this, serving and retired US diplomats felt, was a profound and patronizing contempt for US policy and judgement. Nor was this entirely in their imagination: even today, mention of American approaches to Bosnia provokes tirades from British officials who served on both sides of the Atlantic. At the time, their disregard was manifest, and resented. And whereas Douglas Hurd was unanimously credited with old-world courtesy, the Defense Secretary's style, which, as Marshall Harris and many others recall, 'was more confrontational and had sharper edges',[85] caused widespread offence.

This picture is confirmed by a very well-placed British Nato source. 'Many people in the United States,' he recalls, 'really saw the Brits as Chamberlain-style appeasers. I remember one meeting I went to in the State Department . . . where the anti-British feeling, again Chamberlain/appeasement/Munich, was very strong . . . and I am not talking here about those who, for example, backed Argentina against the UK in the Falklands crisis, I am talking about the European Department of the State Department, with people who had a long tradition of working with Europeans and with the UK, no natural animus. I think they saw the UK as being the one partner that they thought they could count on to make a case for firm action, because that was what the UK had done during the Gulf War, when John Major had been totally supportive, that is what the UK had done regarding the Kurds, [and] we have seen it recently with the air strikes in Iraq. But the one partner that the Americans thought they could rely upon to lobby in Europe for a more robust reaction was in fact as they saw it at the other end of the spectrum, making the case for doing nothing.'[86] The shock was to run very deep.

American officials were mystified as to the motivations of British policy. Some cultivated dark and probably unjustified suspicions about base financial considerations in the higher reaches of politics and officialdom. Others were convinced that Britain sought to contain the rise of German power in the area. Others still believed that Britain viewed the Serbs as 'clients' and that some British politicians were 'pro-Serb'.[87] Routinely, serving US diplomats recall, British diplomats and politicians would claim that 'the Serbs were our allies', 'they fought Hitler' and that 'the Serbs at least had no concentration camps'. At the very least they believed that Britain was 'practically' biased towards the Serbs. In short, as Marshall Harris recalls, 'with the British you had this old, old tangle or every possible objection you could'.[88] All were bewildered and outraged by Britain's determination not merely to avoid intervention against the Bosnian Serbs, but to prevent anybody else from intervening either.

The main problem was that American solicitude for Bosnia cut across a central plank of British policy, which was to force the Bosnians to 'cut a deal'. This was to become particularly evident in 1993–4, but the roots of the estrangement went back to 1992. Lord Carrington, for example, believed that the Americans 'took an extraordinary view' in favour of the Bosnians that summer. 'The Americans,' he claims, 'felt that Bosnia was the downtrodden member of the outfit, and that . . . poor little Bosnia [was] being mucked about by the Serbs and Croats.'[89] Indeed, he blamed them for scuppering an agreement which Jose Cutileiro, a Portuguese diplomat working under his direction, had arranged with all three sides. 'The Americans,' Carrington claims, 'actually sent them [the Bosnians] a telegram telling them not to agree.'[90] 'The Bosnian government,' as Hurd subsequently explained, 'had to be shown that they weren't going to get the UN cavalry coming to the rescue.'[91]

The British were therefore infuriated when the US blew hot and cold over the Vance–Owen plan as unveiled in early 1993. This scheme envisaged the division of Bosnia into a number of autonomous – effectively independent – Serb, Croat and 'Muslim' provinces. It was initially rejected by the Americans on the ground that it *both* ratified ethnic cleansing *and* involved a risky, open-ended and large-scale commitment of US and other western troops to enforce it; it was the worst of all possible worlds. Lord Owen took the American reservations as a personal affront and immediately embarked on a tour of the airwaves to convince Washington that the plan was 'the only game in town'; of all this, more later. The British government, for its part, in what was to become a standard refrain over the next two years, criticized the Americans for damaging the peace process, and endangering British troops, without being prepared to risk its own forces on the ground.

It is certainly true that the Bosnians were heartened by administration and Congressional support and the evident sympathy their cause enjoyed in the United States. 'I don't know what President Clinton and the administration will decide,' the Bosnian leader Alija Izetbegovic remarked in early February 1993, 'But I am now very sure that American public opinion cannot approve any ethnic division of the country and cannot approve ethnic cleansing. I am sure that the American government will follow the American people.'[92] Yet it is a big step from this to say that the Americans 'prolonged the agony' of the Bosnians by encouraging them to hold out for more at the negotiating table or even for belated intervention on their behalf. There is no evidence that the Bosnians would have capitulated without such tepid and inconstant encouragement from the US government as they did receive; and there is, in any case, a lot of evidence to suggest that the Bosnian Serbs were not seriously interested in anything but a maximalist solution prior to the summer of 1995. Quite simply, the Bosnians fought on because they faced extinction if they did not.

Central to the American critique of British policy was their assessment of the military options open to the west. The stark alternative between massive intervention or a purely humanitarian operation was rejected. As one senior diplomat remarked as far back as June 1992, 'The characterisation of the use of force has been too much either/or. Either large numbers of ground forces are sent in, or nobody. There is a range in between that is conceivable. You could talk about actions like knocking out from the air the heavy weaponry that enables the Serbs to lob shells from the hillside with impunity.'[93] And when Douglas Hurd lamented after a meeting of the Contact Group in Geneva in August 1994 that 'We don't have the power to impose a solution' on the Bosnian Serbs, he was reminded by Warren Christopher that the west certainly did have the power, but had decided not to use it.[94] American frustration with British attempts to shrink the military options available was also privately expressed by Clinton's special envoy to the Balkans, Reginald Bartholomew, both in his visit to London in April 1993 and on many subsequent occasions.[95] Instead, the new administration developed an alternative strategy for rolling back ethnic cleansing, or at least forcing the Bosnian Serbs into serious negotiations: lifting the arms embargo on the Bosnian government and launching large-scale air strikes on the Bosnian Serbs. As Tony Lake subsequently explained, the two approaches were complementary: attacking each in isolation was therefore something of a 'straw man'.[96] The debate about 'lift and strike' – for short – was to be at the heart of the Anglo-American rift over Bosnia for the next two years.

Already in 1992, spy-satellite image analysts at the National Security Agency had noted that Serb artillery around Sarajevo was highly vulnerable to air attack. The vast majority of these installations, they argued, might be eliminated in one day.[97] Similarly, the Chief of Staff of the Air Force, General Merrill McPeak, advised the White House throughout 1993 that the Bosnian Serbs could be checked through air power alone: Serb guns, he argued, could be knocked out at 'virtually no risk' to the US aircraft involved.[98] Another supporter of military action was Admiral Boorda, then chief of Nato's Southern Command and later Navy chief.[99] Of course, American political and military opinion was by no means unanimous about the need for and viability of military action in Bosnia. As the Secretary for Defense, William Perry, warned in February 1994, 'The question is, what will the effect be? Not, can we bomb some facilities and kill some people? If air strikes are Act One of a new melodrama, what is Act Two? What is Act Three? What is the conclusion?'[100] The Vice-Chairman of the Joint Chiefs of Staff pointed out that it was 'not a simple or easy thing to use air strikes against guerilla warfare units spread around the countryside'.[101] And the most well-known and influential American general, the Chairman of the Joint Chiefs of Staff, Colin Powell, was sceptical of US interests in Bosnia and vehemently opposed to the dispatch of ground troops. But Powell was inherently a cautious man – he had argued against military action in the Gulf and in favour of continued sanctions against Iraq – and in any case even he endorsed 'lift and strike' as a compromise policy.[102]

This new approach was enthusiastically supported by press and Congressional critics of western inaction. Senator Joseph Biden, a senior Democrat, argued in April 1993 that sending arms to the Bosnians would at least allow them 'to fight and die with a little bit of dignity'. Senator Bob Dole, a longstanding critic of Bush's Bosnia policy, observed that 'If nobody else is willing to defend these people they ought to have a right to defend themselves.'[103] And in early May 1993, forty-six Congressmen wrote to the President urging him to 'enforce the will and conscience of the international community'.[104] As William Safire put it in the *New York Times*, 'The answer is to give bombing a chance.'[105]

Britain, however, was strongly opposed to any sort of military intervention, and in particular to air strikes. From time to time she was publicly prepared to countenance the selective use of air power – as the lesser evil – but in private she consistently sabotaged American initiatives: in February 1993, in April–May 1993, and throughout the following two years.[106] Britain's motivations for so doing were threefold. First of all, British policy-makers feared that air strikes would antagonize the Serbs, encourage the Bosnians to fight on, and generally damage the negotiations at Geneva. Secondly and relatedly, they argued that air attacks would expose British forces on the ground to Serb reprisals. 'We did feel,' as one senior serving British diplomat put it many years later, 'that the US were quite happy putting other countries' troops at risk because they had nothing on the ground themselves.' Thirdly, they did not believe that air power alone could coerce the Bosnian Serbs. Malcolm Rifkind pointed out that air strikes had not sufficed to eject Saddam Hussein from Kuwait. Besides, the 'clear military advice received by the government is that air strikes unsupported by substantial numbers of troops on the ground would be unlikely to be effective given the nature of the conflict, the weapons deployed and the terrain. The chances of civilian casualties would be high.'[107] In April 1993 John Major had asked the Chiefs of Staff to advise on the use of air power to protect the civilian population in Bosnia. The Chiefs recommended that this would not be feasible. They advised that the situation on the ground, the topography of the region and its meteorological peculiarities mitigated against air strikes.[108] We shall return to the question of this military advice in due course.

Moreover, the British argued, air action required troops on the ground, not only to function as forward air controllers, but also in order to consolidate gains made and enforce the peace. It was in this context that the British repeatedly played what they took to be their strongest card: the vulnerability of their own forces with the United Nations relief effort and the unwillingness of the Americans to commit any troops of their own, either to confront the Serbs or to oversee a settlement.[109] When asked about American criticisms, Hurd would reply sharply: 'What is being done on the ground is being done by Europeans.'[110] Likewise, when the British ambassador, Sir Robin Renwick, found himself at odds over Bosnia with incoming Vice-President Al Gore at a dinner party in late 1992, he recalls responding 'that we were risking the lives of British soldiers in Bosnia. This was something the United States was, at the time, unwilling to do, notwithstanding the lectures we received on the subject . . . We would take the Americans seriously on this subject once they were ready to share those risks.'[111] Renwick was later to find himself making similar points in 'lively' debates with American senators. 'The Americans being fair-minded people,' he recalls, 'it was easy enough to win these jousts by pointing out that we would listen to them once they had forces engaged who shared the risks they were taking.'[112] What these ripostes overlooked was that Britain had passionately opposed the use of air power long before her first soldier set foot in Bosnia, and that the humanitarian operation had been intended from the beginning as an ameliorative measure to fend off US-sponsored demands for military intervention.

There was, in any case, a potentially large and highly motivated allied army on the ground: the legitimate army of the state of Bosnia-Herzegovina. It lacked only weapons, denied to it by the arms embargo imposed on the whole of the former Yugoslavia in September 1991 and controversially extended in 1992 to its successor states. As President Clinton's special envoy to the Balkans, Reginald Bartholomew, explained during a fraught visit to London, light arms could be distributed quickly, and the Bosnians could be trained to operate heavier weaponry within seventy-hours.[113] The notion of lifting the embargo on the Bosnian government was floated by Warren Christopher during his confirmation hearings as Secretary of State before the Senate in January 1993.[114] The obvious injustice of the embargo, which, as President Clinton and many others pointed out, 'unfairly and unintentionally penalised the victim of the conflict',[115] made it a prime target of those calling for a change in western policy towards Bosnia. 'The legitimate government,' the *Spectator* argued in January 1993, 'has the men. All it needs are the tools to finish the job.'

The arguments for lifting the embargo were to be rehearsed on many occasions throughout the war, but they were perhaps most cogently advanced by Norman Cigar, Professor of National Security Studies at the US Marine Corps School for Advanced Warfighting in Quantico, Virginia. He pointed out that the embargo copperfastened the decisive superiority of the Serbs in conventional heavy weaponry: 'it has been the regular forces, and particularly the heavy units with their preponderance of heavy equipment and their mobility, which have constituted the Bosnian Serbs' operational centre of gravity.'[116] At the heart of Cigar's analysis was a politico-military assessment of

Bosnian Serb capabilities and psychology. He stressed that the Bosnian Serb army was by no means a formidable fighting machine, but rather dogged by low morale, draft-dodging and desertion. 'The manpower and morale problems,' Cigar argued, 'suggest that the conflict is not likely to develop into an interminable "people's war" on the part of the Serbs if their conventional forces are unsuccessful.' He did not believe that lifting the embargo would bring Serbia itself into the war – any more than she already was. In fact, Cigar wrote, 'The available evidence suggests strongly that both Milosevic and the Bosnian Serb leadership are "rational" in their decision-making . . . and that the Milosevic government, in particular, is quite responsive to a cost–benefit calculus.' Milosevic and the Bosnian Serbs would 'sit down and negotiate, not escalate'. Thus, 'Real peace is likely only if a military balance is established.'[117] Finally, he warned, there was no evidence that lifting the embargo would jeopardize the eastern enclaves: 'Even if the embargo is maintained . . . the Serbs will still try to eliminate as many of the safe areas as possible.'[118]

The arms embargo was not, of course, a solely British preoccupation. Within the Security Council it was supported – for obvious reasons – by the Russian and Chinese, but also by the French and some rotating members. Nevertheless, Britain was rightly singled out by the Americans – and other observers – as the principal obstacle to the lifting of the embargo.[119] As one of Madeleine Albright's aides remarked, 'The British would find the lowest common denominator, the least action possible, knowing that was what the UN would go for.'[120] It was Douglas Hurd who in February 1993 persuaded the German Foreign Minister Klaus Kinkel to back off from his demand that the Bosnians be allowed to defend themselves.[121] It was Britain which threatened to oppose any attempt to lift the embargo in the Security Council; and it was Malcolm Rifkind who travelled to Washington in a last-ditch attempt to win over the US administration.[122] It was Britain that galvanized opposition to the lifting of the embargo at the failed Security Council vote in June 1993. In violation of all common sense and instinctive natural justice, Britain refused to become the 'arsenal of Bosnian democracy'. It did not follow the example of Roosevelt's America, which had revoked neutrality legislation specifically designed to stop the sale of US weapons to belligerents, in order to allow Britain to fight on in 1940. Indeed, Britain elected to prevent – with an almost theological fervour – anyone else from filling that role in her place.

Legally, the British were certainly skating on the thinnest of ice. It was well known that Article 51 of the UN Charter confirmed the 'inherent right of individual or collective self-defence if an armed attack occurs against a member of the United Nations, until the Security Council has taken measures necessary to maintain international peace and security'. This right was an integral part of western political culture, positive international law and natural justice. Indeed, when justifying the intervention against Iraq in the Gulf, Douglas Hurd – writing in 1998 – argued that 'Article 51 of the UN Charter provides an absolute [!] right of self-defence.'[123] It was only the crucial clause 'until the Security Council has taken measures' which prevented Britain from being in direct and incontrovertible violation of the charter. For the duration of the conflict, government lawyers and diplomats were to argue that the intervention of the Security Council had nullified the 'inherent right of self-defence'.

Even legally, this was a shaky construction at best, since the charter also determined that '*nothing in the present charter* shall impair the inherent right of *individual* or collective self-defence'.[124] Moreover, the United Nations General Assembly in 1993–4 twice passed with massive majorities resolutions calling for the embargo to be lifted.[125] Though this was not the first time the General Assembly found itself at loggerheads with the Security Council, or a member thereof, it did suggest a certain tension between legality – if such it was – and legitimacy. But the British defence was in any case totally casuistic, for no reasonable person could argue that – at least by 1993–4 – the UN Security Council had 'taken the measures necessary to maintain international peace and security' which might nullify Bosnia's right to self-defence. This was also the unambiguous view taken by the current Secretary General of the United Nations, Kofi Annan, in his coruscating report of 1999.[126]

But the legal, political and moral ironies did not end there. The British government, as Douglas Hogg put it, did 'not recognise the Federal Republic of Yugoslavia (Serbia and Montenegro)' as the legitimate successor to the old Yugoslavia.[127] By contrast, the Bosnian government in Sarajevo was both legally recognized by Britain and enjoyed *full* representation at the UN in New York, which their tormentors in Pale and Belgrade did not. As a result, the British refused to allow a government they did recognize to defend its people against armed subversion sponsored by a government they did not recognize. Besides, the contemporary case of Angola showed that the notion of distinguishing between a recognized government and an externally sponsored rebel force was not beyond them. In late 1993, the British government announced the selective lifting of the arms embargo on Angola, citing the Angolan government's 'legitimate right of self-defence' against the UNITA rebels of Jonas Savimbi.[128] Thus Douglas Hogg told the House of Commons in January 1995 that 'We observe mandatory embargoes imposed by the United Nations on Iraq, the former Republic of Yugoslavia, Somalia, Liberia, Libya, Rwanda and UNITA [rebels] in Angola.'[129] The (ex-?) communist regime of Angola, which had been loyal to Moscow and Havana in the mid-1970s, and which was not in control of vast tracts of the country, was evidently more legitimate than the Bosnian government in Sarajevo.

Confronted with this fact, David Hannay still saw – even in retrospect – 'no connection or contradiction between sustaining the international arms embargo on the countries of the former Yugoslavia (including Bosnia) and Britain's national decision to lift its embargo on exporting arms to the Angolan government in 1993 (where there had been at no time an international arms embargo and where most other exporters had been exporting arms for a period of years)'.[130] Hannay, of course, was missing the substance of the argument for the legal niceties: in the Bosnian case, Britain was not merely dutifully upholding a Security Council resolution, but was *herself the principal defender of the measure* in the teeth of massive opposition in the General Assembly and from the United States. Moreover, his own former deputy in New York, Tom Richardson, agreed that 'I cannot pretend that the Bosnian government had any different relationship than the Angolan one. They both had lost control of large chunks of their territory and explicitly had a right to action. It is a good comparison.'[131]

British hesitations were not informed by any deep-seated philosophical objections to the international arms trade as such. Quite rightly, the government regarded the responsible supply of weaponry and technology to selected clients as conducive to economic well-being at home and the pursuit of national interests abroad. As David Gore-Booth, the British ambassador to Saudi Arabia and former head of the Middle Eastern Department at the FCO, remarked on BBC Television in April 1994 – at the height of the siege of the underarmed Bosnian garrison at Gorazde – 'You have to factor in the morality [of arms exports] because that is what British public opinion and the British value system demands. But it cannot be the overriding factor because Britain has to survive by exporting.'[132] Indeed, if anything, the administration of John Major tended to err on the side of generosity in the supply of weaponry to crisis areas. The controversy surrounding the 'Arms for Iraq' affair is testimony to that. But when the Labour MP Max Madden asked why 'Her Majesty's Government [were] prepared to breach the arms embargo to allow Iraq to wage war, but now refuse to lift the arms embargo to give the Government Bosnian forces the means with which to defend their independent country', he received an evasive answer.[133] Curiously, as the Labour MP Donald Anderson pointed out, the 'one country to which we have steadfastly refused to sell arms is Bosnia'.[134] Even Jonathan Aitken, then the Minister for Defence Procurement, a man well known for his robust attitude to arms sales, told the House of Commons at the beginning of the first Srebrenica crisis in April 1993 that the government had 'no intention of relaxing the arms embargo in favour of any of its participants'.[135]

Britain advanced many reasons for the maintenance of the embargo, few of them convincing, some bizarre and virtually all disingenuous. Thus Ivor Roberts, the British chargé d'affaires in Belgrade during the second half of the war, argued that 'It is not an embargo on one of the three parties but on them all. As the war has shown, all sides have disposed of large quantities of weapons and ammunition.'[136] This sleight of hand glossed over the fact that the embargo perpetuated the enormous imbalance of weapons in the Serbs' favour at the beginning of the war. Even retrospectively, John Major was to claim that the Bosnians lacked not so much weapons as training. In Major's view, lack of training and discipline in the Bosnian government forces repeatedly gave rise to poorly conceived and disastrous offensives.[137] This was only half untrue, but the Prime Minister's scarcely concealed note of disdain would be more convincing were it not for the fact that his own government was to the forefront of frustrating American and others' plans to provide the Bosnians with the training they needed. It was a short step from this to the odd claim that, as the Bosnian government was already covertly in receipt of enough arms, to end the embargo would be redundant. Thus Baroness Chalker, Minister for Overseas Aid and Development, when challenged about the embargo, denied that 'the Moslems were without arms and unable to fight . . . Whatever else is going on, there is certainly no lack of armaments among the Moslems, the Serbs and the Croats.'[138] To this Lord Mackie of Benshie made the obvious reply, 'My Lords, but that means the embargo is quite useless.'[139] He was not the only observer to marvel that a measure was being defended on the grounds of its ineffectiveness.

In reality, the embargo was all too effective. A steady supply of small arms and ammunition did indeed find its way to the beleaguered Bosnian army, but they remained critically short of heavy weapons. In infantry the government forces outnumbered the Serbs more than two to one (200,000 to 80,000), but could field only forty tanks against the Serbs' 300; the disparity in artillery, particularly of the larger calibres, was equally great.[140] 'The arms embargo,' as Kofi Annan admitted in his subsequent report, 'did little more than freeze in place the military balance within the former Yugoslavia. It left the Serbs in a position of overwhelming military dominance and effectively deprived the Republic of Bosnia and Herzegovina of its right under the Charter of the United Nations to self-defence.'[141]

The effect of this imbalance on the ground was frequently attested to by journalists, combatants and analysts. Already in November 1991, after the fall of Vukovar, the Croatian mayor of the front-line town of Osijek observed that 'In terms of weapons, the army's glass was full and ours was empty when this began. Then Europe imposed an arms embargo, put its hand over the glasses, and ours was left empty.'[142] Similarly, a Bosnian commander complained, 'I am sick . . . of sending my boys into the line with barely a magazine a man, and having to ask them to conserve their fire.'[143] As the British journalist Antony Loyd subsequently wrote, 'the war was an unequal contest. The outgoing fire was only even a fraction of the incoming . . . The government soldiers I met on the lines near our house always complained about how little ammunition they had and most were lucky if they had uniforms let alone boots.'[144] The Bosnian colonel commanding the garrison on Mount Igman overlooking Sarajevo in January 1993 appealed to the west to 'End the arms embargo, give us weapons, ground their helicopters, and the West could shorten the war by several months.'[145] Even 'Kenneth Roberts', a pseudonymous Briton with close links to the intelligence services working for the UN in Bosnia, himself no friend of the Bosnian government, conceded in February 1994 that 'The Muslim Armija long ago came of age as a force capable of inflicting damaging defeats on the Croats, and inferior to the Serbs only in terms of heavy weapons and ammunition. A UN withdrawal would almost certainly see that imbalance redressed by overt or covert military supplies from America or the Islamic world.'[146] Likewise, Milos Vasic, the highly respected and superbly well-informed military analyst with the liberal Belgrade weekly *Vreme*, observed in November 1992: 'A strong armed force in the hands of the legal government of Bosnia-Herzegovina would have deterred much of the fighting. Not arming the legal government has meant more ethnic cleansing, more massacres, more refugees.'[147]

Not only did the British government publicly dispute the effectiveness of the embargo, it even denied that the Bosnian government *wanted* the embargo lifted if this would mean the end of the humanitarian aid effort on the ground. Thus Malcolm Rifkind, speaking in the Commons in July 1995, referred to 'the statement of *fact* that the Bosnian government have said that they would rather that the UN remained in Bosnia than that the embargo should be raised and the UN withdraw. That remains the choice that is available to them.'[148] Douglas Hurd wrote in December 1994 that 'when it came to the point in September, the Bosnian government did not want the immediate lifting of the arms embargo if that meant the withdrawal of UNPROFOR'.[149] Similarly, Ivor Roberts denied that the Bosnians wanted the embargo lifted as a matter of 'justice, fairness, [and] a levelling of the playing field . . . so that they can have a fair chance. They are not particularly interested in buying American arms; they are interested in involving America and in getting their help to [sic] winning the war with whatever American help it takes.'[150] And in retrospect, Douglas

Hurd claimed that 'When those who opposed the arms embargo, notably the US Administration and the Bosnian government, had to choose between ending the arms embargo and continuing the UN force in Bosnia they chose the latter.'[151] Some Foreign Office figures maintain this line to the present day: 'show me a document', one senior official remarked, 'where [President] Izetbegovic publicly and formally asked for a lifting of the arms embargo'. This particular diplomat even denied that President Izetbegovic had ever asked for air strikes in writing. The purpose behind this argument was to show up the alleged bad faith of the Sarajevo government, establish the soundness of British policy and generally reduce the pressure for external intervention.

By dint of repetition, the notion that the Bosnians secretly colluded in the embargo, and had specifically forgone the opportunity to have it lifted, gained widespread acceptance. The *Economist* wrote in December 1994 that 'The Bosnian government, faced earlier this year with the choice between the embargo staying or the UN going, preferred the UN to stay on.'[152] Similarly, the *Daily Telegraph*'s Patrick Bishop commented on the renewed controversy about the embargo in July 1995 thus: 'Weighing the effects of a UN withdrawal, humanitarian as well as military, against its own ability to defend and feed itself, it is not inconceivable that [the Bosnian government] will back off and ask for the embargo issue to be deferred, just as it did a year ago.'[153] Even such a sympathetic and well-informed observer as Martin Woolacott in the *Guardian* believed that the Bosnian government were 'playing the risky game of asking for things they do not want in order to get things they do'.[154]

In this case, the British government was probably not guilty of conscious disingenuity. By early 1995, London had genuinely convinced itself that the Bosnians would not – and never had wanted to – countenance the lifting of the arms embargo at the price of a UN withdrawal. But – leaving aside the ethics of thus blackmailing an embattled nation – it was not so. It is a statement of fact that the Bosnian government unswervingly and sincerely demanded the repeal of the embargo from the very beginning to the very end of the war.[155] Already in August 1992, *before* the arrival of British UN forces, Mohamed Sacirbey, the Bosnian ambassador to the UN, proclaimed that 'We have 50,000 people ready to fight in Sarajevo. We don't want your boys to die in the Balkans, all we need is sophisticated air power to get at the gunners bombing our towns and the other side's air force.'[156] Three months later Mamon Nahas from the Bosnia-Herzegovina Information Centre in London pointed out that 'Our presidency has repeatedly asked not for outside troops but for selective air strikes ... This would be combined with a lifting of the arms embargo against Bosnia. Not a single British life would therefore be at risk.'[157] In January 1993, President Izetbegovic told an Islamic summit in Senegal that 'We have enough boys ready to fight. We don't need any boys from abroad. But we need arms.'[158] Indeed, by the British government's own admission, the lifting of the arms embargo was a matter repeatedly raised by the Bosnian President during his visits to London.[159]

Moreover, the Bosnian government clearly stated – albeit grudgingly – their willingness to trade the humanitarian effort for a lifting of the embargo. In May 1993 the Sarajevo administration had penned a formal letter requesting the withdrawal of the UN presence in order to facilitate an end to the embargo and the defence of Bosnia.[160] It appears to have been withdrawn only because Britain and France were unable to guarantee that the withdrawal of UNPROFOR *would indeed be accompanied by a lifting of the embargo*. A year later, the Vice-President of the Federation of Bosnia-Herzegovina, Ejup Ganic, testified repeatedly before the US Senate Committee on Armed Services that the Bosnian government favoured a UN withdrawal if that was necessary to secure the lifting of the embargo.[161] Not long afterwards, President Izetbegovic publicly accused Britain and France of 'blackmail' over their threat to pull out in the event of the embargo being lifted. Nevertheless, he repeated that he would rather have weapons than a continuation of the UN relief effort.[162] Likewise, Nermin Mulalic, who served as a counsellor in the Bosnian embassy later in the war and who was present at numerous meetings between Haris Silajdzic and the Foreign Office Minister Douglas Hogg, has no recollection of the British government offering any such trade-off. What he does remember very clearly, however, is Silajdzic's consistent demand for the lifting of the embargo, and that he would respond to predictions of UNPROFOR's consequent collapse to the effect: 'Fine, withdraw and lift the embargo.'[163]

Perhaps the most commonly heard arguments against lifting the embargo were that it would intensify the war, leading simply to more suffering on all sides; that it would fuel the Croat–Bosnian split; that Croatian obstructionism would render the supply of arms to the Bosnians impossible; that British forces 'on the ground' would be at the mercy of Serb reprisals; that the Bosnians would be overrun before help could reach them; and that it might well spark a wider war with a Russian-sponsored Serbia proper entering the equation against a US-backed Bosnian–Croat alliance. On this reading, as David Hannay claimed at the Security Council meeting called to discuss the ending of the embargo in late June 1993, the measure was 'a solution of despair . . . such a decision would, in practice, fail to help the people it is designed to assist, the Bosnian Muslims . . . Moreover, a decision to lift the arms embargo would provide a probably irresistible temptation to the Bosnian Serbs and Bosnian Croats to intensify their military efforts and to ensure that, by the time any substantial delivery of weapons was made, the military threat posed to them by the Bosnian Government forces had been neutralised.'[164] Similarly, Douglas Hogg argued in April 1993 that it 'would take time for the arms to be delivered to the Bosnian Muslims and even more time for those people to be trained and expert in their use'.[165] In particular, it was claimed, the safe areas could no longer be protected by UNPROFOR and would be swiftly overrun by a Bosnian Serb army which would cast off all restraint to achieve victory before it was too late. The safe-areas concept and the lifting of the embargo, David Hannay told the Security Council in June 1993, were 'distinct and alternative' policies which could not be combined.[166] Instead, the Prime Minister told the Commons in April of that year, one should 'damp down and not increase the supply of arms'.[167] All in all, Ivor Roberts claimed in 1995, 'If yet more weapons had poured in, many more people – civilians and soldiers, Muslims, Croats and Serbs – would by now have been killed.'[168]

At the same time, the government used the arms embargo debate to stress the complexities of the conflict. Here the Croat–Bosnian split in central Bosnia and in Herzegovina, which had broken out in fits and starts from October 1992 onwards, but escalated seriously in January–February 1993, was fortuitous. Should the embargo be lifted totally, or 'just for the Muslims?' Douglas Hurd asked a critic in April 1993.

'That is the point,' he continued, 'Muslims and Croats were fighting each other in Vitez today. Under the hon. Gentleman's policy, both would be resupplied with arms. Is that really sensible, particularly if the result is that we have to withdraw our troops and stop the humanitarian aid effort?'[169] In the same way, Baroness Chalker claimed that 'one has not only Bosnian Serb fighters fighting Bosnian Moslem people, but Bosnian Croat fighters fighting Bosnian Moslem people and at times the Bosnian Serbs fighting the Bosnian Croats within the area'.[170] In short, as Douglas Hurd famously argued, far from creating a '"level playing field", lifting the embargo would be tantamount to saying "Here are the arms: fight it out." That is the policy of the level killing field.'[171] The Prime Minister liked this phrase so much that he later deployed it against American critics, and it was to resonate on the many subsequent occasions when the arms embargo was debated.[172] Yet 'the level killing field' was no off-the-cuff remark, a forgivable flourish spawned in the heat of argument, but a considered soundbite which Douglas Hurd had tested on his PPS, David Martin.[173]

There was something to be said for these arguments, but not much. It is true that the split between the Bosnian government and Croat nationalists – which cut access to the coast – did seriously complicate the task of supplying the Sarajevo government with arms. But – as the subsequent covert supplies to the Bosnians by air showed – this was not an insuperable obstacle, and it could have been removed by firm political intervention at Zagreb. Certainly, the Croats would have had to 'receive a cut' of any western military aid to the Bosnians as part of a pragmatic strategy against the Bosnian Serbs; no doubt, this approach would not have been without its moral ambiguities. But it is curious that the British apostles of *Realpolitik* in the Balkans, so unshakeably sure of their right to abandon the principal victims to Serb aggression, suddenly became squeamish about the lesser evil of collaboration with the Croats. Besides, the arms embargo itself exacerbated the Croat–Bosnian split. First of all, it reduced the attraction of the integrationist Bosnian ideal to potentially loyal Croats, and Serbs for that matter. Secondly, by reducing the price of betrayal it encouraged Croat nationalists to collaborate with Serb ethnic cleansers in a partition of Bosnia.

The 'troops on the ground' argument against the lifting of the embargo caused massive irritation among Americans. They rejected

Britain's assumption to dictate policy towards Bosnia by deploying inadequate forces for purely palliative purposes.[174] Moreover, many Americans felt that the troops were simply a pretext for inaction. 'Those forces,' as John Fox believed at the time – his direct experience relates to 1992–3 – 'had been put in to forestall real intervention . . . as long as you had UNPROFOR you wouldn't get what the hawks wanted.'[175] Indeed, he recalls that 'this was basically said to me by some of my British interlocutors, that we are going to keep the intervention from happening by the presence of UNPROFOR . . . they would say, "Look the UNPROFOR presence is next to useless, and actually as long as it is there, there won't be an intervention, or as long as the character of UNPROFOR isn't changed. One of the principal arguments for keeping them in is we know it's not a very constructive presence but it keeps you guys out, which is one of our main aims" . . . They really believed that the kind of lift and strike which had been advocated would destabilize the region, force others to take sides, cause all kinds of terrible consequences.'[176]

Similarly, Dr Robert Hunter, who served as Nato ambassador during the second half of the war, remarked that he 'was convinced that one of the reasons the British had troops in UNPROFOR in relationship to bombing was you had troops on the ground, therefore you can't bomb. In other words, to stop bombing was one reason they had troops on the ground . . . We have troops there and that helps stop bombing, not because we have troops there you can't bomb.'[177] The problem was thus one of Britain's own making. The troops were sent in with a humanitarian mandate as a substitute for political and military action; in order to forestall such action by others. To execrate the US for endangering them in the course of reversing this disastrous policy was thus to approach the problem back to front.[178]

Virtually all the other arguments against lifting the embargo were self-contradictory, disingenuous, based on misapprehensions, or otherwise risible. The notions that an end to the embargo might trigger both a wider interminable war and the immediate crushing of the Bosnians were mutually exclusive. Similarly, Douglas Hogg's claim that the end of the embargo would simply mean that 'others would speedily supply arms to the Croats and Bosnian Serbs'[179] without overall benefit to the Bosnian government was a complete sleight of hand. It conveniently overlooked the fact that the Bosnian Serbs were already well supplied, a fact which Hogg himself had carelessly conceded several months before. In a written answer to a query from Sir Russell Johnston, Hogg had responded that 'We have no firm evidence of whether Serbia is continuing to supply arms to the Bosnian Serbs. The Yugoslav authorities deny this. Moreover, the Bosnian Serbs are *already well-equipped; further supplies from Serbia would be unlikely to have a significant effect on their military capacity*.'[180] At a stroke, Hogg had subverted the standard argument that a lifting of the embargo would simply lead to more weapons for the Bosnian Serbs. It was not the first or the last time that a British minister or diplomat was to forget his or her lines.

Similarly, the idea that Serbia proper might be forced to intervene was highly questionable, and, as it turned out, wrong. General Radovan Radinovic, a senior JNA figure close to Milosevic, pointed out in early May 1993 that, while the Yugoslav army regarded a lifting of the embargo as 'unnecessary' and 'negative', it 'would not consider it an act of war'.[181] Oddly, therefore, the British government tried to exaggerate the chances of Serbian cavalry riding to the rescue of Pale, and minimize the chances of the US cavalry arriving over the hills – or perhaps out of the skies – to save Sarajevo. In reality, Belgrade never did intervene openly on behalf of the western Serbs, not in May 1995 when the Croats overran Sector West in Slavonia, not in early August 1995 when the Croats liquidated the rest of the Krajina, nor in September–October 1995 when a Croat–Bosnian offensive and allied air action rolled up the Bosnian Serbs from the west.

The notion of a violent Russian response to a lifting of the embargo was also fanciful. 'We have an interest,' an unusually alarmist Douglas Hurd told the Commons in early May 1995, 'in stopping a war spreading across the map of Europe, particularly a war which would range the US and Russia on different sides.'[182] 'We should not,' he repeated in early July, 'in Bosnia or Yugoslavia, build up a situation in which the NATO powers are on one side and the Russians on the other.'[183] This doomsday scenario was also popular in the press, where Tolstoy's Vronsky was pressed into service to suggest the prospect of a Slav crusade in Bosnia.[184] But the assumption that the Russian government would involve itself in a proxy conflict on behalf of the

Bosnian Serbs or even Serbia itself rested on false assumptions. For one thing, relations between the Serb-dominated Yugoslav military and the Soviets had been poor since Tito had broken with Stalin in 1948. More recently, Slobodan Milosevic had seriously blotted his copybook with Yeltsin by supporting the conspirators during the August 1991 coup.[185]

To be sure, Douglas Hurd was technically justified in claiming that lifting the embargo 'would require Russian consent in a new Security Council resolution'.[186] President Yeltsin consistently indicated that his response to such a measure would be 'negative', and Russian diplomats frequently threatened to use their veto at the Security Council.[187] There may even have been some sense in Hurd's injunction to 'consider the request by the Russian government not to put [further action against the Serbs] to the vote until the end of April [1993]. Our purpose must be to keep Russian consent, because if we lose it, the ability of the Security Council to act effectively will disappear entirely.'[188] And it is also true that the Russian forces serving with the UN in Croatia and Bosnia were characterized as much by their partiality towards the Serbs as they were by their indiscipline and venality.[189]

But in practice the Russians were much less obstructive than they publicly suggested and than the British government wished its critics to believe. They did not block the new sanctions on Serbia imposed in late April 1993.[190] In the arms embargo vote at the Security Council in June 1993, the Russians abstained – along with Brazil, China, France, Hungary, Japan, New Zealand, Spain, and the UK – rather than voted against; this made no difference to the outcome, but was symbolically significant. In February 1994, the Russians reluctantly agreed to the threat of air strikes to protect UN forces, which was a figleaf for an ultimatum to the Bosnian Serbs to compel the withdrawal of their heavy weapons,[191] and in March 1994 they did not object to the shooting down of four Serb jets which had violated the no-fly zone. It was the Duma (the Russian parliament) rather than Yeltsin which reacted with outrage to the unilateral US withdrawal from policing the embargo in November 1994.[192] That same month, the Russians endorsed Nato's air strike against Serb aircraft operating out of Udbina airfield in Serb-occupied Croatia.[193] The Russians finally did veto a UN resolution against the Serbs in December 1994, but they were careful to choose a measure – the restriction of fuel supplies from Serbia proper to the Bosnian Serbs – which had originated with Islamic countries rather than the US. And when in July 1995, the US Congress voted overwhelmingly for a unilateral American lifting of the embargo, the Kremlin merely registered its 'regret', denying any intention to breach UN sanctions against Belgrade in retaliation.[194]

Yeltsin, in truth, was both uninterested in and unsympathetic to the Serb cause. He warned them, once his referendum in April was out of the way, to accept the Vance–Owen peace plan (VOPP), or to risk 'decisive measures to quell the conflict'. 'The Russian Federation,' he announced, 'will not protect those who resist the will of the world community . . . Serbian nationalists and other participants in the conflict who resort to force will come up against a tough rebuff in the United Nations.'[195] Indeed, his special envoy to the former Yugoslavia, Vitaly Churkin, supported the air strikes of April 1994 with the words 'The time has come for Russia to stop all discussion with the Bosnian Serbs. The time for talking is past.'[196] They were, as he memorably put it, 'sick with the madness of war'.[197] His foreign minister, Andrei Kozyrew, recommended 'to the Serbian side not to continue to test the patience of the world community'.[198] And Yeltsin himself noted of the Gorazde crisis that 'the escalation of military actions was inevitable as the Bosnian Serbs did not keep their word'.[199] Underlying all this was a profound sense of exasperation with the Bosnian Serbs who were, as Moscow knew full well, taking them for a ride along with the rest of the 'international community'. 'The Bosnian Serbs,' Vitaly Churkin warned, 'need to understand that they are dealing with a great power in Russia and not with a banana republic.'[200]

Russia's alleged Serbophilia, therefore, was a popular and fringe nationalist phenomenon, not an elite preoccupation.[201] What Russian diplomats *were* interested in was western recognition of an equal voice in Bosnia, something which the British seemed almost determined to foist upon them. For no sooner had Moscow reconciled itself to the enforcement of the VOPP in 1993 than Britain backed down; no sooner had Yeltsin agreed to the Sarajevo ultimatum in February 1994 than the British prevailed upon him to supply Russian forces – 'acceptable to the Serbs' – to police the ceasefire. And no sooner had the Russians vented their frustration at the Serbs over Gorazde by supporting Nato air strikes, than Britain and France yanked her back on to the Serb side by involving her in the Contact Group. Russia's role in these negotiations, as Vitaly Churkin observed in April 1994, meant that it moved from 'an in some sense anti-Serbian position', to a 'more complex manoeuvre' that exploited Russia's (supposed) channels to the Serbs.[202] Decisive here was not Russian attitudes, but the pusillanimity of the west. As the Russian Prime Minister Yegor Gaidar remarked in early 1993, 'The real problem is that the west has not created a strategy to deal with Yugoslavia. Once it is in place, I am sure that the Russian government will support it.'[203]

The Russian government certainly never said publicly that it would supply the Serb side in the event of the embargo being lifted. Indeed, a British diplomat who served in the Moscow embassy during the war, forgetful or perhaps unaware of the standard Foreign Office line, subsequently volunteered that Russian objections played no role in British policy towards the arms embargo. Instead, he explained, it was a question of 'genuine common ground' with Moscow. In short, the Russians simply provided the British government with a convenient smokescreen; indeed, Russian objections were almost encouraged. 'The most useful Russian contribution of all,' a confidential Foreign Office memorandum of 1993 argued, 'has been its firm resistance to US pressure for lifting the arms embargo against the Muslims . . . It has been reassuring to know that when the crunch came, the Russian veto would be forthcoming.'[204] 'In Bosnia,' the Russian expert Anatol Lieven remarked in December 1994, 'Russia is not NATO's enemy but NATO's alibi; if Russia had not existed, then Britain and France would have had to invent it as an excuse for their cowardice and indecision.'[205]

This was also the perception of the Americans. As the State Department lawyer Michael Scharf reports, 'it was not the Russians who were blocking' action at the UN; indeed, the US mission regularly toned down proposals for stiffer action with the comment 'this is the best we can get past the British and the French'. Normally, his erstwhile colleague Paul Williams observes, the US concern at the Security Council was 'how do we get this past the Russians and Chinese?'; over Bosnia, it was a question of 'how do we get this beyond our allies?'.[206] It is thus clear that alleged Russian objections do not explain why

Britain blocked all American attempts to defend the Bosnians, or refused to allow the Bosnians to defend themselves.

The real reason why the British government was so unwilling to lift the embargo was subsequently conceded by Douglas Hurd. Lifting the embargo, he argued, 'would have been to remove any incentive from the Bosnian Muslims to go to the negotiating table. Why should they negotiate when they were going to be helped to win the war on the battlefield? Most people thought that lifting the embargo would be a hindrance to the diplomatic effort.'[207] Likewise, Dame Pauline Neville-Jones, the former Political Director at the Foreign Office, recalls that: 'We thought that the Bosnian Muslims lived under an illusion . . . that if only they could get the Europeans out of the way . . . – or procure circumstances in which the embargo was either ignored or lifted, so that the full might of western armed force could be brought in on their side, in the air, that then they would be in a promised land, because they were bound to win . . . it would have been the total destruction of the policy we were pursuing.'[208] Much better, the argument ran, for the Sarajevo government to abandon all hope of reversing ethnic cleansing and to concentrate on a 'realistic' partitionist solution.

Giving way on the embargo would subvert the standard argument that there was no pragmatic way of checking Serb aggression short of a massive commitment of ground troops. 'The embargo,' as the journalist Martin Ivens remarked, 'is our figleaf for an independent foreign policy. To abandon it now would make Britain's stand on Yugoslavia completely incoherent . . . If the arms embargo is unjust now, then it was unjust to impose it last year.'[209] As the debate on 'lift and strike' reached its crescendo in April–May 1993, this thought was elaborated on by the historian Nikolai Tolstoy. 'Suppose military intervention *were* now to take place *and* to prove effective? It is scarcely necessary to enquire what then would be the moral position of Hurd and Rifkind, *et al.* What is unnerving is the thought [that] the possibility of such a *dénouement* . . . might unconsciously inhibit them from changing their minds now – when it is horribly late, but not still too late.'[210]

To the American critics of British policy it was indeed horribly late by the spring and early summer of 1993. Throughout this period, the pressure in Washington for some sort of military intervention mounted. The draft report of a team of experts sent to the region by President Clinton, prepared in March 1993, called on him to consider the creation of 'safe havens' and air attacks on Serbian artillery.[211] Shortly afterwards a CIA report suggested that continued inaction might embolden further Serbian adventurism and even draw in Albania.[212] On Capitol Hill, Congressional demands for intervention, or at least a lifting of the embargo, grew ever louder; so did the voices within the administration, especially those of Madeleine Albright at the UN and the Vice-President, Al Gore. This theme was taken up by Elie Wiesel in an emotional opening speech directed at Clinton during the opening of the Holocaust Memorial Museum in Washington. And all the while Serb troops tightened the noose on the eastern enclaves: almost hourly western audiences found themselves deluged with television images of terrible suffering of the Bosnian Muslim victims, particularly in Srebrenica.

By late April to early May 1993, US confidence in European policy – and that meant British and French policy – towards Bosnia had completely collapsed. 'The appeasement of the Serbs,' observed Ivo Daalder, who was soon to join Clinton's National Security Council staff, 'has really hurt the image of Britain.'[213] 'There is a belief in Washington,' the American ambassador to Britain, Raymond Seitz, explained in an unusually candid interview, 'much of it unfair, some of it not, that Europe [has] failed.'[214] Al Gore publicly lamented the fact that 'because it's in Europe, it's very difficult for the US to go it alone if our allies are not willing to join with us'.[215] The palpable tension was epitomized by an inadvertent but highly symbolic error of the White House protocol department. Both the British ambassador, Sir Robin Renwick, and the visiting Defence Secretary, Malcolm Rifkind, were turned away from the reception to mark the opening of the Holocaust museum, after failing to persuade guards that they had been left off the list of names by mistake. The ambassador of Belarus was also refused entry, but was admitted after being recognized by a member of the US National Security Council.[216]

Matters came to a head with the famous mission of the Secretary of State, Warren Christopher, to Europe in early May 1993. Christopher had always shown little enthusiasm for military intervention; now his task was to win over the Europeans to the policy of 'lift and strike'. As one American diplomat on the mission recalled, Moscow proved – counter-intuitively – the easiest bit. Next came Paris. By far the most difficult leg of the journey, he recalled, was London.[217] Or rather Chevening, for it was at the country residence of the Foreign Secretary that Douglas Hurd, Malcolm Rifkind, John Major, Christopher and Raymond Seitz assembled to discuss the US initiative. Christopher – under instruction not to lay down the law absolutely or to threaten the end of the Atlantic alliance – lacked all conviction.[218] He had already declined offers of support from the activist Secretary General of Nato, Manfred Wörner, with the words 'I am here in listening mode'.[219] To British observers he was more dead than listening. 'His words,' as the American ambassador recalled in his memoirs, 'had all the verve of a solicitor going over a conveyance deed.'[220] Beneath their reserve, by contrast, the British were full of a passionate intensity. They flatly rejected 'lift and strike' as unworkable and a threat to British forces on the ground.

The British were encouraged in this view by elements in the Pentagon and the State Department opposed to intervention. Raymond Seitz, who accompanied Christopher throughout, candidly admits as much in his memoirs.[221] But there were others. As John Fox recalls, the British 'seemed to be extremely well informed about which officers in which parts of the bureaucracy were putting forward papers . . . and even contemplating doing so'.[222] He was particularly suspicious of the Pentagon and its links with the MoD,[223] and rightly so, for it now transpires, as Renwick's forthcoming memoirs reveal, that the 'Pentagon privately encouraged us to continue resistance to these plans ("save us from ourselves")'.[224]

His duty done, Christopher retreated to Washington to report on this 'exchange of views' with the allies and their objections to American policy. As the former Assistant Secretary of State for Defense, Richard Perle, noted, 'It was an exchange all right: Warren Christopher went to Europe with an American policy, and he came back with a European one.'[225] In the meantime, President Clinton himself – again beset by fears of being drawn into an unwinnable war at the expense of his domestic programme – developed second thoughts about military intervention. 'Holy s—t', the Secretary of State for Defense, Les Aspin, observed, 'He's going south on "lift and strike".'[226] At a post-mortem on 8 May it was decided to call off the policy in the face of allied objections. 'Nobody,' one attendee recalled, 'recommended simply steamrollering the Europeans.'[227] *Telling* the Europeans – particularly the British – what to do, would cause massive resentment, might not work and would make the whole issue an American problem. 'It must have seemed to [Christopher],' Perle recalls, 'that we were [being] given an opportunity to push our way into a quagmire.'[228]

There was, however, no finessing the gulf across the Atlantic, either in the press or among the protagonists themselves. The headlines said it all: 'Bosnia dispute between Europe and US boils over'; 'US and Britain: the rift widens'; and 'War in Bosnia: Hurd tries to bridge rift with America'.[229] Similarly, John Major acknowledged the gravity of the split. He claimed that lift and strike excused the Americans from committing ground forces, while allowing them to moralize.[230] The sense of irritation is still palpable, six years on. 'Whatever the relationship had been before,' the US ambassador commented in his memoirs, after the Christopher mission, 'it wasn't going to be the same again.'[231]

CHAPTER 3

# 'The Real Stumbling Block': Britain Stifles Nato, 1993–1995

By the late summer of 1993, it seemed as if Britain had won the debate and 'converted' the Americans to a policy of non-intervention. Already in February, Whitehall officials were claiming that it was ironic 'to hear Warren Christopher saying things that we were saying already a year and a half ago . . . I hope we can take them along that learning curve quite quickly'.[1] After the collapse of the Christopher mission on 'lift and strike', this hope appeared to become reality. At a fraught meeting at the Goring Hotel in London on 25 July, John Major recalls, the Americans promised British officials that they would now seek to find a 'realistic' – i.e. partitionist – solution to the conflict and support Lord Owen in his peace negotiations.[2] 'Who said Britain no longer has influence?' Hugo Young asked in the *Guardian*. 'Britain, in all her ancestral wisdom, was more influential than any other country in guaranteeing the washing of the hands.'[3] 'At the end of two years of diplomacy,' Boris Johnson observed in the *Sunday Telegraph*, 'the policy of the west has become the policy of Douglas Hurd.'[4] Whatever the pressure from Washington, no matter the outrage at home, the Major administration would not budge on Bosnia. 'The tactic of this government,' one Whitehall official remarked, 'has been to sweat it out.'[5] The worm, it seemed, would not turn.

The Clinton administration, shaken by the vehemence of the British position and divided about the wisdom of unilateral action, backed off with a mixture of reluctance, resentment and relief. Already in late February 1993, Warren Christopher, under severe British pressure not to deliver on Clinton's relatively vague hints of action, remarked that 'I don't suppose you'd want anybody to keep a campaign promise if it was a very unsound policy.'[6] At the end of March 1993, Clinton had described the issue as 'a problem from hell', and the essential ambiguity of the President's own position was reflected in Clinton's famous equivocation of 20 April 1993, when he claimed that 'The US should always seek an opportunity to stand up against – or at least speak out against – inhumanity.'[7] After the failure of the Christopher mission, in any case, the American government temporarily abandoned the activist policy and shared London's desire to keep Bosnia off the agenda. State Department officials such as Marshall Harris – soon to resign in protest at American inaction – found their memoranda were censored and terms like 'genocide' deleted. Indeed, after the 'lift and strike' fiasco in May 1993, bemused State Department officials were asked by Christopher to supply evidence of *Bosnian* atrocities with intent to muddy the waters.[8] The policy itself shifted to one of pure containment: a tripwire force was dispatched to Macedonia and the warnings about Kosovo reinforced. Every effort was made to keep the subject off the TV screens and the front pages. As Warren Christopher told Congressional hearings on 18 May, not long after returning from his disastrous trip to London, Bosnia was 'a problem from hell . . . a morass . . . [with] atrocities on all sides'. He did so in defiance of his State Department briefings, which clearly identified the Serbs as the primary culprits. 'At heart,' Christopher concluded, 'this is a European problem.'[9]

And that, the British government might have been forgiven for thinking, was that. But the war did not, as the realists had predicted, end with a quick Serb victory, or an agreed partition at Bosnian expense. Throughout the darkest days of the autumn and winter of 1993, the Bosnians, outgunned by the Serbs thanks to the arms embargo, beset by internal divisions, and abandoned by the British-led international community, fought on. And, however hard they tried, the Americans proved unable to internalize British arguments about civil wars, quagmires and moral equivalences: an obstinate sense of rationality and fair play prevented them.

Despite the best efforts of the British government, Bosnia continued to force its way on to the international agenda. In late June 1993, not long after the failure of the Christopher mission, it almost derailed the Copenhagen summit of the European Union. Here the German–

American call for the lifting of the arms embargo provoked an unusual display of belligerence from Douglas Hurd. 'We have men there . . . and we pay our dues,' the Foreign Secretary told BBC's *Newsnight*. 'The appeal is addressed to those . . . who are not up to date with their obligations, their money which they owe the Secretary General of the UN for peacekeeping. If he could get his 7,500 men . . . and if he could get, which is just as important, all those countries, including big countries, to pay what they owe, then we could increase the number of lives which are being saved.'[10] This was a thinly disguised attack on the United States for its failure to pay its UN dues or to supply ground forces to UNPROFOR. Bosnia also overshadowed the Tokyo summit of the G7 in July 1993, when both the Americans and the Germans once again publicly called for the lifting of the arms embargo. The result was further bitter exchanges between London and Washington.[11]

As the events following the Christopher mission were to show, damage to the Anglo-American relationship and the Nato alliance was in fact the most serious result of the mishandled Bosnian policy; and secondary detonations were to follow. For if, in Britain, the government managed to hold the line on non-intervention without serious political cost, in the United States, the price of inaction was massive. By late 1993 the Clinton administration was again under severe domestic pressure. Two broadsheets in particular, the *New York Times* and the *Washington Post*, returned to the attack again and again. Government policy was condemned as 'petty and embarrassing' with 'alarming implications';[12] or as a 'farce'. 'America', as the Nobel Prize winner for literature and former Soviet dissident, Joseph Brodsky, argued, 'lies in [a] state-induced moral torpor' over Bosnia.[13] He was contemptuous of British and French objections: 'An ethical man does not need a consensus of his allies in order to act against something he finds reprehensible.' Indeed, William Pfaff wrote in the *Los Angeles Times* that the war was 'accomplishing the destruction of . . . the western European [order and] . . . producing an end to the Atlantic alliance, the moral as well as political-military accord that for decades has guaranteed international order'. 'The project of a common foreign and security policy for Europe,' he continued, 'has been revealed to be a sinister charade.' 'Europe,' in fact, 'has earned the contempt of Americans by its behaviour on Bosnia.'[14]

But it was France and Britain – particularly Britain – which were singled out for the greatest obloquy. Anthony Lewis accused John Major of giving 'a passable imitation of Neville Chamberlain' and of having 'no stomach – no backbone might be a more accurate word – for resistance to the Serbian mass murderers'.[15] Brian Beedham, a Briton writing in the *International Herald Tribune*, summed up a widespread feeling when he observed that 'Britain . . . earns the fewest qualifications to the charge of appeasement . . . it was Britain's foreign minister who always seemed to lead the objections to doing anything more strenuous, and who declined to let arms through to the weakening Muslims because he did not want to "level the killing fields". It was Britain's defense minister who said the "overriding" aim in Bosnia was to protect the foreign soldiers there. Those two remarks will not read well in the history books. If Europe is judged guilty of a historic mistake in the former Yugoslavia, it seems likely that Britain will be considered the intellectual leader of this error.'[16] At the same time, the Congressional critique which had led to the formulation of the lift and strike policy was resumed after the fiasco of the Christopher mission. Joseph Biden, the Democratic Chairman of the Senate Foreign Relations Committee, attacked European policy as a 'mosaic of indifference, timidity, self-delusion and hypocrisy'.[17] And in late July 1993, more than eighty Congressmen signed an open letter to President Clinton calling for an ultimatum to lift the siege of Sarajevo, followed by air strikes.

This critique was not mere media or Congressional froth, but increasingly encompassed large sections of the US foreign policy and national security establishment. Walt Rostow, erstwhile National Security Advisor to Lyndon Johnson, condemned administration 'neurosis' about intervention.[18] The arms control expert Patrick Glynn accused the west of failing 'to understand the basic difference between "good guys" and "bad guys" or to recognise Serbia's policy for what it is – deliberate aggression needing to be countered by force. The result has been the death of a nation and a major blow to the world order.'[19] Even Republican 'realists', from whom a Tory government might have expected some instinctive sympathy, could see that Bosnia was a disaster for western credibility. Donald Rumsfeld, who had served as Defense Secretary under President Ford, and who is currently serving the George W. Bush administration in the same capacity, was a stout supporter of air strikes against the Bosnian Serbs.[20] The same was true for his current deputy, Paul Wolfowitz, a prominent member of the Balkan Action Council, a pressure group for military intervention on the Bosnian side. Henry Kissinger – though generally dismissive of the Bosnian cause – believed that action should have been taken against the Serbs during the Slovenian escapade, or at the very latest during the Croatian war.[21] And Richard Nixon, the most louche and hardboiled of Republican realists, publicly speculated – honourably, if misguidedly – shortly before his death whether the west was not being more tolerant of genocide against Muslims than it would be of the same offence against a Christian minority.[22] For the sad truth was that the west had shown even less interest in the Catholic Croatian victims of Greater Serbia in 1991.

There were, of course, vocal and articulate dissenters. Some – such as Jesse Helms – were opposed to a Balkan intervention on grounds of principle, as were isolationists such as Pat Buchanan.[23] Others, such as Stephen Rosenfeld and A. M. Rosenthal, were sceptical of the Bosnian cause.[24] Others still – especially within the US military – sincerely believed that neither the use of air power nor the lifting of the arms embargo would suffice to contain the Bosnian Serbs.[25] And there were those, such as Edward Luttwak, who simply recommended allowing the war to burn itself out.[26] But the voices of caution and inaction grew ever fainter as the crisis progressed; and the political establishment maintained a sufficiently healthy scepticism of 'expert' advice to escape the sense of paralysis which had infected Whitehall.[27]

At the same time, the US administration came under attack from within the State Department. Already in the autumn of 1992, George Kenney, Deputy Head of Yugoslav Affairs at the US State Department, resigned in protest at the Bush administration's policy towards Bosnia. 'What good is the Conference on Security and Co-operation in Europe if it cannot deal with genocide?' he asked in early September 1992. 'What good is Nato? When military force is not an option for defending freedom in Europe, Nato is a dead letter.' 'The way in which America is handling the Balkan crisis,' he argued soon after, 'is nothing other than classic appeasement policy.'[28] At around the same time, James Hooper, the former Deputy Director of the Office of East European and Yugoslav Affairs, who was intimately involved in Bosnian policy in 1992, unsuccessfully began to agitate for a change of course.[29] By the spring of 1993, the pressure within the State Department had reached boiling point. On 16 April Kenney's successor as country officer for Bosnia, Marshall Harris, sent a stern message directly to Warren Christopher via the 'dissent channel', calling for tougher action.[30] Nine days later, twelve officials signed a letter to the Secretary of State demanding military intervention on the side of the Bosnian government.[31] On 4 August Marshall Harris resigned, followed by Jon Western and Stephen Walker.[32] 'I can no longer serve in a State Department,' Harris wrote in his letter of resignation, 'that accepts the forceful dismemberment of a European state and that will not act against genocide and the Serbian officials who perpetrate it.'[33] And in early 1994, Warren Zimmermann, a senior State Department official and the former ambassador to Belgrade, left after failing to persuade Warren Christopher to change course on Bosnia.

All of this was to harm British relations with the United States in obvious and serious ways. In mid-October 1993, the US President and the Secretary of State launched a ferocious attack on European, and particularly British, policy towards Bosnia in the *Washington Post*. Clinton reproached London and Paris for vetoing his plans for 'lift and strike'. To make matters worse, he claimed that in May 1993 John Major had said that a more forward policy on Bosnia would split his cabinet and possibly bring the government down.[34] If this was intended to be helpful to Major it backfired, for the Prime Minister was acutely sensitive to any suggestion of internal divisions. At the same time, Warren Christopher pronounced the 'special relationship' with Britain and the primacy of the Atlantic alliance over. Europe as a whole, he argued, was not as important as Asia. Moreover, he dismissed European 'blame America' rhetoric which accused Washington of 'not having resolved the problem that Europe failed to resolve itself'. 'Western Europe,' he concluded, 'is no longer the dominant area of the world. There is a lot of criticism coming from western Europe, but I don't see or hear that coming from Asia.'[35] These were extremely harsh words from a normally cautious figure and they betokened a deep and enduring crisis of American confidence in Europe in general and Britain in particular. Such outbursts were the more worrying because they came from two Americans believed 'converted', and at a time when London reckoned the Bosnian issue safely buried.

During 1993–5, in fact, the tone of Anglo-American relations deteriorated markedly.[36] A meeting between the Defence Secretary, Malcolm Rifkind, and Bob Dole in late 1994 on the subject of 'lift and strike' became particularly heated. When – in Dole's eyes – Rifkind warned patronizingly of the dangers of escalation, the Senator could hardly contain himself. 'Don't talk to me about sacrifice,' he responded. Similarly, Senator John McCain, who spent years in a North Vietnamese prison camp, was unimpressed both by British policy and Rifkind's defence of it. One meeting, a staff member recalls, became so heated that he feared that McCain was about to hit the Defence Secretary. Thanks to his confrontational style, American witnesses claim, Rifkind became even more of a hate figure than Douglas Hurd, particularly among members of the Republican national security wing.

Relations were only slightly better at the diplomatic level. As Pauline Neville-Jones, then Political Director for the Foreign Office, recalls, tensions over Bosnia marred 'what was normally a very cooperative relationship' and became 'very painful'.[37] The sentiments expressed by one former British diplomat, Jonathan Clarke, who criticized American foreign policy for its 'fine promises', its 'rhetoric outdistancing deeds', its 'faux Wilsonianism' and its 'chest thumping on Bosnia',[38] certainly reflected the virtually unanimous opinion of his erstwhile colleagues. As one American official recalled, 'Your guys [British diplomats] were usually so refined, but they were going *crazy* on this. I got one pre-emptive visit from a Brit about a memo I hadn't even finished writing! Dammit, someone came up to me in Safeway's and collared me about the arms embargo.'[39] It later emerged that one of these red-faced diplomats was none other than Jonathan Powell, First Secretary at the Washington embassy throughout this disastrous period, and later a confidant of Mr Blair and an ardent advocate of the Kosovo campaign.

But it was at the UN Security Council that the breakdown of relations became most apparent. Here the British permanent representative, Sir David Hannay, repeatedly clashed with Madeleine Albright, most spectacularly in September 1993, after he failed to be moved by one of President Izetbegovic's eloquent pleas on behalf of his country.[40] As James Rubin, who served with Mrs Albright throughout her period on the Security Council, observes, the dispute was not personal – she both liked and respected Sir David – but substantive. 'Her time there and my time there,' he recalls, 'was marked by one of the single weirdest post-war episodes between the US and the British, where the American ambassador sat next to the British ambassador and on every subject except Bosnia they were as one . . . The problem was that most of the time they were talking about Bosnia [and] . . . if you just do the number of meetings at which Bosnia was the topic that dwarfs every other topic.'[41] This divide was epitomized by a famous picture in the *New York Times* which showed her hand raised in favour of lifting the embargo, while Sir David's remained firmly on the table beside her. Indeed, Mrs Albright was so incensed that she stuck that particular photograph on her refrigerator in her apartment.

But it was the 'hostile briefings' behind the scenes which were the most damaging. 'He has made a mess of everything on the foreign policy side – Bosnia, Somalia and now Haiti,' one Whitehall official commented on President Clinton's sallies of October 1993. 'The tone . . . suggests he [Clinton] is trying to defend himself against criticism that in office he had not lived up to what he promised during his election campaign.'[42] Another reported comment from a British official was even more scathing: 'What it betrays is the character of the man, which is a tendency to blame others when things get difficult and to have no understanding of the consequences of his statements . . . People here had few illusions about him as a statesman as it was. But if they had any at all left, they don't now. He's like a little child, saying "I'm not guilty".'[43]

Such briefings became the norm throughout 1994 and 1995. As Andrew Marshall reported in the *Independent* during the Serb assault on the Bihac enclave in November 1994, 'The ghost of Neville Chamberlain is hanging around the elegantly redecorated corridors of the Foreign Office these days whispering that all you can expect from the Americans is words.'[44] Of course, the Americans responded in kind. Ambrose Evans-Pritchard observed during the same period that 'The whispering campaign against Britain is coming out into the open in Washington. Anonymous US officials are now accusing the British government of planting stories about a US covert operation in Bosnia [to supply the Sarajevo government with weapons].'[45] In late February 1995 a senior British diplomat, in what was an increasingly commonplace outburst, exclaimed that 'I feel like saying to the Americans, "Why don't you put your troops where your b—dy mouth is?".'[46] And in June of that year newspaper headlines speaking of 'pro-Muslim elements' in the CIA distorting the evidence on atrocities, and claiming that 'Allies suspect US hawks of increasing risk of war', were supposedly based on 'authoritative diplomatic sources' and 'ministerial' accounts. In other words, both the Foreign Office and the Ministry of Defence were briefing against the Americans.[47]

This decline in Anglo-American relations was of profound concern to the British ambassador, Sir Robin Renwick, not least because his own views tended much more to the US side. Already in October 1991, his forthcoming memoirs reveal, Renwick believed that air power should be used to halt the shelling of Dubrovnik.[48] At that time, he writes, the Serbs 'should have been taught a lesson about western resolve that could have deterred their worst excesses in Bosnia. Instead, they learned the opposite lesson, that there was no western resolve, and they could push as far as their military power would take them.'[49] He was also unpersuaded by the arms embargo, which had been imposed 'with the best of intentions, but without thinking through the consequences of doing so . . . This penalised only the Bosnian Muslims, as the Serbs could rely on the resources of the Yugoslav National Army.'[50] By April 1993 – at the height of the first transatlantic row – he was telling the US National Security Advisor Tony Lake that 'personally, [he] shared his desire to see more effective action taken against the Bosnian Serbs'.[51]

Renwick also believed, as he recently related, 'that the Americans were right in that the heavy use of air power probably could succeed'. He was sceptical of the caution of the British military on this issue, primarily because having 'lived and worked with the US military, [he] probably had a better grasp than some people did of the sophistication of the targeting methods which could now be used in terms of reaching command and control headquarters, field guns and so on'.[52] In short, the very man in the front line of the Anglo-American dispute on Bosnia was himself an ardent supporter of 'lift and strike', provided

UNPROFOR were withdrawn first. And although Sir Robin's erstwhile colleagues furiously deny that he was in any sense a dissenter from the standard British line, Tony Lake himself had 'the sense that Robin was something of a kindred spirit on this issue . . . I definitely got the feeling he was trying to be helpful.'[53]

Renwick's official position, therefore, required him publicly to defend the indefensible.[54] '[British] troops have saved tens of thousands of Bosnian lives,' Renwick told an audience at American University in Washington DC in October 1993, 'but far from being applauded for this risky effort, we are criticised.'[55] The problem was, of course, that such interventions did as much to increase tensions as to defuse them, particularly as they were executed with eloquence and sharpness. As a result, the British ambassador in Washington found himself facing two ways. 'I spent a lot of time in Washington,' Renwick recalls, 'trying to avoid these differences becoming even more detrimental than they were already and trying to gradually get the Americans to accept . . . they were going to have to play a much more direct and positive role . . . and also trying to get my own government to accept that we had to consider taking much more forceful action to bring an end to the conflict.'[56] 'My objective throughout,' he writes in his memoirs, was 'to try to get a new and very uncertain Administration to show effective leadership in dealing with the crisis, given the incapacity of others to do so. As a European, it distressed me that Britain, France and Germany could not themselves display the collective will and unity of purpose needed to deal with the likes of General Mladic. But that, clearly, was not going to happen.'[57]

Sir Robin's assessment of the Major administration's handling of Bosnia was correspondingly bleak. 'Our own government,' he recalls, 'constantly tried to do what it saw as honourable things, but . . . it didn't seem to me to have the full Thatcherite sense of purpose in the sense that she understood the sort of people we were dealing with and that you could only deal with those people one way. It was a long time before "reasonable men" on our side came to that view.'[58]

The transatlantic rift was not confined to Bosnia. The most remarked-on example at the time was the granting of a US visa to the Sinn Fein leader Gerry Adams in January 1994. This move, imposed by the White House over State Department objections, was in clear violation of British national interests as they were then construed, and it was bitterly resented by John Major.[59] Of course, the granting of the visa, a concession to the Irish lobby, was primarily a gambit in American domestic politics; and it is also true that the move was ultimately beneficial to the 'peace process'. Nevertheless, it was only the unprecedentedly low state of Anglo-American relations, in particular those between Warren Christopher and Douglas Hurd, and Bill Clinton and John Major, which permitted such a public gesture of disrespect towards London. Observers were in no doubt that the roots of the row, as the US correspondent of the *Irish Times* put it, 'go back to last spring when Mr Christopher visited London to sell Mr Clinton's proposal to help arm the Muslim-led government of Bosnia'.[60] Likewise, Rupert Cornwell reported in the *Independent*, 'In US eyes, Bosnia is a greater irritant to relations with Britain than the IRA. If Mr Clinton was "punishing" Mr Major, he was doing so for London's brusque dismissal of last spring's US "lift and strike" initiative.'[61] Later on that year, it did not help that the incoming Republican Chairman of the House Foreign Affairs Committee, Benjamin Gilman from New York, was both a strong supporter of the Bosnian government and a leading member of the Irish National Caucus.[62]

In retrospect, the connection made between Bosnia and the Adams visa seems exaggerated. Tony Lake himself, as enthusiastic an advocate of bringing Sinn Fein into the peace process as of 'lift and strike', dismisses any direct link.[63] 'Our differences on Northern Ireland and our differences on Bosnia' were quite separate, he recalls. 'Neither of them infected each other, nor came close to creating a crisis in our relationship, or interfered with our ability to talk all the time, which we did . . . or the work on issues like Iraq.'[64] This does not quite tally with the recollection of other witnesses, such as the State Department official John Fox, who recalls – with reference to the period 1992–3 – that 'US–UK relations were at one point in the balance because of this. That's how Lake felt . . . and many of us in the State [Department] felt.'[65] More specifically relevant to Ireland is the testimony of the US ambassador to Nato, Dr Robert Hunter, who said that the disagreements over Bosnia were 'coupled with Gerry Adams', and that even though the policies themselves ran 'on totally separate tracks', they 'were linked in terms of British perception, that is for sure'.[66] In short, as James Rubin recalls, the two incidents were by no means directly connected, but were linked 'in the press and in the ether out there'.[67]

The most serious consequence of the Anglo-American falling out over Bosnia was the crisis in Nato. 'Dealing with the Europeans was delicate and nettlesome throughout the Bosnia crisis,' Richard Holbrooke recalls, 'and put an unprecedented strain on NATO and the Atlantic Alliance just when the Cold War ties that had held us together had also disappeared.'[68] 'Keeping the Atlantic Alliance . . . from coming apart over Bosnia,' he continued, 'was one of our greatest policy challenges . . . We needed to work in partnership with the alliance on a large number of other issues – the enlargement of NATO, a common policy toward the former Soviet Union, the Mideast and Iran, terrorism and human rights, the environment, and organised crime, – but Bosnia had begun to adversely affect everything.'[69] Indeed, Robin Renwick writes that by 1994 the Bosnian crisis 'had reached a point where it was starting to threaten the fabric of the NATO alliance'.[70] The British notion that Bosnia was merely a regrettable but remote ethnic spat of no importance to the wider world was decisively rejected. Instead, Bosnia was to become a touchstone issue for the future of Nato and the elaboration of a new security architecture for Europe.

Britain was not receptive to the idea of involving Nato in the wars of the Yugoslav secession. 'Nato,' the Foreign Office explained in November 1991, 'will not have a military role in central Europe in the event of instability in the region. Nato is a defensive alliance, and has made clear that none of its weapons will ever be used except in self-defence.'[71] The Foreign Secretary himself was, as officials recall, 'very reluctant' to bring Nato into the equation. Instead, the Foreign Office supported limited action by the Western European Union (WEU), which underwent a brief revival in this period. But, as the British representative at that body recalls, 'the fact was that the WEU, bless their cotton socks, simply didn't have the military wherewithal to compete with the sort of force structures and arrangements which Nato had at its disposal. The WEU was . . . essentially a political organization. It wanted to flex military muscle which frankly it didn't possess.'[72]

The Nato bureaucracy was slow to get involved. At this time, it possessed no political identity or will of its own, although it was to acquire a little of both by the time the war was over. As the Nato spokesman Dr Jamie Shea recalls, 'there was at the beginning a sense of unreality, when the Bosnian conflict first broke out, that this organization need do nothing'.[73] The text of the Rome declaration of November 1991, which added the provision of the 'foundations for a stable security environment in Europe' to Nato's traditional tasks,[74] was blithely penned at the height of the Croatian war, and remained at first a dead letter. Throughout 1992, Nato officials were briefing journalists in much the same way as their counterparts in London did: they emphasized Serb strength, the intractable terrain, and the unpredictability of all the parties.[75] When the chairman of the military committee of Nato, General Vigliek Eide, recommended the dispatch of 40,000 Nato troops in early 1992, he was blocked at the political level.[76] And in June of that year the North Atlantic Cooperation Council's meeting in Oslo merely noted that 'unilateral changes in border, territories or populations achieved through force, violence or faits accomplis are unacceptable'.[77] This injunction – like the signal that Nato was 'prepared to support, on a case by case basis ... peacekeeping activities under the responsibility of the CSCE' – remained without any immediate effect.[78]

By 1993, however, Bosnia began to force its way to the top of the Nato agenda. Tempers flared at a Nato meeting in Brussels in February when Warren Christopher claimed that 'The west missed too many opportunities to prevent or contain this suffering, bloodshed or destruction when the conflict was in its infancy. The lesson to be learned from this tragedy is the importance of early and decisive engagement against ethnic persecution and aggressive nationalism.' Douglas Hurd, against whom these remarks were in part directed, professed himself 'irritated' by the notion that the US 'had just invented the humanitarian effort. A European effort has kept alive many thousands of Bosnians which all predicted would be dead by now.'[79] And in late March 1993, harsh words were exchanged over Bosnia between General Colin Powell, the Chairman of the US Joint Chiefs of Staff, and Air Chief Marshal Sir Peter Harding, Chief of the UK Defence Staff.[80]

Throughout the first two years of the Bosnian conflict, much of the running was made by Manfred Wörner, a former German air force pilot and Minister for Defence. From February 1993 onwards, he regularly signalled his willingness to execute Nato air strikes against Bosnian Serb positions.[81] He was, in the words of two observers who were close to him at the time, in 'crusading mode' on Bosnia. In part, no doubt, the enthusiasm of the Nato bureaucracy for action in Bosnia was part of the search for a new role in the post-Cold War world. But it also reflected profound concern within the security establishment of western Europe about the implications of appeasement and inaction in Bosnia. In an off-the-record interview with the *Washington Times* journalist Georgie Geyer in mid-1993, published a year later after Wörner's death from cancer, the Secretary General condemned the failure to roll back Serb aggression. 'What we are doing,' he argued, 'is simply a cover-up for letting the Serbs win – and NATO will be blamed for it.' Wörner bitterly criticized Britain in particular for the maintenance of the arms embargo, and western leaders generally for obstructing Nato intervention to safeguard democratic values. 'I am the head of the most powerful military organisation in world history,' he lamented, 'and I can do nothing.'[82] Similarly, General Shalikashvili, the Supreme Allied Commander Europe for most of 1993, made no secret of the fact that Nato should intervene militarily in Bosnia, or face complete redundancy; he also believed that Bosnia was 'a lesson to all of us about the price to be paid when American leadership was absent'.[83] Indeed, the feeling in Nato circles was evident from the Labour MP Calum MacDonald's remarks in late July 1993 that a recent visit to the Nato Alliance headquarters in Brussels had left him 'with the clear impression that the most senior officials in NATO were satisfied that intervention was not only feasible and advisable but urgently required. We received a clear impression that there was intense frustration at the failure at the political level to take the steps necessary to resolve the crisis.'[84]

Dr Jamie Shea, the Nato spokesman, was also quick to spot the danger that Bosnia represented to the credibility of the alliance. Already in early 1993, he was warning that 'Alliance members have to face the reality that as fast as they transform the alliance new challenges emerge and new expectations develop. The Cold War is behind us, but in the Balkans a hot war is raging.' 'Violent nationalism in Yugoslavia,' he pointed out, 'may not threaten NATO territory, but left to fester it can only increase insecurity and instability across Europe, eventually provoking the type of international conflict we thought we had put behind us. If the current phase of transition in Europe is not to become a violent historical epoch in its own right, the West's moral authority must be transformed into the hard currency of political authority. In particular, the Alliance must learn to mobilise its resources in a more timely way and concentrated fashion to stop the violence and force the belligerents off the battlefield and towards the negotiating table.' 'Yugoslavia,' Shea concluded, 'is seen as the defining moment for the future of European security, and institutions in Europe will obviously be judged by their success in bringing about a resolution.'[85]

The problem, as Jamie Shea recalls, was not just Nato's role, or lack of one, but its *perceived* weakness. 'We couldn't ignore the problem,' he explains. 'The media were hammering us; even if we weren't ourselves trying to claim a leading role, the media were claiming it for us. And although you know politicians say they don't care what Chip Hogan in the *Washington Post* says or Will Safire in the *New York Times* or Anthony Lewis or any of the others, over a period of hammer, hammer, hammer . . . They were up in arms, the world of the civilized society was putting us under pressure.'[86]

Another worried man at Nato was the British ambassador, Sir John Weston. 'Bosnia,' he recalls, was 'a really important thing to get right – this is the Alliance and if we mess it up . . . nobody's going to believe in Nato again.'[87] Already in late June 1992, Weston was concerned that Nato should not be left on the sidelines of the European security agenda. A year later, Weston took the view that the Secretary General was concerned that Nato was being criticized for failing to achieve things which it had not been asked to take on. This was on top of the broader risk of public disillusionment with the network of international organizations which, for all its strength on paper, was not stemming the bloodshed. Indeed, as Sir John subsequently recalled, 'here we [were] in Nato where we [had] been trying to put flesh on the bones of the new Nato strategy, to rethink and rewrite all the Nato precautionary measures system in relation to international crises, [and] suddenly [there] bowls along a real-life, on your doorstep multifaceted crisis. [This was] a period in which somehow Nato was not involved and that led to great discomfort within Alliance circles because of the perceived risk that the alliance would be found or held to be somehow irrelevant to the new world we were living in.'[88]

The threat to Nato's credibility was increased by the fact that Nato was in the throes of an acrimonious debate on eastward enlargement.[89] In 1991 almost all states in post-Cold War central and south-eastern Europe had wanted to join the alliance, but found little enthusiasm among the existing membership. Many were bitterly opposed to the import of what they regarded as intractable nationality and territorial disputes into their carefully cultivated western European idyll. Existing members also feared provoking Russia, and inflaming nationalists and recidivist communists opposed to President Yeltsin's 'reforms'. Nevertheless, from early 1993, the German government, anxious to escape the role of Nato's front line to the east, and keen to export security and stability to Poland, the Czech Republic, Hungary and possibly even Slovakia and Romania, began to put enlargement on the international agenda.[90] But when the German Defence Minister, Volker Rühe, first formally introduced the idea of Nato enlargement at a lecture in London in March 1993, he was met with widespread scepticism and even hostility from the British security establishment. Indeed, in the summer of 1993, Malcolm Rifkind told a Russian audience that Britain would resist German plans for Nato expansion.[91] The very most Rifkind was prepared to countenance were wholly inadequate association and cooperation agreements, without meaningful obligations on either side. He seemed to regard Nato merely as a glorified insurance company, which wisely refused coverage to those who might need it most.

Throughout 1993, the Clinton administration wrestled with the idea of enlargement. The National Security Council under Tony Lake and prominent figures such as Madeleine Albright were in favour; the Pentagon under Les Aspin and Warren Christopher's State Department were more cautious. Indeed, some senior national security voices, such as Paul Nitze and Brent Scowcroft, were bitterly opposed to enlargement.[92] As one critic later pointed out, 'in view of the Bosnian débâcle . . . the hypothetical possibility of quarrels among these states over the status of minorities should at least be considered before US forces are committed by treaty to the defense of an area where they might arise'.[93]

But by the end of the year, the Americans had come round to the idea of enlargement. In December 1993, the State Department announced that 'The alliance must face a historic choice. That choice is whether to embrace innovation or risk irrelevance.'[94] The British, who now risked isolation, were grudgingly reconciled to enlargement. As Admiral Crowe, who was US ambassador in London during the Nato expansion debate, recalls, the British 'didn't feel that they could oppose us if we were intent on it, and we made clear we were intent on it'.[95]

The ramifications of prospective enlargement for the Bosnian war were considerable. On 4 December 1994 the Foreign Secretary had told a television audience that 'what Nato has been doing for the UN in Bosnia is not part of its basic task and is not a test of its worth.' Now the British ambassador to Nato, Sir John Weston, could remind him that of the four fundamental tasks of the alliance set out in the Strategic Concept, the first listed was to provide for a stable security environment in Europe 'in which no country would be able to intimidate or coerce any European nation or to impose hegemony through the threat or use of force'. As the new Secretary General, Willy Claes, had remarked, the alliance had now moved beyond a purely territorial concept of security towards a more active approach of projecting stability beyond its borders in Europe. The Nato summit of 1994 had committed the alliance to support peacekeeping and other operations outside the authority of the UN Security Council. In the Yugoslav case, Weston believed, Nato had clearly been the victim of the old adage 'you're damned if you do and you're damned if you don't'. In his view, both UN and Nato credibility had taken knocks as a result.[96] Indeed, Sir Richard Vincent, the British Chairman of Nato's Military Committee for most of the war, felt that the west was 'blowing its credibility' over Bosnia.[97] 'I was aware,' he recalls, 'that if this was the best that Nato could deliver at the end of the Cold War what the hell were we paying for?'[98] While neither man makes any claim to having resisted British government policy, both were to become increasingly frustrated and embarrassed at London's attitude.

Another figure in Nato headquarters who had come to the same conclusion was the outspoken and farsighted American ambassador to Nato, Dr Robert Hunter. Even before his arrival in mid-1993, Hunter had signalled the need to move forcefully against the Bosnian

Serbs and their sponsors in Belgrade. He was quick to see the connection between Bosnia and Nato expansion. Already in June 1993, Hunter wrote that ignoring Bosnia 'would dash all hopes of extending the "war-free zone" [in western Europe] in an easterly direction'.[99] 'We had,' he later recalled, 'a new Nato that had to be protective and it wasn't going to be protective if it couldn't take care of a pesky little war down in the Balkans.'[100] Hunter rejected the shallow self-congratulation which characterized some Nato circles in the immediate aftermath of the Cold War. He agreed with those critics who asked, 'What are you talking about Nato's been a success? You've got a war going on in your own backyard. You've failed.' It was the same thinking that led Hunter himself to remark during a discussion on Kosovo, 'The logic is very simple. Nato's about security in Europe. There's a war going on in Europe. Nato hasn't stopped the war. Nato's failed.'[101]

This view resonated widely among Republican security voices in the United States. As Bruce Jackson, a principal fundraiser for the Republican presidential contender Bob Dole and the President of the US Committee on Nato, recalls, the Bosnian war 'completely offended the Republican national security wing'. It was 'a war of aggression . . . [and] aggression appeased'.[102] Failure to act, Jackson added, would undermine plans for Nato expansion and European security. He reminds us that Vaclav Havel's visit to Washington for the opening of the Holocaust museum was accompanied by a personal request to Clinton for Nato enlargement. 'If you are expanding Nato,' Jackson concludes, 'in order to [ensure] the "Never Again" in Europe, you can't . . . have a holocaust break out in Europe. It makes you look like a fool.'[103] Similarly, Richard Perle, former Assistant Secretary of Defense under Ronald Reagan, recalls that 'It was a Nato issue because it was right in the centre of Europe. It was unavoidable because so many countries surrounding the former Yugoslavia were involved, because it had the potential to expand to the east and bring in the Greeks and the Turks in those various ways . . . And at the end of the day, the scale of the atrocity became such that Nato simply couldn't be a passive observer and maintain any credibility.'[104]

This theme was echoed by John Herzberg, a former State Department official who served as a Republican staffer on the Foreign Relations Committee of the House of Representatives from early 1993.

'At that time,' he recalls, 'we were also dealing with Nato enlargement, and we felt that if Nato was going to be at all an organization worthy of any kind of continued support, it had to do things. It had to prove it could handle situations such as that which was going on in Bosnia, and it had to be able to expand to take in new members from central and eastern Europe. And we thought the two things were linked.'[105] Indeed, several close observers of Nato enlargement have remarked that if there had been no Bosnia, or if Nato had failed in Bosnia, there would have been no enlargement.

Many Republican internationalists feared that failure to address the Bosnian problem would not merely undermine Nato but also strengthen the isolationist wing of the party. As Bruce Jackson recalls, 'By 1994 this [Bosnia and Nato expansion] was clearly a fight between the Bob Dole wing and the Pat Buchanan wing of the Republican Party. And . . . the motivation for setting up the US Committee on Nato was explicitly the fact that we lost the first three primaries to Pat Buchanan. People don't remember, but the Senate Leader [Dole] lost the first three times to an isolationist, and there was the huge danger in late 1994, early 1995 . . . that the isolationist party would become ascendant . . . So the Bosnian war really became the battleground for the internationalists versus the isolationists in American politics.'[106]

If much of this debate took place behind the scenes, it soon spilled over into the public domain. Eugene Rostow, the former Director of the Arms Control and Disarmament Agency, observed in July 1993, that unless Nato sorted out Bosnia, 'all that was accomplished by the Gulf War in strengthening the cause of peace will be at risk'.[107] This was also the view of Martin McCusker, the Director of the Defence and Security Committee, North Atlantic Assembly in Brussels, which is made up of parliamentarians from Nato countries. In a strongly worded public letter in late October 1993 he noted that 'Future historians will shake their heads in utter disbelief that so-called civilised Europe allowed such suffering of the innocents to go on so long. And this will occur while our children-scholars will be rewriting the history books that my generation was brought up on, and in which such great stock was placed on the principle of "never again will there be genocide in Europe". It will be perplexing for future generations to reconcile the availability of the greatest multi-national concentration of military force in the history of the world – backed up by economic resources and capabilities – with what they will read about in these new history books. It is on this that our generation, and our leaders, will be judged. The verdict will be damning and shameful.'[108]

Moreover, Richard Lugar, the Republican Chairman of the Senate Foreign Affairs Committee, told the Atlantic Council in December 1993, now that the Cold War was over, 'If only for domestic political reasons, a new rationale . . . revolving around new missions . . . may be essential to halting the erosion in support for NATO in the Congress.'[109] Nato must, as Lugar put it, go 'out of area or out of business'. George Shultz, Ronald Reagan's long-serving Secretary of State, dismissed the west's position on Bosnia in 1994 as 'pathetic, shameful . . . The way you behave in one situation is transmitted all around the world and people take a lesson from your behaviour.'[110] Likewise, the Deputy Secretary of State, Strobe Talbott, linked the case for Nato enlargement directly to Bosnia. 'Many critics have asked,' he wrote in mid-1995, 'why should NATO stay in business at all, to say nothing of expanding, if it can't resolve the conflict in Bosnia?' 'However,' he argued, 'the lesson of the tragedy in the former Yugoslavia is not to retire NATO in disgrace but to develop its ability to counter precisely those forces that have exploded in the Balkans. And many of the nations in the region see NATO as having that potential. Representatives of several Central European states have said publicly that, for them, the Bosnian tragedy is an argument for joining NATO – and for adopting the standards of internal order and external behaviour that will make them eligible.'[111]

In short, by and large, the notion that Nato's credibility was at stake in Bosnia had become something of a consensus on the other side of the Atlantic by late 1993 and certainly by the end of 1994. Most Americans instinctively grasped that inaction in Bosnia was not compatible with the idea of eastward expansion and the ethos on which Nato had been founded. Unlike the British, many Americans realized that simply denying the relevance of Nato did not solve the problem. They rejected the mistaken assumption that an organization could maintain its deterrent credibility in the face of aggression and ethnic cleansing taking place if not within its direct remit then within its immediate vicinity.[112] They realized that this proposition was logically coherent, but untrue in practice. By denying military succour to the victims, the west was not reducing instability but aggravating it, *and* casting doubt over the value of a putative Nato Article V guarantee.[113]

The new states of central and eastern Europe were by no means all sympathizers with the Sarajevo government, but most of them were deeply unsettled by the fiasco of western policy, which left them to seek their own accommodations with potentially rogue states. Ukrainian hesitations about giving up their nuclear weapons were not unrelated to fears of Bosnian-style western inactivity in the event of a Russian invasion or internal subversion.[114] And it was particularly significant that Hungary, a keen advocate of Nato expansion and a ferocious critic of Milosevic, nevertheless informed Nato in mid-1993 that it would not allow the AWACS early warning aircraft currently in its airspace to participate in air strikes against the Bosnian Serbs and began speaking of normalizing relations with Belgrade in early 1994.[115] Soon, Nato would indeed, as Hugo Young put it in the *Guardian*, be 'the club that nobody wants to join'.

The Bosnian war was to affect the fraught triangular relationship between Britain, the United States, and France in curious ways. At one level, predictably enough, transatlantic acrimony furthered the traditional French 'wrecking agenda', by which Paris sought to undermine American leadership within Nato. Thus, in December 1994, at the height of the Bihac crisis, American officials claimed to be in possession of evidence obtained by electronic eavesdropping which suggested that 'Paris might be purposely inflaming tensions over Bosnia to drive a wedge between Britain and the US', and that 'France would like to see Nato broken up and replaced by a European Security Alliance'.[116] Likewise, Richard Perle recalls that Anglo-American friction over Bosnia 'was certainly convenient from a French point of view, because it enabled the French to renew the charge . . . that the US was going to be unreliable or appeared to be unreliable . . . the French made it a point to use almost any American behaviour that could be characterized as failure or otherwise to drive that agenda, which is to diminish the United States in Europe'.[117]

It is certainly true that the French tried to turn Anglo-American friction over Bosnia to their own advantage. 'The conflict in Bosnia,' the French Foreign Minister, Alain Juppé, remarked at the height of the Bihac crisis, 'has shown the necessity to move beyond NATO and American guarantees.'[118] According to one French diplomat, the US withdrawal from policing the arms embargo 'reinforces our argument that NATO needs to break with the tradition of American commanders because they are going to be caught in the dilemmas of conflicting orders'.[119] This argument was implicitly accepted by the British President of the Assembly of the WEU, Sir Dudley Smith, when he remarked, somewhat to the dismay of British officials, that the US decision 'proves just how much Europe needs to be autonomous where intelligence gathering, satellite reconnaissance and logistic support are concerned'.[120] And by January 1995, the British ambassador to Nato believed that while *militarily* the links to the United States remained close, the Bosnian war had raised nagging suspicions that the Americans could no longer be relied on *politically*. Indeed, he felt that the French were more than ready to draw the conclusion that the collective investment in the integrated military structure was not enough to provide for European security in the broad sense defined by Nato's own strategic concept.[121]

Both John Major and Douglas Hurd – Malcolm Rifkind less so – were genuinely committed to closer political and military integration in Europe. They were much more enthusiastic participants in the discussions on the development of a common European security policy and identity than many Eurosceptic critics would have wished. The Anglo-French defence dialogue announced in the autumn of 1994, and solemnized at the summit at Chartres in mid-November 1994, had already begun back in early 1993,[122] at the height of the initial transatlantic recriminations over Bosnia. 'Defence in Europe,' Hurd remarked, 'is not an opt-out subject for us – like the Social Chapter. Working with the French is an important aspect.'[123] In late 1994, France and Britain agreed to establish a joint planning group – to be based in southern England – for their air forces. At the same time, Britain began discussions with Germany, France, Spain, and Italy on the development of the 'Future Large Aircraft', a military transport.[124] Moreover, as Douglas Hurd recalls, 'the experience in Bosnia brought service co-operation between the British and the French to a new post-war high. Suez didn't count because it was short and a disaster.'[125]

Likewise, numerous military sources have testified that working with the French 'on the ground' in Bosnia, often in the 'shadow' of US air strikes, helped to break down barriers between the two armies. And Tom Richardson, who was a mainstay of the Franco-British alliance on the Security Council in New York, thinks that 'the military alliance, for such it was in Bosnia, probably did more to consolidate Anglo-French defence relationships than almost anything else'.[126] The notion that Britain should seek to rely less on a transatlantic chimera and more on her European partners no longer seemed so fanciful.[127]

The cornerstone of this policy was the attempt to entice France back into Nato's integrated military command structure, which de Gaulle had stormed out of some thirty years before. As General Sir Edward Jones, who served as military representative at the WEU and on Nato's military committee throughout the war, recalls, 'there was a real feeling that the French were going to rejoin . . . This wasn't discouraged by the French representative . . . All that was leading us to believe that there was an opportunity here for the French to join the integrated military structure. And that would have been a very considerable prize. My French colleague on the military committee and I used to discuss this regularly, and . . . listening to what he had to say, he certainly gave the impression that this was at least a possibility. And I think that all of us probably paid particular attention to the French position because of the apparent prize that there was at the end of this process.'[128] In accordance with this endeavour, French officers were seconded to the ARRC, the Nato operational level HQ, for contingency planning in early 1995.

Both John Major and Douglas Hurd approached this project without any desire to offend the Americans. Hurd, in particular, denied 'forsaking NATO for some phantom European army'. Rather, he explained, 'We see nothing but advantage in building up a European Security and Defence Identity. Our American friends welcome this . . . Any arrangements must complement NATO's control and command system, and must not undermine or conflict with NATO. It is not as difficult as it sounds.'[129] If Britain could maintain good relations with the US, and at the same time build up a complementary European defence identity and capability, what could be wrong with that?

The problem was not one of intentions, which were good, but of judgement, which was lamentable. For the result of the new British policy was an unprecedentedly close relationship with France at the expense of the United States. At the UN Security Council, the French positions on Bosnia generally dovetailed with those of Sir David Hannay, a dedicated supporter of non-intervention and the arms embargo. Indeed, as diplomats at the UN remarked, 'It is noticeable now that the French support the British on issues where there is no mileage for them, presumably in the hope that it banks goodwill.' Another observed that Bosnia 'forced the British and French into bed together. But now it has spread to other issues and it is based at least partly on the fact that Hannay and Merimée [the French ambassador] actually like one another. Equally clearly, they disdain Mrs Albright.'[130] As British diplomatic sources proudly recall, the very close working relationship between the British and the French over Bosnia was born not in Brussels, but in New York. According to Tom Richardson, 'The cooperation was incredible. We had video conferences the whole time, and an enormous effort was spent in trying to keep alongside the French on policy, on presentation.'[131] The last time Britain and France found themselves so intimately aligned was over Suez in 1956, and the last time before that over Munich in 1938. Against this background, the fact that the French attended their first Nato summit in thirty years in October 1994,[132] not least in order to exploit the Anglo-American rift over Bosnia, should have given pause for thought, not for facile celebrations of a new *entente*.

It soon became clear, moreover, that the British courtship of France in Nato was ill advised. Anything that involved the French was likely to be militarily backward, and politically frivolous. The French had no intention of allowing Nato any kind of veto over European initiatives in the WEU or any other new structure. They were, as the British representative at the WEU recalls, using that body 'as a distraction from Nato. They were trying for their own political ends to enhance the standing of the WEU military committee.'[133] Central and eastern European applicants were encouraged to join the WEU rather than Nato.[134] And the French were only interested in rejoining Nato on their own terms, which would inevitably be anathema to the Americans. 'The extent to which we participate in the alliance,' a French diplomat explained in early 1995, 'will reflect the degree to which it changes.'[135]

The much hoped-for reintegration into the Nato command structure never happened. Moreover, General Jones concluded, 'I don't believe that the French do anything accidentally. And therefore I would conclude personally that this was a deliberate ploy [to destabilize Nato].'[136] In short, the Major administration risked the tried and trusted transatlantic relationship to pursue a Franco-European will-o'-the-wisp.

All the while, Anglo-American relations within Nato deteriorated. As the US ambassador recalls, the atmosphere on Bosnia was 'poisonous . . . this was, I think, the worst moment in Anglo-American relations since Suez'.[137] Some of the difficulties centred on personalities. The American Supreme Allied Commander Europe, George Joulwan, was, as Sir John Weston recalls, 'a lovely chap [but] frankly a bull in the china shop as far as diplomatic niceties are concerned'. But the principal problems, Weston insists, were the 'structural differences', for 'running through many of the debates and arguments in the Nato forum was this sense that the Europeans were trying to bite their tongue all the time, not to make the debating point relentlessly with the Americans, it's all very well for you, you know, you haven't got the guys there – we have and this is what they say'.[138] One very senior British military figure even repeatedly suggested that the US excursion to Somalia was 'in preference to putting feet on the ground in the Balkans'. The Americans in turn tried not to accuse the British of craven capitulation in the face of aggression. Neither side proved very successful in hiding its feelings. There was, Sir John Weston remembers, 'a lot of aggravation in the air'.

One of the most bizarre aspects of all this was that British objections to American-led air strikes exceeded even those of the French. Britain was, Dr Hunter recalls, 'in the final analysis the most reluctant of all the allied states'. For the American mission at Nato headquarters, many of them devout Anglophiles accustomed to a common front with Britain against France, this was a radical and shocking new phenomenon. 'It took me a while to realize that the real stumbling block to the use of air power was Britain,' Hunter recalled, 'and they were doing it from motives that I didn't clearly understand.' 'No matter what the parameters were of the various agreements,' he continues, 'they constantly whittled them back to as little as possible, where they couldn't be defeated altogether.'[139]

Indeed, the Americans found that the French were always willing to come round in the end. As the former senior State Department official James Hooper observes, France has historically taken its objections down to the wire, particularly when the US position is equivocal. But once the US has made its mind up, he suggests, 'the French will be the first' to sign up. 'Once the Americans say they are going to act . . . we say our planes are taking off at 5 a.m., the French will come back and say, well, ours are taking off at 4 a.m.'[140] This is what happened in the Gulf, and the pattern was repeated in Bosnia, where as US officials recall the French blew 'hot and cold' between Serbophile non-intervention and pro-Bosnian activism. 'We found that if we could get the French on board,' Hunter explains, 'that tended to get everybody on board.'[141]

It was, after all, the French who had enthusiastically supported the pre-emptive dispatch of peacekeepers to Croatia and Bosnia in 1991–2. It was the French who provided the critical support for the 'no-fly resolution' in the teeth of British objections.[142] It was the French who in the spring of 1993 were quietly urging the Americans on to military intervention in Bosnia. Yet, as the former State Department official John Fox recalls, 'every time the French would troop in and do this . . . they would be walking out the door and the British would come in the same door saying, "Look, you know our French colleagues, you know how they are, a little up and down, but here's the real take on this". So they were just dumping cold water all over what . . . was being advocated by the French.'[143] And it was the French who delivered the breakthrough which led to the Sarajevo ultimatum of February 1994. 'The French were crucial,' a senior Tory MP remarked at the time. 'We have always been able to argue against the Americans on air strikes by saying we had troops on the ground and they didn't. But we couldn't use that argument once the French wanted air strikes – they have troops closer to Sarajevo than us.'[144] 'The paradox', as the French foreign minister, Alain Juppé, remarked, 'is that it is the country which does the most on the ground that is the most enthusiastic for military action.'[145]

In 1994, therefore, the French were prepared to subordinate their campaign against US dominance in Nato to the cause of rolling back or at least containing Serb aggression in Bosnia; the British, on the other hand, refused to budge, even for the sake of Nato and the transatlantic alliance. In short, over Bosnia, a Conservative, nominally Atlanticist British administration was being more 'French' than France itself.

At one level, the activists in America and the Nato bureaucracy seemed to be winning the argument. On no fewer than three occasions between July 1993 and April 1994, the threat of massive Nato air action was brought to bear on the Bosnian Serbs, and in each case it was effective.

The trigger for the first Nato ultimatum was the progressive strangulation of Sarajevo throughout the summer of 1993, which reached breaking point with the capture of key heights overlooking the city by the Bosnian Serbs. After more than a year of prevarication and deference to the Europeans, the US government finally seized the initiative and declared, as Christopher was to put it, that 'we have concluded that it is in our national interest to prevent the strangulation of Sarajevo'.[146] The Bosnians, he believed, should at least retain a rump state, and the Serbs must be warned not to press on into Macedonia or Kosovo. In late July, the US National Security Advisor, Tony Lake, and the US special envoy to the Balkans, Reginald Bartholomew, flew to London and demanded a clear threat of air action to force the Serbs off Mount Igman. Failure to agree, the British were warned, would turn the Nato summit in January 1994 into a farce, and indeed put the whole future of the organization at risk. 'The pitch,' as Lake recalls, 'was that we had to do something; that we were deadly serious about "lift and strike" . . . I hope that paved the way then for what was . . . people forget this, progress . . . in getting the Sarajevo ultimatum.'[147] Later, this became known – in contrast to Christopher's 'listening mode' – as 'don't ask, tell',[148] but Lake denies this. 'Well, no,' he somewhat implausibly claims, 'I didn't tell Britain what to do certainly. One does not tell one's allies what to do.'[149]

In the face of British misgivings, the North Atlantic Council agreed on 2 August to wide-ranging air strikes to prevent the 'strangulation of Sarajevo'.[150] The French had no objection to air strikes, as such, but violently objected to the operation being under Nato control.[151] In a last-ditch piece of sabotage, however, British officials succeeded in securing a UN veto in the decision-making process. Only if both Nato and the UN Secretary General – acting on advice from UNPROFOR – agreed, could air strikes be launched. The full significance of this infamous 'dual key' was only to become obvious later.[152] For the time being, the Serbs withdrew. The air cavalry had arrived, in the nick of time.

This sequence of events was repeated in February 1994, when the explosion of a Bosnian Serb shell in the market-place at Sarajevo caused horrific loss of life. The graphic footage broadcast across the world galvanized American elite opinion into renewed demands for determined air action. In London, both Douglas Hurd and Malcolm Rifkind were swift to quash suggestions of western intervention: Nato involvement, the Foreign Secretary claimed after initial reports of the outrage, 'is something that is not going to happen'; 'the world cannot send armies into what is a cruel and vicious civil war', said the Defence Secretary.[153] Once again, President Clinton declared the Atlantic alliance in jeopardy if support were not forthcoming.[154] Once again, the London government resisted for as long as it could, but found itself isolated after being abandoned by the French. Once again, Nato threatened massive retaliation unless the Bosnian Serbs withdrew their artillery to designated collection points around the city. Once again – this time after a face-saving interposition by Russian peacekeeping forces – the Bosnian Serbs blinked.

For the British government, the Sarajevo ultimatum was a deeply fraught episode. In order to keep ranks with the Americans as far as possible, it was now forced to admit both that the UN mandate was more extensive than previously claimed, and that the Russians were not the blocking factor they had hitherto made them out to be. 'United Nations Security Council resolution 836,' Malcolm Rifkind conceded to the House of Commons, 'allowed, and indeed encouraged, the consideration of any possible means of ensuring that there was not a stranglehold on Sarajevo [and] . . . I do not believe that it would require a further resolution of the Security Council for the reasons that I have given.'[155] The Russians, in other words, would not be able to exercise a veto. Nor, it emerged, did they want to. At the United Nations meeting of 10 February, the Russian ambassador, Yuli Vorontsov, expressed concern about Nato air action but denied any plans to block it.[156]

But the most embarrassing part for British statesmen and officials was explaining the decision to support the American-led air raids, if necessary, in defiance of their earlier apocalyptic predictions. The newspaper headlines said it all: 'No choice: how Britain was bulldozed into air strikes. Clinton strongarms apprehensive Major', and 'U-turn, what U-turn asks Major'.[157] One British official insisted that 'the difference of approach between Paris and London was never nearly so great as you might think, it is merely that the French thinking surfaced earlier'. 'Sometimes,' said another, 'sadly, it takes a tragic and highly visible single act like this to create a political turning point.' More visible, one might ask, than the bread queue massacre in 1992, the detention camps, the rapes, and the first Srebrenica crisis in 1993? After a clear lead from the Americans, Hurd told reporters that 'The case for air action is very strong, provided we can find a means of doing it which produces more good than harm.' The Foreign Secretary did not reveal why the case was particularly good now, nearly two years into the war, and why the alleged negative factors had so suddenly receded. When challenged on this, an aide to the Foreign Secretary responded that 'I think the effect of these television pictures round the world is greater than you give them credit for.'[158] So much for the posture of not being swayed by media images.

The palpable *volte face* on air strikes offered the opposition something of an open goal in parliament. 'Will the Right Hon. Gentleman explain to the house', the Labour spokesman on Foreign Affairs, John Cunningham, asked, 'why the decision was not taken, as it could and should have been, many, many months ago?'[159] 'Is the Foreign Secretary aware,' the Labour backbencher Dennis Skinner asked, 'that he is engaged in another government U-turn and that he has done it with a look on his face which suggests that his heart is not in it?'[160] The answer from Douglas Hurd was a staggering admission from a man of considerable experience and legendary circumspection. 'At that [Nato] summit,' he said, 'it was very clear that our main allies – and certainly the United States – felt passionately about the Bosnian issue. If we had frustrated yesterday's decision, I do not doubt that we would have administered to ourselves – to our own defence policy – a severe shock. However, as I have said, that would not have been a conclusive argument if we had felt, on listening to our own military advice, that the proposal was unsustainable and untenable.'[161] In

Hurdspeak this meant: we *were* railroaded. This was clearly one of those occasions upon which, as Douglas Hurd recalls, Britain 'went along with Nato escalation' to prevent further damage to transatlantic ties and relationships within Nato.[162]

So concerned was Douglas Hurd about the apparent – and real – inconsistency in the government position, that he sent a letter to MPs enclosing a question and answer brief to help them field enquiries about the ultimatum. In answering the question 'Why air strikes now, not sooner?' the following response was suggested: 'We supported the use of air power in right circumstances for some time. Must consider balance of advantage. Market shelling the last straw. Shocked the world afresh. The balance tipped.'[163] Baroness Chalker had to fight the same battle in the House of Lords. 'I might remind the House,' she said, 'that we have consistently supported the use of air power provided that it would support and not undermine the peace process and the aid effort . . . Our support for air power is not new.'[164]

The third successful threat of Nato air power was made in April 1994 during the siege of the eastern Bosnian enclave of Gorazde by Serb forces. Once again, the British government denied that anything useful could be done or threatened from the air, even after the successful Sarajevo ultimatum. 'The circumstances in Sarajevo were unique,' Rifkind claimed, 'in that artillery was attacking from the heights, which were themselves credible targets for the use of air power.'[165] Leaving aside the fact that the British government had spent one and a half years denying any such thing, the notion that the Serb guns at Gorazde were any less vulnerable than those above Sarajevo betokened a shaky grasp of the local topography. The US Defense Secretary, William Perry, with equally unfortunate judgement but greater candour, publicly affirmed that Nato would not enter the conflict to stop the town from falling. Pin-prick air attacks on individual Serb tanks proved unavailing. But when the collapse seemed imminent, Nato eventually did intervene with the threat of massive air action. Once again, in fact, the British government was forced into an American-sponsored ultimatum at variance with its earlier policy. Once again, the Bosnian Serbs blinked and withdrew.

In the meantime, however, one British Harrier jet had been shot down on its lonely quest for a Serb tank, and one of the courageous

SAS forward air controllers within the pocket had been killed by the Bosnian Serbs. Malcolm Rifkind was quick to interpret this as evidence of the bankruptcy of the air power enthusiasts. The 'facile' suggestion, he remarked on BBC radio, 'that you can bomb all the combatants to the peace table' had thus been 'discredited'. The *Spectator* commented on this strange gloss on the activities of his own armed forces thus: 'While it may seem uncharitable to say that Mr Rifkind was thanking the Serbs for shooting down that plane, the very least that must be said is that he either does not agree with, or does not understand, the policy which his own pilots were risking their lives to execute.'[166] Nor, one might have added, was the Defence Secretary justified in inflating the failure of the pin-prick attacks – which the British supported – into a more general critique of massive aerial threats, which Britain rejected as long as it could, but which delivered the goods on three separate occasions in 1993–4, and finally helped to break the logjam in the autumn of 1995.

Inevitably, the renewed government *volte face* on air power was remarked upon in the Commons. 'As the government seem to accept that when the threat of force was made clear and credible in both Sarajevo and Gorazde it seemed to work,' the Labour MP Clive Soley asked, 'will the right hon. Gentleman tell us why he thinks that it would not have worked 18 months ago?' Douglas Hurd responded: 'I do not believe that 18 months ago the circumstances existed in which it would have worked. We cannot be certain of these things, but that was certainly the advice that we received at the time and the advice on which we and many others acted.'[167] This mysterious 'advice', one can see, was being made responsible for a multitude of sins; of that, more later.

The American alternative strategy for Bosnia was refined in the course of 1994 and 1995. In its essentials, the old 'lift and strike' gambit still stood, albeit with important modifications. The pressure for massive air action was maintained throughout. But instead of confining itself to public calls for the lifting of the arms embargo, the US administration now embarked upon a more discreet course of preparing the Croats and Bosnians for war. General Wesley Clark, the Director of Strategic Plans and Policy on the Joint Staff of the Joint Chiefs of Staff, and a confidant of the President, was dispatched on a mission to Bosnia. The ostensible message he brought back was that the arms embargo should be upheld, as the Bosnian forces were unready for new weapons. In reality, as the 'Senate Select Committee Report on Iran/Bosnia Arms transfers' subsequently established, Clark 'in separate discussions with the head of UNPROFOR and with Bosnian leaders, including President Izetbegovic, moved seamlessly from exploring the implications of a unilateral lifting of the embargo to the question of whether one could rely upon the clandestine flow of embargo-breaking arms and thus avoid UNPROFOR's departure. The officer told the Committee that he had viewed this as an exploration of overt policy options; he had no authority to develop covert action options. But in one of the meetings [Clark] expressed a willingness to encourage greater third-party arms flows in violation of the UN arms embargo and/or to engage directly in covert embargo-busting.'[168]

Little concrete is known about this covert action even today. At the time, UN and European officials – and even some French politicians – routinely accused the Americans of secretly arming 'the Muslims' and of having 'taken sides'. Stories of the provision of US satellite intelligence to the Bosnian government, of nightly resupply missions to airstrips in government-held central Bosnia, proliferated in late 1994 and the first half of 1995.[169] The author is in no position to verify these charges. It is certainly the case that the Clinton administration tolerated supplies of arms to the Bosnians, by the Iranians and others. It is also true that the White House facilitated the activities of MPRI, a highly professional private US military consultancy, in training and reorganizing the Croatian army for the inevitable showdown with the Krajina Serbs. It is further true that the Pentagon, albeit under duress, agreed to draw up a detailed plan for the arming and training of Bosnian government forces; the sums involved were estimated at between $3 and $5 billion.[170]

What is beyond doubt is that all of this contributed to the deterioration of relations within Nato and unprecedentedly bad blood between the US and the British military. This was particularly evident in the angry exchanges of early 1995, when the UNPROFOR spokesman, Lieutenant Colonel Gary Coward, reported numerous sightings of propeller-driven aircraft near the Bosnian government airfield at Tuzla, in violation of the no-fly ban. These were widely believed to be

US or US-sponsored C-130 transports escorted by jet fighters; they were also observed, in the air and on the ground, by British special forces.[171] These allegations provoked a withering response from US and Nato officials who improbably suggested that the observers might have been confused by Serbian civilian flights or Nato training missions.[172] In this atmosphere of claim and counter-claim the report by Robert Block that 'There have been suggestions by some senior UN civilian officials that British and French military officers in Bosnia have been spreading misleading reports about covert US activities in Bosnia to undermine Washington's authority in the debate on the former Yugoslavia' gained some credence.[173]

What is remarkable about all this is not the question of whether or not these American or American-sponsored flights took place, but the undeniable fact that virtually all the Britons interviewed for this study, and most Americans, *believed* that they did. Sir John Weston recalls that 'there were certainly rumours about covert US arms flights to the Bosnians. Some believed them, some not.'[174] Lord Vincent, then Chairman of Nato's Military Committee, speaks of 'the endless drama about these Hercules C-130s landing wherever it was . . . and this did cause great anger through the North Atlantic Council'.[175] Others remember the 'massive pressure' from the Americans to turn a blind eye to the flights.[176] Dame Pauline Neville-Jones remarks that 'it did nothing for confidence between us'.[177] Dr Hunter, the US ambassador to Nato, 'assume[d] that they were either organized or tolerated' by the US government.[178] But since 'in a sense it was consistent with what [he] wanted to see happen', Hunter 'really didn't want to know about it'. Yet there is no reason to doubt Tony Lake's claims before Congress – and since – that these stories were 'simply untrue'.[179] He has no recollection of the matter being raised with him by the British. 'If we were doing it,' he recently remarked, 'and we were lying to our British allies, that would be a rather exceptional event.'[180]

The Americans also became more active on the diplomatic front. In February–March 1994, in a major success which had eluded the Europeans for nearly eighteen months, they knocked Croat and Bosnian heads together to produce the Washington agreement. Under its terms Croatia and Bosnia formed a federation, with the aim of concentrating all their energies on stopping and then rolling back the

Serbs. At the same time, the Americans supported the establishment of a 'Contact Group' on Bosnia, to be made up of representatives from the US, Britain, France, Russia, and Germany. They thus became much more directly involved in the negotiations at Geneva. Tactically, this was useful assistance to the embattled Bosnian government, and vastly improved their negotiating position; strategically, however, it betokened a worrying shift towards a 'European' – that is partitionist – solution, that was to become disastrously obvious at Dayton in October–November 1995.

The British government, of course, welcomed the American diplomatic commitment. On occasion, in fact, British statesmen and officials handsomely recognized the resulting achievements.[181] But as often as not, and with not inconsiderable brass neck, they tried to appropriate these American triumphs for themselves. Thus John Major told the Commons that 'It should not be forgotten by the House or others that we have established a ceasefire between the Croat and Bosnian forces in central Bosnia as well as Sarajevo.'[182] What the Prime Minister had forgotten is that this key achievement was thanks to the activities of US diplomats who brought to an end a split aggravated by British policy. Similarly, Malcolm Rifkind spoke of the 'achievements which General Rose and his colleagues have to their credit in Sarajevo and the Croat and Muslim areas of central Bosnia'.[183] The Defence Secretary carefully concealed the fact that both ceasefires were primarily the result of US diplomacy and a US-sponsored Nato ultimatum. A year later, he was still at it, claiming that 'In a very large part of Bosnia – particularly central Bosnia, which is where the United Kingdom forces are most concentrated – the peace is being kept, and it has been increasingly well kept for the past 18 months.'[184] Another blatant attempt to appropriate American success was made in the same debate by the Foreign Office Minister, Sir Nicholas Bonsor. 'If the British troops . . . were not there . . . I have no doubt whatever that the Muslims and the Croats, who are enjoying a tenuous peace between the two of them, would start fighting within a week . . . It is bad enough having a war between the Serbian side and the alliance, but if there were a three-way conflict, I do not believe that it would be possible for very long to maintain the UN presence there.'[185] Both Rifkind and Bonsor seemed oblivious to the fact that it was not the presence of British troops which was decisive – these had after all been present throughout most of the Croat–Bosnian war – but American diplomacy.

Occasionally, ministers were caught out by parliament. Thus, in late April 1994, the Foreign Secretary tried to suggest that 'the working together of NATO and the UN has already produced peace, or something approaching peace, around Sarajevo and peace, or something approaching peace, in large areas of central Bosnia where, even a few weeks ago, there was very fierce fighting'.[186] Very quickly, he was reminded by the Liberal Democrat MP Menzies Campbell that 'the success of Sarajevo and the Croat–Muslim peace . . . is attributable to the military and diplomatic leadership of the United States'.[187] Hurd was forced to concede that 'The Hon. and learned Gentleman is perfectly right about the crucial role of the United States.' Or, as Dale Campbell-Savours put it brutally later in the debate, 'You have done nothing, Clinton pushed you.'[188]

Even in 2000, Pauline Neville-Jones, who had been Political Director of the Foreign Office during the war, tried to claim the Washington agreement for Britain. According to her, Douglas Hurd had travelled to the American capital in January 1994 with the following message: 'Please stop merely observing the talks in Geneva and get actively involved . . . This invitation resulted in the initiative of Charles Redman, the US envoy, which in turn led to the Washington agreement.'[189] In fact, as Daniel Serwer, who was the American 'Federation Coordinator' from 1994, points out, the British were entirely 'uninterested' in the Bosnian–Croat Federation. 'They thought', he recalled, that it was a 'quixotic multi-ethnic' experiment which 'would fall apart'.[190] And while he gave the British 'some credit' for the 1994 ceasefire, and thought that British forces in central Bosnia did 'a wonderful job' of sustaining it, he was quite clear that the underlying reason for the Croat–Bosnian rapprochement in early 1994 was an American initiative.

If by mid-1994 the British government had been railroaded into three successive and successful ultimata against the Bosnian Serbs, this did not mean that the US had won the argument about the use of force. There was no underlying shift towards *decisive* action. By the end of

1994, in fact, it had become clear that if one or two successful ultimata enhance the credibility of an organization, three or four subvert it. Thanks to consistent British – and variable French – obstructionism, the high ground which Nato had achieved in July 1993, and certainly in February and April 1994, was progressively lost.

This became obvious in the late summer and autumn of 1994 when the negotiations of the Contact Group finally came to fruition. The resulting Contact Group plan unveiled on 6 July 1994 offered the Serbs 49 per cent of territory and the Croat–Bosnian Federation 51 per cent. If the Serbs – who at that time held 70 per cent of Bosnia – rejected the plan, it was hinted that the arms embargo on the Bosnian government would be lifted; if the Bosnians refused to sign, sanctions on Serbia would be eased.[191] In what the British hailed as a major diplomatic breakthrough, President Milosevic endorsed the plan and called upon the Bosnian Serbs to sign up; the fact that he had already done exactly the same thing in May 1993 over the Vance–Owen plan did not dim Foreign Office excitement over their coup. At the same time, London hinted at a willingness to lift the embargo, either to pressure the Bosnian Serbs or to prepare the way for the withdrawal of UNPROFOR, or both. As Douglas Hogg told the House in mid-July 1994 – when the Serbs were still notionally supposed to be considering the plan – in the event of a rejection lifting the embargo would 'probably prove irresistible. We shall have to judge our own policy as the facts develop.'[192] Shortly afterwards, Hurd issued a similar warning that Britain and France might no longer be able to resist US pressure for the lifting of the embargo. This was – of course – a tacit admission that the embargo primarily advantaged the Serb aggressors.[193]

The Bosnians, albeit reluctantly, accepted a plan which ratified ethnic cleansing in large tracts of formerly Muslim north-western and eastern Bosnia. The Bosnian Serbs, unimpressed by western threats and a desultory economic blockade by President Milosevic, rejected the plan outright and refused to use the two weeks' grace until 19 July to reconsider.

All this put western governments in a very awkward position. After all, the Contact Group plan – rather like the final version of the Vance–Owen plan – was not supposed to be another negotiating position. It had been intended as a 'take it or leave it' with specified sanctions for non-compliance. There was no finessing the situation: the Bosnians had taken it, and the Serbs had left it. In London there was some embarrassment, but little real anxiety. After apparently briefly toying with the idea of lifting the embargo and withdrawing UNPROFOR – 'lift and leave' – the Major administration retreated from its earlier insinuations and opposed any lifting of the embargo. It is probably not true, however, that London simply welshed on a firm commitment to lift the embargo. There is no evidence that any promise was made, as opposed to an ostentatious keeping open of options. Thus Sir David Hannay later claimed that there was no formal offer to lift the embargo on the Bosnian government if the Serbs rejected the plan but that the Americans may have given them the impression that this was the case.[194] Likewise British sources close to the Contact Group claim that the stick to be applied in the event of a Bosnian Serb rejection was not a lifting of the embargo but stronger sanctions on Serbia, in order to encourage Milosevic to coerce his former puppets.

For President Clinton, however, the Bosnian Serb rejection was a much more serious matter. Once again, American attempts to secure a better deal for the Bosnians, or at least a levelling of the military playing field, had been frustrated by Serb intransigence and Anglo-French obstructionism. The White House was now under even more sustained attack from internal critics, and the administration was buffeted by yet another wave of critical editorials in the broadsheets.[195] At the same time, the House of Representatives passed a resolution with a bipartisan majority of 244 over 178 votes, that would have ended US support for the arms embargo and authorized up to $200 million in arms for the Bosnian government.[196] This vote – which was taken in the teeth of a major White House lobbying effort – was tentative and non-binding, but it constituted the first concrete sign of the legislative revolt which was ultimately to overturn administration, and indeed western, policy towards Bosnia. In order to head off this growing challenge, Clinton was forced on 10 August 1994 to undertake to give the Bosnian Serbs a final extended deadline: 'If the Bosnian Serbs have not accepted the Contact Group's proposal of July 6 1994,' he promised, 'by October 1994, the President . . . should formally introduce and support a resolution in the UN Security Council . . . to terminate the international arms embargo.'[197]

To the British, this outcome was purportedly to be avoided at all costs. Already in June 1994, shortly after the House vote to lift the embargo, Douglas Hurd visited Washington to plead the case for the status quo.[198] Then in early and mid-September Hurd redoubled his warnings that lifting the embargo was 'bad policy . . . a dangerous policy' which would escalate the war and lead to the withdrawal of UNPROFOR. While he did not threaten to veto the measure in the Security Council, he made clear that 'lift and stay' was not an option.[199] These themes were echoed by Malcolm Rifkind.[200] In order to marshal support in the Security Council against a putative American initiative, the British sought closer ties with Russia during a meeting between Major and Boris Yeltsin. This was yet another indication of the growing perception of a Russian–French–British triple *entente* directed against America.[201]

Then, in late September 1994, the Bosnian government suddenly dropped its demand for an immediate lifting of the embargo. This apparent *volte face* was, of course, a gift to those who argued that the Bosnians had secretly wanted the embargo to be maintained all along, if its lifting would end the humanitarian aid effort. 'British defence officials,' wrote Christopher Bellamy in the *Independent*, 'said the Bosnian government dreaded the withdrawal of the UN and was anxious to comply with UN wishes to keep the force in the area. Lifting the embargo would have forced the UN and aid organisations to withdraw.'[202] Similarly, in July 1995 Malcolm Rifkind was to refer in the House of Commons to the 'statement of fact, that the Bosnian government have said that they would rather that the UN remained in Bosnia than that the embargo should be raised and the UN withdraw. That remains the choice that is available to them.'[203] The Bosnians, in fact, remember no such offer. Douglas Hurd subsequently claimed that 'the Bosnian government came to see us in September 1994 and said "Well, if you really mean that you would pull out if we pressed for the lifting of the arms embargo, we won't any longer press for it." '[204]

The Foreign Secretary's recollection is not incorrect, but it is not the whole truth either. There were some anxieties in Sarajevo about lifting the embargo without the guarantee of air support – for that is what was on offer.[205] But what happened in September 1994 was principally the result not of a Bosnian *crise de foi*, but of pressure from the White House. Terrified that Congress might make good on its threat to pass a binding resolution on lifting the embargo, the Clinton administration asked the Sarajevo government to defer its request for six months only.[206] This picture is confirmed by Sir David Hannay, the British representative on the Security Council, who thinks that 'the Bosnians had temporarily dropped their request for the embargo to be lifted, primarily because the US had asked them to do so in order to avoid a crisis in Nato'.[207] This was not because the Bosnians secretly wanted the embargo maintained, but because they feared losing a powerful friend in Washington, and were mindful of the fact that little serious fighting could be done during the winter; there may also have been a discreet 'sweetener' of covert arms supplies. In this light the sarcasm of John Major's memoirs is not merely unworthy but misplaced. He portrayed President Izetbegovic's request to defer lifting the arms embargo for six months as a humiliating retreat from the lift and strike strategy by its supposed beneficiary, and a tacit admission of its rationality.[208] In fact, the Bosnians asked for a delay because the US President demanded it; Clinton in turn wanted a deferral because he wanted to avoid another row with Britain and France, and probably Russia and China, in the UN Security Council. To infer from this that the Bosnians had secretly favoured the embargo all along is circular, illogical and disingenuous.

At the time, in fact, Douglas Hurd was in no doubt about the circumstances surrounding the Bosnian deferral. In a formal address to the UN General Assembly in New York on 27 September, President Izetbegovic set out his demand for a formal immediate lifting of the embargo to become effective within six months if the Bosnian Serbs did not accept the Contact Group plan; this would give the UN enough time to evacuate before the embargo was actually lifted. The Foreign Secretary told him bluntly before the meeting that the Europeans could not accept this compromise, which would merely delay the showdown by half a year.[209] Two things were remarkable about this exchange. Firstly, that it did not stop British statesmen and diplomats from claiming, even years after the war, that Izetbegovic had never wanted the embargo lifted or formally requested such a thing. Secondly, because it flatly contradicted the British claim that they would agree to the lifting of the embargo so long as the humanitarian effort was wound up.

The Foreign Secretary was right to fear that the issue of the arms embargo – and indeed the whole Bosnian problem – would not go away. In the event he did not have to wait six months for a new round of transatlantic recrimination, fear and loathing. For in the late summer of 1994, the Bosnian government Fifth Corps under the command of Atif Dudakovic launched a highly successful offensive in the Bihac pocket to eliminate the forces of the renegade Muslim leader Fikret Abdic, of whom more later. Within days, Abdic had been utterly defeated and compelled to withdraw to the safety of the Serb-held enclaves in Croatia. Emboldened by this success, desirous to recapture the areas from which many of his soldiers had been brutally expelled at the start of the war and desperate to break the humanitarian stranglehold still exercised by the Serbs on the pocket, Dudakovic pressed on. For a short period the whole Serb position in north-west Bosnia looked imperilled. After some initial victories, however, the superior weaponry and mobility of the Serbs began to take effect and Fifth Corps was soon fighting for its life in and around Bihac itself. The resulting crisis was to be the most serious test of Anglo-American relations and Nato yet.

Under severe American pressure, however, limited air strikes were ordered against the Krajina Serb air base at Udbina, from which Bihac had been attacked. The execution of the raids, in which the runway was neatly cratered but the aircraft themselves carefully spared, was an advertisement both for precision bombing techniques and the absurdity of the western response. American advocates of a firmer stance against the Bosnian Serbs were outraged. 'I went to bed thinking we were actually going to do something serious,' the National Security Advisor Tony Lake recalled, 'and it actually came as a shock to me the next morning – that we had actually waited until the aircraft had left and merely cratered a runway at the insistence of the UN, I understand. And we hadn't known that was going to happen.'[210] Dr Robert Hunter, the Nato ambassador, felt the same way. The Serb advance continued. Some pin-prick air strikes on individual Serb tanks, which was all the UN commanders would sanction, were called off owing to the weather; other Nato air strikes were sabotaged by the failure of the forward air controllers to locate suitable targets.[211] In the end, a truce was brokered by former US president Jimmy Carter and both sides settled down for the winter.[212]

In the United States, the Bihac fiasco triggered yet another assault on the administration's policy and the Europeans, particularly the British. Most worrying of all was that Bob Dole, a longtime critic and now incoming Senate majority leader, was joined by Newt Gingrich, the incoming House majority leader and architect of the Republican victory in the mid-term Congressional elections. Gingrich's conversion to the Bosnian cause was entirely an opportunist stick with which to beat the White House. But his demand for a UN withdrawal, US air strikes, and the arming and training of the Sarajevo government signalled further difficulties ahead.[213]

In order to stave off Congressional demands for more concrete action, the US government unilaterally withdrew from the policing of the arms embargo in mid-November 1994.[214] At first it seemed as if the whole blockade would collapse. Although the Pentagon denied any intention of supplying US arms to the Bosnians, it confirmed that arms for the Bosnian Serbs would be confiscated, whereas those bound for the Sarajevo government would be escorted by US naval vessels to their destination to ensure they were not diverted elsewhere. For a brief moment this conjured up the image of confrontations on the high seas with Anglo-French craft still trying to enforce the embargo. Moreover, the Pentagon also announced that it would not pass intelligence reports of weapons shipments to the Europeans, unless these involved weapons of mass destruction or missiles likely to endanger allied aircraft.[215] It soon became clear that the American move would make little practical difference: very few of the weapons reaching the Bosnians came by sea; only three of the 40,000-odd merchantmen stopped had been carrying arms; and in any case the Europeans could maintain the patrols themselves. Operation Sharp Guard in the Adriatic, and the embargo itself, would continue.[216]

But the political and psychological impact was nevertheless immense.[217] The members of the Western European Union issued a communiqué 'deploring' the US action. The Spanish Foreign Minister, Javier Solana, regretted that 'Washington has signalled the possibility of a military solution to the conflict, a solution we have always refused to recognise'. Indeed, the future Secretary General of Nato during the 1999 bombing campaign in Kosovo continued, 'The unity of the Alliance has been broken because a member of the alliance has broken it.'[218] The British were equally aghast. Douglas Hurd pointed out that the 'worrying' American decision was a violation of a 'mandatory resolution of the Security Council and agreed policy of the [NATO] alliance'. Sir Dudley Smith, the British president of the Western European Union assembly, claimed that 'The withdrawal of US ships and aircraft would make a mockery of the embargo operations.'[219] 'This is a development we could do without,' a British official added, 'it will now make our task harder to persuade the various parties that the best way to end the conflict is through peaceful negotiation, not further bloodshed.'[220] Looking back in January 1995 on the 'baleful' effects of the American move, the British ambassador to Nato felt that it had been merely the culmination of a long-running political haemorrhage within the alliance resulting from their differing policies towards Bosnia.[221] 'Bihac,' as David Owen recalled, 'represented the nadir in UN–NATO and US–EU relations.'[222]

Once again, the London government was excoriated in the broadsheets. 'The British and the French were blockers,' Anthony Lewis argued in the *New York Times*, 'Britain especially: its performance in the destruction of Bosnia has brought back to life perfidious Albion.'[223] The conservative columnist William Safire lamented that 'the sustained fecklessness of Prime Minister John Major has made unspecial the relationship built up by strong British leaders through hot and cold wars'.[224] Nor was this view confined to comment columns. As one State Department official recalled of the Bihac crisis, 'It was getting *very* nasty with the British. America was being called on its position and NATO was falling apart.'[225] Bob Dole, the incoming Republican majority leader in the Senate, blamed France and 'primarily Britain' for obstructing Nato air strikes against the Bosnian Serbs; 'the British', he said, 'are the ones who want to do absolutely nothing'.[226] The ultimate showdown came in the very first week in December when Bob Dole visited London to put his case to the Major government. Here he was subjected to a sustained Foreign Office attempt to 'educate' him in the 'realities' of the conflict. 'We gave him hell,' one very senior British ministerial source recalls. But Dole remained unmoved, and his solitary press conference outside Downing Street, at which he immediately called for 'more strikes', showed that the transatlantic chasm remained as wide as ever. Of course, Bob Dole, a seriously wounded Second World War veteran, a classic Republican internationalist, and a long-term critic of Slobodan Milosevic, needed no education from anyone, neither in military nor in Balkan realities. 'Our worst week since Suez', was how one American official summed up the situation for the Clinton White House.[227] The S-word was back again, and it had not had its last outing for a long time yet.

The damage was not just to Anglo-American relations, but to Nato itself. Bihac, as Ivo Daalder observed, was 'the worst crisis within the Atlantic alliance since 1956'.[228] 'If Nato has to take orders from the United Nations,' Bob Dole complained, 'I don't see any reason for its existence.'[229] This message was relentlessly hammered home by American commentators. 'In Bosnia,' Jim Hoagland argued apropos Bihac, 'the powerful democracies of Europe and North America looked evil in the eye and blinked.'[230] 'What is the purpose,' asked the *Washington Post*, 'of avoiding straight talk about NATO's Balkan performance? An alliance challenged to fulfill a new mission of strengthening European security outside its members' borders failed dismally.'[231] 'Bihac,' Flora Lewis wrote in the *International Herald Tribune*, 'marks the end of pretense that "the international community" is willing to protect the victims.' But it also 'imperilled' Nato. 'Too many members,' she argued, 'have lost a sense of strategy and have tied it in knots to serve short-term political goals and escape hard decisions.' 'The United States,' she concluded, 'would . . . lose a lot if transatlantic ties were broken now. But nobody should count on the need for those ties not arising once more, nor on the United States responding a third time.'[232]

In Britain, the cumulative effect of all this on the Atlantic alliance was beginning to sink in. As Margaret Thatcher pointed out in a well-publicized telephone conversation with Hamdija Kabiljagic, the mayor of Bihac, 'This is in the heart of Europe, and the lack of effective action has robbed NATO of its credibility. You have got to stand up to the Serb aggressor. That is not a matter of opinion. It is a matter of fact. When they do have an air attack, I have never heard anything so absurd as saying "We'll only bomb the runway". You take the airfield out.'[233] This was also the view in much of the British press. 'The damage done by the war in Bosnia seems never-ending,' said the *Economist*. 'To the list of human casualties, add the solidarity of NATO.'[234] A week later it spoke of the 'battle of Brussels, the furious transatlantic war of words over how deeply NATO should be drawn into the Bosnian war. This row could yet, if allowed to escalate again, blow the alliance apart.'[235] 'Pessimists,' Robert Fox wrote in the *Daily Telegraph*, 'predict . . . a terminal split in Nato with the Europeans and the North Americans going separate ways – particularly on European security matters.'[236] Shortly afterwards he suggested that 'The future of Nato itself must be in doubt – it has been shown incapable of metamorphosing itself from a defensive alliance against the Soviet empire to an instrument for Europe's collective security.'[237] The *Independent*'s Andrew Marshall even warned of the possible 'death' of Nato and further Anglo-American estrangement.[238] And *The Times*, in its editorial of 29 November 1994 – 'Ghosts of Suez' – observed that 'Nato has not yet been broken on the Bosnian wheel. But the key agreement that underpins the Alliance is fracturing, and in public view . . . Nato does have a role, and Britain should be exploring with America ways to maximise its impact, rather than blaming Washington for lack of leadership.'[239]

Just how much western and Nato credibility had suffered over Bihac was painfully demonstrated at the Conference for Security and Cooperation in Europe in Budapest in early December. As the *Economist* noted, the summit began with a 'dust-up' between the Russians and the Americans over Nato's eastward expansion, and ended a day later with a 'finger-wagging row' over Bosnia.[240] To the consternation of the assembled dignitaries, the Bosnian president pointed out that 'The entire international community incarnated by the UN and the powerful NATO could not even save a single town.' The result of it all, he continued, would be 'a discredited UN, a ruined NATO and a demoralised Europe, impotent in the face of the first crisis after the Cold War'.[241] Similarly, President Mitterrand noted that none of the many organizations involved, the CSCE, the Council of Europe, EU, CIS, Nato, and the WEU, had been able to end the war. 'What,' he asked, 'are we really useful for?'[242] The war in Bosnia, Izetbegovic had reminded his listeners, was not 'a football match for which [anybody] could blow the final whistle . . . The battle will continue.' Once again, the Bosnian issue had forced itself to the top of the international agenda.

To the embarrassment of all present, the conference broke up in acrimony. No common statement of the fifty-two states attending was agreed, primarily because the Russians vetoed anything which singled out the Bosnian Serbs for blame. Even Chancellor Kohl's impassioned appeal for a separate statement by fifty-one states went unheeded. 'I do not want to go home and answer questions from people who say, What did you do on Bihac?' the Chancellor explained. But he had to do just that. The British Foreign Secretary, on the other hand, was unruffled by this example of Europe's manifest inability to tackle a crisis less than half an hour's flying time from the conference. 'I don't honestly think,' he remarked, 'that many people will be sitting up looking at their watches, asking: "When is the CSCE going to agree on Bosnia?".'[243] The conference did agree, however, to rename itself 'Organisation for Security and Cooperation in Europe', in keeping with its aspiration to 'play an essential role with regard to the problems of the twenty-first century'.

Faced, once again, with a united front of rejection in London and Paris, the United States backed down. Once again, however, the reckoning had merely been deferred. In Congress, Bob Dole tabled the necessary measures to end the arms embargo when the Bosnian ceasefire ran out in the spring.[244] Fearful of damaging the Atlantic alliance still further, National Security Advisor Tony Lake, in principle a firm friend of the Bosnian cause, now insisted that any Congressional vote on the embargo would be met by a presidential veto. Anything else, he explained, would cause 'the worst crisis in Nato's history since Suez';[245] and Nato, the American political establishment from Christopher to Lake agreed, was still 'more important than Bosnia'.[246] For the time being, the Americans would have to accept the Anglo-French strategy of holding on in the hope of the Bosnian capitulation, a benevolent shift in Bosnian Serb behaviour, or of something else turning up. But this strategy could only succeed if the ceasefire itself was maintained, or at least did not break down into renewed and more spectacular disasters.

CHAPTER 4

# 'Let Me Through, I'm a Doctor': David Owen and the Mediation Effort

When challenged by Michael Meacher in the House of Commons to accept 'that a great deal more can be done to aid Bosnia without putting a large army into the field', Mark Lennox-Boyd, the parliamentary Undersecretary of State for Foreign and Commonwealth Affairs, replied that 'The hon. Gentleman would do well to consider the advice of Lord Owen and other such people who are on the spot and know exactly what is going on.'[1] Over the next two and a half years the advice of the 'men on the ground', of the mediators and the military men deployed in Bosnia itself, was repeatedly to be pressed into service in defence of government policy. Lord Owen, General Michael Rose and a large number of colonels, majors and captains were to become not only Britain's public face in the conflict but also, often unintentionally, Whitehall's secret weapon in the attempt to stave off military intervention on behalf of the Sarajevo government.

Lord Owen made his first spectacular intervention on the Bosnian stage in the summer of 1992. On 30 July – outraged by news coverage of Serb concentration camps – he penned a searing letter to the Prime Minister, which was also faxed to the *Evening Standard* and the Press Association. 'It is not an exaggeration,' Owen wrote, 'to say that we are witnessing, 50 years on, scenes in Europe that mirror the early stages of the Nazi holocaust under the dreadful description of "ethnic cleansing". I urge you not to accept the conventional wisdom that nothing can be done militarily . . . The first essential step is to stop by threat of force the use or movement of any military aircraft, tanks, armoured vehicles or artillery in the former territory of Yugoslavia. It is perfectly within the power of NATO to enforce such a ceasefire . . .

If no action is taken now there will be virtually nothing left of Bosnia for the Muslim population to negotiate about.'[2]

When challenged about the practicality of his suggestions, Owen was, initially, largely unmoved. 'Clearly,' he conceded in *The Times* on 4 August, 'Nato aircraft would risk being shot down by Yugoslav army ground-to-air missiles. But they would not face as sophisticated a challenge as presented by the air defences in Iraq.'[3] 'We can also hope,' he repeated, 'that by sharply reducing the use of heavy armaments, the Moslems in Bosnia will be able to hold their ground, so that in any peace talks they have some territory to negotiate over.' He rejected the warning of the Secretary General of the United Nations, Dr Boutros Boutros-Ghali, that Bosnia might become a new Vietnam, as 'nonsense'.[4] On 9 August he demanded that 'we should impose a ceasefire . . . It is vital that we do not allow the annexation of Bosnia and the forcible removal of Muslims from population centres. We have to have a strong European military presence in this and the US must be involved, but only to a lesser extent. The right force is NATO.'[5]

David Owen, in short, was at this stage the leading apostle of precisely the sort of limited but decisive military intervention which Bosnian sympathizers in Britain and the United States demanded throughout the war. It was therefore to general amazement that John Major arranged for Owen's appointment to replace Lord Carrington as the EU negotiator at the International Peace Conference on the Former Yugoslavia (ICFY) at Geneva. He was joined by the American Cyrus Vance, former Secretary of State to Jimmy Carter, whom Dr Boutros Boutros-Ghali had appointed as the UN representative. Not without a certain logic, the Bosnian Serb leader, Radovan Karadzic, objected that 'Since Lord Owen has stated quite categorically that he has no faith in a negotiated settlement without military intervention, and that intervention should be against one side only, he is clearly not in a position to mediate.'[6] Similarly, the *Sunday Telegraph* observed that Owen's statements 'will compromise his position with the Serbs, whose agreement is necessary to any resolution of the conflict'.[7]

For the first ten weeks or so Owen appeared to be on the verge of recommending military intervention against the Bosnian Serbs. When an Italian aircraft carrying humanitarian aid was shot down en route to Sarajevo, killing all eight men on board, Owen warned that the

Security Council would respond with severity. 'There sometimes comes a moment,' he thundered, 'when the world looks at a situation and says that enough is enough. Maybe this might prove to be it.'[8] In the end, it wasn't the moment. In mid-November 1992, Owen made a fine speech in the Security Council where he condemned the fact that Serb leaders 'still appear to want a single geographical [sic] contiguous Bosnian Serbian province. They still espouse the objective of greater Serbia . . . It needs to be said quite clearly, here in the Security Council, that the present Bosnian Serb front line has to be rolled back and that there is no way in which the international community can accept General Mladic's philosophy that might is right and that what they have they hold.'[9] In mid-December he called for 'severe action' to enforce the no-fly zone. 'If we show enough determination that we are going to enforce it,' he told the Commons Select Committee on Foreign Affairs, 'we won't need to enforce it.'[10] It all sounded very promising.

But within six months Owen had transmogrified into a leading critic of the Bosnian government's failure to 'compromise' and of American demands to level the military playing field through the 'lift and strike' strategy. When he finally bowed out in June 1995, Owen was reviled not merely by the Americans and Bosnians, but also by the Germans, the Dutch, the European Parliament, and a substantial proportion of the world's mainstream press. What had happened?

The choice of Lord Owen as EU negotiator raised some eyebrows in Britain. Just as he had destroyed almost every cause he had been in contact with to date, it was surmised, so he would sabotage, either intentionally or unintentionally, any attempt to muster an international intervention against the Bosnian Serbs. It was this legendary tendency towards self-destruction to which *Private Eye* had playfully alluded on its famous cover of August 1992. 'It is a lost cause,' says the bubble emanating from the Prime Minister's mouth; 'I'm your man,' says Owen. And the shadow Foreign Secretary, Dr John Cunningham, was not being entirely humorous when he observed that the Prime Minister's choice 'was regarded as somewhat eccentric by right hon. and hon. Friends and myself – he is known for many qualities, but not as a mediator. Indeed, he has Balkanized a few political parties himself.'[11] Nevertheless, Owen's appointment was not part of an ingenious strategy to wreck the interventionist platform. While it is true that Owen was invariably on the losing side of British politics, this was because he was in many ways ahead of his time. He was a convinced European and a firm supporter of Nato. There was, moreover, nothing in his career before 1992 to indicate the obsessive feuding with Washington which was to become his trademark in 1993–4. Rather, the explanation for Owen's Bosnian fiasco lies in poor judgement, a mistimed exit, a lack of synchronicity between means and aims, and, above all, an obsessively paternal relationship with his progeny, the Vance–Owen peace plan.

Within a very short time of taking on the task of EU mediator it should have been clear to David Owen that the kind of military intervention he had originally demanded was simply not on the agenda in Whitehall; Douglas Hurd had hinted as much at the outset, while the French wished to rule out the threat of force altogether at this stage.[12] Immediately after his 'enough is enough' outburst he was implicitly rebuked by the Foreign Secretary, who observed that it was too easy to demand that 'something' must be done without considering the consequences.[13] Moreover, after intensive briefing and lobbying by government figures and advisors, he increasingly began to question whether such intervention was possible or even advisable. By early December, while insisting that the 'military option must not be excluded', he was warning that 'so-called surgical strikes are never as precise as we anticipate'.[14] Ten days later he condemned 'glib talk' on the enforcement of UN resolutions: 'if we were to start a war in which the UN were seen to be, if you like, actively engaged, then I think we'd see the winter humanitarian effort grind to a halt with tragic consequences for loss of life'.[15] Owen, in short, was already beginning to lapse into the standard government line. Indeed, at his first press conference on the tarmac of Sarajevo airport in December 1992 he warned the Bosnians, 'Don't, don't, don't live under this dream that the west is going to come in and sort this problem out. Don't dream dreams.'[16]

This retreat from the military option went hand in hand with a progressively stronger emphasis on the intractability and complexity of the conflict. 'Within a week of taking the position of Co-Chairman,' Owen subsequently wrote, 'I had come to realize, and to say publicly, that there were no innocents among the political and military leaders in all three parties in Bosnia-Herzegovina. That is not to say that the leaders were the same, and it is mere escapism to pretend that there is no difference between the parties. There is and there remains a quantum difference between the horrors perpetrated by Bosnian Serb leaders and acts committed or authorized by the Bosnian Croat or Bosnian Muslim leaders.'[17] Yet at the time, this valid distinction was increasingly obscured: Owen's initial argument about the peculiar nature of Serb ethnic cleansing and the challenge it posed to the international community became almost inaudible by early 1993. What had once been so clear to him had, by May 1993, become something 'hideously complex with deep historical roots';[18] 'all three constituent nations', he told a London audience of civic and health service dignitaries a month later, 'in Bosnia and Hercegovina fight and cleanse each other . . . It has never been a simple question of invasion and aggression.'[19] And in August 1993, he lashed out at those who 'have exercised their consciences over Bosnia . . . There are elements of aggression, elements of civil war and elements of provocation on all sides.'[20]

The reason for this shift was simple. The immediate cause was the insidious 'education' he received from Whitehall. As Owen relates in his memoir, John Major's private secretary, Stephen Wall, 'patiently . . . explained the fears of the Chiefs of Staff of being sucked into a combatant role in what was essentially a civil war . . . We did not agree, but he undoubtedly dented my arguments.' For, he continues, 'It was clear that, whereas I had come new to the subject, Stephen had been living the issue daily for many months.' Owen recalls that Wall was 'clearly disappointed with my logic and thought I was being self-indulgent and not facing the real issues of government honestly. It was good discipline, for he put me back in the Foreign Secretary's seat and did not allow me the luxury of playing to the gallery. We parted after what diplomats would call a vigorous exchange of views.'[21] But Owen had got the message. In time, the dents in his original argument would become larger, and the exchanges with government less vigorous.

This 'education' was continued on early visits to Sarajevo, by a UN establishment desperate to avoid offending the Serbs, and irritated by the Bosnian government's refusal to see sense and agree to the truncation of their country. They persuaded him that 'The facts were not all as I had first thought. While the terms "aggressor" and "victim" were being brandished as weapons in a propaganda war, the true situation was obviously far more complex than that dichotomy implied – and anyhow, they were terms better avoided publicly by a negotiator.'[22] It was this very same UN bureaucracy which lay behind his outrageous parallel between the Serb besiegers and the desperate attempts of the Bosnian government to staunch the outflow from their capital city. 'In Sarajevo,' Owen writes, 'it became ever clearer that there were in fact two sieges of the city: one by the Bosnian Serb army, with shells, sniper fire and blockades, and the other by the Bosnian government army, with internal blockades and red tape bureaucracy which kept their own people from leaving.'[23] This sense of moral equivalence was reinforced by the briefing he received from the outgoing EU mediator, Lord Carrington. 'We had a very long chat,' Carrington recalls. 'He went in with the idea that the Serbs were the demons . . . And being a highly intelligent man, he wasn't there for more than ten minutes before he realized that it was a great deal more complicated than he realized, and that they were all as bad as each other.'[24] As often during the Bosnian war, the transition from sophisticated qualifications to a generalized condemnation of 'all sides' was almost seamless.

'We delude ourselves,' Owen elaborated later, 'if we think of the issues in simplistic terms, or portray the struggle as one between "good guys" and "bad guys".'[25] Likewise, Brigadier Graham Messervy-Whiting, Owen's military advisor, claimed that the Bosnian Serbs 'all too often [walked] into situations where they ended up being painted as the only cowboys wearing the black hats'; he condemned the American media 'which tended for much of the period to give the impression that the only "good guys" were the Bosnian Muslims, the only "bad guys" – the Bosnian Serbs'.[26] And as if to underline the essential equivalence between the parties, Owen's memoir included three pictures of shattered places of worship: a Catholic church, a Serbian Orthodox church, and a mosque. This was a neat but false symmetry because only the Serbs consistently made it their declared practice to obliterate all cultural and confessional traces of their erstwhile neighbours. Later, Owen explained that he had chosen the pictures to show that 'all sides' had attacked the religious symbols of the others, but he persuasively denied that any qualitative equivalence was intended.[27] If nothing else, this illustrates how easily the quest for balance and objectivity could shade into distortion.

The effect of all this on British perceptions, particularly those of the elite, was pernicious. David Howell, who was chairman of the House of Commons Foreign Affairs Committee throughout the war, remembers the briefings by Carrington and Owen vividly. 'Both those gentlemen,' he recalls, 'conveyed the view that the whole situation was hopelessly confused and muddled and they couldn't trust anybody, and both sides were as bad as the other.'[28]

But Owen's change of heart reflected not merely a progressive disenchantment with the Bosnian cause; there was also a more profound and strategic rationale. He regarded himself explicitly as 'Major's man'. Owen had been one of the few observers with a kind word to say about the Prime Minister's brief tenure at the Foreign Office; he had resoundingly endorsed Major before the April 1992 general election; and he had been Major's first choice for the Governorship of Hong Kong.[29] 'The Foreign Office,' he subsequently pointed out, 'knew that I was considered appointed by John Major . . . of course technically by the EU, but I carry [Major's] imprimatur'; otherwise the Foreign Office would have 'take[n] my legs off'.[30] Major needed and respected Owen's advice on foreign policy, but he was also clear in his rejection of military intervention in support of the Sarajevo government. And he was – as Owen recalls – determined 'not to be edged over into a combatant role under any circumstances'.[31]

As a result, Owen was painfully aware of the political and military constraints under which he was operating: he was merely a mediator, not an arbitrator. As he told the UN Security Council in November 1992, and recalled in his memoir, 'The daunting challenge for the ICFY in November 1992 was whether, armed only with moral authority and weak economic sanctions, and with no credible threat of selective counter-force, we could roll back the Serb confrontation lines and create a new map.'[32] 'The Conference,' he repeated in November 1993, 'has no power of imposition, and so far governments have insisted that any solution must obtain and hold three party agreement.'[33] Whatever powers of enforcement he might have would need to be negotiated afresh whenever an impasse was reached. Only a consensual solution would do, and in the context of Serb ethnic cleansing, this inevitably meant an unfair solution. The west, Owen reminded journalists in August 1993, had repeatedly examined the military option and always rejected it. 'There are consequences of that rejection – I do not criticise them for that rejection – but it limits your influence and power to dictate events.'[34] The resulting emphasis on the essential equivalence between all sides should be seen as an attempt by Lord Owen to justify the injustice to the world, and not least to himself.

In January 1993, the two mediators presented the first draft of their peace plan, the Vance–Owen peace plan, or VOPP, to the world. It was a valiant attempt to square the circle and to rescue what could be rescued. The two underlying principles – that Bosnia should be preserved as a single state and that refugees should be guaranteed the right to return – were commendable. But the practical provisions of the plan suggested something quite different: ten provinces, nine of which would be 'predominantly' either Serb, Croat or Muslim. All real power lay with these units, each of which would enjoy its own legislature answerable to an ethnically cleansed electorate. The central government would have no army and – it seems – no police force. There would be no realistic way of enforcing the legal right of return of refugees. In any case, the effective cantonization of the country on ethnic lines ran totally counter to the multi-ethnic principles to which most of the Sarajevo government still adhered, and which gave the Bosnian cause such resonance in the west. None of the various modifications to the plan between January and May 1993 addressed this fundamental flaw.

Moreover, while the boundaries of the cantons were drawn as skilfully as possible in the circumstances, they still amounted to an endorsement of ethnic cleansing. The Serbs – who made up just over 30 per cent of the population – were awarded about 40 per cent of the surface area, while the 'Muslims' had to make do with about 30 per cent of the surface area on the strength of 40 per cent of the population. Some important towns found themselves on the 'wrong' side of the divide: Gornji Vakuf, for example, had a narrow Muslim majority before the war, but was placed inside a 'Croat' canton. To make matters worse, it soon became clear that the announcement of the VOPP stimulated rather than contained ethnic cleansing. Now that the international community appeared to condone armed separatism, a new wave of attacks was unleashed. In eastern Bosnia the Serbs launched a devastating offensive against the enclaves which soon threatened to overrun Srebrenica and create yet more facts on the ground which the map would have to take into account. By early March 1993, they had overrun the pocket of Cerska, an overwhelmingly Muslim part of eastern Bosnia which was supposed to remain Muslim under the Vance–Owen plan.[35]

But the most disastrous consequence of the VOPP was its effect on the already precarious alliance between the Sarajevo government and the Bosnian Croats. The integrationist and multi-ethnic faction within the political movement of the Bosnian Croats, the HDZ, under Stjepan Kluijc, had been in the ascendant throughout 1992; the proclamation of the Croat separatist statelet of 'Herceg-Bosna' in July 1992 remained without much effect, and Muslims and Croats continued to live uneasily side by side. But as the relentless Serb advance continued, and the flow of Muslim refugees into central Bosnia and Herzegovina threatened to overturn the delicate ethnic balance in key areas, the clamour for the separatist option became ever stronger. Open conflict – which had flared briefly at Prozor in October 1992 – was avoided until the end of the year. Once the last hope that the international community would intervene against the Serbs and restore Bosnia in its old borders had collapsed with publication of the VOPP, the Croats saw a 'green light' from Geneva and there was no stopping them. From mid-January 1993 onwards a new war erupted across central Bosnia and Herzegovina as the Croats scrambled to secure and extend the territory awarded to them under the VOPP.

At the time, Owen himself vehemently denied that his plan had precipitated all-out war between 'Muslims' and Croats; the coalition, he argues, 'had been breaking apart throughout 1992'.[36] Indeed, he now claims most eccentrically that 'The Croat–Muslim war is usually defined as taking place between January and March 1994.' It is easy to see therefore, why he does 'not think there is any link between the VOPP [which had died in mid-*1993*] and the war'.[37] While he acknowledges that there was some 'nasty fighting' which started in January 1993, he insists that 'Even so [the Croat–Muslim] alliance, despite intermittent fighting, continued for most of 1993. The full-scale war developed in late 1993 on the back of Muslim frustrations over Mostar' and disagreements over Bosnian access to the sea.

But the evidence could not be clearer. Colonel Bob Stewart, commander of the British forces in the area, subsequently observed of the fighting in Gornji Vakuf that 'The Croats had apparently decided that, in view of the Vance–Owen plan's intention to make Gornji Vakuf part of a Croat canton, they should have total control over the place immediately. They had demanded the unconditional surrender of all Muslim forces in the town . . . As Gornji Vakuf itself was largely Muslim this ultimatum was hardly reasonable, especially as the Vance–Owen plan had not [yet] been agreed to by the Bosnian government.'[38] After the fighting spread to Vitez, Stewart reflects that 'The deterioration of relationships between local forces had been an increasing phenomenon, particularly since January. I felt sure it was related to the Vance–Owen plan, which divided Bosnian cantons on ethnic lines, and attempts by all sides, particularly the Croats, to get control of as much land as possible.'[39] The British liaison officer, Captain Milos Stankovic – aka Mike Stanley – writes in his memoir, 'I reckon they [the Croats] interpreted the VOPP as a green-for-go: "This'll be a Croat canton. We don't want the Muslims here, so, let's f—k em off before we have to put pen to paper." Well, that's what it looked like at the time, on the ground at any rate.'[40]

Similarly, Angus Boyd-Heron, a British aid worker briefly imprisoned by Croat militias, noted in May 1993 that 'The recent violence between the Croats and Muslims is a direct consequence of the Vance–Owen peace plan. The Croats have been given more than they could have hoped for and in places where they do not even hold a majority. In these areas they are trying to stamp their authority on the Muslims by the slaughter of civilians.'[41] The UN special envoy on human rights, Tadeusz Mazowiecki, issued an outspoken report accusing the Vance–Owen plan of 'stimulating ethnic cleansing'. 'The implementation of the plan,' he claimed, 'stimulated certain acts, designed to create a *fait accompli*, before a final solution.' Moreover, Mazowiecki continued, 'The lack of an effective international response to counter the policy of "ethnic cleansing" perpetrated by Serb forces created the precedent which has allowed them to continue. This encouraged Croat forces to adopt the same policy.' 'The peace plan, according to which Bosnia and Herzegovina would be divided along ethnic lines,' he concluded, 'has been used in order to create ethnically homogeneous areas.'[42] The Bosnian general Jovan Divjak – himself an ethnic Serb – claimed that the Vance–Owen plan 'threatened the fragile unity between Muslims and Croats in Central Bosnia'.[43] And the journalist Janine di Giovanni, who reported from Bosnia for much of the war, recalls that the Vance–Owen plan 'sent the factions into turmoil, trying to carve up as much territory as they could in as short a time as possible'.[44]

Further confirmation of the baleful role of the VOPP is to be found in the memoir of Antony Loyd, who covered the Croat–Muslim war as a journalist. 'The proposed borders,' he writes, 'seemed so ridiculously advantageous to the Bosnian Croats that even they joked that HVO [the acronym for the Bosnian Croat militia force] stood for "Hvala Vance Owen" – thank-you Vance–Owen. Bosnian Croat nationalists in Hercegovina were keen that the land allocated to them in the plan be incorporated into their self-styled state of Herceg-Bosna by force of arms, thinking it would grant de facto credence to the map before anyone had time to change their mind. Much of the area around Stara Bila, including Travnik, was included in the planned Croat sector, so tensions there rose even further, catalysed by the very diplomatic initiative that sought to end it all.'[45] Likewise, the journalist Alec Russell describes how 'The Croats in the south-west saw the plan as a blueprint to enforce their rule on Muslim areas.'[46] Even such a notorious Serb sympathizer as Nora Beloff, who might have been expected to emphasize innate Croat or Bosnian government aggression, accepts that while 'tension between Muslims and Croats frequently erupted', after Bosnia was recognized 'it was the Owen peace plan which was responsible for the all-out 1993–1994 war'.[47] In short, while Owen did not create the Croat–Muslim rift, his peace plan certainly precipitated the outbreak of open and sustained hostilities in the spring of 1993.

The fracturing of the anti-Serb coalition was a gift to both Owenite and British government rhetoric. As one senior Downing Street official subsequently told ITN's Nik Gowing, 'Images [like Croat massacres in Central Bosnia] that complicated the Bosnia-Herzegovina story made it easier for us [to reject air strikes].'[48] It was now possible to argue that the conflict had become too intractable for outside intervention; and the spotlight increasingly fell on the unsavoury phenomenon of Croat opportunism. Thus Owen's military advisor, Brigadier Messervy-Whiting, told visiting British parliamentarians that one of the biggest problems faced by the British army was the Croatian extremist formation HOS, which wore Second World War-style fascist armbands and 'flaunt the Swastika in areas around Mostar'.[49] And when the eyes of the world were once again on Sarajevo and the Serb siege in August 1993, David Owen 'confided' to journalists in Geneva that 'The biggest breach of the ceasefire during this conference has been the Muslim–Croat fighting. Indeed, the greatest tragedy of these last three months has been the unleashing of this inner tension that has always existed between the Croats and Muslims.'[50]

Some Bosnians and Croats believed the conflict between them so opportune to British policy that they suspected London of having deliberately fomented the breach through the Secret Intelligence Services.[51] This is unlikely. There appears to be no evidence to support this allegation, while there is every indication that the 'war within a war' not merely took Owen and the British government by surprise, but was deeply unwelcome, not least because it made the possibility of a negotiated settlement and a UN withdrawal increasingly remote. This comes across vividly in an – admittedly second-hand – account of the high-level meeting at No. 10 on 22 January 1993, at which Brigadier Andrew Cumming, the commander of British forces in Bosnia, was present.

'They're all there [Major, Hurd, Rifkind, Owen],' writes the British liaison officer Milos Stankovic, 'pontificating about how to make the VOPP work and banging on about "lines-to-take" and "ways-forward". They completely ignore Cumming. Eventually, towards the end Cumming is asked his opinion since he is the man on the ground. Cumming tells them straight . . . "As we speak the Croats are pitch-forking to death Muslim farmers around Prozor." Douglas Hurd is incredulous and apparently says, "I don't think we want to hear that." Well, of course they didn't: it blows their plan to bits. But Cumming did say that Hurd approached him afterwards and said, "Is that really what's happening?" Even they couldn't believe that these "allies" were turning against each other.'[52] Interestingly, David Owen's account in *Balkan odyssey* makes no mention of any discussion of the Croat–Muslim split at that meeting, nor did he recall the exchange when subsequently asked.[53] What is striking is the obvious unwillingness of the assembled statesmen to face the truth and absorb the catastrophic effect a well-meant peace plan was having on the ground.

Instead, what preoccupied Lord Owen – and the British government – in the spring of 1993 was the refusal of the Bosnians and the Americans to endorse the VOPP. They objected to 'cantonization', and particularly to the map, as a reward for Serb ethnic cleansing; they (rightly) suspected Croat motivations for instantly accepting the plan; and they doubted that Serb agreement – if forthcoming – would be worth the paper it was written on. In short, as the US National Security Advisor Anthony Lake recalls, 'we didn't think it was viable or made sense, it was so higgledy-piggledy'.[54] Instead, the Americans advanced an alternative strategy for a complete Bosnian victory based on 'lift and strike'. Owen himself was dismissed as an appeaser. The Republican Congressman, James Moran, spoke for many when he claimed that Owen 'seems to be playing the role of Neville Chamberlain'.[55] Owen was outraged: the VOPP itself – and with it any chance of international recognition, perhaps the Nobel Peace Prize – was in danger, and he personally was under attack. With an unmatched passion Owen threw himself into 'selling' the VOPP to American public opinion as 'the only show in town'. In a flurry of dinners, interviews and talk-shows, Owen talked up his plan and rubbished the doubters. He was blatantly discourteous to two senators on television, dismissing their objections as a 'rant': 'you haven't got troops on the ground. I speak for a country that *has* got troops on the ground,' he retorted. When another senator suggested military intervention against the Serbs, Owen – who had previously dismissed Boutros-Ghali's fears of Vietnam as 'nonsense' – responded, 'Do you want another Vietnam?'[56]

Unsurprisingly, Owen's excursion went down very badly with the Americans. As John Fox, a mid-level State Department official intimately involved in Bosnia policy during 1992–3, observed, Owen's personality was 'an unwinning one . . . he might have had some success but he . . . sounded very high-handed, coming in just after the Clinton people took office and essentially asking them to publicly abandon their campaign platform . . . he just got into a series of rows across town, basically'.[57] The Americans were particularly aghast at Owen's evident intention to trade the War Crimes Tribunal for a negotiated settlement. 'He had,' Fox recalls, 'basically been advocating immunity for Milosevic and Karadzic.'

Owen's temperamental unsuitability for a sensitive mission to Washington and New York was later acknowledged by the Foreign Secretary. Douglas Hurd recalls that 'The Americans had a great suspicion of David Owen, which he did nothing to dispel. I was constantly trying to defend him. I knew him reasonably well, and I admired him, but every time he went to Washington he was landing on the beaches and charging up the beach with all guns firing. That's his mode, and they couldn't take it; from that point of view he wasn't an ideal choice, as it turned out.'[58]

Likewise, the British embassy in Washington was profoundly concerned about Owen's poor image. Christopher Meyer felt that Owen 'had – how can I put it? – a more vigorous style than [the Americans] could easily digest'.[59] 'I don't think Owen was well treated by the Americans,' the British ambassador, Robin Renwick, recalls. 'On the other hand, he made some unwise statements about them before he met them.'[60] Senior figures in Whitehall, for their part, were bitterly critical of Renwick's alleged failure to support Owen, and hold him responsible for the failure of the mission.

Owen's principal fear was that the American stance would encourage the Sarajevo government to hold out for peace with justice through victory on the ground. As he told a press conference in New York in mid-February 1993, the Bosnians would never come to terms while there was still hope that the Americans might arm them and redress the military imbalance.[61] He told National Public Radio of the need to 'shatter the Muslims' illusion' of outside aid.[62] In his memoir, Owen referred to 'the effect of the US position on Bosnian President Izetbegovic, Vice-President Ganic and Foreign Minister Silajdzic. There was now not a chance of their accepting the map unless the US position could be dramatically shifted. The renewed talk in the administration of lifting the arms embargo was also bound to undermine our negotiations.'[63] Indeed, as the British ambassador recalls in his forthcoming memoirs, Owen sent him 'a telegram complaining that they [the Americans] were briefing the press in ways that were bound to encourage the Moslems to continue the war'. To hammer the point home, Owen told Johnny Apple, Washington editor of the *New York Times*, that

'Against all the odds, even against my own expectations, we have more or less got a settlement but we have a problem. We can't get the Muslims on board. And that's largely the fault of the Americans, because the Muslims won't budge while they think Washington may come into it on their side any day now. What do they want down there, a war that goes on and on? This [the VOPP] isn't just the best act in town, it's the only act in town. It's the best settlement you can get, and it's a bitter irony to see the Clinton people block it.'[64] Likewise, Owen's military advisor claims that 'many in ICFY felt that some of Izetbegovic's key colleagues were repeatedly able to convince him that he could afford to stall, because they believed that the USA could be induced to commit forces to BiH [Bosnia and Herzegovina], which could then be sucked onto the Presidency's side to "level the battlefield" '.[65]

Eventually, with much bad grace, the Americans backed down, and the Bosnians accepted the plan. Washington did so, not because it was intellectually convinced, but because the alternative appeared to be to precipitate a crisis for which the incoming administration would be blamed. Owen himself believed the virtues of the plan to be beyond question. 'Which negotiations,' he asked that famous New York press conference, 'have ever persuaded an armed force [the Serbs] to withdraw from 24 per cent of the territory they have gained?'[66] In his memoir Owen reminds us of how he 'used to challenge any critic to recall episodes in history when armies that had not been defeated had given up anything like as much territory'.[67] To underline his point he garnishes *Balkan odyssey* with a map showing the impressively large swathes of land the Serbs would have had to evacuate under the VOPP.

There was only one small problem: the Serbs refused to sign, or make the necessary territorial concessions. And when their leader Radovan Karadzic did so under duress of possible [American] air strikes, the Bosnian Serb 'parliament' overturned his decision and was resoundingly endorsed in its stubbornness by a referendum. But Owen – in retrospect at least – never really took in the fact and depth of the Serb rejection of the VOPP: rejection by the assembly at Pale, he said, would be merely a 'temporary setback'.[68] It is revealing that the Bosnian Serb rejection of the VOPP rates no mention in the extremely detailed chronology attached to his memoirs, and in the main text the whole episode rates no more than a brief mention.[69] Owen, in fact, had forgotten that the Bosnian Serb war aim was not to secure a reasonable territorial settlement and constitutional arrangements, but a maximalist programme designed to create an ethnically pure 'Greater Serbia'. The VOPP – for all its inherent flaws and last-minute concessions to the Serbs – was fundamentally incompatible with this project; and the Serbs never did relinquish any of their lands until they had been militarily defeated. To say, as Owen does, that the Vance–Owen plan offered the Bosnian government a marginally better deal than Holbrooke at Dayton in 1995 is missing the point:[70] the territorial provisions of Dayton, lamentable though they are, were superior to the VOPP, because they were actually enforced on a militarily defeated Republika Serbska.

Bizarrely, Owen blamed the failure of the VOPP on the Americans. At the Foreign Affairs Council meeting of the EU in Luxembourg he launched into a carefully scripted attack on Washington: 'It is ironic that the new US administration which for four months from January onwards had been castigating the Vance–Owen plan for favouring the Serbs, for rewarding aggression and for accepting ethnic cleansing, had now gone through a 180-degree turn and was telling Dr Karadzic loud and clear that the pressure from every other country in the world, including the FRY [Federal Republic of Yugoslavia], to withdraw [from lands to be ceded under the VOPP] was being relaxed.'[71] In his memoirs Owen writes that 'the plan had . . . been effectively ditched by the Americans and could never be got back on the road'.[72] Later on he lays responsibility 'clearly at the door of the Clinton administration who, while talking much about morality, had ditched the one plan which could claim to have a moral basis and offered the prospect of actually reversing some ethnic cleansing'.[73] A chapter in his memoir, *Balkan odyssey*, is entitled 'The ditching of the VOPP'. And more recently, five years later, Owen was still speaking of the American administration as 'a nightmare', pursuing a 'one-sided' and 'moralistic' policy which he eventually 'decided to write off' for trying to 'destroy' and 'ditch' the VOPP.[74] Owen, in fact, became a modern-day ancient mariner, trying to get his albatross airborne again. But his refrain lacked the element of self-knowledge that gives the original rhyme its force.

Henceforth, almost every evil was now attributed to this alleged American original sin. 'Only after the US had allowed him to overturn the VOPP in May 1993,' Owen writes absurdly, 'would Karadzic dismiss our complaints about ethnic cleansing without blanching.'[75] He also somehow contrived to blame Washington for the Croat–Muslim split. 'Sadly,' he observed in June 1993, 'the perception ... was that we were accepting the Serbian gains in Bosnian territory. It encouraged the Croats in Mostar to begin taking territory,'[76] seemingly forgetting his standard defence that the Croat–Muslim split long predated the VOPP. And Owen was subsequently to lament that as a result of the collapse of the VOPP 'Milosevic's political influence over the Bosnian Serbs had waned dramatically. This erosion in his authority was the direct consequence of Washington's ditching of the VOPP, which had boosted Karadzic at the expense of Milosevic.'[77] But the *pièce de résistance* must be Owen's claim that 'by August 1995 it was painfully apparent how damaging the US decision to ditch the VOPP in May 1993 had been. The Bosnian Muslims had now been ethnically cleansed from Zepa and Srebrenica and the Croatian Serbs from the Krajina.'[78] So the Americans were to blame for all that, too.

In December 1994, Owen wrote to Hurd to complain of a 'smear campaign about our activity from the US, despite the fact that ... the US have their means of knowing all the facts'.[79] Indeed, in his memoirs Owen gave full vent to what had by now become a generalized anti-Americanism in matters Bosnian.[80] His generic comments on the 'innate decency which characterizes most American attitudes, albeit sometimes overlaid by a vulgarity and loudness that do not truly reflect the inner voice of a fine democracy', were – as he subsequently persuaded me – less hostile and sweeping than they sounded; Owen, after all, is married to an American and entertains strong transatlantic affections.[81] More seriously, he accused the Americans of 'grandstanding with ... a reluctance ... to committing forces on the ground'.[82] 'What the Clinton administration seemed to want until 1994,' he elaborated, 'was power without responsibility.' Thus the Americans betrayed a 'compulsive urge to moralize from the high ground while their military stayed in the air'.[83] Oddly, Owen's version of events gained wide currency both at the time and since. One senior British diplomat, who should have known better, describes being 'particularly aggrieved that the Americans would not support the Vance–Owen peace plan, which was the best hope to get a multi-ethnic Bosnia back on its feet, and which, frankly . . . was a far better plan than the Dayton plan . . . I felt deeply frustrated that the Americans went on and constructed their policy, which was a war policy, not a peace policy.' Sir Christopher Meyer, who was Deputy Head of Mission at the British embassy in Washington at the time, believes that 'the [US] administration was not prepared to put adequate political or military muscle behind it, and so it withered on the vine . . . we couldn't get US support and it died'.[84] Yet another British observer – the former diplomat Jonathan Clarke – attacked the Americans for undermining the plan 'with lofty rhetoric without proposing a practical alternative . . . The effect of this language . . . was that the Vance–Owen plan gradually became a dead letter';[85] this article makes no mention of the fact that the plan was rejected by the Serbs. Likewise, General Rose simply notes that 'the plan eventually fell foul of the US administration in May 1993'.[86] Even such a respected – and otherwise reliable – authority as James Gow holds the US responsible for the failure of the plan.[87]

This was odd, because British ministers themselves were in no doubt that the Bosnian Serbs were the chief obstacles to the VOPP. In January 1993 John Major told the House that it was 'a fair plan. It is a matter of great regret that the Bosnian Serbs are unpersuaded and unprepared to accept it.'[88] Three months later, Douglas Hogg 'welcomed the Bosnian Muslim and Bosnian Croat agreement to the international conference's peace plan for Bosnia. The Bosnian Serbs must now sign. Urgent work is in hand in New York to apply pressure on the Serbs to secure their agreement.'[89] Shortly after that John Major noted that 'The Bosnian Muslims and Croats have signed all the elements of the peace plan. But the Bosnian Serbs refuse to agree the interim government arrangements and the maps. The United Nations Security Council has now adopted a further resolution setting out extremely tough sanctions which will be imposed if they remain intransigent.'[90] And in mid-May Baroness Chalker told the House of Lords that 'We believe that international efforts should now concentrate on pressing the Bosnian Serbs to accept the Vance–Owen peace plan as the only credible proposal for a peaceful settlement.'[91]

Owen's contention that the US – rather than the Bosnian Serbs – had 'killed' or 'ditched' the VOPP hinges on the question of 'implementation'.[92] In his view, the Bosnian Serb rejection should have been met by the progressive implementation of the plan. On the eve of the Athens summit, at which Karadzic had been browbeaten into a signature, Owen had warned of 'stronger measures to be taken if the Serbs fail to implement the peace settlement. Several options are under consideration including military steps.'[93] For Owen had never given up the military option; he was just vehemently opposed to any intervention which was not in support of his own negotiations. His military advisor, Brigadier Messervy-Whiting, prepared a thorough paper which showed that military intervention against the Bosnian Serbs was entirely feasible. In his remarks to EU foreign ministers on 24 April 1993, Owen rejected the lifting of the arms embargo but called for 'authorization to take the necessary measures to interdict the supply lines from the air. Of course this action would not of itself defeat the Bosnian Serbs, but it would tilt the balance in favour of the two armies that have signed up for the peace plan.' Now, he concluded, was the time for 'facing down the Bosnian Serbs' direct challenge to the authority of the Security Council'.[94]

This view has found acceptance from some quarters in Whitehall. 'It is no good just saying,' one senior diplomat argues, '"Oh but Karadzic rejected the plan". Of course he did. But he was the only person who rejected it, and if we had at that stage collectively said "Right, you have rejected it, but . . . we are going to support it until hell freezes over, and by the way, you have six weeks to accept or something very unpleasant will happen", I think we might have got somewhere. But instead of which the Americans managed to torpedo Vance–Owen, they had no confidence in it, they quite disgracefully went around suggesting it was some form of appeasement.' In order to test this view, of course, it is necessary to assess how realistic such an enforcement of the VOPP actually was in May 1993.

Anxious to distinguish his strategy from the standard American programmes for limited intervention against the Bosnian Serbs, Owen stressed the interconnection between military pressure and the negotiations. More recently Owen has claimed that his 'criticism of American policy was much more about their attitude to the VOPP . . . than to their failure to [sic] to impose a settlement'.[95] At the time, however, he attacked the Americans for failing to 'pressurize' or 'even cajole' 'let alone threaten to impose' the various peace plans, particularly the VOPP.[96] 'Instead,' he claimed, 'the US were still hooked on "lift and strike", a policy which the Russians and the main European allies rejected and which bore no immediate relation to a settlement.'[97] He condemned Vice-President Al Gore and Madeleine Albright, 'both of whom seemed to think these issues could be resolved by bombing the Serbs irrespective of where we were in negotiations or the UN were on the ground . . . the White House wanted to practise Realpolitik and simultaneously preach moralism'.[98] 'It seemed odd,' he argued, 'that the US would talk up air power as a response on the battlefield but rule out air power for imposing a settlement stemming from the negotiating table.'[99]

It would indeed be odd, except that the Americans did no such thing. They had always been willing to match military intervention to diplomacy: their objection to the VOPP stemmed from the territorial and constitutional injustice of its provisions, not the measures designed for its enforcement. Owen seems to have envisaged two forms of 'implementation': first, the selective use of air power, and/or – following some suggestions from Belgrade – the progressive implementation and if necessary enforcement of the plan by a large Nato and Russian ground force. 'The VOPP,' he argued, 'should have been imposed along these lines.'[100] It was not America's fault – or at least not exclusively her fault – that neither of these two gambits was tried. There is some confusion about the British refusal to use 'lift and strike' to pressure the Serbs into accepting the VOPP or any other settlement in the calamitous meeting at Chevening in May 1993. But there is no doubt that the idea of 'implementing' the VOPP stage by stage on the ground was rejected not only by the Americans but also by the Europeans, particularly London.

The British were entirely clear on this, both at the time and subsequently. In early May 1993, Hurd stated on the eve of the Bosnian Serb parliament's meeting that 'We certainly would not be putting troops in to push Serbs out of areas which they have to vacate under the Vance–Owen plan. One cannot, of course, guarantee a bullet-free situation, that would be unrealistic, but *we're not talking about an operation for enforcing the Vance–Owen plan.*'[101] When asked in the Commons in mid-June 1993 about plans for 'implementation' of the VOPP, Douglas Hogg responded that there would be 'a series of immediate steps to alleviate the suffering on the ground while work continues to find a lasting and fair political settlement', i.e., business as usual.[102] In his subsequent study on *The search for peace*, Hurd was equally explicit: 'David Owen says that it would have been possible to impose by force the Vance–Owen Plan. I understand why he thinks that, I understand why he is so critical of the Americans for undermining the plan, *I don't believe that it was possible to impose it.*'[103] And most recently, Hurd has reiterated that 'I don't think that he [Owen] could ever have seriously thought that there was any possibility of the [west] imposing a particular solution.'[104] The most the British were prepared to do was send troops to secure 'safe areas' for the Bosnian Muslims which would then be progressively linked up to create a 'leopard spot' solution for the country as a whole.[105] But this was not the same as implementing – i.e. enforcing – the VOPP; here the British took the same view as the American Secretary of State, who confirmed in mid-May 1993 that 'We are prepared to commit our military forces to implement a peace settlement entered into consensually, but we will not use our military forces to impose a settlement in the Balkans.'[106]

There were also serious doubts in parliament as to whether the VOPP could realistically be enforced on the ground. Peter Viggers, a delegate to the North Atlantic Assembly, and a vocal member of the House of Commons Defence Committee, told the House in late April 1993 that 'The imposition of the Vance–Owen peace plan is not on the cards because it is not acceptable to all those who are concerned and the number of troops that it would require is massive. If we tried to impose the plan we would require about ten times the number of troops in Northern Ireland, which means about 250,000 [sic].'[107] Similarly, the Foreign Affairs Committee reported in mid-July that 'We fear that attempting to impose a plan could make things worse', not least because peacekeeping forces could not easily be reconfigured for the new task.[108]

Even the Foreign Office briefing notes on the VOPP, issued in July 1993, are perfectly clear: 'When Radovan Karadzic . . . signed . . . on 2 May 1993, all three sides to the Bosnian conflict . . . appeared to have accepted the peace plan.' But Karadzic subsequently reneged on this, claiming that it was subject to ratification by the Bosnian Serbs' self-styled 'assembly'. This was not forthcoming, and so the peace plan could not be implemented as devised. Indeed, the passage on military preparations notes pointedly that 'The plans were framed on the assumption that the operation was to implement, rather than enforce, the peace plan.'[109]

None of this was any secret to Owen, even though he claimed at the time that the Americans 'wanted to get out of the commitment that Warren Christopher made in February to help with implementation of the peace plan'.[110] In the same document he asked the European leaders to 'determine whether there is still the political will, or the military resources, or the necessary financial support for credible implementation'.[111] The real problem was, as he later admitted in his memoir, that he 'could never get any major government interested in developing a sound counter-force strategy . . . The EC foreign ministers . . . were all hesitant to take up my suggestion to threaten to interdict the Bosnian Serb supply lines from the air.'[112] And when he was recently asked whether the British government would have been ready to *enforce* the VOPP, his answer – after many obfuscations – was essentially 'no'.[113] He explained that both Rifkind and, especially, the Prime Minister were against 'using force to implement it'; John Major was 'always behind the humanitarian mission . . . where he would have difficulty was to committing troops to taking military action'.

One can only speculate why criticism of the failure of his sponsors in London to enforce the VOPP is the only punch left unthrown by Owen in *Balkan odyssey*. Later he repeatedly admitted that he was softer on London and the other EU governments because they were 'employing' him. In a recent letter, Owen asks us 'to remember that [he] was the EU negotiator and felt bound to present the EU in the best light compatible with the truth'. And when challenged on his tendency to 'shield HMG', Owen pointed out that 'because I was not a Conservative I had to be particularly careful not to scapegoat the Conservative government'.[114]

Revealingly, Sir Robin Renwick, who had to defuse the diplomatic fallout as ambassador in Washington, was categorical that the failure of the VOPP should be laid at the door of the Bosnian Serbs. 'The idea that the VOPP failed because of the Americans is a myth,' he insists. 'The VOPP failed because the Bosnian Serbs were never prepared to agree to it and secondly, it was incapable, in my view, of implementation.'[115] 'The idea that the VOPP failed because of the Americans,' he reiterates, 'is a cop-out, quite frankly.'[116]

Moreover, Owen's demand for the enforcement of the VOPP contained a basic logical flaw. He himself had – rightly – stressed that the VOPP's greatest (theoretical) advantage lay in the fact that it involved an *agreed* Serb withdrawal from extensive territorial gains. Likewise, Derek Prag, the Conservative MEP for Hertfordshire, pointed out in late May 1993 that 'The only virtue of the Vance–Owen plan was the possibility that it could stop the fighting. As a long-term solution, it was a cartographer's dream and an administrator's nightmare; a blueprint for further wars.'[117] If the VOPP had to be *enforced*, the plan, with its manifest acquiescence in ethnic cleansing, lost its last shred of justification. It is not hard to see why the British – and particularly the Americans – balked at the idea of committing ground forces, not to secure peace with justice, but to police an unjust and contested settlement. The VOPP – in short – was doubly redundant: it would remain void without the use of force, but if one was prepared to use force, one could have a better plan.

To the surprise of many, Owen did not resign. After all, his original motivations for accepting were never base: he was paid no salary for his work as a negotiator and unlike some figures in the UN and national governments he never profited financially from his involvement in Bosnian misery. Indeed, Owen was to be personally substantially out of pocket for his *pro bono* mediation efforts. He had accepted the post in the full knowledge that it might entail morally dubious sacrifices for the greater good. 'The question,' as he wrote in his memoir, 'was whether to go on being a voice in the wilderness over Yugoslavia or join in the quest for peace;'[118] of course, the desire to play a more active political role may have played a part, though Owen always strenuously denied this. Moreover, Owen was – by his own admission – a serial resigner. He had quit as Labour spokesman on defence in 1972 in protest over Harold Wilson's attitude to the EEC, he left the shadow cabinet over the same issue and over unilateral nuclear disarmament in November 1980 with the election of Michael Foot as leader. He resigned from the Labour Party itself after it rejected 'one member one vote' in February 1981 and he resigned as leader of the SDP when the membership decided to unite with the Liberals.[119] There was nothing to be gained – even personally – from soldiering on, and everything to be said for a grand gesture which would have forced the west to confront the bankruptcy of its own policy. As the late Jill Craigie, wife of Owen's old rival Michael Foot and herself a doughty campaigner for Bosnia, observed: 'David Owen would have emerged as a very great man if he had resigned'; but 'Having said "We are not going to accept aggression, we are not going to accept this, we are not going to accept that", he changed his mind.'[120] 'Had I been younger,' Owen later lamely admitted, 'I would have probably resigned when the Americans ditched the Vance–Owen plan.'[121] He was a man famous for his exits, but he fumbled this one.

There were some good and many bad reasons for not throwing in the towel. First of all, it could be argued that Owen needed to allow his new co-negotiator for the UN, Thorvald Stoltenberg – who had replaced Vance – to find his feet. Secondly, as he wrote in his memoir, 'a resignation over the VOPP would not bring it back to life or change US policy (if one could dignify it with such a name)';[122] the notion of resigning to highlight the conclusive rejection of his plan by the Bosnian Serbs did not occur to him. Instead, he decided to 'stay and live with the partition that was inevitably now going to be part of any peace settlement, in order to rescue as much as I could from the VOPP'. Moreover, since Owen had chosen to construe his primary problem as lying in the US, he was swayed by energetic British and EU attempts to persuade him to stay on; Douglas Hogg was dispatched to Geneva in late May 1993 to ensure just that.

Yet what ultimately damned Owen was not just his decision to stay on, but the way in which he chose to do so. After all, the UN investigator for human rights, the former Polish prime minister Tadeusz Mazowiecki, never felt it incompatible with his task to demand military intervention against the Bosnian Serbs from his appointment in 1992.[123] Then in May–June 1993, Mazowiecki lambasted both the injustices of the VOPP – about the human rights provisions of which he was not consulted – and the total collapse of the west in the face of Serb aggression in May 1993.[124] He stayed on as a highly vocal and effective critic and when he finally resigned after the Srebrenica massacre in 1995, he did so with his reputation intact. But Owen consciously eschewed the Mazowiecki approach: he did not stay on primarily to safeguard the interests of the Bosnian Muslims; he persevered in the hope of mediating a settlement to which all parties would sign and to which he could put his name.

The result was a sorry series of Heath-Robinson schemes based on ethnic partition and constitutional jiggery-pokery. At the same time, Owen increased the pressure on the Bosnian government, now seen as the principal obstacle to a negotiated 'settlement'. One method – long perfected by the London government – was removing all prospect of military succour. Thus, in a spectacularly ill-judged flourish at the Athens summit in May 1993, still hopeful of securing the VOPP, Owen claimed that 'This is a happy day in the Balkans. Now it is time to talk of peace, not war.'[125] 'Look, come off it now,' he told BBC television, 'you've all had your time on bombing. Now let's talk about peace and how you implement a peace plan.'[126] Time and again, in fact, Owen would invoke the 'peace process' as an argument against air strikes. When Nato – with partial success – threatened attacks to prevent the 'strangulation' of Sarajevo, Owen publicly complained that 'The most striking thing is that up until the air strikes came dominating in front of everybody . . . we had a better dialogue than at any time in the last year.'[127] In a confidential cable to EC foreign ministers he argued that while he was not against the use of air power in principle, 'Talk of wide use of air strikes at the present juncture is unhelpful . . . My biggest fear is not how the Serbs are reacting, but that such talk will encourage [Vice-President] Ganic and others [in the Bosnian government] who want to continue with the war that the Americans are about to intervene.'[128] He even threatened publicly that 'If Nato was to go ahead without the support of the UN system, never again in the lifetime of this Secretary General, and probably a lot longer, would Nato be asked to help a UN operation.'[129] It is therefore not surprising to find the Danish foreign minister, Niels Helveg Petersen, arguing that 'My opinion here and now, based among other things on remarks by Lord Owen, is that bombing would disturb the peace process.'[130]

In the same spirit, Owen sought – by his own account – to sabotage calls for Nato air strikes in early 1994 at the time of the Sarajevo market-place massacre. First he rebuked the French foreign minister, Alain Juppé, for 'technically incorrect' talk about 'lifting the siege'.[131] Then he tried to reduce the exclusion zone demanded by the French, made scaremongering predictions of likely Serb retaliation and generally suggested that the threat of Nato action was jeopardizing a peace process once again on the verge of fruition. 'After nearly two weeks of persuasion', he claimed just after the massacre, 'we had reached the point where the Bosnian Serbs were ready to take Sarajevo outside an overall peace settlement and to try to demilitarise it and have UN administration in Sarajevo . . . I am absolutely determined it is not aborted.'[132] Given all that had happened in 1992–3, this determination can only be described as the triumph of hope over experience.

In particular, Owen was obsessed by the precedent of Vukovar, whose fate would be shared by Sarajevo, if the Serbs were excessively provoked by an ultimatum. 'How,' he wondered in the spring of 1994, 'would the Serbs respond if we went ahead with the air strikes . . . ? I used to invoke the famous saying of Aneurin Bevan: "Why look in the crystal ball when you can read the book?" Vukovar had shown us how the Serbs would react: if there had been air strikes, I never doubted that there would be a pounding of Sarajevo that would more than match anything we had seen.'[133] That Vukovar was an eloquent testimony of the military imbalance caused by an arms embargo and the failure to use air power against the aggressor does not seem to have occurred to him. But then, in a typical piece of anti-Americanism, he goes on to subvert his own argument: 'What would have happened,' the same article concludes, 'had President Bush authorized the United States, as a member of NATO, to intervene to stop the bombardment of Vukovar? We will never know. But at the time a critical military threshold was not crossed. It's possible that had that occurred, then the shelling of Vukovar would have been curtailed. There would never have been the same siege of Mostar or Sarajevo.'[134] Quite.

In the end, the Americans and the French largely got their way, and the Serbs got the message. The Serb guns were temporarily withdrawn from around Sarajevo. But lest anybody should think this an endorsement of American strategy, Owen adds: 'Some said this was a vindication of the threat of air strikes and a sign that the Bosnian Serbs would crumble under threat. I felt that it was the Russians who had taken the threat of air strikes seriously and it was their decision to move their troops to Sarajevo which had forced Mladic to hand over his weapons.'[135]

In some cases, Owen rejected air strikes on the grounds that it would be wrong to single out any one party. 'All of them are sinners,' he observed in August 1993, 'there's not one of them out there that's completely guiltless.'[136] At other times, he simply denied the efficacy of air strikes: 'You can possibly tilt the balance,' he claimed in mid-May 1993. 'You can possibly at times help a negotiated settlement. But you will not solve the problem at 10,000 feet'; 'Wars,' he told another audience, 'cannot be won in the air.'[137] Indeed, his practical opposition to air strikes increased as the war dragged on: where he had once endorsed Messervy-Whiting's extensive scheme to level the playing field in favour of the Bosnian government, he now objected to all 'generalized' plans not directly related to 'close support' missions.[138] Thus, in mid-May 1995, he wrote to Hurd arguing that air strikes, as distinct from close air support, meant escalation of the war and UNPROFOR having either to fight or to withdraw.[139] The notion that attacks on Serb heavy weaponry would enable the Bosnians 'to hold their ground so that in any peace talks they would have some territory to negotiate over' – Owen's own words in 1992 – was completely abandoned. He was certainly consistent in trying to deny any practical military help to the Bosnian cause whenever such help was actually on the agenda.

It should come as no surprise, therefore, to find that Owen was resolutely opposed to the lifting of the arms embargo against the Bosnian government. His arguments were familiar: lifting the embargo would escalate the war, open the door to further 'third party involvement', especially that of Russia, would probably bring the Yugoslav army back into the war, and would not lead to a Bosnian military victory in any case.[140] In particular, he was concerned at the supply of 'sophisticated 1990s Soviet weaponry' to the Serbs.[141] Lifting the embargo 'might salve people's consciences for a few weeks', he told EC foreign ministers in April 1993, 'but it could be a fatal step towards a wider Balkan war'.[142] But the principal reason was his fear that lifting the arms embargo – allowing the Bosnians to defend themselves –

would reduce the incentive for the Sarajevo government to agree a settlement. 'Could we really expect the Bosnian Muslims,' he observed in his memoir, 'to start a meaningful negotiation from scratch in the midst of lift and strike which would [sic] give them outright victory?'[143] Indeed, his military advisor, General Messervy-Whiting, candidly admits that opposition to the lifting of the embargo was political and not military-technical in origin. 'On balance,' he says, 'from the point of view of where we stood in the peace conference . . . we felt that the arguments against lifting the arms embargo were stronger than those for lift.' 'We were confident,' he recalls, 'of getting at least partial signatures on aspects of the Vance–Owen plan . . . so it seemed to be not a helpful moment to start radically changing the balance of things on the ground or, indeed, leading one party or another to start recalculating what their chances were of holding out, and, you know, the merits of holding out against reaching an agreement.'[144]

As we have seen in Chapter 2, none of these arguments was tenable. But in Owen's case, his stance on the lifting of the embargo was subverted even by his own testimony and experience. In his memoir, Owen claims that 'so much humbug has been written and spoken about the arms embargo that it is hard for most people outside government to be aware of the facts'. He then reveals, rather grandly, that 'In the Nelson tradition, I was content for a blind eye to be turned' to breaches in the embargo. He admits that he was 'not shocked' to hear that Milosevic, even in late 1994 after he had supposedly broken off all contact with the Bosnian Serbs, was supplying 'key items of equipment and logistical support' to Mladic 'if for no other reason than to keep Mladic apart from Karadzic and as a potential ally'.[145] The fact that this might have facilitated Mladic's genocidal operations against the Srebrenica enclave did not occur to him, apparently. Owen also casually admits that – contrary to his earlier dire predictions – Russian supplies to the Serbs were few, far between and of little importance: 'A number of governments have helped arm the Croats and, through the Croats the Muslims. *The Russian government in comparison by and large maintained the arms embargo against the Serbs . . . Moreover, the Serbs did not need to import more weapons and did not choose to spend their very limited reserves of hard currency on new and sophisticated Russian weapons.*'[146]

Underpinning Owen's analysis was an exaggerated sense of Serb military prowess and innate Bosnian weakness. 'Even if the Muslims fought on indefinitely', he subsequently claimed, 'and made some territorial gains, they could not, in most military experts' view, actually win control of all the territory of Bosnia-Herzegovina.'[147] On the other hand, as he told EU foreign ministers, he genuinely believed that 'the Serbs can take Sarajevo, and could have done so at any time over the last 18 months. It is a political decision not to do so, and I see no evidence to suggest that they have changed their mind.'[148] In fact, the Serbs had tried – and miserably failed – to rush Sarajevo at the outset of the conflict; thereafter, they showed no desire at all to engage with the enemy in street fighting, preferring instead to wear down the defenders through hunger and shelling. But the most peculiar inflation of Serb capabilities lay in Owen's view of General Mladic. 'In one sense,' he recalls, '[Mladic] wanted a real fight, believing that picking off the Muslims was beneath the dignity of the Serbs.' 'Mladic,' he maintained further, 'was widely judged to have fought with considerable skill around Knin,' and 'He never appeared afraid of NATO air strikes or US threats to lift the embargo. Probably he would have welcomed both as getting the politicians off his back and allowing him to wage war with the gloves off.'[149] Of course, this was nonsense: Mladic made his reputation slaughtering lightly armed Croat national guardsmen and defenceless Muslims; and when it was clear that Nato meant business in 1995, he quickly folded. But given the fact that Owen was – according to his own testimony – 'getting the same inputs as ministers' from the MoD,[150] these wildly inaccurate assessments should come as no surprise.

As if all this was not bad enough, Owen also tried to fracture the unity of the Sarajevo government. According to the senior Bosnian negotiator and subsequent ambassador to London, Professor Mohamed Fillipovic, Owen systematically promoted Mate Boban, a Herzegovinian Croat committed to a greater Croatia.[151] Likewise, Lee Bryant, who served on the Bosnian delegation in Geneva in 1993, recalls that Owen began to build up not only the Croats but also President Izetbegovic's old Muslim rival, Fikret Abdic; the Bosnian president was calculatedly treated not as the head of a recognized multi-ethnic polity, but as merely another factional chief.[152] 'Owen,'

Fillipovic claimed, 'created Abdic.' In June 1993, Owen invited the whole presidency to Geneva, including Abdic, whose acceptance undermined Izetbegovic's contention to speak for the country, or even the Muslims, as a whole.[153] As a very senior figure in American intelligence in Europe during the war subsequently told me, if Owen did not 'invent' Abdic, he certainly 'took advantage of him as a Muslim who was prepared to cut a deal'.[154] Matters came to a head in September 1993, when the Bosnians refused to accept the Owen–Stoltenberg plan, which offered them little more than a few Bantustans held together with bits of string. Abdic – whose stronghold of Velika Kladusa in the north-western Bihac pocket would have been one such Bantustan, with himself as the chief – signalled his intention to sign. A UN helicopter was provided to fly him to the decisive meeting with Karadzic in Belgrade which left Izetbegovic isolated.[155] Subsequently, Owen defended his relationship with Abdic as one with a legitimate democratically mandated Muslim leader who was prepared to 'do a deal'.

The result was an open breach between Abdic and the Bosnian army's Fifth Corps, which remained loyal to the Sarajevo government. Now Bihac was the scene of a bitter civil war within a war which dragged on until the late summer of 1995. This was never Owen's intention. As he wrote in his memoir, he 'had urged Abdic to stay in the collective Presidency and warned him that his influence would go if he broke away . . . within the Presidency his influence was legitimate and benefited from his realism'.[156] But having encouraged Abdic, Owen then lost control of him and he cannot escape partial responsibility for what followed. Of course, the 'inter-Muslim' war, just like the Croat–Muslim split, was a gift to those who had always claimed that local complexities precluded armed intervention. David Owen had done it again.

Owen's pressure on the Bosnian government increased sharply in the second half of 1993. When the Serbs and Croats offered a humiliating three-way carve-up in mid-June 1993, he observed that 'The Muslims would be well advised to look very seriously at these proposals and to negotiate.'[157] They should, he insisted in late July 1993, 'face reality'.[158] Mustafa Ceric, the chief Muslim cleric in Bosnia, observed bitterly that: 'Lord Owen is a liar, a liar. Before he became involved in the

Bosnian crisis, he said troops should be sent to crush Serbian aggression. Then he was partner in the Vance–Owen plan and blackmailed the Bosnian Muslims to accept it, although they felt it was unacceptable. He guaranteed that if we accepted this, everything would be OK. And now this week he says that Muslims have to "face the fact" of the conquest of the Serbs and Croats.'[159] In late July Owen repeated the message with even greater emphasis: he warned President Izetbegovic that, unless he negotiated, 'death, destruction and suffering' would follow to an extent to make him 'shudder for the future of your country'. As the *Guardian* observed, this must have been 'the first time in recent history where an intermediary calls for the surrender of one side'.[160]

The notion that the Sarajevo government – rather than the rapacity of the Serbs – was blocking a settlement became something of an idée fixe with Owen in late 1993. In his memoir he attaches particular importance to the failure of the ephemeral 'EU action plan', which 'history may show . . . was a moment when Izetbegovic should have settled'. 'The small independent Muslim state that would probably have emerged,' he explains, 'would have been guaranteed its independence because of the collective guilt of the international community.'[161] The fact that at this late stage Owen should still have considered the 'guilt of the international community' a bankable asset beggars belief. And as if to show how guilty the international community really felt, he began to threaten the Sarajevo government with the end of the humanitarian aid effort. In mid-November 1993 he told the Confederation of British Industry in Harrogate 'not [to] forget we are feeding the warriors, we are interfering with the dynamics of war . . . becoming more and more unjustified as it becomes a battle for smaller elements of territory, smaller elements of principle. There will come a moment when the world community will have to decide how long we can sustain intervention.'[162] Ten days later he told an audience in London's Guildhall that if the Croats or Serbs refused to compromise there should be more sanctions, whereas 'If the Bosnian Muslims fail to compromise I believe government will start to relax their commitment and begin to question the continuation of UN military forces on the ground.'[163] He repeated this threat a year later, for good measure.[164]

If Owen was inclined to bully the principal victims of the war, he went out of his way to cultivate the chief perpetrator, Slobodan Milosevic. 'The key as always,' he told the EU foreign ministers in mid-1994, 'is Milosevic.'[165] His strategy throughout was a 'realistic' one of using the Serbian leader to coerce the Bosnian Serbs into a negotiated settlement. To this end he was prepared to make considerable concessions to the Serb viewpoint in various versions of the VOPP. Under the terms being offered to them in late April and early May 1993, the Serbs were more or less guaranteed that Muslims and Croats would not be able to return to areas from which the Serb armies had withdrawn. In denying that any concessions had been made, Owen was, in the words of the *Economist*, 'being economical with the truth'.[166] Milosevic certainly urged the Bosnian Serbs to sign on the basis that the VOPP effectively ratified most of their gains. For this he was praised by Owen on BBC radio as a man who 'lives in the real world'.[167] 'Milosevic,' Owen opined in early April 1993, 'is now prepared to take on the hard right, he is prepared to deal . . . and he is heading towards leading Serbia back into the European family. I have no doubt of that.'[168] Indeed, according to Sir Russell Johnston, Owen was telling parliamentarians *sotto voce* 'that Milosevic was being quite cooperative, and we should be thinking in terms of progressively reducing sanctions'.[169]

But Milosevic was unable to deliver the Bosnian Serbs in May 1993, and when no military intervention followed, he reckoned it safe to stop trying. This pattern was repeated in 1994 after the rejection of the Contact Group plan. Indeed, giving up the Bosnian Serbs was so easy for the Serbian leader that, rather like other addicts, he did so repeatedly. But as if the promotion of Milosevic himself were not bad enough, Owen also cultivated his transparently deranged wife, Mira Markovic. He told journalists in May 1993 that she was playing a decisive role in undermining the nationalism of the Bosnian Serbs: 'A very significant shift has taken place,' he averred.[170] The feelings were to some extent mutual. When the Croatian envoy Hrvoje Sarinic asked him whether it was true that Owen had written an introduction to a book Mira had published in Russia, Milosevic responded that 'Owen is our good friend, Mira's and mine, but he did not write the introduction, although he did make some suggestions.'[171]

Bizarrely, Owen remains convinced that his close relationship with Milosevic was an important factor in ending the Bosnian war. In his memoirs he rebuked the Americans for their failure to understand 'that splitting the Serbs was a delicate matter requiring some finesse, in part because some of them were obsessed with "getting Milosevic" rather than using his influence for our purposes'.[172] He never understood that Milosevic – who had fomented the wars in Croatia and Bosnia – was the *root* of the problem, not part of any lasting solution.

As a result of all this, Owen came under ferocious attack from critics in the region, the EU and the United States. They saw the whole mediation effort at best as a mere alibi for international inaction, and at worst as a mechanism for legitimating the despoliation of the weaker side. On 15 July 1993, the European Parliament overwhelmingly passed a resolution expressing 'alarm at the pressure of the representative of the EC, Lord Owen, on the government of Bosnia and Herzegovina to accept the plans of Karadzic and Boban backed by Milosevic and Tudjman for a division of the republic into ethnic entities'.[173] The Dutch EC Commissioner for External Affairs, Hans van den Broek, accused Owen publicly of a 'strategy of capitulation' and 'legitimized aggression'. 'As far as I am concerned,' he added, 'Owen and Stoltenberg could well have asked for a tougher mandate when it came to making a credible threat to use force.'[174] In early 1994, the European Parliament even called for Owen's dismissal, by more than two votes to one (160 to 90; there were 13 abstentions).[175] But all this was eclipsed by the avalanche of derision from across the Atlantic. Marshall Harris, who resigned from the US State Department over the 'morally bankrupt' western policy on Bosnia, called for Owen's 'removal' on the grounds that 'He is not fulfilling his function as an impartial negotiator when he treats the Bosnian government neither as a legitimately elected government nor the victims.'[176] He subsequently recalled that Owen had been 'disastrous . . . no matter what happened and no matter what would have happened on the ground in Bosnia, he would still have found a way to try and stop western intervention and try and formulate arguments against it'.[177] The Democratic US senator Frank McCloskey condemned Owen as 'the orchestrator and spokesman for craven EC inaction'.[178] The *Washington Post* compared him to Neville Chamberlain and described him as 'the personification of the West's broad diplomatic failure and moral surrender'.[179] The defence expert and commentator Edward Luttwak spoke of him as 'that most perfect popinjay Lord Owen'.[180]

Owen professed himself hurt but unmoved by the attacks. In his memoir he took comfort from the fact that in the case of the resolution of the European Parliament 'only half the . . . 518-member Assembly had voted and that all the British MEPs, Labour as well as Conservative' had voted for him.[181] Moreover, he adds, 'At least President Izetbegovic was not yet saying that I should be dismissed, commenting wryly that if Lord Owen did not exist, the United Nations and the European Union would have to find another Lord Owen. He said: "We cannot blame the international community's passiveness on only one man. There would be no changes by changing one man. We need to change the policy".'[182] Izetbegovic's reticence was also based on other considerations. As one member of the Bosnian delegation at Geneva observed, Izetbegovic – who was not attuned to the nuances of the English class system – felt a curious deference towards Owen as a peer of the realm and an English gentleman.[183] He felt that the Bosnian delegation should not attack Owen, as 'we are his guests'; he may also have feared that direct confrontation would result in even worse peace terms. In any case, Izetbegovic eventually lost patience with Owen: 'He is an Englishman', the Bosnian president told a German magazine. 'That says everything. Do I need to be more explicit? . . . He is one of the English politicians in the style of Chamberlain.'[184] Mohamed Fillipovic, who dealt with Owen as part of the Bosnian delegation, described him simply as 'a very wicked person . . . a cynic'.[185]

Some of the obloquy directed at Owen was really intended for the British government. As one Bosnian official observed, 'He's just the front man for European policy, especially that of Britain. There's no reason to think that things would change much if he resigned, unless policies changed radically too.'[186] 'Hurd, not Owen is the real target,' argued Boris Johnson in the *Sunday Telegraph*.[187] On this reading, Owen became little more than a stooge in the eyes of his critics. Of course, it is true that Owen was dependent on political support in London – he made no secret of this himself – but 'stooge' is not the right word to describe a relationship that was symbiotic rather than subordinate. When asked whether 'the British government to some extent, because of your British background, still tried to control you?' his response was frank. 'Well, of course,' he answered. 'That's inevitable . . . they gave me intelligence information . . . I was getting the same inputs as ministers. But I don't think anybody ever put what you call pressure on me to adopt a British line.'[188]

Such direct influence was not necessary, however, for Owen had quickly cast off his radical interventionist stance of 1992 and showed every sign of having internalized British government policy by 1993–4. Perhaps the most striking example of how completely Owen had been converted to Hurd's conservative pessimist minimalism is the lecture he gave to the Royal College of Surgeons in Dublin on 8 November 1993.[189] This turned out to be a politico-medical disquisition on the 'risks of intervention', dripping with sonorous sub-Hurdian gravitas. 'As physicians and surgeons,' he argued, 'we have long been aware of the dangers of simply responding to the cry "do something". All too often we know that an illness has to work its way through the system . . . the skill is to appear calm without being complacent, to act unhurriedly but to be decisive even if the decision is to do nothing. Sometimes to look as if one is doing more than one is in fact doing.' 'Governments,' he said, coming to the point, 'similarly face demands for action' and therefore 'politicians need some of the same skills of masterly inactivity as doctors'. 'The answer,' Owen suggested, 'is for politicians to be more open in explaining the limits of any action and the downsides of any intervention . . . politicians will have to show more restraint in calling on the UN to debate and pass resolutions as their equivalent of the pink medicine to delay action.'

Owen did, in fact, rouse himself one last time on the occasion of the Contact Group plan of summer 1994, another unjust partitionist cock-shy, which the Bosnians wearily accepted but which was rejected by the Bosnian Serbs. This was in many ways a déjà vu of the Vance–Owen fiasco in May 1993. 'It seemed to me politically inconceivable,' he wrote in his memoir, 'that these five governments could now just leave such a map on the table. But it was more than conceivable: it was exactly what they did.' Owen then went on to outline his own programme for enforcement: 'I suggested to the ministers that they let the Muslim–Croat Federation know that if they accepted the map and associated constitutional arrangements, and the Serbs did not, the *arms embargo would be lifted* and under UN resolutions NATO *air assets would do all they could* to prevent the Serbs taking military advantage. Most, if not all, UN ground forces and UNHCR personnel would have to be withdrawn during this period.'[190] Just in case anybody thought this a reversal of his position in 1993, Owen added that 'This was *leave* as well as "lift and strike", and it contained two crucial differences from what President Clinton had suggested a year before: first, it would be air action threatened in support of a specific peace plan; and second, it would be air action which had Russian acquiescence, perhaps even Russian support'.[191] The notion that he had thereby sold the pass on the military efficacy not merely of 'strike' – which he had always conceded with qualifications – but also of 'lift', does not occur to him.

The reason why this risky but viable strategy was not adopted was partly because of Russian and French objections, but mainly because the British government – on the advice of the British UNPROFOR commander Michael Rose – feared for the safety of the men on the ground.[192] Their military experts also remained profoundly sceptical about the military viability of 'lift and strike'. The Americans, however, balked at the complete withdrawal of UNPROFOR, which would make them responsible for the end of the humanitarian mission. They believed – correctly as it turned out – that it was possible to consolidate UN forces and continue the mission in Croat and Muslim areas while enforcement actions proceeded against the Bosnian Serbs. Oddly, Owen – whose position was now much closer to Washington's than to London's – wrote a highly coloured memorandum to all EU foreign ministers on 22 July 1994 attacking the Americans. 'The EU,' he wrote, 'is now facing its first real challenge to its CFSP [Common Foreign and Security Policy] over the former Yugoslavia. Letting the VOPP be ditched last May was just about defensible . . . Now in the summer of 1994 allowing the Bosnian Serbs to call our bluff again is far more dangerous.' The 'authority of the EU itself', Owen claimed, was 'on the line', while the 'US, by continuing to advocate lift and strike, have cleverly contrived their own escape hatch'. The danger was, he warned, that the 'US is clearly trying to arrange a progressive pattern of air strikes that seriously risk drawing the UN, and the EU by implication, into a lift, stay and strike policy'.[193]

The rest of the document is a detailed and sound strategy for engaging the Croatian and Bosnian Serbs. He speculated that UNPROFOR might be withdrawn 'so as to free us up to use air power to tilt the balance in favour of the Croatian army within the borders we have recognised for Croatia, and for the Bosnian government army in Bosnia and Herzegovina'. Of course, it went without saying that 'Adopting lift and strike now, as opposed to when the US first proposed it, is a very different strategy.' This was because 'we [now] have a concrete plan to which we can hold the Muslims' and because 'provided air strikes are limited to Bosnian Serb territory, the Russians ought to be able to tolerate them'.[194] Owen concluded that 'It will have to be very clearly stated that NATO will not under any circumstances put troops in on the ground, and that the Muslims and Croats will have to live with the consequences of a strategy which they have asked for, whereby they do the ground fighting, and over which many NATO nations have military doubts as to the efficacy of air strikes. The alternative, in the absence of Milosevic cooperating, is to watch the progressive erosion of the authority of the Contact Group nations and a situation on which the Serbs assert their authority with the world never knowing whether or not the route suggested by the US could have been successful.' Subsequently, of course, Owen never conceded that the American strategy – when tried in 1995 – proved militarily resoundingly successful. In any case, the British, EU and American governments ignored this memorandum, perhaps understandably confused as to which side – apart from his own – Owen was now on in the great transatlantic debate on Bosnia. This did not stop Owen from blaming the failure to enforce the Contact Group plan not on London, Paris or Brussels, but on Washington whose 'advocacy of the lifting the embargo was only for public relations purposes' and which 'preferred posturing'.[195]

By this time, Owen was – as the Director of Information at UNPROFOR recalls – well 'on the way to being sidelined' by the contact group; and he had in any case 'lost heart and was not committed to [the negotiation] in any way.[196] Owen drew attention to himself one last time through his exit, which was conducted in another welter of transatlantic recrimination.[197] By the time he eventually stepped down in early June 1995, Owen had become a marginal figure whose departure, as Edward Mortimer unkindly put it in the *Financial Times* 'may have surprised some who did not realise he was still in the job'.[198]

CHAPTER 5

# 'The Men on the Ground'

If Lord Owen proved to be an effective ally in keeping interventionist demands at bay, the British government found further support among the British UN commanders in Bosnia itself. These 'men on the ground' came to exercise a strange and baleful ascendancy over the imagination of British statesmen, diplomats and commentators. When rejecting military intervention in August 1993, the Foreign Office Minister Douglas Hogg stressed that 'the advice of everyone I met in Bosnia, including the UNPROFOR commander, is that we must be cautious'.[1] David Owen claimed that 'Calls for "robust" or "muscular" action from politicians, retired generals, and commentators in television studios were greeted with hollow laughs by the men on the ground.'[2] Rhetorically, these objections were difficult to gainsay, particularly by those relying only on their common sense rather than supposedly authoritative local knowledge. As Captain Mike Stanley – or Milos Stankovic, a British liaison officer of Serb parentage, who was later arrested and released on charges of spying for the Bosnian Serbs – observed in his memoir *Trusted mole*: 'I've no time for those smart-arsed bastards, those laptop bombardiers, those lizard-like armchair warriors espousing one theory after another from the hushed, cloistered safety of academia, or the sterile environment of ministries. They weren't there.'[3] In the newspapers, in the television studios, in parliament and elsewhere, the importance of 'acting on advice on the ground' was repeated again and again. So much so that in July 1995 *The Times* was not alone in accusing the government of having 'pass[ed] the buck to "the commanders on the ground"'.[4] At times it seemed as if the war in Bosnia was unimportant enough to be left to the soldiers.

For much of the war, General Michael Rose, UNPROFOR commander in Bosnia throughout 1994, was the quintessential 'man on the ground'. From the very beginning Rose cultivated the media,[5] and the British correspondents in theatre – some of whom were indebted to him from reporting earlier conflicts – were initially by and large his faithful supporters.[6] Great things were expected. He was portrayed as 'the most cerebral and least orthodox . . . of the eight Lieutenant Generals in the British Army'. He had narrowly missed a First in PPE at Oxford, and had subsequently served with great distinction in the SAS in Aden, Northern Ireland and the Falklands. It was noted that Rose had had 'surprisingly little direct experience of the conflict between the west and the Soviet Bloc. Consider how he had spent the previous 20 years: he had been involved in nasty little colonial and post-colonial conflicts.' He was, as Milos Stankovic put it, 'an operational soldier, non-Germany, non-NATO, all brush fire wars'.[7] This, it was thought, made him 'well suited to the chaotic post-communist world in which nationality, race and religion were more important than secular ideology, and where terrorism spilled over into civil war and "ethnic cleansing"'[8] As we shall see, this assumption turned out to be mistaken: Bosnia required a more straightforward soldier with an understanding of communist mentalities and of conventional second world warfare. It would also have been helpful to have had a commander more attuned to working with the Americans through multilateral military organizations.

Rose deliberately cultivated an informal, some would say 'cool' or 'macho', style. On their first meeting, his liaison officer, Milos Stankovic, mistook him for one of the bodyguards: 'He was wearing a pair of those green-grey Army issue trainers, faded blue, baggy cotton trousers and a tatty old polo shirt hanging out of his trousers; and he was wearing a pair of ray-bans.'[9] This approach was reflected in the informality of his office in Sarajevo, which he operated 'as though it was a small SAS team'. It was – Stankovic recalls – 'all first name terms except with the general, who was "General", "Sir", or, in the case of his bodyguard, "Boss"'.[10] The salty diction of the general and his entourage was reflected in the forthright and often wounding language used to browbeat uncooperative locals and journalists, including women. The reverse side of all this was a surprisingly thin skin. Rose took criticism badly, and – by his own account – sometimes responded physically. 'I was particularly annoyed', he recalls in his memoir, 'by a TV reporter who accused me during a news report of being "economical with the truth" . . . He was in effect calling me a liar.' Rose, who routinely made such accusations himself, 'responded by dragging him away from his camera team where I challenged him to repeat his accusation. He was in such a state of shock he couldn't speak . . . I told him that if he ever called me a liar again I would tear out his tongue.'[11] As the UNPROFOR Director of Information, Dr Michael Williams, recalls, 'incidents which almost came to blows were not infrequent'.[12]

Rose's cerebrality was impulsive and intuitive, not reflective. He was at his best – such as during the storming of the Iranian embassy in 1980 – when split-second decisions were required. He was at his weakest when the situation called for politico-strategic rather than tactical skills. Calm deliberation was not his forte. One officer who had previously served on his staff told me that Rose was always throwing out ideas, most – but not all – of them 'barking'. More seriously, Rose was notorious for his short attention span: approximately fifteen seconds, he estimated.[13]

It took Rose about that length of time to make up his mind about Bosnia, the Bosnians, and the Bosnian government. He had hardly arrived in the city when he came under fire from Serb guns, allegedly provoked by the Bosnian defenders, on the drive from the airport to Sarajevo city centre. Rose resolved there and then that his 'first task would be to tell President Izetbegovic that this grim strategy of inflicting such horrors on his people would never succeed and that I would do all in my power to prevent the UN from becoming engaged in a war in Bosnia as a combatant'.[14] All of Rose's subsequent policies, his insistence on the essential equivalence between the Bosnian government and its Serb tormentors, his opposition to air strikes, his staunch defence of the arms embargo, his systematic attempts to downplay Serb threats to the safe areas, and his consequent running battles with Nato and the Americans, stemmed from this determination.

Underlying Rose's attitude was a profound distrust for the Bosnian people, particularly their leaders. His memoirs are liberally peopled with Ruritanian villains, such as the Bosnian Vice-President, Ejup

Ganic, whose 'oily charm' was wasted on the general.[15] On the other hand, the American diplomat John Menzies, a strong supporter of the Bosnian government and a critic of British policy, 'had been at school in England and played cricket', so he 'almost became part of the UN team'.[16] When Rose attended a performance of Mozart's *Requiem* in the ruins of the National Library in Sarajevo, conducted by Zubin Mehta, Rose 'wondered if [the Bosnian President] understood the Christian sentiment behind the words and music', which Izetbegovic was no less innately qualified to judge than the conductor.[17] Sometimes, it is true, Rose spoke of the 'simple faith of the people' being 'a source of great inspiration, in direct contrast to the cynicism and venality of their leaders with whom I had to do business'.[18] And sometimes he appealed over the heads of the leader directly to the people. 'I wander around,' he observed in March 1994, 'and talk to them [the people of Sarajevo] and say "Look, if you want this goddam senseless killing to stop it will stop. You must make this plain to your own politicians in as tough a way as we are doing".'[19] But generally he regarded the Bosnians with a cultural, essentially 'orientalist', disdain. 'Shortly after calling the Bosnians [sic] savages during dinner one evening', he recalls, 'I was summoned to the Prime Minister's office and asked why I had done so, when the Bosnians were Europeans like myself. I refrained from replying that, in my view, after the way they had slaughtered each other it would take them at least 500 years to achieve that status.'[20] Later on, he 'wondered how the Balkan [sic] people, who considered themselves modern Europeans, could behave with such savagery'.[21] Indeed, to the Associated Press reporter Maud Beelman, who had ample opportunity to observe Rose throughout 1994, 'He gave every indication that he thought these peoples were savages and deserved the lot that they got and that they were several classes beneath him.'[22]

Nor were these attitudes confined to Rose. Major Vaughan Kent-Payne, who served in the Duke of Wellington's Regiment in Central Bosnia in 1993, described 'the Bosnian people' as 'A race whose only similarity with Western Europeans was physical . . . Mentally, they were poles apart from us and treated each other with a brutality that bordered on the bestial.' The major added, in a nice touch of barrack-room ethnography, that 'the region was where the hot-blooded Latin merged with the brutal Slav and the results were often odious'.[23] Likewise, Lt.-Col. Jonathon Riley, the commanding officer of the Royal Welch Fusiliers in the safe area of Gorazde in 1995, routinely spoke of the 'deceit' and 'ingratitude' of the Muslims.[24] Some of this disdain took on distinctly racist overtones. 'In one British commander's mess,' Noel Malcolm reveals, 'the Bosnian Muslims (and only the Muslims) were jocularly referred to as "the wogs".'[25] In another office, the Serbs were known as 'the Klingons', an obstreperous but noble martial race from the TV serial *Star Trek*; the Muslims, on the other hand, went by the name of 'mutants', that is defective *Untermenschen* with missing limbs and organs.[26]

Many British officers, in fact, harboured Serbophile tendencies or at least felt a curious professional bond with their Bosnian Serb counterparts. When Michael Rose claimed that General Mladic 'generally kept his word', this sounds like a considered tribute of one soldier to another, until one remembers that the exceptions included the 2,000 men and boys of Srebrenica to whom Mladic had publicly promised their lives. Oddly, Mladic's direct responsibility for Srebrenica finds no mention in Rose's memoir *Fighting for peace*, penned in 1998, despite the fact that the author takes detailed issue with the subsequent Nato air campaign. But perhaps the most embarrassing exemplar of British military Serbophilia is that of Lt.-Col. Riley. The Royal Welch Fusiliers CO at Gorazde wrote in his diary: 'I find them [Serb officers] easy to talk to, and most Serb officers are patriotic men of honour, very much aware of the military tradition of the two [sic] world wars fought in alliance with us [sic].'[27] His description of his meeting with the Bosnian Serb commander Ratko Mladic in August 1995, who was then fresh from the Srebrenica massacre and has since been indicted for war crimes, is revealing. 'General Mladic,' Riley wrote in his diary on 28 August 1995, 'is an imposing, indeed dominating, figure both physically and in terms of his personality; it was easy to see why his own men adore him and his enemies fear him. He in turn clearly knew what the Royal Welch had endured, and he was charm itself . . . We then adjourned for some Serb hospitality: a magnificent lunch of barbecued lamb, with the inevitable deluge of plum brandy. I left with a signed photograph of the General.'[28]

All this is rendered the more distasteful by the immediately following account of the desperate attempts by the Bosnian garrison of Gorazde to arm themselves against the next onslaught on their enclave. According to Riley's diary 'a criminal element' now tried to rush the perimeter fence, but was repulsed. Their 'criminal intent' was 'to steal fuel weapons and ammunition' which they so urgently needed. The general tone of disdain and contempt contrasts markedly with the bonhomie previously expressed towards the Serb warlord. Moreover, as my subsequent conversations showed, such attitudes endured among British officers well after the war was over. Indeed, Sandhurst insiders were only slightly exaggerating when they claimed that they had not met a British officer who was not to some extent sympathetic to the Serbs.

This picture is confirmed by the UNPROFOR Director of Information in Zagreb, Michael Williams, who remembers the many trips he undertook with British UN officers to Sarajevo and the Bosnian Serb headquarters at Pale. The meetings with Bosnian government officials would be 'short and crisp', and reflected a mutual disdain. 'And then,' he remembers, 'we'd drive up that hill to Pale, and we'd be lucky to get out before midnight. And you could see the body language sometimes immediately transformed when we went in. Particularly on the military side . . . The Bosnian Serbs would make an entire evening of it, and quite lavish meals with quite a lot of alcohol would be provided. And it was clear there was some sort of general-to-general relationship between Mladic and Rose . . . They [British officers] were very pro-Serb on the whole, and I think there were strong elements of anti-Muslim and anti-Catholic prejudice.'[29]

For many, British military Serbophilia was a puzzling phenomenon. Warren Zimmermann, the last US ambassador to Yugoslavia, observed that 'I still find it perplexing why most UNPROFOR commanders, especially Michael Rose and Canadian General MacKenzie, found the Bosnian Serb army so compatible and its contention that "everybody commits atrocities" so convincing. Was it Serbian military spit and polish when contrasted with the ragtag Bosnians in tennis shoes?'[30] Likewise, Maud Beelman reflects on the contrast between the Bosnian army who were 'wearing red basketball court shoes, and they go to the front line with one bullet', who had 'zero respect in military circles', and the respect shown to the more organized Serbs.[31] And the

Supreme Allied Commander Europe, US General George Joulwan, recalls that 'the preponderance of heavy weapons belonged to the Serbs – they had a military structure, and I think that this appealed to some of the UNPROFOR and NATO commanders because they had an organized force – they'd line up, they'd be in uniform, they'd know how to salute. And I think there was this bias . . . creeping in because there was a proper military on one side and . . . a guerilla movement on the other.'[32] Such instinctive professional fraternalism should not be underestimated. One senior British figure, who had been commanding officer in central Bosnia, recently observed of the Bosnian Serbs, 'of course we naturally respected them as the better army'. 'One can only hope,' the Cambridge historian Joel Dowling remarked, 'that he meant "better than the HVO [the Bosnian Croats] or BIH [Bosnian army]".'[33] Another factor – difficult to calibrate – was the role of the military interpreters, of whom there were only three at the start of the conflict: Milos Stankovic, 'Abbott' and 'Costello'. All three were of Serb background, and two were of Krajina Serb origin.[34] Stankovic acted as interpreter to Brigadier Andrew Cumming, the first British commanding officer in Bosnia, then for Lt.-Col. Bob Stewart of the Cheshires, and finally for UNPROFOR commanders Rose and Smith.

British officers seem to have drawn heavily upon half-remembered military history of the Second World War, in which the Serbs figured as intrepid partisan allies against the Germans: the passage by Lt.-Col. Riley cited above is not untypical. They would have been surprised to learn that, while many Serbs served gallantly in Tito's communist partisans and Mihailovic's royalist Chetniks, many others were loyal to the security forces of General Nedic's collaborationist regime in Belgrade.[35] They would have been even more surprised to hear that Milos Stankovic's father, a member of the Serbian Volunteer Corps – euphemistically described as 'a royalist outfit fighting Tito's communists' – actually served in a collaborationist formation implicated in many German atrocities.[36] Finally, it probably did not help that a battered copy of Rebecca West's rabidly Serbophile travelogue, *Black lamb and grey falcon*, did the rounds of the UN headquarters at Sarajevo with a label warning 'UNPROFOR use only'.[37] As Michael Williams recalls of British officers, 'Their reading was to reinforce their own prejudices. Theirs was a sort of hackneyed, handed-down version of what happened in the Second World War, or didn't . . . they bought into this idea that the Serbs had been our allies in two world wars.'[38]

But a far greater problem than Serbophilia was the ubiquitous doctrine of moral equivalence. Thus, Rose's press officer, Colonel Tim Spicer, claims in his memoirs that 'in the Balkans they are all as bad as each other', and that 'the Serbs and Muslims were just as unpleasant as each other, just as unpleasant and just as ruthless'; indeed, the subtitle of his chapter on Bosnia is 'There are no good guys in Yugoslavia'.[39] Likewise, Lt.-Col. Christopher le Hardy, the Chief of Operations and Intelligence in Sector North-East, denied being 'pro-Serb – far from it, I take the view that all the factional leaders are rotten through and through'. 'It is not our fault,' he explained, 'if the WF [warring factions] wish to carry on fighting. We gave them every chance to come to the table and settle their problems. But you can only lead a horse to water; making him drink is another matter.'[40] Rose himself professed to be in no doubt as to where the principal responsibility for the war lay. 'The Bosnian Muslims,' he writes promisingly, 'became the main victims of a deliberate and systematic policy of ethnic cleansing and in certain areas extermination. Although all three sides were to some extent guilty of war crimes, genocide, as defined by the UN convention on genocide, did not form part of official Bosnian government policy in the way that it so clearly did with the Serbs.'[41] Yet a great deal of his time in Bosnia, and his memoirs, was taken up attacking the Sarajevo government and stressing that 'the Bosnian Serbs were not the sole perpetrators of atrocities'.[42] Thus Rose blamed the Bosnian government for 'launching their successful offensives, which . . . finally derailed the burgeoning peace process'; he claimed that the 'Bosnian government had decided to abandon the peace process'; and he spoke of 'the danger for the USA in pursuing a foreign policy in Bosnia shaped by the propaganda machine of a clever ruthless government'.[43] Like his press officer, Tim Spicer,[44] Rose also routinely accused the Bosnian forces of provoking the Serbs.[45] All this, of course, was grist to the mill of the non-interventionist cabinet and Foreign Office back in London. Dissonant voices supportive of the Bosnian government – such as the first British ambassador to Sarajevo, Robert Barnett, were ignored.[46]

The way in which the British army approached the Bosnian war was inevitably by unfortunate analogy with Northern Ireland, where most soldiers had previously served in one capacity or another. As US General Wesley Clark observes: 'You had in the British army an army very experienced in dealing with Northern Ireland [where you had] seemingly comparable groups of people who stubbornly refused to get along and persistently killed each other . . . each soldier was taught . . . that these two groups are both tomfools and neither side is right and the whole thing is stop the violence, basically.' 'And when they transposed that,' he concludes, 'into Bosnian terms what happened, at least over a period of time, was the UN didn't want to take sides.'[47] Likewise, James Rubin recalls how British soldiers would regularly tell him that '"We're Brits, we're cynical, we've been around a long time. You young naïve Americans just don't understand. This is like Ireland and this is like Cyprus and these little peoples will keep fighting each other, and we're just here to do the best we can given their ancient hatreds". And you could hear the speech start within the first or second or third sentence, and it demonstrated a complete misunderstanding of what was going on and what the proper role for the west is in the post-Cold War world.'[48] And Michael Williams remembers that 'Too often their attitude was we've seen this, we've been there. "It's the Catholics and the Proddies and we have to keep the buggers apart". And it wouldn't have been much more sophisticated than that from Rose and the officers around him.'[49]

Inevitably, the equivalence argument gained ground once the Bosnian army struck back at their Serb and Croat tormentors. The disenchantment produced by the murders at Uzdol in 1993 – perpetrated by Muslims after the Croat massacre of Ahmici – was considerable. 'They can all go and f—k themselves now as far as I am concerned,' one captain remarked. 'Happy f—g Christmas to the lot of them: I'll be at home eating turkey; they can slaughter each other to their hearts' content.'[50] As Christopher Bellamy, the defence correspondent of the *Independent*, subsequently observed, 'When it became obvious there were no "good guys" and "bad guys", the sentiment, in Conrad's words, blazed at you, luminous and terrifying, like a flash of lightning in a serene sky: "Exterminate the brutes". Or, in Bosnia, perhaps, "Let the brutes exterminate each other".'[51] It was thus not surprising to find Lt.-Col. le Hardy observing of the Bosnian offensive in the spring of 1995, designed to recapture ethnically cleansed territory, 'The main perpetrators this time were, at least initially, the Bosnian Muslims. The international media once again attempted to blame the Bosnian Serbs.'[52] Underlying these strictures was the standard desire for a negotiated settlement, however unjust. 'We got,' le Hardy recalls, 'quite p——d off with them constantly attacking and actually ruining the efforts to get to any sort of peace treaty.'[53]

But even where there was no explicit suggestion of equivalence, the men on the ground – much to Whitehall's satisfaction – tended to muddy the waters with the language of complexity and doubt. Reports routinely referred to 'either side', 'warring factions', or some other such permutation; one colonel revealingly referred to 'warring factions, be they the Serb, Croat or Bosnian government authorities [sic]'.[54] 'Bosnia,' Bob Stewart wrote in his memoir, 'is certainly complex beyond anyone's dreams. There are far more sides – Serb, Croat, and Muslim – than we hear about in the media. There are factions within groups and groups within factions.'[55] Lt.-Col. le Hardy, the Head of Operations and Intelligence in Sector North-East towards the end of the war, recalls how 'We all found it very difficult to believe the deviousness of all the warring factions. The Yugoslavs are remarkable in their ability to mislead. And I'm afraid that if you start to believe one side and disbelieve the other, then you are no longer impartial.'[56] This use of language was not malicious – unlike Whitehall, the men on the ground spoke of the 'Muslims' not with political aforethought, but as a convenient, absent-minded shorthand to describe the forces of the legitimate government of Bosnia and Herzegovina.

The result, however, was the same: the fundamental truth that the Bosnians were the principal victims of Serb aggression and Croat scavenging, was lost. Antony Loyd, a British ex-serviceman and astute journalist on the ground in central Bosnia, observed that, 'It was interesting to see the evolution of opinion in the British commanders as the war progressed. Although technically an impartial force, many officers would privately admit to sympathies with the Muslims who were still largely the representatives of a secular ideal, and who were fighting a war against better-equipped forces while crippled by an arms embargo. Later British units, deprived of the opportunity for maverick expression by a revamped UN chain of command, started spouting the organisation's euphemisms that sought to paint every Bosnian side the same shade of guilty grey.'[57] It now became possible to question everything. Strong men began to spout vapid evasions which would not have disgraced a cultural studies department in an American university. 'I learnt one very valuable lesson in the Balkans,' Captain Stankovic/Stanley tells us, 'There is no truth. There is only perception.'[58] Thus the war – or lack of one – made post-modernists of them all.

Part of the problem was the location of the British forces in 1993. They were principally stationed in central Bosnia and Herzegovina, in areas disputed between the Croat separatists and the Sarajevo government. Until 1994, they had relatively few direct dealings with the Serbs; and they had little idea of what had happened and was happening in whole swathes of north-western and eastern Bosnia: in Banja Luka, Prijedor, Sanski Most, Bjelina, Foca and other places where the tide of ethnic cleansing had swept through almost overnight in the summer of 1992. It is significant that Colonel Alistair Duncan, who commanded in central Bosnia from mid-1993, only met Serb officers twice during his tour. 'I know that in other parts of Bosnia,' he added helpfully, 'the Serbs are the main problem.'[59] 'Most British soldiers,' Martin Bell reminds us, 'like most British journalists, never actually met a Serb from start to finish.'[60] What British forces *did* witness very directly in late 1992, and particularly throughout 1993, was the spectacular breakdown of the Croat–Bosnian government alliance and its attendant atrocities. And where the boys went, the media went with them. For example, Brigadier Andrew Cumming, the first British commanding officer in Bosnia, invited visiting journalists to 'get yourself down to Prozor where the Croats are pitchforking to death the Muslim farmers around the town whom they failed to clear out in October'.[61] The media, as one British officer observed, 'were allowed to come and go as they pleased' in the Officers' Mess of the Cheshire Regiment.[62] Indeed, Lt.-Col. Bob Stewart, their commanding officer, was told by the Prime Minister to 'appear as much as possible' on television, and did so.[63] More than anybody else, he put the spotlight on the Croat–Bosnian government war in 1993.

All this was well meant, but was to have a distorting effect on media and public perceptions back in Britain. The broader picture of systematic Serb aggression which had triggered opportunistic scavenging by Croats, and desperate measures by the Muslims, was lost. The argument for complex and intractable hatreds was correspondingly strengthened. Lt.-Col. Alistair Duncan could now plausibly claim that 'alliances could change overnight. There is no logic.'[64] 'Overnight', Martin Bell recalls, the war 'became more complex, harder to reckon on a moral compass, and somehow shaded in grey.'[65] Maggie O'Kane, reporting from Bosnia for the *Guardian*, put her finger on the resulting perspectival problem. 'Is the war in Bosnia centred on Vitez [in central Bosnia],' she asked, 'or is it just being reported that way?' She noted that 'In the past two months, most of the reporting of the war in Bosnia has moved to within a 20-mile radius of the British base at Vitez.' At the same time, she observed, Bosnia as a whole was becoming less newsworthy to an atrocity-fatigued world. The 'men on the ground' became a magnet for the British media because they offered physical protection, and plenty of human-interest stories, particularly about dashing and breathless captains, majors and even colonels.[66] 'The press,' O'Kane observed, 'has settled into an unhappy marriage of convenience and survival with the Brit battalion at Vitez . . . Brit Bat protect us, tell us where they are going, what time they will be home and let us snuggle into the middle of their armoured convoys. In return the reporting of the Bosnian war has become the story of the men of the Prince of Wales Regiment of Yorkshire.'[67]

Sometimes, the focus on the Croat–Bosnian government split was profoundly political in intent. The first initiative by Michael Rose in Bosnia was his attempt to – in his own words – 'engineer a situation in which I could legitimately employ NATO air strikes in order to demonstrate a more robust UN approach to peacekeeping. After some discussion with [the Russian] Viktor Andreev, who firmly supported the idea, I decided that it would be better to launch an air strike against the Croats rather than the Serbs.' The thinking behind this gambit was as follows: 'The Croats were not central to our main effort, and even if they reacted by closing routes, they could not afford to do this for as long as the sizeable Croatian population in the Laskva Valley was wholly dependent on UN aid. Such an attack would send the right signal to Mladic, who would also understand that NATO was not set on destroying the Serbs and that the use of force was impartial.'[68] The attack would indeed have sent a signal to Mladic – a disastrous message that the first UN air strike would have been carried out not against the principal aggressors, the Serbs, but against Croat scavengers. Fortunately, no suitable provocation was offered by the Croats, who may have been forewarned; and another opportunity did not present itself.

If Michael Rose was eager to launch the first Nato air strike ever against the Croats, his reluctance to target the Serbs was palpable. This became clear during the crisis precipitated by the market-place massacre in February 1994. For the first time, it seemed as if Nato would carry the war to the Serb besiegers with massive air strikes. Michael Rose, however, had other ideas. As the UN Secretary General, Kofi Annan, writes in his *Srebrenica report*, the UNPROFOR commander 'opposed this approach, apparently on the grounds that it might "drag the United Nations into war". He endeavoured to convince his own government not to support a wider use of NATO air power designed to force the Bosnian Serbs to the negotiating table.'[69] Rather than allow the Nato ultimatum to be the trigger for a wider rollback of Serb aggression – as later happened in 1995 – Rose sought to harness western military threats to his own much more limited plan for a ceasefire in Sarajevo. This, naturally enough, was bitterly opposed by the Bosnian government, which had seen such ceasefires come and go and now believed military deliverance at hand. In order to break their will, Rose threatened to 'reveal' a now-discredited initial investigation of the cause of the massacre. This is how Rose himself subsequently described the scene: 'Divjak', a Bosnian commander of Serb ethnicity, 'was reluctant to sign up to a ceasefire . . . At this point I sprang a nasty surprise on him. I told him that the first UN examination of the bomb crater in the Markale market place indicated that the bomb had been fired from the Bosnian side of the battle lines.'[70] The Bosnians – terrified of possible adverse publicity – agreed to sign. When the Bosnian government side showed signs of delay or even second thoughts, Rose physically manhandled General Divjak into the signing ceremony. Divjak protested that Rose 'doesn't treat me like an officer in the legitimate army of this country'.[71]

One does not need to have a theological belief in the innocence of the Bosnian government to find this exchange distasteful. It is true, as former Bosnian officials testified to me, that the Sarajevo authorities wilfully hindered the restoration of utilities – water and electricity – for public relations purposes. It is also true that Bosnian forces used hospital positions as firing posts, partly because such buildings were often in the front line, but also in order to provoke graphic Serb retaliation. But these officials thought it most unlikely that Bosnian forces had deliberately and systematically targeted the UN; and they were adamant that the major incidents, such as the bread queue massacre in 1992 and the market-place massacres of 1994 and 1995, were not self-inflicted. Such an operation would, in any case, have been impossible to keep secret in the porous politico-military culture of government-controlled Sarajevo.

Yet even if there was some reasonable doubt of the origin of the market-place shell, it was clear that such contested shells had caused only a tiny fraction of the thousands of civilian casualties in the city. The vast majority of victims incontestably died, individually or in small groups, as the result of indiscriminate Bosnian Serb shelling. Moreover, despite informal attempts to undermine the Sarajevo government with false allegations, the UN never publicly accused the Bosnians of being behind the most contentious episodes, such as the bread queue and Markale market massacres in February 1994.[72] Indeed, General Rose formally stated just after the massacre that he had never seen any evidence that the Muslims had fired on their own people.[73] He noted that the shell was of the same calibre as three indisputably Serb rounds which had killed nine people in a Sarajevo suburb the previous week: 'The world will certainly draw its own conclusions.'[74]

Nevertheless, British-dominated UN headquarters at Sarajevo, and Rose himself, were to spend much of 1994 suggesting or insinuating to journalists and visitors that the Bosnians were shelling themselves.[75] This struck General Wesley Clark, the Head of Policy and Planning at the Pentagon, who had been dispatched by President Clinton on a fact-finding mission, particularly forcefully. Although no uncritical friend of the Bosnian government, he could not fail to notice how 'the Serbophile perspective came out in things like the market place incident . . . when you'd say, "God, how could they do this?" And they'd say "Serbs didn't do it. You know the Muslims are perfectly capable, they fire mortar shells into their own people all the time". "They do? . . . can you prove that?" "No but it's very plausible" . . . I guess it came from somebody in Michael Rose's shop, or some people under Michael Rose maybe. I don't know where it came from.'[76] Similarly, James Rubin remembers that 'military officials from UNPROFOR . . . seemed to go out of their way to speculate with you about how the Muslims might have started something or we couldn't rule out that the Muslims shot first . . . you know, they were so anxious to prove that both sides were bad, that I think they accepted conspiratorial explanations for things that are unknowable.'[77] It must have been briefings such as these which informed Baroness Chalker's statement to the House of Lords in March 1994 that 'on the key issue of culpability [for the market-place massacre], a senior UNPROFOR official has said that the evidence was inconclusive'.[78]

Rose got his ceasefire and some semblance of normality did temporarily return to the streets of Sarajevo. But the cost of this missed opportunity to silence the Serb guns for good was enormous. It was to take another year and a half and another contested massacre before the west generated sufficient political will for the massive air strikes which helped to end the siege and indeed the war itself. Meanwhile, Rose evinced an embarrassing confidence and pride in the effectiveness of the ceasefire. Two stories – artlessly recounted by the General himself – illustrate this point. The first concerns a visit to the battle-scarred suburb of Dobrinja in February 1994. In order to 'demonstrate' the quality of the ceasefire, Rose 'invited' an elderly Bosnian soldier 'to accompany us in our walk across the open ground'. 'To reassure him,' Rose continues, 'I unbuttoned my coat to show that, like him, none of the UN party wore flak jackets. This did not reassure him, but he finally agreed . . . No one said anything until we reached the other side, at which point I took the old man's hand and congratulated him. He replied with a smile that it was the first time in two years that anyone had walked on that ground – and lived . . . I later heard that the old man had walked across the same piece of ground the next day and had been shot in the neck and seriously wounded. At the hospital he was asked why he had been so stupid.'[79] Later that year, a Serb policeman talking to Rose was shot at by a Bosnian sniper. 'The Serb dived for cover and asked me why I had not followed suit. I told him that no one would dare shoot the Commander of UNPROFOR and we all had to demonstrate our faith in the peace process. Sadly, he [the Serb] was killed standing on the same spot the next day.'[80] One senses that the penny has still not dropped.

As they sat on the roof of the British embassy in Sarajevo, listening to the nightly barrage, a British diplomat was startled to hear the general observe 'Ah yes, a city at peace.' 'If you listen out of the window,' Rose told sceptical reporters, 'you might think the third world war was happening. But actually there's an awful lot of firing around this time of night and nothing much ever happens, but we don't go rushing off over-reacting.'[81] Indeed, he told the US diplomat John Menzies in late 1994 that 'the number of civilian deaths by shooting was lower in Sarajevo than in many US cities'. But in other ways, Rose was less sure of the ceasefire than he pretended. In an internal memo, his office stressed 'the need to adopt a more pro-active policy of reporting the qualitative successes of the mission'. For, 'despite numerous successes in the sphere of returning to normality, particularly in Sarajevo, the perceptions, backed up by graphs, were of a slide back to war'.[82] For this reason, as Michael Williams recalls, Rose simply discontinued the reporting of the number of daily firing incidents – usually a standard method of measuring the success of a ceasefire. Whereas the Sarajevo ceasefire had led to a short-term improvement in the quality of life, Williams continues, 'after [the attack on the safe area] Gorazde it went fairly steadily down hill throughout the rest of 1994, so that the firing reports were going up and up and up'. These figures soon found their way to New York and the wider world, and they clearly bolstered the case for further military intervention. 'That,' Williams remarks, 'was the way that Rose saw it, and he changed the way of military reporting, he said look lots of the incidents are simply guys up on the hill, they're drunk and firing in the air, or somebody's had a new baby, or all the rest of it.'[83] Instead, Rose seemed to endorse the official UN line that Sarajevo itself was not – or no longer – under siege. Even his own press officer, Colonel Tim Spicer, wrote that he 'found that position hard to maintain. Sarajevo was under fire from artillery, mortars and snipers; people were being killed every day . . . Every building was pockmarked with bullet holes and no one inside the city was in any doubt that we were under siege.'[84] If, as the UNPROFOR Director of Information, Michael Williams, once wrote, Rose's court resembled Fawlty Towers, then its watchword was, 'Don't mention the siege'.

If Rose had been 'blooded' by the Sarajevo ultimatum, his handling of the Gorazde crisis of April 1994 was to be even more controversial. He failed to anticipate that the terms of his Sarajevo ceasefire allowed the Bosnian Serbs to redeploy their artillery eastwards against Gorazde, the largest of the three surviving enclaves in the Drina valley. This became apparent during the visit of the American Chief of Staff, General Shalikashvili in March 1994, who asked Rose about the likelihood of a spring offensive. 'I told him,' Rose recalls, 'that no side was capable of mounting an offensive campaign that would have any strategic significance.'[85] When the long-expected Serb offensive finally got underway, Rose, suspecting a Bosnian trap to precipitate western intervention, systematically played down the gravity of the situation. Throughout the first week in April, his Sarajevo headquarters sought to obscure the burgeoning military and humanitarian crisis in the enclave. Indeed, he told Charles Redman, the US special envoy to the Balkans, that the fighting in Gorazde, although serious, 'was little worse than elsewhere in Bosnia'.[86] But a leaked report by the embattled United Nations Military Observers (UNMOs) in the pocket left no doubt as to the gravity of the situation. 'From the BBC World Service news of 5 April,' it ran, 'we heard an UNPROFOR assessment that the attack into Gorazde was a minor affair into a limited area. We do not concur with that position. It is a grave situation . . . Saying it is a minor attack into a limited area is a bad assessment, incorrect and shows absolutely no understanding of what is going on here.'[87]

Rose's response was to rubbish the UNMOs and to suggest that Bosnians were provoking the Serbs. He later wrote that 'the statement read as if it had been dictated to the UNMOs by the Bosnian authorities in Gorazde'. He also claims that his liaison officer – Nick 'Costello', of Krajina Serb origin – subsequently found the UNMO team to have been 'completely demoralised . . . In Sarajevo I had suspected from the emotional tone of their reporting that they had ceased to function as a disciplined military unit. A subsequent investigation of their performance revealed that the UNMOs had spent much of their time in the cellars of a bank building, obtaining much of their information from local sources.'[88] At the time, as Williams recalls, Rose grandly reassured them that 'Look, the situation is not that bleak. Of course there is firing into the town. This does not mean that the Bosnian Serbs are necessarily going to up their offensive or are going to seize the town.' In order to obtain what he expected to be a more accurate and less alarmist picture, Rose tried to visit the enclave himself, and, when this was blocked by the Serbs, arranged for an SAS team to be dispatched into the pocket. At this point, however, Rose's memoirs – which are usually frank to the point of self-incrimination – become remarkably coy. He merely notes that his observers' reports 'showed that although there had been some incursions into the enclave, no serious attempt had been made by the Serbs to overrun it or capture the town. Nor did the Serbs ever try to achieve these goals.'[89] As we shall see, this was incorrect.

Subsequently, Rose alleged that the Bosnians had not merely exaggerated the damage to the town, but also deliberately withdrawn in the hope of luring Nato into the war. In an exchange caught on camera, Rose observed of the Bosnian defenders that 'They think that we should be fighting their wars for them. I mean, how the hell they let a tank down that goddamn route. One man with a crowbar could have stopped it. It's a five-mile road down a wooded ravine; they could have just dropped a boulder on it. I think they basically turned and ran and left us to pick up the bits.'[90] It was, perhaps, not inconsistent for a man who supported the arms embargo on the Sarajevo government to expect the Bosnian defenders of Gorazde to stop tanks with boulders and crowbars.

Normally, Rose could have made these claims without fear of contradiction. SAS men are expressly prevented – in the way that UNPROFOR commanders are not – from writing about their experiences; indeed, Rose himself shares the party line that the SAS 'should not go public on operational matters'.[91] In this case, however, we are fortunate to have the account of a retired 'renegade' SAS sergeant, 'Cameron Spence'. Of course, all such sources need to be treated with caution, but discreet enquiries at Hereford, via a senior serving officer, established that 'Spence' had indeed served in this capacity, and that otherwise they did not wish to comment on principle; further discreet enquiries indicated that 'Spence' was an authorial collective made up of several members of the Gorazde team.[92] The memoir, *All necessary measures*, is written on the basis of service in Bosnia in 1994, and the radio conversations and subsequent discussions with the team in Gorazde itself. Gillian Sandford's forthcoming account of the Gorazde crises of 1994, *Wheel of fire*, which is based on documentary and eyewitness evidence, will bear out Spence in most respects.[93] More recently, the memoir of the Harrier pilot downed over Gorazde, Nick Richardson, has also become available. While in no way consciously directed against General Rose himself, both accounts, especially that of Spence, completely contradict his picture of the Gorazde situation.

Both authors are in no doubt that Gorazde was under sustained Serb attack aiming to overrun the enclave. According to Spence's account, the SAS commander, 'Charlie', was warned by a Serb officer just before entering Gorazde, 'You know, Charlie, that Gorazde is not going to be a good place to be in the coming days.' That evening, Spence recalls, the UN spokesman in Sarajevo said that 'Our assessment is that Gorazde is not in any danger of falling.'[94] Both are clear that, while one of the original UNMOs was clearly under great strain, there was no sense of general demoralization. 'Two of them,' Spence relates, 'looked reliable enough.' The reason why they were in the basement of the bank was quite simple: the ferocious shelling meant that it was not safe anywhere else; UNHCR staff had experienced the same problem,[95] and even the SAS team itself was periodically driven to take cover there as well. The pilot who ejected over Gorazde wryly observed that he had imagined the SAS team 'up in the woods, heavily camouflaged and dug in under a pile of earth, I'd thought of [them] living off the land, evading the Serbs, emerging from cover only when NATO's planes came over seeking his guidance. I never thought for a minute that I'd find [them] behind a breakfast bar in a bank in the suburbs of town.'[96]

Their descriptions of the intensity of the fighting are unambiguous. Richardson – who was a direct eyewitness – quotes the SAS commander as saying that 'the Serbs have begun the last stage of their push to take the town'.[97] Spence, who was at Regimental headquarters at Gornji Vakuf, recounts that the SAS commander's 'comments were noted down carefully, then committed to a report that was sent post-haste to General Rose at his forward HQ in Sarajevo. *If the*

*UNPROFOR commander needed evidence of the Serbs' double-dealing in Gorazde, then Charlie's report had it in spades.* Not only were the Serbs advancing on the beleaguered pocket, one of the so-called safe havens, they were now clearly targeting the UN.'[98] He subsequently recounts the words of his colleague 'Kev': 'Intelligence indicates that this isn't some sporadic push on the Serbs' part, it's a *major, precalculated offensive, with the specific objective to capture and hold Gorazde*.'[99] The SAS team also observed the Serbs cold-bloodedly machine-gunning retreating columns of refugees.[100] They described a town 'half-starved to death', around which the Serbs held 'a ring of steel', which they were beginning to 'squeeze tight'.[101] Finally, they were explicit in their demands for more intensive air action. Spence reports that the SAS commander 'got on the radio and told Gornji Vakuf that there was only one thing now that could possibly save Gorazde from a bloodbath as the Serbs swept into the centre of town. At daybreak the next morning they needed air strikes. And they needed them in spades. Force was the only language the Serbs understood.'[102] I am told by informed sources that the transcripts of the communications from the team in Gorazde bear out Spence's account.

The circumstances surrounding the injury and subsequent death of SAS corporal Fergus Rennie and the injury of another SAS man, ambushed in their jeep, are clearly described in both accounts. Both Spence and Richardson agree that the attack was 'a premeditated act of revenge' by the Serbs.[103] The 'spin' placed on the event by UNPROFOR spokesmen, publicly and in unofficial briefings, was rather different. 'Rennie and a fellow SAS man', the press reported, 'were in a bunker outside Gorazde with Muslim troops. With the Serbs only 500 yards from the town centre, the Muslim troops of the Bosnian army exhausted their ammunition and abandoned the bunker, leaving the two British soldiers behind, armed only with pistols. At around 2 pm, the bunker was hit by what a UNPROFOR spokesman later described as "every kind of fire – mortars, heavy artillery, small arms, the lot".'[104] This account insinuates that the SAS men had been left to their fate by the Bosnian defenders.

Yet both Richardson and Spence, especially the latter, repeatedly stress the intense resistance put up by the Bosnian defenders: they had not simply run away, as Rose alleged. In one radio transmission, the SAS commander noted that 'The Muslims are fighting for every house and every street. It's like the last days of the Reich and Beirut on a bad night rolled into one. We are taking a s—tload of incoming [shells]. The defenders are holding out, but only just.'[105] Nor is there any suggestion that the defenders deliberately jeopardized the lives of the SAS men in order to lure Nato into the war. In fact, one of the most moving passages in Spence's account is the exchange which took place between an SAS man and a Bosnian captain whose trench was about to be overrun: 'The interpreter held a hurried exchange with the captain. Then he turned to Glen [the SAS man]. "He says that the Serbs will attack this position now. He says that we should leave. They will be here in minutes." "Tell him we'll do no such thing," Glen said hurriedly. "Tell him we'll stand and fight with him. He can do with the extra men. I know he can." Misha translated while the captain listened, his eyes closed. If this offer had moved him at all, he showed no sign of it. When he spoke again, his voice never wavered from its regular flat monotone. "He says he knows that you are General Rose's men," the interpreter said, more urgency in his voice now. "He says that it is not your job to be here. Your task is clear. Without you, there will be no one to call down the air strikes. The people of Gorazde need you to stay alive to talk to the NATO planes." The SAS men withdrew minutes before the position was overrun. They confessed later that it was the most gut-wrenching moment of their professional lives.'[106]

In fact, the notion that the Bosnians had somehow abandoned the SAS men originated with Rose himself. Michael Williams recalls that 'telephone exchanges were held about the drafting of a statement, and I remember, as was our standard routine, that I as the senior official on the civilian side would draft a statement to be sent to General Rose, and obviously we would discuss it . . . On that occasion he felt strongly that my initial draft put the blame on the Bosnian Serb forces: we spoke about this on the telephone, and he used words to the effect that this was one-sided. We were perplexed, genuinely perplexed, at this stage, although less so as the weeks and months of 1994 [wore on] by his attitude. And then he told me this story which he subsequently told to the press and others I think, that the Bosnian forces had withdrawn . . . very suddenly, and had left these two SAS guys exposed.'

But most remarkably of all, Spence's account shows how the SAS reports were received in Sarajevo. The following three-way exchange between 'Charlie', the SAS commander in Gorazde, 'James' at RHQ at Gornji Vakuf, and 'Richard' at UN headquarters in Sarajevo is worth quoting in full. ' "The pocket has gone, James" [Charlie reports], "It might not fold tonight and it might not fold tomorrow. But the pocket has fallen, mate, believe me. The Serbs will be here any –" "Wait a minute! hold it!" An unfamiliar voice had burst through on the radio . . . I recognised the voice now. It belonged to a Major, a member of the Regiment on Rose's staff in Sarajevo. Just as we were monitoring the transmissions in and out of the pocket so, of course, was UNPROFOR's forward headquarters. This Major, I remembered now, was a liaison officer, an LO on the general's staff. "Charlie, this is Richard at headquarters. Watch your choice of words, man." "What the hell do you mean?" Charlie said. Despite the frailty of the signal you could hear the mixture of astonishment and indignation in his voice. "I'm saying that you should think before you speak. This isn't just a military situation that we have on our hands here. The whole thing is highly politically charged. Gorazde has not fallen, it will not fall." '[107] Evidently, the 'man on the ground' was not saying the right thing.

The SAS team almost failed to make it out of Gorazde. As the Serb tide finally threatened to envelop the pocket, they were instructed by headquarters to allow themselves to be taken captive. 'At the very worst,' Major 'Richard' said, 'you would be treated as prisoners of war, but – and you've got to trust us here, Charlie – we'd fight for your early release. It might take a few months – three or four at the most – but you'll be free before the summer is over, I guarantee you.' The substance of this exchange is confirmed by Nick Richardson, who was himself in the pocket. 'Whatever happens,' he quotes the SAS officer as saying, 'from now on it looks as if we're on our own . . . Sarajevo has ordered us to stay put. There's no magic ending to this story, no rescue plan in the works. They're talking about maybe getting a convoy here in three or four days' time, but frankly that kind of talk just goes to show how out of touch they are with the real situation on the ground. The Serbs have this place sewn up, and in three or four days' time it will all be over. I'm sorry to have to tell you, therefore, that it's all down to us now. We've been left to fend for ourselves.'[108] The suggestion that they allow themselves to be taken captive, of course, was against all the traditions of the SAS. The team, mindful of the deliberate targeting of Rennie and their likely fate, decided to take their chances and break out. Faced with this *fait accompli* – Richardson says that they had 'made it clear we were coming out of the pocket, sh-t or bust' – headquarters in Sarajevo agreed to send a helicopter.[109] When the team – carrying a seriously injured trooper – finally reached the rendezvous, they found no helicopter waiting for them; it had to be summoned *de novo* from Sarajevo to effect the extraction. Richardson observed to the SAS officer that 'They never sent the helicopter because they thought we weren't going to make it. That's the God's honest truth, isn't it?'[110]

This rather unflattering picture of Rose's handling of the Gorazde crisis is confirmed by the testimony of Michael Williams. When he asked Yasushi Akashi, the UN special representative, whether there was anything he held against Rose, Akashi replied, 'Yes, his handling of Gorazde and the way in which the crisis was under-reported.'

In the end, Gorazde held out long enough to allow the Americans to railroad the Europeans into the threat of massive air strikes. The Serbs, so contemptuous of Rose's pin-prick tank-plinking, pulled back. As Aleksander Vasovic, the military correspondent for the independent Belgrade radio station B92, pointed out, the Serbs might prevaricate, but would not take on Nato directly. 'They will withdraw,' he said. 'They just cannot afford the devastating bombing that would occur if they do not.'[111] 'If we have now turned the corner,' observed the outgoing head of UNHCR in central Bosnia, Larry Hollingsworth, 'it is because NATO sent in the bombs, not the UN.'[112] This was also the opinion of UNPROFOR officials, who, as Kofi Annan subsequently wrote in his *Srebrenica report*, 'assessed that the Serbs had advanced in a series of steps, pausing to ascertain whether or not NATO would use force against them. When the Serbs were satisfied that they could move forward without escalating attacks from the air, they did so. UNPROFOR also assessed that, at least in the short term, the NATO ultimatum had put pressure on the Serbs not to press home their attack on Gorazde.'

There were many other cases where Rose or other British officers tried to head off western military intervention on behalf of the Bosnian government. As at Gorazde, they consistently tried to play down the threat from the Bosnian Serbs. Brigadier Andrew Vere Hayes immortalized himself in mid-1993 by claiming that Sarajevo was not really under siege by the Serbs; and he professed to believe that the Serbs had withdrawn their guns in July 1993 in response to UN mediation and not a Nato ultimatum.[113] The visiting Labour MP Calum MacDonald was solemnly assured by a senior British officer that Serb artillery only fired at specific targets in the city.[114] Rose himself carried on the approach perfected at Sarajevo and Gorazde in February and March 1994. He told Douglas Hurd during a meeting at RAF Brize Norton in autumn 1994 that 'much of the bad news concerning the situation in Bosnia was Bosnian government propaganda and that this was often being repeated by the US State Department'.[115]

The men on the ground denied not only the need but also the efficacy of air strikes. Their favourite sport was to ambush American advocates of 'lift and strike' on fact-finding missions to Bosnia. As James Rubin, then a staffer to Senator Joe Biden, reports, 'every time we were with British officers . . . they went into their rap, which was about why the United States should leave this to us and why taking sides was a mistake, and why they were all pretty much backward'.[116] It was, he reflected, 'a remarkable case of where you didn't have to scratch very hard to get political judgements about what one should and shouldn't do, as opposed to military analysis or military capacity'.[117] A particular offender was Brigadier Vere Hayes, who later distinguished himself as the head of the training mission to the Zimbabwean army. 'He was,' Rubin recalls, 'clearly offering the "all sides are guilty" thesis and volunteering it often . . . he was definitely in the "you Americans are naïve and we know better" mode.'[118] Sometimes, as Milos Stankovic relates, these exchanges degenerated into shouting matches, because the Americans allegedly 'weren't interested in what anyone on the ground had to say'.[119] On another occasion he describes the visit of Clinton's special ambassadress Bianca Jagger: 'She announces that she's going to recommend to Clinton that all the bridges over the Drina should be bombed. Can you believe it? The next day we get her up to the base and Phil Jennings disabuses her of this idea – "Drop the

Karakaj bridge and the Muslims in Tuzla get no aid from Belgrade". Her jaw dropped. They just didn't ever realise how complex and interlinked it all was.'[120]

Perhaps the most crushingly negative assessment of the military options open to the west was given by Brigadier Arthur Denaro, who served as Chief of Staff to the United Nations Peacekeeping Force in former Yugoslavia in late 1994 and early 1995. He played down the strength of the incoming Rapid Reaction Force in July 1995 'so as to prevent any expectations of its ability to solve the problems . . . The RRF is not powerful enough . . . to embark on "peace enforcement"; thus protecting "safe areas" is not a viable option and will not suddenly become one. The plain truth is that there is no military solution that the UN can impose on Bosnia; . . . All "positive action" should now be directed towards getting the parties around a table and negotiating a settlement.'[121] It was the same Rapid Reaction Force, of course, which in August–September 1995 – in conjunction with Nato jets – suddenly routed the Serb artillery besieging the 'safe area' of Sarajevo.

Similar sentiments were repeatedly expressed by General Rose himself. The American strategy of 'lift and strike' was dismissed as 'nonsense'.[122] He was particularly scathing about the use of air power. Here the basic problem stemmed from Rose's insistence on refusing all strategic strikes and demanding instant tactical results, one of the things air power cannot necessarily deliver. This did not stop Rose from making sarcastic observations in his memoirs. In the late summer of 1994, he describes calling an air strike on a tank in an orchard: 'in the event, an ageing RAF Jaguar attacked the tank – and missed'.[123] Another attack is described – not without humour – in the following terms: 'the bombs missed their target, although a nearby pigsty received a direct hit. The reason given by NATO was that the sun was shining in the pilots' eyes and they had not been able to see the tank. The UN was beginning to be rather sceptical about the capabilities of NATO aircraft. They could not engage our targets in cloud, in rain, at night, or with the sun in their eyes. They were beginning to sound very like British Rail.'[124] When told that it was too dangerous for Nato jets to fly below 5,000 feet, Rose responded: 'Too dangerous to fly under five thousand feet! We f——g well live below five thousand feet!'[125] This derision is misplaced. The advocates of air power never claimed to be able to turn the tide overnight – or to effect immediate tactical reversals. 'Plinking tanks', as the Commander-in-Chief of Nato's Southern Command, Admiral Leighton Smith, reminded Rose, 'is not warfighting!'[126] Moreover, Rose refused to allow Nato to eliminate Serb anti-aircraft batteries, making low flying even riskier.[127] It was only after Rose left that Nato jets were able to show their true capabilities.

If air power was one target of Rose's scorn, the idea of lifting the arms embargo was the other. Essential to his argument was the systematic denigration of not only the current but also the potential fighting power of the Bosnian army. When in June 1994 the US House of Representatives called on President Clinton – by a large majority – to lift the arms embargo, Rose immediately sought to dampen Bosnian expectations: 'Their view that "give us the tools and we'll finish the job" is fairly widespread. But my own view is that it takes a lot more than just being given equipment to win a war, and that there's a whole level of training and integration needed after the actual lifting of the embargo.'[128] He wheeled out a hapless young Bosnian soldier to persuade the visiting US General Galvin that 'most of the assumptions that would justify "lift and strike" were false . . . that the Bosnian army was in no military position to defeat the Serbs in battle, no matter how many weapons were parachuted into Bosnia. The Bosnian army was a gallant, though ad hoc, group of fighters capable only of skirmishing at company level and conducting old-fashioned trench warfare.'[129] Indeed, Rose argued that 'UNPROFOR was able to demonstrate to the US that the lifting of the arms embargo would result in the defeat of the Bosnian army and the probable deployment of US troops to defend the state.'[130] Of course, when the Bosnian government – under severe US and British pressure – temporarily deferred its request for the lifting of the embargo, Rose felt vindicated: this had, he claimed, 'given the lie to [his] critics'.[131]

One of the striking aspects of Rose's rhetoric was the consistent slighting of Bosnian commanders. Colonel Bob Stewart had had the courtesy to acknowledge that 'Few of them are professional soldiers but they are all brave men. They've been under fire much more than I have in all my career.'[132] Milos Stankovic writes of the legendary Bosnian commander in Bihac, General Dudakovic, that his 'tactical handling of Fifth Corps throughout the war was extraordinary'.[133]

Rose writes simply that 'I was beginning to suspect that somewhere in Tito's Yugoslavia there had been a school producing standard army generals on the Soviet model: short, fat, arrogant and brutal. Dudakovic was no exception . . . I found him an unpleasant man.'[134] Indeed, Rose seemed to have an *idée fixe* about the supposed Soviet–Yugoslav connection. 'Most of the officers in the former Yugoslav army had been Serbs,' he writes, 'and they had been well educated by their Soviet masters in the art of manoeuvre, the mass application of fire and how to concentrate their forces for a decisive attack.' 'The Bosnians, on the other hand,' this fantasy continues, 'had received no military training.'[135] Rose seemed unaware of Tito's split with Stalin in 1948 and the fact that the JNA had spent the past forty years preparing for a Soviet invasion. He also seemed to be under the impression that Bosnian Serbs and Bosnian Muslims had been conscripted into different armies prior to 1992.

There were, in any case, inconsistencies and hypocrisies in Rose's assessment of the Bosnian army. When the Bosnian Foreign Minister, Haris Silajdzic, lamented the failure of the latest offensive, Rose replied that the Bosnian commander, Delic, 'had not had the privilege of training at the British Staff College. He was however always welcome.'[136] This was a particularly self-defeating piece of rhetoric, because of course the one thing Delic – or any other Bosnian soldier – was *not* offered was British training to defend his country. But Rose could never resist the temptation to lecture the Bosnians. He subsequently relates how he advised them to abandon futile offensives and 'follow a longer-term strategy and wait until their people were no longer reliant on UN aid and the new Federation had built sufficient military strength before aiming at all-out victory [sic]'.[137] Just how this little homily could be reconciled with his condemnation of a similar US strategy, with his demands for a negotiated settlement, and his rejection of arms supplies, is not clear.

Equally unfortunate was Rose's tendency to impugn the courage and motives of his critics at home; this formed a standard part of the 'men on the ground rhetoric'. 'If the international community had abandoned the peacekeeping mission,' he writes, 'then it might well have become necessary for Noel Malcolm himself, who once signed a letter in *The Times* under the banner of "The Alliance to Defend

Bosnia", to take up a rifle rather than a pen.' Mark Almond, who had the temerity to criticize Rose in the *Daily Mail*, was dismissed as sitting in a 'comfortable book-lined study'.[138] Rose, on the other hand, grandly claimed in his memoirs – the inside jacket cover of which shows him in a book-lined study – that if the west were really to go to war on Bosnia's behalf, he would be the first to sign up.[139] And yet, when Nato finally did make the move to enforcement in August–September 1995, there was no sign of the general returning to make good his pledge. This was a pity, since his undoubted physical courage and tactical panache would have been extremely useful to the Rapid Reaction Force as it grappled with Serb artillery around Sarajevo, and even more to Dudakovic's company commanders in north-western Bosnia as they struggled to keep up with their allies, the US-armed and trained Croatian regular army.

Underlying much of Rose's policy was a burgeoning anti-Americanism which both reflected and contributed to the broader transatlantic malaise in Whitehall. In his memoir, he speaks of 'the role played by America . . . in prolonging the war in pursuit of a "just" solution, which was only partly redeemed by its – allegedly belated – intervention to bring the war to an end'.[140] Much of this was alarmingly attributed to the baleful 'Jewish influence on current events' in the US and the 'powerful Jewish lobby behind the Bosnian state'.[141] Rose also repeatedly criticizes the refusal of the Americans to commit ground forces. 'Without such a commitment,' he writes, 'President Clinton was, in effect, playing with the lives of soldiers of other nations.'[142] His relations with the US ambassador, Victor Jackovitch – 'a cool man with a thin black moustache and a secretive manner' – were famously poor.[143] He was also convinced, not only that elements within the State Department were trying to undermine his peacekeeping efforts, but that the US military was intercepting his communications and bugging his headquarters. When he challenged the Americans, Rose claims, 'they never denied it'.[144]

Similar antagonisms were becoming routine further down the line. The British Chief of Staff of UN forces in Bosnia, Brigadier Vere Hayes, was widely reported when he demanded to know what President Clinton 'thinks he's up to' with his threats of air strikes, adding that 'air power won't defeat the Serbs'.[145] Rose's liaison officer, Milos

Stankovic, refers warily to John Menzies, the number two in the US embassy, as 'A man whose only vice was Diet Coke, Menzies was something of a fanatic[al] State Department apostle and an advocate of the wider bombing of the Serbs.'[146] When there was public discussion of American help to extract the UN force in December 1994, one British officer was cited as having pointed to the friendly-fire cases in the desert: 'They'd be a disaster. This isn't the desert. Tell them to go away.'[147] As one former serving soldier told me, these incidents 'are *always* cited as reasons why the Americans cannot be trusted in *any way*'.[148] Indeed, Philip Corwin, a senior American UN civilian official in Sarajevo, himself no friend of the Bosnian cause, noted in his diary in 1995 that 'The Brits, with the notable exception of General Smith, flaunt their anti-Americanism whenever they can.'[149] Even after the war, senior British officers criticized 'the attitude of the Americans and the media', for 'dividing the people into two groups: the goodies and the baddies . . . Just like a western film [with] White Hats and Black Hats.'[150]

One bone of contention was the suspected electronic surveillance of UNPROFOR headquarters by US agencies. Milos Stankovic refers to 'the troglodytes, the American NATO cave-dwellers in the annex. The Hidden Ones. You don't think their forest of antennae and funny boxes were for show, do you?' One of them, he adds indignantly, 'wasn't even US army. He was a Langley [CIA] bloke dressed up as a soldier.'[151] Stankovic consoled himself with the thought that 'It's a huge American weakness, their total and utter reliance on technology. They base everything on electronic emissions – it's their God, but it's their eternal Achilles' heel. They're useless at Humint, human intelligence. That's where the real art is – what you read in someone's eyes, in the catch in their voice, in their nervous mannerisms. Those are the real point-scorers. They had none of it and we had it all and it drove them mad.'[152]

Another source of tension was the alleged American covert supply operation to the Bosnians. Milos Stankovic reports that in February 1995 'the covert landings of large, blacked-out transport aircraft touching down on Tuzla's secondary runways were observed and reported by UN personnel . . . NATO denied that any aircraft had been over Bosnia on either occasion and even sent an American-led "investigation" team over to Bosnia whose line of questioning seemed determined to debunk anything observers had seen. It was a messy, shallow and shabby attempt to conceal what was widely believed to be the covert re-supplying of arms to the Muslims in defiance of the UN embargo.'[153] At least one British officer, Lt.-Col. le Hardy, the Chief of Operations and Intelligence in Sector North-West, became involved in an acrimonious exchange with Americans on this subject. This was the same le Hardy whose father, Wing Commander Tony le Hardy, had directed RAF fighters in support of Tito during the Second World War and later became a forceful advocate of aerial intervention on behalf of the Bosnian government.

This lamentable political anti-Americanism should be seen in perspective. Rose has close family ties to America: in cultural terms, he was no more anti-American than David Owen, who is himself married to an American. It is also true that many American military men – particularly in the army – had 'gone native', were critical of the administration's forward policy on Bosnia, entertained a sneaking regard for the Bosnian Serbs, and sympathized with General Rose.[154] There can be no suggestion that the close military relationship nurtured during the Cold War disintegrated in Bosnia. Nevertheless, it is true that – as Sandhurst insiders told me[155] – the British forces have long despised the Americans for their alleged unwillingness to engage 'on the ground' and for their exaggerated faith in air power. They begrudged the Americans their demonstrably superior technology and level of physical comfort in the field. This budget envy can be seen in Stankovic's panegyric on the British grasp of 'human intelligence', which contrasted with American reliance on 'bristling antennae'; this is perhaps just as well, given that British army radios are obsolete and the SA80 rifle has a tendency to jam.

Like the officials at Whitehall, British diplomats in Washington and at the Security Council in New York, and Lord Owen, Rose made strenuous efforts to 'educate' the Americans. 'I had to educate the Americans,' he subsequently claimed, 'before they understood what the mission in Bosnia was about.'[156] The key to this, of course, was stressing the 'complexity' of the conflict, by obscuring the difference between aggressor and victim. Apart from journalists, Rose's particular targets were visiting senior American military. These would be carefully treated to helicopter flights over areas devastated by one side or the other during the Croat–Bosnian government war, in order to relativize the guilt of the Bosnian Serbs. Rose hit the jackpot during the visit of Admiral Leighton Smith, the Nato CinCSOUTH. A Muslim farmer – paraded in front of the admiral at his request – serendipitously turned out to have served in Paulus's Sixth Army at Stalingrad, and had then – as Stankovic relates – 'proceeded to prove it by throwing up his arm in a Nazi salute and screaming "Heil Hitler! Heil Hitler!" '[157] The effect was so satisfying that Rose later directed General John Galvin, the Supreme Allied Commander in Europe, to the same spot and more salutes.[158] But perhaps his greatest coup was the visit of General Wesley Clark – apparently at Rose's instigation and certainly against the express advice of local US diplomats – to General Mladic, which ended in an embarrassing photograph of the two wearing each other's caps that nearly ended Clark's career.[159] Indeed, far from being 'appalled' at his acceptance of an engraved pistol from Mladic, Clark claims that Rose 'sort of encouraged me to do it'.[160]

Rose's difficulties with the Americans were part of his wider feud with Nato. Foreign Office, Nato, and UN sources all spoke freely of his stand-up rows with the Supreme Allied Commander Europe, General Joulwan. The US ambassador to Nato, Dr Robert Hunter, recalls that 'there were suspicions that the British officers serving with UNPROFOR were doing what they could to frustrate the decision of the Nato council. Whether they did it on their own, or did it under direction from London was not clear.' Indeed, Rose's memoirs are peppered with Natophobic statements which sound extraordinary on the lips of a British general. At first, he merely criticizes 'the need for NATO to "maintain its credibility" ', which meant that 'NATO often seemed to advocate taking disproportionate action against the Serbs, while ignoring violations on the side of the Muslims'.[161] He refers – mildly enough – to his efforts 'in trying to steer NATO and the Americans away from their determination to end the war in Bosnia by bombing the Serbs'.[162] But very soon he is speaking of 'hawks in NATO' who were trying 'to push the peacekeeping operation towards war'.[163] Of the Supreme Allied Commander in Europe, he had this to say: 'Joulwan came across as a bully . . . Joulwan seemed to have difficulty accepting that NATO was in a supporting role to

UNPROFOR in Bosnia and that both were engaged in a mission where there were no enemies or victories.'[164] As Joulwan recalls, Rose's suspicion ran so deep that he tried to pass off Serb heavy weapon emplacements as 'rusted hulks', lest the American should be 'pounding on his desk for air strikes'.[165] Indeed, Rose says straight out that 'given NATO's apparent wish to find an excuse to bomb the Serbs', he 'did [not] altogether trust the organisation'.[166] At the time, Rose was even more scathing in his views. The *New York Times* correspondent Roger Cohen describes Rose as 'barking questions, pouring scorn on what he viewed as America's guilt-ridden attachment to Bosnia's Muslims, [and] muttering about Muslim plots to lure NATO into the war'.[167] In short, Rose's liaison officer, Milos Stankovic, was not exaggerating when he repeatedly referred to an 'insidious dirty stag fight between NATO and the UN'.[168]

Of course, none of this prevented Rose or other British military sources from getting the credit for American or Nato initiatives. T. D. Bridge, writing in the *Army Quarterly and Defence Journal* of January 1995, argues that 'by force of personality Michael Rose arranged a ceasefire which has largely held' in Sarajevo; no mention was made of the Nato ultimatum.[169] Rose himself claimed that 'Whole areas of central Bosnia have been successfully transported from a situation of civil war to one of comparative peace.'[170] The fact that the crucial element was US diplomacy, and that the two sides had been killing each other for more than a year in spite of the presence of British forces, does not seem to have occurred to him. Similarly, Colonel Peter Williams, just back from commanding the First Battalion of the Coldstream Guards in Bosnia, spoke of a 'UN-brokered peace accord' between the Croats and the Bosnian government.[171] And Rose claims that in April 1994 the Nato ultimatum at Gorazde cut across UN efforts to mediate an end to the Serb attacks and thus 'became a problem rather than the supportive measure it was intended to be'.[172]

One of the more bizarre results of the Anglo-American military tension was Rose's cordial relations with the Russians, which mirrored the *entente* at diplomatic level over Bosnia. His closest confidant within the UN civilian bureaucracy was certainly the Russian Viktor Andreev, the same man who had enthusiastically endorsed his plans for a first strike against the Croats. At times, Russian warmth embarrassed even Rose himself. He notes how 'Zotov, the Russian member of the Contact Group, was an old-style Soviet diplomat . . . he kept smiling encouragingly at me, as if I were some kind of fellow-traveller.'[173] In general, Rose tried to play down the significance of Russian involvement. When the historian Mark Almond accused him in the *Daily Mail* of letting the Russians into Europe's backyard to police the Sarajevo ceasefire in February 1994, he responded: 'Perhaps no one had told him that the cold war was over.'[174] But the effect of this riposte was spoiled by other contemporary and subsequent statements. Thus, in May 1995, he claimed that Bosnia 'is in a position where east meets west and it could have turned into a major conflict between major powers had the UN not intervened to contain the situation'.[175] Rose, in fact, was quite happy to don the mantle of the cold warrior when it suited him. Thus he notes that 'Russian positions between the Serb and Bosnian trenches in Sarajevo began to resemble the fortified border between East and West Berlin'; and 'when the [Russian] deputy commander embarked on a long diatribe against the Muslims . . . I cut him short . . . and reminded him that he was attending a peacekeeping conference of the UN, not a meeting of the Soviet Praesidium'.[176]

Throughout the war, British officers professed themselves seriously constrained by their UN mandate. Major Bryan Watters, who served as second in command of the Cheshires in central Bosnia, wrote in 1994 that 'We are powerless under the present mandate to prevent this genocide taking place on a holocaust-like proportion.'[177] Major Vaughan Kent-Payne, who served around Vitez in 1993, writes that 'We did what we could but were constantly hampered by the mandate and the lack of a clear statement of exactly what we were there to do. We did not have the backing, or teeth, to peacekeep and the locals knew this.'[178] Lt.-Col. Jonathan Riley, who commanded the Welch Fusiliers at Gorazde in 1995, wrote in his diary that 'the UN is not in former Yugoslavia to enforce anything'.[179] Rose himself told BBC's *Panorama* that 'We are not under [UN resolutions] 824 and 836 here to protect or defend anything other than our own selves and our own convoys, and of course everyone has a right of self-defence.' (Though not the Bosnian government, apparently.) 'We are here to deter attacks against [safe areas] and that is a very different thing.'[180] 'There is,' he claimed at the height of the Bihac crisis in late 1994, 'a limit to how much force we can use in a peacekeeping mission. We should only use force when there is direct targeting of the civilian population or my own troops in the Bihac pocket.'[181] 'The United Nations,' he cautioned, 'has never said it would defend anything'; and when Bosnian Serb forces transgressed the boundaries of a designated safe area, Rose merely explained that 'There's nothing sacrosanct about that line.'[182] Indeed, he later argued, 'UNPROFOR was never there to protect one party from another. Even though one may be a legitimate sovereign power and the other one may be a renegade regime. That's not what peacekeeping is about. The dangers are that you lose sight of what you are here to do because you are sucked in and you get manipulated by internal and external pressures. Then you lose your mission and cross the "Mogadishu Line" using more force than you should and end up with the sort of disaster we saw in Somalia.'[183] Indeed, American diplomats and military men remember Rose's Venn diagrams on the 'Mogadishu' were received with a blend of hilarity and irritation in Brussels and Sarajevo.[184]

Instead, British officers developed what Rose called 'a new approach to peacekeeping and new concepts of operation . . . a new doctrine of peacekeeping'. What developed was a hybrid between peacekeeping and peace-making, the nonsense of 'Chapter VI½'. However, it was stressed that the forces on the ground were neither peace-makers nor combatants: 'minimum force only can be employed to achieve a specific aim', Rose writes, 'combatancy' should be avoided.[185] It was vital, argued Colonel Peter Williams, commander of First Battalion, Coldstream Guards in Bosnia, to adhere to 'the over-arching principles of impartiality and consent'.[186] For this reason, Colonel Allan Mallinson, the custodian of British army peacekeeping doctrine in 1995, defended the refusal to escalate air strikes at Gorazde in April 1994: 'If the strikes had continued to push back the Serbs the UN would have become a combatant, and a military target.'[187] Once you cross the 'Mogadishu Line', he claimed, 'you are crossing the River Styx, the river of Hades – and you can't get back'. This new orthodoxy was enshrined in Lt.-Col. Charles Dobbie's manual *Wider peacekeeping* in early 1995.

All this may have made sense to the men on the ground at the time, but it was not what the UN resolutions actually said. The UN knows no formal distinction between 'peacekeeping' – or 'wider peacekeeping' – and 'peace-making'; it distinguishes between 'consent' mandates issued under Chapter VI and 'enforcement' mandates issued under Chapter VII of the UN Charter.[188] All the crucial resolutions issued on Bosnia – 757 (May 1992), 770 (August 1992) and 836 (June 1993)[189] – were under Chapter VII. Indeed, they had induced considerable unease from the Chinese representative on the Security Council, who believed resolution 770 'tantamount to issuing a blank cheque'. General George Joulwan felt it was 'a very robust mandate', but that 'their [UNPROFOR's] interpretation of their mission was in many cases different than what was written'.[190] In other words, the men on the ground had the international legal authorization to use military means to force through convoys or deter attacks on the safe areas.[191] Senior British officers were perfectly aware of this, but advanced pragmatic rather than legal reasons for caution. When he was asked why he didn't simply sweep away roadblocks, Rose responded, 'Of course, we could do that. I mean, we could put in APCs or even get the Danish tanks to come in, we could even use . . . air strikes. Of course, it would be totally counter-productive to the overall quality of the mission. It would stop all convoys running throughout the length and breadth of the country.'[192]

Similarly, Lt.-Col. Bob Stewart, who commanded the Cheshires in central Bosnia in late 1992 and early 1993, writes that 'Taken literally we could have simply put a Warrior at the front and back of each UNHCR convoy and tried to escort the column to its destination. Some UN contingents might indeed interpret the mission in that way. It would have been taking the Security Council exactly at its word. But that was not the way either I, or for that matter, my superiors in the British chain of command interpreted what was required. I felt that the mandate must be interpreted in a much more wide-ranging way than that.'[193] Similarly, his successor, Colonel Alistair Duncan, writes that 'Military force is a very blunt instrument . . . For example, if I smashed through a road barrier with a warrior (easy to do), I would not get through the next day. But negotiation through that same barrier could get us through for the next three weeks.'[194] He assumed considerable latitude in the execution of his mandate: 'My task was to provide an escort to the convoys . . . In addition, we were to provide assistance to endangered people as required. That was all. There was no further close direction either from the United Nations or from the British Government or Military. Strange though it may seem, I was quite delighted with that because my hands were entirely free to deal with the problem as I saw fit.'[195]

Indeed, it is significant that when the Defence Secretary, Malcolm Rifkind, visited the Cheshires and asked Stewart whether he 'had any problems with [his] mandate . . . I replied that I had not and explained how I looked at problems in simple terms of whether an action was essentially right or wrong. He agreed with my approach . . . Never again did I concern myself with worries about the mandate.'[196] He was doing the very thing that Rose subsequently described as the general response to the Bosnian war, which was 'to pluck from the often contradictory United Nations Security Council Resolutions (743–990) their *own* mission statement . . . to sustain the people of Bosnia in the midst of three-sided civil war, try and bring about the conditions necessary for a peace agreement and to maintain the conflict within Bosnia'.[197] The apparent confusion when Stewart writes soon after that he 'had no mandate for forcing a passage through regardless' thus resolves itself: Stewart is no longer referring to the UN mandate but his own constructed mandate.

Part of the problem, as Michael Williams recalls, was that 'there isn't much of a mandate, of instruction that is given to the principal civilian officer in the UN mission and the force commander, from the secretariat. The resolutions are passed by the Security Council and then faxed down to the mission in country X, or whatever. Not much guidance is given from New York: in fact quite the opposite. It is left to those on the ground to interpret the implementation of those resolutions. So in fact quite extraordinary leeway and power is given to the individuals on the ground.' It was in no way wrong in principle for British officers to interpret their mandate in a pragmatic way, but they would then have to be judged by results. To hide behind the mandate when criticized – as many of them did – was to have their cake and eat it. It is no wonder that Michael Williams, UNPROFOR Director of Information at Zagreb for most of the second half of the conflict, subsequently spoke of 'a growing rift between UNPROFOR's civilian and military personnel, and between the military and other civilian actors such as NGOs, most of whom believed that the military were not doing enough to implement the operation's mandate'.[198] In any case, just how minimalist and problematic Rose's interpretation of the mandate was is shown by the policy pursued by his successor, Lt.-Gen. Sir Rupert Smith, in 1995 without any new UN mandate. Of this, more later.

In the meantime, what 'wider peacekeeping' and 'keeping within the Mogadishu Line' meant in practice soon became clear. Rose bowed to the Serbs because he felt he had to, and bullied the Bosnians because he thought he could.[199] In the autumn of 1994 he even threatened the Bosnian government forces around Sarajevo with air strikes after blaming them for renewed fighting.[200] The journalist Robert Block noted drily that 'General Rose's threat to the Muslims – while the UN has done little more than condemn the Serbs for the evictions of at least 1000 Muslims across confrontation lines – raises questions over the UN's handling of the conflict'. Rose also tried to highlight Bosnian government violations of the demilitarized zone. Indeed, the largest-scale UN operation to date – ordered by Rose – was the use of armoured vehicles, rockets, and cannon fire in October 1994 to clear hundreds of Bosnian troops off the hills south-west of Sarajevo; NATO had refused to do the job with air power.[201] The gusto with which this operation was executed shocked many observers. One UN official remarked that 'I don't believe there is any precedent for this kind of thing against the Serb side'. 'It's perverse,' a western diplomat argued. 'UNPROFOR knows that the Serbs can and will hit back and hurt them, but that even if the Bosnians can, they won't.'[202]

All this struck Wesley Clark very forcibly. 'You don't know where it is coming from really,' he subsequently observed, 'but it's a sort of moral neutrality in which the UN force is more or less the buffer force and so the logic of it is: . . . the Serbs are shooting at us and they're shooting at the Muslims, there's no point in us shooting back at the Serbs because . . . we've got to have a meeting with them and talk this thing through . . . if we get a war with the Serbs then they're not going to come to our meetings, so then where will we be?' 'When the Serbs pressed hard,' Clark elaborates, 'UNPROFOR said, "Well, you Muslims have to give in, I mean, you're provoking this artillery fire.

Your snipers are up there on the roofs, there shooting, they fired first" . . . so what you had was a case where the weaker party was bullied not only by the stronger party but by UNPROFOR, at least that was their perception. It had to be that way because UNPROFOR wasn't capable of doing much to physically oppose the Serbs.' 'What is interesting,' he concluded, 'is the mentality. Because no matter what the Serbs did it was always provoked by the Muslims.'[203]

Clark was sceptical about Rose's claims to robustness. 'Michael Rose,' he recalls, 'was describing how they'd taken out a sniper, he said: "Look we're being criticized for not returning fire, I want you to know we returned at that building right there." I said, "What did you do?" He said, "There was fire coming, we fired back." I said, "Did you fire one round or what?" He said, "No, we fired several rounds. I can't tell you how many rounds," he said, "but we fired several rounds." I said, "Well, did you go clear the building and sort of run through, get rid of the snipers?" He said, "Oh no, I don't think we did that".' "He was brave enough to shoot back,' Clark adds, 'but not brave enough to go through and do a real close and destroy the enemy.'[204]

By the end of 1994, on the other hand, Rose had virtually given up threatening the Serbs. Even such a sympathetic observer as Patrick Bishop, writing in November of that year, conceded that 'Rose has opposed anything but the most symbolic use of force against Serb transgressions'.[205] This reluctance was graphically illustrated by an embarrassingly humble letter – subsequently leaked – from Rose himself to the Bosnian Serb commander Ratko Mladic during the Bihac crisis. 'I would like to confirm,' he wrote, 'that the UN always regrets the need to use force . . . I fully agree with you that we must, in future, avoid all situations which necessitate the use of force . . . We can only do this through closer liaison and cooperation . . . It is not part of our mission to impose any solution by force of arms. We are neither mandated nor deployed for such a mission . . . These are difficult times for everyone, and we must not allow local tactical-level incidents to undermine the road to peace.'[206] Three weeks later, at the height of the Bihac crisis, the Serbs warned Rose through his liaison officer: 'Don't mess with us . . . Don't f—k with us.'[207] So he didn't.

Rose's many critics highlighted the mismatch between Rose's

rhetoric and performance and the increasing contrast between his appeasement of the Serbs and bullying of the Bosnians. The patience of the Sarajevo government finally snapped in the autumn of 1994, when all eight Bosnian parties, supported by several ministers, called for his resignation.[208] This demand was repeated on the other side of the Atlantic, where Rose's criticisms of the US policy and the Atlantic Alliance caused outrage. In November 1994, Bob Dole spoke of the 'breakdown' of Nato and called for Rose's replacement.[209] William Safire referred to him as 'the reincarnation of Neville Chamberlain',[210] whose 'repugnance at war-making when UN havens become war zones symbolizes Britain's least fine hour'. Anthony Lewis called him 'a symbol of the sellout'.[211] And Charles Forrest, an American liaison officer at the UN Office for the Special Coordinator for Sarajevo, revealed after his resignation in early December 1994 that he had 'heard Rose express contempt for the Bosnians. I believe he felt that Bihac deserved to fall because the Bosnians had dared to launch an attack against the Serbs from the pocket.'[212] Even sympathetic senior American officers described Rose as 'self-serving'.[213] The scale of the disenchantment was proportionate to the extraordinary level of expectation which had accompanied his arrival. 'Who killed Sir Michael Rose?' wondered the famous American columnist Georgie-Anne Geyer.[214] In ten months, as Patrick Bishop wryly observed, Rose's reputation had 'sunk from *preux chevalier* to Eurowimp'.[215]

Rose was also coming under fire in Britain. The BBC journalist Martin Bell – generally a partisan of the 'men on the ground' – observed that 'By the time he left, there was little muscular or robust about the force he led, or his leadership of it.'[216] Criticism within UNPROFOR, particularly the civilian operation, also mounted, fuelled partly by his autocratic style and partly by outrage at his appeasement of the Serbs. 'When he came here,' one UN official observed, 'he was a man of action. But he's learnt very quickly and he's now very sensitive to what his political masters want.'[217] And even in Whitehall, which was the greatest beneficiary of Rose's activities, irritation with his behaviour and high profile was widespread.

Rose himself was aware of and resented these voices. In his memoirs he candidly describes 'the venomous way I treated anyone I thought was obstructing the peace process. On one occasion I accused the head of the UN information service in Zagreb not only of being incapable of doing his job, but also of actively undermining the work of UNPROFOR by repeating Bosnian propaganda'. He also felt that 'civil servants were still pushing the old US line on lift and strike', and that he was 'being targeted by my own side' for causing tension with the Americans.[218] Rose was, in fact, increasingly isolated and under serious strain. 'The only people I felt at ease with,' he admits, 'were my own team and particularly Viktor Andreev, whose familiar cure of iced Vodka and caviar always seemed to make me feel better.'[219]

But perhaps the most serious threat to Rose came from within the British military establishment itself. Some of the irritation was with the personality cult surrounding the general, and there was also annoyance at the way in which Rose had bounced the MoD into the dispatch of more reinforcements.[220] His handling of the Gorazde crisis – too activist for some, too restrained for others – increased anxieties in Whitehall. 'The difficulty,' one official remarked at the time, 'is that Rose is politically isolated and militarily vulnerable. If things get worse, people will want a scapegoat, and he is an obvious choice.'[221] Nor was this unease confined to civilians. The British Chairman of Nato's Military Committee, General Vincent, condemned UNPROFOR for 'going soft' and tolerating unacceptable behaviour by the Bosnian Serbs.[222] Subsequently, Vincent criticized Rose as 'one who did not see . . . the Serbs as the principal offenders', and who 'became less and less willing to use the resources [i.e., air power] that were in theory made available for him to enforce . . . what he was trying to achieve. I don't think he actually came out of it with great credit.'[223] One admiral said that Rose was becoming 'too proprietorial regarding the peace process', and that he had – again – 'gone soft on the Serbs'.[224] Nor was Rose at all reassured when he was told by the Chief of the Defence Staff, Peter Inge, that he 'still had the confidence of everyone back in London'.[225]

The British defence establishment was right to be concerned about the effect of the Bosnian war on the army. Many soldiers were 'Balkanized' and even 'demoralized' by the Bosnian experience. This is illustrated by a revealing anecdote in Major Vaughan Kent-Payne's memoir, *Bosnia warrior*. He describes the scene that greeted him on arrival in the officers' mess of the Cheshires at Vitez, a luridly decorated former disco well away from the perimeter wire. Over a can of Boddington's, he sizes up his surroundings. 'The more I looked,' he writes, 'the more some of them appeared to be decidedly odd. One fellow came up to me and introduced himself as one of the LOs [liaison officers]. He was wearing a pistol in a shoulder holster over the top of his jumper . . . I just couldn't take my eyes off it. It wasn't the fact that I was talking to someone silly enough to parade around the mess wearing a pistol, it was the size of the magazine on the weapon. Normally, the 9 mm Browning takes a thirteen round magazine, which fits snugly into the butt. This guy had a mag which, he proudly told me, held twenty-five rounds and was several centimetres longer than normal. Every time he turned around it bumped against the corner of the bar with an audible clank. However, he was totally oblivious to the fact that he looked a complete prat. He was posing around with this thing with not a word said by anyone. Above all, however, the oddest fact was the huge amount of drink that everyone was consuming.'

Such 'macho' postures – anathema to British army culture – also characterized the court of Sir Michael Rose in the 'Residency' at Sarajevo. It is perhaps no coincidence that his liaison officer confused the commander with his bodyguard.[226] Nor is it accidental that Rose's press officer – Colonel Tim Spicer, who prided himself on being an 'unorthodox soldier' – made a point of wearing his pistol during his briefings. Nor should we be surprised by the casual violence of one of his bodyguards. 'When a civilian parked his car in front of the Residency,' the General writes, 'and refused to move it, after twice being asked to do so, [he] dragged him out of his car and knocked him unconscious.'[227] The verbal – and occasionally physical – coercion which the general himself admits to using on his critics inevitably rubbed off on his surroundings. Eyewitnesses have described the unpleasant and intimidatory atmosphere in Rose's headquarters, sustained by copious amounts of alcohol and indiscriminate obscenities hurled at men and women alike. The overall impression, as Michael Williams later related, was a cross between a third-rate public school and a brothel.[228] 'Rose,' he recalls, 'always seemed to cultivate that. I think part of him thought that it would look better to the press.'[229] In general, the men with whom the General surrounded himself confused their carefully cultivated eccentricities with inner strength, their orientalist babblings with true insight.

Visiting American soldiers were appalled by what they saw. Milos Stankovic describes the scene in his account of Wesley Clark's visit to Sarajevo: 'Clark was quickly ushered into Rose's office . . . Clark's MA and ADC, Pentagon staff officers with field satchels hanging properly from their shoulders, were stiff and subdued, probably shocked by their peculiar surroundings. Jon Ellis (Victor Andreyev's MA) was bellowing down the telephone to someone in Muratovic's office (Bosnian Minister of UN affairs), "This isn't a f——g taxi service!", Carmella (another of Andreyev's staff) was calmly filing (nails not papers), Jean quietly swearing at her computer . . . all presided over by the passably seductive nude over Colonel Daniell's desk. A perfect nuthouse. A somewhat stilted ten minutes passed. The expressions of mild dismay and revulsion on the Americans' faces betrayed their secret thoughts.'[230] Much more worrying than this attractive scene of anarchy, was the simultaneous erosion of warfighting attitudes. When Wesley Clark visited UN positions at Sarajevo he almost flummoxed the French commanding officer by asking him to solve – theoretically – a straightforward military problem. However, it is the response of the British liaison officer Stankovic which is the most revealing: 'Oh that's a bit low. But typical. Fighting's all they know.'[231]

The mismatch between the mandate – as it was interpreted by British officers on the ground – and traditional military tasks was obvious. As Major Kent-Payne writes, 'Our work for the UN in Bosnia was a totally new environment for most of us. We'd trained to kill the Queen's enemies and the tasks we were required to perform were alien to us.'[232] Trained men were forced to sit idly by while ethnic cleansing raged around them, or its detritus was decanted on to their doorsteps. They resented, as one journalist put it, 'being asked to act like superannuated traffic cops', shepherding humanitarian aid.[233] Some of the disappointment and discomfort which servicemen felt at their new tasks is reflected in Cameron Spence's account of his initial briefing. 'In the confusing picture that had developed,' he recalls, 'it was the Serbs who had emerged as the main aggressor. I hoped, therefore, that Phil was about to give us some juicy tasking to take out a local Serb warlord or an arms dump crucial to the Serb war effort.'[234] Instead, much to his disappointment, Spence is assigned the task of mapping the ceasefire lines between the Croats and the Bosnian government. Later, Spence reflects that 'If the objectives were strictly military, we could crack the nut, however tough it was . . . But drop us into a situation where the problems were socio-political, not military, and I began to wonder whether using the SAS was ever going to be the answer.'[235]

Old certainties went by the wayside. Observing the shambles of Gorazde, Cameron Spence hints darkly that he 'felt sure that the flabbiness existed higher up the chain, higher probably than the most senior echelons of the Regiment itself. The SAS had a long history of delivering the impossible. It was also known for looking after its own. The sense I was getting was that nobody was keeping an eye on either of these two vital facets of our past.'[236] But perhaps the classic example of the collapse of good practice was the unprecedented instruction from Sarajevo headquarters to the SAS team in the pocket not to break out but to surrender to the Serbs and allow their release by negotiation.[237] This was so contrary to SAS traditions that Cameron Spence writes, 'I, too, couldn't believe what I was hearing.' Spence elaborates, 'This was not the Regiment I knew. This wasn't the Regiment at all. It was as if I'd slipped into a parallel universe.'[238]

Perhaps the most problematic 'parallel universe', however, was that of the liaison officers. Bosnia, it is sometimes said, was a 'captain's war',[239] in which young officers found themselves thrust into positions of considerable political responsibility. Milos Stankovic, of course, was an extreme case, but some of the phenomena he describes have a wider application. He had, he writes of the Serbs, to 'get into their mentality and into their minds . . . Trouble is, once you're in their minds, they're in yours too.'[240] What this meant is unambiguously spelt out by Stankovic: 'Lying, cheating, deception, manipulation and a belief in the rule of force was the lingua franca of the warring factions. Unless you're able to speak that same language you'll get absolutely nowhere.'[241] Less floridly and less reflectively, Lt.-Col. Alistair Duncan, the commanding officer in central Bosnia during the second half of 1993, effectively described his own Balkanization at the hands of Bosnian commanders. 'I had,' he recalls, 'what was by any standards an extraordinary relationship with them. It became very personal – I would threaten them, I would flatter them, I would embarrass them, I would annoy them, I would cajole them.'[242]

War always involves agonizing choices, but Bosnia inflicted a peculiarly debilitating set of moral quandaries on the British Army. In a typical incident, Lt.-Col. Alistair Duncan of the Prince of Wales Regiment of Yorkshire, shortly after becoming the new commander of the British forces in central Bosnia, suddenly found himself in the media spotlight in June 1993. Following regulations, though perhaps not his own claimed mandate of 'providing assistance to endangered people as required' – he refused sanctuary to nearly a hundred men, women and children who had fled to his base after a Croatian mortar attack. Lower ranks, the press reports, were 'so embarrassed that they apparently defied their officers and crept out to distribute food and blankets to the survivors huddled outside in the early hours'.[243] Indeed, 'One unidentified officer, pushing his hand over a television camera, said: "We are not responsible for the area outside the camp. You are the responsibility of the local authorities. There is nothing I can do".' A nearby captain 'explained that the role of the army was only to escort aid . . . Another kept repeating: "We are here to protect the UNHCR convoys [only]".' It was widely believed that their imagined powerlessness in the face of terrible crimes had psychologically damaging effect on British soldiers; counselling was arranged to deal with this problem.[244]

As we have seen, the resulting frustration was often vented on the Bosnian victims rather than the Serbian aggressors. UNPROFOR soldiers, as one senior American diplomat, who observed British forces in Bosnia throughout most of Rose's tenure, has speculated, suffered from pronounced 'cognitive dissonance'. They were decent men, and brave men, and their natural instinct was to help. They knew what they should do, but felt they couldn't do it. Instead, they accused the Bosnians of 'whingeing' and indeed of self-inflicted wounds, consoling themselves with the thought that the Serbs were at least 'more like an army'. But others were more self-knowing. One British officer, writing home in 1993, wondered 'how we will be judged by history or, closer to home, how my children will regard our role in this genocidal conflict. How did we stand by and watch the systematic destruction of Sarajevo by Serb artillery? Why did we prevaricate while Sarajevo burned?

What did we think while we watched entire communities dispossessed and flee into a cauldron of shellfire to die on the streets of some further besieged village of cold and neglect?'[245]

The fundamental problem was that British soldiers found themselves in the middle of what they had been told to think of, and generally regarded as, 'another man's war'. Since no government minister had tried to explain the British national interest in stopping ethnic cleansing, Rose's bodyguard Goose could be forgiven for regarding 'the situation in Bosnia as something of an incomprehensible joke'.[246] Many officers and men saw the humanitarian action – itself only a palliative – as a worthwhile end; others found it difficult to justify the loss of British life on an internationalist whimsy. One lieutenant commander told me of the words of his rating the moment Yugoslav radar 'locked on' to his vessel during Operation Sharp Guard in the Adriatic: 'I don't want to die for this.'[247] Nick Richardson, the pilot downed over Gorazde, recites a similar exchange on board ship when 'Wren Alexander' asks him, 'What are we doing, sir? What is Bosnia to us? I don't understand, do you?' When Richardson tells her that 'We're part of a force that is trying to prevent a humanitarian tragedy from taking place,' she merely asks, 'Do you believe that, sir?'[248] Later, within the pocket of Gorazde one of the UNMO team suggests surrendering to the Serbs forthwith: 'It's not our b——y war anyway.'[249]

But perhaps the most vivid illustration of this attitude was the speech addressed by the SAS commander in Gorazde to the Bosnian mayor of the town, who had accused him – not unjustly – of planning to leave the enclave. 'Let's pretend for a moment that our positions are reversed,' he says. 'Let's pretend that this is Liverpool, a famous English city, and that an aggressor is on our doorstep, shelling the s——t out of us. Then let's advance this scenario further. Let's say we appeal to you, the Bosnian Muslims, for assistance, because the people of Liverpool are dying and the city is about to be overrun. Would you come to our assistance? Would you?'[250] Given the gravity of his situation, the exasperation of this officer is easy to understand, but his analogy was less of a knock-out argument than he – or the other British witnesses – fondly imagined. The Bosnian mayor might have responded that his country did not have a superb warfighting machine, was not a permanent member of the UN Security Council, was suffering under an arms embargo enforced by the SAS officer's government and that he himself was not a highly trained special forces soldier, but a civilian official in a pocket about to be overrun by rapists and murderers. But because he had a lot of other things to do, the mayor said nothing, turned around and left.

The notion that it was 'not our war', of course, corresponded to the Whitehall agenda and was espoused at the very highest levels in the British Army on the ground. Michael Rose, after all, had accused the Bosnian army at Gorazde of 'wanting us to fight their war for them', though that didn't stop him from supporting an arms embargo designed to prevent the Bosnians from fighting their own war. Less controversially, but equally emphatically, Lt.-Col. Alistair Duncan, the most senior British commander in central Bosnia from mid-1993 onwards, explained that 'I was well aware that the war in Bosnia was not my war. It was someone else's war and I was there to prevent strife if I could, but only where possible.'[251]

Most British officers were not themselves to blame for their predicament. As Major Kent-Payne adds in his account of the gun-toting Cheshire: 'Roy [his companion] and I discussed this and we decided that many of them appeared to have gone barking mad. We reflected that it must be down to poor leadership and that there was no way we would become like that. What a naïve and pretentious sentiment this proved to be.'[252] For, as the rest of the memoir makes clear, it is not the Cheshire Regiment which was responsible for this shambles but the nature of the situation: highly trained and motivated men thrown into the middle of a horrific conflict whose outcome their political masters had forbidden them to change. Similar frustration was voiced by RAF crews policing the no-fly zone over Bosnia. John Nicol left the service after Bosnia because its role there had been a 'joke'. 'We were supposed to be monitoring the no-fly zone,' he recalls. 'But we were being ignored and were left flying around in circles watching helicopters landing and then villages burning and pretending it wasn't happening. Putting our lives at risk so that the politicians back home could make it look like our men and women were doing something.'[253]

When Sir Michael Rose stood down as UNPROFOR commander in late January 1995, he could look back on real achievements in the field of humanitarian relief; and he could be sure of some domestic press adulation of 'the man on the ground'.[254] But the overwhelming impression was of a Balkanized political-military shambles. The new man, General Rupert Smith, the *Telegraph* assured its readers, was 'from the same mould'.[255] Here, however, the newspaper had been let down by its contacts within the services. The two men, as Christopher Bellamy wrote, 'could not have been more different'.[256] This was partly a matter of temperament. Rose corresponded more typically to an 'Elizabethan' type or that of a 'new Brit': physically brave, arrogant, magniloquent, querulous, outspoken, baroque, demonstrative, self-dramatizing, melancholic, and short-tempered. Smith, on the other hand, resembled much more the archetypal nineteenth- or early twentieth-century Briton: outwardly temperate, austere, reserved, forbearing, quietly courageous, and implacable. But the two were also very different types of soldier. Rose, it will be remembered, was largely non-Nato, a veteran of brush-fire wars. In more than thirty years of service, he had spent barely half an hour inside a tank.[257] Smith – who served in Northern Ireland and who had to master the political complexities of the 1979 settlement in Zimbabwe/Rhodesia – was no stranger to 'small wars and insurgencies'.[258] But Smith was *also* an expert in conventional warfare involving large formations, and as a Gulf War commander he had the experience of dealing with Britain's American allies which Rose so fatally lacked.

The departure of Rose, as Michael Williams recalled, led to an almost instantaneous transformation in the culture of the Sarajevo headquarters.[259] 'With the arrival of General Smith,' Stankovic writes, 'it became clear that things were going to change. The Outer Office would become a more recognisable, military body. No more nicknames or first names . . . A new broom was sweeping away the dust of Rose's term from the Outer Office.'[260] 'General Smith,' he continues, 'brought with him a measure of military calm and order. His edict to refer to proper military ranks was symptomatic of a need to change chaos into near-order, at least in the Outer Office and among the Team. It's hardly surprising that the newcomers came in and' – not unlike those fastidious American visitors – 'boggle-eyed, found the remnants of those of us who'd stayed behind close to a state which they referred to as "out of control".' Indeed, Stankovic's account – which for all its bravado is highly self-knowing – is so revealing about the strange, almost demented, atmosphere in Rose's court at Sarajevo that the rest of the passage is worth quoting extensively: 'If we'd been out of control it's simply because there'd been little or no control exerted.' Under Smith, on the other hand, 'The wilder excesses of the Old Order and its collective behaviour had all but disappeared . . . although the situation was deteriorating, there reigned a thoughtful calmness which took a longer view, and was less knee-jerk and less driven by immediate crises . . . The New Order brought in military sensibility' – by which he presumably means sensible military practice – 'and ousted the ghosts of an ego-driven cult of the personality, during which we'd become lackeys: unquestioningly, unthinkingly, spaniel-like, pursuing every order and instruction, however absurd – zealots all, driven by a mesmerising, masochistic and self-flagellating fascination with the personality. In many respects we'd become an extension of that ego, aping its ways, accepting as perfectly normal behaviour what was not just unorthodox but, worse still, beyond orthodoxy itself.' (Whatever that may mean.) '. . . In a perverse and nostalgic way I missed the abuse. I was adrift. Being treated normally came as an immeasurable shock. I don't think I ever really got used to it, which put me at loggerheads with the New Order. I suppose the only way to explain what happened to us collectively out there is to suggest that every war throws up its very own Kurtz. Bosnia's and ours had been the Old Order. When it departed it took with it, and, in part, left behind, the tattered vestiges of what amounted to near-pagan ideology. Small wonder then that outsiders peering in through the looking glass were aghast at what they found in Bosnia's heart of darkness – Horror! The horror! . . . of our mad souls.' Enough said.

What effect the new man would have on the political situation was not at all clear. As Assistant Chief of the Defence Staff (Operations) in London since 1992, he had had plenty of time to form a view of the conflict. But unlike Rose, he preferred to bide his time and keep his own counsel. Nobody yet knew – indeed Smith did not know yet himself – just what a decisive effect this general was to have on the course of the war.

The Bosnian war was a huge missed opportunity for the British army. Prior to 1995, tens of thousands of highly skilled and experienced soldiers were wasted on essentially alien humanitarian tasks. They were forced to negotiate with murderers and rapists, and they were often put in moral quandaries more terrible than those common to conventional warfare: their morale and warfighting capacity decayed correspondingly. This was primarily the fault of the politicians who had sent them there. But the men on the ground were in some ways complicit in this process: their preoccupation with local factors reinforced the doctrines of moral equivalence emanating from Whitehall; and they both underestimated the potential of air power and exaggerated the fighting strength of the Bosnian Serb army. They came to exemplify a 'can't do' attitude. At the time and for long afterwards, this puzzled many, since the reversal of ethnic cleansing could have been construed as a welcome new task for the services after the end of the Cold War.

In fact, senior military men were alert to the possibilities of Bosnia. Sandhurst insiders have spoken of the high level of bitterness and disillusionment among men returning with their heads held high from the Gulf in 1991–2, only to find that their regiments were being abolished or amalgamated. They did not believe the Bosnian Serbs could be defeated; and for obvious reasons they had little use for an American-style 'lift and strike' strategy, which did not involve them. A manpower-intensive humanitarian operation, on the other hand, was an ideal way of staying the axe. It both saved cap-badges and – it was thought – avoided a quagmire. As the columnist Boris Johnson observed in one of his few astute comments on Bosnia: 'The concept of peacekeeping has replaced deterrence as the central justification for the £25 billion of our money that is still spent on the Armed Forces . . . If you go to the Ministry of Defence, all discussion circles proudly back to Bosnia . . . At £186 million for the financial year 1994–1995, and a further £400 million for the new deployment, the UNPROFOR mission is a vast Keynesian employment scheme. That is why it is so important to maintain a peacekeeping operation, when there is no peace to keep.'[261] This agenda chimed neatly with that of Glynne Evans' UN Department at the FCO, which sought a new global role for the British Army in peacekeeping.[262] This strategy was not unsuccessful: one of the triumphs which Bob Stewart records in his memoirs was the abandonment of the proposal to amalgamate the

Cheshires with the Staffordshire Regiment.[263] And it was certainly a subtext of Rose's constant demands for reinforcements that the number of redundancy notices – many of them being issued to soldiers serving in Bosnia – should be reduced.[264]

More than a dozen British soldiers died in Bosnia, and hundreds of others were injured, some seriously. They ensured the passage of aid, saved lives, and temporarily delayed the deaths of many more. They reflected credit on themselves, their regiments and their country through many acts of kindness and courage. But their overall role was baleful. Their very presence provided Whitehall with a figleaf to conceal its politico-military unwillingness to confront Bosnian Serb aggression. Even more seriously, the 'men on the ground' – who were highly vulnerable to Serb reprisals – became the strongest argument against the American strategy of 'lift and strike', or the move to the enforcement of the UN mandate. It is certainly a terrible irony that the most decisive British military move of the war was the rapid extraction of the Royal Welch Fusiliers – potential hostages – from Gorazde in August 1995. This finally allowed Nato to launch the massive air strikes which the Americans had always argued would help to bring the Bosnian Serbs to the negotiating table.[265] Lt.-Col. Alistair Duncan was thus rather too quick to claim that British troops 'got the job done';[266] they got in the way, which is not quite the same thing.

CHAPTER 6

# The Hour of the Experts

From the beginning of the Bosnian war, the British government was adamant that military intervention on the side of the Sarajevo government would not succeed without a massive commitment of ground forces and the likelihood of heavy casualties. It was equally insistent that the use of air power and the arming and training of the Bosnian forces would not suffice to reverse, or even stem, the Serb tide. In November 1992, for example, the Defence Secretary, Malcolm Rifkind, warned that a military solution in Bosnia would involve 'hundreds of thousands of troops . . . the probability if not the certainty of very large casualties . . . a massive commitment of a kind the world has not seen before'.[1] Shortly afterwards, he spoke of the 'ability of the inhabitants of Bosnia of all backgrounds to indulge in guerrilla war. We are conscious that these are tough people who have a strong tradition of fighting skills.'[2]

When challenged on their policy, government figures invoked expert advice. 'Clear military advice received by the Government,' Malcolm Rifkind told the Commons in April 1993 at the height of the first Srebrenica crisis, 'is that air strikes unsupported by substantial numbers of troops on the ground would be unlikely to be effective given the nature of the conflict, the weapons deployed and the terrain'; he also pointed out that air strikes on their own had not worked in the Gulf.[3] In February 1994, Alistair Goodlad, the Minister of State at the Foreign Office, said that 'Military commanders, whether in NATO, the United Nations or the United Kingdom, have consistently advised that a generalised policy of strategic air strikes would not end the war. It could make the situation worse by bringing the United Nations into the conflict and disrupting humanitarian relief . . . It has not hitherto been military advice that air strikes would help the situation.'[4] The following day, Malcolm Rifkind rebuffed a call for air strikes on the grounds that the 'suggestion goes against all military advice and military common sense'.[5] Not long afterwards, Douglas Hurd claimed that 'When an historian looks at the archives, he will find over and over again that the possibilities of military action were considered not just by us, but by the allies. He will find the advice which we received.' Hurd spoke of the 'responsibility which falls on those who neglect . . . advice and who set off on enterprises to gain applause without a proper judgement of the consequences. That is why, in all our discussions in different places – particularly during the past few days – we have put the emphasis on the need for military advice.'[6]

Subsequently, both the Prime Minister and the Foreign Secretary were to reiterate this emphasis on the importance of expert military advice for the decisions over Bosnia. In his autobiography, John Major writes of the six-hour emergency meeting in the COBRA Room beneath Downing Street in August 1992. At that meeting, he had asked his Chiefs of Staff the number of troops needed to keep the three warring parties apart. The answer was some 400,000; more than double the size of the British army.[7] In April 1993 he asked them whether bombing could be used in the defence of civilians, but was told that it was more or less ruled out both by Bosnia's climate and geography and by difficulties in defining clear targets.[8] Similarly, Douglas Hurd later claimed that 'there was never a moment when in my view or the view of my colleagues . . . it was feasible to support the imposition of any particular peace plan by force on the warring combatants. I choose my words carefully, because when you consider these things, you have military advice: military advice was always extremely cautious.'[9] Two years later, well after the war, he wrote that 'If the firm and rapid use of military force would have stopped the fighting we would have agreed it . . . But professional advice allied to common sense repeatedly indicated that this was a hallucination.'[10] This theme – 'military advice was against it' – was also a constant refrain in my interviews. In short, Douglas Hurd, Malcolm Rifkind, and John Major all hid and still hide behind the experts. At times it seemed as if British policy was being made not by the politicians, but by the experts.

Unfortunately, this author has no access to the archives – for good reasons these are closed for thirty years, perhaps longer – and is unable to follow Hurd's injunction to examine the mountain of expert advice contained therein. Formal enquiries to the Foreign Office were met with informal discouragement. One way around this – *faute de mieux* – is to infer this advice from actions and statements, and from contemporary briefings. This is, however, risky, not least because it is unclear exactly what question the Chiefs of Staff were asked at what point. With expert military advice, as one British officer told me, 'a lot depends on how the question is phrased'. But what one can already say at this stage is that if the Chiefs of Staff believed that there was a viable and reasonably uncostly strategy for the defeat of the Bosnian Serbs, they kept quiet about it in public, and allowed the politicians to suggest otherwise.

We know even less about the role played by the intelligence services during the Bosnian war. This is in marked contrast to the situation in the United States, where the role of the CIA was widely discussed at the time, and subsequently became the object of press attention and Congressional scrutiny. It is now clear that the CIA accurately predicted the collapse of the Yugoslav federation, obtained satellite and other intelligence on Bosnian Serb atrocities long before they became public, and assisted or tolerated a covert campaign to arm and train the Croat and Bosnian armies.[11] We also know that US military intelligence – which, as General Wesley Clark relates, was heavily Serbophile[12] – generally forecast that western intervention would fail to contain the Serbs and merely inflame the situation; that Croatian attempts to retake the Krajina would be militarily repulsed; and that, in any case, a successful Croat–Bosnian offensive would probably bring the regular Yugoslav army back into the war.[13] Whether GCHQ, SIS (MI6) or DIS possessed comparable information and made similar misjudgements is not known to the author and must remain the subject of another book. If the recollection of the renegade agent Richard Tomlinson is a reliable guide – and there is no reason to believe that it is – then the picture for MI6, at least, is vaguely reassuring. Any service which plots the assassination of Slobodan Milosevic and which allows its field officers to recycle Bosnian government propaganda cannot be all bad.[14]

We do know what the Defence Intelligence Staff (DIS) was prepared to place in the public domain. Its unclassified briefings on Bosnia give some indication of expert advice on the effects of the arms embargo. In an annex to its 'background' paper of June 1994, it noted that 'Serbia, Montenegro and the Serb-occupied parts of Bosnia and Croatia possessed substantial stocks of weaponry from the former Yugoslav army. Moreover, Serbia has the industrial capacity to produce the majority of the Serbs' arms requirements. The embargo has thus only had a limiting [sic] effect on them.' It is striking that the briefing made no mention of Russian arms supplies as a factor. On the other hand, it stressed that 'The arms embargo has been most "successful" [sic] in preventing virtually all heavy weaponry from reaching the mainly Muslim Bosnian government. The main effect of the embargo has been to ensure the military weakness of the RBH [Republic of Bosnia-Herzegovina] compared with the Croats and Serbs in the Bosnian war.' Only after the (US-brokered) Bosnian Federation Agreement of 1994, the paper concludes, did the Sarajevo government begin to receive arms through Croatia.[15] Interestingly, in the virtually identical section in the DIS update of February 1995, the sarcastically quoted 'successful' had been dropped.[16]

In other respects, however, the DIS and other military briefings were notable for their inadequacy. For example, even the accompanying caveats cannot dispel the amateur, almost 'orientalist' generalizations in Annex A of 'Background briefs Yugoslavia', which were 'based on the lengthy personal experience of those who have lived and worked in the region, and who continue to visit'. 'The Serbs,' we are told, 'are assertive and resilient. They can be moody, unreliable, devious and untrustworthy. They are quick to take offence, bear grudges with relish and prefer revenge to sainthood – as a Serb saying has it. They have a tendency to idleness. They can be brutal and cruel – as the last two years have shown – yet at other times warm-hearted and incorrigibly romantic; passionate and compassionate. They would not see themselves as particularly sophisticated.' 'The Croats,' on the other hand, 'are more sophisticated, self-possessed and urbane. They are individuals and slightly suspicious of the motivations of others. Their ability to deceive is more accomplished than that of the Serbs.' The Muslims, interestingly, rate the shortest and mildest entry in the DIS briefing: 'The Serbs and Croats together consider the Muslims as second class citizens, untrustworthy, conspiratorial and disloyal to the extent that they are labelled as traitors for having converted to Islam under Ottoman pressure. The Bosnian Muslims are Europeans first and Muslims second, although the conflict is increasingly changing this.'[17] If taken seriously, such briefings might explain the attitudes which soldiers brought to the war zone.

Indeed, many of the soldiers going out to Bosnia complained about the level of briefing received. Sir Michael Rose, for example, describes how he 'spent the fourth day of [his] final week before going to Bosnia in the Ministry of Defence in London, which I remember more for the general messages of goodwill than for any specific instructions or advice, let alone intelligence, about the warring parties.'[18] Perhaps this was just as well, because the fuller the briefing, the more likely it was that misconceptions and relativizations would creep in. The way in which the former SAS sergeant Cameron Spence describes his briefings is highly instructive. His initial sympathies had been very much on the Bosnian government side. The impact of his briefing was correspondingly greater: 'There was a hell of a lot to learn,' Spence wrote subsequently. 'We listened up.' He came away with the overwhelming impression that 'the former Yugoslavia was totally screwed up and always had been . . . The various factions had been killing each other since the dawn of the day of time. Like clinical madness, it was in the genes.'[19] Not for the first time, official sources had succeeded in sowing confusion and doubt where there had previously been a clarity that was much closer to the truth.

Moreover, the briefings dwelt at length on the history of the Second World War, often imperfectly understood. This is illustrated by the following passage from Spence: 'During the Second World War, I remembered from our int[elligence] briefs, the Croatians had done things that had even unsettled their allies, the Nazis . . . They started with the Serbs, moved on to the Jews (to please the Nazis), then set about the Communists. Finally, it became the turn of the Greek Orthodox Christians [sic]. The Ustasha or Croat secret police, made the burning of churches, complete with their congregations, a speciality. And – in a telling indication that nothing much had changed over the past half-century – their unlikely bedfellows in all of this? None other than the Muslims, who were also supported by the Germans in the collective fight against the mostly Communist Serbs [sic].'[20] What matters here are not so much the errors produced by Spence's own recollection, as the distortions and omissions which clearly characterized the original briefing. Judging from my own conversations with British officers, Spence's experience was by no means unusual.

Part of the problem was the unpreparedness of such centres as Sandhurst during a period of post-Cold War disorientation and spending cuts. It is common knowledge in military education circles that when the Major government took the decision to intervene in Bosnia, British military education was approaching a nadir. The certainties of the Cold War had reduced 'education' to instruction, employing lists of principles and templates. Indeed, the academic departments at Sandhurst narrowly avoided being abolished in early 1991. The army which went into the Balkans in 1992 was singularly ill-prepared for such an operation. Insofar as expertise did exist, I was told, it tended to see the region within a Serbophile, anti-German, and essentially Second World War paradigm.

The lack of sensitivity in official circles to Serbophile propaganda was demonstrated by the case of John Zametica, a Yugoslav-born British resident of mixed German and Muslim parentage. Despite his background – he was born 'Omar' – Zametica was a pro-Serb historian and Balkan security analyst, who for some time lectured in European security at the University of Westminster.[21] This did not stop the army from employing him as an 'independent expert' on training courses long after the start of hostilities.[22] Nor did it stop the *Independent* from describing his pamphlet 'The Yugoslav conflict', published by the International Institute for Strategic Studies in mid-1992 – which dismissed plans for military intervention as the preserve of a few 'hotheads' – as 'authoritative'. Even more worryingly, some of his views were 'endorsed . . . by defence sources'.[23] Sir Michael Rose, whose liaison officer was later to be at the receiving end of some unscholarly language from him, says that Zametica had 'written a perceptive paper on the history of the Balkans for the International Institute for Strategic Studies in London'.[24] He later came out as 'Jovan' Zametica, an advisor to the Bosnian Serb leader Radovan Karadzic; he has since disappeared from public view.

*

We are on safer ground with arguments made by experts in the public domain. Take, for example, the prestigious International Institute for Strategic Studies. In February 1993 its Deputy Director, Colonel Michael Dewar, penned an influential article entitled 'Intervention – the case against'. At the outset he insisted – reasonably enough – that 'difficult political decisions cannot . . . be taken on the basis of emotion. They can only ever be taken on the basis of more coldly calculated criteria. Will a given response – for example, military intervention – work? Is it in European and/or British interests to intervene? Is a vital interest involved? Is military intervention legal? What cost, in particular in this case in terms of British lives, is politically and morally acceptable?' So far, so good, although he then adds a little unnecessarily that 'it is easy for those of us who do not have to take these complex and difficult decisions to take a high moral tone. The reality is often very different.'

What then, according to Michael Dewar, was the reality? He condemned the 'siren voices' calling for a military intervention which would only cause 'more deaths and increased misery for the survivors'. There was, he argued, a limit to what outside forces could do. And although a military victory 'of sorts' could be won, he asks, 'at what cost?' Given all its other commitments, 'Britain is in no shape to provide anything but a token force of a few thousand troops'. 'Although it is difficult to make precise estimates as to what force levels would be required to undertake effective military intervention in Bosnia,' he continues, 'the defeat of the Serbian militias in Bosnia and the subsequent military occupation of Bosnia and Hercegovina would require something in the order of 500,000 men. It would have to be assumed that regular Serbian forces would also be involved in hostilities. But it is not so much the defeat of all opposition that would be the most manpower-consuming; rather the subsequent peace-enforcement exercise throughout the whole of Bosnia in every city, town and village. And that is assuming Serbia [proper] remained neutral.' He did not say how many troops it would take to defeat Greater Serbia, but, extrapolating from the Bosnian case, he must have had a truly astronomical figure in mind. It is not hard to see why he concluded – somewhat sinisterly – with the injunction 'to ease the passage of history, not to try and reverse it'.[25]

Three months later, Dewar addressed himself to the question of the arms embargo. This, he told the *Guardian*, was the only issue on which he agreed with Margaret Thatcher, 'In fact, I suggested that as an option six months ago. A sovereign nation recognised as such should have the right to defend itself, and we have got to the stage where we should lift the arms embargo. I believe a level killing field is better than a bumpy one. We should think in terms of arming the Bosnians, if necessary with defensive weapons, in order to salve our consciences. One would hope that international opinion could be persuaded and it could be done within the bounds of the UN. If the Russians were completely intransigent I would recommend governments to ignore their veto.'[26] But within five days Dewar seemed to have got cold feet. He conceded that the Bosnians were 'presently [sic] at a serious disadvantage having virtually no heavy weapons'; and he still accepted that 'the provision of arms to the Muslims, despite the risks, is probably the most militarily efficient way to prevent further Serb aggression'. 'However,' he argued, 'Russia would be most unlikely to agree to a reversal of the UN arms embargo; even if it did, it would take time to supply enough arms to make a difference and more to train the recipients how to use them. Arguably it would encourage the Serbs to seek more arms, though they already have more than they need.' There then followed the routine warnings of UN withdrawals and widening conflicts. 'Unfortunately,' Dewar concluded, 'there are no effective military solutions to the Bosnian crisis. Studied indifference is, of course, another possibility . . . Doing nothing might allow a "natural" solution to emerge more quickly.' Indeed, 'perhaps the unpalatable truth is that when a people are determined to fight each other there is precious little that the outside world can do to help'.[27]

These words were not those of a remote academic or organizational apparatchik, but of a distinguished soldier with a string of respected publications on modern warfare to his name. After service as Commanding Officer of the Royal Green Jackets, Dewar had been Chief of Operations of 1 (British) Corps in Germany, before becoming Deputy Director of the International Institute for Strategic Studies. An expert in low-intensity warfare and counter-insurgency, his better-known books were *Brush fire wars* (1984), *The British army in Northern Ireland* (1985), and *Defence of the nation* (1989). One would naturally assume that he knew what he was talking about.

The notion that Serbian partisan warfare would prove an insuperable obstacle to western military intervention was elaborated in some detail by Charles Dick, lecturer at the Royal Military Academy at Sandhurst, in December 1992. Unlike many commentators, he rightly discounted any threat of involvement by the rump Yugoslav army in Serbia proper. Instead, he predicted that 'The Serbs will be prepared to defend their gains, seen by them as their rightful homeland, through partisan warfare of indefinite duration.'[28] Indeed, 'The will of Yugoslavia, and of the ethnic Serbs outside its borders, should not be underestimated . . . the Serbs are a warlike, intensely nationalistic people easily mobilised and persuaded to endure great hardships and casualties to resist what they see as unjustified aggression against their homelands. The pain threshold of the Serbs is very high, and even the sort of destruction visited on Iraq is unlikely to do other than unite the people and stiffen resolve.'[29] There then followed a detailed account of how the guerillas would benefit from secure resupply in Serbia and Montenegro, as well as from Russian, Romanian, Ukrainian and Greek benevolence; of how – using plans and training from Titoist times – they would be ubiquitous in harassing refugees and western soldiers, exploiting mountainous terrain. Finally, Dick warned of the 'possible sparking off a general Balkan war and a spate of terrorist attacks on the interventionist's homeland'.[30] All this was garnished with confident generalizations about national character and Serb resilience. 'The Slavic nationalities of former Yugoslavia,' Dick claimed, 'are tribal societies, governed more by their emotions than their intellects.'[31]

Slightly less dire predictions of Serb partisan prowess and of the limitations of air power were made by other experts. Paul Beaver, the editor of *Jane's Defence Weekly*, argued in October 1992 that 'There are no standard military solutions. You can't bomb Serbian gun positions because you don't know where they are.' He also called to mind the Second World War, when 'The German army had 60 [sic] divisions tied down in Yugoslavia from 1943 to 1945.'[32] Similar objections were put forward in the *International Defense Review*, where Rupert Pengelley claimed in late 1992 that 'There are no targets of substance for aircraft to hit, since guerillas don't deploy in tidy lines, they do not often mass, and the existence of so many factions among the combatants implies that there is in reality no command chain to demolish.'[33] Brigadier Michael Harbottle – the Director of the Centre for International Peace-building at Chipping Norton and erstwhile Chief of Staff of the UN peacekeeping force in Cyprus 1966–8 – wrote that 'If one draws on the German army's failure in the Second World War to subdue the partisans, divided as they were, it is difficult to believe that a mixed UN force would be any more successful at overcoming the opposition in Bosnia today. It is certainly improbable that such a military intervention would deter the Serbian forces.'[34] The retired Air Chief Marshal Sir Michael Armitage even believed that between 500,000 and 1 million troops would be needed to stop the fighting.[35]

A similarly cautious note was sounded by John Keegan, the respected defence correspondent of the *Daily Telegraph*, formerly senior lecturer in military history at Sandhurst. For much of the war, he echoed the widespread belief in the warrior qualities of the present-day Serbs and their proficiency in guerilla warfare. In August 1993 Keegan dismissed the notion that the credible threat of massive air strikes would bring the ethnic cleansers to heel. 'The Serbs,' he wrote, 'have given evidence of being very tough-minded indeed. They glory in their episodes of national suffering – the death march to Corfu in 1915, the internal war of 1941–1944, when half a million of them died. They are suffering now, both in Serbia proper, where sanctions have brought down the economy, and in Serbian Bosnia, where their young men are dying. An unused threat seems unlikely to shift them.' Keegan – whose politico-military stance on the problem remained ambivalent until coming down firmly on the side of military intervention in 1995 – was not dogmatically opposed to confronting the Bosnian Serbs. But at this stage he insisted that nothing short of either a punitive attack by ground forces on the besiegers of Sarajevo, or a Gulf War-style demolition of Serbia's infrastructure, would do the trick.[36]

Keegan was sceptical of the idea of a full-scale ground war. 'Some estimates,' he argued – presumably referring to Dewar's calculations – 'of the numbers required go as high as 500,000.' Moreover, 'Even if the Bosnian Serbs prove a paper tiger, as some think, they would not melt away when beaten but almost certainly revert to the partisan tactics at which they have an historic expertise. Bosnia would then become a giant Ulster.'[37] He returned to this theme ten months later when he remarked that 'If a hundred IRA men can require Crossmaglen to be re-supplied by helicopter, imagine what thousands of Serb "fighters" could achieve.'[38]

He resolutely rejected the American-sponsored scheme of 'lift and strike'. An unsupported Nato air attack would simply lead to the concealment of Serb guns, the killing of forward air controllers, direct attacks on the UN, and assaults on the safe areas, which would 'heighten the conflict to no one's advantage but the Serbs'.[39] 'Air strikes on the Sarajevo hillsides,' Keegan wrote in February 1994, 'will make magnificent television but, even with precision weapons, are unlikely to end the torment of the city below . . . Not only will the surviving artillery be relocated,' he assured us, 'but the Serbs have simply got better as the war has dragged on. The best training for war is war, and the Serbs, like the rest of the combatants, have now had 18 months' intensive practice. If they were ever a soft option, they have ceased to be one.'[40] Indeed, Keegan expressed himself almost apocalyptically about the consequences of Nato's decision. 'The military prospect,' he wrote, 'is dark. The omens are horribly reminiscent of the time before the United States took the decision for "limited" intervention in Vietnam . . . the probability is that, against its members' better judgment and with no real will for the fray, NATO, as the UN's agent, is now about to do something. Past indulgence in empty threats has driven it to this extremity. What a calamity. Why did no one remember that, if people choose to fight a civil war [sic], it is almost impossible to stop them?'[41]

Nor did the success of the ultimatum change Keegan's mind. 'Heavier air strikes,' he argued later that year, 'would make things worse. Delivered at the outset, they might have taught the Serbs a lesson. Now they are likely to be both provocative and ineffective. The Germans defended Italy, similar terrain, for two years in 1944–45 under the flail of allied air power. It budged them from their chosen positions not at all. In Bosnia, air strikes merely provoke the Serbs to take UNPROFOR troops hostage.'[42]

He also would not hear of lifting the arms embargo. 'This,' he wrote in April 1993, 'is the cry of the moment. It promises to be as disastrous as it has always looked.' The result, Keegan claimed, would be that

'The Muslims, had they any military sense, would use heavy weapons not merely in defence but to open up fronts where the Bosnian Serbs are weak, particularly in the north-west. The war would widen, perhaps drawing in Serbia itself. A geographically limited horror would become a genuine Yugoslav civil war, far more terrible than anything yet seen.'[43] He later expanded his objections in one of the odder arguments advanced by any military expert during the war. 'The battle lines,' he wrote in early December 1994, 'have not shifted since the war began two years ago. The Serbs, who have heavy weapons, have not succeeded in capturing more territory with them.' The inference that the Serb failure to break the deadlock proved the redundance of heavy weapons ran counter to the generally accepted, and correct, view that the only reason for the initial Serb gains, and their ability to hold on to them, was their monopoly on heavy weapons. It also co-existed uneasily with Keegan's earlier fears that the Bosnians would be successful in setting up new fronts with their new weapons. Even more eccentrically, Keegan added that 'Giving heavy weapons to the Bosnian government forces would not alter the balance to their advantage. It would merely make for heavier fighting, and more suffering, on the lines that have been drawn. It might actually work to the Serbs' advantage. They are better fighters and are more than capable of capturing the weapons that the lifting of the embargo would put into Bosnian government hands.'[44]

Underlying Keegan's view was his 'anthropologization' of the war, which he expounded on a number of occasions. 'The war,' he argued, 'is understood by no-one – perhaps not even by the Bosnian Serbs themselves – and defies comprehension in conventional terms . . . In so far as it can be given a name, it is a primitive tribal conflict, of a sort known only to a handful of anthropologists.' The various Bosnian Serb transgressions, such as territorial displacement and, of course, mass rape 'might be taken from a field report on the Yanomano, one of the [most] primitive and savage tribes known'.[45] Indeed, in his 400-page *History of warfare*, penned in 1994 as the war raged, Bosnia merited only a short and slighting reference along the same lines: 'The peoples of former Yugoslavia whom Tito sought to unite [are] bloodying their hands against each other in a struggle reminiscent of nothing so much as the "territorial displacement" anthropologists identify as the underlying logic of much "primitive" warfare in tribal society.'[46]

The notion that there were 'no front lines' in Bosnia and that Bosnia was not really a war at all, and certainly not a winnable one, recurs in the rhetoric of anti-interventionists. It was most succinctly and trenchantly stated by the Prime Minister himself in a letter to David Owen in August 1992, when the war was still largely a two-way fight between the Bosnian Croats and the Bosnian government on the one side and Serbs on the other. 'We are not dealing with an orthodox war,' John Major wrote, 'a single enemy, a front line, or clearly identifiable targets.'[47] 'Because of [the] patchwork quilt of peoples,' Michael Dewar wrote in early 1993, 'there is no simple front line but rather a complex pattern of conflict for the control of individual towns, villages and even fields. An international force attempting to stop the fighting would have to separate feuding factions [sic] all over the country and negotiate with, or impose a military defeat on, numerous local militia commanders whose control over his own men is often incomplete.'[48] Similarly, Brigadier Graham Messervy-Whiting, military advisor to Lord Owen at Geneva, wrote in 1994 of the 'essentially tribal nature of the campaigns; the resultant importance of particular *opstinas*, particular villages and particular local military leaders, often under very loose central control'.[49]

This general impression of bewildering military complexity and fragmentation was often supported by the 'men on the ground'. 'The differentiation between military and civilian is impossible,' Colonel Bob Stewart wrote in 1993. 'Bosnia is undergoing a classic civil war, fought by civilians against civilians. A civilian one minute is a soldier the next.'[50] This, of course, is true of all wars fought, as most European twentieth-century wars have been, by conscript armies. The waters were muddied in a different way by his successor, Colonel Alistair Duncan, who claimed that 'on the ground things were not quite so clearly defined. Of the three groups – Serb, Muslim, or Croat – at any stage in time or in any area of Bosnia two of them could be allied against the third. In addition, alliances could change overnight. There is no logic.'[51]

To a considerable extent, the defence correspondents of national broadsheets, whether in London or on assignment in Bosnia, appeared to take their cue from Whitehall, the experts, and the military. For the most part, they too systematically minimized the chances of successful military intervention against the Bosnian Serbs.[52] They were particularly scathing about American demands for air strikes. The *Sunday Telegraph*'s Christy Campbell feared that one might be 'blundering towards a big new European conflict – pushed this time by an ill-thought through American plan for an air war in Bosnia'.[53] 'Nobody,' he added, 'ever surrendered to a bomber circling at 2,000 feet'[54] (until Milosevic did in 1999). Similarly, Andrew Hogg in the *Sunday Times* stressed 'the limitations of war from the air in this mountainous region' and claimed there were so 'few targets that present a realistic chance of success to allied aircraft' that 'military analysts' were sceptical of 'selective bombing' of Serb supply routes. Indeed, 'inside their labyrinthine tunnels, it is believed that the Serbs possess enough fire-power and ammunition to wage war for another two or three years . . . Row upon row of the Serbs' 600 tanks are hidden in the bowels of the mountains. They are safe from even a nuclear strike.' Moreover, the five Bosnian Serb corps headquarters were not only well fortified, but mutually independent: 'A successful attack on any one of them would be unlikely to disrupt matters in the field. Military power in Bosnia long ago devolved to local commanders.'[55]

Christopher Bellamy of the *Independent* was no less discouraging when – basing his estimates on official briefings – he calculated that 100,000 men would be needed just to secure the opening of a land corridor from Split to Sarajevo, plus another 50,000 men solely to ensure the safety of the Bosnian capital.[56] He was also sceptical of lifting the arms embargo. The use of multiple rocket-launchers on both sides in central Bosnia, he argued, 'cast doubt on the view that the Muslims lack heavy weapons'; moreover, while 'anyone able to read a map and use a compass should be able to direct artillery fire', he queried whether the Bosnians would 'be able to exploit more sophisticated methods of seeking targets: artillery- and mortar-locating radars, for example'. In any case, he concluded, even if the arms embargo were lifted, there still remained severe practical problems in supplying the Bosnian forces.[57] Two years later, Bellamy warned that 'Even if the UN arms embargo were now lifted and supplies of heavy weapons brought in, it would take months for the

BIH to learn the complex techniques of "combined arms warfare".'[58] In the meantime, it was feared, the Bosnian Serbs might overrun the eastern enclaves in a last push. Indeed, Bellamy advanced the legendary commander of Srebrenica, Naser Oric, in support of this argument in late May 1995. 'If you lift the arms embargo', he was quoted as telling a UN commander, 'we die. Sixty thousand of us (the population of the enclave) will die.'[59] Less than six weeks later, with the arms embargo still firmly in place, 7,000 of them were to die anyway.

The influence of the 'men on the ground' on the defence correspondents was pervasive. Even such critical observers as Bellamy were sometimes sucked into the orbit of Sir Michael Rose. Some would argue that this was evident in his depiction of the Croat–Muslim ceasefire of February 1994 as the result of British mediation on the ground, rather than simply an offshoot of the fundamental shift in relations brought about by American diplomacy.[60] More seriously, Bellamy wrote after the war that safe areas 'have to be large and well defended to survive while isolated with a guarantee of whatever further support is necessary from the international community to ensure their survival, even in the face of mind-boggling incompetence by their own commanders . . . The half-hearted Bosnian Muslim defence of Gorazde in April 1994, which Lieutenant-General Rose ridiculed in a private interview, disgracefully leaked, is an example.'[61] Indeed, Bellamy even went so far as to deliver a Roseite homily on how the Bosnian army could do better: 'Despite the Bosnian government's criticism of the UN and NATO for allegedly not doing enough to prevent the fall of Bihac, it has not itself initiated any strategic plan to draw Serb attention away from the enclave. It is as if the five Bosnian government "corps" – each maybe 5,000 strong – fight their own war, and the other corps care little about those in Bihac. Rather than blaming the UN, the Bosnian government might have tried to impose more unity on their disparate forces.'[62]

A more worrying phenomenon was the tendency of some British defence analysts to indulge Serbian allegations that the Bosnian government was shelling its own side. Thus, Paul Beaver, the editor of *Jane's Defence Weekly*, thought Serbian protestations about the market-place massacre not unreasonable. 'I find it difficult to contemplate,' he told the *Independent*, 'that a 120-mm mortar could cause this number of casualties even in a confined space like a market . . . 68 dead is theoretically possible but in practice I'm not aware of such a high number ever having been killed by a single shell.'[63]

Much expert military commentary on Bosnia was in conscious contradiction to the Americans. The 'simplistic' US view of the conflict as a morality play, with the Serbs as the 'baddies', was said to be mirrored by the US obsession with 'doctrine', 'crusades', 'warfighting', and 'overwhelming force'. The British, by contrast, were seen as the inheritors of a 'small war' tradition, with a nuanced view of success and failure. John Keegan, for example, described Bob Dole's plans for 'lift and strike' as 'very American'. Quoting the American soldier J. B. Motley, he noted that the US was committed to 'an all or nothing approach. That is to say, total victory over the enemy in an ideological crusade.' On the other hand, Keegan argued, 'Britain and France, old imperial powers with a long experience of combating disorder in violent areas of the world, take a much more gradualist view. In North Africa and in India they were accustomed to dealing with armed dissidents always ready to go to war when weakness or the chance of advantage was scented. They had the opposite of "an all or nothing approach" and did not hope for total victory. They accepted the wickedness of the world and sought to contain it by a whole spectrum of means, including the cultivation of personal relations and the use of bribery, as well as threat and punishment. It might be called the "political officer" method. It has had a revival in Bosnia. General Sir Michael Rose has, indeed, been acting as a political officer on a national scale.'[64] As we have seen, much the same sentiments, in less sophisticated terms, were being expressed by Milos Stankovic, Michael Rose himself and other 'men on the ground'.

Another critic of US military strategy towards Bosnia was Philip Towle of the Centre of International Studies in Cambridge, a respected expert on air power. He too saw the analogies between Bosnia and colonial 'small wars'. After all, he wrote, 'what is peace-keeping, but imperialism with a multinational and humanitarian face?'[65] He also invoked historical examples such as the Korean War as a 'salutory reminder that it is far easier to intervene, to become embroiled, than it is to extricate forces without humiliation and demoralisation'.[66] Mindful of the experiences in the Falklands and the Gulf, he sought to dispel any 'false impression of the efficacy of conventional military power'.[67] He contrasted the near-consensus in Britain on the inadequacy of air power with American proposals for 'lift and strike'. 'It may be indeed,' he wrote, 'that US emphasis on air strikes consciously or unconsciously reinforced British reluctance to become involved in an American-led campaign against Serbia. Those taking the crucial decisions had come of age in the 1960s when the predominant image was of US air operations in Vietnam.' Moreover, Carter's failure to rescue the hostages in Iran and Clinton's fiasco in Somalia had tended to 'reinforce' the 'assessment that the American armed forces were incapable of waging low-key operations'.[68]

Other experts were less subtle about alleged American shortcomings. Paul Mansell, a major in the Royal Marines, who served on the British defence staff at the embassy in Washington, was dismissive of the fact that 'because of media pressure, governments are forced into reactive gestures that have no long-term utility but, as in the case of air strikes and food drops in Bosnia, do quench the public's thirst for an early, visually impressive and safe option'.[69] He also noted – not incorrectly – that 'In Bosnia . . . President Clinton has not been willing to uphold the principles of democracy through the commitment of ground forces';[70] that Bosnian democracy might better be served through air power and arms supplies than through no military help at all, he would not allow. Similarly sharp criticism was voiced by the London International Institute for Strategic Studies in its annual review in 1994. 'The United States,' it argued, 'even more than usual, does not seem to be following a steady compass'; President Clinton, in particular, was 'blowing a very uncertain policy trumpet'. 'By the end of the year,' it concluded in a Keeganesque vein, 'the US was insisting on no open-ended commitments, assurance of victory without casualties, and exit strategy. These are awesome guarantees to ask for in today's uncertain world.'[71]

All of this had a profoundly sobering effect on the British debate on military intervention. It became almost impossible to argue against the serried ranks not only of the 'men on the ground', but also of the experts. Newspaper reports routinely cited the resistance of 'defence sources' and 'military analysts' to action against the Bosnian Serbs.[72] Even those in favour of intervention felt compelled to exaggerate the dangers, lest their optimism be used to dismiss their analysis out of hand as 'unrealistic'. Thus the columnist Hugo Young, himself a consistent and intelligent advocate of intervention, spoke in April 1993, at the height of the first Srebrenica crisis, of the 'scenario [painted] by the International Institute for Strategic Studies: 500,000 troops committed to Yugoslavia for 10 years'; two years later he was citing Philip Towle on 'the limitations on the ability of outsiders to limit the damage'.[73] Michael Dewar's assessment obviously underlay the claim of the peer and columnist Woodrow Wyatt (Lord Wyatt of Weeford) that 'if you were to keep the peace in Yugoslavia, you would have to send in at least half a million troops and you would have to keep them there for 30 years'.[74] Dewar's judgement was also explicitly invoked by Cyril Townsend, a Tory MP with strong military connections. 'Colonel Michael Dewar,' he pointed out, 'Deputy Director of the International Institute for Strategic Studies, has estimated that effective military intervention in Bosnia, including the defeat of the Serb militias and military occupation, would require something like half a million men, and it is almost certain that regular Serbian forces would become involved.'[75] And if Michael Clarke, the head of the Centre for Defence Studies at King's College London, was clear that 'the consequences of non-involvement on Bosnia are worse than the dangers of involvement', he also insisted that it would require 60,000 troops just to open two land corridors to Sarajevo. 'I am not so sure,' he added, 'there is the political will to commit such levels of manpower.'[76] Wittingly or unwittingly, the 'experts' had succeeded in pricing Britain out of the intervention market.

Britain was no better served on the civilian side. The advent of the Bosnian war found the Foreign Office unprepared. There was, as the retired head of the Diplomatic Service, Sir John Coles, has admitted, too much routine work and not enough time for policy thinking. 'We were trying,' he writes, 'to do too much of everything – and the casualty was policy. I believe that if we had had more time and better mechanisms for strategic thinking, policy would have been better conceived. We would have addressed the fundamental issues arising from the disintegration of Yugoslavia more effectively.'[77] There was also a shortage of regional expertise, caused by lower staffing levels and cuts. 'Geographical departments in the Foreign Office,' Coles points out, 'which often handle situations of considerable significance for British interests, such as the Gulf War, the Arab–Israeli dispute and Bosnia, are very much smaller than they were twenty years ago and command much less genuine regional expertise.'[78]

Those regional experts who were available tended to be pro-Serb, supporters of engagement with Milosevic (i.e., appeasement), or at least equally sceptical of all sides. Thus Sir Peter Hall, the ambassador to Belgrade and later an advisor to Lord Owen, told John Major at the outset of the conflict: 'Prime Minister, the first thing you have to know about these people is that they like going around cutting each other's heads off.'[79] His successor in Belgrade since March 1994, Ivor Roberts, was a prominent advocate of a 'deal' with Milosevic and a well-known Serb empathizer. He was famous for his lack of sympathy with peripheral nationalisms, and was even unfairly reputed once to have fallen asleep in the company of the leader of the Albanian passive resistance in Kosovo, Ibrahim Rugova.[80] Yet he was a frequent and attentive visitor to the Serbian leader and their late-night conversations were legendary in the diplomatic community in Belgrade. Indeed, as sources within the Serbian government have told me, Roberts was so widely believed to be in Milosevic's confidence that he was regularly importuned by foreign journalists in search of information. His forthcoming memoir of this period, in a neat echo of Milovan Djilas' earlier volume on another and altogether more terrifying dictator, is to be entitled *Conversations with Milosevic*.

The Serbophilia of the Belgrade embassy and the 'old Balkan hands' was sometimes remarked upon by visiting journalists. Alec Russell reports how, early on in the conflict, before the tenure of Ivor Roberts, he dined with the 'resident British diplomat' on his way back from Bosnia: 'For two hours he steadfastly highlighted misdoings by the Croats and Muslims.' He seemed incapable, Russell relates, of grasping that this was a case of 'the hyena devouring the scraps left by the big cats'. 'The more the diplomat talked,' he concluded, 'seemingly treating the Serbs' aggression as a given factor, the more credence I attached to a prevalent conspiracy theory that early in the conflict the Foreign Office took a conscious decision to back the Serbs.'[81] 'Backing the Serbs', in this context, meant something less sinister than it sounded. For British policy did not aim – as some conspiracy theorists thought – at a Greater Serbia. Instead, it sought some form of negotiated solution through the good offices of a 'strong' Serbia. Essential to the execution and legitimacy of such a strategy was some degree of understanding of Serb claims, and confidence in President Milosevic's ability and intention to help bring a compromise settlement about.

Ivor Roberts himself – who was only executing government policy – claims that he was engaging in 'analysis' not 'apology'. Roberts was instructed, as he put it, 'to get inside Milosevic's head and find out what his real bottom lines were'. 'Now to some people,' he recalls, 'particularly the Americans, this was regarded as supping with the devil, outrageous behaviour.'[82] Of course, the line between analysis and apology, though quite distinct, can sometimes be a fine one. Indeed, to Richard Holbrooke, the American negotiator of the Dayton accord, it seemed that the Serbs had got inside Roberts' mind. For while there is some dispute as to whether the British diplomat wrote a passionate letter about the 'historic Serb sense of injustice', or merely made animated verbal entreaties on their behalf, the nub of his message was not in doubt.[83]

Yet the criticism – and the defence – both miss the point. The problem was not the apologia, or the morality, but the analysis, which hinged on the assumption that Milosevic – who was primarily responsible for the wars in Croatia and Bosnia – *could* be corralled into some sort of acceptable behaviour, and that he *might* be part of a stable solution, however unjust. It is true that the Americans were, for a considerable time, disastrously persuaded of the need to work through Milosevic. But there is no evidence that the Serbian leader delivered the Bosnian Serbs to anything more than the success of the allied air campaign in 1995 and the Croat–Bosnian government advance forced upon them in any case. And as the events of 1998–9 in Kosovo were to show, Milosevic was the most disruptive force in the Balkans, not the guarantor of stability, just or unjust.

There were deeper structural reasons for the Serb affinities of the 'old Balkan hands'. In his paper 'Why are British ambassadors at Belgrade pro-Serb?', Sir Reginald Hibbert, a senior retired diplomat and sometime ambassador to Paris, explains how Britain and the

Foreign Office 'were historically committed to Yugoslavia and to Serbia as the dominant component of Yugoslavia'.[84] Moreover, he continues, British diplomats, 'knew Belgrade, hardly knew Zagreb, had almost no idea what Sarajevo represented, and had not heard of Pristina'. There was also, Hibbert explains, 'a general, inherited, belief in London that Yugoslavia, and within Yugoslavia, Serbia, held the key to stability (i.e., the status quo) in the Balkans'.

Likewise many Americans who dealt with the Foreign Office over Bosnia recall that British diplomats were mired in a traditional Serbophile paradigm. 'I always thought,' James Woolsey, the Director of Central Intelligence, remembers, '[that] there was some faint echo of history, [that] the Serbs had been good allies against the fascists in the war.'[85] The State Department official John Fox, who spent several years in British education as a schoolboy, undergraduate, and graduate student, felt that 'there was almost a schoolboy quality to their expertise . . . in these meetings they were actually saying [mimicking Bismarck] "not worth the bones of a Pomeranian grenadier"'. 'My favourite,' he continues, 'was the Fitzroy Maclean argument, that the Bosnian Serbs are ten feet tall, and they defeated the Germans, this is a quagmire, so watch out, the next Vietnam, so watch out.' It was all, Fox thought, 'biased ententist thinking, very old school . . . the "traditional ally" and the rest of it'.[86] Some of this came across in public pronouncements, such as when Sir David Hannay prefaced an admonition via the UN Security Council with the words 'My government has no quarrel with the people of Serbia. They have been our allies in war; we have worked with them in peace; and we have nothing but respect for them.'[87]

In this scheme of things, the embattled new state of Bosnia could not rate highly. Indeed, some observers interpreted the dispatch of a relatively junior diplomat, Robert Barnett, belatedly to open the Sarajevo embassy in the spring of 1994, as a deliberate attempt to minimize the importance of the mission. In fact, Barnett – who had been intimately involved in Bosnian policy back in the Foreign Office – courageously volunteered for this dangerous assignment.[88] He was no straightforward partisan of the Sarajevo government, but he did stand out from the rest of the Foreign Office through the clarity of his interpretation and the depth of his commitment to the Bosnian cause.[89]

Barnett threw himself into the task of putting Sarajevo back on the cultural map, not least by organizing and funding a film festival: he attempted, as he put it, to lift not only the 'siege of the stomachs' but also that of 'hearts and minds'. For this he was ridiculed by Rose's liaison officer as 'a Mr Bean type, whose sole interest seemed to be running the Bosnian–British friendship society at the embassy on Monday evenings'.[90] All this cut little ice in London. 'I don't think,' Douglas Hurd recalls, 'I would have felt that [Barnett] was supremely qualified to comment on the origin and basic status of the war, but his views were . . . an important part of the picture. He was the man on the spot. The fact that he was stationed in Sarajevo didn't give him a supreme view of the origins and nature of the war.'[91] This time, the 'man on the ground' was saying the wrong thing.

Very soon, Barnett found himself at loggerheads with Sir Michael Rose, whose Panglossian view of the ceasefire and jaundiced attitude to the Bosnian government he did not share. According to UN officials, Rose regularly boasted of his ascendancy at Whitehall. 'Look,' he would say, '[Barnett's] reports go back to London and mine go back to London, and I know which ones are trashed.'[92] It was an unequal contest: Rose's strategy corresponded more closely to the Whitehall agenda, and the General succeeded in sidelining Barnett until he was eventually moved – in effect, sacked – to a posting in Germany.

The driving force behind FCO thinking on Bosnia during the early stages of the war was not the regionally relevant 'Eastern Adriatic' section, but the United Nations Department.[93] This was a direct result of the tendency in Whitehall to regard the war as a humanitarian rather than a political problem. The head of the department was Glynne Evans, whose frequent courageous visits to Sarajevo sucked her into the orbit of the 'men on the ground'; Michael Rose refers to her as 'my chief ally in the Foreign Office'.[94] Foreign Office officials told me that she made no great secret of her desire to construct a great humanitarian empire, policed by British forces under United Nations auspices. She appeared to have no sense at all of the broader strategic and political implications of allowing Serb aggression to run unchecked in Bosnia. Indeed, she routinely suggested at briefings throughout the war that all sides were more or less equally culpable.[95] It therefore comes as no surprise to read in Michael Rose's memoir that 'Glynne

Evans . . . reassured me that there was a growing awareness among the Europeans of how brilliantly the Bosnian Muslims had been playing the Americans and that a widening of the air campaign by Nato would be tantamount to a declaration of war.'[96]

Later, the conduct of British policy towards Bosnia within the FCO fell increasingly to the political director, Pauline Neville-Jones.[97] For most of the conflict, as attenders at briefings recall, she maintained the standard government line of equivalence 'between the parties'. Nor was she ever, as Michael Rose claims in his memoirs, a closet air striker, eager to pursue a 'war policy'.[98] Yet it is probably true that, as Neville-Jones herself recalls, she was 'never entirely happy about the human rights side of the whole thing, and I didn't like our stand on it'. Indeed, she claims that 'there are bits of paper . . . inside the machine' which show that her 'position was never quite what it was thought to be'.[99] But it was only as the war dragged on that the political director progressively moved towards military intervention, hamstrung mainly by Douglas Hurd's indecision and the behaviour of Michael Rose on the ground.

The net result of all this was that, until shortly before the end, official advice from the Foreign Office was consistently sceptical about the need for, and viability of, military intervention against the Bosnian Serbs. The problem was an early false diagnosis, which reverberated in official thinking long after the war had escalated. Sir Percy Cradock, who advised the Prime Minister on foreign policy, writes candidly and self-critically of his own paper in September 1991 on the war in Croatia: 'I came to the unsatisfactory conclusion that while we were ready to concede that the federation was irretrievably fragmented, we still recoiled from the conclusion that international aggression was occurring . . . As we saw it, British interests were not seriously threatened.'[100] By the time that the reality of Serbian aggression in Croatia, and later in Bosnia, had become too obvious to finesse,[101] the FCO had convinced itself that military obstacles to intervention were insuperable.

This line was summed up in the briefing paper 'The case against intervention' of October 1992, which stressed the disastrous German experience in the Second World War, the difficulty of the terrain and many other familiar themes.[102] 'The fighting in Bosnia', it was claimed, 'is not the result of an invasion by a foreign power but is inter-ethnic.' 'The most likely outcome of international military intervention,' therefore, 'would be more deaths and increased misery for the survivors.' Besides, the paper continued, 'there is no single front line but many many pockets of fighting where people fight for the control of individual towns, villages and even fields'. In spite of outlining the sanctions imposed on rump Yugoslavia, the paper was quite unable to point the finger at any primary responsibility of the Bosnian Serbs and their backers in Belgrade. Instead of describing the practice of ethnic cleansing, the document simply notes how 'atrocities by extremists in all the factions have turned them into implacable opponents and fuelled the bitterness of the fighting'.[103]

The comparison with the role of the US State Department is striking. Here the pusillanimity and inconsistency of government policy produced anger and despair. By late 1992, as serving officials recall, nearly everybody involved in Bosnia policy at working and mid-level had become a dissident. There was at least one major 'revolt' in 1993, and several smaller insurrections throughout the war, as well as numerous 'back channel' memoranda sent directly to the Secretary of State. Four mid-level officers resigned in 1993, and one senior officer – the former ambassador to Belgrade, Warren Zimmermann – resigned in 1994.[104] None of these men were 'serial dissenters'.[105] Moreover, many of those who remained, such as Peter Galbraith, the ambassador to Croatia, Victor Jackovitch, the ambassador to Sarajevo, John Menzies, his successor, and many others, were outspoken supporters of military intervention on behalf of the Sarajevo government.

By contrast, British policy on Bosnia provoked virtually no dissent within the Foreign Office. There were no resignations, and apart from Robert Barnett apparently no protests worth speaking of. Partly, as senior officials explained to me, this was a question of tradition and culture: diplomats were merely executors of policy.[106] There were also more mundane pressures. As Martin Bell writes, 'It has been my general experience that British diplomats engaged on the issue, who are intelligent men and women with at least some sense of the realities on the ground, have had little enthusiasm for the policy – perhaps even the policy vacuum – which they were required to defend and promote. [But] none of them had resigned. I asked one who wished to why he hadn't. His answer wasn't principled, but frank. It was a matter, he said, of boarding-school allowances.'[107]

If some British diplomats were deeply troubled by having to defend policy on Bosnia, others threw themselves into the task with gusto. Perhaps the most prominent defender of the Whitehall position was Sir David Hannay, the formidable permanent representative on the United Nations Security Council. He was suspected by some Americans, including Vice-President Al Gore's National Security Advisor, Leon Fuerth, of 'impeding' even initiatives which had been agreed between Bill Clinton and the British Prime Minister.[108] Many noted the 'cold legalism' with which Hannay rejected Bosnia's right to defend itself.[109] The result was a series of running battles on the Council with the redoubtable Madeleine Albright, a battleship whose big guns were sometimes unable to depress sufficiently to engage the impish and subversive Sir David. To quote one of his greatest admirers, Sir Michael Rose, Hannay 'possessed all the necessary wit and experience to keep Britain at the centre of the international decision-making process'. Sir Michael even adds an example of this wit: 'When debating Bosnia in the Security Council, Madeleine Albright had quoted Karl von Clausewitz's remark that "after all, war is merely an extension of politics by other means". "Yes Madeleine," David replied, "that is exactly what Clausewitz said. But he was a German, and the Germans listened to him. Look what happened to them, twice!".'[110] This was a knock-down argument. 'It does very good things for my morale,' said Bob Peirce, the First Secretary covering UN policy, 'to know that the cleverest chap on the Security Council is our man.'[111]

For the rest, Hannay executed – and still defends – the standard British and FCO viewpoint on Bosnia. He criticized the 'German-led drive towards the early recognition not only of Slovenia and Croatia but also of Bosnia and Macedonia' as 'premature' and responsible for undermining Lord Carrington's negotiation efforts.[112] He stressed the importance of 'clientitis' in the former Yugoslavia and suggested that 'the relationship between modern Germany and Croatia' shows that the lessons of history have not been learned'.[113] At the same time, Sir David worked diligently to restrict the UN mandate as much as possible. He tried to blunt the safe areas resolution in 1993 by insisting that air power was to be used to defend the soldiers sent to deter attacks, not to protect the safe areas themselves.[114] Despite the fact that the UN mission enjoyed an enforcement mandate under Chapter VII, and notwithstanding 'the undoubted primary responsibility of Milosevic and of the Bosnian Serbs', he insisted that Bosnia was not 'a black and white issue calling for enforcement action'.[115] Indeed, I found throughout my researches that British diplomats in general *still* routinely tried to deny the existence of a mandate for the use of force, until chapter and verse were cited.

But perhaps the most striking thing about British diplomats throughout the war was their increasingly anti-American tone. Even today, the rift with the Americans rankles: Sir David still claims, in spite of the manifest ultimate success of a variant of 'lift and strike', which had been on the table since 1993, that the Americans had 'no alternative policy to offer in Bosnia' before 1995.[116] Partly, this is out of sympathy for Lord Owen, whose peace plan, as David Hannay writes, 'was allowed to wither on the bough . . . the new US administration just didn't know what was going on'.[117] More generally, Hannay condemned the fact that 'The Americans have felt it politic to pass over in something close to silence the debt owed to the UN, and in particular to UNPROFOR for four hard years of slog in a pretty smelly quagmire.'[118] His then deputy in New York, however, recalls that 'If I am honest with myself, I think that the Americans were on the right track, and that some form of collective Nato action was necessary earlier in the day. But that wasn't where we were starting from.'[119]

The Foreign Office, of course, was not entirely dependent on its own expert resources. At many stages during the disintegration of Yugoslavia, particularly at the outset, the advice of various outside experts was sought. Yet, as with military advice, so with all other: a great deal depends on how the question is framed. It is clear from the activities of the Commons Committee on Foreign Affairs that the principal preoccupation of the FCO, and certainly of the parliamentarians, was not the Yugoslav crisis itself, but whether the violence would spread throughout the region. Repeatedly, the experts were asked whether the Yugoslav problem was *sui generis* or betokened some wider conflagration. 'It is very important,' the Chairman, David Howell, MP, remarked, 'to have the views of all of you on this. Is it containable *sui generis* or is it contagious and is it going to spread? That is our big thought on which we should like to have your views.'[120]

The answer was reassuring. 'Yugoslavia,' an FCO memorandum to the Foreign Affairs Committee argued in November 1991, 'is a case *sui generis*; the tragedy there has lessons to teach, but though there are evident dangers of contagion there is no necessary reason why the crisis in Yugoslavia should generate widespread regional instability.'[121] Similarly, the preamble to a submission of the Centre for Defence and International Security at Lancaster spoke of having been 'encouraged to make comment upon the likelihood of civil war in the region [central and south-eastern Europe] in the light of the current conflict in Yugoslavia, particularly with reference to selected potential 'flash-points'. Again the message was reassuring: war, while 'not entirely impossible' was 'unlikely'.[122] Dr Jonathan Eyal, Director of Studies at the Royal United Services Institute, drew hope from the fact that 'perhaps for the first time in the Balkan history [sic] there are no great vultures around the area trying to create spheres of influence'.[123] He added that he thought 'the Yugoslav crisis is rather unique . . . and I think that trying to associate the problem of Yugoslavia and project it to the entire European continent was probably what paralysed us from the beginning in our handling of the problem and it was one of the most mistaken assumptions.'

All this was received with palpable relief by the parliamentarians. As the Conservative MP James Lester observed, 'I think that both the Foreign Office, and, indeed, the Yugoslav ambassador told us that he thought that events in Yugoslavia were very particular to themselves and were not likely to be repeated in other countries.'[124] Here the experts were absolutely right, but the unintended effect was to suggest that the Yugoslav crisis was a containable aberration. Moreover, what neither the FCO nor more than a handful of the experts predicted was that the Yugoslav war *on its own* would be enough to unleash the most sustained crisis in the forty-year history of the Atlantic alliance. Nor was there – yet – clarity or unanimity about the driving force behind the war. Some, such as Dr David Dyker from the University of Southampton, unambiguously stated that 'it is the "Serbs" who are smashing up parts of Croatia, not Croats who are smashing parts of Serbia', and both Mark Wheeler and James Gow emphasized the importance of 'Greater Serbia'.[125] But the overwhelming impression of the discussion on the responsibility for the war in Croatia is of complexity. Much of it was *pointilliste* and characterized by sterile *Besserwisserei*, so much so, indeed, that the chairman of the Foreign Affairs Committee had to ask the contributors to stop speaking over one another. It is unlikely that the parliamentarians were left much the wiser on the question of war guilt. Their puzzlement was summed up by Ted Rowlands, MP, who observed that 'The message we are getting is very much the mirror image, that is, that you look in the mirror and see the same image.'[126] This impression – once gained – later proved very difficult to shake off.

A comparison between two of the experts consulted by the Foreign Office, Dr James Gow of the Department of War Studies at King's College London and Dr Jonathan Eyal, is instructive.

As a proficient Serbo-Croat linguist and expert on the Yugoslav army, James Gow was supremely qualified to analyse the Bosnian war. Nearly everything he said about the crisis was of a very high standard and has stood the test of time well. He consistently argued that the main, though not the only, destabilizing factor in the region was Serb nationalism, that Yugoslavia could not be kept together as a single state, that military intervention to curb Serb aggression was not only inevitable but desirable, that the British government exaggerated Bosnian Serb strength and that the charge of 'premature recognition' levelled at Germany was unjustified.[127] He also criticized the arms embargo on the grounds that 'an international community not prepared to act itself should have revoked the arms embargo as it affected Bosnia. At the very least it was hard to imagine how doing this could really have made the situation there any worse.'[128] While well aware of the many complexities, Gow resisted the tendency to complicate the war unnecessarily and cloud the issues at stake. 'In reality,' he later wrote, 'much about the war was far more simple and straightforward than the obfuscatory and confusing pattern of rival narratives suggested.' The 'real nature of the war', he pointed out, 'was a clash of state projects'.[129]

Some of Gow's advice – from the perspective of hindsight – was slightly wide of the mark. Thus, in late 1991 he thought it 'unlikely that Tudjman will remain in office long; if openly fascistic elements do not gain power immediately, there will be Croat–Croat civil war once there is peace with the Serbian coalition, if not before'.[130] At the time, of course, this was far from a fanciful prediction. But it does give an insight into the widespread official and expert preoccupation with Croatian fascism, a dog which in reality resolutely refused to bark in Zagreb. At around the same time – during the Croatian war, but before the outbreak of hostilities in Bosnia – Gow was much less forthright about the arms embargo. When pressed on the subject by the Foreign Affairs Committee, Gow responded that 'I do not know whether it is right or wrong. It added to an already existing asymmetry . . . I do not have a clear opinion on this. I can only reiterate what I just said, that is, that there are cases to be made both ways . . . I think that it is an important question that everybody has to decide for themselves.'[131] There is nothing wrong with admitting uncertainty, but the notion that a major politico-strategic issue was something that 'everybody has to decide for themselves' seems uncharacteristically evasive. Moreover, Gow was later slightly too quick to criticize the Americans for their 'diplomatic immaturity', for 'killing off' the Vance–Owen plan in May 1993, and for drawing back from lifting the arms embargo in September 1994.[132]

But the principal problem with Gow was the respectful blandness which results from an advisory capacity, however unofficial. In order to maintain his credibility, even the most scrupulous of experts is compelled to calibrate his advice according to the circumstances and the prevailing orthodoxy. Perhaps Gow wanted to escape the fate of the Oxford historian Mark Almond, whose forthright critique of western policy during the war – *Europe's backyard war* – was, as Gow himself relates, rejected by officials 'because of its tone'.[133] The difficulties of trying both to analyse and mould policy comes across strikingly in some of Gow's own subsequent reflections. He writes that 'One aspiration' of his book *Triumph of the lack of will* 'is to provide an account which, among other things, reveals an understanding of the problems which would not offend foreign ministers and officials but might still suggest those aspects of failure for which they could be expected to acknowledge responsibility'.[134] Perhaps it was for this reason that Gow reproached Noel Malcolm, whose analysis by and large he shared, for being excessive and simplistic in his 'admonishment

[sic]' of the international community.[135] And perhaps it was for this reason also that Gow argues within one and the same book both that the arms embargo was wrong and that 'Most of the UK's "objections" over the issues surrounding the use of force (including the arms embargo) were founded on sound analysis of the circumstances.'[136]

All this points to a broader problem with the official advisory process. As one MoD source told me, Whitehall has contractual relationships with certain university departments, such as War Studies at King's College London and the University of Southampton. Academics at these institutions inevitably become part of the official culture and the formal process of deliberation. 'They know what we want,' I was told, 'and they give it to us.' This is often a good thing, as it enables efficient communication and rigorous focus on practical issues. But there are situations – and Bosnia may have been one of them – where the advisors become too caught up in official 'group-think' to break ranks, or – as was perhaps the case with some – are understandably fearful of giving offence, and thus losing influence without having advanced their argument. This has been the excuse of the advisor down the ages, of course, but that does not make it any less true.

Jonathan Eyal's contribution to the Bosnian debate was more prominent, but also more uneven. Initially, the standard of his analysis was very high indeed: a savage pamphlet published in early 1993 mercilessly laid bare the deficiencies of European, and particularly British, policy during the Slovenian and Croatian wars. He recognized that Yugoslavia was doomed much earlier than most experts, and he did not seek to pin its demise on the Germans or other improbable conspirators. 'Those who are still suggesting that Yugoslavia must be kept together at all costs,' he wrote in May 1991 before the outbreak of open hostilities, 'fail to draw a distinction between the desirable and the possible.'[137] 'The maintenance of Yugoslavia,' he continued, 'as one state under Serbian domination will ultimately be more destabilising than the country's disintegration.'

Nor could Eyal be faulted for his broader view of central and eastern Europe throughout 1993–5. He could not have been clearer about the consequences of western failure in Bosnia. 'Today's western politicians,' he wrote in May 1993, 'labour under the same mentality that produced the disaster of the Thirties . . . they believe that it is still possible to confine collective security to a prosperous west.' He rejected public opinion as 'the excuse, rather than the reason for inaction'. 'It may come as a revelation to John Major and his colleagues, but the role of governments in a democracy is both to guide and to articulate public opinion at the same time.' Nor did he pull his punches with Douglas Hurd, whose pretension to 'punch above his weight' for Britain was roundly criticized. 'Flabby paunch above a thin waist is a more accurate description,' he wrote.[138] Eyal was also rightly sceptical of any supposed Russian sympathies with the Bosnian Serbs.[139] He had – and has – a lot of sensible things to say about the need to integrate eastern Europe, Nato expansion, and the dangers of unstable buffer zones.

His grasp of specifically Bosnian matters, on the other hand, was much shakier and became increasingly so as the war dragged on. There were already signs of this during the initial debate on military action in 1992. Eyal poured scorn on the advocates of 'all-out military intervention'. 'Their arguments,' he claimed, 'appear compelling: aggression must not be allowed to succeed, and Serbia must be taught a lesson. Yet their practical options usually amount to little more than an intellectual balancing act between a guilty conscience and a blissful ignorance of Balkan realities.' The reality, in Eyal's view, was that the war was 'not an apocalyptic struggle between light and darkness', but a conflict with 'overlapping historic, ethnic, religious, territorial and economic grievances, amenable to careful handling rather than clear solutions'. More specifically, Eyal was highly sceptical of the '"surgical" strikes currently being weighed by every armchair strategist'. Only full-scale intervention on the ground would do the job, otherwise it would be best to 'recognise that the original Bosnia is finished and Serbia's aggression has achieved its broad aims'. 'Any other supposed third way,' he concluded, 'remains a path covered with slippery fig leaves.'[140]

This set the scene for Eyal's subsequent analyses, which focused heavily on the inadequacy of air power and its American advocates. He rejected the threat of Nato air strikes in August 1993 – which drove the Serbs off Mount Igman – as 'too little, too late, and hardly relevant'.[141] In April 1994, during the Gorazde crisis, he condemned the 'aerosol approach to international relations': 'if you don't like what some nations do to each other, but don't consider your own interests vitally affected, spray the guilty parties with some bombs from the air'.[142] Eyal was particularly critical of the Americans. 'Senator Dole,' he wrote at the height of the Bihac crisis in December 1994, 'and those of his compatriots who are now so keen to criticise the alliance, would do well to remember that the United States is largely responsible for pushing NATO into the air strikes policy only to discover what any cadet at a military college knows already: that air power alone, "awesome" as it may be, is no substitute for ground troops.'[143] Some months later, during the hostage crisis of May 1995, he declared that 'The main culprits for the impasse are the Americans, who pushed for the air strikes last week without thinking ahead.'[144] Here, however, Eyal overlooks the fact that those air strikes were primarily the initiative of General Rupert Smith.

Indeed, much of Eyal's commentary was characterized by an undercurrent of anti-American animus. In early 1993, for example, he sneered at 'The ever-young republic that does not tolerate ethnic cleansing (as every native American Indian [sic] can testify).'[145] Two months later, he rejected American criticism that the Europeans had failed to solve conflicts on their own continent. 'Presumably,' he asked, 'they should have learnt from the way America solved the problems of Cuba, Haiti, Nicaragua and Panama?'[146] In August 1993, he condemned not merely Bill Clinton as the 'can talk, can't do' president, but also American policy on Bosnia as a whole. 'Spraying people with bombs from the comfort of a Washington chair,' he wrote, 'is a tactic that failed in Vietnam, Cambodia, Iraq and Somalia, but the Europeans were expected to believe it would somehow succeed to perfection in Bosnia . . . Bombs with no responsibility is what Washington wants.' 'Barking from the sidelines,' he added, 'never inspires respect, and arguments do not become more convincing simply because they are shouted louder.'[147] After a decent interval, he returned to the same theme in October 1993. 'The Americans', he claimed, 'are singularly ill-equipped to handle such conflicts' as Bosnia. 'Instead of proposing the use of moderate force, the Pentagon suggested the application of firepower without the slightest idea of what this was meant to achieve. Its policy was to . . . zap Slobodan Milosevic from the comfort of a Washington armchair.'[148]

Increasingly, Eyal's own recommendations began to dovetail with the Whitehall agenda. He strongly opposed the lifting of the arms embargo. 'They ask for arms in the full knowledge that this is the one way to draw western forces in,' he claimed in April 1993. 'Arming the Muslims might salve the conscience of the West,' he continued, 'but it would achieve nothing except more slaughter. Would it expiate the West's guilty conscience to see Serbian children as well as Muslim children being killed?'[149] The arms embargo issue, of course, also enabled him to indulge his critique of the Americans still further. In 1995, for example, he condemned Congressional plans for a lifting of the arms embargo as 'a disaster for the Balkans'. Following the standard military view, he claimed that 'The Muslims do not lack small firearms . . . The Sarajevo government does need heavy weapons, but handling them requires training . . . The question, then, is not whether arms can be supplied, but who will provide the Muslims with the time to train.' Picking up an earlier theme, he argued that 'The Bosnian leaders are requesting weapons not because they believe they can win, but because they assume that once the Americans become engaged, they will be sucked further into the conflict.' He also claimed – somewhat at variance with his earlier claims of Russian indifference towards Serbia – that 'Russia will start supporting the Serbs directly, and the area will be divided into spheres of influence, a proxy war in which the superpowers play games on the backs of little nations that matter little on their own.'[150]

But Eyal's sympathy for the little nations had its limits. He mocked the Bosnian ambassador to the UN, Mohamed Sacirbey, for his telegenic appearance: 'a handsome face, a good suit complete with floral tie, perfect one-liners delivered in fluent English and a determination to appear on every television programme in defence of his beloved "Baasnia"'.[151] Why Eyal should have felt the need to highlight Sacirbey's assimilatory endeavours is not clear. More seriously, Eyal joined in the clamour from Whitehall, Lord Owen, and others, for the Sarajevo government to 'see sense' and agree to a partitionist settlement. If there was to be no 'massive military intervention', he wrote in December 1992, 'then it would be better to opt for the creation of a smaller, but viable Muslim state'.[152] 'All those involved in the conflict,' he argued in April 1994, 'must be brought together to negotiate, and they should negotiate frontiers – not some hazy ideas about new confederations that nobody is prepared to enforce. True, this means that the West will participate in further ethnic cleansing. But is it preferable to watch while the Serbs perform the same task in a piecemeal but even crueller fashion?'[153]

If such brutal realism seemed harsh, Eyal comforted himself and his readers by questioning the victim status of the Bosnian government. 'The Bosnian Muslims,' he observed in May 1994, 'are not entirely the blameless characters the western media make them out to be.' Indeed, he reproaches the Bosnian garrison in Gorazde for having maintained a weapons manufacturing ability, and for 'deliberately exaggerating' the casualty figures. 'It would be a brave western leader,' he adds, 'who would have suggested that the Bosnians had exaggerated the extent of the tragedy.' Eyal clearly knew no such fear, though he might have if he had known the truth of what the SAS observers were reporting to Sarajevo. In any case, Eyal noted, 'It is the Muslim government, not the rebel Serbs, which now refuses to sign a general ceasefire in Bosnia.'[154] Almost exactly a year later, he condemned Bosnian forces trying to recapture ethnically cleansed territory as 'responsible as much as the Serbs for the current fighting'.[155]

The language of brutal *Realpolitik* was also the preferred medium of Sir Laurence Martin, the Director of the Royal Institute of International Affairs at Chatham House. In the summer of 1993 he welcomed 'the carve-up engineered between Croatia and Serbia' as the 'only concession to reality'. 'Moreover, to be even more brutally realistic,' he continued, 'the reason why that carve-up has some plausibility is that it has been arrived at by force and power executed by people on the scene, and not legislated by remote theorists.'[156] He saw no merit in the Bosnian position, simply by virtue of their having been attacked; nor did he distinguish between a preplanned campaign of ethnic cleansing and the desperation of a state on the verge of annihilation. 'What the United Nations is doing in effect,' he argued, 'is refusing to let the weaker side lose. Public sympathy and consequent UN interventions will indeed probably always be on the weaker, and thus, according to a common popular presumption, the virtuous side. In practice, determining where the balance of virtue lies is rarely easy and often impossible. But the simplifications of the media and the sense of moral certainty that the public finds comforting drive debate towards black and white conclusions. As a result Croatians and Muslims have quite literally got away with murder in recent months, though there is no need to dispute that opportunity has almost certainly given the Serbs the chance to behave even worse.'[157]

But the man who was probably most in the public eye as a Balkan expert was Misha Glenny, well known to British listeners as the BBC World Service's central Europe correspondent at the beginning of the crisis. Within a very short time, Glenny had to 'retool' himself as an authority on the former Yugoslavia, a process he candidly hinted at himself. 'I understand politburos and the means of production,' he wrote in early 1993. 'I monitor the progress of political prisoners and the repression of minority rights. I know about east–west relations and the Hallenstein [sic] doctrine. [But] Guns, bullets, slaughter? What is all this about?'[158] His books *The rebirth of history* and *The fall of Yugoslavia* were widely read and he was a regular contributor to *The Times*, the *New York Review of Books*, the *London Review of Books*, and other publications. Glenny's influence, not merely on public but also on political and military perceptions of the war, was considerable. Sir Michael Rose, for example, writes how 'From time to time I also enjoyed sensible debates about what was happening in Bosnia with visitors like Misha Glenny, whose book *The Fall of Yugoslavia* had contributed so much to my understanding of the Balkans.'[159] Similarly, Lord Owen, when lamenting that nobody had noticed his success in facilitating a Zagreb–Belgrade rapprochement – prospective carve-up might be a better word – noted that 'One exception was Misha Glenny, whose book *The Fall of Yugoslavia* is the most outstanding account of the Serbo-Croat war and required reading for any serious student.'[160]

In later years, Glenny was to wonder why the inhabitants of the Balkans are 'seen either as congenitally irrational and bloodthirsty mobs, never happier than when they are slitting the throats of their neighbours, or as incompetent clowns in fanciful uniforms that mysteriously invoke a medieval past? It would be hard to find academics or Balkan specialists who take the view that the collapse of Yugoslavia was a product of ancient hatreds. But this belief is stubbornly held by the Western media and Western policy-makers.'[161] It is a curious fact, however, that Glenny himself was a major contributor to such beliefs.

Already in August 1991 he was speaking of 'the irrational logic that provoked the fighting' between Serbs and Croats, and saying that 'the same irrational belief that drives Serbs to repeat crimes against their opponents in almost predictable historical cycles is shared by all its neighbours'.[162] In *The fall of Yugoslavia* he pronounced that 'for Balkan politicians it is axiomatic that the only truth is a lie'.[163] He also describes a meeting with Serb peasants: 'the faces confronting me were those of the peasantry. They were round, wide-eyed with large amounts of roughly-trimmed hair – demons with the trigger, but no Einsteins.'[164] Confronted with these and other sentiments, the usually temperate Cambridge historian Dr Catherine Simpson observed that 'some of Glenny's writing would in a different context be described as racist'.[165]

Over the years, Glenny's credentials as a Balkan historian have been repeatedly eviscerated by scholars.[166] But – speaking from a non-specialist standpoint – some of this criticism is a little harsh. Most historians make mistakes of some sort, and writing history for a general readership inevitably involves greater exposure to factual error. All things considered, Glenny's recent history of the Balkans, which genuinely tried – consciously or unconsciously – to make amends for earlier excesses, probably did more good than harm. What is far more worrying is the consistent weakness of Glenny's *political* analysis and judgement. Glenny, after all, was highly conscious of his role as a prescient sage. 'Insofar as I enjoy a reputation as a journalist in eastern Europe,' he wrote in early 1993, 'this is largely due to my doom-laden warnings, during 1990 and 1991, about the coming carnage in Yugoslavia. With ever greater clarity, I could make out the ghastly outline of the four horses of the apocalypse, dashing through the skies. But what reputation is this, which stands atop a mountain of newly dismembered flesh and blood?'[167]

One of Glenny's obsessions was the role of Germany and the Catholic Church, whose baleful 'premature recognition' of Slovenia and Croatia he bitterly criticized at the time[168] and subsequently held responsible for the descent into bloodshed.[169] He denied that 'recognition will lead to a swift end to the war in Croatia'; instead, he argued that it opened up 'the possibility of arms sales to Croatia by Germany', which would 'intensify' the fighting between the Croats and the Serbs. This did not happen: recognition shocked Belgrade and the Krajina

Serbs into accepting a ceasefire mediated by Cyrus Vance. Glenny seemed closer to the mark on Bosnia: recognition might 'extend the war southwards into Bosnia-Herzegovina and Macedonia . . . Using the Serbian population in both states as its agent, the JNA will take the war to these two republics. Recognition of Croatia and Slovenia will definitely mean war in Bosnia and probably in Macedonia.'[170] German recognition, he later claimed, 'finally provoke[d] the war in Bosnia': it 'effectively signed the death warrant for Bosnia-Herzegovina'.[171] Glenny also censured the London government for its alleged willingness to trade their opposition to recognition for Slovenia and Croatia for concessions on the Maastricht treaty. 'After all,' he told the readers of the *London Review of Books*, 'what matters the fate of four million people inhabiting a far away country of which we know f—k all, if we can save a few bob for our ailing small businesses?'[172] Glenny was partly right: war in Bosnia did follow, but he seems curiously blind to the possibility that the Serb campaign of ethnic cleansing might have deeper roots than a knee-jerk response to German initiatives.

Glenny's preoccupation with German interference was exceeded only by his conviction of imminent breakdown and full-scale war in Macedonia. Already in August 1992 he wrote that 'For the sad Macedonians, once again attempting the Sisyphean task of asserting their independence against the wishes of two powerful neighbours, the bell now seems to toll. Those who wish to anticipate the next stage of the current Balkan crisis would be well advised to mug up on the 36 years of history in south-eastern Europe that followed the Berlin conference of 1878. History is about to repeat itself.'[173] A year later he warned the readers of the *New York Times* to 'Demilitarize Bosnia or the storm will spread south',[174] and he repeated the message in March 1995 in an article entitled – without obvious irony – 'Here we go again. Misha Glenny on the coming Balkan war'.[175]

But none of this happened: the long-predicted conflagration in Macedonia resolutely refused to break out, not even during the depths of the Kosovo crisis in 1999. By 2000, Glenny had stopped predicting war in Macedonia. In March 2001, the country was convulsed by clashes between ethnic Albanian guerillas and the Macedonian security forces. Glenny might have repeated himself, but history did not.

Perhaps slightly embarrassed by the perpetual postponement of the Macedonian apocalypse, Glenny added a defensive passage to the third edition of *The fall of Yugoslavia*. 'My obsession with Macedonia,' he wrote, 'and the regional stability of the southern Balkans would sometimes provoke amused comments from some of my colleagues, who believed that I was unnecessarily alarmist about the country. At times I did exaggerate the immediate threat to peace in the Southern Balkans, but I did so in order to try to shake the complacency which assumed that Bosnia-Herzegovina was a specific problem which existed outside the wider context of Balkan stability.'[176] This statement is an interesting insight into the tension between dispassionate analysis and policy prescription which affects all experts to a greater or lesser degree.

During the early stages of the conflict, interestingly enough, Glenny was by no means completely dismissive of military intervention; and some of his pieces can still be read with profit.[177] But as the war dragged on, bad commentary increasingly drove out good. The chief characteristic of Glenny's analysis was his belief that the Serbs were not merely being misunderstood but underestimated as well. He came to reject military intervention against them as unjust, impractical and totally counter-productive. In early 1993, he was still arguing that 'We cannot know for certain what the reaction of the Serbs would be' to intervention.[178] Four months later, he had thrown caution to the winds. He rejected the notion that 'the Serbs are inveterate cowards . . . the history of the last two centuries would tend to favour the private assessment of Cyrus Vance's deputy, Herbert Okun. He maintained that "the Krajina and Bosnian Serbs kill without compunction and die without complaint".' (This turned out to be only half true.) 'General Ratko Mladic has promised to lay waste large parts of the northern Balkans in the event of air strikes against his forces. I take his threats seriously.'[179] In 1994, when writing about Nato ultimata, he assured his readers that 'The Serbs were ready to face the air strikes. The idea, widely regarded throughout the world as unshakeable truth, that Serb bravado crumbled when a credible threat was issued, does not stand up to scrutiny.'[180] And in May 1995 he opined that 'Five minutes in the company of the Bosnian Serbs will show that these people – not just their leaders – are ready to fight to the death, glorying in their fatalist mythology of martyrdom. But they will make sure they take the rest of the Balkans with them.'[181]

For this reason, Glenny was a steadfast opponent of 'lift and strike'. 'Lifting the arms embargo or bombing the Serbs,' he wrote in November 1993, 'would have led to increased conflict and destruction throughout eastern Europe.'[182] Six months later he expanded on this theme: 'The Muslims cannot win the war alone because of their inferiority in weaponry . . . The idea that the "playing fields would be evened" by lifting the arms embargo fails to take aspects of the war into account. Firstly, the Muslims are already receiving substantial amounts of weaponry [from Saudi Arabia, Iran and Pakistan]. They are not nearly at such a great disadvantage militarily as sometimes appears from afar.'[183] The fact that such a military disadvantage is asserted in one of his own preceding sentences, does not seem to have occurred to him. And towards the end of 1994, he asked rhetorically: 'How can the west help? Not by dropping bombs.' 'To offer large-scale military support to the Bosnian government,' he claimed, 'would trigger a ferocious response from Belgrade.'[184]

His opposition was part of a broader critique of US policy towards Bosnia and an impatience with the 'special relationship'. 'The United Kingdom,' he demanded in February 1994, 'must begin to pay more attention to Germany and concentrate less on the special relationship with the United States (which looks more like a tired anachronism every day).'[185] Even today, Glenny still argues that 'While clothed in lofty rhetoric about the right of a nation to defend itself and the need to halt Serb atrocities', US military proposals were 'a device whereby the Americans could appear to be doing something without risking the lives of their servicemen and women'; instead of becoming involved, they 'carped from the sidelines'.[186] But Glenny's was no knee-jerk anti-Americanism. Interestingly, he was highly laudatory of US initiatives in the 'southern Balkans', particularly towards Macedonia.[187]

Underlying much of Glenny's commentary was a fundamental and increasing suspicion of the Sarajevo government. Thus he responded to television pictures of preparations for a Bosnian offensive – to retake ethnically cleansed areas – with the following sour observation: 'Had it been the Serbs who were openly boasting about offensives under preparation, the massed ranks of the international media would have been crying foul. But the response was muted when the Bosnian government trashed its solemn commitments to the international community.'[188] But perhaps the most striking sign of Glenny's byzantinism and moral equivalence was the credence he lent to the notion that the Bosnians might be shelling their own people. 'I imagine,' he wrote about the Sarajevo bread-queue massacre of May 1992, 'that about ten people know the truth of the matter and they are unlikely to tell the story. Or if they did, who would believe them?'[189] 'It is important to note,' he observed of the market-place massacre of February 1994, 'that the United States acted upon the effects of a lone mortar whose origin officially remains unknown.'[190] After all, Glenny had claimed in October 1991, 'Lying is not just a national passion in Yugoslavia, it is the truth.'[191]

Just how absurd this invincibly sceptic stance could become is illustrated by an exchange between Glenny and the new Assistant Secretary of State, Richard Holbrooke, in the US State Department at the height of the Serb attack on Bihac in late 1994. 'So whaddya think?' Holbrooke asks upon hearing news of Serb breakthroughs, 'Should we bomb them around Bihac?' Glenny's response was to ask whether the reports had been confirmed.[192] After Sarajevo, Foca, Bjelina, Gorazde, the first Srebrenica crisis, and many other cases, after more than two years of war, tens of thousands of casualties, and millions of refugees, Glenny still required confirmation of Serb attacks.

Instead, Glenny told the Sarajevo government to settle while it still could. He roundly condemned the US for 'encouraging' Alija Izetbegovic to hold out in the expectation of western help.[193] Rather he 'must recognize that he has lost the war against the Serbs and negotiate accordingly'.[194] Consequently, Glenny condemned 'The rejection of the Owen–Stoltenberg peace plan by the Bosnian parliament', which 'appeared to bury the possibility that an unjust but necessary peace settlement would be made'.[195] As the war dragged on, the Bosnians refused to settle, and outside intervention gradually increased, Glenny slipped more and more into the role of a Cassandra. He spent much of early 1995 predicting disaster in the Krajina. A Croatian attempt to recapture the area, he claimed, would place Belgrade 'under overwhelming domestic pressure to send troops to support the Krajina Serbs'.[196] He ridiculed Tudjman's military pretensions and his 'claims that Serbia and the Yugoslav army are too weary and battered to fight on behalf of their Krajina brethren'. Not only, Glenny argued, should Tudjman – whom he lampooned as a 'supremely sagacious military historian' and 'perspicacious president' – realize that 'the Krajina Serbs are no pushover', but that they could also call on the Bosnian Serb army. In any case, he pronounced, 'far from sounding sheepish and weary', Belgrade had signalled that it would come to the aid of the Krajina Serbs.[197]

Much of what the experts argued was contested at the time. As we have seen, it was not true that Germany precipitated the war in Bosnia by forcing through the recognition of Slovenia and Croatia as part of a broader hegemonic design. Observers could also see that the notion of a rough moral and political equivalence between the two – later three – sides was entirely misleading. The Bosnian presidency was the internationally recognized government of the country, the Bosnian Serbs and subsequently the Bosnian Croats were illegal separatists. Even more to the point, there was no comparison between the essentially reactive crimes perpetrated by Bosnian forces and the calculated policy of ethnic displacement pursued by the Bosnian Serb regime. For one military expert to write that 'The media suggested and the majority of the public accepted the view that most of the murders, rapes and tortures had been carried out by Serbs. This simplified picture was threatened by reports of Muslim massacres,'[198] is misleading. It would have been wrong to claim that *all* the crimes were committed by one side; to argue that *most* of them were the responsibility of the Bosnian Serbs was no more than the truth. This is an example of yet another *déformation professionelle* among experts: the yen to suggest that things are more complicated than they really are.

Nor did the various historical analogies hold water. This time, the experts were guilty of over-simplification. The notion that dozens of German divisions had been held down by doughty Serb partisans, while the Croats and Muslims collaborated, should have been recognized as a complete distortion at the time. It overlooked the inconvenient facts that the genocidal Croatian Ustasha regime which took power in 1941 was largely made up of rank outsiders, that many Croats, including President Franjo Tudjman himself, had fought against the Nazis, and that the Serbs themselves had spawned a puppet regime in Belgrade – under General Milan Nedic – with deep roots in the pre-war Serbian establishment.[199] Resistance in Serbia proper between the failure of the rising of 1941 and the arrival of the Red Army in 1944 was minimal.[200] Indeed, many Serbian nationalist 'Chetnik formations' were collaborationist. And while the overstretched German army did make heavy weather of suppressing the partisans, it is also true that German combat fatalities during the initial invasion of Yugoslavia were in the hundreds, not many more than the western coalition suffered in the Gulf War.[201]

The safest thing to say about historical analogies between the situations in the Second World War and the early 1990s is that they are (mostly) not helpful. They certainly did not suggest that intervention, even of a limited nature, would necessarily fail. On the contrary, the experience of 1941–4 showed that forces operating under much more difficult conditions than the Bosnian government forces were in 1992–5 could be supplied from the air. Nor did this experience necessarily suggest the inefficacy of air power. As Wing Commander Tony le Hardy, commander of the Forward Fighter Sector on Vis island and liaison officer at Tito's headquarters for much of 1944, remarked fifty years later: 'The very reason why the German occupation of Yugoslavia failed to subdue the partisans was just because they did not have air superiority – let alone supremacy. Certainly, from January 1944 ... Allied aircraft roamed at will over Yugoslavia without opposition from the Luftwaffe.' 'Indeed,' le Hardy continued, one major German offensive in May 1944 supported by tanks and paratroops 'was brought to a standstill *solely by air strikes*.' Finally, the wing commander remarked, 'Germans involved at the time have since recorded that the constant allied air attacks, or the fear of them, were as destructive of morale as the fear of attack by the partisans. It is this psychological factor which seems to have been entirely overlooked by the "armchair" strategists (and politicians) who have consistently argued that air strikes will not help to lift the siege of Sarajevo or of the other so-called UN safe areas in the country.'[202]

There were other veterans and experts who were optimistic about the chances of a successful military intervention, even a limited aerial action, against the Bosnian Serbs. They were certainly contemptuous of historical analogies. 'It is utterly different to when the Germans were there,' argued General Sir Anthony Farrar-Hockley, sometime Commander-in-Chief of Allied Forces in northern Europe. 'If the Germans had had the sort of helicopters we've now got, Tito would never have lasted . . . you can't hide people and guns in woods any longer.'[203] He estimated that two or three divisions, or about 30–40,000 men, with maritime air cover would be sufficient to take on the Serbs. He also rejected the argument that lifting the arms embargo would 'simply lead to more deaths'. This was only partly true: 'more Serb invaders would be killed, but fewer Bosnian Muslim and Croat civilians would be killed . . . An arms embargo favours only the oppressors.'[204] This view was echoed by Colonel Michael Dewar in late October 1992, whose better judgement was not always crowded out by sonorous semi-official negativity. He reckoned that Serb militias could be defeated by 50–100,000 men using carrier groups in the Adriatic: 'You could create conditions which really do change Serbia's mind.'[205] Even such a sceptic as Fitzroy Maclean agreed that whereas air attacks 'were never decisive' during the Second World War, 'air-strikes, as delivered by Nato's powerful air force half a century later, would be infinitely more effective and could well give the Serbs, both in Bosnia and Belgrade . . . a sufficient jolt to bring them to their senses, or at any rate to the conference table'.[206]

Perhaps the most persistent and informed advocate of an alternative strategy was Edward Cowan, a retired colonel in the Black Watch and the British Defence Attaché to Yugoslavia from 1987 to 1990. In a series of detailed articles and briefings, Cowan showed how the Bosnian Serbs could be confronted and repulsed. 'Throughout the conflict,' he argued in April 1993, 'there has been a tendency to over-emphasize the military capabilities of the combatants, and hence to argue that an outside intervention force would be sucked into a quagmire.' Indeed, he pointed out that 'a large-scale, high-intensity operation undertaken by NATO, backed by a sufficiently strong UN mandate, would quickly overwhelm serious resistance by Bosnian Serb forces or those of the FRY, and could be carried out with relatively minor casualties'.[207] And while he had reservations about the unsupported use of air power, Cowan was an enthusiastic supporter of US-backed Nato ultimata. 'The American plan would have a dramatic impact,' he continued. 'For the first time Serb forces would face widespread disruption and suffer severe casualties. This action alone might be sufficient to induce a more compliant [Serb] attitude.'[208]

But the only *official* argument by a serving officer for air strikes was made in April 1993, by Lord Owen's military advisor, Graham Messervy-Whiting.[209] This remarkable document came to light when Owen's *Balkan odyssey* was published and was based on, though not necessarily in tune with, advice taken by the author from air power experts at the MoD.[210] 'Many of the heavy weapons,' he pointed out, 'cannot be quickly and effectively moved.' These could be 'degraded' or even destroyed. The effectiveness of mobile weapons could be greatly disrupted by air attacks. Ground forces could confine themselves to 'specialist intelligence, targeting and communications teams'. 'Attacking aircraft would of course be vulnerable to ground fire,' he conceded, 'but vulnerability can be minimised by the expert offensive air planners; use of a judicious mix of surprise, electronic warfare measures, medium-altitude attack with laser designation and single-pass attacks at low altitude.' Moreover, he added, many Serb formations had 'long and vulnerable LOC [lines of communication]'. 'Interdiction of the road[s] . . . would undoubtedly affect the Bosnian Serb army's offensive capability.'[211] Later, in fact, Messervy-Whiting was to claim – with qualifications – that other 'experts at the time were perhaps overestimating the effectiveness of the Bosnian Serb army once they had been engaged with decisive power'.[212] He was stating no more than the obvious.

What is clear is that the notion that the Americans were culturally and intellectually indisposed to tackle 'small wars' with possibly imperfect outcomes does not apply to Bosnia. It was, indeed, the Americans who advocated a 'limited' war, based on aerial and logistical support for a sympathetic government; it was the British who demanded guarantees of total success. It was the Americans who felt that if helping the Bosnians militarily was something worth doing, it was worth doing badly; it was the British who at all times counselled perfection – and consequently inaction. To reverse these alignments – as so many experts and commentators did – was pure psychological 'projection'.

Nor was the Bosnian conflict so difficult to understand militarily. It was a highly conventional war. With the exception of the Bosnian government enclaves in the east, there was practically no guerilla warfare. All sides, particularly the Serbs, tended to fight unimaginatively with the aim of taking and holding identifiable pieces of ground. Victory in these battles generally went to the side strongest in conventional heavy weaponry such as tanks and artillery – usually the Serbs. Moreover, with the temporary exception of sectors of the Croat–Bosnian government war in central Bosnia and Herzegovina, there were definite front lines. Nobody was ever in any doubt as to whether they lived on the Serb, Croat, or Bosnian government side of the line. Indeed, throughout the war the front lines were clearly visible on a map on an almost daily basis in western newspapers; they rarely changed until the successful Croat–Bosnian government offensive in late 1995. Messervy-Whiting was quite clear about this. 'There were front lines,' he recalls, 'you were very conscious there were front lines . . . you were certainly very conscious when you went from one *side* to the other *side*.'[213] In short, in military terms Bosnia was a conventional, if incompetently executed, war. All arguments to the contrary reflected not a serious military assessment, but a psycho-political need to marginalize the conflict.

But on the substantive issues – the role of air strikes, the potential strength of the Croatian and Bosnian armies, the true fighting power of the Serb armies – the jury was still out in 1992–5. Of course, there was already a strong case to suggest that the threat of serious air power could have a moderating effect on the Bosnian Serbs. Their withdrawals following Nato ultimata in July 1993, February 1994, and April 1994 showed this; but these successes were sufficiently obscurable by the role of UN or UNPROFOR mediators or the Russians to undermine any broader claims made on their behalf. There was a lot of contemporary journalistic and circumstantial evidence for the efficacy of military threats.[214]

There were some contemporary observers who rejected the orthodox view of Serb military prowess. The Liberal Democrat leader, Paddy Ashdown, himself a former Royal Marine, pointed out that 'The massive misjudgment the Government is making is that these people are not the IRA, they are not the Vietnamese; I've watched these people; they are local town thugs. They are not trained, they are not fit, they are not prepared to close with the enemy. They run whenever somebody actually fires back at them; they are cowards, most of them.'[215] David White, defence correspondent of the *Financial Times* and by no means an enthusiastic interventionist himself, stressed in April 1993 that whereas 'outside military intervention . . . is a daunting prospect for a number of reasons, . . . the sophistication of Bosnian Serb forces is certainly not among them'. He outlined their shrinking level of manpower, low morale, poor training and general lack of cohesion.[216] Similar assessments were made by the defence correspondent Chris Bellamy, who firmly parted company with official orthodoxy on this issue, the historian Mark Mazower, and the journalist Martin Bell.[217]

In the United States, in fact, this view was something of an orthodoxy. As the new Chairman of the Joint Chiefs of Staff, General John Shalikashvili, argued in August 1993, 'We are not fighting a first-rate, fully combat-capable outfit. Never underestimate the mess and nastiness you get into, but I think we've had too much overestimating.'[218] General William Nash, commander of the US armoured division which went into Bosnia in late 1995 as part of the Dayton settlement, remembers that he 'had no particular respect for the capacities of the Serbs . . . The equipment certainly didn't impress me . . . I'm not too impressed by armies that make their reputation on attacking civilians.'[219] James Woolsey, the Director of Central Intelligence, recalls that 'we knew all along, and were not particularly impressed by, the Bosnian Serbs' military capabilities'.[220] Similarly, Richard Holbrooke later rejected the much-invoked analogy with Vietnam. 'The comparison,' he writes, 'was dangerously misleading: Bosnia was different, and so were our objectives. While we had to learn from Vietnam, we could not be imprisoned by it. Bosnia was not Vietnam, the Bosnian Serbs were not the Vietcong and Belgrade was not Hanoi. The Bosnian Serbs, poorly trained bullies and criminals, would not stand up to NATO air strikes the way the seasoned and indoctrinated Vietcong and North Vietnamese had.'[221] Indeed, the whole American strategy of 'lift and strike' – as discussed in Chapter 2 – hinged on the assumption that a US-armed and trained Bosnian and Croatian force supported by Nato jets could defeat the over-rated Serb armies, or at least force them to the negotiating table.

Even Philip Corwin, an American UN official who was no friend to the Bosnian government and who bitterly opposed Nato air strikes on the Bosnian Serbs, later had this to say about their army: 'At some point in the future, historians will write about the true nature of the BSA. The common perception of it as a ruthless and efficient military machine ... was hardly accurate. Ruthless, yes, but efficient and well-trained, not necessarily. Many of their soldiers were ... undisciplined fun-loving farmers who preferred brandy and women to war. During the whole of the Bosnian conflict there were very few examples of hand-to-hand combat, guerilla operations, or sabotage behind the lines. Bayonets and other paraphernalia of close combat were almost unknown. The Serbs set up their artillery on mountain tops and shelled villages until the civilians decided to leave. Then the BSA swooped in [and] "cleansed" the village by massacring enough of the locals still present to convince the rest to leave ... This war was one of artillery and massacre. The BSA did not want an infantry war because it was outnumbered and did not have the morale to fight such a war. They preferred long-distance shelling to hand-to-hand combat.'[222]

But prior to the late summer of 1995 these were judgements, not findings of fact; and in some cases they may well have been coloured by hindsight. For most of the war, British and American 'experts' found themselves debating a question to which there might have been a common-sense answer, but no theoretical resolution. How effective massive air strikes could be, and how formidable the Serb army actually was, could only be established on the battlefield itself.

The doubts and hesitations sown by the experts reinforced the British government's determination to avoid military intervention. But there was a considerable circularity in this process. It is true that senior military experts appeared sceptical about intervention against the Bosnian Serbs. Thus, when the British Chairman of Nato's Military Committee, Field-Marshal Sir Richard Vincent, announced in April 1993 that 'The first principle of war is: for God's sake decide what you're trying to achieve before you go out there and start doing it', this was not unreasonably taken by the defence correspondent of the *Telegraph* to mean that he 'continue[d] to urge a cautious approach to the use of force in former Yugoslavia'.[223] But in fact, Field-Marshal

Vincent was criticizing the lack of political direction. Of course, as Nato sources recall, Vincent was cautious in the military advice he gave. But what the government did not want to hear was Vincent's view that intervention was not only possible but necessary, even at great cost. He privately compared the western response to Bosnia to the appeasement of Nazism in the 1930s, and he felt that the number of troops needed to implement the peace plans, to seal the Serb border, or to secure Sarajevo had been exaggerated. 'I am old enough to remember Munich,' Vincent subsequently remarked. 'My father took me to Heston airport to see Neville Chamberlain coming back.'[224] He adds that 'I think the UK did drag its feet unduly' and that 'I think we could have done it quicker and saved one hell of a lot more lives if we had made up our minds somewhat earlier.' The Bosnian Serb threat he dismissed as a 'spectre'. Indeed, so strongly did Vincent feel about all this at the time that, as he later recalled, he 'did seriously consider how long professionally I could go on living with this total strategic discontinuity myself . . . we were losing credibility.'[225]

Vincent was by no means alone. Senior military figures back in London observed the palpable 'drift' in British policy with increasing dismay. They respected the Foreign Secretary's intellect, but found him a 'prevaricator'. They felt that the politicians were 'hiding behind the military'. They were also openly contemptuous of the general lack of direction 'typical of the Major government'. The dilemma of British military experts was graphically described by the Nato spokesman Jamie Shea. 'The thing about military people,' he pointed out, 'is that they don't want to give politicians the impression that there's an easy option, you know, just let us bomb and within twenty-four hours we've solved your problem for you . . . because politicians will too easily allow the military to bomb and then turn around and say well you promised us it was going to work, you gave us bad advice, you let us down, it's your fault.' For this reason, he concludes, 'it became this dreadful vicious circle where the military . . . weren't allowed to come up with the grandiose options. They were being asked to develop a way to make military force effective in a very microscopic kind of framework.'[226]

The military were not blameless in this. As Nato sources recall, any time the politicians asked for estimates for a ground operation, the military came up with inflated figures: 'we probably could have done it with 20,000 . . . [but the military men] over-egged the pudding, they came out with these unbelievable numbers, which then scared the politicians, and completely devalued the notion that there was a ground option, and then everybody said well, therefore we can only do it by air, but air's not going to win, therefore there is no option'. Moreover, as Jamie Shea remembers, the prevailing view on air power was 'clearly too cautious. I heard many briefings on the fact that air strikes would not work, the hilly terrain, the fog, [and] the difficulty of selecting targets accurately.'[227] Likewise, Douglas Hurd remembers that 'the military were certainly against military intervention on the ground to impose a solution. They were constantly saying that wasn't possible. I think they may find they over-estimated the sticking power of the Bosnian Serbs.'

Misgivings about government policy at the highest levels of the British military soon began to circulate at Westminster. Thus, on 22 July 1993 the Labour MP Andrew Faulds claimed that 'the Government have consistently misrepresented the view of the military both in Britain and at NATO about the feasibility of effective action in that country'.[228] This theme was taken up by no fewer than four MPs in the debate of 26 July. 'I have talked to soldiers, diplomats and journalists,' the Tory MP Patrick Cormack remarked. 'I do not want to break confidences or embarrass people, but suffice it to say that I am not persuaded – how shall I word this carefully – that what has been said in the House entirely reflects the advice that I am told has been given at a lower level. Perhaps that advice has not permeated to the top and, if that is the case, there is something wrong with the system. There is an appreciation among diplomats and those responsible in NATO and elsewhere that there is something that should and could be done.'[229] Later on, the Labour MP Chris Mullin spoke at some length of dissenters within the British military and diplomatic corps for whom government policy was 'a diplomatic and strategic disaster with major implications for western security'. Indeed, he continued, 'Our diplomats and military personnel have been misled by Ministers about the state of public opinion and, perhaps, the state of opinion in this House. I think that they have been told not even to contemplate anything that involves military action, because the British public will not wear it and

Members of Parliament will not support it.' Clare Short and Malcolm Wicks spoke in similar terms.[230]

The implications of all this were drawn out by Andrew Marr in a fascinating article in July 1993: 'The Foreign Office insists that, as far as ministers are aware, the military advice has been unanimous and unequivocal against intervention. But military men and diplomats who favour intervention have complained privately that they have been warned by MPs not to speak out because their views are not welcome.'[231] Indeed, James Gow was later to reveal 'that intervention was possible and necessary at different levels . . . That opinion could still be heard from many, if not all corners of officialdom, both civilian and military, in private discussion. The assessment was that politicians were the major constraint on policy.'[232] The Prime Minister's contention that no advice had been received 'either from senior diplomats or from military figures that a solution could be imposed by military force' thus cannot be true, even if it was made in good faith.[233]

All this was summed up by none other than Colonel Michael Dewar, the Deputy Director of the International Institute for Strategic Studies. 'My view,' he said in late October 1992, 'is that military intervention is perfectly feasible from a military point of view and that Douglas Hurd and others, for entirely political reasons, are fighting shy of saying that it is viable. What they mean is that it is not politically desirable.'[234] This time, he knew what he was talking about.

CHAPTER 7

# 'Emulsifying the Whole Affair': Parliament and the Public Sphere

In late July 1995 the US Senate, the upper house of the legislature of the most powerful nation on earth, convened for a dramatic session. It took place in the terrible aftermath of the Srebrenica massacre, during which the Bosnian Serbs had killed more than 6,000 Muslim men and boys while UN peacekeepers stood idly by. The immediate subject was the lifting of the arms embargo on the Sarajevo government, but the resulting debate was essentially on American and European policy towards the problem as a whole. To be sure, some of those attacking the administration were opportunist Republicans seeking to damage President Clinton. But the vast majority of those present were motivated by genuinely bipartisan considerations. The co-sponsors of the bill were the Senate majority leader, Bob Dole, a Republican who had been a critic of the senior Bush administration's policy back in 1991–2, and Senator Joe Lieberman of Connecticut, a centrist Democrat, who later became the Vice-Presidential candidate in 2000. And while emotions ran high, the general tenor of the discussion befitted the representatives of a great nation deliberating a matter of enormous international importance.

This debate was the outcome of a long Congressional and media campaign against Bill Clinton's Bosnia policy. It was the culmination of a relentless synergy between politics and civil society. It was a revolt of large elements of the political elite, a 'revolution from above', as one of its protagonists called it. The gravity of the Congressional initiative should not be underestimated: the presidential prerogative in foreign policy was being directly challenged in a way unknown since the end of the Vietnam War. Far from being careless of the consequences of their actions, American lawmakers – and their allies in the media and the foreign-policy establishment – knew very well what they were doing. It is a testimony to the strength of their beliefs on Bosnia that they were prepared to press matters to the sticking point. Even though the distances were greater, Bosnia was no small far-off country for them.

No such debate took place in Britain. The Establishment remained – as we have seen – almost unanimously supportive of government policy. Nor was there any sustained challenge from within the political nation: from the two houses of parliament. The very organs which should have driven a critique of the executive, the national broadsheets, did more to obscure the issues involved than to promote their careful consideration. At the same time, many British intellectuals eschewed the engagement of their counterparts across the Atlantic and across the Channel, preferring instead to add a veneer of intellectual coherence to governmental policy. The synergy between civil society and political nation manifest in Washington, and evident in British policy during the Falklands and Gulf crises, was painfully absent.

In part, the lack of debate was due to the Major administration's determination to keep the issue off the political agenda. It was only at the repeated prompting of the Conservative MP Patrick Cormack – an honourable and eloquent critic of his own government's policy – that a debate on the former Yugoslavia eventually took place on 12 December 1991 at 3.21 a.m. By then, of course, nearly one-third of Croatia had been occupied, hundreds of thousands of people, mainly Croats, expelled, and the Slavonian city of Vukovar had been levelled by Serb and 'Yugoslav' artillery. The absurdity of debating such a major issue in the early hours of the morning in front of a largely empty House struck George Robertson, later Defence Secretary during the Kosovo War and now Secretary General of Nato. 'The hon. Gentleman,' he observed, 'is not to blame for the procedures that the House has foisted upon itself. Having spent 13 years in this place, I still find it truly remarkable that, with regard to such important issues – Croatia is receiving perhaps its first real airing in the House since the tragedy began to unfold – we are having this debate at 3.35 a.m. The House should not be proud of that.'

This provoked the Minister of State at the Foreign and Commonwealth Office, Douglas Hogg, to express his 'distaste for these early-morning debates'. 'We are discussing a matter of considerable importance,' he conceded. Indeed, Hogg continued, 'it is difficult to think of a matter of greater importance at the moment in central Europe – yet my hon. Friend has been obliged to raise it at an hour that is inappropriate for a matter of such gravity. My hon. Friend deserves our congratulations and thanks for having raised it, but the systems and procedures of the House should not have obliged him to do so at this time – or obliged us to be here at 3.47 a.m. to deal with a matter of such moment . . . I wish that we would put an end to such proceedings. They do the House no good whatsoever.'[1] Why it should have been left to Patrick Cormack to secure a debate, Douglas Hogg, the responsible serving minister in HMG, did not say.

In any case, by May 1994, more than two years and many massacres later, Patrick Cormack was still lamenting 'the fact that the House has not been given the opportunity more often to debate the crisis in the former Yugoslavia and, in particular, the terrible events in Bosnia. Throughout the whole of this long, tragic saga, we have hardly had an opportunity to debate the issue exclusively. We had a brief, three-hour debate introduced by the Liberal Democrats on a Supply day. If my memory serves me correctly, we have had one or two foreign affairs debates in which it has been germane to mention the matter, but the House has not focused its attention on these matters as much as it should have done.' 'When the House neglects to debate these matters,' he added forlornly, 'it marginalises itself, because what is happening in the Balkans is of enormous significance to us all.'[2]

Cormack's prescient call for the government to recognize that 'something more must be done to identify the aggressor and to hold him to account' and to 'stop acting as an honest broker between victim and aggressor',[3] went unheeded. Nor did the opposition call for a division on Bosnia. Indeed, the only division of the war was at the request of the Liberal Democrats, in November 1992. The motion – condemning government action as 'too little, too late' – was defeated by 166 votes to 37.[4] Only 206 MPs actually voted. Patrick Cormack was the only Conservative MP to vote against the government.

There was, in fact, remarkably little constructive criticism of government policy on Bosnia in parliament. Sir Patrick Cormack was the only Conservative MP who consistently supported the Sarajevo government. There was a small number of other Tories whose common sense and decent instincts revolted at the arms embargo. Winston Churchill, for example, asked pertinently whether it was not 'unprecedented for the United Nations to impose an arms embargo on the victim of military aggression – in this case, the Bosnian Muslims?'[5] By the end, the most senior critic of the arms embargo was Iain Duncan Smith, the secretary of the Foreign Affairs Committee and a man with a military background himself.[6] The number of Labour critics was rather larger and included Peter Mandelson, Peter Hain, Clare Short, Calum MacDonald, Max Madden, Malcolm Wicks, and Kate Hoey. They harried the government as best they could; but they were never more than a doughty minority, even in their own party. Among the Liberal Democrats, the most effective and coherent critic of government policy was their deputy leader, Sir Russell Johnston.[7] Until 1995, it was essentially this same band which returned to the fray time and again.

Comparatively few members could be classed as pro-Serb, but they inflicted damage out of all proportion to their numbers. Their principal spokesman was Bob Wareing – affectionately known as 'Slob-a-Bob' – a leading light of the all-party group on Yugoslavia and its chairman from February 1994.[8] He took a keen interest in the economic aspects of Anglo-Yugoslav relations.[9] Some thought him an authority on account – as the Conservative MP David Tredinnick put it in September 1992 – of his service 'in Yugoslavia during the Second World War'.[10] In fact Wareing, who was born in 1930, played no part in that conflict, and has never claimed to. The strategy pursued by Wareing and like-minded members such as Harold Elletson (Con.), John Reid (Lab.) and John Townend (Con.) was transparent but clever. At every point in the debate they sought to play down the level of Serbian atrocities, to blacken the Croats and the Sarajevo government, to demand the 'demilitarization' of safe areas – i.e. to render them totally defenceless – and generally to obscure the difference between the principal victims, the Bosnians, and their chief tormentors, Bosnian Serb separatists.

A typical example of this approach is John Reid's comment of May

1993, made at the height of the transatlantic 'lift and strike' debate, on the basis of a visit organized by the Bosnian Serbs. He used the example of an alleged massacre by Croats against Serbs as an 'illustration of the fact that atrocities are being committed by all sides'. 'Will the government,' he continued, 'maintain the even-handed approach that they have sensibly deployed over the past few months and resist any pressure from sections of the media to turn this into a holy war for the Serbs?'[11] Another instance would be Bob Wareing's speech of 29 April 1993. 'There is no nationality of Bosnian,' he told the House. 'They are Serbs, Croats and Muslims. Even the Muslims are Serbs. They are the descendants of those who converted from the Orthodox religion to the Muslim religion during the time of the Ottoman Empire.' Wareing then – rather startlingly for a Labour MP of the old school – claimed that the Serbs 'owned' more than 60 per cent of the land in Bosnia. For good measure he also repeated the canard that it had been 'discovered that the attack on a bread queue [1992] in Sarajevo was by Muslims'.[12] Later that year Wareing was to reject accusations of being 'pro-Serb', and advanced his own criticisms of Serb paramilitary atrocities in Croatia in his defence;[13] but his highly controversial trip to Serb-occupied Bosnia in late July 1995, just after the Srebrenica massacre, which culminated in a meeting with Ratko Mladic and Radovan Karadzic, showed where his true sympathies lay.[14]

It came as no surprise when, after the war, Wareing was suspended by his own party in 1997 for failing to declare payments made by Serbian companies in consideration of his activities as a lobbyist.[15]

These exercises in obfuscation had their humorous side. In late April 1993, Harold Elletson wanted to know what 'appropriate response' the UN Security Council intended to make to 'Croat aggression against Muslim civilians in Bosnia-Herzegovina';[16] he never showed such solicitude when it was a question of Serb aggression against Muslim civilians. Bob Wareing, on the other hand, discovered a sudden tenderness for the Bosnian Croats from mid-1993.[17] In both cases, the intention was to blur distinctions and tarnish those victims who were now belatedly and effectively fighting back.

Most parliamentarians, however, were committed to neither side. Many, particularly fellow Conservatives, agreed with Nicholas Budgen's repeated assertion that there was no British interest at stake in Bosnia. Already in June 1992 he was asking Douglas Hurd to 'explain how the sad fighting in Yugoslavia affects British national interests. Or is it the case that we have taken on the role of some sort of second-class world policeman, whenever we can find a similar policeman among what he grandly calls the international community?'[18] He rejected the idea that 'discussion of the details of this horrible civil war and all this grand but ineffectual lecturing give the impression that we are responsible for these horrible events'.[19] 'What we lack,' Budgen claimed, 'is a Disraeli. There is a case for inaction and, now, disengagement, but it has never been put.'[20] Similarly, Terry Dicks (Con.) observed that 'People are sick and tired of having British forces at risk when there is no British interest there at all.'[21] Andrew Robathan (Con.), himself a former soldier, stressed the 'very different' nature of the Bosnian conflict when compared with the Gulf and the Falklands. 'It is difficult,' he argued, 'to see a clear national interest for us, or a clear aim . . . There is no obvious British national interest, so why are our troops in the area?'[22] And Nigel Forman (Con.) spoke for many when he demanded 'a policy based on our national interest – after all, this is the British House of Commons and our first responsibility is to our voters and our people – in an area where our national interest is not greatly engaged in the outcome'.[23] On a more mundane level such scepticism was reflected by the Conservative David Wilshire, who reported that 'not a single one of my constituents has written to me, telephoned me, come to my surgery, or tracked me down in the street to say that they support sending troops to Bosnia either at the beginning or now'.[24]

At the very least, most MPs accepted the government's contention that British interest in the area exhausted itself in containing the conflict and supplying humanitarian aid. The notion that there might be a British security interest in stopping aggression and ethnic cleansing within her European sphere of influence, and in maintaining relations with the US, occurred to few of them, and even then only to be rejected. As Cyril Townsend observed in the Commons in early February 1993, 'the Conservative side of the House in particular is anxious that Britain should continue to be seen as a reliable ally of the United States. We are aware, too, that pressure for Britain to give up its permanent seat on the United Nations Security Council would be increased by a clear refusal to take a more active role in the former Yugoslavia – *but the arguments on the other side are stronger*.'[25]

Few parliamentarians questioned the prevailing governmental and expert view about the dangers of air strikes and lifting the arms embargo. Air strikes, the Conservative Bill Walker claimed, 'may sound grand' but would 'only escalate the conflict' if unsupported by ground troops.[26] Lifting the arms embargo, John Home Robertson (Lab.) told the House, 'would certainly lead to pre-emptive strikes by those who have heavy weapons – not only the Bosnian Serbs, but the Croatian forces'.[27] Variations on this theme dominated parliamentary debates on Bosnia throughout the war.[28] Many MPs were correspondingly scathing about Lady Thatcher's dramatic demands for air strikes and the lifting of the arms embargo. Harold Elletson called on the Defence Secretary to 'treat the recent comments of Baroness Thatcher with the contempt that they deserve'.[29] Malcolm Rifkind, who had just dismissed her reasoning as 'emotional nonsense', needed little encouragement to do just that. Other MPs called upon the government to distance themselves from the former Prime Minister.[30]

MPs were equally contemptuous of American policy, and for the same reasons. Some of the criticism came, predictably enough, from Labour backbenchers. Mike Gapes asked the House if it was not 'about time that we told those carping and whining voices in Congress that some of us in Europe are getting fed up getting advice and condemnation when they are not prepared to put people's lives at risk?'[31] Later that year he demanded a 'categorical assurance that our Government will not give way to misguided pressure from the American Congress and President Clinton, but will work with others to stop the lifting of the arms embargo'.[32] Nor does it come as any surprise to find the veteran anti-American Tony Benn calling upon the Foreign Secretary to 'make clear to the Americans' British opposition to 'lift and strike'.[33] To Benn, US policy was the more sinister in the light of American global arms sales, which – he told the House – amounted to more than two-thirds of the global trade and which fuelled the vast majority of contemporary conflicts: 'I have always thought the arms trade the most criminal in the world.'[34] On this reading, of course, lifting the arms embargo was nothing more than a transparent attempt by the American military-industrial complex to line its own pockets on the back of

Balkan misery. Even some pro-Bosnian MPs found it difficult to shake off the anti-American reflexes of their adolescence and early adulthood. 'The Americans,' Chris Mullin observed in April 1993, 'have always been very keen on bombing, mainly because they have never been bombed themselves.'[35]

But many Tories, now able to vent their suppressed anti-Americanism for the first time since Suez in 1956, were just as acerbic. Sir Peter Tapsell accused President Clinton of being 'more interested in New Hampshire than old Sarajevo', and of advocating 'a Balkan policy of bombing Serbia back to the stone age from a very safe height'.[36] Sir Nicholas Bonsor warned the House during the Bihac crisis of 1994 about the danger 'that the Americans might take further action that would appear to be partisan on the part of the Muslim Bosnians and therefore jeopardise the safety of UNPROFOR forces'.[37] David Sumberg called upon the government to 'make it clear to the American authorities that our troops, not theirs, are at risk daily in Bosnia, and that lifting the arms embargo will mean the immediate withdrawal of those troops'.[38] And Nigel Forman was confident enough to suggest that 'we must resist military escalation, which I believe may mean the necessity for firm, quiet private advice from our Prime Minister to the President'.[39]

As one might expect, the intense strains within the Nato alliance itself were also reflected in parliamentary debate. When Iain Duncan Smith, a respected national security Conservative backbencher and secretary of the Foreign Affairs Committee, proclaimed in November 1994 that 'Bosnia is becoming the anvil upon which Nato is being broken', the seriousness of the breach was evident. 'The recent decision of President Clinton to do what Congress has been demanding and lift the arms embargo on the Bosnian Muslims has caused a wave of speculation about the differences between the US and Europe. It has even led to absurd talk of the need for a single European response rather than involving the US. At stake is the possibility that the US decouples from Europe, assisted by disagreement over the failure of policy over Bosnia.'[40] While Duncan Smith had evidently confused withdrawal from *policing* the embargo with lifting the embargo itself, there was no confusing the sense of crisis surrounding the Nato alliance.

None of this, of course, prevented some MPs from appropriating the successes of US diplomacy. John Home Robertson quite overlooked the crucial American contribution to the Croat–Bosnian government *rapprochement* in central Bosnia and Herzegovina, which he attributed solely to a 'United Nations-sponsored truce on 23 February 1994'.[41] The doughty left-winger and Yugo-nostalgic Alice Mahon, on the other hand, acknowledged the American role, but could not quite bring herself to welcome it. 'Surely,' she told the House in early March, 'if we are to have a lasting peace in Bosnia, agreement such as that declared today between the Croats and Muslims should occur after consultation with, and the agreement of, all five permanent members of the Security Council . . . Does that not make affairs much more difficult in that area, especially for the Russians?'[42] She seemed to think that the Americans needed Russian permission on the Security Council to make peace between the Sarajevo government and Croatian separatists.

If irritations with the US were powerful, they paled into insignificance behind the wave of Germanophobia the war in Bosnia unleashed among some MPs. The ostensible cause of this was the notion of the 'premature recognition' of Slovenia and Croatia in 1991 and 1992, into which Britain had been 'bounced' by Germany and which had 'precipitated' the war in Bosnia.[43] This erroneous belief was genuinely held by the vast majority of parliamentarians, most of whom were not necessarily anti-German in the general sense. But the tendency of many parliamentarians to go well beyond what even the most negative plausible interpretation would allow shows that deeper sentiments were clearly in play. Thus, in December 1991, the Conservative MP Bowen Wells argued wildly in the Foreign Affairs Committee that 'Austria and Germany have . . . armed Croatia and have therefore enabled it to resist'.[44] Another committee member called upon Douglas Hurd to recognize that 'the German-led policy is the height of folly . . . Can we be sure that if this goes wrong and there is military involvement . . . we will not be involved on the coat-tails of the Germans?'[45] Underlying some of this was a fear of a US–German axis on Bosnia. Bernard Jenkin (Con.) suggested in July 1994 that 'the speeches by President Clinton proposing a leadership role for Germany oversimplify foreign policy in Europe and are rather more reminiscent of Joseph Kennedy than of JF Kennedy'.[46] Others criticized Germany more for her reticence. 'It appears,' the Conservative Julian Brazier claimed, 'that the Germans, who are leading the calls for "intervention", would once again be prevented from participating by a constitution which they appear less than enthusiastic to amend.'[47]

But by far the most strident attacks came from the longstanding Labour Germanophobe, Dennis Skinner. He repeatedly called upon the government to admit that Slovenia, Croatia, and Bosnia were recognized 'because Germany twisted the British government's arm and a quid pro quo deal was done on the two opt-outs for Maastricht'. British troops in Bosnia, he argued, were merely 'carrying out the wishes of the German nation'.[48] This argument neatly skewered two principal enemies in Skinner's phantasmagoric universe, the Fourth Reich and its cats-paw, the hated European Union.

Much parliamentary discussion was larded with quaint and repetitive reference to the military experience of MPs, however irrelevant. Cyril Townsend drew on his status as 'a former regular soldier' and 'an ex-military man' to lend authority to his sceptical view of air power.[49] Similarly, the Labour MP Tam Dalyell frequently adverted to his national service in the 1950s.[50] Members tended to be scornful of 'armchair generals'. Sir Anthony Grant (Con.) congratulated the government on resisting 'the military ambitions of some American and other television armchair warriors'.[51] Another parliamentarian condemned those who 'start talking from the comfort of another place about military intervention'.[52] Philip Oppenheim (Con.) derided 'those Johnny-come-lately, get-tough-from-afar proponents of action'.[53] In the same vein, Matthew Banks (Con.) asked John Major to affirm that 'contrary to the advice of the armchair generals and pseudo-defence experts [on air power], all suggestions of substantial military action in the Bosnian region should be totally resisted as in that terrain it would lead to guerilla warfare'. The Prime Minister had no difficulty in stating that he understood 'the point that my hon. Friend makes and agree[d] with him'.[54]

One particularly vociferous defender of government policy and critic of armchair generals was the late Alan Clark, a military historian and periodic Conservative MP fabled for his indiscretion and wealth. Although notorious for his robust attitude to the sale of (British) arms overseas, Clark never questioned the legitimacy or even the economics of the arms embargo on the Bosnian government. Instead, he saturated the airwaves and the television screens with horror stories about the historic Serb capacity for guerilla warfare. But his attempts to puncture advocates of military intervention sometimes misfired. In late July 1995 he dismissed one such call as emanating from 'the security of a job in the EC in Brussels', and from a man who 'has never been in combat, heard young men crying from their wounds, or seen how the neck is arched back in the seconds before dying',[55] a subject on which Clark spoke, like most of us, with more feeling than first-hand knowledge. As it transpired, his target, Graham Andrews, was a freelance writer who has never worked for an EC institution and who – as a young man growing up in Belfast – had been badly injured in a bomb explosion and caught up in several others. Andrews emphasized, with understandable asperity, that he needed 'no lectures from anybody on the subject of violent death'.[56] In itself, the exchange was of no consequence, but it did illustrate the discourteous and unnecessary abandon with which opponents of intervention accused their critics of physical cowardice.

Much parliamentary thinking derived from half-remembered history and strongly held but erroneous generalizations. One of the more diverting barrack-room historians in the House was Tam Dalyell. 'Is it ethnic cleansing?' he asked the House during the hostage crisis of May 1995. 'Are we quite sure about that, because the history of those particular Muslims is not ethnic? I return for a moment to Baghdad, where the Sunnis and Shiites, when asking about Bosnia, say, "These particular Muslims are not quite our kind of Muslims". They are the grandchildren and great-grandchildren of Serbs who tried to ingratiate themselves with the Ottoman Turks by embracing the religion of the Ottoman Turks, often in order to gain position in the Turkish empire and get some kudos from Constantinople, or Istanbul. I am against massacres, but we should not think it is straightforward ethnic cleansing. They are interacting tribal affairs and ancient rivalries.'[57] More pertinently perhaps, Dalyell was convinced that the Yugoslav People's Army was 'the most formidable, expert, tough guerilla army in the world . . . In that terrain, how on earth are we ever going to have military success against people who feel that they have great causes?'[58]

Accompanying all this was a portentous respect for Serbian arms which often shaded into muddled Serbophilia. Julian Brazier, MP for Canterbury and a frequent contributor to defence debates, warned in September 1991 that 'the Serbs have earned a formidable reputation over the centuries: even the massed armour of the Wehrmacht was badly shaken 50 years ago'.[59] A year later he reminded 'the swelling chorus of those calling for military intervention that the Serbs believe they have a cause. They would fight for it and would do so on their own terrain.'[60] All this could just about be defended as dispassionate analysis, albeit a mistaken one. But the boundary to obscurantism was clearly crossed by Sir Peter Tapsell in his curious eulogy of May 1995, delivered at the height of the hostage crisis. 'The west,' he told the House, 'has consistently under-estimated the Serbs. They are one of the fiercest, bravest and most patriotic races on earth, and always have been . . . Greater Serbia is a dream that will never die, however many Serbs may die in its pursuit. Anyone who has read Balkan history . . . will tell us that.'[61]

The Croats, on the other hand, found few champions in the House. They were indelibly associated with the alliance between Germany and the Croatian Ustasha movement during the Second World War; and Germany's role in securing recognition of Croatian independence in 1991–2 only reinforced this image. 'Is this not the same Croatia,' Dennis Skinner asked, 'which supported Hitler in the Second World War and was responsible for slaughtering hundreds of thousands of Serbs?'[62] Derek Prag, the Conservative MEP for Hertfordshire, cited in May 1993 'The horrors of the Serbs' fight for freedom against the Nazis and their murderous puppet state of Croatia in the 1939–1945 war, in which most Bosnian Muslims sided with the Germans.'[63] 'If you are a Croat,' Nicholas Budgen confidently wrote in 1995, 'you can remember that your father fought with the Germans.'[64] Much of the animus was directed against the unlovely Croatian President, Franjo Tudjman. For Mike Gapes, praise for Tudjman from the war criminal Dinko Sakic, commander of the Second World War camp at Jasenovac, was condemnation enough.[65] The supposed irony of inviting the Croatian President over for the fiftieth anniversary of Victory in Europe Day to 'commemorate the victory over fascism' was much remarked on. Paddy Ashdown, famously seated next to Tudjman at the Guildhall dinner, noted in his diary on 6 May 1995: 'Somebody in the Foreign Office with a sense of humour! Particularly since he wasn't on our side during the war.'[66] The joke was indeed on him, for Franjo Tudjman, who spent the latter part of the war risking his life in Tito's partisans, had a much better anti-fascist pedigree than many western leaders, including President Mitterrand.

On the whole, in fact, the collective military experience of the House was of little help in its deliberations on Bosnia. What is one to make, for example, of Tam Dalyell's contention that imposing a solution would 'involve more than the 37 German Panzer divisions tied down during the war'?[67] For – with the exception of the spring of 1941, when Hitler overran Yugoslavia with fewer than 200 casualties – there were never more than two Panzer divisions stationed in the Balkans at any one time, and these were deployed to deter a seaborne invasion by the western allies. If the Germans had really possessed thirty-seven Panzer divisions in one place at any one time, it is most unlikely that the Westminster parliament would have survived for Tam Dalyell to ventilate his adolescent reading in 1995. But the prize for the choicest contribution to the military debate on Bosnia must go to the Conservative Peter Viggers. A national serviceman in the RAF and former member of the Territorial Army, delegate to the North Atlantic Assembly, and thus a man not without experience in the area of defence, Viggers seems to have thought the lifting of the arms embargo almost redundant. 'The Muslims,' he observed in May 1995, 'have taken the opportunity to rearm, and it is clear that they are re-equipped and rearmed with all that they need apart from tanks, heavy armour and aircraft.'[68] In the circumstances this was rather like a builder saying that a house was ready except for the roof, front door, and walls.

Underlying parliamentary opposition to military intervention against the Bosnian Serbs was a deepseated anti-quagmire reflex. During the first debate on Bosnia, the Labour MP David Winnick, later an enthusiastic convert to the interventionist position, asked the Foreign Secretary to 'accept that there is almost unanimous opinion in the House – and, in my view, in the country at large – that no military force should be used by outside countries, certainly not by Britain, and that British troops should under no circumstances get involved in such a vicious Balkan civil war'.[69] Peter Viggers told the Defence Secretary 'that if the cabinet commits further troops for use in Bosnia it will not have the support of many members on my side of the House'.[70] Cyril Townsend made a Miltonian plea to avoid further involvement 'in this treacherous Bosnian bog'.[71] The Conservative MP Jacques Arnold warned that 'If we were to intervene militarily ... we should run the risk of becoming bogged down in the Balkans, something which successive British governments have avoided for a century.'[72] 'The people who are crying for military intervention,' Geoffrey Dickens predicted, 'would soon be crying for the bodies of our men and women if they were returned in body bags.'[73] 'I hope,' Winston Churchill said of the British troop deployment in September 1992, 'that we are not blundering into a situation that will prove to be a costly can of worms ... It is plain that 1,800 troops cannot possibly hope to fight their way through an area which 30 [sic] Nazi divisions failed to control in the Second World War.'[74] And, of course, Bismarck's wisdom that 'the Balkans were not worth the bones of a single Pomeranian grenadier', was repeatedly pressed into service.[75]

British parliamentarians were particularly wary of civil wars. Sir Dudley Smith, Chairman of the WEU Defence Committee and later Chairman of the WEU Assembly, told the House in late April 1993 that it 'would be unwise for western nations to become involved in a civil war unless that specific civil war posed a threat to the integrity of one of the union's number'.[76] Some reference was made to Vietnam – Nicholas Budgen noted that 'many Conservative Members fear that we are slowly becoming embroiled in something not unlike a British Vietnam'.[77] Others thought of the Lebanon. Andrew Robathan pointed out 'as a former soldier' that 'there is a chaotic mixture of antagonists, indistinguishable to a British soldier, leaders who have questionable authority over their forces and very disparate aims amongst the forces involved. If you want a parallel, I suggest Beirut.'[78] But the principal fear, which explicitly or implicitly informed most of the debates on Bosnia, was, of course, that of another Northern Ireland. Thus, William Powell warned that 'surely we have had enough experience of Northern Ireland to realise that military intervention does not necessarily solve problems as easily as those who enter into such engagements might imagine. We have surely enough experience of Northern Ireland to know that the difficulties of reconciling what appear to outsiders to be irreconcilable divisions are considerable.'[79]

The attitude of the Northern Irish parliamentarians is therefore particularly instructive. 'In Northern Ireland,' the Ulster Unionist MP for Strangford, John Taylor, told the House in May 1995, 'people have taken and continue to take a considerable interest in the affairs of Bosnia. There are many reasons for that ... First, we live on an island, part of which was able to break away in 1921 and exercise its right of self-determination – something that we understand. Secondly, we live in a society that has grievously suffered from ethnic, cultural and religious divisions and, therefore, we recognise more clearly than others the kind of problems that exist in the Balkans.'[80] Some Ulstermen, such as the Democratic Unionist leader Ian Paisley, rejected calls for intervention as part of an EC – and therefore presumably popish – agenda. 'I think it's a matter for the EC, and the leaders of the EC who say they're the only people who can bring peace in Europe. They're the ones flying the flag for European unity, let them do it.'[81] And when James Molyneaux, leader of the Ulster Unionist Party, objected that 'the United Nations is in breach of its charter when it interferes in the internal affairs of any member state', he was clearly fearful of setting precedents for Northern Ireland.[82]

By far and away the most striking objections to military intervention came from John Taylor. Some of these simply echoed similar arguments being made on all sides of the House. Thus Taylor was concerned not to allow Bosnia to jeopardize 'one of the top priorities of British foreign policy', namely, 'the continuing improvement of relations between Russia and the United Kingdom'.[83] He also questioned, routinely enough, whether it was sensible to ask British troops 'to carry out humanitarian work in the midst of a civil war in which, politically, we are seen to be actively opposed to one of the participants'.[84] Yet John Taylor's impassioned condemnation of the bombing which led to the hostage crisis of May 1995 showed that his thinking on Bosnia was guided by much deeper preoccupations. He condemned 'without hesitation', 'the bombing of the Serbs' – ordered by General Sir Rupert Smith – which he 'knew' to have been American-inspired. 'Above all,' he continued, 'we should understand that – it is perhaps also because I come from Ireland that I know this – one cannot bomb nationalism out of a people, whether they are Serbs, or in Ireland, or Chechens. We condemned the Russians for bombing the people of Chechnya, yet now the Americans urge the bombing of the people in Serbia. It is incredible.'[85] It was indeed incredible to see a senior Ulster Unionist MP unable to distinguish between IRA bombings of civilians, indiscriminate Russian bombing in Chechnya, and air strikes on ammunition dumps in Pale, ordered by a British general in order to deter the shelling of a safe area.

But Taylor was to say more incredible things still. The 'fundamental problem', he claimed, was that 'Bosnia is a failed entity, which had and still has little cohesion as a nation state'. 'New international boundaries,' he continued, 'must be agreed within the former states of Yugoslavia; and those boundaries must be related to the ethnic groups that live in those areas.'[86] The phrase 'failed entity', which Taylor used repeatedly in debates on Bosnia,[87] is a resonant one in Ulster, for it is usually used by Irish nationalists of all stripes to dismiss the legitimacy of the Northern Irish state.

His vanquisher as leader of the Ulster Unionist Party, David Trimble, responded very differently to Bosnia. He immediately saw that the root cause of the conflict was the radical nationalist agenda in Belgrade. Already in June 1991, he was pressing the government to recognize the 'parallel between the position of the northern republics of Yugoslavia and that of the Baltic states. In both cases, democratic Governments are trying to break free from former communist states, and the former communist states are using force to prevent that. Is it not sad that in both cases this government [is], in effect, lining up behind the former communist regime to obstruct democracy?'[88] A year later, when the magnitude of Serbian intransigence was beginning to sink in with the government, Trimble welcomed 'the condemnation of the expansionist policies of the Serbian leadership, which were clearly demonstrated years ago when it overthrew autonomy in Kosovo and Vojvodina. Its intention to create a greater Serbia was clearly signalled last year and it is a matter of regret that the international community did not respond quickly enough, because the tragedies might have been averted.'[89] And in early November 1992 he pointed out that the government, 'in view of the Foreign Office's crazy idea of ethnic cantonisation, which was put forward by Lord Carrington some time ago, have some responsibility for encouraging the development of the war there'.[90] Nor did Trimble confine himself to grand speeches: he was also active in demanding the freezing of Yugoslav assets in Britain, and financial assistance to Slovenia to enable her to deal with Croat and Bosnian refugees.[91]

Constitutional nationalists, on the other hand, remained almost entirely silent on Bosnia. Neither John Hume nor his deputy, Seamus Mallon, saw fit to comment in public.

Because most parliamentarians saw Bosnia essentially as an intractable civil war, they were highly susceptible to governmental suggestions that there was not much to choose between the sides. 'The information I have,' Peter Viggers told the House in late April 1993, 'shows that there is little difference between the atrocities committed by all three parties to the conflict, the Serbs, the Croats and the Muslims in Bosnia. I say that on the basis of a visit there in February and some discussions. I agree that the Serbs are responsible for most of the aggression, but that does not mean that they commit the majority of the atrocities.'[92] This curious argument was simply factually wrong, as the Serbs clearly had committed the largest proportion of crimes. More vague but equally pernicious were the musings of Nigel Forman. 'Who really are the aggressors?' he asked during the same debate. 'Is Serbia the only aggressor? Obviously that is not the case. There are many other aggressors and no one is really clean.'[93] This argument was immensely helped, of course, by the outbreak of the Croat–Bosnian war from early 1993. 'Soldiers,' Andrew Robathan noted pointedly, 'would have no idea whom they were meant to be curbing, nor would they have any idea who would be shooting at them. The death of Lance Corporal Edwards was not due to a Serbian bullet.'[94]

This doctrine of equivalence, which took its cue from ministerial briefings and from the 'men on the ground', went hand in hand with a cultural relativism not usually associated with the Tory benches. 'Why,' Sir Peter Tapsell asked repeatedly in the May 1995 debate, 'are we not sending troops to Angola, Rwanda, Cambodia, Kurdistan, Tibet and Chechnya, to mention just a few? What is so very different about Bosnia?' When Sir Patrick Cormack made the obvious point that Bosnia was in Europe, Tapsell continued, 'Yes, Bosnia is at the heart of Europe, but I suspect that many people throughout the world will say that what is so very different about Bosnia is that its people are white.'[95] When Cyril Townsend asked what was 'so unique about this one conflict, one of 25 in our modern world',[96] it was with less multicultural *brio*, but similar intent. After rehearsing a list of the usual lost causes, Townsend moved in for the kill. 'In Angola,' he explained, 'we all know that Unita lost the election but is now back fighting its corner. Is there a call in the House to take action against Unita? I do not think so.'[97] The force of this argument was somewhat dented when HMG lifted the arms embargo on the Angolan government later that year, precisely so that it could more effectively fight Unita.

It is often said that the standard of speeches in the House of Lords is higher. This was marginally true of the Bosnian debates, where critics of government policy such as Lord Renfrew of Kaimsthorn, Lord Beloff, Lord Mackie, Lord Hylton, and Baroness Blackstone were periodically ascendant.[98] But the overall picture differed little from the Commons. The American strategy of lift and strike encountered the same objections as in the other place, even from peers well-disposed to the Bosnian cause;[99] the usual canards about German 'unilateral recognition' were trotted out;[100] there were the same objections, to quote Lord Chalfont (Ind.), to 'interfering in the affairs of sovereign nations' or civil wars;[101] there was the same determination, in the Labour Lord Healey's words, to 'beware the temptation to oversimplify the conflict and paint the Bosnian Serbs as the only aggressors';[102] and the same portentous warnings from former soldiers against, as Lord Hailsham put it, 'listening to those with loud mouths and no military experience'.[103] On the whole, the House of Lords seems to have agreed with the sentiments of the opposition leader, Lord Richard, themselves a clear echo of Douglas Hogg's mantra, that 'Nobody is going to come in on a white charger and sort out the problems of Yugoslavia. Those problems will have to be sorted out by the Yugoslavs themselves, though I think that the international community as a whole will do its very best to aid the process and indeed to emulsify [sic] the whole affair.'[104] The policy of whitewashing ethnic cleansing could not have been more elegantly described.

There were also the same powerful irritations with the Americans. Lord Richard believed that 'there has been perhaps too much lecturing from across the Atlantic and not sufficient action on behalf of the United States'.[105] Lord Callaghan of Cardiff, the former Labour Prime

Minister, seemingly unaware that the air strikes had been at the initiative of a British general, could not 'forget that it was the bombing by the American air force which led to the Royal Welch Fusiliers being taken hostage'; he also called upon the government to resist the 'something must be done school' to avoid slipping 'deeper into a morass'.[106] Lord Monkswell noted that the US was 'not prepared to deploy troops on the ground, but it is happy to bomb from the air and to see an unremitted arms supply to the Balkan theatre'.[107] Similarly, Lord (Merlyn) Rees (Labour) observed that 'The Americans talk glibly in the UN about long distance strikes . . . that would look good on television but there are some matters for which there are no solutions';[108] no doubt the conservative pessimist 'realism' underlying his remarks being not unrelated to his spell as Northern Ireland Secretary in the 1970s. But perhaps the most persistent and obsessively anti-American peer on Bosnia was Lord Kennet, who had been SDP spokesman on defence and foreign affairs in the 1980s, sometime member of the WEU Assembly who later, ironically enough, went on to become a member of the North Atlantic Assembly. Throughout 1994–5 he made a particular point of criticizing the United States, especially its covert support for the Croats and Bosnian government and the 'US unilateral defection from the UN [arms] embargo'.[109] He even went so far as to ask whether the 'Saudi Arabia decision to buy aircraft from the Boeing company was in any way related to the United States' decision to allow United States forces to be deployed in Sarajevo'.[110]

As in the Commons, the debate on Bosnia in the Lords was characterized by moments of extreme eccentricity and ignorance. The most dramatic instance was Lord Carver's observation in May 1995 that 'The United Nations force's humanitarian mission in Bosnia and Croatia has dragged it into a muddled form of Chapter VI action; but it is perfectly clear that the Security Council has never authorised Chapter VII action and has no intention of doing so.'[111] There followed a little tutorial on the differences between 'consent'-based operations under Chapter VI of the charter and enforcement operations under Chapter VII. As a Second World War hero, former Chief of the General Staff and eminent military historian, Field-Marshal Lord Carver was, of course, a man of the utmost distinction, but in this case he was simply mistaken. For, as we have repeatedly noted, the relevant

Security Council resolutions expressly cited Chapter VII authority to push aid convoys through by 'all necessary measures' and to deter attacks on safe areas.

Other interventions were odder still, if well-meant. Lord Annan, for example, spoke in mid-April 1993 of 'the possibility of designating an agricultural area devoid of population, 20 miles outside Belgrade, and sending a large bomber force to saturate the area. It might persuade the Belgrade government that the injuries that have been inflicted upon the women and children in Srebrenica and Sarajevo could well be inflicted on the civilian population, were the western powers so to decide.'[112] Baroness Strange (Con.), for her part, stressed the need 'to cut off the Bosnian flames from the rest of the world'. 'We are only too aware,' she continued, 'of the fireball that engulfed the civilised world following the assassination in Sarajevo in 1914.' Hence the west should 'contain the fire until such time as it has died down, when we can go in to feed the hungry, succour the children and old people, and once more help to build a safe world from the ashes'.[113] These remarks, which seemed to blend harsh *Realpolitik* with the solicitude of the chatelaine at a village teaparty, were less reassuring than they were intended to be.

There were very few challenges to the party line on the Conservative side. A small number of MPs, such as Tony Marlow, Bill Cash and John Gorst, spoke out against appeasement. Most of them came from the right of the party; but there was no particular connection between factional affiliation and individual stances on Bosnia. Thatcherites, in particular, were to be found on both sides of the divide. The only Conservative MP to threaten a full-scale revolt on Bosnia was Patrick Cormack. 'It is an urgent matter,' he warned the House in December 1992. 'I know that I have gone on about it at some length, and that I have raised it many times in the House. I hope that my colleagues will forgive me, but I feel deeply about the matter – so deeply that I must tell my right hon. Friend the Leader of the House that the government cannot be sure of my vote on anything if something is not done about Bosnia.'[114]

One senior Tory in parliament did intermittently challenge the government on Bosnia. This was David Howell, the Chairman of the

Foreign Affairs Committee. But his interventions lacked force and coherence. Throughout 1992–5, Howell's position on Bosnia meandered back and forth. He had little to say throughout 1992 when a stiff parliamentary challenge was most needed: at that time, by his own subsequent admission, he believed that the war was simply a routine and containable Balkan fracas. Then in April 1993, under the impact of the first Serb assault on Srebrenica, he broke ranks with the government. 'Very, very reluctantly', Howell announced, he now felt that the west should intervene militarily, 'even if it is not in [its] direct, narrow interest'.[115] Shortly afterwards, he became more definite, when he spoke of the need to impose 'some check . . . on the Serbian-driven expansionism and aggression, which we are presently witnessing, and which is leading to all the blood and slaughter'.[116] And later that month, he was to make a speech of Churchillian potential. 'I confess,' he told the House, 'that I used to think that this was just another Balkan mess, that they have been at it for hundreds of years . . . and if we could somehow put a ring fence around all that, we could stand aside and walk away from it. The truth, which has gradually dawned on the policy makers and perhaps on all of as well, is that we cannot possibly walk away. We have already been dragged in.' 'The choice,' he concluded, 'is not between involvement and non-involvement, but between action now and far more involvement later.'[117] All this sounded very promising, even more so when Howell indicated his support for air action to cut off Bosnian Serb supply lines.

But no sooner had Howell found the plot than he lost it. He greeted the collapse of the Vance–Owen plan with condemnation, but no concrete proposal for action.[118] And in late July 1993 he specifically rejected the use of western air power, while recognizing the need to lift the arms embargo. For the rest, despite the accompanying outrage, his views essentially reflected the standard government line that Bosnia could no longer be restored as an independent state within its pre-war boundaries, that misjudged intervention would impede the aid effort, and that talk of intervention merely encouraged the Bosnian government to continue a hopeless struggle.[119] For more than a year thereafter, Howell said virtually nothing on Bosnia, until in late November he switched back to supporting air strikes. Europe, he demanded, should take 'a resolute stand of principle' by supporting the lifting of the arms embargo and 'intensify' aerial bombardments until the Serbs agreed to the Contact Group plan.[120] The Bosnian presidency, on the other hand, should be told that 'they will be on their own, unless they too call it a day and negotiate'. This was a peculiar demand given the fact that Sarajevo had already accepted the Contact Group plan, an unjust partitionist solution which the international community had presented on a 'take it or leave it' basis.

His handling of the Foreign Affairs Committee was no less suspect. In its deliberations on the Croatian war, the Committee failed – partly perhaps because it was poorly advised – to put its finger unequivocally on the root cause of the conflict: Serb separatism directed from Belgrade. His overall concern at that time was to establish whether there was a broader danger to European security, or whether Yugoslavia was *sui generis*. The report of the Committee in early 1992 was definite and reassuring about this: 'The dissolution of Yugoslavia is unlike anything else going on in Central Europe.'[121] This was not wrong, and there is no sense that the Committee was being excessively complacent in the broader sense – indeed, the concern it showed for unrest elsewhere in eastern Europe was probably exaggerated – but nor was there any understanding of the implications that war and ethnic cleansing within Yugoslavia would have *in and of itself* for British interests and Britain's status in international organizations. For the next three years, moreover, the Committee does not seem to have engaged with the issue at all. 'I think,' Howell recalls, 'that [the Committee] was generally resigned to the fact these were squabbling Balkan tribes, and we just somehow had to keep the peace between them. I don't think the Committee got very focused or aligned, really.'[122] 'I don't think [Bosnia] was ignored,' Howell continues, 'but . . . the Foreign Affairs Committee . . . was cautious about being the fifth wheel on the coach, it was a very current issue, being voted in the Chamber and everything else [BS: in fact, there was only one division on Bosnia], we thought our job was to look at the things which lay ahead. So we may have said "It's too current, too hot for prolonged enquiry, we'll just keep the ball rolling".'[123]

The result was that Howell, who was instinctively looked to for guidance by some members of the House, remained curiously muted. Instead, parliament was treated to lengthy and inconclusive disquisitions. 'We . . . are listening with bated breath,' as the Labour MP Chris Mullin eventually remarked in exasperation, 'to find out what the right hon. Gentleman suggests is the solution to this terribly complex problem. As he is Chairman of the Select Committee on Foreign Affairs, we treat his views with particular respect. He has been speaking for nearly 20 minutes, but we still do not have a clue.'[124] The general sense was of a man of decent instincts but uncertain direction.

Another challenge which failed to ignite was that of the Liberal Democrat leader, Paddy Ashdown. He is generally credited with having had a 'good war' over Bosnia, and in relation to the vast majority of his parliamentary colleagues, and certainly to other party leaders, that is not incorrect. But closer examination shows his stance to have been confused and inconsistent.

Throughout the war, Ashdown was a familiar voice lambasting the government in and out of parliament. In mid-summer 1992 he noted that western aircraft could and should stop the shelling of Sarajevo 'at little risk and modest expense' if mandated to do so by the UN, and in December 1992, he called for a redefinition of the UN mandate and 'drawing a line on the Serbian advance', even if it meant 'embarking on a Cyprus-style operation, possibly even for a number of years'.[125] By January of 1993, he was criticizing the Major administration for its failure 'to understand that conflict in the Balkans had implications for the wider stability of South-East Europe and the security of the whole continent'. 'The outcome,' he pointed out, 'will send a signal across the whole of Eastern Europe.'[126] At the Liberal Democrat party conference in September 1993, the Tories were condemned for a policy that was 'cynical . . . short-term [and] lacking in honour'. It was, he concluded, 'called appeasement'.[127] He even showed some signs of challenging the hegemony of the 'experts' and the 'men on the ground'. 'The Secretary of State,' he told the House in April 1993, 'says that military commanders have advised against what I propose. I tell him that there are times when politicians, who have to take account of wider considerations, have to disagree with military commanders.'[128] All this was very promising.

What those speeches and articles did not vouchsafe was any concrete strategy for bringing the Bosnian Serbs to heel. There was talk of 'penalties', of UN standing armies, of the great work of the troops 'on the ground', but on the key issues of 'lift and strike', there was a marked reticence. The once wholehearted support for the use of air power against Serb artillery was heavily qualified. In April 1993, Ashdown opposed the Labour leader's demand for an ultimatum to the Bosnian Serbs, to be followed by air strikes on their supply line, if necessary. 'Nobody who has seen the position on the ground,' he claimed, 'would recommend this action . . . They don't need supplies from Serbia . . . There would be nothing better calculated to strengthen the Serbs in worsening this conflict.'[129] In this way, Ashdown appropriated precisely the same 'men on the ground' rhetoric which bedevilled the whole Bosnian debate. He also vigorously opposed the lifting of the arms embargo as 'the single action best calculated to ensure the widening of the war'.[130] Only ground troops, he insisted, could deliver effective intervention.[131] The Americans were roundly condemned for refusing to 'put US troops on the ground, while promoting a hawkish agenda that puts those who are there at greater risk'.[132] It was not until 1995 that Paddy Ashdown became an advocate of 'lift and strike' (along with almost everybody else).

Underlying Ashdown's position was a surprising uncertainty about the origins of and responsibility for the war. In mid-August 1992 he wrote that 'This is a war of minorities. They are all – Serb, Croat, Muslim, Orthodox or Catholic – national minorities in Bosnia-Herzegovina: which may help to explain why they exercise a local majority they enjoy with such ferocity.'[133] This suggested a symmetry between Serb separatist and Bosnian government behaviour which simply did not exist. And in April 1993 he made the extraordinary claim that even if the Serbs were now the principal offenders 'a powerful case can be made that the aggression in Bosnia-Herzegovina was started by the Muslims as much as by the Serbs'.[134]

Perhaps it was for this reason that his preoccupations were more humanitarian than strategic. Throughout 1992–3 he called for the establishment of 'safe havens', and his advocacy of air power and troop reinforcements was almost invariably in the context of protecting these Muslim reservations from further Serb attack.[135] In the context of 1992–3, of course, this was much better than nothing. But what is striking is that Ashdown *never* called for military intervention, limited or otherwise, to re-establish a multi-ethnic Bosnia within its internationally recognized boundaries. By a considerable irony, therefore, the most prominent parliamentary critic of government policy on Bosnia inadvertently furthered Whitehall's attempts to 'humanitarianize' the conflict.

The most striking thing about the parliamentary response to war and ethnic cleansing in Bosnia was the absence of any concerted attack by the opposition on government policy. Instead, during the early stages, the Labour party was a *retardative* factor. As the shadow Foreign Secretary Gerald Kaufman remarked in early June 1992, 'The right hon. Gentleman has not mentioned the use of force and I welcome that. The situation is far too confused for forcible intervention from outside to do any positive good.'[136] Three months later his successor, John Cunningham, said that 'The Foreign Secretary rightly ruled out military solutions to these complex problems, at least for the moment.' 'British military involvement,' he added, 'must not be allowed to escalate into such a quagmire and we do not believe that escalation is inevitable.'[137] And the shadow Defence Secretary argued during the same debate that 'In no way can we give the Government a blank cheque for further escalation. To extend military participation further would be extremely dangerous, if not foolhardy. The terrain is ideal for hit-and-run attacks. The old Yugoslav army, many of whose remnants are now fighting in Bosnia, was trained specifically for that task and we simply must not get drawn into a conflict on one of the various sides.'[138] No doubt, the party was positioning itself to capitalize on the government's difficulties, if intervention failed or resulted in heavy casualties.

The Labour front bench also went well beyond Douglas Hurd in its condemnation of supposed German provocations. Thus, the shadow Foreign Secretary Gerald Kaufman criticized Hurd for 'unwise[ly]' trading the recognition of Slovenia and Croatia in return for an 'opt-out' on the Social Chapter of the Maastricht Treaty. As a result, he claimed, 'the German government began cashing cheques that the British government owed them . . . The Foreign Secretary, against his will and against his wiser instincts, was dragged along behind the German government on agreeing a date for the recognition of the Yugoslav Republics.'[139] Just over six months later, Kaufman returned to this theme when he referred to the 'unwise capitulation . . . to the insistence of the German government that every little self-declared republic in what was Yugoslavia should be given international recognition'. 'The European Community,' he added, 'should have no military role in this conflict or indeed in any other. The need is not to extend the conflict but to maintain it [sic].'[140]

For the most part, however, Labour policy and rhetoric was indistinguishable from that of the Major administration. The notion that all sides to the conflict were more or less equally guilty found widespread acceptance. Already in June 1992, Gerald Kaufman was telling parliament that 'The Foreign Secretary is equally right to make it clear that the Serbs are not the only guilty party – that others share that guilt.'[141] And even if his successor noted that 'the Serbs are the principal aggressors', this was followed by the usual qualifying clause that 'The reality is that among political leaders as well as among the military leaders in Bosnia there are no innocents. They all bear a grave responsibility for continuing the slaughter in the way that they do.' When challenged on the use of 'Muslim' to describe the legitimate Bosnian government and to recognize its right to self-defence, Cunningham pointedly responded: 'I accept that civil war is going on in Bosnia, and I also accept that Serbian aggression is taking place.'[142] Later on in the same debate he was to repeat that 'political leaders on all sides of the conflict are willing to continue to wage war. I do not believe that in those circumstances there are any innocents.'[143]

For this reason, the Labour Party opposed military intervention during most of the war. It was particularly supportive of the international arms embargo. Lifting the embargo, Jack Cunningham told the House in April 1993, would 'extend and exacerbate war and conflict'.[144] David Clark elaborated on this standard argument when he claimed that 'It has always seemed to us rather crazy to try to douse a fire with petrol.'[145] It was particularly supportive of the arms embargo. Even the Labour leader, John Smith, who was broadly sympathetic to the Bosnian cause, opposed the lifting of the embargo on the grounds that it would 'merely intensify the conflict'.[146] A year later, during the debates on the Contact Group plan, the shadow Foreign Secretary, John Cunningham, hoped that Hurd would 'be successful in impressing on the combatants that this is perhaps their last opportunity for a negotiated settlement. It is sad that the current offer to the Bosnian government is worse than was available when they had the opportunity to reach a settlement in 1992 [sic].' He also demanded an assurance that 'there will be no early abrogation' of the arms embargo on Bosnia or the economic embargo on Serbia.[147] The extent to which Cunningham accepted Douglas Hurd's stated strategy of using the embargo to pressure the Bosnian government into a partitionist settlement is obvious.

For a brief moment in April–May 1993, at the height of the 'lift and strike' debate, Labour broke ranks with the government. John Smith asked the Commons whether it was 'not now necessary for a clear ultimatum to be issued to the Serbs that they will not be allowed to continue their aggression unchecked and that, if they continue that aggression, their lines of supply within Bosnia will be subject to air attack'.[148] A week later the Labour leader announced that 'if the Serbs are to be stopped, they must be given an ultimatum that is backed by a credible threat to their lines of communication and supply in Bosnia'.[149] Even John Cunningham demanded that the 'Government should support in the Security Council the issuing of an ultimatum to the Serbians. If the ultimatum is not complied with, selected air strikes should follow.'[150] But his heart was clearly not in it, for during the same debate he rejected the notion that there was any quick military solution which would not simply provide the Serbs with an incentive to seize more land.[151] In any case, Cunningham queried the idea 'that we have a moral duty to intervene in Bosnia. No one talks about our moral duty to intervene in Angola, where nearly three times as many people have been killed in a bloody civil war.'[152] This classic piece of Hurdite rhetoric shows the remarkable extent to which Cunningham's thinking was interchangeable with that of the Major administration.

The Labour policy on Bosnia which emerged under Tony Blair and the new shadow Foreign Secretary, Robin Cook, in 1995 was a great improvement on that of 1992–4, but it lacked the clarity and steely resolve which became the hallmark of their Balkan stance in the late 1990s. Indeed, Tony Blair's only public contribution to the debate in 1992–4 concerned the plight of refugees.[153] This interest, while welcome and honourable, inadvertently tended to reinforce the 'humanitarianization' of the conflict promoted by the Major administration. And Robin Cook's early sallies were not confidence-inspiring, either. 'All the troops we have to spare,' he wrote in late May 1995, 'will not be enough to keep apart the warring parties in Bosnia, so long as they are bent on ethnic confrontation.'[154] The casual failure to distinguish between the right of a legitimate government to self-defence and the violence of separatist rebels illustrates just how successful Whitehall was in framing the terms and language of the Bosnian debate. Instead of military intervention to reverse ethnic cleansing, which would 'address only the symptoms of ethnic hatred', Cook called for 'a mass propaganda effort . . . to combat the twisted nationalism from which the local warlords draw their power'. Hence, as he had explained a fortnight earlier, 'we must support the citizen groups and civic forums which are bringing together different ethnic groups [and] . . . Most of all, we must encourage and insist upon a free media.' 'The power base of Milosevic and Tudjman,' he stressed, 'is that they both have total control over television, which has 90 per cent penetration throughout the countries. That gives them a more powerful weapon than tanks and heavy artillery.'[155] Later on, of course, he was to argue, more plausibly, that the best way of combating the propaganda from the Belgrade television station was to destroy it with guided missiles.

For most of the war, in short, and certainly between mid-1993 and mid-1995, the Labour Party did not try to make political capital of governmental mishandling of the war. Indeed, Labour prided itself on not turning Bosnia into a party-political issue. Looking back at three disastrous years, David Clark claimed to 'know that the House will appreciate that the Opposition have not tried to make political capital out of this matter'.[156] 'This is not,' as Robin Cook put it with statesmanlike candour during the same debate, 'a failure for which we can pass the parcel of blame between the political parties. We all have a share in the responsibility for the failure of the international community.'[157] Labour complicity in government policy throughout most of the conflict could not have been more succinctly described. Of course, such misplaced bipartisanship was to be ill repaid by the Conservatives during the Kosovo war and since.

Unlike the United States, the British government did not come under sustained and irresistible pressure from the press. At first sight, this seems surprising. Bosnia was the best-reported war in history. Journalists such as Ed Vulliamy and Maggie O'Kane for the *Guardian*, Janine di Giovanni for the *Sunday Times*, Alec Russell for the *Daily Telegraph*, and many others told the story more or less as it was. They uncovered the camps, they highlighted the misery of Mostar and Sarajevo, and they helped to expose the untruths on which western policies were founded. Sometimes, indeed, as with the reports of widespread destruction in Dubrovnik (October–November 1991), their accounts were 'clearer than the truth'.[158] It is no coincidence that more journalists were killed in Bosnia than in any previous war. Nor should it surprise that the customary proportion of dead journalists to western military fatalities should have been reversed; as many observers have pointed out, journalists were combatants, and more effective ones than the UNPROFOR mission they had come to cover.

There was, therefore, no shortage of excellent information reaching the principal broadsheets. What was in short supply was sensible analysis. As the Cambridge historian Joseph Pearson, who has made a detailed study of the response of the British press to the outbreak of war in 1991–2, points out, reportage on Croatia and Bosnia was often at complete variance with editorial policy.[159] For every Alec Russell, there was a Max Hastings, for every Maggie O'Kane, there was a Peter Preston. The element of doubt and equivocation which characterized much media analysis throughout the war was thus metropolitan in origin; it did not come from their 'men on the ground'.

Some broadsheets were quick to understand the implications Bosnia had for western interests. Charles Moore's *Sunday Telegraph* and Andrew Neil's *Sunday Times* were among the first. Likewise, after some hesitation, *The Times* became and remained a firm supporter of limited military intervention to contain the Bosnian Serbs. So were individual columnists, such as Hugo Young, Martin Woolacott, Martin Walker, and – in time – Andrew Marr. But the most vocal supporter of the Bosnian cause was the *Independent*, which did more than any other paper to keep the war on the media agenda after the fiasco of May 1993, even if, as we shall see, the editorial line was less consistently helpful throughout the war than one might think. Much of the press, however, remained confused, ill-informed, and in the grip of Whitehall 'spin'. It would be tiresome to repeat all the misapprehensions here, which mirror those we have already surveyed in earlier chapters: a small sample will suffice.

The most obvious analytical flaw was the widespread insistence on the moral equivalence of the antagonists. Thus in April 1993, the *Sunday Telegraph*'s commentator Con Coughlin claimed that 'such is the obsession of the media with the Nazi-style tactics of the Serbs in their determination to create a "Greater Serbia" that scant regard is paid to the fact that the Serbs are not the only ones intent on genocide.' He criticized the 'portrayal of the Serbs as the demons', stressed that the reality was 'infinitely more complex than the television pictures would have us believe', and praised the Foreign Secretary's wisdom in rejecting military intervention. It was not so much that the Serbs were unjustly maligned, he claimed, rather that 'the other participants in the conflict have not been subjected to the same intensity of exposure'.[160] Three months later, he repeated his view that 'many western leaders, particularly the new American president, laboured under the misapprehension that the Serbs were the primary villains of the piece';[161] in fact, he suggested, the Croats were equally guilty. The choice of words here is significant: Coughlin was not merely denying that the Serbs were the 'only' villains, he was even denying that they were the 'primary' culprits.

This view, moreover, was contradicted by reporters 'on the ground'. Thus when the *Observer*'s Victoria Clark recounted the story of a short Croatian offensive in January 1993 under the headline 'No nice guys left as patience runs out', the main text of the article left the reader in no doubt of the fact that the Serbs were the original and primary aggressors. 'If Croats have learned to lie,' she wrote, 'it could be because they have noticed that lying has worked a treat for Serbia,' and, she asked, 'Would the Croats be so warlike now if the world had rescued them from Serb aggression in 1991?'[162] Similarly, when the *Guardian*'s Ian Traynor investigated claims that the Bosnian government was resorting to ethnic cleansing in its turn, he found isolated murders, but no systematic policy of massacre and expulsion.[163] As Martin Bell, who reported for BBC Television throughout much of the war, subsequently explained, it was right to note 'the shades of grey' and the fact that the 'Serbs also suffered' as 'part of the whole picture'. But, he stressed, context was even more important. 'The Serbs,' Bell writes firmly, 'had begun this war, they alone could end it.'[164]

The notion than Bosnia was merely a nasty civil war with few broader implications for British or western interests also found wide acceptance. According to Alistair Burnet, the war was nothing more than a 'nasty local brawl' in which there was no British interest; the Foreign Secretary was thus 'right' to stay out. 'The Serbs,' he remarked truthfully, 'are not building their Greater Serbia by force and threat because they want to dominate Europe. They cannot do this.' The war, he stressed, would only 'become unmanageable when great powers get engaged'.[165] Indeed, the *Mail on Sunday*, citing 'defence experts', warned that 'the experience of Northern Ireland' showed 'the dangers of sending troops in without being able to pull them out'. British troops, it feared, might have to be 'stationed for the remainder of this century and beyond', and it noted that 'The men and women in our armed forces joined up to protect this country, not to police the world's trouble spots.'[166] Even such generally astute commentators as Anne Applebaum, who had previously seen 'at the very beginning, a western strategic interest, and a British strategic interest' that 'borders in Europe should not ever be changed by force', argued that there was 'no longer a western interest in this war'.[167] Why the western interest in reversing ethnic cleansing should be any less vital than preventing it was not satisfactorily explained.

Perhaps the most striking feature of most broadsheet discussion of Bosnia was the virulence with which the strategy of 'lift and strike', in sum or in its component parts, was rejected. The *Guardian* spoke of 'American petrol, [and] Bosnian flames',[168] and of a 'wild idea';[169] the *Observer* was also violently opposed.[170] The arguments were the familiar ones: such action would sabotage the 'peace process', expose UNPROFOR to Serb reprisals, jeopardize ceasefires, infuriate the Russians, and encourage the Bosnians to continue their 'hopeless' struggle. But at least the *Guardian* and the *Observer* were consistent in their refusal to countenance military action on Bosnia's behalf or even to allow the Bosnians to defend themselves.

The same cannot be said of the *Daily Telegraph*, and certainly not of the *Independent*, whose editorial line was to meander back and forth throughout the conflict. The *Daily Telegraph* reacted to the outbreak of the war with a profound analysis from which it beat a lamentable retreat in the course of the next three years. 'It was never going to be possible,' the editorial of 13 June 1992 argued, 'for the great powers to stand aside as one and a half million people were driven from their homes in southern Europe.' 'Understandably, perhaps,' it continued, 'the Foreign Office, the State Department and the Quai d'Orsay have sought to avoid entanglement in Yugoslavia by presenting the conflict as a tribal feud of limited strategic interest or moral significance. This approach was flawed from the beginning. It is now discredited. As we have argued repeatedly, however badly the Croats or Muslim Slavs may have behaved 50 years ago, the essential cause of the current civil war is the pocket imperialism of Greater Serbia, pursued with methodical cynicism by president Slobodan Milosevic.' Moreover, the *Daily Telegraph* noted, 'If the Muslims had had a modest amount of weaponry three months ago they might have been able to defend themselves, and hold on to most of their ancestral lands. But the United Nations, although it has recognised Bosnia-Herzegovina as an independent member state, has not only failed to provide any protection, it has actually assisted the Serb aggressor by imposing an arms embargo on both sides of the conflict. This embargo . . . amounts to a unilateral blockade of Bosnia. The Milosevic regime does not need to import arms. As the inheritor of the Yugoslav federal army it already has more weapons than it can use, as well as vast stocks of ammunition. While there is a strong case for avoiding the proliferation of arms in the Balkans, we question whether the United Nations has any moral justification for preventing the people of Bosnia from obtaining the arms they so desperately need from friendly nations abroad.' Finally, the editorial concluded that 'The whole multinational operation is ill conceived because it is trying to keep a peace which is not there. Its purpose should be not to hold the ring, but to stop Serbian aggression.'[171]

By August 1994, however, the *Daily Telegraph* was arguing that the arms embargo should be maintained. It advanced all the usual reasons: Douglas Hurd's phrase of a 'level killing field', the editorial warned, 'is as good today as it was two years ago'. Indeed, the paper claimed rather audaciously that 'this American enthusiasm for lifting the embargo is now a more considerable threat to the unity of the five power contact group than the mild pro-Serb statements made by the Russians'. As for arming the Bosnians, the argument ran, 'It will take years before they can match the Bosnian Serb forces'. Since these words were written in late 1994, more than two years after the outbreak of hostilities, it is striking that the paper did not wonder whether the process might have been started a little earlier.[172] Towards the end of the month, this argument was further elaborated when the *Daily Telegraph* predicted that the 'lifting of the arms embargo against the Bosnian government would run the risk of accelerating and widening the conflict'.[173] And a week later the same paper demanded that 'The Clinton Administration should be left in no doubt that if it brings the issue before the United Nations Security Council . . . it will face a British veto.'[174]

A more remarkable sequence of reversals was executed by the *Independent*. Thus the editorial of 11 August 1992 welcomed the drafting of a Security Council resolution to allow the use of 'all necessary means' to force through aid convoys. 'What is taking place in Bosnia,' it observed, 'is not a civil war in the normal sense. The movement of populations is not a product of fighting . . . but the primary purpose of a campaign of terror and territorial annexation', which was 'practised mainly by the Serbs'. Moreover, the *Independent* continued, the west was wrongly 'trying to salve public opinion by dealing with humanitarian aspects while failing to live up to the root cause: the policy of ethnic cleansing directed from Belgrade'. For this reason, it was argued, 'With the UN arms embargo perpetuating the Serbs' huge military superiority, [the Bosnian] plea for weapons also deserves sympathy, as Baroness Thatcher has been underlining with commendable forcefulness in the US.'[175]

Throughout 1993 the *Independent* more or less maintained a strongly pro-Bosnian stance. But in early 1994, the first fissures began to appear. In January of that year, the editorial argued that 'Unfortunately, the Bosnian forces are no longer fighting for a multi-ethnic state . . .[but] a "cleansed" Muslim state. That is the cause the West would be espousing if it channelled weapons to the Muslim side.'[176] By September 1994, the *Independent* had turned viciously on the Bosnians. Looking back on the responses of 1992 it noted scornfully that 'Demands for action were swift, the remedies proposed sometimes simplistic'. This can only be read as self-criticism, for the editorial went on to argue that lifting the embargo would inevitably lead to an

UNPROFOR withdrawal. 'The Bosnian government,' it warned with the same candour as scores of British officials beforehand, 'should reflect on that grave possibility.' The *Independent* then took aim at President Izetbegovic and 'his sloganeering Prime Minister, Haris Silajdzic' for having 'too often presumed on the guilt of Europe'. 'The Bosnian government,' it pronounced with something amounting to contempt, 'has been not merely outgunned, but outgeneralled and outfought as well.' For this reason, the *Independent* concluded, 'all the outside powers, especially nations with troops in Bosnia, should read the riot act to the Bosnian government'.[177] At this point, let it be remembered, the Serbs were defying the international community by rejecting the Contact Group plan.

By 1995, in fact, it appeared that the *Independent* was ingesting Whitehall spin no longer by osmosis but by direct injection. When the hostage crisis broke out in late May 1995, it counselled the immediate resumption of talks with Slobodan Milosevic and warned that 'escalating military action is out of the question because this would threaten NATO's relations with Russia, and the Russians are still our best hope of persuading the Serb leadership to reach a peaceful settlement'. 'When the best is not readily available,' the editorial concluded with Hurdite sagacity, 'avoiding the worst is still a worthwhile goal.'[178] But the most striking example of the *Independent*'s conversion to the Major administration's conservative pessimist realism came two days later in an editorial in which the notion of primary Serb responsibility for the war had been all but abandoned. It sneered at the 'gung-ho merchants of two years – the apostles of "surgical strikes" . . . [and] the "remember appeasement" school of historical over-simplification', who were now 'metamorphosing into a new "troops out" movement'. The rest of the argument was pure Hurd. 'Bosnia is the long haul,' it concluded. 'It could be a generation until – as in Northern Ireland or Lebanon – the sides sicken of pointless aggression. To persevere in a messy and often terrible world, at risk to yourself, takes courage and patience. So far we have shown these qualities, we should not now give in to moral cowardice or cheap demagoguery.'[179]

Some seventy years ago the French writer Julien Benda published *La Trahison des clercs* – 'the treason of the intellectuals'. It was a searing indictment of the way in which European – and especially French – intellectuals had abandoned the universal values of the Enlightenment in favour of nationalism, racism and the exaltation of the strong over the weak. 'The "clerks"' (that is, the intellectuals), he lamented, 'praise attachment to the particular and denounce the feeling of the universal'; they 'praise attachment to the practical, and denounce love of the spiritual'. Benda criticized 'The affirmation of the rights of custom, history, the past . . . in opposition to the rights of reason.' Intellectuals, he observed, were no longer the custodians of moral values but stimulants and celebrants of the 'game of political passions'.

Similar criticisms might be made of the response of many British intellectuals to aggression and ethnic cleansing in Croatia and Bosnia. Of course, it is true that many British novelists, political philosophers, and historians came out clearly against the projects of a 'Greater Serbia' – and to a lesser extent 'Greater Croatia'. In some cases, no doubt, this stance was no different from the reflexive – and unreflective – solidarity they showed with what they regarded as comparable causes the world over: East Timor, Nicaragua, Tibet, the Kurds, and so on. But there was a substantial, vocal, and highly influential minority of British intellectuals who regarded the principal victims of the war – the Muslims, loyal Croats, and loyal Serbs of Bosnia-Herzegovina – not merely with indifference, but with suspicion and hostility. Their stance may have been reinforced by a certain cussedness, a determination to swim against what they saw as the current of media-driven 'hysteria', yet their motivations in opposing any intervention on behalf of the victims of aggression and ethnic cleansing were much more complex.

'Treasonable clerks' were to be found on the left, on the right and in the centre of the political spectrum. For some left-wing intellectuals, the Yugoslavs were suspect by virtue of their 'nationalism', which was held to be a retrogression from the socialist federalism of the former Yugoslavia. These intellectuals contrasted what they regarded as the historic, constitutional, progressive, and inclusive nationalism of western Europe with what they took to be the racist, regressive, malevolent, immature, dictatorial, and thoroughly pernicious nationalism of the successor states in eastern Europe.[180] 'Like all of Eastern Europe,' Mary Kaldor claimed at the outset of the conflict, 'Yugoslavia is a patchwork of tribes . . . and all of Yugoslavia has experienced long, bitter and bloody histories of conflicts between different cultural, religious, linguistic or ethnic groups.'[181] What this interpretation failed to address was the *root cause* of the problem in the Greater Serbia project: the generalized disdain for 'nationalism' blurred any distinction between victim and perpetrator. It was an intellectualized version of Whitehall's classic 'moral equivalence' argument.

Closely related to the blanket condemnation of 'nationalism' was a deep sense of moral relativism, which was often part of a wider scepticism towards the west – specifically the United States – and western values. 'Americans,' the broadcaster and social historian Michael Ignatieff wrote, 'are especially prone to assuming that the Yugoslav nightmare is a morality play which pits Serb aggressors against blameless Croats and innocent Muslims.'[182] 'If the Americans allow the arming of the Muslims,' he continued, 'they will soon find themselves complicit in ethnic cleansing, for that is what the Muslims are certain to do.' Instead, he advocated 'a policy of even-handed dislike for the work of all parties'. The motivation here was the desire to avoid a 'simplistic' reading of the conflict in favour of an interpretation which acknowledged only quantitative but no qualitative differences between aggressor and victim. Later, Ignatieff was to come out much more strongly against the Greater Serbia project: indeed, by 1999, he was the leading intellectual defender of the Nato action over Kosovo.

But perhaps the strongest force behind left-wing indifference to Bosnia was a principled hostility to western intervention or other 'neo-colonial' enterprises. Thus John Pilger, while professedly sympathetic to the Bosnians, refused to countenance the use of air power on their behalf. 'The threat of western bombing,' he wrote, 'adds a grotesque, if predictable, dimension to an often secret western policy of dividing Yugoslavia along ethnic lines, dismantling it and eventually recolonising it.'[183] Indeed, the memory and the rhetoric of Vietnam sometimes led to an instinctive sense of solidarity with the putative victims of US air power. 'We are not America,' wrote the columnist and popular historian Edward Pearce, 'ready to bomb troublesome gooks back into the stone age.'[184] Another example of this pervasive anti-Americanism would be the remarks of the radical leftist Chris

Harman: 'for three bitter years we have been denouncing the governments of Serbia and Croatia, but also refusing to fall into the trap of believing that somehow western intervention can do any more good in former Yugoslavia than it did in Central America, Lebanon, the Gulf or Somalia'.[185]

Sometimes, the 'humane and sceptical' opponents of intervention themselves resorted to the language of brutal *Realpolitik*. 'Wars end when one side is beaten,' the *Times* columnist and author Simon Jenkins wrote. 'Most of the killing takes place between the moment when defeat is certain and the moment when the defeated accept it. Outside intervention usually prolongs that killing gap: as I fear is the case in Srebrenica.'[186] This view could be criticized on *a priori* grounds, for it made no distinction between aggressor and victim; but it was also suspect on empirical grounds. In his last sentence – which was written in early 1993 – Jenkins left a cruel hostage to fortune. For when in 1995 the outgunned defenders finally 'accepted' defeat as they were urged to do, the *real* killing began as the men of Srebrenica were led off by the Serbs to mass execution.

Underlying the attitude of many left-wing intellectuals towards aggression, ethnic cleansing and intervention in Bosnia was a deep-seated satisfaction at the collapse of the 'New World Order' ordained by President Bush after the western triumphs of the Gulf War and the fall of communism. Perhaps the best example of this was the outburst by the radical feminist writer Beatrix Campbell: 'What is this war telling us about the New World Order?' she asked. 'First that the West, in its rush to rid itself of the Communists, assumed that its values would triumph. It assumed that the white West would rule the world. But those values had been sustained by the drama of the Cold War. European conservatism is sliding into crisis in the wake of European communism's collapse. The great white West will not inherit the world.'[187]

It was the perfect formula for having it every way, an invincibly sceptic critique of the New World Order. If the US was about to intervene, this was symptomatic of western hubris; if she did not, this proved that the war on Iraq had been waged solely for oil. The Croats and the Bosnians were thus the victims of a profoundly postmodern malaise among British intellectuals. To have forced a settlement on the Bosnian Serbs would have been to act the 'world policeman'. Above all, to intervene would have meant transcending their own nagging sense of political, moral and cultural relativism.

Interestingly, a strong moral relativist – and anti-American – streak can also be found among right-wing opponents of intervention. The Cambridge English don John Casey, for example, condemned the United States for its 'moralizing' stance on Bosnia in the following terms. For the Americans, Casey wrote, 'Foreign policy is part of the endless struggle between freedom and tyranny, good and evil. When President Bush ludicrously described the Gulf War as a defence of freedom, he was using the only language Americans know.'[188] A similar moral relativism – and an oddly left-wing universalism – underpinned the arguments of the conservative biographer Allan Massie. He rejected any suggestion that Europeans bore a greater responsibility for the Bosnians than for any other wretched of the earth. 'There is a nasty whiff to this argument,' he observed. 'It verges on racism, as if brutalities committed by Europeans on Europeans are somehow more brutal and more deplorable than brutalities inflicted by Chinese on Tibetans, Cambodians on Cambodians or Somalis on Somalis.'[189] Here the rhetoric of universalism was being deployed not in defence of human dignity but to justify its betrayal.

But the root cause of the right's intellectual hostility to Bosnia was their opposition to the bogey of 'political correctness'. If some left-wingers were prepared to abandon Bosnia out of their own cultural diffidence and indifference in the face of the Greater Serbia project, then these conservatives rejected Bosnia as a politically correct illusion. 'Bosnians are Muslims,' the columnist and popular historian Paul Johnson argued, 'and all non-Christians are in the eyes of the left goodies until proved otherwise. Moreover, Muslims tend to be non-white too, and the fact that Bosnian Muslims are white is a point that, in the interests of Political Correctness, can be overlooked.'[190] Similarly, the conservative columnist Michael Wharton lampooned the fact that '"Bosnia" has become a dream country, an ideal realm where before the irruption of the fiendish Serbs multi-culturalism flourished . . . a prime example for "multi-racial Britain" and a pattern for the world-wide multi-racial order of the future.'[191] Every Serb blow against the concept of a secular, multi-ethnic Bosnia thus became a blow on the home front against a multi-cultural Britain.

In short, British intellectuals found many reasons to release themselves from their universalist obligations towards the Croat and Bosnian victims of ethnic cleansing. If conservatives rejected any such obligation outright, left-wingers invoked moral relativism, anti-imperialism, the spectre of nationalism, and a host of other rhetorical ploys to justify inaction. Indeed, Bosnia became the scene of a war by proxy in the struggle for cultural hegemony in Britain: the issues involved were interpreted in the light of existing debates; these intellectuals made little attempt to understand the conflict on its own terms.

But perhaps the most powerful argument of all was common to both the left and the right. This was the alleged Nazi past, not merely of individual Croats and Bosnian Muslims, but of the two peoples as a whole. According to this interpretation, the events of 1941–4 showed that the Croats tended to be genocidal Ustasha sympathizers, who had collaborated with the Germans. John Pilger, for example, spoke of 'Croatia's historical fascism'.[192] By the same token, the Bosnian Muslims were regarded as eager auxiliaries of their Croat and German masters. Thus Melvyn Hiskett, a former lecturer at the School for Oriental and African Studies in London, dilated on the SS Muslim division Handschar, which was 'reputed to have massacred 700,000 Serbs'. On this reading, the Serbs – irrespective of their present misdeeds – were at least partly acting out of self-defence. 'Having been subjected to massacre in the last war,' wrote Edward Pearce, 'they are not minded to be tractable.'[193] Similarly, Allan Massie spoke of 'vivid memories of their sufferings at the hands of Germans and Croats during the Second World War'.[194] For some conservatives the Serbs were also victims of a communist-inspired British betrayal of the royalist partisans. When Germany – the historic foe of two world wars – recognized the breakaway Croat republic in 1991 the lesson seemed clear: once again the Serbs – genocidal victims but also victors of the last war – had lost the peace.

The result of this was a kind of renewed Grand Alliance between intellectuals of the left and the right. By redefining the current conflict as a continuation of the last war, they were able to justify their own inaction. Yet the intellectual sleight of hand involved was obvious. Even if the historical record of Croats and Bosnians was as straightforward as they claimed, this could not possibly justify the present-day massacre of their children and grandchildren. After all, nobody would claim that the existence of the Pétainist regime in Vichy – of which François Mitterrand was once a faithful servant – would have justified the murder and expulsion of hundreds of thousands of Frenchmen in the mid-1990s. The fact that some intellectuals – especially on the left – were prepared to 'understand' Serb aggression and ethnic cleansing in the light of 'history' is a striking example of the 'treason' described by Julien Benda some seventy years earlier: the abandonment of universalist values for a worldview based on 'custom, history, the past . . . in opposition to the rights of reason'.

Perhaps the most treasonable clerk of all was Conor Cruise O'Brien, author of an acclaimed biography of the great eighteenth-century Anglo-Irish political thinker Edmund Burke – *The great melody* – and a renowned international sage. One might have thought that O'Brien, guardian of enlightened values and custodian of the Burkeian legacy, would have been the first to champion the victims of ethnic cleansing. Instead, O'Brien deliberately forsook the rich rhetoric of anti-appeasement left by his hero Burke and took refuge in cultural pessimism and moral relativism. 'Ethnic cleansing,' he wrote, 'is not just a Serbian idea. It is a fancy recent label for standard practice in a Balkan Civil War.'[195] Bosnia was recognized, he lamented, in the 'days of democratic triumphalism, after the wall came down. Democracy was about to triumph everywhere including Bosnia.'[196] Rather than exhorting his audience to greater efforts on behalf of the victims, he donned the mantle of realism. Rejecting American proposals for 'lift and strike', he insisted that there was no 'kind of quick military fix';[197] indeed, western policy could and should be no more than a few humanitarian 'charades, designed to keep the children quiet';[198] non-intervention would ensure that the conflict would burn itself out more quickly. Any analogies with appeasement were explicitly ruled out. 'Comparisons with Hitler are intoxicating,' he wrote, 'and should be avoided. It was by seeing Nasser as Hitler that Anthony Eden got Britain into Suez';[199] moreover, Bosnia differed from, say, Abyssinia because 'Here there is no limited form of intervention available that could resolve the crisis.'[200]

There were two reasons why O'Brien steadfastly refused to address the major points of political principle involved in the war, and opted for a stance that was at best wearily cynical and at worst openly hostile to the principal victims. The first was a deepseated sense of cultural pessimism about what he called the 'terminal' condition of an 'enlightenment tradition' under threat from both Islamic and Roman Catholic fundamentalism. He even raised the possibility that 'the Pope, in the year 2000 [might] announce his acceptance of the Koran and summon the faithful, through the papal muezzin, to join him in prayer at the mosque of St Peter' (in *On the eve of the millennium*). Indeed, long before the Bosnian war, O'Brien had been quite explicit about his hostility towards the Islamic world. In an article in *The Times* in 1989 he wrote: '[Muslim society] looks repulsive because it *is* repulsive from the point of view of Western post-enlightenment values . . . It remains true that Arab and Muslim society is sick and has been sick for a long time.'[201] Strikingly, O'Brien makes no effort to distinguish between moderate and fundamentalist Islam. Hence, in the Bosnian Muslims he could see not the upholders of an enlightened secular multi-ethnic ideal, but only the grave-diggers of the Enlightenment who were about to stretch their hands to the clerical-fascist Croats in what would amount to a religious Hitler–Stalin pact. The second source of O'Brien's blindness on Bosnia was a pathological fear and hatred of Germany. Some three years earlier the prospect of German unification had famously prompted him to predict that statues of Hitler would be constructed all over Germany within a decade. Unsurprisingly, O'Brien saw in Germany's belated support for Croat and Slovene separatism sinister evidence of expansionism. In short, O'Brien was the ideal of the treasonable clerk: his cumulative phobias produced an intellectual short-circuit of monumental proportions.

Throughout the Bosnian war, the political nation and the public sphere never generated enough interest and momentum to overturn government policy. Unlike the United States, there was no revolt of 'civil society', no revolution of the elites. Instead, parliamentary and public discussion tended to reinforce existing historical preconceptions, to perpetuate the notion of moral equivalence, to express ill-considered polemics against the Americans, to defer to 'the men on the ground', and generally – as the late Lord Richard put it – to 'emulsify the whole affair'.

CHAPTER 8

# The Reckoning

By early 1995, British policy on Bosnia had reached a complete dead end. London continued to argue that the Bosnians should not be allowed to protect themselves because that would endanger the troops sent to protect them, but who had failed to do so. Indeed, the Major administration insisted that Britain should not only abandon the legitimate Bosnian government to its fate, but that it should do all in its power to prevent the Americans from coming to its aid, even at the price of a catastrophic transatlantic rift. Bizarrely, while there was allegedly no British national interest in saving the Bosnians from aggression or ethnic cleansing, there seemed to be great reserves of political will and invective to prevent the Americans from doing so. But this strategy was getting nowhere. The Bosnians had resolutely refused to 'see sense' and agree to the truncation of their country. They had not capitulated in the dark days of 1993 and they were unlikely to do so now.

Yet, as the Nato spokesman Jamie Shea has observed, the west, and particularly Britain, was now mired in a '*Bridge over the River Kwai* syndrome'. In this famous novel and film set in wartime Burma, imprisoned British officers build a bridge for the Japanese which they subsequently refuse to blow up. Similarly, the British presence in Bosnia was increasingly determined by the need to accommodate the Serbs, to maintain the myriad of small and debilitating compromises without which, they believed, the humanitarian effort would collapse completely to be followed by even greater bloodshed. It was, Shea claimed, a 'logic . . . totally determined by the microcosm of the situation'.[1]

One obvious way out was through withdrawal, which British sources periodically threatened in various permutations.[2] But Britain would need a pretext and a scapegoat upon whom the subsequent carnage could be blamed. From the autumn of 1994 it appeared that the Congressionally sponsored campaign to lift the arms embargo might provide one. Throughout late 1994 British diplomats 'grudgingly' began to talk up the possibility of a lifting of the embargo preceded by the withdrawal of UNPROFOR. 'Imagine the television pictures,' one British official told interlocutors. 'We pull out in the depths of a Balkan winter, under fire. Muslim women lie in the snows begging our soldiers not to leave. What would we do? We would tell people where the blame lay: with the American Congress.'[3] 'So it might still be lift and withdraw,' another senior British diplomat observed. 'Arm the Bosnians and let them fight it out while the United Nations cuts and runs. It may well come to that – but it's worth trying anything to avoid it.' Douglas Hurd warned that 'lifting the embargo may become inevitable . . . but it is not compatible with keeping our troops there'.[4] And John Major warned that 'It is conceivable that events will force us down this path [of lifting the embargo], but we will not go down it willingly.'[5] 'Armageddon,' Andrew Marr shrewdly predicted, was being 'pencilled in for December . . . the chorus would go up: it was not us, it was the Americans.'[6]

But the Clinton administration was not stupid. It was wary of any unilateral act which might damage US-sponsored embargoes against Iraq, North Korea, and other rogue states,[7] and it knew well that such a move would turn Bosnia into a US rather than a British problem. For a precipitate and contested withdrawal of UNPROFOR would involve hazardous commitments of US transport and ground troops to cover the retreat: western European militaries had persuaded governments and themselves that they could not do the job on their own. Neither London nor Washington was prepared to move first in this debilitating game of political chicken.[8] And so, as Matthew Parris noted wearily in *The Times*, 'We stay as one stays in a late night bus queue ages after the bus has failed to come and suspicion has grown almost to a certainty that it won't be coming at all – but no one else in the queue has quit and there has been no announcement.'[9]

In the spring of 1995 the Bosnian government launched a series of tactically successful offensives, including the capture of the crucial

Mount Vasic feature in central Bosnia. In May the rearmed and retrained Croatian army overran 'Sector West', one of the Serb-held areas in Slavonia, with surprising ease. Around the same time the Serbs restarted the shelling of Sarajevo in earnest, thus escalating a siege partially lifted by the Nato ultimatum of February 1994. This was a direct challenge to the new UNPROFOR commander, General Rupert Smith, who responded by destroying two Bosnian Serb ammunition dumps at Pale, the first 'strategic' strikes of the war. The Bosnian Serbs retaliated by shelling the safe areas – leading to massive civilian loss of life outside a café in Tuzla – and by taking several hundred UNPROFOR troops hostage, including dozens of Britons. These were then dispersed in the vicinity of strategic installations such as television masts and barracks. The humiliating footage was instantly beamed around the world. The Bosnian crisis was back at the top of the international agenda.

But it was to get much worse. British officers had been warning of the threats to the eastern enclave of Srebrenica since early 1995. In late February, Lt.-Col. C. A. le Hardy, head of intelligence at UNPROFOR HQ Sector North East, expressed the view that 'Srebrenica has to be dealt with before the situation further deteriorates.' He warned that 'The Safe Area declaration in itself will not guarantee stability in or around Srebrenica.' Indeed, he noted that 'the Srebrenica Safe Area has to be secured from external, BSA [Bosnian Serb army], attacks. If the BiH [Bosnian army] have given up their arms, the UN has to secure the safety of the enclave. This may call for (1) further UN troop contributions to the enclave, (2) the credible use of CAS [Close Air Support] and Air Strikes by NATO/UN.' In short, he concluded, 'Srebrenica will not simply go away. It needs high level attention.'[10]

Now in mid-July 1995, the Bosnian Serbs contemptuously elbowed aside the Dutch force in Srebrenica and rapidly overran the enclave. A belated pin-prick air strike, which was all that the UN bureaucracy would authorize, made no impact at all. Tens of thousands of wretched Bosnian Muslim refugees were decanted into Tuzla; some 7,000 males were summarily massacred and dumped in mass graves. It was by a considerable margin the biggest single war crime in Europe since 1945. Zepa fell soon after. For years, the opponents of intervention had argued that 'lift and strike' would trigger attacks on the eastern enclaves; now they had been overrun anyway. Moreover, as we now know, the SAS observers inside the pocket stood aside, powerless.[11] Much to the embarrassment of the government, all this happened in the immediate aftermath of the sumptuous celebrations held to mark the fiftieth anniversary of VE Day.

In Britain, the hostage fiasco and the Srebrenica massacre provoked public horror, political mortification, and important operational changes, but no fundamental change in government policy. Rupert Smith was ordered to desist from air strikes while the release of the hostages was negotiated, and the supreme UN commander in the region, General Janvier, also appears to have promised General Mladic that no further attacks would take place. The only new departure was the dispatch of substantial Anglo-French reinforcements, including artillery, as part of a 'Rapid Reaction Force'. Despite the change from white-painted to camouflaged vehicles, Lord Henley, the Parliamentary Undersecretary of State for Defence, announced that the force 'will be serving very much in a blue beret role and will be wearing blue berets'.[12] The Armed Forces Minister, Nicholas Soames, was even more explicit. 'The theatre reserve force,' he told the BBC, 'is designed to do one thing and one thing only, and that is to protect troops of UNPROFOR . . . and to enable them to carry out their humanitarian and peacekeeping mission . . . The mandate remains exactly as it was . . . Talk of rapid reaction forces, to be frank, goes a bit further than we would like. They are a theatre reserve force . . . We are not there to war-fight. They are there to keep the peace.'[13] The true mission was widely believed to be covering an imminent withdrawal, and for this reason the Sarajevo government was slow to facilitate its deployment.[14] In short, as far as London was concerned, the RRF was not a first step towards grasping the nettle of enforcement, but rather the last gasp of a 'humanitarian' strategy designed to stave off military intervention against the Bosnian Serbs.

Nor did Srebrenica lead to a change of heart. As the former UNPROFOR Director of Information Michael Williams noted in the immediate aftermath of the massacre, 'the silence' of the British government on the safety of the remaining 'safe areas' was 'stunning'. He criticized London for still clinging 'obstinately to the idea of impartiality in the face of savageries perpetrated by the Bosnian Serbs, an attitude which has led to the paralysis of UNPROFOR'.[15] 'There is no clear destination on this particular mission,' Nicholas Soames reiterated on television in late July, 'this is a humanitarian mission.'[16] British 'sources' continued to blame the Bosnians for their own fate.[17] A London conference of all the major Nato and UN players was summoned by the British government in the immediate aftermath of the massacre. Sometimes regarded as a turning point in British policy, it was, in fact, no such thing.[18] Nor – in logic – was there any reason why it should have been. Why make Srebrenica the turning point after all the previous massacres, the detention camps, and the rapes? Had Douglas Hurd and Malcolm Rifkind not prided themselves on remaining unswayed by the latest atrocity?

Instead, the London conference – described by one very senior British military man present as 'dreadful' – was primarily designed to deflect demands for even stronger action and to guarantee the safety of British forces. 'The current Bosnian Serb offensive,' the attendees eventually agreed, 'and the continuing siege of Sarajevo must be met with a firm and rapid response . . . The meeting therefore warned that in order to deter any attack on Gorazde, any such action will be met with a substantial and decisive response. There was strong support for this to include the use of air power, but there was also great concern expressed. Countries are conscious of the serious risks involved in this course of action. We emphasized that the United Nations must not go to war, but needs to support realistic and effective deterrence.'[19] Nobody could consider this a charter for air power; indeed, it was a public confirmation, if any was needed, that the west remained profoundly divided. For the communiqué guaranteed the defence of Gorazde, but said nothing about recovering Srebrenica, defending Zepa, then in its final death throes, and, more to the point, gave no indication of what was to be done about the imminent Serb attack on Bihac. As Bob Dole observed, 'The conferees wrote off Srebrenica and Zepa, vowed to protect Gorazde at some point, that point not being clear, and declined to respond to the dramatically changing situation in Bihac and Sarajevo.'[20] This view was effectively endorsed by one senior British participant, when he noted that 'the purpose of Lancaster House was to avoid the British facing what the Dutch had faced at

Srebrenica. It is quite clear in my view that this was a way to save the British face in Gorazde. That is why it only talks about Gorazde in the original statements.'

The British strategy was simple: allow the Americans to let off steam, abolish the dual key for Gorazde only, where it could be used to protect the Welsh garrison, and rely on the sclerotic Janvier, an Americanophobe who lived in terror of Mladic, to keep further US demands at bay. It looked as if London was going to have to be dragged kicking and screaming into enforcement action.

Accompanying all this was a final luxuriant efflorescence of press, expert, and parliamentary opinion. David Owen, in his parting shot as EU negotiator, warned that British forces were being 'sucked ever more into a Balkan war'.[21] Peter Viggers, a senior Conservative MP, and leading light of the Commons Defence Committee, lashed out against the Americans during the hostage crisis. He claimed that a CIA report accusing the Bosnian Serbs of having committed 90 per cent of atrocities in Bosnia conflicted with the Committee's own experience on the ground, where it was clear that ethnic cleansing had been carried out by 'all sides'.[22] This was an unnecessary and distortive gloss on a report which spoke only of the 'principal' rather than the 'sole' blame of the Bosnian Serbs, but it was a typical example of parliamentary attempts to blur the distinction between aggressor and victim.

A similar testiness underlay much of the press response. 'No government,' warned *The Times*, 'has an electoral mandate to go beyond the present humanitarian operation, however much the American Congress and the Muslim side urge a partisan military response . . . Britain, like other western allies, will not risk its men's lives in an internecine tribal feud. But nor will it be driven from its international responsibilities by terrorism. That message must be forced through, even into narrow Balkan minds.'[23] As ever, the United States was a favoured target for editorializing. 'Its support for the Muslim leadership of Bosnia', the *Independent* claimed at the height of the hostage crisis, was 'so misleading to that optimistic government that it bordered on the callous'.[24] Further military action was widely rejected. 'Whatever these strikes do,' the *Independent* announced, 'they won't force a solution, and it is folly to encourage the Bosnian Muslim fantasy that we might ever be able or willing to do that.'[25] The *Observer* warned its readers to 'Beware the siren calls to war'.[26] And the left-leaning *Independent on Sunday* dismissed air strikes on Bosnian Serb strategic targets as 'ineffective and dangerous'. 'The awful truth,' it concluded with brutal *bien pensant Realpolitik*, 'is that the quickest way to end wars, short of piling in on one side or the other, is to stand by and let the victors take their spoils.'[27]

The Srebrenica massacre provoked loud editorial condemnation, generalized demands for 'action not words', or for lines in the sand, but little support for a realistic limited military intervention against the Bosnian Serbs.[28] 'As we have said a hundred times in the past three years,' the *Guardian* wrote, 'air power is no substitute for sufficient troops on the ground.' It defended 'the struggle to maintain a neutral role with humanitarian aid', and questioned whether 'we really want this to become a Nato war against the Serbs'.[29] Indeed, the *Guardian* warned that 'An exclusive Nato war in Bosnia would destroy the concept of peacekeeping everywhere.'[30] The *Daily Telegraph* continued to fear that western arms supplies to the Bosnians would provoke the Russians to do likewise.[31] And the *Observer*, writing in the aftermath of photographs of mass graves at Srebrenica released by the US, lashed out at the Americans for having 'ceased all efforts at impartiality' and insisted that 'the idea of a multi-ethnic [Bosnian] state is dead. What we are now talking about is the degree of separation.'[32]

The experts, of course, were in much demand throughout mid-1995. John Keegan showed himself relatively unruffled during the hostage crisis; indeed, he was already beginning to adopt a more realistic view of Serb capabilities. 'The Serbs,' he pointed out, 'have not yet had to fight a real war and it is unlikely that they will bite the bullet now.'[33] At the same time, the quality of his political analysis was already showing a marked improvement. He condemned the Serb tactic of 'us[ing] blockades as a means to blackmail the legitimate Bosnian government into granting concessions'. Even more promisingly, he added that 'This is a European problem. If the effective European members of the UN, who are also members of Nato, wish to preserve the military credibility and moral integrity of both nations, they must go forward.'[34] But accompanying all this was still a worryingly paranoid view of US policy and intention. He still roundly rejected the strategy of 'lift and strike', which, he wrote at the height of the hostage crisis, 'appears to have supporters in the Central Intelligence Agency, who are allegedly in direct touch with Muslim elements in the Bosnian government, offering them assurance of American backing and doctoring intelligence assessments to justify the Lift and Strike policy'.[35] These suggestions – which Keegan had the sense to preface with 'allegedly' – were pure Whitehall spin.

Misha Glenny was more strident. He pronounced that 'Those who ordered airstrikes last week on Bosnian Serb positions around Pale bear direct responsibility for the deaths of dozens of young people in Tuzla when the Serbs retaliated and for the subsequent fate of the UN hostages.' Glenny warned that the 'West must understand that the [Yugoslav army] leadership will not hesitate to enter a war with NATO and the Bosnian government'. 'Disaster,' he concluded, 'is therefore looming. It is the result of a disgraceful, macho policy, egged on by western opinion makers from across the ideological spectrum.'[36] Others saw no sign of the military stalemate breaking. Chris Bellamy confidently claimed in early May 1995, shortly after the Croatian recapture of Sector West, that 'The war in Bosnia and the neighbouring Serb-held areas of Croatia is the kind that goes on for decades – and probably will . . . and it is probable that Croatia will avoid attacking elsewhere [in Serb-held Croatia] for fear of provoking Serbia into joining the Bosnian Serbs, and thus precipitating a wider war.'[37]

Across the Atlantic, the cumulative effect of the hostage crisis and Srebrenica on the political establishment was seismic. Malcolm Rifkind had hoped that the hostage crisis would 'still' the 'siren voices' from Congress.[38] The opposite was the case: in the eyes of most American politicians and commentators, the policy of refusing military support for the Bosnian government by 'humanitarianizing' the conflict, with its attendant risks to British servicemen, had now finally been discredited. Indeed, as the *Washington Post* pointed out, the crisis was also an 'utter public humiliation' for the United States and its 'leadership'.[39] Moreover, as the former head of the US National Security Agency pointed out at the height of the hostage drama, the general implications for Nato were catastrophic: 'If the alliance cannot deal effectively with Bosnia, questions will arise about its effectiveness in the face of the challenges of potential instability in Central and Eastern

Europe.'[40] Finally, there was general dismay at what Richard Holbrooke calls the 'substantial, if circumstantial evidence of secret deals between the UN and the Bosnian Serbs' to secure the release of the hostages. 'A suspicion spread rapidly,' he adds, 'that the Serbs and the local UN commanders had made a deal never to use NATO airpower in Bosnia again.'[41] As Newt Gingrich, the Republican leader of the House of Representatives and a late convert to the Bosnian cause, told the International Republican Institute in early June 1995, 'When you are weak and confused on Bosnia, the North Koreans are watching.'[42]

Srebrenica was the last straw. A final unstoppable wave of outrage and derision now descended on the White House and the Europeans. Newt Gingrich lamented that 'the entire world's honour' was being ruined in Bosnia. 'The notion of a small band of Barbarians directly taking on the civilised democracies and winning is a threat to the entire survival of stability on this planet,' he fumed, 'and we should respond to it with whatever level of coercion is ultimately required.'[43] 'When all options are dangerous,' suggested Robert Kagan, a senior State Department official during the Reagan administration, 'choose the honourable one.'[44] 'Let Bosnia defend itself,' demanded the *New York Times*.[45] Jeane Kirkpatrick, erstwhile ambassador to the United Nations under Reagan, claimed that 'Multi-lateralism can't do the real job' and dismissed the 'endless conversations' of the Contact Group, the European Union, Nato and the UN. Even the normally staid *Wall Street Journal* remarked that 'the geopolitical consequences of western humiliation in the Balkans will be enormous. Bullies and thieves the world over will be encouraged.'[46] The post of 'Leader of the Free World' was now vacant, claimed Zbigniew Brzezinski, formerly National Security Advisor to the Democratic President Jimmy Carter. 'The result,' he argued, was 'a moral and political calamity of historic proportions.'[47]

All of this sent Nato into what appeared to be an existential crisis. The UN rapporteur on Human Rights, the former Polish Prime Minister Tadeusz Mazowiecki resigned in protest after Srebrenica. 'If NATO cannot even protect Srebrenica,' he asked, 'what can it do?'[48] 'Can I, in Poland,' Mazowiecki elaborated, 'feel secure in the wake of these events? The towns of Srebrenica and Zepa have been abandoned. Who says Poland won't also be abandoned one day?'[49] David Warzawski, the editor of the leading Warsaw paper *Gazeta Wyborcza*, noted that Poles 'saw Bosnia as a test-case for the functioning of the international community' and pointed out that 'Partnership for Peace' offered Poland 'far weaker guarantees than those which the UN had promised the inhabitants of Sarajevo, Zepa, Srebrenica and Bihac'.[50] Zbigniew Brzezinski lamented that 'both the unity and credibility of our alliance are now at stake. Nato's inability to act assertively is generating increasing tensions within the alliance itself. It would be ironic if Europe's longer-range security and stability were to join the growing list of victims of the unchallenged aggression in Bosnia.'[51]

Britain was a particular target of these attacks. 'What Bosnia has done is expose the myth and illusion of the special relationship in a cruel way,' observed Owen Harries, editor of the conservative *National Interest*, and no interventionist himself.[52] And Richard Perle wrote how Congress was 'appalled' to hear from London that lifting the embargo would 'merely prolong the war and increase the suffering'. 'They remember,' he remarked pertinently, 'that the same argument could have been made in 1940 when Lend Lease [an arrangement by which America kept Britain supplied with essential military equipment] "prolonged" a war that might have been ended quickly by British surrender or a Nazi victory.'[53] All this reflected a wider transatlantic malaise at governmental, diplomatic, and military level which had been mounting since 1993.

In short, by mid-1995, as Ivo Daalder, then a staffer on the National Security Council, noted, 'the impact of the Balkan conflict on NATO's credibility and even its continued viability had become too great'.[54] 'The issue dominated every NATO meeting,' he wrote, 'but none concluded with a clear consensus on how to proceed. Over time, NATO's failure to end a brutal war on its doorstep had a profound impact on both the alliance's viability and the credibility of the United States.'[55] Indeed, the Bosnian issue threatened to crowd out the many other important topics on the administration's agenda. As Richard Holbrooke, Assistant Secretary of State since September 1994, recalled, 'there was rarely a day when Bosnia did not overwhelm every other issue, never a day when we did not feel that we were, at best, only one more disaster from the abyss.'[56] This was demonstrated during President Chirac's first visit to Washington in June 1995. 'The trip,' Holbrooke writes, 'was supposed to be one in a series of semi-annual US–EU summits, and Chirac was accompanied by Jacques Santer, the new President of the European Union. But it quickly turned into a Bosnia crisis session and the rest of the agenda – including economic, trade, law enforcement and environmental issues, was swept away.'[57]

Two problems now served to concentrate the mind of the White House. The first was that the Srebrenica massacre was quickly followed on 26 July by an overwhelming and veto-proof Congressional vote to lift the arms embargo on the Bosnian government. This was the greatest slap in the face for presidential authority since the War Powers Act, passed in 1973 towards the end of the Vietnam War. As Elizabeth Drew writes, Bill Clinton certainly saw it as a 'frontal assault on the authority of the President to conduct the foreign policy of the United States'.[58] The second and related headache was that US troops would be needed to implement a Nato plan to cover an UNPROFOR withdrawal precipitated by the lifting of the embargo, or some other development. Quite apart from the danger it posed to Clinton's re-election the following year, such a commitment commanded very little support in Congress. Not unreasonably, it was dismissed by Bob Dole and others as a reinforcement of the failed Anglo-French policy at considerable risk to American lives. William Pfaff observed bitterly that one would think '20,000-plus European professionals, reinforced by the two largest and best armies and navies in Western Europe, the British and French, better able to look after themselves, as they flee the Serbs, than those Bosnian refugees trying to escape the collapse of enclaves where, until now, those same Europeans had promised them protection'.[59] But the appalling vista was there: refusal to extract the Europeans in UNPROFOR, however justified, would deal the Atlantic alliance a body blow. As the *Economist* noted, 'Honoring the promise to the allies could cost [Clinton] the 1996 presidential election. Breaking it could shatter NATO.'[60] Something would have to give.

Srebrenica and the arms embargo vote finally tipped the balance within the Clinton administration in favour of the interventionists. Bosnia, as Vice-President Al Gore pointed out, 'goes to [the heart of] the kind of people we are'.[61] Tony Lake, the National Security Advisor, reiterated that 'This is larger than Bosnia . . . Bosnia has become and is the symbol of US foreign policy.'[62] The president himself remarked immediately after the massacre that 'I don't like where we are now . . . This policy is doing enormous damage to the United States and to our standing in the world . . . The Europeans could bring forces to bear but they prefer to whine at us.'[63] In short, as one former National Security Council staffer recalled, Bosnia 'was a cancer threatening to metastasize and envelop not only the Clinton presidency but also American foreign policy on a broad scale'.[64]

In late July, Clinton finally swung behind Tony Lake's 'endgame strategy', by which the Europeans were to be pressured into an enforcement operation against the Bosnian Serbs. Shortly after the evasions of the London conference, the US ambassador to Nato compelled the North Atlantic Council to extend the Gorazde warning to all the safe areas, including Sarajevo. Moreover, not only was the notorious 'dual key' now abolished, but it was agreed that air strikes would continue even if hostages were taken. 'After Srebrenica,' Shea recalls, 'we got the key back, so we no longer had to worry that if we wanted to use force the UN would veto us.'[65] And in late July and early August, Warren Christopher and Tony Lake were dispatched to London to lay down the law on the massive use of air power. In contrast to the last Christopher mission of May 1993, the Americans were no longer in 'listening mode': 'don't ask, tell', was the new slogan. As Holbrooke writes, 'Despite the rule changes for bombing that came out of the London conference, I have no doubt the Europeans would have blocked or minimized the bombing were it not for Washington's new resolve.'[66]

At around the same time, the new French government under President Jacques Chirac broke ranks with London. Speaking on Bastille Day in Paris, he condemned the west's reaction to the fall of the enclave as 'keeping things in proportion, a bit like the talks that Chamberlain and Daladier' had held with Hitler at Munich.[67] Failure to act, he added, would make the UN 'accomplices to ethnic cleansing', and in a barbed reference to Britain, he suggested that the west 'should at least guarantee the Safe Zone of Gorazde, where the British troops are deployed, by defending it properly'.[68] 'If such a military action proved impossible,' Chirac's statement warned, 'France would be bound, in conjunction with its partners and the UN Secretary-General, to draw all the relevant consequences'[69] – in other words to withdraw, blaming the British. An infuriated Malcolm Rifkind struck back with the charge that 'President Chirac has so far given a lot of fine words but no proposal.'[70] Not content with trading insults with Washington and putative ideological soulmates in the Republican Party, Rifkind now entered the lists against the French as well, and against a French conservative at that. The new *entente* over Bosnia had proved remarkably fragile.

Britain was now well and truly isolated. Simply toughing it out, as so many times before, was no longer an option. For, however insubstantial Chirac's posturing might be, the defection of the French had demolished that last and trusted British line of defence: that Britain had troops on the ground while the US had not. Moreover, there was now a real danger of a *rapprochement* between Paris and Washington on Bosnia at London's expense. 'There was only one thing the British feared,' one US diplomat recalled, 'a Franco-American alliance that left them out . . . We said to Holbrooke "If you want to do something about London, go to Paris".'[71] The French connection could be used to lever the British out of their old rejectionist stance. 'The British,' as the US ambassador to Nato recalls, 'did not want to get left behind.'[72] As one senior Nato source remembers, 'The idea of the French and Americans forming an alliance with the UK left out . . . helped to shift things in London in 1995 considerably.' Similarly, James Rubin remembers that 'the British were desperately afraid of falling behind a Franco-American axis . . . The American side began to think more boldly about how to proceed, and the French and the Americans essentially took over the policy, and the British were in the second-fiddle category and the last thing they wanted to do was to lose this special relationship with the United States, and the idea of the French and Americans on one side and the British and the Russians on another was unthinkable, and so the British went along with pretty much everything the French and Americans wanted.'[73] For all the wrong reasons, therefore, London now felt it had no choice but to accept an enforcement strategy.

So when the US National Security Advisor, Tony Lake, finally persuaded President Clinton to move towards an enforced 'endgame' strategy after Srebrenica and the Congressional revolt, he found that the British had deserted the positions defended with such bitterness since early 1993. 'I was quite disappointed,' Lake later recalled with some irony, 'because I had thought this was going to be 1993 again . . . I thought this was going to require some spectacular act of diplomacy and advocacy . . . and it turned out it was not as hard as I thought it would be. So while I would like to have convinced myself that it was a stunning act of effective diplomacy, in fact I was walking through a nearly open door.'[74] Britain would certainly not initiate air strikes, but she would no longer obstruct them at every turn, either.

Moreover, the Americans now had an ally within the British camp: General Rupert Smith, the commander in Sarajevo. Ever since his time as Assistant Chief of the Defence Staff in London, he could see that there was no overall strategy in place, merely a series of palliative devices. Smith shared the view that UNPROFOR had reached the end of the road, and was determined to 'break the machine': to escape the vicious circle of appeasement, vulnerability and inaction which had dogged the operation from the start.[75] Faced with the impasse of 1995 he proceeded to do something quite remarkable. He would fulfil his mandate by deterring attacks on the safe areas and ensuring the passage of humanitarian aid. And if necessary, after taking advice,[76] he would use all the powers entrusted to him – and to his predecessors – under Chapter VII of the UN Charter, to enforce this programme on the Serbs. Otherwise, he would go home.

His predecessor, General Rose, had been handicapped by a background in the special forces and the infantry. Rather than using massive Nato air strikes against strategic Bosnian Serb targets such as ammunition dumps, as American commanders repeatedly urged, he employed penny-packets of aircraft against individual tanks or guns; and when these proved difficult to destroy or even locate, Rose advanced this fact as evidence of the ineffectiveness of air power. Unlike Rupert Smith, who had commanded an armoured division in the Gulf and was familiar with the principles of second-world conventional warfare, Rose was essentially a tactical-level infantry commander with extensive experience of counter-insurgency in Northern Ireland and the Third World. He was consequently out of his depth in what was essentially, despite all its oddities, a conventional

European conflict with aggressors and victims, and a straightforward military solution. A little knowledge of 'intractable situations' can be a dangerous thing.

Smith, on the other hand, possessed both the background and the judgement to meet the military challenges in Bosnia. His response was a radical breach with traditional British wisdom on the use of air power. The enclaves, he believed, were indefensible with the available ground forces. Nor would the kind of close air support occasionally sanctioned by Rose during 1994 suffice. Only wide-ranging and massive air strikes which targeted command and control centres far from the enclaves themselves would do the job.[77] Unlike his predecessors and the military advisors in London, Smith had a very realistic sense of the fighting power of the Bosnian Serb army and the devastation Nato could wreak upon it. Moreover, he saw clearly that the UN garrisons scattered the length and breadth of Bosnia were not only insufficient to deter Serb attacks, but a hindrance to the use of Nato air power.

As we have seen, the first attempt to implement the new strategy ended in the disaster of the hostage crisis. Smith was effectively disowned by London and the United Nations in New York, and under his supreme commander, General Janvier, the old UN 'machine' was temporarily patched up. Smith's own career hung by a thread, and he very seriously considered resignation.[78] Instead, he hung on, bided his time and continued to press the government for enforcement action. Immediately after the hostage crisis, Philip Corwin, the Chief UN Political Officer in Bosnia, noted in his diary how 'Smith is the best general that the Bosnian government has, and they know it . . . and he is even driving policy in London, not vice versa as is the usual scenario.'[79] The political director at the Foreign Office, Pauline Neville-Jones, a former stalwart of the appeasement policy, who was now gravitating towards enforcement,[80] kept him abreast of developments in London.

Once the London government decided to go along with an enforcement strategy, Smith was able to 'break the machine' once and for all. UNPROFOR troops were progressively and unobtrusively withdrawn to the relative security of Federation territory. The Welch Fusiliers in Gorazde were extracted across Serb lines with some difficulty. After years of arguing that only ground troops could do the job, the government announced that Gorazde would be defended as the US had always demanded – by the threat of heavy attack from the air and by its Bosnian garrison.

Everything now happened very quickly. Having overrun Zepa and backed off Gorazde – henceforth protected by the threat of massive air strikes – Bosnian Serb and Croatian Serb forces converged on Bihac, the last Bosnian stronghold in the north-west and a bone in the throat of a Greater Serbia. It proved to be an enclave too far. Now that brainchild of US diplomacy, the Croat-Bosnian government alliance of convenience, came into its own. In a surprise operation in late July, Croatian regulars and Bosnian Croat forces effortlessly pushed the Serbs out of Glamoc and Bosansko Grahovo in Herzegovina. Several days later, in early August, the Croatian President Tudjman launched 'Operation Storm', a ferocious and carefully coordinated assault on Serb-occupied territories within Croatia, the Krajina. Like the defenders of Vukovar back in 1991, the Serbs were outnumbered. Unlike them, they were well supplied with heavy weapons and enjoyed excellent fortified positions in the mountains. Instead of fighting, they chose to flee and within a very short time more than 150,000 refugees, most of them innocent Serb women and children, were on their way to an uncertain future further east. The few who remained behind were subjected to terrible abuses.

All this took western opinion completely by surprise. Even as late as 5 August 1995, the defence correspondent of the *Independent*, Christopher Bellamy, was writing that 'The Croatian assault on Serb-held Krajina has conformed so far to all the stereotypes of the civil war in neighbouring Bosnia: heavy shelling, followed by committing a few tanks, but with little sign of determined infantry attack.' Indeed, Bellamy confidently stated, 'there was little sign . . . of a slick new model army'. 'So far,' he insisted, 'the fighting has preserved the half-hearted character of most battles of the war. There have been no large-scale clashes and movement has been slow and predictable.'[81] Instead, as the *Daily Telegraph* noted just two days later, the Croats 'proved conventional wisdom about the war in Yugoslavia wrong on a number of counts': that the Yugoslav army would inevitably come to the aid of the Krajina Serbs and that any attempt to provide limited military assistance to the Croats and Bosnians would inevitably end in disaster.[82] Tudjman's success also led to further transatlantic recrimination, as the British accused the Americans of facilitating, or at least endorsing, ethnic cleansing.[83]

Shortly afterwards, the Serbs fired a shell too many at Sarajevo. The resulting massacre was a direct challenge to the resolutions of the London conference, as amended by the US, and reinforced by the new Franco-American axis. At the very end of August, taking advantage of Janvier's absence, and without consultation with his UN superiors or with any of the troop-contributing countries – Smith struck.[84] In Operation 'Deliberate Force', Serbian artillery around Sarajevo found itself under sustained attack both from the Rapid Reaction Force and from the air. Serb ammunition dumps, communications centres, and bridges were destroyed. British journalists on the ground watched, almost mesmerized. 'I just stood and gaped, unbelieving,' Martin Bell recalled. 'This was the option that for three and a half years the policy makers had told us was inconceivable, the road they could not go down . . . And through the jaded press corps in the battered hotel there spread a feeling new to all of us – a sense of awe and wonderment.'[85] Taking advantage of Serb disarray, Croatian and Bosnian forces now attacked on several fronts. Huge swathes of north-west Bosnia, from which Croats and Muslims had been expelled in 1992, were wrested back. The Serbs bolted. Belgrade did not intervene. One French jet was shot down, but there were no western fatalities at Serb hands. The Serbs were bombed to the negotiating table, as the 'armchair generals' had always said they would be. The siege of Sarajevo was lifted, totally and for good. The Russians rolled with the punch. 'Lift and strike' had worked. All this – as Kofi Annan pointedly noted – was undertaken on the strength of the existing mandate.[86]

As Nato bombers finally went into action, the Cassandras enjoyed one last outing. Jonathan Steele condemned the use of air power as a 'slippery slope'; indeed, he felt that there was 'something inherently cowardly and heavyhanded about the choice of bombs'. 'Europeans,' he concluded, 'are right to be nervous of letting the Bosnian crisis slip into the hands of people with a trigger happy tradition and their own agenda.'[87] The *Guardian* fretted that cruise missiles were 'a blunt instrument in a complex war'.[88] Julian Brazier, an MP with a longstanding interest in defence and eastern Europe, feared that 'The Balkans could be the catalyst for pushing Russia over the brink into a hostile extremism, heavily armed and much less stable than its Soviet forerunner.'[89] The *Independent on Sunday* believed it unlikely that raids would 'do anything to secure an early peace'.[90] Jonathan Eyal lampooned the 'smack the Serbs brigade' and 'the reasoning of western governments [that] once the Serbs understand that they cannot win, they will be forced to negotiate. But the only certainty in the Balkans now is that the outcome will be precisely the opposite.' The result of this 'petulant' Nato action, he predicted, 'may not be an equitable peace, but a division of the Balkans into western and Russian spheres of influence, each continuing a proxy war on Bosnia's soil. Nato's offensive will be remembered not as an exercise in western decisiveness, but as a textbook case of what happens when emotions overcome rationality and force is used to no particular end.'[91] Instead, Eyal was himself a textbook example of an expert unable to grasp that the interpretation he had been defending for so long was disintegrating around him. Even as he wrote, Serb positions were being obliterated before his very eyes, the Croats and Bosnians were about to unleash an irresistible assault, and the Serbs were within weeks of suing for a ceasefire.

But not everybody was so obtuse. Now the ground began to writhe with turning worms. Support for a limited US enforcement strategy, once a tiny trickle, now turned into a veritable geyser of approval. John Keegan gave fulsome praise to the Croatians for their unexpectedly rapid victory, and by the end of the year he was rejecting comparisons between Bosnia and Vietnam, quite rightly, as 'shallow'.[92] The *Daily Telegraph* now argued that those 'urging . . . the Bosnian Croat and Bosnian government forces to halt offensives against the Bosnian Serbs betray[ed] a wish to settle even if it means letting the aggressors off the hook.' Indeed, it concluded, 'The goal of a viable, multi-ethnic Bosnia must be kept in mind as the [US] president wrestles with pressures from the warring parties, Russia and his own Congress. Anything less will condemn the Balkans to further war and provide a green light to ethnic cleansers in other parts of the world.'[93] The sentiments and language of this editorial, though belated, were most welcome. Likewise, the *Guardian*, a longtime sceptic, conceded that

Nato air strikes 'will be seen to have "worked" and a future threat to employ air power will acquire greater credibility'.[94] And the *Independent*, whose stance had meandered back and forth throughout the conflict, told the government not to 'wobble' on Bosnia, by letting the Serbs off the hook.[95]

All this was exploited by Richard Holbrooke, the US Assistant Secretary of State and the man charged by President Clinton with the task of producing a negotiated solution backed by the threat or use of force. Clinton was genuinely concerned to bring about a settlement, but there is no doubt that his primary motivation was domestic. The aim, as serving US diplomats recall, was 'the quickest possible resolution of the conflict, which does not necessarily mean a lasting peace'. Indeed, as Holbrooke's deputy, Bob Frasure, was heard to remark, the new initiative was about getting Bosnia off the front page. 'This isn't about US policy,' he claimed, 'it's about Bill Clinton being re-elected.'

This does not mean that Holbrooke was a mere opportunist. He had been a longstanding critic of western appeasement in Bosnia, which he described in early 1995 as 'the greatest collective security failure of the west since the 1930s'.[96] It was not long before Holbrooke had taken the measure of the Pale Serbs: 'headstrong, given to empty theatrical statements, but in the end, essentially bullies when their bluff was called. The western mistake over the previous four years had been to treat the Serbs as a rational people with whom one could argue, negotiate, compromise and agree. In fact, they respected only force or an unambiguous and credible threat to use it.'[97] He now elbowed aside the Europeans and used Bosnian Serb disarray to enforce the Dayton settlement which brought the war to an end.

Holbrooke's relations with the British were cool. He seems to have held both David Owen and Michael Rose in low regard.[98] In Belgrade he found himself up against Serb empathizers such as the British Chargé d'Affaires Ivor Roberts, who implored Holbrooke not to push the Serbs into a corner.[99] He treated other British diplomats, especially Pauline Neville-Jones, with unconcealed disdain. Nor did the new Foreign Secretary, Malcolm Rifkind, get much change out of Holbrooke on his trip to Belgrade in mid-September. 'I was so tired,' Holbrooke recalls, 'I fell asleep while we were talking, but Rifkind graciously pretended not to notice. I even dozed off while answering a question.'[100] And – this was the unkindest cut of all – the Serbian leader now looked to the Americans rather than the British who had so assiduously courted him. 'Milosevic,' as one British diplomat recalled ruefully, 'wasn't interested in talking to us.'

The manifest success of the American enforcement strategy put the protagonists of the old system on the back foot. A variety of apologetic gambits have been advanced to obscure this fact.[101] The most obvious and least persuasive is simply to deny that air power had made any decisive difference in 1995. 'Any air interdiction campaign,' Rose wrote in his memoirs, 'was likely to have a limited effect, as was proved when NATO finally did launch an air bombardment against Bosnian Serb positions in 1995, and the military effect of some 3,500 sorties was judged by commentators to be negligible.'[102] In fact, no serious analyst takes this view.[103] On the contrary, both the airmen themselves, and, more importantly, Croat, Bosnian, and Serb officers on the ground stress the immediate impact 'Deliberate Force' had on Bosnian Serb command and control systems. Even Misha Glenny, from the perspective of the year 2000, writes of the 'NATO bombing campaign against Bosnian Serb positions . . . that culminated in a strike of thirteen Tomahawk Cruise missiles on the Bosnian Serb Army's command and control centre. *As a consequence*, the Serb defences in western Bosnia collapsed and the Muslim and Croat armies filled the vacuum.'[104] David Owen expressed himself in the same vein, albeit grudgingly.[105]

Others, such as Dame Pauline Neville-Jones and former UNPROFOR officers interviewed for this study, stressed the role of the Rapid Reaction Force on the ground in engaging Serb artillery around Sarajevo.[106] Ironically, sources which had spent the previous three years arguing that an army of 500,000 was needed to do the job now claimed that a few thousand men plus a handful of guns had turned the tide. No doubt, these men played their part, but it was largely confined to Sarajevo and had little effect on the progress of the war in north-west Bosnia.

Perhaps the most plausible military objection was that it was the Croatian victory in the Krajina, followed by Bosnian and, particularly, Croat advances in September–October 1995, not Nato air power, which turned the tide. There is something in this, but this gambit has the unintended effect of endorsing the covert US support to the Croats and Bosnians which made the successes of 1995 possible. Ironically, it is often advanced by those who were most vociferous about Croatian and Bosnian incompetence and the impracticality of waging a 'proxy war'. In any case, as a claim designed to undermine the retrospective credibility of 'lift and strike', the argument is entirely self-contradictory, for it hinges on the assumption that some combination of air power and US-sponsored ground troops prevailed.

Douglas Hurd, on the other hand, still stands resolutely by the arms embargo. 'I cannot be sure,' he reflects, 'no one can be sure, whether other policies would have worked better, or whether eventual policies could have been put into effect earlier without disaster. It would be perverse to be dogmatic about this either way, though I am clear that some of the alternatives proposed, such as relaxing the arms embargo on the parties, would have prolonged rather than curtailed the disaster.'[107] The structure of the argument is crafty. First, philosophically irrefutable sagacities – 'no one can be sure' – designed to cast doubt on air power, followed by dubious certainty on the arms embargo. Hurd's evasions contrast strikingly with the way in which the Roseite loyalist Milos Stankovic reflects on Deliberate Force. He tells us of how Rupert Smith 'called the Serbs' bluff and spoke their lingo: force'. 'Just a moment, Milos,' his interlocutor responds. 'Earlier you seemed to come out against the use of air strikes. They weren't complementary to the peace effort is what you said. Aren't you contradicting yourself?' 'Of course I am,' Stankovic replies. 'All I can do is make observations. But so what if I'm contradicting myself? That war was laced with contradictions and hypocrisy . . . mainly western.'[108] Yet even Stankovic had his 'let-out' clause: the political legacy of the Dayton agreement, which perpetuated ethnic division and permitted the survival – albeit reduced – of Republika Srbska. 'That's no great measure of success,' Stankovic concludes, 'no great vindication of bombing. Now you can do the hard work and try and resolve that contradiction.'[109]

The appropriation of Dayton is, in fact, the apologists' last and most formidable line of defence. It underpins John Major's own apologia. Confronted with the embarrassingly rapid success of the 'deliberate force' strategy, John Major claimed that while technical problems with air power persisted, everything else had substantively altered. He pointed, in particular to a colossal injection of equipment and training received by the Croatian army. The fact that this mysterious immaculate arming was conducted in defiance of an embargo he had stoutly supported, Major conveniently ignores. Moreover, the argument continues, the Bosnian Serbs had 'lost the sponsorship' of Belgrade and Moscow, not least thanks to the rigorous sanctions imposed by the UN. Major's conclusion was that air strikes were not the key reason the Serbs were pushed back. This success was attributable to political negotiating as much as to military intervention.[110] Pauline Neville-Jones was to make the thrust of the final argument more specific when she stressed the 'belated, but very welcome, US willingness to deal seriously with Belgrade'.[111]

All this was designed to effect three things: to discredit 'lift and strike', to validate the strategy of engagement with Milosevic, and to suggest that it was not British obstructionism but 'waiting for the Americans' that had held everything up.[112] On this reading, in fact, the Americans could even be blamed for the slight reduction in Bosnian territory between the Vance–Owen plan and the Dayton settlement. Of course it is true that Dayton offered Sarajevo less land than was theoretically on offer in the VOPP. The crucial difference is that the Serbs rejected the former, whereas the latter was forced upon them. John Major is thus quite wrong to suggest that the *deus ex machina* of a consensual plan made the difference. After all, more or less the same territorial arrangements as Dayton had been on offer in July 1994 in the Contact Group. But on that occasion London had obstructed any attempts at military enforcement. Nor can the estrangement between Belgrade and the Bosnian Serbs have been decisive, for that had begun in May 1993 and was already complete in mid-1994. And even when Pale was offered additional constitutional inducements to sign up in 1995, these proved insufficient too.[113] The Bosnian Serbs, in short, were bludgeoned into accepting Dayton by a combination of western air power and US-sponsored Bosnian–Croat advances on the ground. This crucial order of events is reversed, not coincidentally, in John Major's interpretation.

Stankovic, Owen, and the rest are right about one thing. Dayton was a shabby retreat by the Americans from the principle of a unitary and ethnically diverse Bosnia. For 1995 had seen the triumph not only of a – sound – American military strategy, but the acceptance of deeply unsound European political strategy. Instead of stepping up the pressure, and retaking Bosnia up to the Drina, the American negotiator, Richard Holbrooke – much to the bafflement of all on the ground and to his own palpable subsequent regret – proceeded to throw away the military advantage gained.[114] He told the Bosnians to settle for the 51 per cent of territory originally guaranteed under the Contact Group plan. The Croats and Bosnians, who had been on the verge of capturing Banja Luka and other towns, complied. Holbrooke gave and Holbrooke took away; blessed be the name of Holbrooke. The resulting agreement followed the partitionist, ethnically exclusive, and 'realistic' paradigms which had characterized all previous European – particularly British – solutions. The Americans, as one very senior British diplomat remarked with *Schadenfreude*, had thus 'put water in their own milk'. The Serbs, apparently on the verge of total defeat, rejoiced.[115] Those American diplomats who had backed military intervention in support of Bosnian unity were sidelined. Indeed, as Ed Vulliamy succinctly put it, the Americans had 'finally bombed the Serbs into a European solution'.[116]

Now American troops were sent by a casualty-averse administration to oversee an unjust peace. By their very presence they were to disrupt subsequent attempts, not least by the British, to implement Dayton's provisions on the arrest of war criminals. Having for three years prevented the Americans from doing what they were good at, namely large-scale bombing and the supply of weapons, London and Paris now insisted on US involvement in a peacekeeping operation to which they were manifestly ill suited. Politically and diplomatically, the Americans also signed up to a disastrous four-year reliance on Milosevic as the guarantor of stability in the Balkans. In the topsy-turvy world of Britain's Bosnian policy, all this was reckoned a major victory for Foreign Office diplomacy and for common sense generally.

How much more honest the assessment of one of Martin Bell's interviewees, an 'upwardly mobile staff officer' who had 'held a senior position in the UN's Bosnia command and had defended the bunker-based caution then in fashion'. After 'Deliberate Force', Bell asked the 'inevitable' question: 'Couldn't this have been done years before?' 'Yes,' the officer answered, 'I think it could have been.'[117]

British policy towards the former Yugoslavia achieved, or appeared to achieve, some very important things. Millions of Bosnians were fed by the humanitarian aid effort carried out under the aegis of UNPROFOR; an unquantifiable number of Bosnians were saved by individual interventions 'on the ground'. The war, whether through luck or judgement, did not escalate into a general Balkan conflagration. Milosevic was gradually weaned away from the Bosnian Serbs. The peace process which eventually achieved the 'realistic' partitionist solution of Dayton, was Britain's brainchild if it was anybody's.

But the overwhelming impression is of disastrous and comprehensive failure. The former head of the Diplomatic Service, Sir John Coles, includes Bosnia, along with Suez and the intelligence failure over the Falklands as 'episodes regarded as failures of foreign-policy making'.[118] Even John Major damns himself with the faintest of self-praise. Four years on, he still felt that there was no alternative to the policy he had pursued. He accepted his share of the blame for the failure of the international community over Bosnia, but demanded recognition too of what he saw as Britain's laudable efforts in response to the crisis.[119]

It is true: Britain did do more than most. She seized the reins of policy and refused to surrender them. 'The most impressive thing about this period,' one senior Foreign Office official recalled without irony, 'whatever you think of the policies, was how tough the British government was at sticking to its guns.' More than any other major western country, including even France, Britain consistently refused to go to the military aid of an embattled member of the United Nations. She tenaciously obstructed all attempts by other countries – especially the United States – to provide such help. Indeed, thanks to her determined advocacy of the international arms embargo, Britain would not even allow the Sarajevo government to defend itself. A vital European partner, Germany, was scandalously scapegoated for the failure to forestall Serb ethnic cleansing in Bosnia. Above all, Britain's policy on Bosnia led to a sustained rift on the UN Security Council and in Nato with her most important ally, the United States. A potentially catastrophic outcome to this was averted only by the narrowest of margins in 1995. What proportion of the tens of thousands of murdered Bosnian civilians and millions of refugees should be attributed to this mistaken policy is unknowable, but certainly substantial.

Sustaining all this were several logical sleights of hand. On the one hand, British statesmen, diplomats, and experts dismissed talk of 'aggressors' and 'victims' as 'simplistic'. On the other hand, they frequently dispensed with crucial distinctions to condemn 'all sides' as 'more or less equally bad'. On the one hand, the Bosnian Serb army was typecast as a formidable and malicious foe which could not be defeated except at great cost and at the risk of a Third World War. On the other hand, these same formations besieging the safe areas were spun as either too ramshackle to overrun weakly defended enclaves, or as too restrained to want to do so. On the one hand, the Bosnians were told in the language of brutal *Realpolitik* to make their accommodation with Milosevic, the Bosnian Serbs, and with military realities generally through an unjust peace; on the other, the British government was fastidious in its refusal to regard Franjo Tudjman as a potentially useful and effective military ally of the Bosnian government. On the one hand, the British accused the Americans of 'refusing to get their hands dirty', on the other, London steadfastly refused to countenance any strategy in which total victory and a safe exit route were not guaranteed.

Even some of the supposed successes of British policy do not bear closer scrutiny. The notion that British diplomacy somehow 'contained' the conflict rests on the false supposition that Milosevic planned to attack neighbouring Albania, Bulgaria, or Hungary. In fact, the war took place precisely in those areas of Croatia and Bosnia that Milosevic wanted. If it took some time to spread into Kosovo, this was thanks to Washington's 'Christmas Warning' in 1992, and the Albanian leadership's perseverance with non-violent protest. Moreover, the vaunted contribution of British forces to UNPROFOR is vitiated by two tragic ironies. In general, the Serbs did not take aid workers hostage, but rather the men who were supposed to be guarding them. And while the British army lost eighteen men conducting a three-year humanitarian operation, the brief enforcement campaign – effectively a war – against the Bosnian Serbs was carried off without a single fatality. In any case, the role of British troops on the ground cannot be separated from their alibi function in the broader scheme of British policy. They were originally sent to pre-empt demands for military intervention by Britain; they later became an argument against military intervention by the United States. They did far more harm than good.

Britain, in short, sat astride the international management of the Bosnian war like an enormous dog in the manger, by turns resentful and self-congratulatory, firmly blocking any attempt at an alternative strategy. It was a particularly pernicious case of misplaced pseudo-activism. 'Punching above one's weight' is no virtue when so much is at stake. Contenders who feel themselves outclassed should make way for heavier-weights. Instead, to extend the boxing analogy so beloved of British statesmen, the British government held the ring, and administered balm and ice-packs, while a vastly superior adversary knocked the stuffing out of a victim who maddeningly refused ever to be quite out for the count.

The fundamental problem was the 'humanitarianization' of the war, assiduously promoted by Whitehall, Westminster, and the pre-Smith military presence. This allowed the government to suppress the existence of a major strategic and political crisis in the middle of Europe. It also, as one senior British military critic observed, meant that all efforts were directed towards 'ameliorating' the consequences of the problem, rather than addressing the problem itself. And – to quote Kofi Annan – 'The problem, which cried out for a political/military solution, was that a Member State of the United Nations, left largely defenceless as a result of an arms embargo *imposed upon it by the United Nations* was being dismembered by forces committed to its destruction. This was not a problem with a humanitarian solution.'[120]

Of course, the Americans made mistakes too. The Bush administration was far too slow to realize that it was dealing with a full-blown security crisis in Europe. The initial comments by the Secretary of State, James Baker, that the US 'had no dog in this fight' were rightly condemned by Richard Perle as 'one of the most appalling statements from somebody who claims to be a leader'.[121] The attempts by his successor, Lawrence Eagleburger, to play down reports of Serb atrocities in the summer of 1992 were equally disgraceful. President Clinton and Warren Christopher's half-hearted sallies on behalf of 'lift and strike' in 1993 were also far from confidence-inspiring. On at least two occasions, moreover, the US Defense Secretary, William Cohen, inadvertently gave the green light for attacks on a safe area. First of all, in April 1994 when he announced that the US 'will not enter the war', to prevent the fall of Gorazde; secondly, and more allusively, in November 1994 over Bihac.[122]

By comparison with Britain, however, US policy was a model of good sense. Some of the initial and most of the later hesitation was in response to European – particularly British – objections. Moreover, the alternative American strategy was straightforward, if risky: ground troops were rejected in favour of a calibrated use of air power and arms supplies. This was much less than needed to guarantee victory, but it was better than nothing. The British, on the other hand, were opposed to any military support for the Bosnian government. Moreover, American political opinion proved capable of developing. Many of those who came round to some form of military intervention in 1994–5, such as John McCain, had been sceptical in 1991–3. In Britain, the attitudes of 1992 became set in stone and needed the cataclysmic events of mid-1995 to dislodge them. Of course, some of the American interest in Bosnia was political posturing and opportunism. But that in itself is significant, for virtually no British statesman, politician, or expert saw any merit in breaking ranks with the stifling consensus in London. The Americans, in short, were at least half right on Bosnia; Britain was consistently wrong. 'We on our worst day,' as one US diplomat recalled, 'were better than you on your best day.'[123]

Moreover, the American military-strategic analysis was borne out by events. Despite British warnings about Croatian and Bosnian unpreparedness and incompetence, it proved possible to wage a successful proxy war against the Bosnian Serbs, and to do so without causing a Third World War, without triggering the capture of the remaining safe areas, or any of the other horror scenarios advanced by London. In the event, it was not even necessary to terminate the humanitarian operation altogether while the west belatedly moved to fulfil its United Nations mandate. The Serbs were bombed, UNPROFOR stayed, and the sky did not fall on everybody's heads. So the Americans had been right about this, too.

As we have seen, Britain's failure over Bosnia was not confined to government. Unlike their American counterparts, parliament and the opposition failed to mount any significant challenge to the executive. Similarly, much of the press remained for far too long in the grip of Whitehall spin and distortion about the origins and course of the war. Many British intellectuals, instead of puncturing the contradictions and shortcomings of British policy, actually defended it. Moreover, British mediators and military men such as Lord Carrington, Lord Owen, and Sir Michael Rose played a particularly baleful role in the international response to the war. Without them, Britain could not have kept international pressure for military intervention at bay for as long as it did. Above all, Britain was let down by its experts. For three years regional and military pundits spewed out a torrent of nonsense. The risks of action were systematically exaggerated; those of inaction minimized. The political intentions of Milosevic and his Bosnian Serb allies were misjudged; their military capabilities were preposterously inflated.

The British position on Bosnia was thus rhetorically and philosophically a 'closed system'. It could not be overturned on *a priori* grounds. Practical challenges had to penetrate at least four lines of interlocking defences: the United Nations Security Council, with its imagined Russian and actual Franco-British veto; NATO's North Atlantic Council in Brussels; the British-dominated international mediation effort; and the 'men on the ground', whose fear of Serb reprisals kept US aircraft out of play for most of the war.

Of course, experts are right to be sceptical and cautious, especially where military action is concerned. But caution and scepticism are elements of judgement, not substitutes for it. We will respect a builder for a realistic estimate which takes account of reasonable costs and unforeseen problems. But we will not thank one who gives us such an inflated figure that the whole project has to be called off. In such situations, of course, the householder can use common sense and seek another opinion. In the case of great matters of state, this is not so straightforward, because there is a monopoly on advice. But it is not impossible: as we have seen, there were other sources of advice even within Britain, and there was certainly a wealth of US expertise which suggested that a relatively small engagement could turn the tide against the Bosnian Serbs.

There is no such thing as a controlled experiment or secure knowledge in military and international affairs. Once a particular option has been tried – whether or not it has succeeded – there is no way of definitively determining what the alternative policy might have achieved. We cannot rerun the same situation with the same variables: whatever we have done first will have changed the original problem. There is therefore no way of proving conclusively that air strikes would have worked in 1993–4, although they played an important role in 1995, and no way of proving that lifting the arms embargo would have speeded Bosnian Serb defeat, although it is hard to deny that the Croats would not have been able to defeat the Krajina Serbs and the Bosnian Serb army in north-west Bosnia without US weapons and training. Nevertheless, the military success of Operations Storm and Deliberate Force in August–September 1995 suggest that 'lift and strike' should have been tried earlier.

Of course, it is easy to be wise with hindsight. It could not necessarily be foreseen that the Bosnian Serbs would behave so murderously, that British inaction would lead to such friction with the United States, and that the Bosnian Serbs would fold so quickly under pressure. But then what are advisors for? And what is judgement, if not advice ratified by hindsight? Anybody can go into the library and read Fitzroy Maclean or Rebecca West on Serb national myths and guerilla prowess; anybody can surf the internet or just leaf through *Jane's Defence Weekly* for details of Yugoslav and Bosnian Serb military strength. What the intelligence services and regional or military experts are paid to tell us is what their actual intentions and capabilities are. Normally, intelligence services are reasonably accurate about the latter, but tend to misjudge the former. In this case, they failed miserably on both counts.

Of course, we all make mistakes. Very few Sovietologists predicted the fall of the Berlin Wall and the disintegration of the Eastern Bloc. The present author would have staked his reputation – if he had one – on the outbreak of a diversionary war in Montenegro in the autumn of 2000; and in the light of recent events it is possible that he was too optimistic about Macedonia.[124] A certain humility about individual fallibility and the vagaries of the advisory process is therefore appropriate. But the failure of the experts over Bosnia was of a fundamentally different and more debilitating nature. It was not just a temporary blip or aberration; it was not just a matter of forgivable confusion about the character of the war in 1991–2. British experts persisted in their error throughout 1993–5, long after the main contours of the Serb project had become plain for all to see.

Yet in the end, the root of the problem lay with the politicians. Foreign Office and military sources were unanimous in their view that British policy towards Bosnia was primarily driven by Douglas Hurd's determination to stay out of the war. In part, senior military men and diplomats felt, this reflected the fragility of the Major government and its general lack of direction. The contrast with Margaret Thatcher and her resolute stand over the Falklands, the Gulf, and Bosnia also struck American conservatives such as Richard Perle. 'It was nothing like the Thatcher administration,' he remarked apropos Bosnia. 'The Major government was a very weak government.'[125] Many British diplomats and military personnel interviewed for this study felt the same way. Of course, an enforcement strategy might have led to disaster; it might have embroiled Britain in an interminable and unwinnable Balkan partisan war. But this is no excuse. Conservatives – rightly – delight in the fact that they deal with the world as it is, not as it might or should be.

Compounding this was an unsustainably narrow conception of the national interest. British statesmen were certainly right to be selective. Britain cannot act everywhere at once, and therefore should not do so. It is true that Bosnia was by no means as straightforward as the Falklands or the Gulf. And it was at least plausible to fear that military intervention in Bosnia would embroil Britain in an unwinnable partisan war without any obvious aim or exit strategy. Where Douglas Hurd, Malcolm Rifkind, and John Major failed was in their inability to grasp the extent to which an apparently 'peripheral' issue could mutate into a major threat to the national interest; and in their obtuse refusal to accept that a military solution would be quicker and much less costly than they had convinced themselves it would be. It might not have been obvious that Bosnia would lead to an escalating transatlantic split, to profound fissures within Nato, and to a grievous loss of British prestige, but it should have been foreseen. That is what judgement is about: it cannot be learned, it cannot be inferred from first principles, or from precedent, but statesmen are expected to have it.

It is this lack of judgement which stood out in 1996, when a freshly retired Douglas Hurd, now acting as deputy chairman of Natwest Markets, visited Belgrade in pursuit of a lucrative contract to advise on the privatization of Serbian utilities. The real problem was not so much the block-headed insensitivity of appearing to profit from his connection with Milosevic, but that of judgement. For Hurd defended himself with the argument that it was 'in the interest of the west' for Serbia 'to liberalise and privatise'.[126] In fact, Milosevic was simply flogging off state assets in order to prop up his rule, and in the end he went for an Italian consortium prepared to pay cash 'up front'. Today, both Hurd and Neville-Jones still maintain that Milosevic 'had the option' of turning towards the west. Neville-Jones speaks of 'an opportunity for Milosevic to get himself into better standing again by modernizing, democratizing and dealing with the Kosovo problem . . . He chose not to.'[127] 'Milosevic had a window after Dayton,' Hurd argues. 'He could have turned back, in which case he could have been rehabilitated.'[128] Yet if that statement is to have more than mere tautological meaning, it must suggest that Hurd believed there was a realistic chance of Milosevic going straight – and there was never any likelihood of that.

Just how different British policy could be was demonstrated by Tony Blair after May 1997. The attitude changed almost overnight. 'I think,' James Rubin recalls, '[that] the arrival of Robin Cook and the Blair government on the scene was a breath of fresh air to Madeleine Albright and the rest of us, because we had to push and prod and argue our way through every day with the Major government on Bosnia.'[129] The footdragging on the arrest of war criminals ceased; the casualty-shy Americans now became the major retardative factor. But by far the most striking difference was the determined way in which the new Labour government handled the Kosovo problem in 1999. Now it became clear what the diplomats and military men who had let Britain down so badly over Bosnia were capable of under a new management.

Of course, the Kosovo war was in many ways very unsatisfactory. The operation was sloppily conceived and – at least initially – executed with a curious languor. The idea of forcing a Serb withdrawal from the province through an air campaign unsupported on the ground was only vindicated by the slenderest of margins. The likelihood of a mass deportation of the Albanian population in response to Nato intervention was either not foreseen or foolishly ignored. Nor can anybody be proud of the unintended consequence of victory, namely the 'reverse ethnic cleansing' of the Serb minority. But by contrast with Britain's conduct during the Bosnian war, the trio of Prime Minister Tony Blair, Foreign Secretary Robin Cook, and Defence Secretary George Robertson proved extremely impressive. Unlike in Bosnia, intervention was relatively swift; and there were no western military fatalities at the hands of the enemy. Unlike the surviving Muslims of Banja Luka, Zvornik, and Srebrenica, the Albanian refugees have been able to return. And while the expulsion of the Serb population was entirely wrong, it was preferable – for there was no alternative – to a Serb victory and all that would have entailed. The Conservatives, by comparison, still showed themselves to be floundering over Kosovo. They could have called on Tony Blair to commit the resources necessary for victory. Instead, William Hague demanded a guarantee that no ground troops be sent, a stance which might have positioned them to profit from a Nato defeat, but left them in complete disarray after Milosevic's capitulation.

Similarly, the Labour administration's handling of the insurgency in Macedonia has been moderately reassuring so far, though much more should be done to support the Macedonian government, if necessary through the dispatch of British troops to disperse Albanian rebels. John Major, Douglas Hurd, and Malcolm Rifkind would no doubt have clapped an arms embargo on 'all sides', told the government in Skopje to cut the best deal it could with the rebels, and generally inadvertently signalled her neighbours to help themselves.

Last but not least, the Blair government's decision to subvert Milosevic's hold on power by helping the Serb opposition and indicting him for war crimes has been vindicated. At the time, this was dismissed by the Conservatives, and particularly by Douglas Hurd, as a meaningless piece of Labour 'spin', likely only to strengthen the dictator. But this particular vapidity was to be exposed, as all previous ones had been, by events. Far from making Milosevic more stubborn, his indictment appears to have hastened the Serb retreat from Kosovo. Defeat in that war did not reinforce his position but severely undermined it. Moreover, the Serbian revolution of October 2000 was a tribute not merely to the courage of the democrats and nationalists who took to the streets, but to the western experts who advised and financed them. By a delicious irony, the dramatic events in Belgrade took place on the very day that the Conservative leader, William Hague, gave his much-trumpeted 'keynote address' at the party conference at Bournemouth. Incredibly, in his whole speech Hague made no mention at all of events in Serbia. But perhaps this is not surprising, for the events which pushed William Hague off the news bulletins that evening and off the newspaper headlines the following day comprehensively rubbished ten years of Tory policy on the Balkans. The 'realist' strategy of engagement with Milosevic, Douglas Hurd's efforts to 'democratize' Serbia through specious privatization schemes, the argument that Kosovo had merely strengthened the Serbian dictator, all this was finally laid to rest.

To many, these outcomes were counter-intuitive. Labour had not indulged in oppositional grandstanding on Bosnia; its firmness of purpose on Kosovo while in government came as a complete surprise. Others had written off Tony Blair as a pseudo-messianic charlatan, his Defence Secretary as a trade union thug, and his Foreign Secretary as an opinionated popinjay. But men should be judged by their actions, not their appearances.

At the time of writing, Serbia remains desperate to rejoin the west, opinion polls indicate majority support for Nato's surrogate, Partnership for Peace, and there is even a substantial caucus in favour of Nato membership, which is inevitable in the long run.

Once toppled, there was widespread speculation that the former Serbian president would be arrested, tried in Serbia, and extradited to stand trial at the International Court at The Hague. Yet when the police came to arrest him at his suburban mansion, Milosevic did not – as widely expected – take his own life or go out in a defiant blaze of gunfire. Nor – and here Milosevic was typical of the broader bombast underlying the whole Greater Serb project – had he ever had any intention of doing so. He had been bluffing all along. He had bluffed in 1991 over Vukovar and Dubrovnik. He had bluffed throughout the

Bosnian war. And he had bluffed over Kosovo in 1999. His Bosnian Serb allies, of course, were the biggest bluffers of all. For three years they persuaded the west that they were the invincible heirs of historic Serb partisan prowess, who could only be brought to heel at huge military cost and at the risk of provoking a Third World War.

But the British had been bluffing, too. Douglas Hurd and Malcolm Rifkind's calculated caution and gravitas, the sage warnings, and the weighty caveats: this was all bluff. The authoritative Foreign Office briefings: more bluff. The military pundits who spewed out wild distortions about the relative capabilities of Serbians, Croats and Bosnians: bluff again. The barrack-room historians and ethnographers in parliament and the press: bluffers all. None of them had the faintest idea what they were talking about.

And yet the implications of all this have not sunk in at Whitehall and Westminster. In the aftermath of the Kosovo campaign, the Conservative foreign affairs spokesman John Maples called for a parliamentary inquiry into the government's handling of the conflict. Given his own party's record during the earlier part of the decade, the request showed a lack of self-knowledge bordering on autism, and he was duly punished for it by Robin Cook at the dispatch box. But the idea of a parliamentary inquiry into Britain's handling of the Bosnian war has much to recommend it. After all, previous disasters, such as the intelligence failure before the Falklands, have been thoroughly investigated, and the French parliament, the US Congress, and the United Nations have all conducted their own inquiries into individual aspects of the war.[130] Such an inquiry might be expected to examine the role of expert advice, what happened at Gorazde, the transatlantic split, and, of course, the formulation of government policy in general.

The short-term consequences of Bosnia have been extensively described; the long-term effects are much more difficult to determine. Philip Gordon, a highly respected US defence analyst, wrote in the spring of 1996 that 'There was a Berlin crisis to remind us of the need for the alliance after Suez, but there may not be an equivalent after Bosnia.'[131] He could not have foreseen that the success of the Kosovo campaign, and Britain's crucial role therein, would limit the damage done in 1993–5. 'Were it not for Tony Blair and the British,' James

Rubin recalls, 'I don't believe we could have maintained the alliance unity we needed to win the war in Kosovo.'[132]

Yet there was considerable hidden damage. Transatlantic irritations originating in Bosnia persist. The most striking consequence of Bosnia was the growth of British support for a European defence identity, conventionally dated to the famous St Malo summit in 1998, at which Britain abandoned its long-held objections to a European Defence Identity. 'Something happened before St Malo,' the President of the US Committee on Nato surmises, 'which probably encouraged the British state to . . . redefine its relationship with America . . . I suspect that the precondition for St Malo in 1998 is back in the alienation of 1994–5.'[133] Likewise, Douglas Hurd claims that Bosnia was 'a prelude to St Malo. There is now a much closer relationship between our [French and British] armed forces than there used to be, and that is the result of Bosnia.'[134]

To that extent, Jonathan Eyal was prescient when he wrote in November 1994 that 'the true implications of America's behaviour in the Balkans' were that 'from now on, the Europeans face tough security decisions and more often these will have to be taken without US cooperation . . . All Europeans must conclude that they can no longer rely on US support and that, ultimately, Nato may be unreformable . . . Military contacts between France and Britain, hitherto at the opposite ends of the European military debate, will be further cemented . . . The Europeans are acquiring a new unity of purpose.'[135] 'The rows over Bosnia,' *The Times* suggested in September 1995, 'do not demonstrate the inadequacy of international institutions so much as the diverging interests among the members of the UN Security Council. Britain should clearly proclaim its interests and look for closer defence cooperation with allies in Europe.'[136]

Unfortunately, Tony Blair squandered much of the American goodwill he had built up over Kosovo through his well-meant support for European defence integration outside of Nato. The European Rapid Reaction Force was finally created in 2000, with Major-General Graham Messervy-Whiting, the erstwhile advisor to Lord Owen, who had been a forlorn voice of reason on the efficacy of air power in April–May 1993, as its first commander. It caused widespread unease across the Atlantic.[137] Now the public was treated to the ultimate irony of Conservatives, media pundits, and military sources attacking the Labour administration for jeopardizing transatlantic military and political ties.[138] *The Times*, which in September 1995 had called for Britain to 'look for closer defence cooperation with allies in Europe', now spoke of a 'Phantom Army' and an 'unwarranted risk with European Security'.[139] John Major, whose administration had done so much damage to Nato and transatlantic ties in the mid-1990s, and who had pursued a French will-o'-the-wisp at US expense, condemned Tony Blair for playing into French hands and undermining the primacy of Nato. 'The French have had their own agenda in NATO since the time of de Gaulle,' Major wrote, 'they are now semi-detached from the Alliance and would dearly love the rest of Europe to share their policy.'[140]

Both Douglas Hurd and Malcolm Rifkind, the two men who bear the greatest responsibility for Britain's disastrous Bosnian policy, were ardent disciples of Edmund Burke. 'No one,' the Defence Secretary quoted to the House of Commons, 'makes a greater mistake than he who does nothing because he, himself, can do only little.'[141] Yet Rifkind was strident in his belief that it was better to do nothing to help the Bosnian government militarily than to do something, however inadequate. Likewise, Douglas Hurd recently recommended Burke's *Reflections on the Revolution in France* as an 'anchor of belief' to save politicians from being 'at the mercy of every gale'. 'So many errors,' he believed, 'from the Poll Tax to the campaign to ban fox hunting could be avoided if every Prime Minister re-read Burke before each election.'[142]

There is no doubt that both Hurd and Rifkind were well read and historically aware men. Yet this did not help them to deal with Bosnia. In fact, as we have seen from the various false historical analogies employed – from the Eastern Question, through the origins of the First World War, Suez, Vietnam, and Northern Ireland – it was a hindrance. 'We do not,' Burke reminds us in the *Reflections*, 'draw the moral lessons we might from history. On the contrary, without care it may be used to vitiate our minds and to destroy our happiness. In history a great volume is unrolled for our instruction, drawing the materials of future wisdom from the past errors and infirmities of mankind. It may, in the perversion, serve for a magazine. Wise men will apply their remedies to vices, not to names; to the causes of evil which are permanent, not to the occasional organs by which they act, and the transitory modes in which they appear. Otherwise you will be wise historically, a fool in practice.'

# Notes

## Preface to the Paperback Edition

1. *Unfinest hour* was reviewed positively by: Mark Mazower, 'How Britain got it wrong in Bosnia', *Evening Standard*, 29.10.2001; Branka Magas, 'Shaking hands with the butcher of the Balkans', *The Tablet*, 3.11.2001; Martin Woolacott, 'Wrong wars', *Guardian*, 3.11.2001; Nick Cohen, 'Betrayal in the Balkans', *Observer*, 4.11.2001; Melanie McDonagh, 'Conservative pessimism', *New Statesman*, 12.11.2001; Marcus Tanner, 'Britain's low dishonest Balkan decade', *Independent*, 13.11.2001; Cal McCrystal, 'Lest we forget', *Financial Times*, 17/18.11.2001; Eamon Delaney, 'Myths and diplomacy', *Irish Times*, 1.12. 2001; Noel Malcolm, 'Britain's fatal foreign policy', *Sunday Telegraph*, 9.12.2001; Adam LeBor, 'The slow turning of the battleship', *Literary Review*, 12.2001/1.2002. Overwhelmingly positive but with some serious reservations: Alan Judd, 'Did British involvement help to destroy Bosnia?', *Sunday Times*, 4.11.2001. Guarded but on balance positive were: Stephen Robinson, 'Britain was indifferent', *Daily Telegraph*, 27.10.2001; Sir Reginald Hibbert, 'Unfinest hour', *The World Today*, 12.2001. The only negative reviews were: Air Marshal Professor Sir Timothy Garden, 'Aims fuzzied by the hatred', *Times Higher*, 2.11.2001; Lord Hurd, 'The war we steered clear of', *The Scotsman*, 3.11.2001, S2; 'On its head', *Economist*, 17.11.2001; Lord Hannay, 'Bosnian blame game', *Prospect*, 12.2001. At the time of writing (late February 2002) no review had appeared in the *Spectator*, *Times Literary Supplement* or the *London Review of Books*. *Unfinest hour* received favourable mention in various 'Books of the year' or 'Christmas books' listings: *Sunday Times* (compiled by Andrew Holgate), *Guardian*, 8.12.2001 (Francis Wheen), *Observer*, 25.11.2001 (Geoffrey Robertson) and the *Sunday Telegraph* (my colleague John Adamson). There was also some discussion in the news sections and commentary: John Phillips, 'British role in Bosnia was its "unfinest hour"', *The Times*, 20.10.2001; Michael Gove,

'Colonialism is alive and well in the Middle East', *The Times*, 4.12.2001; Henry Porter, 'The triumph of reason', *Observer*, 23.11.2001. The only major broadsheet in which the book was neither discussed nor reviewed was the *Independent on Sunday*. *Unfinest hour* has not yet been distributed in the United States.

2. Alan Judd, 'Did British involvement help to destroy Bosnia?', *Sunday Times*, 4.11.2001.

3. E.g., Ian Traynor, 'Trying the tyrant we helped to create', *Guardian*, 16.1.2002; and Hugo Young, 'It's sick to ignore our part in the making of Milosevic', *Guardian*, 14.2.2002. On the general background to the War Crimes Tribunal up to 1999 see Geoffrey Robertson, *Crimes against humanity: The struggle for global justice* (London, 1999), pp. 264–99.

4. The International Criminal Tribunal for the Former Yugoslavia, Case No. IT-01–51–I: 'The Prosecutor of the Tribunal against Slobodan Milosevic. Indictment: The Prosecutor of the International Criminal Tribunal for the former Yugoslavia, pursuant to her authority under Article 18 of the Statute of the International Criminal Tribunal for the former Yugoslavia, charges: Slobodan Milosevic with Genocide, Crimes against Humanity, Grave breaches of the Geneva Conventions and Violations of the Laws or Customs of War' (point 5).

5. In addition to *Unfinest hour*, *passim*, see Timothy Mak, 'The case against an International War Crimes Tribunal for the Former Yugoslavia', *International Peacekeeping*, 2/4 (Winter 1995), p. 556; and Yves Beigbeder, *Judging war criminals: The politics of international justice* (Basingstoke, 1999), p. 146. For a more positive view of the British role see Rachel Kerr, 'International judicial intervention: The International Criminal Tribunal for the former Yugoslavia', *International Affairs*, xv, 2 (August 2000), p. 18; and 'Operational justice: The reality of War Crimes Prosecutions in the International Criminal Tribunal for the Former Yugoslavia' (review article), *International Journal of Human Rights*, 5/4 (Winter 2001), p. 112.

6. Article IX of the Dayton Agreement reads: 'The parties shall cooperate fully with all entities involved in implementation of this peace settlement, as described in the Annexes to this Agreement, or which are otherwise authorized by the United Nations Security Council, pursuant to the obligation of all Parties to cooperate in the investigation and prosecution of war crimes and other violations of international humanitarian law.'

7. Lord Hurd, 'The war we steered clear of', *The Scotsman*, 3.11.2001, S2; 'On its head', *Economist*, 17.11.2001; Lord Hannay, 'Bosnian blame game', *Prospect*, 12.2001; Air Marshal Professor Sir Timothy Garden, 'Aims fuzzied by the hatred', *Times Higher*, 2.11.2001. Somewhat mysteriously, Garden's

byline observed that he had 'had no role in Bosnia policy and operations during his military career'. I attempt to deal with the critics, some of whom – including the former Defence and Foreign Secretary Sir Malcolm Rifkind – made a number of interesting points, in my forthcoming article 'Paradigm shift: Britain and the Bosnian War' in the *Journal of Southeast European and Black Sea Studies*, 4 (2002).

8. Sir Ivor Roberts to author, 26.10.2001, Dublin; Sir Ivor Roberts to author, 9.1.2002, Dublin.

9. Needless to say, the author has no ambitions to serve either the Liberal Democrats or the new High Representative in any capacity whatsoever.

10. Gillian Sandford, 'Canada's unsung "superhero"', *National Post* (Canada), 12.1.2002. The subsequent quotations are all taken from this article.

## Preface

1. See Julius Strauss, Philip Sherwell and Joe Murphy, 'Milosevic: I'll name British leaders who helped me', *Sunday Telegraph*, 1.7.2001, and Michael Evans, 'Britons deny secret deal', *The Times*, 2.7.2001.

2. See Fiachra Gibbons, 'Free Milosevic says Pinter', *Guardian*, 26.7.2001.

## 1 'No Intervention': Defining Government Policy

1. Kofi Annan, *Report of the Secretary-General pursuant to General Assembly Resolution 53/35 (1998)* [*Srebrenica report*], p. 6 et passim.

2. Ibid., p. 107.

3. Ibid., p. 111.

4. Ibid., p. 109.

5. Ibid., p. 112.

6. See David Leigh and Ed Vulliamy, *Sleaze: The corruption of parliament* (London, 1997), p. 118.

7. Ibid.

8. For example, by Martin Ivens, 'Whitehall at war', *The Times*, 30.12.1992.

9. See Niall Ferguson, 'How to stop the drift – Mr Hurd's departure is a chance to form a proper foreign policy', *Sunday Telegraph*, 25.6.1995; Boris Johnson, 'The Tory leadership: exit the flannel-suited statesman', *Daily Telegraph*, 24.6.1995; and Philip Stephens, 'Statesman soothes the waves', *Financial Times*, 4.10.1993.

10. *The Times*, 30.1.1993.
11. Robert Hardman, 'Commons sketch', *Daily Telegraph*, 26.9.1992.
12. Peter Riddell, 'Government fights a holding action', *The Times*, 20.4.1993.
13. Hansard, 24.5.1993, col. 580.
14. *Daily Telegraph*, 1.1.1992.
15. See Michael Libal, *Limits of persuasion: Germany and the Yugoslav crisis, 1991–1992* (Westport, Conn., 1997), p. 54.
16. Cited in Sarah Helm, 'Yugoslavia's divisions expose conflict and confusion within the EC', *Independent*, 6.8.1991.
17. David Usborne, 'EC pulls back from sending troops to Yugoslavia', *Independent*, 20.9.1991.
18. See Boris Johnson and Michael Montgomery, 'Europe drops Croatia buffer force plan', *Daily Telegraph*, 2.9.1991; David Usborne, 'Hurd calls for caution on use of troops', *Independent*, 21.9.1991.
19. Annika Savill, Steve Crawshaw and Andrew Marshall, 'Britain isolated over Yugoslavia: France, Italy, and the US back use of military force as Serbian tanks join fierce fighting in Sarajevo', *Independent*, 8.7.1992.
20. Anthony Bevins and Annika Savill, *Independent*, 16.12.1992.
21. Iain Guest, *On trial: The United Nations, war crimes and the former Yugoslavia* (Refugee Policy Group, Center for Policy Analysis and Research on Refugee Issues, Washington, DC, 1995), p. 119.
22. See James Gow, *The triumph of the lack of will: International diplomacy and the Yugoslav war* (London, 1997), p. 182.
23. Cited in Boris Johnson, 'How the "war party" lost: Right or wrong, Hurd got his "do nothing" way on Bosnia', *Sunday Telegraph*, 13.6.1993.
24. George Soros, 'Bosnia and beyond', *NYRB*, 7.10.1993.
25. Cited in Gow, *Triumph of the lack of will*, p. 175.
26. See London Briefing, Bosnia-Herzegovina Information Centre, 1.12.1994, 3–4.
27. Guest, *On trial*, p. 122.
28. Jim Muir, 'Is Bosnia biting the hand that feeds them? Plan to sue Britain for genocide could backfire', *Sunday Telegraph*, 21.11.1993. But see also the pertinent remarks by Margaret Thatcher's confidant Robin Harris, 'War crimes: look who's guilty now', *Sunday Telegraph*, 16.7.1995.
29. Interview, James Rubin, 8.2.2001, fo. 18.
30. Quoted in Martin Bell, 'Conflict of interest', *Guardian*, 11.7.1996. Likewise, *The Times*, leading article, 30.1.1993, saw him as an essentially pragmatic Palmerstonian, rather than a Gladstonian.
31. Douglas Hurd, 'Keeping our heads in a nightmare', *Guardian*, 1.7.1993.
32. Hansard, 25.4.1994.

33. Quoted in Michael Sheridan, 'A decisive week with no clear outcome', *Independent*, 3.6.1995.
34. Hansard, 14.7.1993, col. 967.
35. Quoted in the *Daily Telegraph*, 29.9.1993.
36. Extracts of the speech printed in Douglas Hurd, 'Britain's role in fighting the New World Disorder', *Daily Telegraph*, 30.1.1993.
37. See Christopher Bellamy, 'Army cuts "limit ability to intervene in Bosnia"', *Independent*, 26.8.1992. Alex Renton and Christopher Bellamy, 'Nato obligations would force halt to army cuts', *Independent*, 4.5.1993.
38. As quoted in George Jones, Peter Almond, and Stephen Robinson, 'Hurd rejects intervention in Bosnia war', *Daily Telegraph*, 28.1.1993.
39. Hansard, oral answers, 25.2.1993, col. 1000.
40. Ibid., col. 1001.
41. Quoted in the *Sunday Telegraph*, 6.9.1992.
42. Quoted in the *Independent*, 9.7.1992.
43. Quoted in *The Times*, 1.7.1993.
44. Douglas Hurd, 'We can, at least save civilian lives', *Independent*, 12.12.1994. On the notion of 'imperial responsibility' see also Peter Howard, 'The Jane's interview [with Douglas Hurd]', *Jane's Defence Weekly*, 10.7.1993.
45. Quoted in David Usborne, 'EC pulls back from sending troops to Yugoslavia', *Independent*, 20.9.1991. See also Hella Pick, 'Britain acts to deter armed intervention', *Guardian*, 16.9.1991: 'The British tactic is to deter the allies by highlighting the difficulties and warning that intervention might lead to a Northern Ireland situation.'
46. As cited in Gow, *Triumph of the lack of will*, p. 305.
47. Hurd, 'Lessons of Bosnia: A British overview of the conflict', All Souls Foreign Policy Studies Programme lecture, 8.3.1996, p. 5.
48. Ibid.
49. Douglas Hurd, *The search for peace. A century of peace diplomacy* (London, 1998), p. 107.
50. Hansard, 19.4.1993.
51. Hurd, *The search for peace*, p. 90.
52. Hansard, 29.4.1993, col. 1246.
53. Minutes of Foreign Affairs Committee, 6.11.1991, p. 57.
54. See Hella Pick, 'Hurd urges EC to act on Yugoslavia', *Guardian*, 10.5.1991.
55. Minutes of Foreign Affairs Committee, 6.11.1991, p. 57.
56. Michael Sheridan, 'A change of heart', *Independent on Sunday*, 23.7.1995.
57. Interview with Lord Carrington, *Mendoza transcripts*, London, 20.2.2001, fos. 1–2.

58. *Diplomatic List*, HMSO, London, 1993, p. 56.
59. *Diplomatic List*, HMSO, London, 2000, p. 119.
60. Letter to Charles Crawford, Director South East Europe Department, FCO, 9.11.2000.
61. Interview, Sir Ivor Roberts, 3.1.2001, Dublin, fo. 7.
62. Interview, Lord Hurd, 24.1.2001, London, fos. 2–3.
63. Hansard, 27.6.91, cols. 1137–8.
64. Reginald Hibbert, 'War among the South Slavs in the wider Balkan context', *International Relations*, 1994, pp. 4–8.
65. House Foreign Affairs Committee, 'Examination of witnesses', 14.1.92, p. 188.
66. Douglas Hurd, 'Developing the Common Foreign and Security Policy', *International Affairs*, 70, 3 (July 1994), pp. 421–8.
67. Hurd, *The search for peace*, p. 96.
68. Ibid., p. 98.
69. *Daily Telegraph*, 29.7.1993.
70. Hurd, *Ten minutes to turn the devil*, pp. xiv–xv.
71. Ibid., p. 20.
72. Ibid.
73. Ibid., pp. 33–4.
74. Ibid., pp. 34–5.
75. Foreign Affairs Committee, 'Examination of witnesses', 6.11.1991, p. 67.
76. Cited in Philip Johnson, 'Britain is ready to send 1800 troops to Bosnia', *Daily Telegraph*, 19.8.1992.
77. John Major, *The autobiography* (London, 1999), p. 111.
78. Ibid., p. 514.
79. Ibid., p. 532.
80. See David Wastell, 'The do-nothings versus do-littles', *Sunday Telegraph*, 2.5.1993; Donald Macintyre and Christopher Bellamy, 'Major shifts on troops for Bosnia', *Independent*, 4.3.1994.
81. Interview with Lord Carrington, *Mendoza transcripts*, London, 20.2.2001, fos. 2, 5, 11.
82. Tony Barber, 'Yugoslavia's last chance', *Independent on Sunday*, 8.9.1991.
83. Lord Carrington, 'Turmoil in the Balkans: development and prospects', *RUSI*, October 1992, p. 1.
84. Quoted in Andrew Marshall, 'Twelve certain to recognise Croatian independence', *Independent*, 12.10.1991.
85. E.g. Anthony Seldon, *Major: A political life* (London, 1997), pp. 504–5.

86. See Gow, *Triumph of the lack of will*, pp. 166 ff., 62, 65 on this.
87. See Foreign Affairs Committee, Minutes of Evidence, 14.1.1992, p. 181.
88. Misha Glenny is fully aware of this fact: 'Bosnia: the last chance?', *NYRB*, 28.1.1995.
89. Lord Carrington, 'Turmoil in the Balkans: development and prospects', *RUSI*, October 1992, p. 1. On the FCO see 'Memorandum submitted by the FCO to the Foreign Affairs Committee', 15.1.1992, p. 194, which speaks of the 'Yugoslav federal army's cynical aggression against Dubrovnik and the obstructive tactics employed by Serbia at the October discussions'.
90. As cited in Gow, *Triumph of the lack of will*, p. 64.
91. See House Foreign Affairs Committee, 'Examination of witnesses', 6.11.1991, p. 61.
92. See the very clear-headed analysis by James Gow, 'Nervous bunnies: the international community and the Yugoslav war of dissolution, the politics of military intervention in a time of change', *Political Quarterly*, 1994, p. 22, on this.
93. Cited in the *Daily Telegraph*, 24.4.1992.
94. See the critique by Branka Magas, 'Letter to the editor: Carrington's conflicting claims', *Daily Telegraph*, 27.7.1992.
95. Interview with Lord Carrington, *Mendoza transcripts*, London, 20.2.2001, fos. 2, 5, 11.
96. Cited in Magas, 'Letter to the editor'.
97. Quoted in Steve Crawshaw, 'Search for the peace principle', *Independent on Sunday*, 23.8.1992.
98. See 'Britannia rules the waverers: Britain has had the chance to take a lead in the world's response to the upheaval in ex-Yugoslavia. It is making the worst of it', *Economist*, 15.8.1992.
99. Interview, Dame Pauline Neville-Jones, *Mendoza transcripts*, London, 20.2.2001, fo. 2.
100. Major, *The autobiography*, p. 537.
101. On this see Libal, *Limits of persuasion*, p. 99.
102. Ed Vulliamy, 'Tragic costs of allies' hidden hostility', *Guardian*, 21.5.1996.
103. Hansard, 13.1.1993, col. 902.
104. Hansard, 25.9.1992, col. 186.
105. Quoted in Anna Pukas, 'We should have been tougher, says disillusioned aid chief', *Sunday Times*, 17.4.1994.
106. See leading article, 'Mud and tears', *Guardian*, 24.9.1992.
107. *Independent*, 16.9.1992.
108. *Daily Telegraph*, 11.9.1993.

109. Hansard, 14.4.1993, col. 838.
110. Hansard, 29.4.1993, col. 1245.
111. See Con Coughlin, 'Carter enters where wise men fear to tread', *Sunday Telegraph*, 18.12.1994; Richard Dowden, 'Boutros-Ghali accepts UN's limitations', *Independent*, 27.4.1994; Emma Daly, 'UN chief meets wall of insults in Bosnia', *Independent*, 1.12.1994.
112. Annika Savill, Christopher Bellamy, and Robert Block, 'Muslims call for western intervention as enclave burns', *Independent*, 5.5.1993.
113. Cited in the *Independent*, 25.11.1994.
114. John Sweeney, 'UN cover-up of Srebrenica massacre', *Observer*, 10.9.1995.
115. Robert Fox, 'Nato postures as Sarajevo suffers', *Sunday Telegraph*, 25.9.1994; Mike O'Connor, 'Bosnian Army sniped at own people, UN unit says', *Herald Tribune*, 2.8.1995.
116. Robert Fisk, 'Tormented UN Sector North goes native', *Independent*, 19.12.94.
117. See Norman Cigar, *Genocide in Bosnia. The policy of 'ethnic cleansing'* (College Station, Tex., 1995).
118. Quoted in the *Daily Telegraph*, 3.7.1991. I thank Joseph Pearson for drawing this quotation to my attention. In the same vein later: Hansard, 3.5.1995, col. 329.
119. Hansard, 14.10.1991, cols. 40, 44.
120. Hansard, 20.11.1991, col. 1004.
121. Hansard, 18.12.1991, col. 184.
122. (Mr Richardson), S/PV.3269, 24.8.1993, p. 56. For more 'all parties' rhetoric see the remarks of Sir David Hannay in Security Council, 3369th meeting, 27.4.1994, S/PV.3369, p. 3; Security Council, 3434th meeting, 30.9.1994, S/PV.3434, p. 8; Security Council, 3521st meeting, p. 6.
123. 'Eye of the storm' (interview), *Crossbow* (magazine of the Conservative Bow Group), February 1994, p. 4.
124. Hansard, 18.4.1994, col. 647. For similar language re 'factions' see Archie Hamilton, the Minister of State for the Armed Forces, Hansard, 2.2.1993, col. 303 ('although all three factions have agreed').
125. Hansard, 7.12.1994, col. 942. In the same vein also Baroness Chalker 28.2.1994, col. 812, and Lord Cranborne, 10.3.1994, col. 1540.
126. Hansard, 23.11.1993, col. 315.
127. Hansard, 19.7.1995, col. 1782.
128. Hansard, 14.2.1994, col. 76.
129. Major, *Autobiography*, p. 543.

130. Hansard, 7.2.1994, col. 20.
131. Hansard, 14.1.1993, col. 1066.
132. Hibbert, 'War among the South Slavs', p. 5.
133. Hansard, 1.4.1993, col. 498. For a much defter muddying of the waters see the repeated remarks of Sir David Hannay, Sec. Cnl. pp. 42–3, 30.5.1992; Security Council, 3428th meeting, S/PV.3428, p. 32.
134. Hansard, 19.10.1993, col. 498. See also in Hansard, 14.2.1994, cols. 26–7, same vein: Hansard, 14.4.1993, col. 1108.
135. Hansard, 18.4.1994, col. 656.
136. Hansard, 22.6.1995, written answer, col. 324. See also the Prime Minister, 9.2.1993, col. 821 on the need to 'increase the pressure on the parties'.
137. Hansard, 10.2.1994, col. 454.
138. As paraphrased by Annika Savill, *Independent*, 9.2.1994.
139. Cited in Noel Malcolm, 'The whole lot of them are Serbs', *Spectator*, 10.6.1995.
140. Patrick Bishop, 'Bosnian victims blamed for war', *Sunday Telegraph*, 4.12.1994.
141. Patrick Bishop, 'Bosnian Muslims biggest losers in battle for Bihac', *Sunday Telegraph*, 4.12.1994.
142. As paraphrased in the *Daily Telegraph*, 18.7.1992.
143. Cited in the *Guardian*, leading article, 4.8.1993.
144. Hansard, 10.2.1994, col. 450.
145. Hansard, 12.7.1995, col. 957.
146. As described by Christopher Booker, *Sunday Telegraph*, 16.8.1992.
147. Hansard, 14.7.1993, col. 976.
148. Douglas Hogg, *Independent*, 6.8.1993.
149. Douglas Hogg, 'Central Europe, the new security relationships', *RUSI*, August 1994, p. 16. Earlier variants of these remarks were cited in the *Economist*, 21.5.1994, and Mark Almond, 'A faraway country . . .', in Ben Cohen and George Stamkoski (eds.), *With no peace to keep: United Nations peacekeeping and the war in the former Yugoslavia* (London, 1995), p. 131.
150. Robert Block and Annika Savill, 'Despairing West gets ready to leave Bosnia', *Independent*, 9.7.1993.
151. Cited in the *Financial Times*, 20.11.1993. See also Alan Osborn and Alan Philps, 'Queen's speech debate: Hurd's hint of withdrawal shocks MPs', *Daily Telegraph*, 20.11.1993; *Independent*, 2.2.1994; Peter Almond, '"Time not right" for British withdrawal', *Daily Telegraph*, 9.12.1994.
152. See *Daily Telegraph*, 22.11.1993.
153. 'Major to give warning of Bosnia withdrawal', *Daily Telegraph*, 8.7.1994.

154. Paddy Ashdown, 'Abandoning Bosnia to its fascist fate', *Guardian*, 17.12.1993.
155. Hogg, 'Central Europe, the new security relationships', p. 16.
156. Hansard, 4.3.1993, col. 450.
157. Security Council, 3247th meeting, 29.6.1993, S/PV.3247, p. 132.
158. Hansard, 6.7.1993, col. 86.
159. Hansard, 1.3.1994, col. 786.
160. Hansard, 2.2.1994, col. 880.
161. See Leonard Doyle and Tony Barber, 'Islamic plea to UN over Bosnia's Muslims', *Independent*, 16.5.1992; Robert Fisk, 'Arab passions fired by Bosnia', *Independent*, 31.8.1992; Annika Savill and Hugh Pope, 'Turkey defends Balkan meeting', *Independent*, 24.11.1992; Ahmed Rashid, 'Blonde Muslims find shelter in Pakistan', *Independent*, 26.6.1993.
162. Andrew Hogg, 'Arabs join in Bosnia war', *Sunday Times*, 30.8.1992; Andrew Hogg, 'Terror trail of the Mujaheddin', *Sunday Times*, 27.6.1993; Marcus Tanner, 'Muslim refugees threaten Sarajevo's tradition of tolerance', *Independent*, 5.10.1993; Charlotte Eager, 'Muj more fun if you're a cool dude in Bosnia', *Observer*, 7.11.1993; Emma Daly, 'Imam tries to ban beer and bacon', *Independent*, 12.10.1994; Ian Traynor, 'Sarajevo turns an illiberal face to the world', *Observer*, 15.10.1994.
163. Alec Russell, *Prejudice and plum brandy: Tales of a Balkan stringer*, (London, 1993), p. 285.
164. Douglas Hogg, 'Three good reasons to exercise caution', *Independent*, 6.8.1993.
165. Hansard, 14.4.1993, col. 829. In similar terms see Douglas Hurd: 'The Serbs clearly bear the greatest share of the blame for starting the war and for the atrocities that it has produced, but they are not uniquely guilty. The recent carnage in central Bosnia committed by the Croats and occasional evidence of Muslim atrocities against both Serbs and Croats vividly illustrate that no side has the monopoly on evil.' Hansard, 29.4.1993, col. 1167.
166. Hansard, 14.4.1993, col. 1109.
167. Hansard, 18.1.1993, col. 15.
168. Hansard, 19.4.1993, col. 28.
169. Russell, *Tales of a Balkan stringer*, p. 280.
170. As cited in Robert Block and Donald Macintyre, 'Bosnia: end fighting by force, says UN commander', *Independent on Sunday*, 6.12.1992.
171. Leading article, *Guardian*, 7.12.1992.
172. Dr Alain Destexhe, letter to the editor, *Independent on Sunday*, 13.12.1992.
173. As cited in Martin Bell, *In harm's way: Reflections of a war zone thug* (London, 1996), pp. 190–1.

174. Cited in the *Independent*, 6.8.1993.
175. David Grubb, letter to the editor, *Guardian*, 26.7.1995.
176. Anna Pukas, 'We should have been tougher, says disillusioned aid chief', *Sunday Times*, 17.4.1994.
177. Hansard, 26.7.1993, col. 868.
178. Cited in the *Sunday Telegraph*, 15.8.1993.
179. See Barbara Trapido, 'Irma's death is a sad symbol of our failure on Bosnia', *Guardian*, 7.4.1995; Nick Cohen, 'Little Irma, symbol of the west's failure, is dead', *Independent on Sunday*, 2.4.1995.
180. Report in the *Economist*, 21.11.1992.
181. Douglas Hurd, 'Controls and compassion', *Guardian*, 18.9.1992.
182. I requested clarification of this passage from Lord Hurd and am awaiting a reply.
183. R. D. Wilkinson to Nora Beloff, FCO, 4.6.1993 (photocopy in possession of the author) (emphasis added).
184. Hansard, 25.9.1992, cols. 125–6.
185. Douglas Hurd, 'Keeping our heads in a nightmare', *Guardian*, 1.7.1993.
186. Hansard, 14.4.1993, col. 834.
187. Hansard, 29.4.1993, col. 1193; in the same vein see 18.4.1994, col. 649.
188. Hansard, 18.4.1994, col. 648.
189. Hansard, 19.7.1995, col. 1741.
190. Hansard, 24.5.1993, col. 574.
191. Ibid., col. 577.
192. Hansard, oral answers, cols. 391–2.
193. Hansard, 15.12.1994, col. 1066.
194. Hansard, 7.12.1994, cols. 940 and 942.
195. Major, *Autobiography*, p. 545.
196. Hansard, 13.11.1991, col. 1208.
197. Hansard, 7.12.1994, col. 940.
198. See Michael Scharf and Paul Williams, 'The letter of the law', in Ben Cohen and George Stamkoski (eds.), *With no peace to keep: United Nations peacekeeping and the war in the former Yugoslavia* (London, 1995), p. 35.
199. See Stephen Robinson and Jon Hibbs, 'Draft resolution opens door to the use of force', *Daily Telegraph*, 11.8.1992.
200. As cited in Scharf and Williams, 'The letter of the law', p. 38.
201. 'Former Yugoslavia: the UN mandate', Briefing note, Foreign and Commonwealth Office, November 1992.
202. As cited in Marc Weller, 'Peace-keeping and peace-enforcement in the Republic of Bosnia and Herzegovina', *Zeitschrift für ausländisches öffentliches Recht und Völkerrecht*, 56, 1–2 (1996), p. 107.

203. Hansard, 24.2.1994, col. 317.

204. Peter Pringle, 'UN chief earns White House praise', *Independent*, 20.4.1994.

205. Interview, Sir David Hannay, 20.11.2000, London.

206. Hansard, 19.4.1993.

207. Richard H. Ullman (ed.), *The world and Yugoslavia's wars* (New York, 1988), p. 40.

208. As cited in Weller, 'Peace-keeping', pp. 108–9.

209. Cited in *The Times*, 7.8.1992.

210. Hansard, 26.7.1993, col. 871.

211. Annika Savill, 'Looking after the little things', *Independent*, 12.8.1993.

212. Background interview.

213. Hurd, *The search for peace*, p. 99.

214. Nick Cohen, Stephen Castle and Patrick Cockburn, *Independent on Sunday*, 18.4.1993.

215. Cited in *Independent on Sunday*, 16.8.1992.

216. Joseph Sanders Pearson, 'British press reactions to the onset of war in ex-Yugoslavia' (PhD dissertation, University of Cambridge, submitted 2001), pp. 222–3.

217. Peter Riddell, 'Government fights a holding action', *The Times*, 20.4.1993.

218. Cited in the *Independent*, 21.2.1994.

219. Cited in the *Observer*, 23.7.1995. I thank Joseph Pearson of Cambridge University for collating all the relevant polls in easily digestible form.

220. John Coles, *Making foreign policy* (London, 2000), p. 200.

221. Hansard, 14.4.1993, col. 1105.

222. Hurd, 'Lessons of Bosnia', p. 4.

223. Bell, *In harm's way*, p. 41.

224. Interview, Lord Hurd, 24.1.2001, London, fos. 7–8.

225. Annika Savill, 'Looking after the little things', *Independent*, 12.8.1993.

226. Rt Hon. Douglas Hurd, 'Inaugural Douglas Hurd lecture at Oxford Brookes University', 12.3.1993, p. 1 (emphasis in original).

227. See edited extract in Douglas Hurd, 'War of the words', *Guardian*, 17.9.1993. See also Nicholas Jones, *Soundbites and spin doctors: How politicians manipulate the media – and vice versa* (London, 1995), pp. 25–6. For a 'media' response see Maggie Brown, 'Hurd rebuked for attack on BBC news. Leading journalist defends standard of Bosnia coverage', *Independent*, 17.9.1993, and Hugo Young, 'Hurd's world in camera, not in the camera's eye', *Guardian*, 14.9.1993.

228. Miles Hudson and John Stanier's *War and the media: A random searchlight* (1998), takes its subtitle from Hurd's phrase.

229. See the *Independent*, 18.9.1993.
230. See Francis Wheen, 'Winners in a war of words', *Guardian*, 2.8.1995.
231. See Vladimir Lojen, 'A letter to the BBC World Service', *Bosnia Report*, September–December 1995, p. 11.

## 2 'The Lowest Common Denominator': Britain Stifles America, 1991–1993

1. I would like to express my sincere thanks to my doctoral student Alan Mendoza for allowing me to use the transcripts of interviews he conducted for his PhD on Anglo-American relations during the Bosnian war.
2. John Nott, 'America is right about Bosnia', *The Times*, 1.12.1994.
3. Donald Macintyre, 'Thatcher fighting for Croatia', *Independent on Sunday*, 27.10.1991.
4. See Margaret Thatcher, 'We must act now before it is too late', *Guardian*, 7.8.1992; letter, 'Thatcher plea on Bosnia', *The Times*, 14.8.1992; Anthony Bevins and Stephen Goodwin, 'Thatcher warns of "Holocaust" risk in Bosnia appeal', *Independent*, 17.12.1992; Philip Webster and Robert Morgan, 'Thatcher says massacre brings shame on west', *The Times*, 14.4.1993; Peter Riddell, 'The Thatcher intervention', *The Times*, 14.4.1993; George Jones and Stephen Robinson, 'Major faces the fury of Thatcher', *Daily Telegraph*, 15.4.1993; Julie Kirkbride, 'Thatcher hits out again over Bosnian plans', *Daily Telegraph*, 15.6.1993; Margaret Thatcher, 'Stop the Serbs with air strikes and arms for their adversaries', *New York Times*, 5.5.1994; and Margaret Thatcher, 'Bosnia; a tragedy of broken principles' [extracts from her memoirs], *Sunday Times*, 4.6.1995.
5. Thatcher, 'We must act now before it is too late'.
6. Thatcher, 'Stop the Serbs with air strikes and arms for their adversaries'.
7. As cited in Bevins and Goodwin, 'Thatcher warns of "Holocaust"'.
8. See 'Profile: mother of all the battlers', *Observer*, 18.4.1993, and Jones and Robinson, 'Major faces the fury of Thatcher'.
9. As reported in Webster and Morgan.
10. As quoted in Atticus, *Sunday Times*, 2.5.1993.
11. David Wastell, 'Special report on Bosnia's agony: The grand old lady stirs it up – The cry for action: Lady Thatcher's intervention prompts fresh Balkans debate. Margaret Thatcher speaks out and shows that overseas issues can still be harnessed as a popular cause', *Sunday Telegraph*, 18.4.1993.
12. See Peter Riddell, 'Churchill's champion churns up the "level killing

field"', *The Times*, 14.4.1993; Ralph Atkins, 'Parliament and politics: Thatcher rekindles her old fire', *Financial Times*, 15.4.1993.

13. Atkins, 'Parliament and politics'.

14. Thatcher, 'Bosnia: a tragedy of broken principles'.

15. Major, *Autobiography*, p. 497.

16. Ibid., p. 540. In the same vein: Interview, Lord Owen, London, 18.5.2000, *Petersen transcripts*, fos. 1–2.

17. Robin Renwick, *Fighting with allies: America and Britain in peace and war* (Basingstoke, 1996), p. x.

18. Interview, Sir David Hannay, London, 21.11.2000.

19. Percy Cradock, *In pursuit of British interests: Reflections on foreign policy under Margaret Thatcher and John Major* (London, 1997), p. 191.

20. Richard Holbrooke, *To end a war* (New York, 1999 edn), p. 361.

21. Interview, Professor Anthony Lake, Washington, 10.1.2001, fo. 21 (and again fo. 3 on the dangers of precipitating 'the worst crisis since Suez, I think worse than Suez'). In the same vein also the US Ambassador to Nato, Dr Robert Hunter, 10.1.2001, fo. 11: 'In a word it was not a happy family . . . it [was] not of the order of Suez, but there hadn't been anything in between that would have been serious like this', and similarly fo. 10.

22. Raymond Seitz, *Over here* (London, 1998), p. 327.

23. Quoted in Vulliamy, 'Tragic costs of allies' hidden hostility'. For comparisons with Suez see also the contemporary assessments by Andrew Marr, 'A British tail wagging the American dog', *Independent*, 29.4.1993; 'America and Europe: a ghost at the feast', *Economist*, 19.2.1994; Vincent Cable, 'Europe and the US: the rift is growing wider', *Independent*, 28.7.1995; 'EU and the scholarly assessment' in Gow, *Triumph of the lack of will*, p. 245.

24. See Wayne Bert, *The reluctant superpower: United States policy in Bosnia, 1991–1995* (Basingstoke, 1997), pp. 133, 137.

25. Ed Vulliamy, 'Hard truths swept under the carpets', *Guardian*, 22.6.1996.

26. See Ed Vulliamy, 'Secret War. The transatlantic war (USA 2)', full transcript.

27. Holbrooke, *To end a war*, p. 29.

28. Interview, Bruce Pitcairn Jackson, Washington, 7.1.2001, fo. 9.

29. Interview, Richard Perle, Chevy Chase, Md., 8.1.2001, fo. 1.

30. On this see, generally, Wayne Bert, *The reluctant superpower*, p. 105.

31. Ibid., p. 159.

32. As reported in Hella Pick, 'Hot blood and cold feet. The west at last has reacted to the Yugoslav crisis with sanctions but is this too little too late?', *Guardian*, 1.6.1992.

33. As cited in Mark Danner, 'The US and the Yugoslav catastrophe', *NYRB*, 20.11.1997.
34. As cited ibid.
35. Interview, Dr John Fox, Washington, 11.1.2001, fo. 12.
36. Robin Renwick, *Memoirs* (forthcoming), p. 237.
37. See remarks quoted in Patrick Cockburn, 'US to offer gradual end to Serb sanctions', *Independent*, 18.4.1994, and Rupert Cornwell, 'US torn over response to "cowardly act"', *Independent*, 7.2.1994.
38. Quoted in Anne Applebaum, 'Therapeutic bombing', *Spectator*, 7.8.1993.
39. Cited in the *Independent on Sunday*, 9.8.1992.
40. Cited in Holbrooke, *To end a war*, p. 42.
41. Bert, *Reluctant superpower*, pp. 86–9.
42. See 'Lexington: A puzzled people. America and Bosnia', *Economist*, 8.5.1993.
43. Elizabeth Drew, *On the edge: The Clinton presidency* (New York, 1994), p. 150.
44. See Nik Gowing, 'Real-time TV coverage from war: Does it make or break government policy?', in James Gow, Richard Paterson, and Alison Preston (eds.), *Bosnia by television* (London, 1996), esp. p. 85.
45. Interview, Bruce Pitcairn Jackson, Washington, 7.1.2001, fo. 18.
46. Interview, James Rubin, London, 8.2.2001.
47. On this see the pertinent remarks of Wayne Bert, *Reluctant superpower*, p. 85.
48. *Independent on Sunday*, 9.8.1992.
49. Holbrooke, *To end a war*, p. 34.
50. Ibid., p. 42.
51. Ibid., p. 39.
52. Interview, Dr John Fox, Washington, 11.1.2001, fo. 2.
53. See Drew, *On the edge*, p. 145.
54. As cited in Colin Brown, 'Serbs seize weapons', *Independent*, 23.1.1993.
55. As cited in Drew, *On the edge*, p. 139.
56. Interview, Professor Anthony Lake, Washington, 10.1.2001, fo. 5.
57. Holbrooke, *To end a war*, p. 50.
58. Ambrose Evans-Pritchard, 'Will Clinton keep it special?', *Sunday Telegraph*, 21.2.1993. See also Seitz, *Over here, passim.*
59. Interview, Professor Anthony Lake, Washington, 10.1.2001, fo. 1. See also James Adams, 'That special relationship', *Sunday Times*, 31.1.1993.
60. On the continued violation of the zone, principally by the Serbs, see Joris Janssen Lok, 'Serbia continues combat sorties', *Jane's Defence Weekly*, 26.9.1992.

61. As cited in the *Daily Telegraph*, 15.12.1992. For Serb threats against UNPROFOR in the event of an enforcement of the no-fly zone see Tony Barber, 'Bosnian Serbs warn west', *Daily Telegraph*, 17.12.1992.
62. As cited in Annika Savill, 'West intensifies the pressure over Bosnia', *Independent*, 17.12.1992.
63. Quoted in James Adams and Michela (sic) Wrong, 'Americans bring Manna from 10,000 ft', *Sunday Times*, 28.2.1993.
64. See the MoD sources cited in Trevor Fishlock, David Wastell, and Robin Lodge, 'Major agrees two-week Bosnia deadline: British troops could face action in New Year', *Sunday Telegraph*, 20.12.1992.
65. Tim Lankester, 'An overwhelming sense of a city slowly dying', *Independent*, 11.12.1992.
66. Renwick, *Memoirs*, typescript, p. 239.
67. Interview, Professors Michael Scharf and Paul Williams, Cambridge, 16.12.2000.
68. Guest, *On trial*, p. 53.
69. Ibid., p. 79.
70. As cited in Bass, *Stay the hand of vengeance*, p. 213.
71. 'Former Yugoslavia: War Crimes Implementation of Resolution 808. Comments and Observations of the United Kingdom', reproduced in full in annex 2 of Guest, *On trial*, p. 181.
72. Ibid., p. 184.
73. Ibid., pp. 9, 120 *et passim* and Scharf, *Balkan justice*: *The story behind the first international war crimes tribunal since Nuremberg* (Durham, NC, 1997), pp. 40–1.
74. Hansard, 10.2.1993, col. 976.
75. Interview, Mr Tom Richardson, London, 20.2.2001, *Mendoza transcripts*, fo. 16.
76. Scharf, *Balkan justice*, p. 77.
77. Quoted ibid., p. 76.
78. Quoted ibid.
79. Interview, Sir David Hannay, London, 21.11.2000.
80. As cited in Mark Almond, 'Doing business with war criminals', *Spectator*, 15.5.1993.
81. Interview, Dr John Fox, Washington, 11.1.2001, fo. 6.
82. Ibid., fo. 13.
83. Ibid., fo. 1.
84. Ibid., fo. 3.
85. Interview, Marshall Freeman Harris, Washington, 9.1.2001, fo. 18.
86. Background interview.

87. Interview, John Herzberg, Washington, 9.1.2001, fo. 8.
88. Interview, Marshall Freeman Harris, Washington, 9.1.2001, fo. 6.
89. Interview, Lord Carrington, London, 22.2.2001, *Mendoza transcripts*, fo. 5.
90. Ibid.
91. Interview, Lord Hurd, London, 5.4.2000, *Petersen transcripts*.
92. Cited in *The Times*, 7.2.1993.
93. Annika Savill, 'The dangers of "doing something"', *Independent*, 2.6.1992.
94. 'More poker in the Balkans', *Economist*, 6.8.1994.
95. David Wastell and Toby Helm, 'Get tough on Serbs, Major told', *Daily Telegraph*, 18.4.1993.
96. Interview, Professor Anthony Lake, Washington, 10.1.2001, fol. 12 (see also fo. 11).
97. Vulliamy, *Sleaze*, p. 114.
98. Cited in Bert, *Reluctant superpower*, p. 174.
99. Ed Vulliamy, 'Tragic costs of allies' hidden hostility', *Guardian*, 21.5.1996.
100. Cited in Tony Barber, 'West's inaction caused by uncertain aims', *Independent*, 8.2.1994.
101. Maurice Weaver, 'Battle for Clinton's ear. President faced with tough policy decision as US military interventionists battle with the cautious to influence strategy', *Daily Telegraph*, 29.4.1993.
102. Ivo Daalder, *Getting to Dayton: The making of America's Bosnia policy* (Washington, DC, 2000), p. 15.
103. Weaver, 'Battle for Clinton's ear'.
104. As cited in Colin Smith, 'Vietnam ghosts return to haunt America', *Observer*, 2.5.1993.
105. William Safire, 'Bosnia: the answer is to give bombing a chance', *International Herald Tribune*, 10.8.1993.
106. See Vulliamy, 'Tragic costs of allies' hidden hostility'; James Adams and Andrew Grice, 'Britain vetoes US plan to arm Bosnian Muslims', *Sunday Times*, 2.5.1993.
107. Hansard, 14.4.1993, cols. 830, 839.
108. Major, *Autobiography*, p. 541.
109. E.g., George Jones and Stephen Robinson, 'Rifkind stirs Bosnia row with Clinton. Rift over troops deepens as Major prepares to meet US President', *Daily Telegraph*, 19.2.1994.
110. Andrew Marshall, 'Serbia offered sanctions trade-off', *Independent*, 23.11.1993.
111. Renwick, *Memoirs*, typescript, p. 238.

112. Ibid., pp. 245–6.
113. As reported in Wastell and Helm, 'Get tough on Serbs, Major told'.
114. *Independent*, 23.1.1993.
115. Cited in Soren R. Bollerup, 'UN conflict management: the case of Bosnia-Herzegovina' (MPhil dissertation, University of Cambridge, 1996), p. 42.
116. Norman Cigar, *The right to self-defence: Thoughts on the Bosnian arms embargo*, Institute for European Defence and Strategic Studies, Occasional paper 63, London, 1995, p. 8.
117. Ibid., pp. 12, 16, 28, 37, 28, 2.
118. Ibid., p. 31.
119. E.g. Bill Clinton in the *Washington Post*, 6.4.1993. Quoted in Gow, *Triumph of the lack of will*, p. 175.
120. As cited in Vulliamy, 'Tragic costs of allies' hidden hostility'.
121. Robin Gedye, 'Bonn backs down on arms embargo', *Daily Telegraph*, 18.2.1993.
122. Andrew Marr and Marcus Tanner, 'UK and France beg Clinton not to arm Bosnian Muslims as British colonel denounces civil war', *Independent*, 22.4.1993; Andrew Marr, Colin Brown, and David Osborne, 'Britain set to break with US over Bosnia', *Independent*, 29.4.1993; Adams and Grice, 'Britain vetoes US plan to arm Bosnian Muslims'.
123. Hurd, *Search for peace*, p. 92.
124. Emphasis added. On this see the reflections of Daniel Patrick Moynihan, himself an erstwhile US Ambassador to the UN Security Council, in Kathy Sawyer, 'Bomb Serb bridges, Moynihan urges in attack on U.S. policy', *International Herald Tribune*, 25.4.1994: 'It's a question of law', he added, 'We [the United States] have the inherent right under Article 51 to lift the embargo.'
125. Rupert Cornwell, 'US ponders Bosnia arms-ban snub', *Independent*, 5.11.1994. See 20.12.1993: 109 for lifting, 57 abstentions, 0 against; 3.12.1994: 97 for, 61 abstentions, 0 against.
126. Annan, *Srebrenica report*, p. 109.
127. Hansard, 5.7.1995, col. 260. On this question see Michael P. Scharf, 'Musical chairs: the dissolution of states and membership in the United Nations', *Cornell International Law Journal*, 28, 1 (winter 1995), pp. 29–69, esp. pp. 30, 59.
128. As reported in the *Independent*, 10.8.1993; Hansard, 10.2.1994, col. 63.
129. Hansard, written answers, 16.1.1995, col. 283; see also Holbrooke, *To end a war*, p. 5.
130. Interview, Sir David Hannay, London, 21.11.2000 and subsequent correspondence.

131. Interview, Mr Tom Richardson, London, 20.2.2001, *Mendoza transcripts*, fo. 22.
132. As cited in the *Financial Times*, 28.4.1994.
133. Hansard, 10.11.1992, col. 740.
134. Hansard, 21.6.1994, col. 118.
135. Hansard, 1.4.1993, col. 501.
136. Ivor Roberts, 'Bosnia: a British perspective', *Review of International Affairs*, 46, 1032, 15.5.1995, p. 21.
137. Major, *The autobiography*, p. 544.
138. Hansard, 10.1.1994, col. 9.
139. Ibid.
140. Tony Barber, 'Muslim numbers make up for forces' lack of weapons', *Independent*, 24.6.1993 (quoting James Gow).
141. Annan, *Srebrenica report*, p. 109.
142. Quoted in Marc Champion, *Independent*, 16.11.1991.
143. Quoted in Antony Loyd, *My war gone by I miss it so* (London, 1999), p. 33.
144. Ibid. See also in the same vein Janine di Giovanni, *The quick and the dead: Under siege in Sarajevo* (London, 1994), p. 72 *et passim*.
145. As cited in the *Sunday Telegraph*, 3.1.1993.
146. 'Kenneth Roberts', 'Salving consciences in Hampstead', *Spectator*, 5.2.1994.
147. Ian Traynor, 'Bosnia's looking-glass war', *Guardian*, 3.11.1992.
148. Hansard, Commons, 12.7.1995 (emphasis added).
149. Douglas Hurd, 'We can, at least, save civilian lives', *Independent*, 12.12.1994.
150. Roberts, 'Bosnia, a British perspective', p. 21.
151. Hurd, *The search for peace*, p. 103.
152. *Economist*, 17.12.1994.
153. Patrick Bishop, 'Apocalypse postponed', *Daily Telegraph*, 28.7.1995.
154. Martin Woolacott, 'Striking a balance', *Guardian*, 28.7.1995.
155. Interview, Professor Mohamed Fillipovic, London, 2.10.2000, fo. 20.
156. Cited in the *Independent*, 10.8.1992.
157. Mamon Nahas, letter to the editor, *Independent*, 25.11.1992.
158. Quoted in Hugh Pope, 'Turks call for arms from Islamic nations', *Independent*, 12.1.1993.
159. Hansard, 8.7.1993, col. 237.
160. See also Graham Messervy-Whiting, *Peace conference on former Yugoslavia: The politico-military interface*, London Defence Studies, 21, Centre for Defence Studies, London, 1994, p. 42 on Silajdzic's letter of 13.5.1993: 'the request was speedily withdrawn'.

161. Hearing, Committee on Armed Services, US Senate, 103 Congress, second session, 23.6.1994, pp. 22, 43, 58, 62. Cited in Bert, *Reluctant superpower*, pp. 177 and 273.

162. See Andrew Marshall and David Usborne, 'US move to arm Bosnia horrifies Europe', *Independent*, 12.9.1994.

163. Interview, Nermin Mulalic, London, 5.9.2000, fo. 6.

164. David Hannay to UNSC, 29.6.1993, p. 132.

165. Hansard, 14.4.1993, col. 820.

166. S/PV. 3328, 4.6.1993, p. 57.

167. Hansard, 15.4.1993, col. 944.

168. Roberts, 'Bosnia: a British perspective', p. 21.

169. Hansard, 19.4.1993, col. 32.

170. Hansard, 6.5.1993, col. 814.

171. Douglas Hurd, letter to the editor, Jakarta, Indonesia, *Daily Telegraph*, 5.4.1993.

172. Patricia Wynn Davies, 'Major warns of "killing field" if Bosnians armed', *Independent*, 2.12.1994.

173. See Mark Stuart, *Douglas Hurd. The public servant. An authorised biography* (Edinburgh and London, 1998), p. 339.

174. On this see the various quotations in Ambrose Evans-Pritchard, 'Will Clinton keep it special?', *Sunday Telegraph*, 21.2.1993.

175. Interview, Dr John Fox, Washington, 11.1.2001, fo. 4.

176. Interview, Dr John Fox, Washington, 4.4.2001, *Mendoza transcripts*, fos. 9–10.

177. Interview, Dr Robert Hunter, Pentagon City, 10.1.2001, fo. 14.

178. On this see Brendan Simms, 'Why America is right about Bosnia', *Independent*, 2.12.1994.

179. Hansard, 14.4.1993, col. 820.

180. Commons written answers by Douglas Hogg, 27.10.1992 (emphasis added).

181. Cited in 'Bosnia Serbs wait in vain for the cavalry', *Independent*, 1.5.1993.

182. Emma Daly, 'UN loses face over mission impossible', *Independent*, 10.5.1995.

183. Hansard, 5.7.1995, col. 377.

184. E.g., with varying plausibility: Ian Traynor, 'Belgrade tries to divide Russians from the west', *Guardian*, 15.12.1992; Marcus Warren, 'Russians revive the Slavic brotherhood', *Sunday Telegraph*, 18.4.1993; Andrew Higgins and Colin Brown, 'Major feels the chill in Moscow', *Independent*, 16.2.1994; and Susan Richards, 'There's more to it than Slav fellow feeling', *Independent*, 15.2.1994.

185. See Andrei Edemski, in *International perspectives on the Yugoslav conflict*, p. 32.
186. Hansard, 19.4.1993, col. 22.
187. See the huffing and puffing reported in: 'Russia to bar arms to Muslims. Veto is pledged on any UN move to lift Bosnia embargo', *International Herald Tribune*, 30 June or July 1993; Andrew Marshall, Tony Barber and Helen Womack, 'Bomb the Serbs, says EU', *Independent*, 8.2.1994; Stephen Robinson, 'Summit hugs fail to hide rift over Bosnia', *Daily Telegraph*, 28.9.1994; Rupert Cornwell, 'Bill gets a bear hug from big buddy', *Independent*, 29.9.1994.
188. Hansard, 14.4.1993, col. 821. See also Hurd's fears as reported in Alan Philps, 'West fears orthodox bloc led by Russia could divide Europe', *Daily Telegraph*, 6.1.1993.
189. See Louise Branson, 'Fury over UN's Russian troops', *Sunday Times*, 21.2.1993.
190. Indeed, Yeltsin's envoy Churkin had announced on 18 April 1993 that 'Should Srebrenica fall, all sorts of bad things will be happening . . . We would certainly be supportive of a Security Council vote [on tougher sanctions],' *Daily Telegraph*, 18.4.1993. In the end Russia abstained.
191. See Colin Smith, 'US boosts fleet as Russia agrees to "protective" hits', *Sunday Times*, 13.2.1994. There were some noises off from within the government and from the nationalist opposition: Tony Barber, 'Threat to "Slavic Allies" unites parties in Russia', *Independent*, 10.2.1994.
192. Richard Beeston, 'Duma accuses Clinton of sowing chaos', *The Times*, 12.11.1994.
193. Christopher Bellamy and Emma Daly, 'Nato jets blast Serb air base in Croatia', *Independent*, 22.11.1994.
194. Michael Evans, 'Allies say vote to scrap weapons ban will send wrong signals', *The Times*, 28.7.1995.
195. See also Imre Karacs, 'Victorious Yeltsin joins the anti-Serb chorus', *Independent*, 28.4.1993. See also Mark Frankland, 'Russia shuts its ears to pleas of Serb nationalism', *Observer*, 23.5.1993.
196. Quoted in Andrew Marshall and Tony Barber, 'Russia joins west in condemning Serbs', *Independent*, 19.4.1994.
197. As quoted in 'Bluff called', *Economist*, 23.4.1994.
198. Quoted in Helen Womack, 'Kremlin set to ditch Serb ally', *Independent*, 20.4.1994.
199. As quoted in 'Quotes of the week', *Independent*, 20.4.1994.
200. As quoted ibid.
201. See Helen Womack, 'Eddie's right-wing chapter shocks Russian readers',

*Independent on Sunday*, 24.1.1993, and, on Vladimir Zhirinovsky, Robert Block, 'Russian bad boy falls flat during "ego-trip" to Serbia', *Independent*, 31.1.1994.

202. For the quotations and perceptive analysis see Mark Frankland, 'Make or break for Russia', *Observer*, 17.4.1994.

203. Quoted in Julian Nundy, 'Gaidar glimpses silver in the Russian clouds', *Independent*, 7.2.1994.

204. Quoted in Noel Malcolm, 'Bosnia and the west: a study in failure', *National Interest*, spring 1995.

205. Anatol Lieven, 'Don't bait the bear', *The Times*, 6.12.1994.

206. Interviews, Professors Paul Williams and Michael Scharf, Cambridge, 16.12.2000.

207. Douglas Hurd, *Lessons of Bosnia*, p. 22.

208. Interview, Dame Pauline Neville-Jones, London, 20.2.2001, *Mendoza transcripts*, fo. 11. Dame Pauline adds: 'we didn't actually believe that you could bomb people to the negotiating table . . . What we thought was, we'd have a roaring war in the Balkans, then we'd have the Serbs invading elsewhere as well. So we thought we'd have a bigger and wider war . . . and we did not believe that the Americans could put troops on the ground, and we did not see how you could ever do anything unless you were prepared to put troops on the ground. So we thought that the whole thing was a snare and a delusion for the Muslims.'

209. Martin Ivens, 'Defy the Hurd instinct', *The Times*, 24.6.1993.

210. Nikolai Tolstoy, letter to the editor, 'Blood in Bosnia', *Spectator*, 24.4.1993.

211. Michael Gordon and Stephen Engleberg, 'Experts urge US to intervene in Bosnia', *Guardian*, 12.4.1993.

212. David Usborne, 'Clinton "must decide" ', *Guardian*, 26.4.1993.

213. As cited in Evans-Pritchard, 'Will Clinton keep it special?'

214. Interview by Dominic Lawson, 'Bosnia is Europe's problem', *Spectator*, 8.5.1993.

215. Rupert Cornwell, 'US contemplates military options to punish Serbs', *Independent*, 17.4.1993.

216. David Usborne, 'White House snub for Rifkind', *Independent*, 24.4.1993.

217. As quoted in a conversation with His Excellency Mr Osman Topcagic, the ambassador of Bosnia-Herzegovina, 23.3.2000.

218. Drew, *On the edge*, p. 156.

219. Daalder, *Getting to Dayton*, p. 16.

220. Seitz, *Over here*, p. 329.

221. Ibid.
222. Interview, Dr John Fox, Washington, 11.1.2001, fo. 1; Seitz, *Over here*, p. 329.
223. Ibid., fo. 3.
224. Renwick, *Memoirs*, typescript, p. 242.
225. Cited in Marshall Freeman Harris, 'Diplomatic differences in Bosnia', *Foreign Service Journal*, April 1997.
226. Quoted in Drew, *On the edge*, p. 157.
227. Quoted ibid., p. 158.
228. Interview, Richard Perle, Chevy Chase, 8.1.2001, fo. 4.
229. Andrew Marshall, 'Bosnia dispute between Europe and US boils over', *Independent*, 12.5.1993; 'US and Britain: the rift widens', *Daily Telegraph*, 19.5.1993; and 'War in Bosnia: Hurd tries to heal rift with America', *Daily Telegraph*, 20.5.1993.
230. Major, *Autobiography*, p. 540.
231. Seitz, *Over here*, p. 330.

## 3 'The Real Stumbling Block': Britain Stifles Nato, 1993–1995

1. See Annika Savill, 'UK officials "convert" US on Bosnia plan', *Independent*, 12.2.1993.
2. Major, *Autobiography*, p. 543.
3. Hugo Young, 'The west stands back while the world gets mugged', *Guardian*, 24.6.1993.
4. Boris Johnson, 'How the "war party" lost: right or wrong, Hurd got his "do nothing" way on Bosnia', *Sunday Telegraph*, 13.6.1993.
5. Annika Savill, 'No arms from Britain for the Muslims. Government will "sweat out" pressure to intervene in the war in Bosnia', *Independent*, 7.4.1993.
6. Quoted in Drew, *On the edge*, p. 139.
7. Ibid., p. 153.
8. Guest, *On trial*, p. 110.
9. Bert, *Reluctant superpower*, p. 105; Drew, *On the edge*, p. 162.
10. As reported by Annika Savill, *Independent*, 24.6.1993.
11. John Dickie, *'Special' no more: Anglo-American relations, rhetoric and reality* (London, 1994), p. 253, comments that 'After more than 50 years of close co-operation, both the Americans and the British had come to the end of the road in their joint endeavour.'
12. E.g., 'Bosnia's cruel mirror', editorial, *Washington Post*, 24/25.7.1993;

'Bosnia policy is a farce', editorial, *Washington Post*, 11.8.1993. Also George Zarycky, 'Bosnia: ominous scandal for the west', *Washington Post*, 27.7.1993; 'For US clarity on Bosnia', editorial, *Washington Post*, 18.8.1993; and 'High time to get tough', editorial, *New York Times*, 4.8.1993.

13. Joseph Brodsky, 'Enough of this unnecessary carnage in the Balkans', *Herald Tribune*, 5.8.1993.

14. William Pfaff, 'Sarajevo: Great powers play out the tragedy again', syndicated in *International Herald Tribune*, 14/15.8.1993.

15. Anthony Lewis, 'A disaster slogging towards a climax', *New York Times*, 14/15.8.1993; Anthony Lewis, 'Will the west stop playing fool with Serbian aggressors?', *International Herald Tribune*, 10.8.1993.

16. Brian Beedham, 'Now let us write the painful Bosnian postmortem', *International Herald Tribune*, 17.8.1993.

17. Quoted in 'Into Bosnia? Europe and America squabble over tactics to end fighting in Bosnia', *Economist*, 15.5.1993.

18. As quoted by Ambrose Evans-Pritchard, *Sunday Telegraph*, 2.5.1993.

19. Patrick Glynn, 'The Sarajevo fallacy lives on', *Sunday Telegraph*, 22.8.1993.

20. See Thomas E. Ricks, 'Rumsfeld, Bush agendas overlap little', *Washington Post*, 11.1.2001.

21. See the paraphrase in Martin Ivens, 'A statesman looks at the new world chaos', *The Times*, 1.6.1994.

22. See the paraphrase in 'Is the west blinded by religion?', *Los Angeles Times*, 3.5.1994.

23. See the quotations in Ambrose Evans-Pritchard, 'Clinton "unfit for office"', *Daily Telegraph*, 20.11.1994, and Hugh Davies, 'Clinton chiefs blame the UN', *Daily Telegraph*, 30.5.1995.

24. See, e.g., A. M. Rosenthal, 'It's time to tell Bosnians their fate is up to them', *International Herald Tribune*, 31.5.1995; A. M. Rosenthal, 'A callous west cheers the bombing of the Serbs', *International Herald Tribune*, 9/10.9.1995; and Stephen S. Rosenfeld, 'Krajina offensive reveals the Balkans' true colours', *International Herald Tribune*, 14.8.1995.

25. E.g., Patrick Cockburn, 'US pilots "cannot find Serb targets"', *Independent*, 3.12.1994.

26. Edward N. Luttwak, 'Meddling by outside powers', *International Herald Tribune*, 11.8.1995.

27. On Madeleine Albright's famous views see Michael Doobs, *Madeleine Albright: A twentieth-century odyssey* (New York, 1999), p. 360.

28. George Kenney, 'Time to start up the tanks', *Guardian*, 4.9.1992; 'Bewaffnet die Bosnier', *Die Zeit*, 11.9.1992. See also in the same vein George

Kenney, 'Die Diplomaten verzweifeln', *Die Zeit*, 20.8.1993. Later, in 1994–5, he was inexplicably to change tack and argue for non-intervention.

29. Interview, James Hooper, 9.1.2001, Washington, fos. 3–4.

30. Guest, *On trial*, p. 110.

31. Daalder, *Getting to Dayton*, p. 15.

32. Interview, Marshall Freeman Harris, Washington, 9.1.2001, fos. 2–3.

33. Quoted in Peter Pringle, 'US voices raised for taking decisive action', *Independent*, 6.8.1993.

34. See also Warren Christopher, 'Bringing peace to Bosnia', in *In the stream of history. Shaping foreign policy for a new era* (Stanford, 1995), p. 346, in which Major's claim is quoted again.

35. As reported extensively in Stephen Robinson and George Jones, 'US anger erupts against Britain: frustration over Bosnia leads White House to question historic ties', *Daily Telegraph*, 18.10.1993.

36. For a contemporary look at the transatlantic malaise see Richard Latter, *A new transatlantic bargain*, Wilton Park paper 77, HMSO, November 1993, 21–22 (re Bosnia) et passim and Andrew Marr, 'A special relationship? Don't mention it', *Independent*, 24.2.1994.

37. Interview, Dame Pauline Neville-Jones, London, 20.2.2001, *Mendoza transcripts*, fo. 15.

38. Jonathan Clarke, 'Rhetoric before reality. Loose lips sink ships', *Foreign Affairs*, September–October, 1995, 2–5.

39. Quoted in Vulliamy, 'Tragic costs of allies' hidden hostility'.

40. As reported in the *Daily Telegraph*, 10.9.1993. Interview, Sir David Hannay, 21.11.2000. On the differences between Sir David and Mrs Albright generally see Francis Harris, 'Our man and their woman fall out at UN', *Sunday Telegraph*, 5.12.1993. See also his clash with US Admiral Boorda, as described in Vulliamy, 'Tragic costs of allies' hidden hostility'.

41. Interview, James Rubin, London, 8.2.2001, fo. 7.

42. Quoted in Stephen Robinson and George Jones, 'US anger erupts against Britain: frustration over Bosnia leads White House to question historic ties', *Daily Telegraph*, 18.10.1993. See also Philip Johnston, Alan Philps and Suzanne Lowry, 'Whitehall takes action to limit the damage', *Daily Telegraph*, 19.10.1993.

43. Annika Savill, Colin Brown and Leonard Doyle, 'Britain hits back at US over Bosnia policy attack', *Independent*, 19.10.1993.

44. Andrew Marshall, *Independent*, 28.11.1994.

45. Ambrose Evans-Pritchard, 'It's America first', *Sunday Telegraph*, 20.11.1994.

46. Quoted in the *Economist*, 25.2.1995.

47. See Noel Malcolm in the *Spectator*, 10.6.1995, on this.
48. Renwick, *Memoirs*, typescript, p. 235.
49. Ibid., p. 236.
50. Ibid., p. 237.
51. Ibid., p. 241.
52. Interview, Lord Renwick, London, 27.11.2000, fo. 6.
53. Interview, Professor Anthony Lake, Washington, 10.1.2001, fo. 6. Interview, Dame Pauline Neville-Jones, London, 20.2.2001, *Mendoza transcripts*, fo. 16: 'I do not recall at any stage him putting forward an alternative policy. And if he is suggesting that somehow (a) he had one, and (b) he made his reservations known – pull the other leg!'
54. Interview, Professor Anthony Lake, Washington, 10.1.2001, fo. 6: 'He was', as Tony Lake recalls, 'a very disciplined professional diplomat' who would never behave 'disloyally' or 'fail to convey what the official policy was'.
55. Cited in Heather Bruce, *The American*, 5.11.1993, reporting a speech of 26 October. Cited in John Baylis (ed.), *Anglo-American relations since 1939. The enduring alliance* (Manchester and New York), p. 229.
56. Interview, Lord Renwick, London, 27.11.2000, fos. 1 and 8 (in the same vein).
57. Renwick, *Memoirs*, typescript, p. 251.
58. Interview, Lord Renwick, London, 27.11.2000, fo. 7.
59. Interview, Professor Anthony Lake, Georgetown, 10.1.2001, fo. 1.
60. Conor O'Cleary, '"Special relationship" breaks down. Clinton is now more committed to Irish interpretation of Northern Ireland conflict', *Irish Times*, 5.2.1994.
61. Rupert Cornwell, 'Britain not so special for the US. Row over Gerry Adams's visa puts relationship with UK in perspective', *Independent*, 4.2.1994.
62. See Martin Walker, 'Europe braces for more rows with US', *Guardian*, 12.11.1994.
63. Interview, Professor Anthony Lake, Georgetown, 10.1.2001, fo. 2: BS: 'Was there any link between disagreements over Bosnia [and Northern Ireland]?'; AL: 'No, I never saw one. I mean there were never those arguments where here's where we disagree on Bosnia . . . and how about Northern Ireland. No.'
64. Interview, Professor Anthony Lake, Georgetown, 10.1.2001, fo. 21. I hope I have thus discharged my obligation to Professor Lake: 'If you are going to quote me, if you can get any balance I have here right and not pluck out one side or another of what is probably a very contentious issue.'
65. Interview, Dr John Fox, Washington, 11.1.2001, fo. 8.
66. Interview, Dr Robert Hunter, Pentagon City, 10.1.2001, fo. 10.

67. Interview, James Rubin, London, 8.2.2001, fo. 9.
68. Holbrooke, *To end a war*, p. 83.
69. Ibid., p. 84.
70. Renwick, *Memoirs*, typescript, p. 245.
71. FCO memorandum, 'Recent developments in Eastern Europe with special reference to Yugoslavia', 6.11.1991, House of Commons Foreign Affairs Committee, vol. II, CE 17. See also FCO memorandum, 'Developments in Central Europe: mechanisms of security and co-operation', Foreign Affairs Committee, Minutes of Evidence, House of Commons, 1991–2, 15.1.1992, Appendix 13.
72. Interview, General Sir Edward Jones, London, 24.1.2001, *Mendoza transcripts*, fo. 2.
73. Interview, Dr Jamie Shea, Brussels, 24.11.2000, fo. 5.
74. On this see Field Marshal Sir Richard Vincent, 'Nato – where next?', *RUSI*, 138, 6 (December 1993), p. 9.
75. As reported in Judy Dempsey, 'Balkan minefield for the west: pressure is mounting for some form of military intervention to support the Yugoslav relief effort', *Financial Times*, 8.8.1992.
76. As claimed by Calum MacDonald, Kate Hoey and Malcolm Wicks, 'Sarajevo: we are still not doing enough', *Independent*, 20.10.1993.
77. Quoted in Jane Sharp, 'If not NATO, who?', *Bulletin of the Atomic Scientists*, 8 (October 1992).
78. NAC communiqué of June 1992 as cited in S. Nelson Drew, *NATO from Berlin to Bosnia: Trans-Atlantic security in transition*, McNair Paper 35, January 1995, Institute for National Strategic Studies, National Defense University, Washington, DC, p. 9.
79. As reported by Boris Johnson, 'Christopher blames EC for Balkan crisis', *Daily Telegraph*, 27.2.1993.
80. See James Adams, 'Bosnia mission causes NATO row', *Sunday Times*, 28.3.1993.
81. Robin Gedye, 'Shrinking NATO is urged to play active role over Bosnia', *Daily Telegraph*, 8.2.1993; Andrew Marshall, 'NATO chief favours action in Bosnia', *Independent*, 22.4.1993.
82. Georgie-Anne Geyer, 'How the conscience of the west was lost', in Stjepan Mestrovic (ed.), *The conceit of innocence: Losing the conscience of the west in the war against Bosnia* (College Station, Tex., 1997) (article reproducing syndicated coverage of the war).
83. See reports in the *Sunday Telegraph*, 29.8.1993 and 'Britain in Bosnia: Shali, new chairman of US joint chiefs of staff', *AQDJ*, 123, 4 (October 1993), p. 385.

84. Hansard, 26.7.1993, col. 838.
85. Jamie Shea, 'NATO's eastern dimension: new roles for the alliance in securing the peace in Europe', *Canadian Defence Quarterly*, March 1993, pp. 55–6. Oddly, Shea has more recently said that he 'didn't think there was ever a sense of an existential crisis for NATO over Bosnia . . . there wasn't [a] spirit that Bosnia would make or break NATO', Interview, fo. 6, but these remarks seemed to have been made in the context of the truly existential crisis represented by Kosovo.
86. Interview, Dr Jamie Shea, Brussels, 24.11.2000, fo. 21.
87. Interview, Sir John Weston, Richmond, 23.11.2000, fo. 12.
88. Ibid., fos. 1–2.
89. On Nato enlargement in general see James Goldgeier, *Not whether but when: The decision to enlarge Nato* (Washington, DC, 1999), which says little about the Bosnian dimension, pp. 3, 63, 86.
90. On this see Ulrich Weisser, *Sicherheit für ganz Europa. Die Atlantische Allianz in der Bewährung* (Stuttgart, 1999), p. 25 *et passim.*
91. See ibid., p. 38.
92. For opposition to enlargement, including some twenty distinguished signatures, see R. T. Davies (ambassador to Poland 1973–8), 'Should NATO grow – A dissent', *NYRB*, 21.9.1995, and 'No rush to expand NATO', leading article, *New York Times*, 1.12.1994. For a contrary view see William Pfaff, 'The new job for NATO should be security eastward', *International Herald Tribune*, 8.12.1994.
93. Davies, 'Should NATO grow – A dissent'.
94. As cited in Weisser, *Sicherheit für ganz Europa*, p. 57.
95. Interview, Admiral Crowe, Washington, 4.4.2001, *Mendoza transcripts*, fo. 15.
96. Interview, Sir John Weston, Richmond, 23.11.2000, fos. 3–4.
97. Interview, Lord Vincent, London, 19.1.2001.
98. Interview, Field Marshal Lord Vincent, London, 28.2.2001, *Mendoza transcripts*, fo. 15.
99. For a public statement of Hunter's prescient views see Robert E. Hunter, 'Notfalls mit Gewalt. Amerika's Führungsstärke ist gefragt um den Krieg auf den Balkan zu beenden', *Die Ziet*, 12.6.1993.
100. Interview, Dr Robert Hunter, Pentagon City, 10.1.2001, fo. 15.
101. Ibid., fo. 21.
102. Interview, Bruce Pitcairn Jackson, Washington, 7.1.2001, fo. 4.
103. Ibid., fo. 16.
104. Interview, Richard Perle, Chevy Chase, 8.1.2001, fo. 2.
105. Interview, John Herzberg, Washington, 9.1.2001, fo. 5.

106. Interview, Bruce Pitcairn Jackson, Washington, 7.1.2001, fo. 3.
107. Eugene V. Rostow, 'On waging war in the pursuit of peace', *International Herald Tribune*, 2.7.1993.
108. Martin McCusker, letter to the editor, *Independent*, 1.11.1993.
109. Quoted in Jonathan Clarke, 'Beckoning quagmires: NATO in Eastern Europe', *Journal of Strategic Studies*, 17, 4 (December 1994), p. 43.
110. As quoted in William Shawcross, 'Around the world in eighty briefings', *Spectator*, 9.7.1994.
111. Strobe Talbott, 'Why NATO should grow', *NYRB*, 10.8.1995, p. 28.
112. Although as Bert, *Reluctant superpower*, points out, this view was not uncommon in the US during the early stages of the crisis.
113. E.g., Stephen S. Rosenfeld, 'If NATO won't save Bosnia, why would it save central Europeans?', *International Herald Tribune*, 3/4.12.1994.
114. See Helen Womack, 'Kiev and Moscow risk "a Bosnia in Crimea"', *Independent*, 24.5.1994, and 'Sicherheitsgarantien für die Ukraine gefordert', *Frankfurter Allgemeine Zeitung*, 30.7.1993.
115. See Elizabeth Nash, 'Hungary seeks shelter', *Independent*, 17.5.1993; 'Hungary puts Nato on the spot', leading article, *Independent*, 18.5.1993; Viktor Meier, 'Serbischer Macht hilflos ausgeliefert. Ungarn im osteuropäischen Sicherheitsvakuum', *Frankfurter Allgemeine Zeitung*, 7.7.1993; Mathias Rüb, 'Nach dem Ausritt nach Belgrad der Musterknabe auf Abwegen. Die ungarische NATO-Politik gerät ins Schlingern', *Frankfurter Allgemeine Zeitung*, 17.2.1994; Charles William Maynes, 'Both options in NATO's Bosnia dilemma look bad for NATO', *International Herald Tribune*, 28.7.1994.
116. As cited in Patrick Cockburn, 'French "plot to split NATO over crisis"', *Independent*, 6.12.1994.
117. Interview, Richard Perle, Chevy Chase, 8.1.2001, fos. 7–8.
118. As quoted in William Safire, 'Arm Muslim fighters and bomb Serbian positions', *International Herald Tribune*, 29.11.1994.
119. As cited in *International Herald Tribune*, 12/13.11.1994.
120. Quoted in Ian Black and Martin Walker, 'Hurd irate as alliance falls apart. Russia joins EU protests against US move on Bosnia', *Guardian*, 12.11.1994. In a similar vein see Jonathan Eyal's hysterical 'Broken ranks, stronger bonds', *Independent*, 16.11.1994: 'All Europeans must conclude that they can no longer rely on US support and that, ultimately, NATO may be unreformable.' At the same time Eyal was arguing, laudably, for Nato expansion.
121. Interview, Sir John Weston, Richmond, 23.11.2000, fo. 5.
122. See William Wallace, 'Hurd fails in the sunset', *Guardian*, 31.1.1995.

123. As cited in George Jones and Peter Almond, 'Interview with Douglas Hurd', *Daily Telegraph*, 11.11.1994.
124. On all this see the extremely useful report, 'The defence of Europe – it can't be done alone', *Economist*, 25.2.1995.
125. Interview, Lord Hurd, London, 24.1.2001, fo. 23. See also Interview, Lord Hurd, London, 14.3.2001, *Mendoza transcripts*, fo. 13: 'On military matters the Anglo-French axis is the natural one.'
126. Interview, Tom Richardson, London, 20.2.2001, *Mendoza transcripts*, fo. 1.
127. For an intelligent, sympathetic but ultimately wrong-headed discussion of this tendency see Michael Howard, '1945–1995: reflections on half a century of British security policy', *International Affairs*, 71, 4 (1995), pp. 705–15, esp. pp. 713–15.
128. Interview, General Sir Edward Jones, London, 24.1.2001, *Mendoza transcripts*, fo. 4.
129. Douglas Hurd, 'NATO's new horizons', *Sunday Telegraph*, 4.12.1994.
130. As cited in Harris, 'Our man and their woman fall out at UN'.
131. Interview, Tom Richardson, London, 20.2.2001, *Mendoza transcripts*, fo. 20.
132. See Christopher Lockwood, 'France warms to Claes' NATO', *Daily Telegraph*, 30.9.1994.
133. Interview, General Sir Edward Jones, London, 24.1.2001, *Mendoza transcripts*, fo. 3.
134. See Ulrich Weisser, *Sicherheit für ganz Europa*, p. 39.
135. Cited in 'The Defence of Europe – it can't be done alone', *Economist*, 25.2.1995.
136. Interview, General Sir Edward Jones, London, 24.1.2001, *Mendoza transcripts*, fo. 4.
137. Interview, Dr Robert Hunter, Pentagon City, 10.1.2001, fo. 10.
138. Interview, Sir John Weston, Richmond, 23.11.2000, fo. 8.
139. Interview, Dr Robert Hunter, Pentagon City, 10.1.2001, fos. 1–3.
140. Interview, James Hooper, Washington, 9.1.2001, fo. 16.
141. Interview, Dr Robert Hunter, Pentagon City, 10.1.2001, fo. 2.
142. See Alan Philps, 'Britain wins a breathing-space before no-fly action', *Daily Telegraph*, 19.12.1992.
143. Interview, Dr John Fox, Washington, 11.1.2001, fo. 7.
144. As cited in Michael Prescott et al., 'Clinton strongarms apprehensive Major', *Sunday Times*, 13.2.1994.
145. As cited in Boris Johnson and Christopher Lockwood, 'West ready to

launch air strikes against the Serbs: massacre in Sarajevo market was turning-point, says Hurd', *Daily Telegraph*, 8.2.1994.

146. As cited in Peter Pringle, 'Nato "to keep up pressure of attack"', *Independent*, 13.8.1993.

147. Interview, Professor Anthony Lake, Georgetown, 10.1.2001, fo. 4.

148. On the new departure see Jim Hoagland, 'If the Serbs defy Clinton in Sarajevo', *International Herald Tribune*, 4.8.1993; Jim Hoagland, 'In Bosnia, Christopher learned bitter lessons', *International Herald Tribune*, 18.8.1993.

149. Interview, Professor Anthony Lake, Georgetown, 10.1.2001, fo. 4.

150. Barbara Starr and Charles Bickers, '"Deny flight" forces posed for Bosnia strikes', *Jane's Defence Weekly*, 14.8.1993.

151. See Francis Harris, 'War in Bosnia: America pushes for intensive air strikes', *Daily Telegraph*, 4.8.1993.

152. As described in Daalder, *Getting to Dayton*, pp. 21–3. See also, contemporaneously, Andrew Marshall, 'NATO unclear on plans for attack', *Independent*, 7.8.1993.

153. As reported in the *Sunday Times*, 13.2.1994.

154. See report in Robert Block, Donald Macintyre and Helen Womack, 'Shelling shatters UN truce after blue helmets move in', *Independent*, 11.2.1994: 'Amid growing signs in Whitehall that Britain had bowed to strong pressure from the US and France to back the air-strike ultimatum, President Clinton was said to have made it clear to Mr Major on Wednesday that the alliance would be under severe threat if Britain did not support Washington. Downing Street last night fiercely denied Mr Major was "leaned on".'

155. Hansard, 8.2.1994, col. 134.

156. As reported by Robert Block, Donald Macintyre and Helen Womack, 'Shelling shatters UN truce after blue helmets move in'.

157. *Sunday Times*, 13.2.1994.

158. As reported in Annika Savill, 'Hurd feels his way to air strikes', *Independent*, 9.2.1994.

159. Hansard, 10.2.1994, col. 449.

160. Ibid., col. 456.

161. Ibid., col. 453.

162. Interview, Lord Hurd, London, 24.1.2001, fo. 8.

163. See Philip Johnston and George Jones, 'Public backs Bosnia action', *Daily Telegraph*, 12.2.1994. See also 'Saving NATO or people', leading article, *Independent on Sunday*, 13.2.1994.

164. Hansard, 14.2.1994, col. 72.

165. Hansard, 18.4.1994, col. 645.

166. See 'Hobbled Harriers', leading article, *Spectator*, 23.4.1994.

167. Hansard, 4.5.1994, col. 711.

168. 'United States actions regarding Iranians and other arms transfers to the Bosnian Army, 1994–1995', *Report of the Senate Committee on intelligence, United States Senate, together with additional views*, November 1996, p. 5.

169. See Robert Block, 'US winks at Iranian arms for Bosnia', *Independent*, 3.6.1994; *Economist*, 19.11.1994; Peter Beaumont, 'US gives Muslim army satellite aid on Serb positions', *Observer*, 13.11.1994; Askold Krushelnycky and Ian Mather, 'America has joined war in Bosnia', *The European*, 18–24.11.1994; Tony Barber and David Usborne, 'France accuses US of arming the Muslims', *Independent*, 1.7.1995; Ed Vulliamy, 'America's secret Bosnia agenda', *Observer*, 20.11.1994; Tom Rhodes, 'US accused of organising arms supplies to Muslims', *Independent*, 29.7.1995. On the SACEUR's apprehensions, Interview, General George Joulwan, Virginia, 3.4.2001, *Mendoza transcripts*, fo. 12.

170. Con Coughlin and Ambrose Evans-Pritchard, 'US set to train Bosnian forces', *Sunday Telegraph*, 13.11.1994; Emma Daly, Richard Dowden and Julian Nundy, 'Serb jets drop napalm on Bihac', *Independent*, 19.11.1994; Rupert Cornwell, 'US "secretly agreed Iran arms for Bosnia"', *Independent*, 6.4.1996.

171. On this see the account by 'Cameron Spence', *All necessary measures*, pp. 87–8, 101–2, whose sympathy for the supply operation is sometimes visible.

172. Peter Almond, 'US angry over Bosnia arms delivery claim', *Daily Telegraph*, 4.3.1995; Julian Borger, 'Bosnians "are being covertly armed"', *Guardian*, 25.2.1995.

173. Robert Block, 'US accused of aiding Bosnian forces', *Independent*, 12.11.1994.

174. Interview, Sir John Weston, Richmond, 23.11.2001, fo. 17.

175. Interview, Field-Marshal Lord Vincent, London, 28.2.2001, *Mendoza transcripts*, fo. 11.

176. Interview, Michael Williams, London, 22.11.2000. Williams was UNPROFOR Spokesman in Zagreb at the time.

177. Interview, Dame Pauline Neville-Jones, London, 20.2.2001, *Mendoza transcripts*, fo. 12. Douglas Hurd, though aware of the flights, decided simply to turn a blind eye: Interview, Lord Hurd, London, 14.3.2001, *Mendoza transcripts*, fo. 5.

178. Interview, Dr Robert Hunter, Pentagon City, 10.1.2001, fo. 18.

179. Interview, Professor Anthony Lake, Georgetown, 10.1.2001, fo. 18.

180. Ibid., fo. 20.

181. Security Council, 3344th meeting, 49th year, 4 March 1994, p. 9.

182. Hansard, 19.4.1994, col. 735.
183. Hansard, 18.4.1994, col. 655.
184. Hansard, 31.5.1995, col. 1100.
185. Ibid., col. 1041.
186. Hansard, 25.4.1994, col. 24.
187. Ibid.
188. Ibid., col. 29.
189. Pauline Neville-Jones, 'Dayton, IFOR and alliance relations in Bosnia', *Survival*, 38, 4 (winter 1996–7), p. 46.
190. Daniel Serwer, telephone conversation, Washington, January 2001.
191. 'Another map for Bosnia: but, whatever they say, the belligerents are not yet in the mood for peace', *Economist*, 9.7.1994. See also Tony Barber, 'Clinton "might ease" sanctions against Serbia', *Independent*, 10.6.1994 and Tim Judah, 'Serbs keep allies waiting with secret reply to peace plan', *The Times*, 20.7.1994: 'The Bosnian Serbs have been told that one of the consequences of rejection would be the lifting of the arms embargo on the Muslims.'
192. Hansard, 13.7.1994, col. 980. See also Tony Barber, 'Britain ready to end ban on arms for Bosnia', *Independent*, 29.7.1994; David Wastell, 'Major to back down on Bosnia arms ban', *Daily Telegraph*, 31.7.1994.
193. This point is made by Patrick Bishop, 'Hurd's threatening bluster is unlikely to ruffle the bully of Bosnia', *Daily Telegraph*, 16.7.1994.
194. Interview, Sir David Hannay, London, 20.11.2000, and subsequent correspondence; Interview, Professor Anthony Lake, Georgetown, 10.1.2001, fo. 15.
195. E.g., *New York Times*, 9.9.1994 and 13.9.1994, and *Washington Post*, 13.9.1994.
196. See Paul F. Horvitz, 'House demands Clinton allows arms for Bosnia', *International Herald Tribune*, 10.6.1994.
197. As cited in William Safire, 'The clock is ticking on Bosnia', *International Herald Tribune* (*New York Times*), 16.9.1994. See also Douglas Jehl, 'Bosnian crisis hangs over Clinton like a darkening cloud', *International Herald Tribune*, 9.9.1994, and David Usborne, 'Clinton sets deadline to lift Bosnia arms embargo', *Independent*, 12.8.1994.
198. As described in George Brock, 'Faltering White House leaving gap at the heart of its foreign policy', *The Times*, 28.9.1994.
199. Interview, George Jones, 'Hurd says Clinton Bosnia policy is dangerous. US warned that troops will pull out if arms embargo is lifted', *Daily Telegraph*, 7.9.1994.
200. Michael Evans, 'Rifkind prepared for rift with US over Bosnia arms', *The Times*, 13.9.1994.

201. Alan Philps, 'Major relishes chance to meet Siberian leader out of his lair', *Sunday Telegraph*, 25.9.1994.
202. Christopher Bellamy, 'Nato adopts tougher line over attacks on UN forces', *Independent*, 30.9.1994.
203. Hansard, 12.7.1995, col. 965.
204. Hurd, 'Lessons of Bosnia', p. 12.
205. Interview, Jennifer Brush, Washington, 29.3.2001, *Mendoza transcripts*, fo. 17.
206. For an excellent account see Ian Williams, 'USA: the arms embargo and the man', *War Report*, October–November 1994, p. 7.
207. Interview, Sir David Hannay, London, 20.11.2000, and subsequent correspondence.
208. Major, *Autobiography*, p. 544.
209. See James Bone and Eve-Ann Prentice, 'Britain rejects Izetbegovic plea to set arms ban deadline', *The Times*, 28.9.1994; Stephen Robinson, 'Embargo deal falls through', *Daily Telegraph*, 28.9.1994; 'Only postponing. Diplomacy "triumphs" in Bosnia', *Economist*, 1.10.1994.
210. Interview, Professor Anthony Lake, Washington, 10.1.2001, fo. 8.
211. On this see Ed Vulliamy, 'How the CIA intercepted SAS signals', *Guardian*, 29.1.1996, and the testimony of the UNPROFOR Spokesman, Dr Michael Williams, London, 22.11.2000.
212. Emma Daly, 'Doubts linger over Carter-brokered truce', *Independent*, 21.12.1994.
213. See the comments cited in Andrew Marshall, 'Milosevic supports peace moves', *Independent*, 5.12.1994; Ambrose Evans-Pritchard, 'Empty threat of US action over Bosnia', *Sunday Telegraph*, 11.12.1994; Emma Daly and Rupert Cornwell, 'Bihac awaits its fate as defences fail', *Independent*, 28.11.1994.
214. Stephen Robinson, 'Clinton lifts blockade on Bosnia arms', *Daily Telegraph*, 12.11.1994; Con Coughlin, 'US moves to calm allies over end of Bosnia arms ban', *Sunday Telegraph*, 13.11.1994.
215. See the accounts in Martin Fletcher and Michael Evans, 'US abandons Bosnia arms blockade', *The Times*, 12.11.1994, and Joseph Fitchett, 'Allies are worried after US calls off policing the ban on arms to Bosnia', *International Herald Tribune*, 12/13.11.1994.
216. James Adams, 'Arms row turns to farce as US mollifies allies', *Sunday Times*, 13.11.1994. Conversation, Lt.-Commander RN, 25.10.2000.
217. On this see Interview, General George Joulwan, Virginia, 3.4.2001, *Mendoza transcripts*, fo. 12.
218. Cited in Sarah Lambert, 'NATO plays down US embargo effect', and

Richard Dowden, 'Facing up to life without Uncle Sam', *Independent*, 15.11.1994. See also George Graham, Laura Silber and Chrystia Freeland, 'US moves to ease Bosnia arms ban angers NATO allies', *Financial Times*, 12/13.11.1994.

219. See Ian Black and Martin Walker, 'Hurd irate as alliance falls apart. Russia joins EU protests against US move on Bosnia', *Guardian*, 12.11.1994; George Brock, 'US condemned for undermining transatlantic solidarity', *The Times*, 12.11.1994; Robert Fox, 'NATO split looms over US end to arms embargo', *Daily Telegraph*, 12.11.1994.

220. Cited in Con Coughlin, 'US moves to calm allies over end of Bosnia arms ban', *Sunday Telegraph*, 13.11.1994.

221. Interview, Sir John Weston, 23.11.2000, Richmond, fo. 4.

222. Owen, *Balkan odyssey* (London, 1995), p. 307. For a contemporaneous view see Andrew Marr, 'Battles that history will heed', *Independent*, 24.11.1994.

223. Anthony Lewis, 'The shame began with George Bush's decision to do nothing', *International Herald Tribune*, 3/4.12.1994.

224. William Safire, 'Arm Muslim fighters and bomb Serbian positions', *International Herald Tribune*, 29.11.1994.

225. Vulliamy, 'Tragic costs of allies' hidden hostility'.

226. As cited in Richard Dowden, '"More strikes", Dole tells Downing Street', *Independent*, 1.12.1994.

227. As cited in James Adams, John Davison and Michael Prescott, 'Ties that unwind', *Sunday Times*, 4.12.1994.

228. Daalder, *Getting to Dayton*, p. 33.

229. As quoted in Rupert Cornwell, 'Dole's trip likely to sow more seeds of disunity', *Independent*, 26.11.1994.

230. Jim Hoagland, 'In sum powerful democracies looked evil in the eye and blinked', *International Herald Tribune*, 1.12.1994.

231. 'Straight talk about NATO', leading article, *International Herald Tribune*, 5.12.1994. See also in the same vein: Diane Kunz, 'Are we hammering the nails into NATO's coffin?', *Sunday Times*, 27.11.1994.

232. Flora Lewis, 'The world "community" is betraying the victims', *International Herald Tribune*, 1.12.1994.

233. As cited in Dowden, '"More strikes", Dole tells Downing Street'.

234. 'Patching up NATO: the western alliance has become another victim of Bosnia's war', *Economist*, 19.11.1994.

235. 'The consequences of Bosnia', *Economist*, 3.12.1994.

236. Robert Fox, 'Nato split looms over US end to arms embargo', *Daily Telegraph*, 12.11.1994.

237. Robert Fox, 'Let's get out of this trap: this week it has become all too clear that the western alliances do not have the will to sustain their peace-keeping efforts in Bosnia', *Daily Telegraph*, 20.11.1994.
238. Andrew Marshall, 'What could die at Bihac', *Independent*, 28.11.1994.
239. 'Ghosts of Suez. Britain and America are moving still further apart', leading article, *The Times*, 29.11.1994. See also Fox, 'Nato split'; 'Meanwhile, back at the ranch . . .', leading article, *Independent*, 3.4.1995 (lifting the embargo 'probably would have caused the worst crisis in NATO since Suez').
240. 'Europe's post-post-cold-war defences wobble into action. Europe talks about security', *Economist*, 10.12.1994.
241. Text of President Alija Izetbegovic's address to the CSCE summit, Budapest, 5.12.1994.
242. As cited in Daniel L. Cruise, 'The OSCE and the future of European security arrangements. Bosnia and beyond' (MPhil dissertation, University of Cambridge), 1997, p. 14. See also 'Ambushed in Budapest', leading article, *International Herald Tribune*, 8.12.1994.
243. As described and cited in Andrew Marshall, 'Fiasco as summiteers fail to agree', *Independent*, 7.12.1994, and Patrick Bishop, 'Europe split on Bosnia after Yeltsin uses veto', *Daily Telegraph*, 7.12.1994.
244. Rupert Cornwell, 'Republicans move to lift arms embargo', *Independent*, 5.1.1995.
245. Donald Macintyre and Rupert Cornwell, 'Britain and US hope Major visit will heal rifts', *Independent*, 3.4.1995.
246. On this see, *inter alia*, Interview, Dr Jamie Shea, Brussels, 24.11.2000, fo. 2.

## 4 'Let Me Through, I'm a Doctor': David Owen and the Mediation Effort

1. Hansard, 7.12.1992, col. 589.
2. Lord Owen to John Major, London, 30.7.1992, quoted in full in Owen, *Balkan odyssey*, pp. 14–16.
3. David Owen, 'When it's right to fight', *The Times*, 4.8.1992, p. 8. See also Andrew Billen 'Interview: Lord Owen', *Observer*, 2.8.1992.
4. As quoted in Colin Brown, 'Appeals for UK military action in Bosnia rejected', *Independent*, 4.8.1992.
5. Martin Wroe, Andrew Gliniecki and Edward Pilkington, 'The Bosnia crisis: should we send in the troops?: And if so, what should be their

aim? The 16 people in our survey were divided', *Independent on Sunday*, 9.8.1992.

6. Tony Barber, 'Impartiality of Owen challenged', *Independent*, 27.8.1992.

7. 'To the point', *Sunday Telegraph*, 30.8.1992.

8. Tony Barber, 'Enough is enough – Owen. UN concludes Sarajevo aid flight was shot down', *Independent*, 5.9.1992.

9. S/PV.3134, 13.11.1992, New York, pp. 26, 28.

10. Nicholas Timmins, 'UN may have to use force in Bosnia, Owen warns', *Independent*, 11.12.1992.

11. Hansard, 25.9.1992, col. 132.

12. Interview, Lord Owen, London, 19.1.2001. See also the remarks by the Dutch MEP Arie Oostlander, as cited in Boris Johnson, 'Hurd, not Owen, is the real target', *Sunday Telegraph*, 23.1.1994: 'After Owen was given his mandate, Douglas Hurd told him that military intervention could never be proposed.'

13. David Wastell, 'Hint to Owen on the UN's limits', *Sunday Telegraph*, 6.9.1992; Stephen Castle, 'Hurd opposes increasing UN deployment', *Independent on Sunday*, 6.9.1992.

14. Quoted in Hella Pick, 'Fighting to give peace a chance', *Guardian*, 5.12.1992.

15. Annika Savill and Tony Barber, 'West intensifies the pressure over Bosnia', *Independent*, 17.12.1992.

16. Cited in Mark Danner, 'Clinton, the UN, and the Bosnian disaster', *NYRB*, 18 (1997).

17. Owen, *Balkan odyssey*, p. 45.

18. Rupert Cornwell, 'US blames allies for Bosnia delay', *Independent*, 10.5.1993.

19. Lord Owen, 'Lessons the world must learn from Yugoslavia', edited text of his address to the annual City of London Lord Mayor's lecture, *Daily Telegraph*, 19.6.1993.

20. Michael Sheridan, '"No easy way out of the conflict". Lord Owen says that use of military force is not the solution to a war with no clear distinction between aggressor and victim', *Independent*, 7.8.1993.

21. Owen, *Balkan odyssey*, pp. 16–17.

22. Ibid., p. 27.

23. Ibid., pp. 59–60.

24. Interview, Lord Carrington, London, 28.2.2001, *Mendoza transcripts*, fo. 10.

25. Owen, *Balkan odyssey*, p. 341.

26. Graham Messervy-Whiting, *Peace conference on former Yugoslavia: the*

*politico-military interface*, London Defence Studies 21, Centre of Defence Studies, 1994, p. 18.

27. Interview, Lord Owen, London, 19.1.2001.

28. Interview, Lord Howell, London, 28.2.2001, *Mendoza transcripts*, fo. 9.

29. See Andrew Billen, 'Lord Owen: interview', *Observer*, 2.8.1992.

30. Interview, Lord Owen, London, 18.5.2000, *Petersen transcripts*.

31. Owen, *Balkan odyssey*, p. 103.

32. Ibid., p. 67.

33. Lord Owen, 'Yugoslavia', Churchill Lecture, Guildhall, London, 25.11.1993, p. 21.

34. Michael Sheridan, 'No easy way out of the conflict. Lord Owen says that use of military force is not the solution to a war with no clear distinction between aggressor and victim', *Independent*, 7.8.1993, p. 6. In the same vein also Michael Sheridan, 'I'm no Neville Chamberlain says Owen', *Independent on Sunday*, 15.8.1993: 'Look, rightly or wrongly the world's political leaders have decided they do not wish to be combatants.'

35. See Chuck Sudetic, *Blood and belonging*, on this; also David Crary, 'UN warns of massacre at Cerska', *Independent*, 3.3.1993.

36. Owen, *Balkan odyssey*, p. 59.

37. Lord Owen to author, 31.1.2001.

38. Bob Stewart, *Broken lives: A personal view of the Bosnian conflict* (London, 1993), p. 216.

39. Ibid., p. 283.

40. Milos Stankovic, *Trusted mole: A soldier's journey into Bosnia's heart of darkness* (London, 2000), p. 77.

41. Angus Boyd-Heron, 'At the mercy of men with black cigarette holders', *Observer*, 2.5.1993.

42. As cited in Michael Binyon, 'Vance–Owen plan blamed for "ethnic cleansing"', *The Times*, 20.5.1993, and Marcus Tanner, 'Bosnian Serbs "ready to agree peace"', *Independent*, 20.5.1993.

43. Cited in di Giovanni, *The quick and the dead*, p. 88.

44. Ibid., p. 92; see also pp. 44 and 106.

45. Loyd, *My war gone by*, p. 86.

46. Russell, *Prejudice and plum brandy*, p. 286.

47. See Nora Beloff's review of *Balkan odyssey* in *Times Literary Supplement*, 24.11.1995.

48. As cited in Nik Gowing, 'Real-time TV coverage from war: does it make or break government policy?', in James Gow, Richard Paterson, and Alison Preston (eds.), *Bosnia by television* (London, 1996), p. 88.

49. See the comments of Bob Wareing, Hansard, 29.4.1993, col. 1231.
50. As cited in Michael Sheridan, 'Brutality of factions brings devastation' (the unspecific inanity of the headline shows the extent to which Owen was successful), *Independent*, 17.8.1993.
51. Private conversation. See also Mark Almond, *Europe's backyard war: The war in the Balkans* (London, 1994), p. 324.
52. Stankovic, *Trusted mole*, pp. 85–6. He bases his account on the testimony of Brigadier Cumming, who was present.
53. Owen, *Balkan odyssey*, pp. 102–3.
54. Interview, Professor Anthony Lake, Georgetown, 10.1.2001, fo. 7.
55. As cited in Annika Savill, 'Hurd to press US over Bosnia plan', *Independent*, 6.2.1993.
56. As cited in: Peter Pringle, 'Owen set for Bosnia showdown with US', *Independent*, 3.2.1993; Geordie Greig, '"Dr Death" takes on America – but will it backfire? Snub for Bosnia peace plan kindles his rage', *Sunday Times*, 7.2.1993; and Henry Porter, 'Owen lords it on prime time', *Sunday Telegraph*, 14.2.1993.
57. Interview, Dr John Fox, Washington, 11.1.2001, fo. 8.
58. Interview, Lord Hurd, London, 24.1.2001, fo. 14. Lord Hurd adds that 'he was very well qualified in other ways'.
59. Interview, Sir Christopher Meyer, Washington, 2.4.2001, *Mendoza transcripts*, fo. 5.
60. Interview, Lord Renwick, London, 27.11.2000, fo. 10.
61. As described in Henry Porter, 'Owen lords it on prime time', *Sunday Telegraph*, 14.2.1993.
62. As cited in Cohen and Stamkoski, *With no peace to keep*, p. 131.
63. Owen, *Balkan odyssey*, p. 102.
64. As cited in ibid., p. 110. See also Renwick, *Memoirs*, typescript, pp. 239–40, for his account of the meeting.
65. Messervy-Whiting, *Politico-military interface*, p. 18.
66. As cited in Peter Pringle, 'Owen set for Bosnia showdown with US', *Independent*, 3.2.1993.
67. Owen, *Balkan odyssey*, p. 91.
68. As cited in the *Economist*, 8.8.1993.
69. Owen, *Balkan odyssey*, p. 154. Owen, it appears, did not compile the chronology himself, Interview, Lord Owen, London, 19.1.2001.
70. Owen to author, House of Lords, 31.1.2001, p. 1.
71. Cited in Owen, *Balkan odyssey*, p. 180. See also p. 166 et passim.
72. Ibid., p. 172.
73. Ibid., p. 192.

74. Interview, Lord Owen, London, 18.5.2000, *Petersen transcripts*.
75. Owen, *Balkan odyssey*, p. 55.
76. As cited in Sarah Lambert, 'EC "must be ready to go it alone"', *Independent*, 9.6.1993.
77. Owen, *Balkan odyssey*, p. 295.
78. Ibid., p. 184.
79. Ibid., p. 311.
80. See, in addition to the examples cited in the text, ibid., pp. 163, 169, 173, 176, 192, 253, 254, 365 et passim.
81. Ibid., p. 113.
82. Ibid., p. 130.
83. Ibid., pp. 366–7.
84. Interview, Sir Christopher Meyer, Washington, 2.4.2001, *Mendoza transcripts*, fo. 5.
85. Jonathan Clarke, 'Rhetoric before reality. Loose lips sink ships', *Foreign Affairs*, September–October 1995, p. 7.
86. Michael Rose, *Fighting for peace: Bosnia 1994* (London, 1998), p. 256.
87. See Gow, *Triumph of the lack of will*, pp. 1, 241, 248–53, 259.
88. Hansard, Oral answers, 12.1.1993, col. 764.
89. Hansard, Written answers, 14.4.1993, col. 576.
90. Hansard, Written answers, 22.4.1993, col. 194.
91. Hansard, Written answers, 18.5.1993, col. 85.
92. On 'progressive implementation' see also the interview with Messervy-Whiting, fo. 19 and Messervy-Whiting, *Politico-military interface*, pp. 6, 38.
93. As cited in *The Times*, 3.5.1993.
94. Owen, *Balkan odyssey*, p. 142.
95. Owen to author, 31.1.2001, House of Lords, p. 2.
96. Owen, *Balkan odyssey*, p. 364.
97. Ibid., p. 159.
98. Ibid., pp. 198–9.
99. Ibid., p. 281.
100. Ibid., pp. 158–9.
101. As cited in Robert Block and Anthony Bevins, 'Serbs close to accepting peace', *Independent*, 6.5.1993 (emphasis added).
102. Hansard, 16.6.1993, col. 638.
103. Hurd, *The search for peace*, p. 7 (emphasis added).
104. Interview, Lord Hurd, London, 24.1.2001, fo. 12.
105. Francis Harris, Alan Philps and Stephen Robinson, 'War in Bosnia: moving the spots on the leopard – The peacemakers: tougher UN approach', *Daily Telegraph*, 21.5.1993.

106. Cited in the *Daily Telegraph*, 19.5.1993.
107. Hansard, 29.4.1993, col. 1233.
108. See Roger Mathews, 'Parliament and politics: Bosnian peace plan "misconceived"', *Financial Times*, 16.7.1993.
109. See FCO background brief, 'Former Yugoslavia: the Vance–Owen peace plan', July 1993, pp. 1, 3.
110. See Owen, *Balkan odyssey*, p. 180.
111. Ibid., p. 181.
112. Ibid., pp. 136–7. In the same vein also p. 103.
113. Interview, Lord Owen, London, 18.5.2000, *Petersen transcripts*.
114. Interview, Lord Owen, London, 19.1.2001 and Owen to author, London, 31.1.2001, p. 3.
115. Interview, Lord Renwick, 27.11.2000, London, fo. 9.
116. Ibid. See in the same vein also his draft *Memoirs*, pp. 239–40: 'The real problem with the plan was that it was simply unworkable, incapable of implementation ... It was in the end the Serbs, not the Moslems, who scuppered the Vance–Owen plan.'
117. Derek Prag, letter to the editor, *Independent*, 26.5.1993.
118. Owen, *Balkan odyssey*, p. 23.
119. As described ibid., pp. 174–5.
120. As cited in Charlotte Eagar, 'Foot names guilty men of Bosnia', *Observer*, 1.1.1995.
121. Cited in Nigel Farndale, 'Doctor knows best', *Sunday Telegraph Magazine*, 3.1.1999.
122. Owen, *Balkan odyssey*, p. 175.
123. E.g. Leonard Doyle, '"Use troops to stop atrocities": investigator urges UN to intervene, not write reports, over human rights abuses in Bosnia', *Independent*, 1.9.1992.
124. See Annika Savill, 'Peace envoys set to bale out', *Independent*, 26.5.1993, and Guest, *On trial*, p. 50 (on tensions between Owen and Mazowiecki).
125. As cited in Michael Binyon, Tim Judah and Nicholas Wood, 'Bosnian Serbs threaten to block UN peace deal', *The Times*, 3.5.1993.
126. As cited in Annika Savill, David Usborne, Anthony Bevins and Robert Block, 'Owen begs US to hold its fire in Bosnia', *Independent*, 3.5.1993.
127. As cited in Annika Savill, 'Nato resolve will be put to the test', *Independent*, 7.8.1993.
128. Owen, *Balkan odyssey*, p. 205.
129. As cited in Annika Savill, 'Allied machine primed but may not fly', *Independent*, 11.8.1993.
130. As cited in ibid.

131. Owen, *Balkan odyssey*, p. 258.
132. As cited in Andrew Marshall, Rupert Cornwell, Helen Womack and Colin Brown, 'Allies split over response to market massacre', *Independent*, 7.2.1994.
133. David Owen, 'The fall of Vukovar', *Granta*, 47 (spring 1994), p. 194. In the same vein see Owen, *Balkan odyssey*, p. 259.
134. Owen, 'The fall of Vukovar', p. 195.
135. Owen, *Balkan odyssey*, p. 268.
136. As cited in Michael Sheridan, Patricia Wynn Davies and Annika Savill, 'Bosnia time bomb is ticking', *Independent*, 4.8.1993.
137. Rupert Cornwell, 'US blames allies for Bosnia delay', *Independent*, 10.5.1993; Lord Owen, 'Lessons the world must learn from Yugoslavia', *Daily Telegraph*, 19.6.1993.
138. See Owen, *Balkan odyssey*, p. 247.
139. Owen's own paraphrase from *Balkan odyssey*, p. 322.
140. See Annika Savill, 'US envoy goes to ground over arming Bosnia's Muslims', *Independent*, 16.4.1993; Lord Owen, '1993 Churchill Lecture', delivered 25.11.1993, Guildhall, London, pp. 3–4; and Owen, *Balkan odyssey*, pp. 45, 252.
141. See Lord Owen, The Eighth Annual Distinguished International Health Lecture, Royal College of Surgeons in Ireland, Dublin, 8.11.1993, p. 3.
142. Owen, *Balkan odyssey*, p. 142.
143. Ibid., p. 161.
144. Interview, General Messervy-Whiting, London, 17.1.2001, fo. 6.
145. Owen, *Balkan odyssey*, p. 352.
146. Ibid., p. 349 (emphasis added).
147. Ibid., p.252.
148. As cited ibid., p. 205.
149. See ibid., pp. 77–8, 156–7.
150. Interview, Lord Owen, London, 18.5.2000, *Petersen transcripts*.
151. Interview, Professor Mohamed Fillipovic, London, 2.10.2000, fo. 3.
152. Lee Bryant, conversation, London, 7.7.2000.
153. 'Direr and emptier. Carving up Bosnia', *Economist*, 26.6.1993.
154. Private conversation, 13.5.2000.
155. Guest, *On trial*, pp. 103–4. Interview with Professor Mohamed Fillipovic, London, 2.10.2000.
156. Owen, *Balkan odyssey*, p. 222.
157. Annika Savill and Giles Elgood, 'Lord Owen admits his peace plan has failed. Mediator urges Bosnian Muslims to consider three-way carve-up of Yugoslavia proposed by presidents of Serbia and Croatia', *Independent*,

18.6.1993. See also Michael Sheridan, 'Bosnians under strong pressure to accept "reality"', *Independent*, 25.6.1993.

158. As cited in Michael Sheridan, 'Izetbegovic told to "face reality" and cut deal', *Independent*, 29.7.1993.

159. As cited in Robert Fisk, 'Bosnian imam rails against the West's injustice', *Independent*, 12.7.1993.

160. 'Dead-end diplomacy', leading article, *Guardian*, 23.7.1993.

161. Owen, *Balkan odyssey*, p. 241.

162. Tony Jackson, 'Owen queries Bosnia action', *Financial Times*, 16.11.1993.

163. Owen, '1993 Churchill Lecture', p. 21.

164. Michael Sheridan, 'Owen hints at UN Bosnia pull-out', *Independent*, 11.11.1994: 'The world may well question the resources devoted to this dispute.'

165. As cited in Owen, *Balkan odyssey*, p. 287.

166. See the analyses in *Economist*, 8.5.1993, 'Bosnia's Serbs against the world', and 15.8.1993, 'Slobo's slide: pressures on Serbia's president'.

167. As cited in Mark Almond, 'Doing business with war criminals', *Spectator*, 15.5.1993.

168. Cited in Almond, *Europe's backyard war*, p. 293.

169. As paraphrased by Sir Russell, Hansard, 26.7.1993, col. 847.

170. Boris Johnson and Michael Montgomery, 'War in Bosnia, Owen's praise for Serb first lady – President Milosevic plays "decisive role" in the peace effort as fighting continues in Mostar', *Daily Telegraph*, 11.5.1993. See also Janine di Giovanni, 'Milosevic family values', *Night and Day*, 24.11.1996.

171. As cited in 'Further adventures of Hrvoje Sarinic in the land of the Serb aggressor', *Bosnia Report*, 9/10, April–July 1999, p. 34.

172. Owen, *Balkan odyssey*, p. 136.

173. As cited from a letter by Mamon Nahas, Bosnia-Herzegovina Information Centre, *Independent*, 14.8.1993.

174. As cited in Owen, *Balkan odyssey*, p. 213.

175. See 'Im Europäischen Parlament nimmt die Kritik an Lord Owen zu', *Frankfurter Allgemeine Zeitung*, 16.9.1993. Letter from Bernard Besserglik, *Independent*, 22.1.1993.

176. Ian MacKinnon and Phil Reeves, 'American critics call for Owen to resign', *Independent*, 12.8.1993.

177. Interview, Marshall Freeman Harris, Washington, 9.1.2001, fo. 9.

178. Gordon Martin and F. Harries, 'Geneva talks resume', 10.8.1993.

179. Michael Sheridan, 'Mediators demand Serbs withdraw today', *Independent*, 12.8.1993.

180. Edward Luttwak, 'Arm the Bosnians at last', *International Herald Tribune*, 17.7.1995.
181. Owen, *Balkan odyssey*, p. 251.
182. Ibid., p. 210.
183. Lee Bryant, conversation, 7.7.2000.
184. As cited in Alan Philps and Francis Harris, 'War in Bosnia: "sound-bite" is no basis for military action says Hurd', *Daily Telegraph*, 10.9.1993, and Steve Crawshaw, 'A delayed victory for Hitler', *Independent*, 18.8.1993.
185. Interview, Professor Mohamed Fillipovic, London, 2.10.2000, fos. 2–3.
186. As cited in Jim Muir, 'Talk of pull-out piles on despair. Sarajevans now fear a bloodbath if UN troops go', *Sunday Telegraph*, 23.1.1994.
187. Boris Johnson, 'Hurd, not Owen is the real target. Germans think the envoy is a stooge', *Sunday Telegraph*, 23.1.1994.
188. Interview, Lord Owen, London, 18.5.2000, *Petersen transcripts*.
189. Lord Owen, The Eighth Annual Distinguished International Health Lecture, Royal College of Surgeons in Ireland, Dublin, 8.11.1993.
190. Owen, *Balkan odyssey*, p. 282 (emphasis added).
191. Ibid. (original emphasis).
192. Ibid., p. 284.
193. Lord Owen, *Personal for foreign ministers only. Subject: Bosnia*, 22.7.1994, reproduced ibid., pp. 287 ff.
194. Ibid.
195. Owen, *Balkan odyssey*, p. 290.
196. Interview, Dr Michael Williams, London, 22.11.2000, fo. 22.
197. Ian Black, 'Conflict a bridge too far for Owen', *Guardian*, 1.6.1995.
198. Edward Mortimer, 'Lord Owen: interview. An exit with one regret', *Financial Times*, 2.6.1995.

## 5 'The Men on the Ground'

I thank Joel Dowling and Gillian Sandford for their extremely useful comments on earlier versions of this chapter.

1. Douglas Hogg, 'Three good reasons to exercise caution', *Independent*, 6.8.1993. See also Rifkind, Hansard, 12.7.1995, col. 955, who hides behind the recommendations of local UN force commanders and Douglas Hurd's remarks cited in the *Independent*, 12.6.1993.
2. Owen, *Balkan odyssey*, p. 354.
3. Stankovic, *Trusted mole*, p. 440.
4. *The Times*, leading article, 17.7.1995. See in the same vein Hugo Young,

'Sabres rattle on in a world out of control', *Guardian*, 1.6.1995. He speaks of an 'abdication of decision to "the commanders in the field" . . . Instead of democratic leaders deciding their objective and finding the means to achieve it, the generals are to tell them what can be done, and it will then be the duty of the politicians to go thus far and no further'; and Hugo Young, 'Bosnia marks a final failure of political will', *Guardian*, 20.7.1995; 'Mr Major isn't even prepared to take responsibility for deciding to keep British troops in the UN force, telling Parliament that naturally he must bow to the military experts "on the ground".'

5. On Rose and the press see Bell, *In harm's way*, p. 185.

6. See, for example, Charlotte Eagar, 'Rose brings hope to city of despair', *Observer*, 13.2.1994.

7. Stankovic, *Trusted mole*, p. 229.

8. 'Profile: Lt.-Gen. Sir Michael Rose, UN peace-seeker in Bosnia', *Independent*, 19.2.1994.

9. Stankovic, *Trusted mole*, p. 217.

10. Ibid., p. 230.

11. Rose, *Fighting for peace*, p. 64.

12. Interview, Michael Williams, London, 22.11.2000, fo. 16.

13. Conversation with a serving senior officer, November 2000.

14. Rose, *Fighting for peace*, p. 18.

15. Ibid., p. 26.

16. Ibid., p. 217.

17. Ibid., p. 146.

18. Ibid., p. 92.

19. As cited in Patrick Bishop, 'Peace lies in the people's hands', *Sunday Telegraph*, 6.3.1994.

20. Rose, *Fighting for peace*, p. 72.

21. Ibid., p. 98.

22. Interview, Maud Beelman, Washington, 4.4.2001, *Mendoza transcripts*, fo. 11.

23. Vaughan Kent-Payne, *Bosnia warrior: Living on the front line* (London, 1998), p. 353. See also p. 222 for further shaky generalizations: 'All Bosnians seemed to be the same: when their side is on the up they behave like swaggering bullies. As soon as they are losing, they become servile and pleading.'

24. Jonathan Riley, *White Dragon: The Royal Welch Fusiliers in Bosnia* (Wrexham, 1995), CO's diary, 15.8.1995, p. 65.

25. Noel Malcolm, 'The whole lot of them are Serbs', *Spectator*, 10.6.1995.

26. See Noel Malcolm's letter in the *Spectator*, 1.7.1995.

27. Riley, *White Dragon*, p. 14.

28. Ibid., CO's diary, Gorazde, 28.8.1995, pp. 66–7.
29. Interview, Dr Michael Williams, London, 22.11.2000, fo. 25.
30. Warren Zimmermann, *Origins of a catastrophe: Yugoslavia and its destroyers* (New York, 1996), p. 224.
31. Interview, Maud Beelman, Washington, 4.4.2001, *Mendoza transcripts*, fo. 13.
32. Interview, General George Joulwan, Virginia, 3.4.2001, *Mendoza transcripts*, fo. 4, and fo. 17 in the same vein.
33. Communication from Joel Dowling, 5.12.2000, Beckenham, Kent.
34. See Stankovic, *Trusted mole*, pp. 55, 59.
35. See Philip Cohen, *Serbia's secret war: Propaganda and the deceit of history* (College Station, Tex., 1996).
36. Stankovic, *Trusted mole*, p. 40.
37. See the pertinent remarks by Mark Mazower, 'Europe's failure' (a review of the memoirs of Michael Rose and Carl Bildt), *Times Literary Supplement*, 12.2.1999.
38. Interview, Dr Michael Williams, London, 22.11.2000, fos. 23–4.
39. Tim Spicer, *An unorthodox soldier: Peace and war and the Sandline affair* (Edinburgh and London, 2000), pp. 130, 137, 123.
40. Lt.-Col. C. A. le Hardy, Lecture to the British embassy, The Hague, 11.1.1996.
41. Rose, *Fighting for peace*, p. 35.
42. Ibid., p. 35. In the same vein p. 198.
43. Ibid., pp. 218, 141, 68.
44. Spicer, *An unorthodox soldier*, p. 135: 'The Muslims needed to keep themselves in the eye of the international community as the injured parties . . . even creating incidents that put them in a good light.'
45. E.g. Robert Block and Donald Macintyre, 'Serbs "going to the brink" as trickle of guns are handed in', *Independent*, 14.2.1994.
46. Conversations with a senior official of the Bosnian Foreign Ministry during the war, 23.3.2000 and 7.11.2000.
47. Interview, General Wesley Clark, Washington, 11.1.2001, fo. 9.
48. Interview, James Rubin, London, 8.2.2001, fo. 3.
49. Interview, Michael Williams, London, 22.11.2000, fo. 25.
50. Cited in Loyd, *My war gone by*, p. 141.
51. Christopher Bellamy, *Knights in white armour: The new art of war and peace* (London, 1996), p. 32.
52. Lt.-Col. le Hardy, Lecture to the British embassy.
53. Interview, Lt.-Col. C. A. le Hardy, 13.2.2001, *Mendoza transcripts*, fo. 15.
54. See 'The Haniste Patrol, Lt. John Owens', in Riley, *White Dragon*, p. 27.

For a classic example of 'warring faction' tropes see Col. P. G. Williams, 'Liaison: the key to success in Central Bosnia', *Army Quarterly and Defence Journal*, 124, 4 (October 1994), pp. 389–92 (the quotation is on p. 390).

55. Stewart, *Broken lives*, p. 318.

56. Interview, Lt.-Col. le Hardy, 13.2.2001, *Mendoza transcripts*, fo. 5.

57. Loyd, *My war gone by*, p. 94.

58. Stankovic, *Trusted mole*, p. ix. He expressed similar sentiments in an interview with Tim Sebastian.

59. Col. Alistair Duncan, 'Operating in Bosnia', *RUSI Journal*, 139, 3 (June 1994), p. 14.

60. Bell, *In harm's way*, p. 151.

61. Cited in Stankovic, *Trusted mole*, pp. 77–8.

62. Kent-Payne, *Bosnia warrior*, p. 34.

63. Stewart, *Broken lives*, p. 175.

64. Duncan, 'Operating in Bosnia', p. 11.

65. Bell, *In harm's way*, p. 151.

66. The classic 'human interest' story was Anna Pukas's piece on Bob Stewart – 'A very British warrior' – in the *Daily Mail*, reprinted in *Army Quarterly and Defence Journal*, April 1993, pp. 133–5.

67. Maggie O'Kane, 'White warriors lost in the ether', *Guardian*, 19.6.1993. In the same vein see also Bell, *In harm's way*, p. 151: 'Colonel Bob and his men did indeed accomplish some heroic things, but these were achieved essentially in the margins of someone else's war. Yet to British journalists they were the main event'; and 'Kenneth Roberts': 'The war has been covered by the British press almost exclusively from the media village by the British base in Vitez', as cited in Aernout van Leyden, letter, *Spectator*, 24.7.1993.

68. Rose, *Fighting for peace*, pp. 36–7.

69. Annan, *Srebrenica report*, p. 32.

70. Rose, *Fighting for peace*, p. 48.

71. Cited in Charlotte Eagar, 'Rose brings hope to a city in despair', *Observer*, 13.2.1994.

72. On these accusations see, for example, Leonard Doyle, 'Muslims "slaughter their own people". Bosnia bread queue massacre was propaganda ploy, UN told', *Independent*, 22.8.1992; the article by the UN bureaucrat and British intelligence operative 'Kenneth Roberts', 'Glamour without responsibility', *Spectator*, 5.3.1994; and the journalist Janine di Giovanni, who reported from Sarajevo throughout the siege, *The quick and the dead*, p. 115, on UN accusations that the Bosnians shelled themselves to get world attention.

73. As reported in Robert Block, 'Irony of a twisted myth lost on Serbs', *Independent*, 7.2.1994.

74. Tony Smith, 'Injured fly out on a day of mourning', *Independent*, 7.2.1994.
75. Interview, Jennifer Brush, Washington, 29.3.2001, *Mendoza transcripts*, fo. 14.
76. Interview, General Wesley Clark, Washington, 11.1.2001, fos. 8–9.
77. Interview, James Rubin, London, 8.2.2001, fos. 4–5.
78. Hansard, Written answers, 3.3.1994, col. 83.
79. Rose, *Fighting for peace*, p. 63. Rose adds that the man replied that 'unless people demonstrated confidence in the peace process, the country would be permanently at war. He would do it again when he recovered.'
80. Ibid., pp. 130–31.
81. Cited in Charlotte Eagar, 'Rose can only pray for winter snow as he fires barrage of optimism', *Observer*, 13.11.1994.
82. Cited ibid.
83. Interview, Michael Williams, London, 22.11.2000, fos. 13–14.
84. Spicer, *An unorthodox soldier*, p. 130.
85. Rose, *Fighting for peace*, p. 96.
86. Ibid., p. 104.
87. Ibid., p. 103.
88. Ibid., pp. 120, 121.
89. Ibid., p. 103.
90. As cited in Emma Daly, 'Diplomacy takes off as need for air attacks fades', *Independent*, 28.4.1994 and (more fully) in Bell, *In harm's way*, p. 184.
91. As cited ibid.
92. Repeated attempts to contact 'Spence' directly were unsuccessful.
93. Gillian Sandford, *Wheel of fire* (forthcoming).
94. See Spence, *All necessary measures*, pp. 160–61.
95. See the report by Tony Barber, 'Rose accuses Muslims of trickery over Gorazde', *Independent*, 29.4.1994: 'UN officials said yesterday the battle had rapidly become so intense that UNHCR staff in Gorazde had been prevented from leaving their shelters to verify casualty numbers.'
96. Nick Richardson, *No escape zone* (London, 2000), p. 168.
97. Ibid., p. 193.
98. Cameron Spence, *All necessary measures* (London, 1998), p. 171 (emphasis added).
99. Ibid., p. 203 (emphasis added).
100. Ibid., p. 191.
101. Ibid., p. 189.
102. Ibid., p. 238.
103. Richardson, *No escape zone*, p. 192. See also Spence, *All necessary*

*measures*, p. 239: 'the Serbs had given a clear indication that Fergie's death might not have been altogether an accident'.

104. Pukas, 'SAS death marks the grave of UN hopes'.

105. Spence, *All necessary measures*, pp. 240, 233–4 et passim.

106. Ibid., pp. 208–9.

107. Ibid., pp. 240–1. Subsequently (p. 255) Spence refers to Major 'Richard' as 'the LO in Sarajevo who had told Charlie, as the fur was flying all around him, that he was forbidden to allude to the fact that Gorazde was falling'.

108. Richardson, *No escape zone*, p. 198.

109. Ibid., p. 208.

110. Ibid., p. 227.

111. Cited in Emma Daly, 'Retreating Serbians keep tight grip on besieged Gorazde', *Independent*, 26.4.1994. See also Spence, *All necessary measures*, p. 289.

112. As quoted in Anna Pukas, 'We should have been tougher, says disillusioned aid chief', *Sunday Times*, 17.4.1994.

113. As reported by Colin Smith, 'Seeing ourselves as America sees us', *Observer*, 22.8.1993.

114. See Noel Malcolm, 'The whole lot of them are Serbs', *Spectator*, 10.6.1995.

115. Rose, *Fighting for peace*, p. 178.

116. Interview, James Rubin, London, 8.2.2001, fo. 3.

117. Ibid., fo. 4.

118. Ibid., fos. 5–6.

119. See Stankovic, *Trusted mole*, p. 143.

120. Ibid., p. 169.

121. Brigadier A. G. Denaro, letter to the editor, *The Times*, 14.7.1995.

122. Cited in Owen, *Balkan odyssey*, p. 284.

123. Rose, *Fighting for peace*, p. 162.

124. Ibid., p. 177. See also in the same vein Stankovic, *Trusted mole*, p. 322.

125. Cited in Stankovic, *Trusted mole*, p. 323. See also p. 359 for similar sentiments.

126. Cited ibid., p. 323.

127. Jim Muir, 'Peacekeepers divided over use of air power', *Sunday Telegraph*, 27.11.1994.

128. Cited in Tony Barber, 'Rose cool on lifting the arms embargo', *Independent*, 11.6.1994.

129. Rose, *Fighting for peace*, p. 83.

130. Ibid., p. 251.

131. Ibid., p. 181.

132. Cited in Anna Pukas, 'A very British warrior', *Army Quarterly and Defence Journal*, 123, 2 (April, 1993), pp. 133–5.
133. Stankovic, *Trusted mole*, p. 436.
134. Rose, *Fighting for peace*, pp. 98–9.
135. Ibid., p. 198.
136. Ibid., p. 154.
137. Ibid., p. 202.
138. Ibid., pp. 152, 153.
139. Ibid., p. 189: 'If the peace process finally failed, and NATO sent troops to fight a war to impose a just peace in Bosnia, I told him that I would be the first to volunteer for the mission.'
140. Ibid., p. 9.
141. Ibid., p. 5.
142. Ibid., p. 60.
143. Ibid., pp. 147–8.
144. See the charges made by Rose to Michael Evans, 'US bugged me in Bosnia, says General Rose', *The Times*, 10.11.1998.
145. As reported in Phil Reeves and Annika Savill, 'Squabble exposes Bosnia tensions', *Independent*, 19.8.1993.
146. Stankovic, *Trusted mole*, p. 388.
147. Christopher Bellamy, 'UN troops laugh off prospect of American rescue', *Independent*, 10.12.1994.
148. Private conversation.
149. Philip Corwin, *Dubious mandate: A memoir of the UN in Bosnia, summer 1995* (Durham, N.C. and London, 1999), p. 54.
150. See Lt.-Col. le Hardy, lecture to the British Embassy, p. 3.
151. Stankovic, *Trusted mole*, p. 251.
152. Ibid., p. 252.
153. Ibid., p. 418. See also p. 144.
154. Private conversation with US military. See also Stankovic, *Trusted mole*, p. 296.
155. Private conversation.
156. Evans, 'US bugged me in Bosnia, says General Rose', *The Times*, 10.11.1998.
157. Stankovic, *Trusted mole*, p. 243.
158. Rose, *Fighting for peace*, p. 83. The accounts of Rose (pp. 82–3) and Stankovic (pp. 243–4) differ and are contradictory in certain respects. The above is my own interpretation of chronology and motivation.
159. Stankovic describes how the meeting came about: 'Rose had obviously cast a fly at Clark on the way back. Clark, it seemed, had bitten. It was peculiar

how everyone wanted to meet "the man the whole world loves to hate".' Rose's Military Assistant tells Stankovic: 'The General's very keen for Clark to see Mladic.' *Trusted mole*, pp. 292–3. Clark, however, claims that the visit was entirely his own idea: Interview, General Wesley Clark, 11.1.2001, Washington, fo. 5. On the warnings issued by the US embassy in Sarajevo, see Jennifer Brush, Interview, Washington, 29.3.2001, *Mendoza transcripts*, fos. 10–11.

160. Interview, General Wesley Clark, Washington, 11.1.2001, fo. 7.

161. Rose, *Fighting for peace*, p. 52. The need to 'maintain credibility' was emphasized by the Nato commander General Joulwan.

162. Ibid., p. 64.

163. Ibid., p. 118.

164. Ibid., pp. 122–3.

165. Interview, General George Joulwan, Virginia, 3.4.2001, *Mendoza transcripts*, fo. 4.

166. Rose, *Fighting for peace*, p. 123.

167. Cited in Noel Malcolm, review of *Fighting for peace*, *Sunday Telegraph*, 22.11.1998.

168. Stankovic, *Trusted mole*, p. 438. See also p. 367.

169. T. D. Bridge, 'Success: Trafalgar to Sarajevo and Haiti', *Army Quarterly and Defence Journal*, 125, 1 (1995), p. 2.

170. Sir Michael Rose, 'The British Army in Bosnia: facing up to new challenges', *Army Quarterly and Defence Journal*, 125, 2 (1995), p. 136.

171. Colonel P. G. Williams, 'Liaison – The key to success in central Bosnia', *Army Quarterly and Defence Journal*, 124, 4 (1994), p. 389.

172. Rose, *Fighting for peace*, p. 118.

173. Ibid., p. 195.

174. Ibid., p. 61.

175. Sally Weale, 'Optimistic Rose warns against over-reaction', *Guardian*, 31.5.1995.

176. Rose, *Fighting for peace*, p. 87.

177. Cited in Bell, *In harm's way*, p. 193.

178. Kent-Payne, *Bosnia warrior*, p. 352.

179. CO's diary, Gorazde, 14.5.1995, in Riley, *White Dragon*, p. 41.

180. BBC, *Panorama*, 23.1.1995, transcript.

181. As quoted in Adrian Brown, Jim Muir and Christy Campbell, 'Serbs set to sweep into Bihac', *Sunday Telegraph*, 27.11.1994.

182. As cited in William Pfaff, 'The death of an ideal darkens Europe', *International Herald Tribune*, 1.12.1994, and Emma Daly, 'Six towns protected only by paper shield', *Independent*, 26.11.1994.

183. Cited in Tim Ripley, 'Peacekeeping with a war machine: interview with General Rose', *International Defense Review*, 1 (1995), p. 11. On 'Mogadischu Line' see also Rose, *Fighting for peace*, p. 126.

184. Interview, Jennifer Brush, Washington, 29.3.2001, *Mendoza transcripts*, fo. 13; Interview, General George Joulwan, Virginia, 3.4.2001, *Mendoza transcripts*, fo. 3.

185. Rose, 'The British Army in Bosnia: facing up to new challenges', *Army Quarterly and Defence Journal*, 125, 2 (1995), p. 134.

186. Colonel P. G. Williams, 'Liaison – The key to success in Central Bosnia', *Army Quarterly and Defence Journal*, 124, 4 (1994), p. 390.

187. As cited in Robert Fox, 'Peacekeepers draw the line at fighting warlords', *Sunday Telegraph*, 26.3.1995.

188. See Williams and Scharf, 'The letter of the law', p. 36.

189. See Weller, 'Peace-keeping and peace-enforcement', pp. 95–7.

190. Interview, General George Joulwan, Virginia, 3.4.2001, *Mendoza transcripts*, fos. 1–2.

191. For a robust (airman's) view of the mandate see Group Captain A. D. Sweetman, 'Close air support over Bosnia-Hercegovina', *RUSI Journal*, 139, 4 (August 1994), pp. 34–6.

192. BBC, *Panorama*, 23.1.1995, transcript.

193. Stewart, *Broken lives*, p. 316.

194. Duncan, 'Operating in Bosnia', p. 16.

195. Ibid., p. 11.

196. Stewart, *Broken lives*, p. 317.

197. Sir Michael Rose, Liddell Hart Lecture, 1999, p. 3 (emphasis added).

198. Michael C. Williams, *Civil-military relations and peacekeeping*, Adelphi Paper 321 (1998), p. 26.

199. Here I follow the elegant formulation of Emma Daly, 'UN General shrugs off call to resign', *Independent*, 27.10.1994. See also Robert Block, 'UN General under fire for kid glove approach to Serbs', *Independent*, 22.9.1994.

200. See Robert Block, 'UN blames Muslims for Sarajevo battle', *Independent*, 20.9.1994; Rose, *Fighting for peace*, p. 163.

201. Rose, *Fighting for peace*, p. 187.

202. As cited in Ian Traynor, 'UN forces use heavy muscle on Bosnians. Rose under fire for not using the same tactics on Serbs', *Guardian*, 8.10.1994.

203. Interview, General Wesley Clark, Washington, 11.1.2001, fos. 9–11.

204. Ibid., fo. 14.

205. Patrick Bishop, 'Built up and knocked down', *Spectator*, 19.11.1994.

206. The whole letter is printed in Eve-Ann Prentice, 'Rose letter informs Serbs he wants to avoid air strikes', *The Times*, 2.11.1994.
207. This famous recorded exchange is cited, *inter alia*, in Charlotte Eagar, 'West leaves Bihac to its grim fate', *Observer*, 27.11.1994.
208. See Emma Daly, 'Bosnian MPs tell Rose to go', *Independent*, 26.10.1994. See also Ian Traynor, 'Bosnia's whipping boy stands firm', *Guardian*, 30.9.1994.
209. Rupert Cornwell, 'Dole deepens rift over Bosnia', *Independent*, 28.11.1994.
210. William Safire, 'Arm Muslim fighters and bomb Serbian positions', *New York Times*, 29.11.1994.
211. Anthony Lewis, 'The shame began with George Bush's decision to do nothing', *New York Times*, 3/4.12.1994.
212. Charles A. Forrest, 'The United Nations and NATO have a responsibility to save Bosnia', *International Herald Tribune*, 8.12.1994.
213. Private conversation, May 2000.
214. See Geyer, 'How the conscience of the west was lost', p. 102 et passim.
215. Patrick Bishop, 'Built up and knocked down', *Spectator*, 19.11.1994.
216. Bell, *In harm's way*, pp. 199–200. See also Tony Barber, 'Few cheers for Rose as he bows out of Bosnia', *Independent*, 24.1.1995.
217. As cited in Emma Daly, 'UN General shrugs off call to resign', *Independent*, 27.10.1994.
218. Rose, *Fighting for peace*, p. 169.
219. Ibid., p. 216.
220. James Adams, 'Rose the people's hero rocks on his pedestal', *Sunday Times*, 17.4.1994.
221. As quoted ibid.
222. See Rose, *Fighting for peace*, p. 142.
223. Interview, Lord Vincent, London, 19.1.2001.
224. As cited in Rose, *Fighting for peace*, p. 181.
225. Rose, *Fighting for peace*, p. 203.
226. Stankovic, *Trusted mole*, p. 217.
227. Rose, *Fighting for peace*, p. 117.
228. Interview, Michael Williams, London, 22.11.2000, fo. 13.
229. Ibid.
230. Stankovic, *Trusted mole*, pp. 290–1.
231. Ibid., p. 291.
232. Vaughan Kent-Payne, *Bosnia warrior*, pp. 11–12.
233. See Tim Butcher, 'When duty means traffic patrol', *Sunday Telegraph*, 23.1.1994.

234. Spence, *All necessary measures*, p. 8.
235. Ibid., pp. 114–15.
236. Ibid., pp. 203–4.
237. Ibid., p. 255.
238. Ibid., p. 256.
239. The phrase is Chris Bellamy's, *Knights in white armour*, p. 164. See also Duncan, 'Operating in Bosnia', p. 13.
240. Stankovic, *Trusted mole*, p. 35.
241. Ibid., p. 436.
242. Duncan, 'Operating in Bosnia', p. 12.
243. Nick Gordon, 'British offer Bosnians no hiding place. New commander defends actions', *Sunday Times*, 6.6.1993.
244. E.g. Peter Almond, 'Horror leaves mark on British soldiers', *Daily Telegraph*, 22.4.1993. See also Duncan, 'Operating in Bosnia', p. 18.
245. As cited in Bell, *In harm's way*, p. 136.
246. Rose, *Fighting for peace*, p. 22.
247. Confidential conversation.
248. Richardson, *No escape zone*, p. 68.
249. Ibid., p. 195.
250. Ibid., p. 200.
251. Duncan, 'Operating in Bosnia', p. 15.
252. Kent-Payne, *Bosnia warrior*, p. 34.
253. As cited in Maggie O'Kane, 'Top-flight entertainer', *Guardian*, 7.12.2000.
254. E.g., editorial, *Daily Telegraph*, 23.1.1995. For a more critical view see Robert Fox, 'A man of peace quits the battle. But Bosnians say "good riddance"', *Daily Telegraph*, 23.1.1995.
255. Editorial, *Daily Telegraph*, 23.1.1995.
256. Christopher Bellamy, 'New British general gets tougher on Serbs', *Independent*, 26.5.1995. See also the profile by Mark Almond in the *Daily Mail*, 24.7.1995, and the very full and illuminating profile of Rupert Smith, 'In the line of fire', *Sunday Telegraph*, 28.5.1995.
257. By his own account. See the review of Patrick Wright, *Tank* (London, 2000) in *The Times*, 25.10.2000.
258. I am grateful to members of Sir Rupert's staff for underlining this point to me.
259. Interview, Michael Williams, London, 22.11.2000.
260. Stankovic, *Trusted mole*, pp. 440–1.
261. Boris Johnson, 'The importance of peacekeeping missions to the survival of the army', *Spectator*, 3.6.1995. See also John Keegan, *Daily Telegraph*, 19.11.1992.

262. Interview, Michael Williams, London, 22.11.2000.
263. Stewart, *Broken lives*, pp. 246–7.
264. Christy Campbell, 'Front bench versus front line. The success of a British general in Bosnia has embarrassed the government', *Sunday Telegraph*, 6.3.1994. On redundancy notices see Gwynneth Dunwoody, Hansard, 14.12.1992, col. 67, and John Spellar, Hansard, 9.2.1993, col. 808.
265. On this great achievement see Riley, *White Dragon*, pp. 69–70. He has still not quite understood the obvious – confirmed to me by one of his company commanders and by aid workers in Gorazde – that the Bosnian defenders, although determined to relieve the Royal Welch Fusiliers of whatever hardware they could, were eager to see the back of them in order to clear the decks for Nato.
266. Duncan, 'Operating in Bosnia', p. 18.

## 6 The Hour of the Experts

1. Quoted in Christopher Bellamy, 'Our lads should take on Serbia: a month's visit has convinced Christopher Bellamy that the UN could fight – and prevail', *Independent*, 26.11.1992.
2. Hansard, 14.1.1993, col. 1064. For further examples see above, Chapter 1.
3. Hansard, 14.4.1993, cols. 830, 839.
4. Hansard, 7.2.1994, cols. 20–4.
5. Hansard, 8.2.1994, col. 127.
6. Hansard, 10.2.1994, col. 456. For further examples of Hurd and the invocation of expert advice: Hansard, 4.5.1994, col. 706 and Hansard, 19.4.1993, col. 23.
7. Major, *Autobiography*, p. 535.
8. Ibid., p. 541.
9. Hurd, 'Lessons of Bosnia', p. 7.
10. Hurd, *The search for peace*, p. 99.
11. See, e.g., Charles Lane and Thom Shanker, 'Bosnia: what the CIA didn't tell us', *NYRB*, 9.5.1996.
12. Interview, General Wesley Clark, Washington, 11.1.2001.
13. Daalder, *Getting to Dayton*, p. 83; Holbrooke, *To end a war*, pp. 62, 159.
14. See Richard Tomlinson, *The big breach: From top secret to maximum security* (Moscow, 2001).
15. See Defence Intelligence Staff, 'Unclassified background brief no. 9: Yugoslav [sic] update', 10.6.1994, annex C, p. 24.

16. See Defence Intelligence Staff, 'Unclassified background brief no. 22: Former [sic] Yugoslavia update', 17.2.1995, annex C, p. 24.
17. See Defence Intelligence Staff, 'Unclassified background brief no. 9: Yugoslav [sic] update', 10.6.1994, annex A, pp. 19–20.
18. Rose, *Fighting for peace*, p. 16.
19. Spence, *All necessary measures*, p. 33.
20. Ibid., pp. 42–3.
21. John Zametica, 'First steps to freedom, but can they avoid civil war?' [on Albania], *The Times*, 10.7.1990. His byline describes him as 'a historian and specialist on the Balkans'. For a short profile see Eve-Ann Prentice, 'Cambridge man gives Karadzic a lifeline to the west', *The Times*, 20.7.1994. See also D. C. Watt's trenchant 'You are a liar and an outcast', *Observer*, 30.7.1995.
22. See Noel Malcolm, 'The whole lot of them are Serbs', *Spectator*, 10.6.1995.
23. Chris Bellamy, 'Military intervention "not a viable option"', *Independent*, 5.8.1992. John Zametica, 'The Yugoslav conflict', Adelphi Paper 270 (Brassey's/IISS, 1992).
24. Rose, *Fighting for peace*, p. 195.
25. See Michael Dewar, 'Intervention in Bosnia – the case against', *The World Today*, February 1993, pp. 32–4.
26. As cited in David Sharrock, 'Allies at home offer "sympathy"', *Guardian*, 15.4.1993.
27. Michael Dewar, 'Bosnia every which way but win', *Guardian*, 20.4.1993.
28. C. J. Dick, 'Serbian responses to intervention in Bosnia-Hercegovina', *British Army Review*, 102 (December 1992), p. 21.
29. Ibid., p. 22.
30. Ibid., p. 24.
31. Ibid., p. 18.
32. As cited in Catherine Bennett, 'Paralysed with fear', *Guardian*, 23.10.1992.
33. Rupert Pengelley, 'Into the quagmire', *International Defense Review*, 9 (1992), p. 799.
34. Brigadier Michael Harbottle, Letter, *Independent*, 11.8.1992.
35. As cited in Bennett, 'Paralysed with fear'.
36. See John Keegan, 'Only a short, sharp shock will end their defiance', *Daily Telegraph*, 10.8.1993.
37. See John Keegan, 'What can be done?', *Daily Telegraph*, 15.4.1993.
38. John Keegan, 'It'll make good TV but . . .', *Daily Telegraph*, 8.2.1994.
39. Ibid.
40. Ibid.

41. Ibid.
42. John Keegan, 'He doesn't understand', *Daily Telegraph*, 2.12.1994.
43. Keegan, 'What can be done?'.
44. Keegan, 'He doesn't understand'.
45. John Keegan, 'A primitive, tribal conflict only anthropologists can understand', *Daily Telegraph*, 15.4.1993.
46. John Keegan, *A history of warfare* (London, 1994), pp. 55–6.
47. Cited in Owen, *Balkan odyssey*, p. 18.
48. Dewar, 'Intervention in Bosnia – the case against', p. 33.
49. Messervy-Whiting, *Politico-military interface*, p. 27.
50. Stewart, *Broken lives*, pp. 318–19.
51. Duncan, 'Operating in Bosnia', p. 11.
52. For classic examples see David Fairhall, 'Nightmare in a no-go zone', *Guardian*, 2.6.1992, and 'Intervention risks all too clear', *Guardian*, 15.12.1992.
53. Christy Campbell, 'Ground forces hold key to US air strikes', *Sunday Telegraph*, 2.5.1993.
54. Ibid.
55. Andrew Hogg, 'No easy targets for an allied strike', *Sunday Times*, 18.4.1993.
56. See Christopher Bellamy, 'Nato ponders how to turn words into action', *Independent*, 12.8.1992.
57. See Christopher Bellamy, 'Practical problems hinder call to arms', *Independent*, 17.4.1993.
58. Christopher Bellamy, 'Medieval armies jousting in a half-hearted conflict', *Independent*, 2.5.1995.
59. Cited in Christopher Bellamy, 'Jets launch new attack on Serb "capital"', *Independent*, 27.5.1995.
60. See Christopher Bellamy, 'How to outmanoeuvre the west', *Independent*, 17.4.1994, and 'Turning point on an open road', *Independent*, 8.11.1994. See also Bellamy, *Knights in white armour*, pp. 112, 121, 149.
61. Bellamy, *Knights in white armour*, p. 169.
62. Bellamy, 'When winter failed to do its worst', *Independent*, 29.11.1994.
63. Quoted in Robert Block, 'Sarajevo bomb suspects protest their innocence', *Independent*, 9.2.1994.
64. Keegan, 'He doesn't understand'.
65. Philip Towle, 'British debate about intervention in European conflicts', *The Political Quarterly*, 1994, p. 103.
66. Ibid., p. 105.
67. Ibid., p. 94.

68. Ibid., p. 102.
69. Paul Mansell, *The ambivalence of the US to United Nations peacekeeping operations*, London Defence Studies 24, Centre for Defence Studies, London, November 1994, p. 17.
70. Ibid.
71. As cited in Leonard Doyle, 'Moral tone irks Europe', *Independent*, 30.5.1994.
72. E.g., Peter Beaumont, 'Armed and ready for Nato', *Observer*, 13.2.1994: 'British defence sources and military analysts say a Nato bombing raid would bring a high risk of casualties among pilots and civilians.' Also: Michael Evans, 'Argument for action hardens', *The Times*, 1.6.1992, and Michael Evans, 'Yugoslav peacemakers must wait in line for British military help', *The Times*, 2.7.1992 (re manpower requirements); Annika Savill, 'The dangers of "doing something"', *Independent*, 2.6.1992 and Annika Savill, 'Looking after the little things', *Independent*, 12.8.1993, for a 'military analyst close to the government'. The defence analyst and Balkan expert James Gow, 'Nervous bunnies: The international community and the war of Yugoslav dissolution, the politics of military intervention in a time of change', *Political Quarterly*, 1994, p. 26, writes that 'it was thought that, to be successful, the scale of intervention would have to be prohibitively large – the troop numbers discussed never fell below 120,000 and were more usually in the region of 400–500,000'.
73. Hugo Young, 'Hesitant west a spectator at the slaughter', *Guardian*, 13.4.1993; Hugo Young, 'The hard, slow road from apocalypse', *Guardian*, 13.7.1995. For another outing for Dewar's *World Today* article see Tony Barber, 'Bosnia's year of agony and division', *Independent*, 3.4.1993.
74. Hansard, 31.5.1995, col. 1161.
75. Hansard, 2.2.1993, col. 301.
76. As cited in Judy Dempsey, 'Balkan minefield for the west: pressure is mounting for some form of military intervention to support the Yugoslav relief effort', *Financial Times*, 8.8.1992.
77. Coles, *Making foreign policy*, p. 205.
78. Ibid., p. 147.
79. Quoted in Seldon, *Major*, p. 506.
80. See 'Ambassador Ivor Roberts on Kosovo', *Albanian Life*, 62 (winter 1997), p. 28.
81. Russell, *Prejudice and plum brandy*, p. 283.
82. Interview, Sir Ivor Roberts, Dublin, 3.1.2001, fo. 13.
83. See Holbrooke, *To end a war*, p. 110. Interview, Sir Ivor Roberts, Dublin, 3.1.2001, fos. 7–8.

84. Sir Reginald Hibbert, 'Why are British ambassadors at Belgrade pro-Serb?', no date. The accompanying letter from Sir Reginald, Frondeg, Powys, 23.12.2000.
85. Interview, James Woolsey, Washington, 29.3.2001, *Mendoza transcripts*, fo. 7.
86. Interview, Dr John Fox, Washington, 4.4.2001, *Mendoza transcripts*, fos. 6 and 3. In the same vein see also Interview, Dr John Fox, Washington, 11.1.2001, fo. 2 (conducted by author) and background interviews with serving State Department officials.
87. S/PV.3082, 30.5.1992, p. 43.
88. Robert Barnett to the author, Maugersbury, Glos., 4.1.2001. I thank Mr Barnett for his detailed statement on his time in Sarajevo and his willingness to talk to me on the telephone.
89. As recalled by Jennifer Brush: Interview, Jennifer Brush, Washington, 29.3.2001, *Mendoza transcripts*, fo. 19.
90. Stankovic, *Trusted mole*, p. 232.
91. Interview, Lord Hurd, London, 24.1.2001, fo. 18.
92. Interview, Dr Michael Williams, London, 22.11.2000, fo. 17.
93. Also noted by Martin Bell, *In harm's way*, p. 38.
94. Rose, *Fighting for peace*, p. 70.
95. Interview, Dr Michael Williams, London, 22.11.2000.
96. Rose, *Fighting for peace*, p. 119.
97. Interview, Sir Ivor Roberts, Dublin, 3.1.2001, fo. 3.
98. Rose, *Fighting for peace*, p. 69.
99. Interview, Dame Pauline Neville-Jones, London, 20.2.2001, *Mendoza transcripts*, fos. 3–4.
100. Cradock, *In pursuit of British interests*, p. 187.
101. See, e.g., the forthright words in 'Developments in central Europe: mechanisms of security and cooperation' (CE 129), memorandum submitted by the FCO, Foreign Affairs Committee, 1992, p. 194.
102. Referred to in Gow, 'Nervous bunnies', p. 25.
103. *The case against international military intervention in Bosnia*, 'The former Yugoslavia: briefing note', Foreign and Commonwealth Office, October 1992. See also the equally unhelpful *Britain's peace-making role in former Yugoslavia: questions and answers*, 'Former Yugoslavia: a briefing note', FCO, February 1993.
104. Warren Zimmermann, *Origins of a catastrophe: Yugoslavia and its destroyers* (New York, 1996), pp. 226–8.
105. Interviews with Marshall Harris, James Hooper, and other (serving) State Department officials who prefer to remain anonymous.

106. Interview, Pauline Neville-Jones, London, 20.2.2001, *Mendoza transcripts*, fo. 13: 'You don't on the whole go out and resign or argue a lot.' This sentiment was echoed by numerous serving and retired diplomats.
107. Bell, *In harm's way*, p. 40.
108. Interview, Professor Leon Fuerth, Washington, 4.4.2001, *Mendoza transcripts*, fo. 9.
109. Recollection of Dr Richard Caplan of debates between Hannay and Mohamed Sacirbey in 1994.
110. Rose, *Fighting for peace*, p. 15.
111. Cited in Ruth Dudley Edwards, *True Brits: Inside the Foreign Office* (London, 1994), p. 157.
112. David Hannay, 'The UN's role in Bosnia assessed', *Oxford International Review* (Spring 1996), p. 5.
113. Ibid., p. 10.
114. See Vulliamy, 'Tragic costs of allies' hidden hostility'.
115. Hannay, 'The UN's role in Bosnia assessed', p. 5.
116. Interview, Sir David Hannay, London, 21.11.2000, and subsequent correspondence.
117. Hannay, 'The UN's role in Bosnia assessed', p. 6.
118. Ibid., p. 4.
119. Interview, Tom Richardson, London, 20.2.2001, *Mendoza transcripts*, fo. 4.
120. Foreign Affairs Committee, 27.11.1991, p. 94.
121. 'Memorandum submitted by the Foreign and Commonwealth Office', CE 17, 6.11.1991, House of Commons Foreign Affairs Committee, vol. II, p. 19.
122. 'Memorandum submitted by the Centre for Defence and International Security Studies, Lancaster University, 20.11.1991', Foreign Affairs Committee, Developments in Central Europe, Minutes of Evidence, 14.1.1992, House of Commons, 1991–2, Appendix 13, p. 244.
123. 'Developments in Central Europe', Foreign Affairs Committee, 4.12.1991, Mrs J. Sharp, Mr A. Smith, Dr J. Eyal and Dr L. Roucek, p. 122.
124. Foreign Affairs Committee, 4.12.1991, p. 125.
125. 'Minutes of Evidence', Session 1991–2, 27.11.1991, Foreign Affairs Committee, Dr James Gow, Dr David Dyker, Dr Mark Wheeler and Dr Stevan Pavlovitch, pp. 89, 71, 78.
126. 'Minutes of Evidence', Foreign Affairs Committee.
127. E.g., during the war: James Gow, 'Deconstructing Yugoslavia', *Survival*, 33, 4 (July/August 1991), pp. 291–311; and 'Nervous bunnies', pp. 14–33. See also *Triumph of the lack of will*, which was published after the war but

drew heavily on critiques which appeared during the conflict itself: pp. 62, 65, 166 (re recognition), p. 181 (re Bosnian Serb strength) et passim.

128. Gow, *Triumph of the lack of will*, p. 89.

129. James Gow, 'After the flood: literature on the context, causes and course of the Yugoslav war – reflections and refractions', *SEER*, 75, 3 (July 1997), p. 447.

130. 'Minutes of Evidence', Session 1991–2, 27.11.1991, Foreign Affairs Committee, pp. 73, 90, 92.

131. Ibid., p. 93.

132. See Gow, *Triumph of the lack of will*, pp. 146 and 242 (re general critique of US), and 'Nervous bunnies', p. 21 (re VOPP), p. 220 (re September 1994).

133. See Gow, 'After the flood', pp. 458–9.

134. Ibid., p. 459.

135. Ibid., p. 473.

136. Gow, *Triumph of the lack of will*, p. 181. Compare this passage with p. 89.

137. Jonathan Eyal, 'Balkan states crack on rock of reality', *Guardian*, 10.5.1991.

138. Jonathan Eyal, 'Europe's future is fraying fast', *Independent*, 31.5.1993.

139. E.g., Jonathan Eyal, 'Another walk-on part for Moscow', *Independent*, 27.4.1994; 'From bad to worse to Bosnia', *Spectator*, 17.6.1994.

140. Jonathan Eyal, 'Lessons in Balkan reality', *Guardian*, 13.8.1992.

141. Jonathan Eyal, 'Betrayed Bosnians await their fate', *Sunday Times*, 8.8.1993.

142. Jonathan Eyal, 'Where are our principles now?', *Independent*, 19.4.1994.

143. Jonathan Eyal, 'Which way will Europe go?', *Independent*, 5.12.1994.

144. Jonathan Eyal, 'Contact Group posturing fails to conceal lack of unity and resolve', *The Times*, 29.5.1995.

145. Jonathan Eyal, 'A guilt trip with photo opportunities', *Independent*, 18.3.1993.

146. Jonathan Eyal, 'Peace, or myth wrapped in a folly?', *Independent*, 4.5.1993.

147. Jonathan Eyal, 'A "can talk, can't do" president', *Independent*, 19.8.1993.

148. Jonathan Eyal, 'Big words, small deeds', *Independent*, 19.10.1993 (this piece was also directed against US policy in Somalia).

149. As cited in Michael Evans, 'Plea for weapons "a Muslim strategy to draw in Western troops"', *The Times*, 15.4.1993.

150. Jonathan Eyal, 'Doling out arms is no answer', *The Times*, 28.7.1995.

151. Jonathan Eyal, 'Dustbin for a world of dirty politics', *Independent*, 6.5.1994.
152. Jonathan Eyal, 'The West's cynical game is up', *Independent*, 17.12.1992.
153. Eyal, 'Where are our principles now?'
154. Eyal, 'Dustbin for a world of dirty politics'.
155. Eyal, 'Contact Group posturing fails to conceal lack of unity and resolve'.
156. Sir Laurence Martin, 'Peacekeeping as a growth industry', *The National Interest*, 32 (Summer 1993), p. 6.
157. Ibid., p. 7.
158. Misha Glenny, 'Apocalypse now', *New Statesman and Society*, 19.2.1993.
159. Rose, *Fighting for peace*, p. 54.
160. Owen, *Balkan odyssey*, p. 52.
161. Misha Glenny, 'Only in the Balkans', *London Review of Books*, 29.4.1999 (reviewing Vesna Goldsworthy, *Inventing Ruritania* and Maria Todorova, *Imagining the Balkans*).
162. Misha Glenny, 'War returns to Europe', *New Statesman and Society*, 9.8.1991.
163. Misha Glenny, *The fall of Yugoslavia* (1992 edition), p. 99.
164. See the painful demolitions by Ivo Banac, 'Misreading the Balkans' (review article), *Foreign Policy*, 93 (Winter 1993–4), pp. 177–8, and Attila Hoare, 'Misha Glenny and the Balkan mind', *Bosnia Report*, March–May 1998, p. 17.
165. Catherine Simpson, review of Stevan Pavlovitch, *Tito, Yugoslavia's great dictator: A reassessment* and Misha Glenny, *The fall of Yugoslavia, Historical Journal*, 38, 2 (1995), pp. 787–90, at p. 790.
166. E.g., Hoare, 'Misha Glenny and the Balkan mind', pp. 17–19.
167. Glenny, 'Apocalypse now'. For further musings on his own prescience see Misha Glenny, *The Balkans, 1804–1999: Nationalism, war and the great powers* (London, 1999), p. 634, and Roland Keating, 'When reporters go over the top', *The Times*, 18.1.1993.
168. Misha Glenny, 'The massacre of Yugoslavia', *NYRB*, 30.1.1992.
169. Misha Glenny, 'Nehmt euch Tito zum Vorbild!', *Die Zeit*, 6.8.1993.
170. Misha Glenny, 'Germany fans the flames of war', *New Statesman and Society*, 20 and 27.12.1991.
171. Misha Glenny, 'Bosnia: the last chance?', *NYRB*, 28.1.1993, 'What is to be done?', *NYRB*, 27.5.1993.
172. Misha Glenny, 'Here we go again. Misha Glenny on the coming Balkan war', *LRB*, 9.3.1995.

173. Misha Glenny, 'The wheel of history turns full circle', *New Statesman and Society*, 28.8.1992.
174. Misha Glenny, *International Herald Tribune*, 31.7.1993 – 1.8.1993. See also Glenny, 'The return of the great powers', *New Left Review*, May–June 1994, and 'Yugoslavia: the great fall', *NYRB*, 23.3.1995.
175. See n. 172.
176. Glenny, *Fall of Yugoslavia*, 3rd edn (1996), p. 248.
177. Such as Misha Glenny, 'On the brink', *New Statesman and Society*, 5.6.1992, and, particularly, 'Yugoslavia: the revenger's tragedy', *NYRB*, 13.8.1992. 'Yugoslavia: the great fall' is not bad either.
178. Glenny, 'Bosnia: the last chance?'.
179. Glenny, 'What is to be done?'.
180. Glenny, in 'The return of the great powers', p. 128.
181. Misha Glenny, 'Disaster lurks in West's folly of macho vengeance', *The Times*, 30.5.1995.
182. Misha Glenny, 'Bosnia: the tragic prospect', *NYRB*, 4.11.1993.
183. Glenny, 'The return of the great powers', p. 127.
184. Misha Glenny, 'How can the west help? Not by dropping bombs', *International Herald Tribune*, 8.12.1994.
185. Misha Glenny, 'Getting it wrong' (review of Timothy Garton Ash, *In Europe's name*), *LRB*, 24.2.1994.
186. Glenny, *The Balkans*, pp. 640, 642.
187. E.g., Misha Glenny, 'Heading off war in the southern Balkans', *Foreign Affairs* May–June 1995, pp. 98–108.
188. Glenny, *The fall of Yugoslavia*, 3rd edn, pp. 265–6.
189. Cited in Hoare, 'Misha Glenny and the Balkan mind', p. 18.
190. Glenny, 'The return of the great powers', p. 125.
191. Misha Glenny, 'Bluff and double bluff', *New Statesman and Society*, 25.10.1991.
192. Glenny, *Fall of Yugoslavia*, 3rd edn, p. 271.
193. E.g. Misha Glenny, 'Why safe zones are a recipe for anarchy', *Observer*, 30.5.1993, and 'The return of the great powers', p. 126.
194. Misha Glenny, 'Impose corridors in Bosnia and arrange a settlement', *International Herald Tribune*, 30.7.1993.
195. Glenny, 'Bosnia: the tragic prospect'.
196. Misha Glenny, 'A chance for Croats and Serbs to avert the approaching explosion', *International Herald Tribune*, 17.3.1995.
197. Glenny, 'Here we go again. Misha Glenny on the coming Balkan war'.
198. Towle, 'British debate', p. 101.
199. See Cohen, *Serbia's secret war*, on this.

200. On Serbian military prowess generally see the rather bleak assessment in 'Warrior nation or paper tiger? Serbia and her ground wars', *Bosnia Report*, 9/10 (April–July 1999).
201. On this see Norman Stone, 'Of pundits and partisans', *Salisbury Review*, December 1992, pp. 30–1.
202. Wing Commander Tony le Hardy, 'Wartime lessons on air supremacy' (letter), *Independent*, 12.2.1994 (original emphasis).
203. As cited in Bennett, 'Paralysed with fear'.
204. See the discussion in Anthony Farrar-Hockley, 'Serbia must be beaten back', *Independent on Sunday*, 13.12.1992.
205. As cited in Bennett, 'Paralysed with fear'.
206. Sir Fitzroy Maclean, 'Enemies must find their own salvation', *Observer*, 2.5.1993.
207. Edward Cowan, 'The price of intervention', *Independent*, 30.4.1993. See also Briefing Paper no. 33, International Security Information Service (ISIS). See also Cowan, 'Should we intervene?', *Sunday Times*, 9.8.1992, 'West must bomb now', *Sunday Times*, 8.8.1993, 'Sarajevo could yet be saved', *Independent*, 10.8.1993, and 'What it takes to save Bosnia', *Independent*, 26.4.1994.
208. Cowan, 'West must bomb now'.
209. This came to light when David Owen published extensive extracts from this memorandum in *Balkan odyssey*, pp. 290–2. Messervy-Whiting himself made no reference to the paper in *Politico-military interface*.
210. Interview, Major-General Graham Messervy-Whiting, London, 17.1.2001.
211. Owen, *Balkan odyssey*, pp. 290–2.
212. Interview, Major-General Messervy-Whiting, London, 17.1.2001, fo. 3.
213. Discussion on 'front lines', Interview, Major-General Messervy-Whiting, fos. 25–8.
214. See, for example, the reporting of John Simpson, himself no committed interventionist: 'Back to Baghdad?', *Spectator*, 19.2.1994, and 'A sense of proportion', *Spectator*, 14.8.1993. Likewise, the comments of Karadzic and the Bosnian Serb Vice-President, Professor Nikola Koljevic, as quoted in Marcus Tanner, 'Karadzic offer to withdraw from captured mountains', *Independent*, 6.8.1993, and (for Koljevic) as quoted in Corwin, *Dubious mandate*, p. 166.
215. As quoted in Anthony Bevins, 'British military intervention in Bosnia ruled out', *Independent*, 4.12.1992.
216. See David White, 'No early end to bloodshed: proposals for outside military intervention all have their risks', *Financial Times*, 16.4.1993.
217. See Chris Bellamy, 'Our lads should take on Serbia', *Independent*,

26.11.1992; Mazower as cited in Tony Barber, 'Bosnian Serbs warn the west', *Independent*, 17.12.1992; Tony Barber, 'West's aid could turn the tide of war', *Independent on Sunday*, 20.12.1992; Martin Bell, *In harm's way*, p. 108.
218. As quoted in Ambrose Evans-Pritchard, 'New man takes charge', *Sunday Telegraph*, 15.8.1993. In the same vein, the Supreme Allied Commander Europe, General George Joulwan, Interview, Virginia, 3.4.2001, *Mendoza transcripts*, fo. 17.
219. Interview, General William Nash, Washington, 3.4.2001, *Mendoza transcripts*, fo. 2.
220. Interview, James Woolsey, Washington, 29.3.2001, *Mendoza transcripts*, fo. 4.
221. Holbrooke, *To end a war*, p. 93.
222. Corwin, *Dubious mandate*, pp. 202–3.
223. Peter Almond, 'The first principle of war', *Daily Telegraph*, 29.4.1993.
224. Interview, Field-Marshal Lord Vincent, London, 19.1.2001.
225. Ibid.
226. Interview, Dr Jamie Shea, Brussels, 24.11.2000, fo. 17.
227. Ibid.
228. Hansard, 22.7.1993, col. 508.
229. Hansard, 26.7.1993, col. 844.
230. Ibid., col. 861.
231. See Andrew Marr, 'Politicians "let NATO down" over Bosnia', *Independent*, 22.7.1993, on the circularity of the arguments against military intervention.
232. See Gow, 'Nervous bunnies', p. 30.
233. Hansard, 12.7.1993, col. 682.
234. As cited in Bennett, 'Paralysed with fear'.

## 7 'Emulsifying the Whole Affair': Parliament and the Public Sphere

1. Hansard, 12.12.1991, col. 1165.
2. Hansard, 25.5.1994, col. 349.
3. Hansard, 12.12.1991, col. 1160.
4. 'Air strikes ruled out in Bosnia', *Guardian*, 17.11.1992.
5. Hansard, 14.4.1993, col. 835.
6. See his remarks in Hansard, 31.5.1995, col. 1009.
7. See Sir Russell Johnston, letter to the editor, 'Who should intervene in Yugoslavia?', *The Times*, 3.12.1991, and Hansard, passim.

8. See *Times* diary, 24.2.1994. On the Serb lobby in parliament see Carole Hodge, *The Serb lobby in the United Kingdom*, The Donald W. Treadgold Papers, no. 22, Henry M. Jackson School of International Studies, Washington State, 1999, and Vulliamy and Leigh, *Sleaze*, pp. 110–18.
9. See his question on wine imports, Hansard, 12.3.1992, col. 624.
10. Hansard, 25.9.1992, col. 171.
11. Hansard, 6.5.1993, col. 288.
12. Hansard, 29.4.1993, col. 1232.
13. Hansard, 26.7.1993, col. 864.
14. See Philip Johnston, 'MP and Peer in Serb trip row', *Daily Telegraph*, 31.7.1995; Adrian Lithgow, 'Labour MP and Bosnia's butcher', *Daily Mail*, 30.7.1995.
15. See Philip Webster and Andrew Pierce, 'Bar on MP who failed to declare £6000', *The Times*, 30.7.1997; Christian Wolmar, 'Labour MP "was profiting from Serb link"', *Independent*, 20.6.1997.
16. Hansard, 28.4.1993, col. 431. Also 30.4.1993, col. 586.
17. E.g., Hansard, 14.6.1993, col. 476.
18. Hansard, 2.6.1992, col. 718. In the same vein: 19.4.1993, col. 30; 14.7.1993, cols. 966–7 and 'Our troops must leave Bosnia', *Independent*, 31.5.1995. See also Sir Peter Tapsell, 31.5.1995, Hansard, col. 1053.
19. Hansard, 3.5.1995, col. 330.
20. Nicholas Budgen, 'What's it got to do with us?', *Guardian*, 4.4.1993.
21. Hansard, 18.4.1993, col. 651.
22. Hansard, 31.5.1995, cols. 1077–9.
23. Hansard, 29.4.1993, col. 1230.
24. Hansard, 31.5.1995, col. 1051.
25. Hansard, 2.2.1993, col. 300 (emphasis added).
26. Hansard, 7.2.1994, col. 23.
27. Hansard, 4.7.1995, col. 127.
28. E.g., Hansard, 15.2.1994, col. 803 (Mr Butcher).
29. Hansard, 14.4.1993, col. 838.
30. Ibid., col. 819. See also Stephen Goodwin, 'Inside Parliament: Thatcher casts her shadow over Commons', *Independent*, 15.4.1993.
31. Hansard, 25.4.1994, col. 28.
32. Hansard, 13.7.1994, col. 983. In the same vein (Gapes) 31.5.1995, col. 1084.
33. Hansard, 29.4.1993, col. 1172.
34. Hansard, 31.5.1995, col. 1021.
35. Hansard, 29.4.1993, col. 1204.
36. Hansard, 31.5.1995, col. 1054.

37. Hansard, 21.11.1994, col. 343.
38 Hansard, 6.5.1993, col. 287.
39. Hansard, 29.4.1993, col. 1230.
40. Iain Duncan Smith, 'The anvil upon which Nato is being broken', *Independent*, 28.11.1994.
41. Hansard, 31.5.1995, col. 1028.
42. Hansard, 2.3.1994, cols. 926–7.
43. E.g., Duncan Smith, 'The anvil upon which Nato is being broken'; Edward Heath, interview, *Crossbow*, October 1994, p. 15; and Hansard passim.
44. Foreign Affairs Committee, Minutes, 11 December 1991, p. 149.
45. Hansard, 18.12.1991, col. 261 (Mr Rees).
46. Hansard, 13.7.1994, col. 974.
47. Julian Brazier, letter to the editor, *The Times*, 25.9.1991.
48. Hansard, 13.1.1993, col. 901; 11.6.1993, col. 563; 7.2.1994, col. 26.
49. Hansard, 31.5.1995, col. 1067.
50. Hansard, 19.7.1995, col. 1776.
51. Hansard, 24.5.1993, col. 575.
52. Hansard, 14.4.1993, col. 826 (Mr Dickens).
53. Hansard, 4.5.1994, col. 705.
54. Hansard, 15.4.1993, col. 946.
55. *Guardian*, letter from Alan Clark, 26.7.1995.
56. *Guardian*, letter from Graham Andrews, 5.8.1995.
57. Hansard, 31.5.1995, col. 1049.
58. Hansard, 19.7.1995, col. 1777. See also 31.10.1995, col. 1050, 19.4.1995, col. 32, et passim.
59. Julian Brazier, letter to the editor, *The Times*, 25.9.1991.
60. Julian Brazier, letter to the editor, *The Times*, 13.8.1992.
61. Hansard, 31.5.1995, col. 1054.
62. Hansard, 13.1.1993, col. 901. In the same vein, but intelligently couched, see the observations by Tait on the Foreign Affairs Committee, 6.11.1991.
63. Derek Prag, letter to the editor, *Independent*, 26.5.1993.
64. Nicholas Budgen, 'Our troops must leave Bosnia', *Independent*, 31.5.1995.
65. Hansard, 3.5.1995, col. 331 (also re irony of inviting Tudjman 'to commemorate the victory over fascism').
66. Cited in extracts from *The Ashdown Diaries, Volume I* (London, 2000), *The Times*, 26.10.2000.
67. Hansard, 31.5.1995, col. 1050.
68. Hansard, 31.5.1995, col. 1063.

69. Hansard, 2.6.1992, col. 720. See also Peter Fry, 13.11.1991, col. 1202, Peter Temple-Morris, 13.1.1993, col. 903, Sir James Spicer, 29.11.1994, col. 1074.
70. Hansard, 31.5.1995, col. 1059.
71. Hansard, 25.4.1994, col. 28.
72. Hansard, 8.2.1994, col. 127.
73. Hansard, 14.4.1993, col. 826.
74. Hansard, 25.9.1992, col. 162.
75. John Biffen, Hansard, 12.7.1995, col. 953. See also the echo by Sir Peter Tapsell, 13.7.1995, cols. 1084–5.
76. Hansard, 20.4.1993, col. 175.
77. Hansard, 31.5.1995, col. 1075. See also 2.6.1992, col. 716.
78. Andrew Robathan, letter to the editor, *The Times*, 1.2.1993.
79. Hansard, 14.12.1992, col. 70. See also Don Anderson, 5.3.1992, col. 466, et passim.
80. Hansard, 31.5.1995, col. 1042.
81. Cited in 'Opinions are divided over whether Britain should use military force and send troops to try to end the bloodshed in Bosnia-Herzegovina', *Independent*, 16.12.1992.
82. Hansard, 25.4.1994, col. 25.
83. Hansard, 12.4.1994, col. 27.
84. Hansard, 13.1.1993, col. 904.
85. Hansard, 31.5.1993, col. 1043.
86. Ibid., cols. 1043–4.
87. Ibid. (twice), and on 14.12.1994, col. 922.
88. Hansard, 27.6.1991, col. 1139.
89. Hansard, 2.6.1992, col. 719.
90. Hansard, 5.11.1992, col. 432.
91. Hansard, 2.6.1992, col. 359, 9.6.1992, col. 87.
92. Hansard, 29.4.1993, cols. 1232–3.
93. Ibid., col. 1229. See also Robathan, 31.5.1995, col. 1078, in the same vein.
94. Andrew Robathan, letter to the editor, *The Times*, 1.2.1993.
95. Hansard, 31.5.1995, col. 1053. See also col. 1009.
96. Hansard, 29.4.1993, col. 1191.
97. Ibid.
98. See for example, Hansard, 10.1.1994, cols. 6–9. See also the very prescient questions of Lord Hylton, 17.5.1991, Written answers, 77 and Lord Hylton, letter to the editor, 'Successful military intervention is possible', *Financial Times*, 5.12.1992.

99. E.g., Baroness Blackstone and Lord Bonham-Carter, Hansard, 31.5.1995, cols. 1166, 1264. Also Lord Bonham-Carter, 4.4.1993, col. 1103.
100. E.g., Lord Bruce of Donington, Hansard, 19.10.1993, col. 498.
101. As cited in 'Should we use force in Bosnia: interviews by Bill Frost and Julia Llewellyn Smith', *The Times*, 20.4.1993.
102. As cited ibid.
103. As cited ibid.
104. Hansard, 20.11.1991, col. 1003.
105. Hansard, 31.5.1995, col. 1122.
106. Ibid., 31.5.1995, col. 1131.
107. Ibid., 31.5.1995, col. 1151.
108. Hansard, 14.4.1993, col. 1107.
109. Hansard, Written answers, 5.12.1994, 65, 66. See also ibid., 55.
110. Hansard, Written answers, 21.4.1994, 18.
111. Hansard, 31.5.1995, col. 1138.
112. Hansard, 19.4.1993, col. 1272.
113. Hansard, 31.5.1995, cols. 1154–5.
114. Hansard, 14.12.1992, col. 59.
115. As quoted in Philip Johnston, 'Senior Tory calls for military intervention', *Daily Telegraph*, 7.4.1993.
116. Hansard, 14.4.1993, col. 833.
117. Hansard, 29.4.1993, col. 1205, also col. 1209.
118. See the remarks quoted in Louise Branson, 'Golden highway makes a joke of Bosnia blockade', *Sunday Times*, 23.5.1993.
119. See the comments quoted and paraphrased in 'Interview: David Howell MP tells Tony Barber that Bosnia cannot be restored as a state', *Independent*, 28.7.1993.
120. David Howell, 'It's time to call it a day and negotiate', *Independent*, 28.11.1994.
121. Report of the Foreign Affairs Committee, presented 14.1.1992, HMSO, Section IV: Yugoslavia, p. xxiv.
122. Interview, Lord Howell, London, 28.2.2001, *Mendoza transcripts*, fo. 3.
123. Ibid., fo. 8.
124. Hansard, 26.7.1993, col. 852.
125. Paddy Ashdown, 'Dress rehearsal for a global strategy', *Guardian*, 4.8.1992; 'Only delaying the inevitable', *Guardian*, 15.12.1992.
126. Paddy Ashdown, 'We cannot turn our backs on Bosnia', *Observer*, 17.1.1993.
127. As quoted in Stephen Goodwin, 'Ashdown maps out path for party in the big time', *Independent*, 24.9.1993.

128. Hansard, 29.4.1993, col. 1196.
129. As quoted in Colin Brown, 'Ashdown urges more UN troops for Bosnia', *Independent*, 21.4.1993.
130. Hansard, 29.4.1993, col. 1194. In the same vein also 12.7.1994, col. 826 et passim.
131. Ibid., col. 1196.
132. Paddy Ashdown, 'Too little, too late, too bad for all our Bosnias', *Observer*, 27.11.1994.
133. Paddy Ashdown, 'We are making Europe's Palestinians', *Independent*, 13.8.1992.
134. Hansard, 29.4.1993, col. 1189.
135. See Paddy Ashdown, 'When will you act?', *Guardian*, 13.8.1992; 'Interview: "Put Muslim-led areas into UN protectorate"', *Independent*, 29.7.1993; 'Bosnia: heroism betrayed', *Independent*, 5.8.1993.
136. Hansard, 2.6.1992, col. 715.
137. Hansard, 25.9.1992, col. 132.
138. Ibid., col. 180.
139. As cited in Stephen Goodwin, 'Parliament and politics: Hurd defends joint EC action over Yugoslavia', *Independent*, 20.12.1991.
140. Hansard, 2.6.1992, col. 715. He means 'contain', presumably.
141. Ibid.
142. Hansard, 29.4.1993, col. 1178.
143. Ibid.
144. Ibid., col. 1180.
145. Hansard, 14.4.1993, col. 831.
146. Hansard, 29.4.1993, col. 1147.
147. Hansard, 13.7.1994, col. 975.
148. Hansard, 20.4.1993, col. 179.
149. Hansard, 29.4.1993, col. 1147. Indeed, Smith was to maintain this muscular approach right up to his death in 1994 (e.g., Hansard, 22.2.1994, col. 143, where he calls for 'the threat of military action . . . to end the sieges of Tuzla, Zepa, Gorazde, Srebrenica and Bihac').
150. Hansard, 29.4.1993, col. 1184.
151. Ibid., col. 1181.
152. Ibid., col. 1180.
153. E.g., Hansard, 5.11.1992, col. 425 and 30.11.1992, col. 31.
154. Robin Cook, 'Sending a message to the Serbs', *Independent*, 30.5.1995.
155. Robin Cook, 'Peace moves in Bosnia', *Guardian*, 15.5.1995.
156. Hansard, 19.7.1995, col. 1778.
157. Ibid., col. 1746.

158. See Joseph Sanders Pearson, 'British press reactions to the onset of war in ex-Yugoslavia' (PhD dissertation, University of Cambridge, 2001), pp. 124–5.
159. Ibid., passim.
160. Con Coughlin, 'TV throws up screen against truth about Bosnian conflict', *Sunday Telegraph*, 11.4.1993.
161. Con Coughlin, 'West plans to leave Bosnians to their doom', *Sunday Telegraph*, 11.7.1993.
162. Victoria Clark, 'No more nice guys as patience runs out', *Observer*, 31.1.1993.
163. Ian Traynor, 'Claims of genocide on all sides deserve closer examination', *Guardian*, 18.6.1993 (as reprinted in *The Irish Times*).
164. Bell, *In harm's way*, pp. 52, 131.
165. Alistair Burnet, 'Outsiders should beware of risks in nasty local brawl', *Sunday Times*, 31.1.1993.
166. 'Opinion', leading article, *Mail on Sunday*, 4.4.1993.
167. Anne Applebaum, 'It's time to get the troops out of Bosnia – all of them', *Daily Telegraph*, 30.5.1995.
168. 'American petrol, Bosnian flames', editorial, *Guardian*, 14.9.1994.
169. *Guardian*, editorial, 7.2.1995.
170. 'No time to give up on Bosnia', editorial, *Observer*, 31.7.1994. See also in the same vein Adrian Hamilton, 'A bloodbath in Europe', *Observer*, 18.9.1994.
171. 'Havens from terror', editorial, *Daily Telegraph*, 13.6.1992.
172. 'Arms and consequences', editorial, *Daily Telegraph*, 1.8.1994.
173. 'Serbian divisions', editorial, *Daily Telegraph*, 29.8.1994.
174. 'Lack of conviction', editorial, *Daily Telegraph*, 7.9.1994.
175. 'The crossing of a Rubicon', editorial, *Independent*, 11.8.1992.
176. 'We must not abandon Bosnia', editorial, 21.1.1994.
177. 'A long battle for peace in Bosnia', editorial, *Independent*, 12.9.1994.
178. 'Still no way out of Bosnia', editorial, *Independent*, 29.5.1995.
179. 'The siren call of Little England', editorial, *Independent*, 31.5.1995.
180. See Tom Nairn, 'Demonising nationalism', *LRB*, 25.2.1993.
181. Mary Kaldor, 'Long divisions of the Balkan mind', *Guardian*, 21.6.1991, as cited in Pearson, 'British press responses', p. 96.
182. Michael Ignatieff, 'They are all baddies in Bosnia', *Observer*, 31.1.1993.
183. John Pilger, 'The west is guilty in Bosnia', *New Statesman*, 7.5.1996.
184. Edward Pearce, 'Bosnia is best left alone', *Guardian*, 3.12.1994.
185. Chris Harman, letter, *LRB*, 27.1.1994.
186. Simon Jenkins, 'They die so that we feel better', *The Times*, 17.4.1993.

187. Beatrix Campbell, 'The new world order of intimate warfare', *Independent*, 28.4.1993.
188. John Casey, 'In the name of mercy, no mercenaries', *Sunday Telegraph*, 30.8.1992.
189. Allan Massie, 'War will not bring peace to Bosnia', *Sunday Telegraph*, 20.12.1992.
190. Paul Johnson, 'Is the life of the *Independent* moving aggressively to a close?', *Spectator*, 14.8.1993.
191. Peter Simple [Michael Wharton], 'To arms', *Sunday Telegraph*, 8.8.1993.
192. Pilger, 'The west is guilty in Bosnia'.
193. Pearce, 'Bosnia is best left alone'.
194. Massie, 'War will not bring peace to Bosnia'.
195. Conor Cruise O'Brien, 'We enter Bosnia at our peril', *Independent*, 23.4.1993.
196. Conor Cruise O'Brien, 'Ritual humiliation at the UN', *Independent*, 4.6.1993.
197. O'Brien, 'We enter Bosnia at our peril'.
198. Conor Cruise O'Brien, 'There will be no Nuremberg here', *Independent*, 26.2.1993.
199. O'Brien, 'We enter Bosnia at our peril'.
200. O'Brien, 'Ritual humiliation at the UN'.
201. As cited in Michael Sells, *The bridge betrayed* (Berkeley and London, 1996), p. 203.

## 8 The Reckoning

1. Interview, Dr Jamie Shea, Brussels, 5.3.2001, *Mendoza transcripts*, fo. 14.
2. E.g. Mr Gomersall, United Nations Security Council, 3522, New York, 21.4.1995, p. 21. See in the same vein the fleshing out of an exit strategy in United Nations Security Council, 3521, 19.4.1995, and the quotations in Andrew Marshall, 'Major warns British troops may quit Bosnia', *Independent*, 6.12.1994.
3. Quoted in George Brock, 'Faltering White House leaving gap at the heart of its foreign policy', *The Times*, 28.9.1994.
4. As quoted in Robert Fox and Christy Campbell, 'Foreign Focus', *Sunday Telegraph*, 4.12.1994.
5. Quoted in George Jones and Ashmed Rashid, 'Hurd says Clinton Bosnia policy is dangerous', *Daily Telegraph*, 7.9.1994.

6. Quoted in Michael Binyon, 'Major confirms Britain near to Bosnia pullout', *The Times*, 7.12.1994.
7. Andrew Marr, 'Hurt British feelings are the least of it', *Independent*, 15.9.1994.
8. On this see Kathy Sawyer, 'Bomb Serb bridges Moynihan urges in attack of US policy', 25.4.1994, *International Herald Tribune*, 25.4.1994.
9. Matthew Parris, 'Must politicians wait for events to demonstrate that they are in the wrong when they know it already?', *The Times*, 8.5.1995.
10. HQ Sector North East, BHC, UNPROFOR, 'Srebrenica', An analysis by Lt.-Col. C. A. le Hardy and Captain H.-C. Hagman, 24.2.1995.
11. See Michael Evans, 'SAS looked on helplessly as thousands were killed', *Independent*, 12.7.2000, and Tom Walker, 'SAS book on Bosnia blocked', *Sunday Times*, 9.7.2000. Le Hardy and Hagman, 'Srebrenica', notes that 'JCOs [SAS teams] . . . have been deployed to the enclave'.
12. Hansard, 31.5.1995, col. 1171.
13. As cited in Mark Almond, 'A faraway country . . .', in Cohen and Stamkoski, *With no peace to keep*, p. 131. See also Weller, 'Peace-keeping and peace-enforcement', pp. 152–3, on the restrictive way in which the RRF's mandate was interpreted.
14. See Tim Ripley, 'A "Deliberate Force" on the mountain', *International Defense Review*, 10 (1995), p. 28.
15. Michael Williams, letter to the editor, *The Times*, 17.7.1995.
16. As cited in Anne Applebaum, 'Military fiction that spells more misery for Bosnia', *Daily Telegraph*, 25.7.1995.
17. *The Times*' editorial of 14.7.1995 refers euphemistically to 'western intelligence'. It doesn't mean the CIA.
18. Contra Seldon, *Major*, p. 593, whose account has, it would appear, been 'spun' by Mr Major.
19. As cited in Weller, 'Peace-keeping and peace-enforcement in Bosnia and Herzegovina', p. 154.
20. As cited in Elizabeth Drew, *Showdown: The struggle between the Gingrich Congress and the Clinton White House* (New York, 1996), p. 251.
21. As cited in Donald Macintyre, '"Britain sucked into war". Grim warning from Owen as he quits Bosnia role', *The Times*, 1.6.1995.
22. As paraphrased by George Jones, 'Evidence builds up of Muslim bias by CIA', *Daily Telegraph*, 3.6.1995. See also George Jones and Suzanne Lowry, 'Allies suspect US hawks of increasing risk of war', *Daily Telegraph*, 2.6.1995.
23. 'Confronting terror', *The Times*, 29.5.1995.
24. 'At last some sense from Washington', *Independent*, 2.6.1995.
25. 'The United Nations in chains', *Independent*, 27.5.1995.

26. 'Beware the siren calls to war', *Observer*, 4.6.1995.
27. 'A defeat for good intentions', *Independent on Sunday*, 28.5.1995.
28. 'Drawing a line in the sand', editorial, *Independent*, 21.7.1995; 'Stand up to the Serb bully', *Observer*, 16.7.1995. An exception was 'We must not be disgraced', *Sunday Telegraph*, 4.6.1995.
29. 'A day of feeble hints', editorial, *Guardian*, 22.7.1995.
30. 'Bosnia's last tomorrow', editorial, *Guardian*, 20.7.1995.
31. 'A widening war', editorial, *Daily Telegraph*, 28.7.1995.
32. 'The Balkan pot boils over', editorial, *Observer*, 13.8.1995.
33. John Keegan, 'Why taking hostages could backfire', *Daily Telegraph*, 30.5.1995.
34. John Keegan, 'UN faces clear choice between positive action and retreat in Bosnia', *Daily Telegraph*, 29.5.1995.
35. John Keegan, 'Point the way out for the Serbs with a mailed fist', *Daily Telegraph*, 2.6.1995.
36. Misha Glenny, 'Disaster lurks in west's folly of macho vengeance', *The Times*, 30.5.1995.
37. Christopher Bellamy, 'Medieval jousting in a half-hearted conflict', *Independent*, 2.5.1995.
38. Hansard, 31.5.1995, col. 1096.
39. 'A debacle for Clinton', leading article, *Washington Post*, 31.5.1995.
40. William E. Odom, 'Send in ground troops, 100 000 or more', *New York Times*, 2.6.1995.
41. Holbrooke, *To end a war*, p. 64.
42. Cited in Drew, *Showdown*, p. 248.
43. Martin Fletcher, 'Gingrich crusades to rid the world of barbarians', *The Times*, 20.7.1995.
44. Robert Kagan, 'When all options are dangerous, choose the honourable one', *International Herald Tribune*, 19.7.1995.
45. 'Let Bosnia defend itself', *New York Times*, 28.7.1995.
46. 'Clinton's hostage crisis', editorial, *Wall Street Journal*, 19.7.1995.
47. Zbigniew Brzezinski, 'Give them arms and dignity', *Independent*, 21.7.1995.
48. Cited in Jeane Kirkpatrick, 'The United Nations stands accused of betrayal', *International Herald Tribune*, 22.8.1995 (*Los Angeles Times*).
49. Bernard Osser and Patrick de Saint-Exupery, 'The UN's failure: an interview with Tadeusz Mazowiecki', *NYRB*, 21.9.1995.
50. David Warzawski, 'Menetekel für Osteuropa. Der Bosnien-Konflikt führt den Polen die Unsicherheit der eigenen Lage vor Augen', *Die Zeit*, 28.7.1995.

51. Zbigniew Brzezinski, 'Give them arms and dignity', *Independent*, 21.7.1995.
52. As cited in Ambrose Evans-Pritchard, 'Bosnia burn-out hits NATO. Crisis deepens rift "more serious than Suez"', *Sunday Telegraph*, 30.7.1995.
53. Richard Perle, 'Let the Bosnians arm, and bring the UN forces out', *International Herald Tribune*, 20.7.1995.
54. Daalder, *Getting to Dayton*, p. vii.
55. Ibid., p. 164. See also in the same vein p. 187.
56. Holbrooke, *To end a war*, p. 59.
57. Ibid., p. 67. For contemporary perception of how Bosnia overshadowed all other international agenda see Michael Sheridan and David Usborne, 'Congress rebuffs Europe on UN funds', *Independent*, 16.6.1995, and Michael Sheridan, 'Not so Magnificent Seven', *Independent*, 17.6.1995.
58. Drew, *Showdown*, p. 249.
59. William Pfaff, 'As of now, Serbia wins, Europe loses and the future is dark', *Los Angeles Times* (*International Herald Tribune*), 17.7.1995.
60. Cited in *International Herald Tribune*, 18.7.1995.
61. As quoted in Bob Woodward, *The choice* (New York, 1996), p. 263.
62. As quoted ibid., p. 262.
63. As cited ibid., p. 261.
64. Daalder, *Getting to Dayton*, p. 189.
65. Interview, Dr Jamie Shea, Brussels, 24.11.2000, fo. 3.
66. Holbrooke, *To end a war*, p. 103.
67. As cited in Christopher Bellamy, Tony Barber, and Donald Macintyre, 'Serb attacks pile on the misery', *Independent*, 15.7.1995.
68. As cited in Mary Dejevsky, 'France throws down gauntlet', *Independent*, 15.7.1995. See also Eve-Ann Prentice and Jill Sherman, 'Second safe area under attack. Chirac appeasement gibe at Major', *The Times*, 15.7.1995.
69. As cited in 'Allies told: fight or get out. Rifkind plays for time as President Chirac issues Bosnia ultimatum to NATO', *Guardian*, 14.7.1995. See also Daniel McGrory and Jon Craig, 'Major wars with Chirac', *Daily Express*, 15.7.1995.
70. As cited in Marcus Warren, 'The west dithers', *Sunday Telegraph*, 16.7.1995. See also Michael Sheridan, 'Anglo-French discord leaves Rifkind out in the cold', *Independent*, 18.7.1995.
71. As cited in Vulliamy, 'Tragic costs of allies' hidden hostility'. For Holbrooke's assessment of the French change of policy see *To end a war*, p. 84.
72. Interview, Dr Robert Hunter, Pentagon City, 7.1.2001, fo. 13.
73. Interview, James Rubin, London, 8.2.2001, fo. 16.

74. Interview, Professor Anthony Lake, Georgetown, 10.1.2001, fo. 13.
75. On this see the fascinating article by Mark Danner, 'Bosnia: breaking the machine', *NYRB*, 19.2.1998.
76. For an unsympathetic but revealing account of this process see Philip Corwin, *Dubious mandate*, p. 206. See also pp. 43–4.
77. See the briefings summarized ibid., pp. 57, 69, 153, 114, and, particularly, 149 and 152.
78. See Bell, *In harm's way*, p. 264.
79. Corwin, diary entry, 9.6.1995; *Dubious mandate*, p. 42.
80. For varying views of Pauline Neville-Jones see Owen, *Balkan odyssey*, p. 277, Rose, *Fighting for peace*, p. 178, and the rather negative assessment of the Bosnian ambassador in 1995, who thought her 'definitely' unsympathetic to his cause: Interview, Professor Mohamed Fillipovic, London, 2.10.2000, fo. 20.
81. Christopher Bellamy, 'A gamble calculated to take Serbs to the brink', *Independent*, 5.8.1995.
82. 'Final settlement', editorial, *Daily Telegraph*, 7.8.1995.
83. See Michael Sheridan, 'Britain angry after US denies "ethnic cleansing"', *Independent*, 9.8.1995, and Gerald Butt and Marcus Warren, 'Britain leads criticism of Zagreb's offensive', *Daily Telegraph*, 5.8.1995.
84. See Annan, *Srebrenica report*, points 439 and 441.
85. Bell, *In harm's way*, p. 281.
86. Annan, *Srebrenica report*, point 452, citing Safe Area Resolution 836: 'Despite earlier having argued that the more general use of force would require a new mandate from the [UN Security] council, and that resolution 836 (1993) gave UNPROFOR a mandate to use force essentially only in self-defence, the Secretariat now took a different line reflecting the change of political will in the international community.'
87. Jonathan Steele, 'Americans eager to bomb and talk', *Guardian*, 7.9.1995.
88. 'Not so smart weapons', editorial, *Guardian*, 12.9.1995.
89. Julian Brazier, letter to the editor, *The Times*, 12.9.1995. See also Anne Applebaum, 'As the cruise missiles fall, expect Moscow mischief', *Daily Telegraph*, 12.9.1995.
90. 'Bloody mark of failure', editorial, *Independent on Sunday*, 3.9.1995.
91. Jonathan Eyal, 'How Nato prolonged the war', *The Times*, 31.8.1995. In a similar vein see also Jonathan Eyal, 'Nato's "successful" offensive will encourage more violence', *The Times*, 2.9.1995. For other examples of expert pessimism about 'Deliberate Force' see Richard Norton-Taylor, 'Nato "would take weeks" to damage Serbs', *Guardian*, 7.9.1995.
92. John Keegan, 'Croatian victory shifts power in Bosnia', *Daily Telegraph*,

9.8.1995, and 'Nato should gain upper hand in Bosnia's military labyrinth', *Sunday Telegraph*, 10.2.1995.

93. 'Glimmer of Balkan hope', leading article, *Daily Telegraph*, 18.9.1995. See also 'Retaliation at last', leading article, *Daily Telegraph*, 31.8.1995, and 'A step towards peace', *Daily Telegraph*, 9.9.1995.

94. 'Whose peace in Bosnia?', editorial, *Guardian*, 16.9.1995.

95. 'Do not wobble over Bosnia', editorial, *Independent*, 14.9.1995.

96. Holbrooke, *To end a war*, p. 21. See also p. 54.

97. Ibid., p. 152.

98. See Glenny, *Fall of Yugoslavia*, p. 270.

99. Holbrooke, *To end a war*, p. 110.

100. Ibid., p. 137.

101. For a particularly frantic apologia see Corwin, *Dubious mandate*, pp. 232–3. A measured but none the less entirely misleading apologia can be found in Major, *Autobiography*, p. 545. See also Rose, *Fighting for peace*, epilogue, passim and Glenny, *Fall of Yugoslavia*, pp. 289–90.

102. Rose, *Fighting for peace*, p. 6.

103. On the effect of 'Deliberate Force' see Tim Ripley's massively researched *Operation Deliberate Force: The UN and NATO campaign in Bosnia 1995* (Lancaster, 1999).

104. Glenny, *The Balkans*, p. 651 (emphasis added).

105. Owen, *Balkan odyssey*, p. 336.

106. See Pauline Neville-Jones, 'Dayton, IFOR, and Alliance relations in Bosnia', *Survival*, 38, 4 (winter 1996–7), pp. 45–65.

107. Hurd, *Ten minutes to turn the devil*, p. xv.

108. Stankovic, *Trusted mole*, p. 437.

109. Ibid., p. 437 and, in the same vein, p. 322.

110. Major, *Autobiography*, p. 545. In a similar vein, Glenny, *Fall of Yugoslavia*, p. 290.

111. Neville-Jones, 'Dayton, IFOR, and Alliance relations in Bosnia', p. 48.

112. E.g., Interview, Dame Pauline Neville-Jones, London, 20.2.2001, *Mendoza transcripts*, fo. 20, and Owen, *Balkan odyssey*, p. 330. See also the claims in Stuart, Hurd, *passim*, *Sunday Telegraph*.

113. Contra Owen, *Balkan odyssey*, p. 330.

114. See, for example, Tim Judah, 'Bosnian Serbs rejoice at US peace plan', 10.9.1995, and Holbrooke, *To end a war*, pp. 153, 160.

115. E.g., Judah, 'Bosnian Serbs rejoice at US peace plan'.

116. Vulliamy, 'Tragic costs of allies' hidden hostility'.

117. Bell, *In harm's way*, p. 293.

118. Coles, *Making foreign policy*, p. 34.

119. Major, *Autobiography*, p. 549.
120. Annan, *Srebrenica report*, point 491 (original emphasis).
121. Interview, Richard Perle, Chevy Chase, 8.1.2001, fo. 3.
122. See the remarks quoted in 'Darkness at dawn', *Economist*, 16.4.1994; Christopher Bellamy, 'US stands aloof as Serb guns batter Gorazde', *Independent*, 4.4.1994, and Richard Dowden, Andrew Marshall and Patrick Cockburn, 'West clutches at straws over Bihac debacle', *Independent*, 29.11.1994.
123. Ed Vulliamy, 'Secret war: The transatlantic war' (uncut version of newspaper articles).
124. E.g., Brendan Simms, 'The unanswered question', *Times Higher Education Supplement*, 3.3.1999.
125. Interview, Richard Perle, Chevy Chase, 8.1.2001, fo. 5.
126. See Tim Judah, 'Banker Hurd to fund "Butcher of Belgrade"', *Sunday Telegraph*, 1.9.1996; Douglas Hurd, letter to the editor, *Sunday Telegraph*, 8.9.1996; 'Slobodan can't bank on Hurd', *Observer*, 29.12.1996.
127. Interview, Dame Pauline Neville-Jones, London, 20.2.2001, *Mendoza transcripts*, fo. 6.
128. Interview, Lord Hurd, London, 14.3.2001, *Mendoza transcripts*, fo. 8. In the same vein also Interview, Lord Hurd, London, 24.1.2001, fos. 24–7.
129. Interview, James Rubin, London, 8.2.2001, fo. 17.
130. E.g., 'Paris: Inquiry into Srebrenica massacre', *The Times*, 15.12.2000, and Congressional inquiries into breaches of the arms embargo.
131. P. H. Gordon, 'Recasting the Atlantic Alliance', *Survival*, 38, 1 (spring 1996), p. 34.
132. Interview, James Rubin, London, 8.2.2001, fo. 17. See also Interview, Marshall Freeman Harris, Washington, 9.1.2001, fo. 17: 'I think that if there was any damage or some ill will [over Bosnia] then that [Blair and Kosovo] helped to heal it.'
133. Interview, Bruce Pitcairn Jackson, Washington, 7.1.2001, fo. 5: the original has 'predicate', not 'precondition'.
134. Interview, Lord Hurd, London, 14.3.2001, *Mendoza transcripts*, fo. 11. See also Michael Evans, 'Balkans led to new thoughts on NATO', *The Times*, 23.11.2000, citing British military sources.
135. Jonathan Eyal, 'Broken ranks, stronger bonds', *Independent*, 16.11.1994.
136. 'The British interest', *The Times*, 2.9.1995.
137. One of the more restrained critiques was by William S. Cohen, outgoing US Secretary of Defense, 'Preserving history's greatest alliance', *Washington Post*, 8.1.2001.

138. E.g., Michael Gove, 'An army fit for a Third World War', *The Times*, 4.1.2000; Iain Duncan Smith, 'Euro army wants to be separate from NATO', letter to the editor, *Daily Telegraph*, 6.12.2000; Viscount Cranborne, 'Truth about European defence plans', *Daily Telegraph*, 7.12.2000; and, for the response of Tory MPs, Greg Hurst, 'Euro army sparks an outbreak of hostilities. Prime Minister's questions', *The Times*, 23.11.2000.
139. 'Phantom army', editorial, *The Times*, 21.11.2000.
140. As cited in Tony Paterson, 'French plan "will kill NATO", claims top German general', *Sunday Telegraph*, 27.5.2001.
141. As quoted in Hansard, 31.5.1995, col. 1096.
142. Douglas Hurd, 'A guide to life', *Sunday Telegraph*, 1.4.2001.

# *Sources and Bibliography*

## Interviews conducted by the author

General Wesley Clark, Chief of Plans for the US Joint Chiefs of Staff 1994–5, Washington, DC, 11.1.2001

Professor Mohamed Fillipovic, Bosnian Ambassador to Britain 1995, London, 2.10.2000

John Fox, US State Department 1992–3, Washington, DC, 11.1.2001

Georgie-Anne Geyer, syndicated columnist, Washington, DC, 11.1.2001

Sir David Hannay, Permanent Representative at the United Nations 1990–95, London, 21.11.2000

Marshall Freeman Harris, US State Department 1992–3, Washington, DC, 9.1.2001

Professor Adrian Hastings, Chairman, Alliance to Defend Bosnia-Herzegovina, Cambridge, 6.9.2000

John Herzberg, US State Department 1991–3, Staff, House of Representatives, Foreign Relations Committee, Washington DC, 9.1.2001

James Hooper, US State Department 1991–3, Washington, DC, 9.1.2001

Dr Robert Hunter, US Ambassador to Nato 1993–5, Pentagon City, 10.1.2001

Rt. Hon. Lord Hurd of Westwell, Secretary of State for Foreign and Commonwealth Affairs 1989–95, London, 24.1.2001

Bruce Pitcairn Jackson, President, US Committee on Nato, Washington, DC, 7.1.2001

Dr Jeane Kirkpatrick, Ambassador to the UN under President Reagan, Washington, DC, 10.1.2001

Professor Anthony Lake, National Security Advisor to President Clinton 1993–6, Georgetown, 10.1.2001

Major-General Graham Messervy-Whiting, Military advisor to Lord Owen 1992–3, London, 17.1.2001

Mr Nermin Mulalic, Attaché, Consular Section, Bosnian Embassy London 1994–6, Bosnian Institute, London, 5.9.2000

Lord Owen, EU mediator, International Conference on the Former Yugoslavia 1992–5, London, 19.1.2001

Richard Perle, Assistant Secretary of State under President Reagan, Chevy Chase, Md., 8.1.2001

Lord Renwick, Ambassador to Washington 1991–5, London, 27.11.2000

Sir Ivor Roberts, Chargé d'Affaires in Belgrade 1994–6, Dublin, 3.1.2001

James Rubin, Advisor to Madeleine Albright, US Mission to the UN 1993–5, London, 8.2.2001

Michael Scharf, Attorney Advisor for UN Affairs, Office of Legal Advisor, US State Dept 1992–3, Cambridge, 16.12.2000

Dr Jamie Shea, Nato spokesman, Nato HQ, Brussels, 24.11.2000

General Sir Rupert Smith, Commander UNPROFOR 1995, Brussels, 24.11.2000

Mr Edgar Vanderputte, Nato Defence Planning, Nato HQ, Brussels, 24.11.2000

Field-Marshal Lord Vincent, Chief of the Defence Staff 1991–2, Chairman of the Military Committee, Nato, 1993–6, London, 19.1.2001

Sir John Weston, Ambassador to Nato 1992–5, Richmond, 23.11.2000

Dr Michael Williams, UNPROFOR Spokesman Zagreb 1994–5, London, 22.11.2000

Paul Williams, Attorney Advisor for European and Canadian Affairs, Office of Legal Advisor, 1991–3, US State Dept Legal Advisor to Bosnian Government, 1994– , Cambridge, 16.12.2000

Mr Tim Winter, President, UK Friends of Bosnia-Herzegovina, Cambridge, 5.10.2000

## Interviews conducted by Benedikte Malling Petersen (*Petersen transcripts*)

Mr Andrew Bretnall and Mr Geoff Dean, Ministry of Defence, London, 22.5.2000

Sir Peter Hall, Ambassador to Yugoslavia 1989–92, London, 11.5.2000

Lord Hurd, London, 5.4.2000

Mr Michael McLay, Special Advisor to the Foreign Secretary 1993–5, London, 18.5.2000

Dame Pauline Neville-Jones, Deputy Under-Secretary for Overseas and

Defence Cabinet Office 1991–4, Chairman Joint Intelligence Cttee 1993–4, Political Director, FCO 1994–6, London, 26.5.2000
Lord Owen, London, 18.5.2000

## Interviews conducted by Alan Mendoza (*Mendoza transcripts*)

Maud Beelman, Associated Press, Washington, DC, 4.4.2001
Jennifer Brush, US embassy in Sarajevo, 1994–5, Washington, DC, 29.3.2001
Lord Carrington, EC negotiator, International Peace Conference on the Former Yugoslavia, 1991–2, London, 28.2.2001
Sir Patrick Cormack MP, London, 30.1.2001
Admiral Crowe, US ambassador to Britain 1994–6, Washington, DC, 4.4.2001
Ambassador Eldon, New York, 22.3.2001
Dr John Fox, Washington, DC, 4.4.2001
Professor Leon Fuerth, National Security Advisor to Vice-President Al Gore, 1993–2000, Washington, DC, 4.4.2001
Dr Jeffrey Gedmin, New Atlantic Initiative, Washington, DC, 27.3.2001
Sir David Hannay, London, 30.1.2001
Lt.-Col. C. A. le Hardy, Head of Intelligence, UNPROFOR Sector North East, 1994–5, 13.2.2001
Marshall Freeman Harris, Washington, DC, 3.4.2001
Lord Howell of Guildford, Chairman, House of Commons Foreign Affairs Committee, 1987–97, London, 28.2.2001
Rt. Hon. Lord Hurd of Westwell, London, 14.3.2001
General Sir Edward Jones, UK Military Representative, Nato HQ 1992–5, London, 24.1.2001
General George Joulwan, Supreme Allied Commander Europe 1993–5, Virginia, 3.4.2001
Dr Jeane Kirkpatrick, Washington, DC, 26.3.2001
Professor Anthony Lake, Washington, DC, 29.3.2001
Sir Christopher Meyer, Deputy Head of Mission, British Embassy, Washington, DC, 1992–4, Washington, DC, 2.4.2001
General William Nash, Washington, DC, 3.4.2001
Dame Pauline Neville-Jones, London, 20.2.2001
Thomas Richardson, Deputy Permanent British Representative to UN 1989–94, London, 20.2.2001
Dr Jamie Shea, Brussels, 5.3.2001
General Sir Rupert Smith, SHAPE, Mons, 5.3.2001

Field-Marshal Lord Vincent, London, 28.2.2001

James Woolsey, Director, Central Intelligence Agency 1994–5, Washington, DC, 29.3.2001

## Official documents

Annan, Kofi, *Report of the Secretary-General pursuant to General Assembly Resolution 53/35 (Srebrenica Report)* (New York, 1998)

*Defending our future: statement on defence estimates*, Defence White Paper (HMSO, London, 1993)

Hansard, *Parliamentary Debates*, 1991–5

*The International Conference on the Former Yugoslavia. Official Papers*, 2 vols, edited by B. G. Ramcharan (The Hague, London and Boston, 1997)

Specter, Arlen, et al., *Senate Select Committee report on Iran/Bosnia arms transfers*, Washington, DC, November 1996

*United Nations Security Council provisional verbatim record* (New York, 1991–5)

United States Congressional Record, 1992–5

*Wider peacekeeping* (HMSO, London, 1995)

### HOUSE OF COMMONS, FOREIGN AFFAIRS COMMITTEE

Foreign Affairs Committee, *Soviet Union/Development in Central Europe.* Minutes of Evidence, 6.11.1991 (HMSO, London), including:

'Recent developments in Eastern Europe with special reference to Yugoslavia', Memorandum submitted by the Foreign and Commonwealth Office (CE 17)

'Examination of witnesses'

Foreign Affairs Committee, *Developments in Central Europe*, Minutes of Evidence, 14.1.1992 (HMSO, London)

Foreign Affairs Committee, *Central and Eastern Europe: problems of the post-communist era*, vol. 2, 6.2.1994 (HMSO, London)

### FOREIGN AND COMMONWEALTH OFFICE (FCO) BRIEFING NOTES

*The case against international military intervention in Bosnia*, October 1992

*Former Yugoslavia: the UN mandate*, November 1992

*Britain's peace-making role in former Yugoslavia: questions and answers*, February 1993

*British aid to the former Yugoslavia*, October 1994

## DEFENCE INTELLIGENCE STAFF (DIS) BRIEFINGS

Defence Intelligence Staff, Unclassified Background Brief no. 9: Yugoslav update, 10.6.1994

Defence Intelligence Staff, Unclassified Background Brief no. 9: Former Yugoslav update, 17.2.1995

## PARLIAMENTARY BRIEFINGS

Richard Ware, *The end of Yugoslavia*, Background Paper 290, 15.6.1992, International Affairs and Defence Section, House of Commons Library

Fiona Watson and Richard Ware, *Bosnia, the UN and the NATO ultimatum*, Research Paper 94/33, 17.2.1994, International Affairs and Defence Section, House of Commons Library

Fiona Watson, Tom Dodd and Richard Ware, *Bosnia: the 'Sarajevo Formula' Extended*, Research Paper 94/62, 29.4.1994, International Affairs and Defence Section, House of Commons Library

Fiona M. Watson and Tom Dodd, *Bosnia and Croatia: the conflict continues*, Research Paper 95/55, 1.5.1995, International Affairs and Defence Section, House of Commons Library

Richard Ware, Fiona M. Watson and Tom Dodd, *Bosnia: update and supplementary information*, Research Paper 95/69, 30.5.1995, International Affairs and Defence Section, House of Commons Library

Tom Dodd, *War and peacekeeping in the former Yugoslavia*, Research Paper 95/100, 12.10.1995, International Affairs and Defence Section, House of Commons Library

Fiona M. Watson, *'Not peace, but a big step forward': Bosnia in October 1995*, Research paper 95/102, 16.10.1995, International Affairs and Defence Section, House of Commons Library

## NEWSPAPERS AND MAGAZINES

*Daily Telegraph*

*Economist*

*Financial Times*

*Guardian*

*Independent*
*Independent on Sunday*
*International Herald Tribune*
*London Review of Books (LRB)*
*New Statesman and Society*
*New York Review of Books (NYRB)*
*Observer*
*Spectator*
*Sunday Telegraph*
*Sunday Times*
*The Times*
*Times Literary Supplement (TLS)*

## BOOKS AND ARTICLES

Almond, Mark, *Europe's backyard war. The war in the Balkans* (London, 1994)

Almond, Mark, 'A faraway country . . .', in Cohen and Stamkoski, pp. 125–67

Ash, Timothy Garton, *History of the present: Essays, sketches and dispatches from Europe in the 1990s* (London, 1999)

Badsey, Stephen (ed.), *The media and international security* (London and Portland, Oreg., 2000)

Bass, Gary Jonathan, *Stay the hand of vengeance: The politics of war crimes tribunals* (Princeton and Oxford, 2000)

Baylis, John (ed.), *Anglo-American relations since 1939: The enduring alliance* (Manchester, 1997)

Bell, Martin, *In harm's way: Reflections of a war zone thug* (London, 1996)

Bellamy, Christopher, *Knights in white armour: The new art of war and peace* (London, 1996)

Bert, Wayne, *The reluctant superpower: United States' policy in Bosnia, 1991–1995* (Basingstoke, 1997)

Bet-El, Ilana, *Playing to different audiences: The UN and the media in the Bosnian war*, Reuter Foundation Paper 106, Green College, Oxford, no date

Blackman, Ann, *Seasons of her life: A biography of Madeleine Korbel Albright* (New York, 1998)

Boatswain, Tim and Neville, Peter (eds.), *The Balkans crisis*, Contemporary History: Sources and Debates, 1 (Luton, 1995)

Bollerup, Soren R., 'UN conflict management: the case of Bosnia-Hercegovina', MPhil dissertation, University of Cambridge, 1996

Bridge, T. D., 'Success: Trafalgar to Sarajevo and Haiti', *Army Quarterly and Defence Journal*, 125, 1 (January 1995)

Brock, Peter, 'Dateline Yugoslavia: the partisan press', *Foreign Policy*, 93 (winter 1993–4), pp. 151–72

Brzezinski, Zbigniew, *The grand chessboard: American primacy and its geostrategic imperatives* (New York, 1997)

Calvocoressi, Peter, *Discordia demens or What next in the Balkans*, David Davies Memorial Institute of International Studies Occasional Paper 6, London, 1994

Caplan, Richard and Feffer, John (eds.), *Europe's new nationalism: States and minorities in conflict* (Oxford, 1996)

Caplan, Richard, 'The European Community's recognition of new states in Yugoslavia: the strategic implications', *Journal of Strategic Studies*, 21, 3 (September 1998), pp. 24–45

Carrington, Peter, 'Turmoil in the Balkans: developments and prospects', *RUSI*, 137, 5 (October 1992), pp. 1–4

Carruthers, Susan, *The media at war: Communication and conflict in the twentieth century* (Basingstoke, 2000)

Christopher, Warren, *In the stream of history: Shaping foreign policy for a new era* (Stanford, Calif., 1998)

Cigar, Norman, *The right to self-defence: Thoughts on the Bosnian arms embargo*, Institute for European Defence and Strategic Studies, Occasional Paper 63, London, 1995

Clarke, John N., 'Ethics and humanitarian intervention', *Global Society*, 13, 4 (1999), pp. 489–510

Clarke, Jonathan, 'Beckoning quagmires: NATO in Eastern Europe', *Journal of Strategic Studies*, 17, 4 (December 1994), pp. 42–60

Clarke, Jonathan, 'Rhetoric before reality. Loose lips sink ships', *Foreign Affairs*, September–October 1995, pp. 2–7

Cohen, Ben and Stamkoski, George (eds.), *With no peace to keep: United Nations peacekeeping and the war in the former Yugoslavia* (London, 1995)

Cohen, Philip, *Serbia's secret war: Propaganda and the deceit of history* (College Station, Tex., 1996)

Cohen, Roger, *Hearts grown brutal. Sagas of Sarajevo* (New York, 1998)

Coker, Christopher, *Western intervention in the Third World*, Security Policy Library 10, 1993

Coles, John, *Making foreign policy* (London, 2000)

Connaughton, Richard, 'Trying to clear the doctrine dilemma', *Jane's Defence Weekly*, 7.4.1994

Conversi, Daniele, *German-bashing and the breakup of Yugoslavia*, Donald W. Treadgold Papers 16, Seattle, 1998

Cook, Mark, *Promise of hope* (London, 1994)

Corwin, Philip, *Dubious mandate: A memoir of the UN in Bosnia, summer 1995* (Durham, NC, and London, 1999)

Coward, Gary, 'Feeding the reptiles', *International Affairs*, April 1999

Cradock, Percy, *In pursuit of British interests: Reflections on foreign policy under Margaret Thatcher and John Major* (London, 1997)

Cruise, Daniel L., 'The OSCE and the future of European security arrangements. Bosnia and beyond', MPhil dissertation, University of Cambridge, 1997

Cushman, Thomas and Mestrovic, Stjepan (eds.), *This time we knew: Western responses to genocide in Bosnia* (New York and London, 1996)

Cyr, Arthur I., *After the Cold War: American foreign policy, Europe and Asia* (London, 1997)

Daalder, Ivo H., *Getting to Dayton: The making of America's Bosnia policy* (Washington, DC, 2000)

Danchev, Alex and Halvesen, Thomas (eds.), *International perspectives on the Yugoslav conflict* (Basingstoke, 1996)

Danner, Mark, 'Bosnia: the great betrayal', *NYRB*, 26.3.1998

Dewar, Michael, 'Intervention in Bosnia – the case against', *The World Today*, February 1993, pp. 32–4

Dick, C. J., 'Serbian responses to intervention in Bosnia-Hercegovina', *British Army Review*, 102 (December 1992), pp. 18–25

Dickie, John, *'Special' no more: Anglo-American relations. Rhetoric and reality* (London, 1994)

Dobbs, Michael, *Madeleine Albright: A twentieth-century odyssey* (New York, 1999)

Drew, Elizabeth, *On the edge: The Clinton presidency* (New York, 1994)

Drew, Elizabeth, *Showdown: The struggle between the Gingrich Congress and the Clinton White House* (New York, 1996)

Drew, S. Nelson, *Nato from Berlin to Bosnia: Trans-Atlantic security in transition*, McNair Paper 35, Institute for National Strategic Studies, National Defense University, Washington, DC, January 1995

Duncan, Alistair, 'Operating in Bosnia', *RUSI*, 139, 3 (1994)

Dunn, John F., *Europe's troubled corner: How to overcome instability and tensions in the Balkans*, Wilton Park Paper 66, HMSO, 1993

Dyker, D. A. and Vejvoda, I. (eds.), *Yugoslavia and after: A study in fragmentation, despair and rebirth* (London, 1996)

Edwards, Ruth Dudley, *True Brits: Inside the Foreign Office* (London, 1994)

Freedman, Lawrence, 'Why the west failed', *Foreign Policy*, 97 (winter 1994–5), pp. 53–69

Freedman, Lawrence (ed.), *Strategic coercion: Concepts and cases* (Oxford, 1999)

Fugate, Jessica S., 'NATO enlargement: US policy toward creating a new European security architecture', MA dissertation, Boston University, 1998

Geyer, Georgie-Anne, 'How the conscience of the west was lost', in Mestrovic, pp. 74–119

Giovanni, Janine di, *The quick and the dead: Under siege in Sarajevo* (London, 1994)

Glenny, Misha, *The fall of Yugoslavia: The Third Balkan War* (London, 1992) (3rd edn with a new epilogue published 1996)

Glenny, Misha, 'The return of the great powers', *New Left Review*, 205 (May–June 1994), pp. 125–30

Glenny, Misha, *The Balkans 1804–1999: Nationalism, war and the great powers* (London, 1999)

Glover, Stephen (ed.), *Secrets of the press: Journalists on journalism* (London, 1999)

Goldgeier, Jim, *Not whether but when: The decision to enlarge Nato* (Washington, DC, 1999)

Goldsworthy, Vesna, *Inventing Ruritania: The imperialism of the imagination* (New Haven and London, 1998)

Gordon, Philip H., *France, Germany and the western alliance* (Boulder, San Francisco and Oxford, 1995)

Gow, James, 'Deconstructing Yugoslavia', *Survival*, 33, 4 (July–August 1991), pp. 291–311

Gow, James, 'Nervous bunnies: The international community and the Yugoslav war of dissolution, the politics of military intervention in a time of change', *Political Quarterly*, 1994, pp. 14–33

Gow, James, 'After the flood: literature on the context, causes and course of the Yugoslav war – reflections and refractions', *SEER*, 75, 3 (July 1997), pp. 446–84

Gow, James, *Triumph of the lack of will: International diplomacy and the Yugoslav war* (London, 1997)

Gow, James and Freedman, Lawrence, 'Intervention in a fragmenting state', in Nigel S. Rodley (ed.), *To loose the bands of wickedness: International intervention in defence of human rights* (London, 1992), pp. 92–132

Gow, James, Paterson, Richard and Preston, Alison (eds.), *Bosnia by television* (London, 1996)

Guest, Iain, *On trial: The United Nations, war crimes and the former Yugoslavia*, Refugee Policy Group, Center for Policy Analysis and Research on Refugee Issues, Washington, DC, 1995

Hannay, David, 'The UN's role in Bosnia assessed', *Oxford International Review* (Spring 1996), pp. 4–12

Harbottle, Michael, *New roles for the military: Humanitarian and environmental security*, Conflict Studies 285, Research Institute for the Study of Conflict and Terrorism, London, 1995

Hastings, Adrian, *SOS Bosnia*, 3rd edn (Leeds, 1994)

Hibbert, Reginald, 'War among the South Slavs in the wider Balkan context', *International Relations*, 1994, pp. 4–8

Hibbert, Reginald, 'Why are British ambassadors at Belgrade so pro-Serb?', unpublished mss

Hoare, Quintin and Malcolm, Noel (eds.), *Books on Bosnia: A critical bibliography of works relating to Bosnia-Herzegovina published since 1990 in west European languages* (London, no date)

Hodge, Carole, *The Serb lobby in the United Kingdom*, Donald W. Treadgold Papers 22, Henry M. Jackson School of International Studies, Seattle, 1999

Hogg, Douglas, 'Central Europe: the new security relationships', *RUSI*, 139, 4 (August 1994), pp. 15–19

Holbrooke, Richard, *To end a war* (New York, 1999)

Hopkinson, Nicholas, *The media and international affairs after the Cold War*, Wilton Park Paper 74, HMSO, August 1993

Howard, Michael, '1945–1995: reflections on half a century of British security policy', *International Affairs*, 71, 4 (1995), pp. 705–15

Hughes-Wilson, John, *Military intelligence blunders* (London, 1999)

Hurd, Douglas, 'Inaugural Douglas Hurd Lecture at Oxford Brookes University', Oxford, 12.3.1993

Hurd, Douglas, 'Developing the Common Foreign and Security Policy', *International Affairs*, 70, 3 (July 1994), pp. 421–8

Hurd, Douglas, 'Lessons of Bosnia: A British overview of the conflict', All Souls Foreign Policy Studies Programme, 8.3.1996 (verbatim text of lecture)

Hurd, Douglas, *The search for peace: A century of peace diplomacy* (London, 1997)

Hurd, Douglas, *Ten minutes to turn the devil: Collected short stories* (London, 1999)

Ignatieff, Michael, *Blood and belonging: Journeys into the new nationalism* (New York, 1993)

Ignatieff, Michael, 'The seductiveness of moral disgust', *Index on Censorship*, 5/1995, pp. 22–38

Ignatieff, Michael, *The warrior's honor: Ethnic war and the modern conscience* (London, 1999)

Jones, Nicholas, *Soundbites and spin doctors: How politicians manipulate the media – and vice versa* (London, 1995)

Judah, Tim, *The Serbs: History, myth and the destruction of Yugoslavia* (New Haven and London, 1997)

Keegan, John, *A history of warfare* (London, 1994)

Kent, Sarah A., 'Writing the Yugoslav wars: English-language books on Bosnia (1992–1996) and the challenges of analyzing contemporary history', *American Historical Review*, 102, 4 (October 1997), pp. 1085–114

Kent-Payne, Vaughan, *Bosnia warrior: Living on the front line* (London, 1998)

Kumar, Radha, *Divide and fall? Bosnia in the annals of partition* (London and New York, 1997)

Lane, Charles and Shanker, Thom, 'Bosnia: what the CIA didn't tell us', *NYRB*, 9.5.1996

Latter, Richard, *A new transatlantic bargain*, Wilton Park Paper 77, HMSO, November 1993

Libal, Michael, *Limits of persuasion: Germany and the Yugoslav crisis, 1991–1992* (Westport, Conn., 1997)

Loyd, Antony, *My war gone by I miss it so* (London, 1999)

MacDonald, Calum, 'Rose tinted spectacles', *Bosnia Report*, 9 (1995), pp. 5–6

Magas, Branka, *The destruction of Yugoslavia: Tracking the break-up 1980–1992* (London and New York, 1993)

Magas, Branka and Zanic, Ivo (eds.), *The war in Croatia and Bosnia-Herzegovina, 1991–1995* (London and Portland/Ore., 2001)

Major, John, *The autobiography* (London, 1999)

Malcolm, Noel, *Bosnia: A short history* (London, 1994)

Malcolm, Noel, 'Bosnia and the west: a study in failure', *National Interest*, spring 1995, pp. 3–14

Malcolm, Noel, 'The whole lot of them are Serbs', *Spectator*, 10.6.1995

Mandelbaum, Michael, *The dawn of peace in Europe* (New York, 1996)

Mansell, Paul, *The ambivalence of the US to United Nations peacekeeping operations*, London Defence Studies 24, Centre for Defence Studies, London, November 1994

Martin, Lawrence, 'Peacekeeping as a growth industry', *The National Interest*, 32 (summer 1993), pp. 3–11

Mayall, James (ed.), *The new interventionism, 1991–1994: United Nations experience in Cambodia, former Yugoslavia and Somalia* (Cambridge, 1996)

Mazower, Mark, *The war in Bosnia: an analysis*, Action for Bosnia, London, December 1992

Mendoza, Alan, 'Anglo-American relations during the Bosnian war', MStud. dissertation, University of Cambridge, 2001

Messervy-Whiting, Graham, *Peace conference on former Yugoslavia: The politico-military interface*, London Defence Studies 21, Centre for Defence Studies, London, 1994

Mestrovic, Stjepan G. (ed.), *The conceit of innocence: Losing the conscience of the west in the war against Bosnia* (College Station, Tex., 1997)

Mousavizadeh, Nader (ed.), *The Black Nook of Bosnia* (New York, 1996)

Muravchik, Joshua, *The imperative of American leadership: A challenge to neo-isolationism* (Washington, DC, 1996)

Neville-Jones, Pauline, 'Dayton, IFOR and Alliance relations in Bosnia, *Survival*, 38, 4 (winter 1996–7), pp. 45–65

O'Brien, Conor Cruise, *The great melody: a thematic biography and commented anthology of Edmund Burke* (London, 1992)

O'Brien, Conor Cruise, *On the eve of the millennium* (New York, 1994)

O'Shea, Brendan, *Crisis at Bihac: Bosnia's bloody battlefield* (Stroud, Glos., 1998)

Owen, David, 'Yugoslavia', 1993 Churchill Lecture, Guildhall, London, 25.11.1993

Owen, David, 'The Fall of Vukovar', *Granta*, 47 (1994), pp. 194–5

Owen, David, 'The Eighth Annual Distinguished International Health Lecture, Royal College of Surgeons in Ireland, Dublin, 8.11.1993

Owen, David, *Balkan odyssey* (London, 1995)

Palubiak, Holly C., 'The post-Cold War transatlantic security relationship and NATO's Combined Joint Task Forces', MPhil dissertation, University of Cambridge, 1998

Parsons, Anthony, *The Security Council: An uncertain future*, David Davies Memorial Institute of International Studies, Occasional Paper 8, November 1994

Parsons, Anthony, *From Cold War to hot peace: UN interventions, 1947–1994* (London, 1995)

Peach, Stuart William, 'Air power in peace support operations: coercion versus coalition' (MPhil dissertation, University of Cambridge), 1997

Pearson, Joseph Sanders, 'British press reactions to the onset of war in ex-Yugoslavia' (PhD dissertation, University of Cambridge), 2001

Pengelley, Rupert, 'Into the quagmire', *International Defense Review*, 9 (1992)

Petersen, Benedikte Malling, 'A tale of two interventions: British policy in the Bosnian and Kosovo crises compared' (MPhil dissertation, University of Cambridge, 2000)

Prentice, Eve-Ann, *One woman's war: Life and death on deadline* (London, 2000)

Pukas, Anna, 'A very British warrior', *Army Quarterly and Defence Journal*, 123, 2 (April 1993), pp. 133–5

Ramet, Sabrina Petra, *Balkan Babel: The disintegration of Yugoslavia from the death of Tito to ethnic war* (Boulder, Color., 1996)

Renwick, Robin, *Fighting with allies: America and Britain in peace and war* (Basingstoke, 1996)

Renwick, Robin, *Memoirs* (forthcoming)

Richardson, Nick, *No escape zone* (London, 2000)

Rifkind, Malcolm, 'Peacekeeping or peacemaking? Implications and prospects', *RUSI Journal*, 138, 2 (April 1993), pp. 1–6

Riley, Jonathan (ed.), *White Dragon: The Royal Welch Fusiliers in Bosnia* (Wrexham, 1995)

Ripley, Tim, *Air war Bosnia: UN and NATO airpower* (Shrewsbury, 1996)

Ripley, Tim, *Operation Deliberate Force: The UN and NATO campaign in Bosnia 1995* (Lancaster, 1999)

Ripley, Tim, 'Peacekeeping with a war-machine: interview with General Rose', *International Defense Review*, 1 (1995)

Roberts, Ivor, 'Bosnia: a British perspective', *Review of International Affairs* (Belgrade), 46, 1032 (May 1995), pp. 19–22

Robinson, Michael, *Managing Milosevic's Serbia*, RIIA Discussion Paper 54 (1995)

Rossanet, Bertrand de, *Peacemaking and peacekeeping in Yugoslavia*, Nijhoff Law Specials, Vol. 17 (The Hague, London and Boston, 1996)

Rossanet, Bertrand de, *War and peace in the former Yugoslavia*, Nijhoff Law Specials, Vol. 33 (The Hague, London and Boston, 1997)

Rose, Michael, *Fighting for peace: Bosnia 1994* (London, 1998)

Rose, Michael, 'The British army in Bosnia: facing up to new challenges', *Army Quarterly and Defence Journal*, 125, 2 (spring 1995)

Rose, Michael, 'A Liddell Hart approach to peacekeeping', Annual Liddell Hart Centre for Military Archives Lecture, King's College, London, 18.1.1999

Russell, Alec, *Prejudice and plum brandy: Tales of a Balkan stringer* (London, 1993)

Ryan, R. d'Arcy, *The guerilla campaign in Yugoslavia*, Strategic Studies Institute Occasional Paper 6, Camberley, 1994

Sacco, Joe, *Safe area Gorazde: The war in eastern Bosnia, 1992–1995* (Seattle, 2000)

Scharf, Michael, 'Musical chairs: the dissolution of states and membership in the United Nations', *Cornell International Law Journal*, 28, 1 (winter 1995), pp. 29–69

Scharf, Michael, *Balkan justice: The story behind the first international war crimes tribunal since Nuremberg* (Durham, NC, 1997)

Scott, C. M., 'Forcing the peace', *Air Power Review*, 2, 1 (spring 1999), pp. 26–39

Seitz, Raymond, *Over here* (London, 1998)

Seldon, Anthony, with Lewis Baston, *Major: A political life* (London, 1997)

Sells, Michael, *The bridge betrayed* (Berkeley and London, 1996)

Sharp, Jane, 'If not Nato, who?', *Bulletin of the Atomic Scientists*, 48 (October 1992), pp. 29–32

Sharp, Jane, *Honest broker or perfidious Albion? British policy in former Yugoslavia*, Institute for Public Policy Research, London, 1997

Shaw, Martin, *The global state and the politics of intervention*, Centre for Global Governance at the London School of Economics Discussion Paper 13, December 1994

Shawcross, William, *Deliver us from evil: Warlords and peacekeepers in a world of endless conflict* (London, 2000)

Silber, Laura and Little, Allan, *The death of Yugoslavia* (London, 1995)

Simms, Brendan, *Bosnia: the case for intervention*, Bow Group Paper P706, May 1993

Simpson, John, 'An Englishman in Sarajevo – Rose's war', transcription of BBC *Panorama* programme, 23.1.1995

Simpson, John, *Strange places, questionable people* (London, 1998)

Smith, Mark A., *Attacks on Gorazde: Russian perceptions and their implications*, Conflict Studies Research Centre, RMAS, Occasional Brief 30, May 1994

Spence, Cameron, *All necessary measures* (London, 1998)

Spicer, Tim, *An unorthodox soldier: Peace and war and the Sandline affair* (Edinburgh and London, 2000)

Stankovic, Milos, *Trusted mole: A soldier's journey into Bosnia's heart of darkness* (London, 2000)

Stewart, Bob, *Broken lives: A personal view of the Bosnian conflict* (London, 1993)

Stone, Norman, 'Of pundits and partisans', *Salisbury Review*, December 1992, pp. 30–1

Stuart, Mark, *Douglas Hurd. The public servant: An authorised biography* (Edinburgh and London, 1998)

Sudetic, Chuck, *Blood and belonging. One family's story of the war in Bosnia* (NY and London, 1998)

Sunley, Jonathan, 'Sold on Serbia. Anatomy of a strange British attraction', *Bosnia Report*, 16 (July–October 1996), pp. 15–17

Tanner, Marcus, *Croatia: A nation forged in war* (New Haven and London, 1997)

Thompson, Mark, *A paper house: The ending of Yugoslavia* (New York, 1992)

Thornberry, Cedric, 'Saving the War Crimes Tribunal', *Foreign Policy* (fall 1996), pp. 72–85

Tomlinson, Richard, *The big breach: From top secret to maximum security* (Moscow, 2001)

Towle, Philip, 'The British debate about intervention in European conflicts', *Political Quarterly*, 1994, pp. 94–105

Tucker, Robert and Hendrickson, David C., 'America and Bosnia', *The National Interest* (Fall 1993)

Udoviciki, Jasminka and Ridgeway, James (eds.), *Yugoslavia's ethnic nightmare: The inside story of Europe's unfolding ordeal* (New York, 1995)

Ullman, Richard H. (ed.), *The world and Yugoslavia's wars* (New York, 1996)

Urban, George, *Diplomacy and disillusion at the court of Margaret Thatcher: An insider's view* (London and New York, 1996)

Vincent, Richard, 'NATO – where next?', *RUSI Journal*, 138, 6 (1993), pp. 8–12

Vulliamy, Ed, *Seasons in hell: Understanding Bosnia's war* (London, 1994)

Vulliamy, Ed, 'Secret war: The transatlantic war' (uncut version of newspaper articles)

Vulliamy, Ed and Leigh, David, *Sleaze: The corruption of parliament* (London, 1997)

Weisser, Ulrich, *Sicherheit für ganz Europa. Die Atlantische Allianz in der Bewährung* (Stuttgart, 1999)

Weller, Marc, 'The international response to the dissolution of the Socialist Federal Republic of Yugoslavia', *American Journal of International Law*, 86, 3 (July 1992), pp. 569–607

Weller, Marc, 'Peace-keeping and peace-enforcement in the Republic of Bosnia and Herzegovina', *Zeitschrift für ausländisches öffentliches Recht und Völkerrecht*, 56, 1–2 (1996), pp. 70–177

Willcocks, Mike, 'Future conflict and military doctrine', *RUSI Journal*, 139, 3, pp. 6–10

Williams, Ian, 'USA: the arms embargo and the man', *War Report*, 29 (October–November 1994)

Williams, Michael, *Civil-military relations and peacekeeping*, International Institute of Strategic Studies Adelphi Paper 321, London, 1998

Williams, Michael, 'Perceptions of the war in Bosnia', *International Affairs*, 75 (April 1999)

Williams, Paul and Scharf, Michael, 'The letter of the law', in Cohen and Stamkoski, pp. 34–41

Williams, P. G., 'Liaison – The key to success in central Bosnia', *Army Quarterly and Defence Journal*, 124, 4 (October 1994)

Wilson, T. R., 'Should NATO involve itself in wider peacekeeping operations?', *British Army Review*, 111 (December 1995), pp. 74–86

Woodward, Bob, *The Choice* (New York, 1996)

Woodward, Susan L., *Balkan tragedy: Chaos and dissolution after the Cold War* (Washington, DC, 1995)

Zametica, John, 'The Yugoslav conflict', International Institute of Strategic Studies Adelphi Paper 270, 1992

Zimmermann, Warren, *Origins of a catastrophe: Yugoslavia and its destroyers* (New York, 1996)

# Index